HOW I FOUND
LIVINGSTONE
IN CENTRAL AFRICA

Henry M. Stanley

DOVER PUBLICATIONS, INC.
Mineola, New York

Published in Canada by General Publishing Company, Ltd., 895 Don Mills Road, 400-2 Park Centre, Toronto, Ontario M3C 1W3.

Published in the United Kingdom by David & Charles, Brunel House, Forde Close, Newton Abbot, Devon TQ12 4PU.

Bibliographical Note

This Dover edition, first published in 2001, is an unabridged republication of *How I Found Livingstone: Travels, Adventures, and Discoveries in Central Africa, Including Four Months' Residence with Dr. Livingstone,* published by Sampson Low, Marston & Company, London, in 1895.

Library of Congress Cataloging-in-Publication Data

Stanley, Henry M. (Henry Morton), 1841–1904.
    [How I found Livingstone]
    How I found Livingstone in Central Africa / Henry M. Stanley.
      p. cm.
    Originally published: How I found Livingstone. London : Sampson Low, Marston & Co., 1895.
    Includes index.
    ISBN 0-486-41953-3
    1. Africa, Central—Description and travel. 2. Livingstone, David, 1813–1873. I. Title.

DT351 .S786 2001
967—dc21

                    2001042397

Manufactured in the United States of America
Dover Publications, Inc., 31 East 2nd Street, Mineola, N.Y. 11501

TO

JAMES GORDON BENNETT, ESQ.,

(PROPRIETOR OF THE 'NEW YORK HERALD,')

THIS RECORD OF THE

EXPEDITION SENT IN SEARCH OF DOCTOR LIVINGSTONE

AND OF

TRAVELS, ADVENTURES, AND DISCOVERIES IN CENTRAL AFRICA,

Is Respectfully Dedicated,

AS A TRIBUTE

TO THE GENEROSITY AND THE LIBERALITY WHICH ORIGINATED, SUSTAINED, AND CROWNED THE ENTERPRISE,

BY HIS GRATEFUL SPECIAL CORRESPONDENT

HENRY M. STANLEY,

LATE COMMANDER NEW YORK HERALD' EXPEDITION.

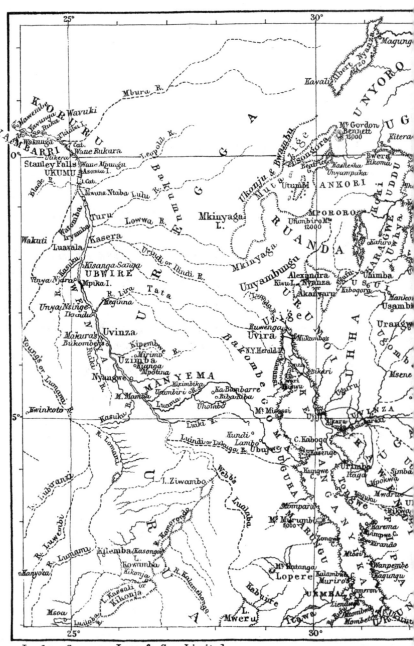

London, Sampson Low & Co., Limited.

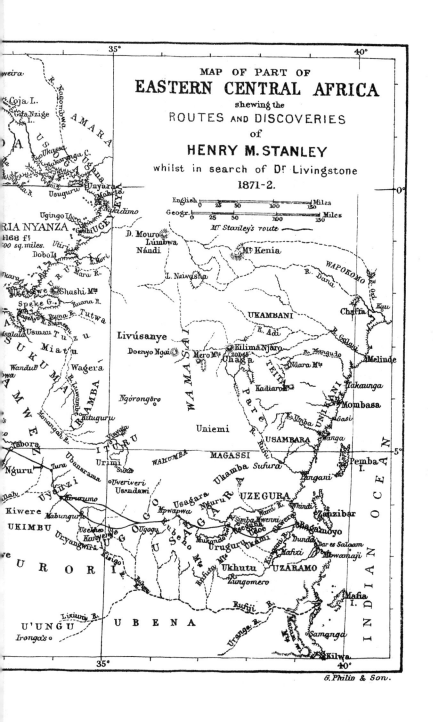

CONTENTS.

CHAPTER VII.

CHAPTER VIII.

CHAPTER IX

CHAPTER X.

CHAPTER XI.

CHAPTER XII.

CHAPTER XIII.

CHAPTER XIV.

CHAPTER XV.

CHAPTER XVI.

LIST OF ILLUSTRATIONS.

MEMOIR OF LIVINGSTONE

THE great African traveller, the search for, and relief of whom this book describes, was born near Glasgow, March 19th, 1813. At the very early age of ten he was employed in a factory as a " piecer," by which he earned sufficient money to contribute his mite towards the support of his family. A portion of his wages he was permitted to devote to the purchase of books, whereby he laid the foundation of a useful and sound knowledge. At sixteen he was pretty well acquainted with the writings of classic authors. Horace and Virgil were favourites, but his readings were not limited to this branch of education, they ranged over every field of literature save fiction. Books of travels were especially delightful to him ; scientific works, books on natural history, medicine, and theology served not only to lighten tedious hours at the spinning jenny, but to fit him for the career for which he was destined, and which he has since pursued with honour to himself and credit to the family from which he sprung.

At nineteen years of age he was promoted to a cotton

spinner, in which capacity he obtained a higher wage, which enabled him to support himself while attending the Greek and Medical classes, as also Divinity lectures during the winter in Glasgow. After confining himself to the study of Medicine and Divinity, with a view to offer himself, by the advice of friends, as a Missionary Physician for service, under the auspices of the London Missionary Society, in China, at twenty-five years of age he was summoned to undergo the necessary examination, out of which test he emerged as a Licentiate of Faculty of Physicians and Surgeons.

He was then sent as a Probationer to the establishment of the Rev. Mr. Cecil, at Chipping Ongar, in the county of Essex.

About the time he became qualified for the vocation for which he had been preparing himself, the Chinese Opium War broke out, and it became inexpedient for him to proceed to China. For such reason his services were diverted to South Africa, for which Mission-field he embarked, after a short course of theological training, in the year 1840.

The Rev. David Livingstone, M.D., landed at the Cape of Good Hope, after a voyage of three months from England, in his twenty-eighth year. He proceeded into the interior, viâ Algoa Bay, and arrived, after a journey of 700 miles, at the Mission Station of Kuruman, which had been established thirty years before by Messrs. Hamilton and Moffat.

After a nearly five years' residence at Kuruman, he became united in marriage to the daughter of Robert Moffat—from whom, in course of time, were born Robert

Moffat Livingstone, Thomas Steele Livingstone, Agnes Livingstone, and W. Oswell Livingstone.

During his preparatory labours at the Kuruman Mission, which extended from 1840 to 1845, that spirit to explore which has since distinguished him, developed itself. In the year 1845 he proceeded to Chonuane, and thence to Kolobeng, where he established a mission house, cultivated a vegetable garden, and a farm, besides ministering to the spiritual necessities of the Bechuana population which surrounded Kolobeng.

This post was the most advanced in the missionary field, and David Livingstone was the vanguard of the soldiers of the Cross, who were marching northward into the African interior to attack the stronghold of barbarism.

It was at Livingstone's house that enterprising travellers, lured to this far region by the report of multitudes of large game, while on their way to the game countries beyond, halted to refit. Here they stored their supplies, to this house they returned to rest from their sport; and of the humble missionary's house, and the kindly hospitality they received, Gordon Cumming, Mr. Oswell, Mr. Webb of Newstead Abbey, Major Frank Vardon—all great hunters—speak and write in terms of enthusiastic praise.

Years roll by, the Christian congregations flourish under his careful supervision and constant labour, and he begins to move onward towards the North. He has heard of a lake situated beyond the desert of Kalahari : no white man has ever seen its shores; and seeking a site whereon to build a new mission and sow the seed of the Gospel, he determines to go and search for it.

The very name of a lake of fresh waters and numerous streams had a charm for him, dwelling as he was within a thirsty and dry region. Water was precious at Kolobeng. The Bechuana believed that if they had but plenty of water, the neighbourhood of Kolobeng could not be excelled for the salubrity of its climate and fertility of its soil. The Kalahari desert was crossed by Livingstone, Oswell, and Murray, and the Lake Ngami was discovered by the three friends on the 1st of August, 1849.

From this discovery Livingstone returned to Kolobeng, where he arrived on the 10th of October, having been absent on his first expedition of exploration four months and ten days.

Lake Ngami lies between south latitudes 20° and 21°, and near the 20° longitude. It is from fifty to seventy miles in length, and is 2,825 feet above sea level. For this discovery Livingstone was awarded half of the usual premium placed at the disposal of the Royal Geographical Society by the Queen.

In April, 1850, the second journey of exploration was undertaken by Livingstone, this time taking with him his wife and three children, Robert, Thomas, and Agnes. Taught by experience, derived from his first expedition, of the obstacles to be met, he selected a feasible route presenting but few difficulties as far as the Zouga River. Crossing the river, the family proceeded up the northern bank, with the intention of going to Linyanti, where Sebituane, chief of the Makololo tribe, resided. But he

was unable to proceed beyond the Zouga, and he was reluctantly compelled to forego his intention. Livingstone's
uprightness of character, however, soon won the heart of
the warrior Lechulathebe, who at once tendered his
friendship, and assistance for the furtherance of his
labours, in proselytising the heathen under him. He
was not able to avail himself of the offer for any length
of time, as the lives of his wife and children were
threatened by the terrible fever of the country, and
he was compelled to return in consequence to Kolobeng.

Early in 1857 he began his third journey, accompanied
by his wife, children, and Mr. Oswell the hunter. On
the arrival of the party at Linyanti, the great chief
Sebituane warmly received them, offered to replace the
cattle slain by the tsetse fly, and in other ways manifested the interest he felt in them.

During Dr. Livingstone's residence with the Makololo,
Sebituane died. His nominee to the chieftainship was a
daughter, but she disclaimed the supreme authority
in favour of a younger brother called Sekeletu, then aged
nineteen, who was at once recognised by the Makololo, as
their chief.

The chapters of 'Missionary Travels,' relating to his
life and labours among the Makololo, are among the most
interesting which Livingstone ever wrote.

Alarmed by the weak health of Mrs. Livingstone
and of his children, he returned once more to Kolobeng,
and finally concluded to escort his family to the Cape of
Good Hope, and see them embark for England.

From the Cape of Good Hope he started on his journey

alone back to Linyanti, whence with the brave band of
Makololo, that Sekeletu the chief supplied him, he
proceeded to St. Paul de Loanda on the West Coast
of Africa, where he arrived at the house of a Mr. Gabrielle,
sick almost to death.   But his strong constitution
triumphed over the disease, and after a few months' stay
at Loanda, he returned to the interior to Linyanti.
From Linyanti he proceeded eastward, during which
travels he discovered the great Victoria Falls of the
Zambezi, and finally emerged on the East Coast of Africa
near Kilimane in 1856.

From 1840 to 1856 are sixteen years of hard labour, as
a missionary and traveller.   In what a brief sentence can
we sum up so much earnest, hearty work, so many
fatigues from marches, privations consequent upon in-
salubrious climates ; fevers, the result of rain and
marshes ; dangers which at all times surround the
explorer in Africa !

Livingstone left Kilimane on the 12th of August, 1856,
and proceeded to Mauritius, where he was most hospitably
received by Major-General C. M. Hay, who constrained
him to remain with him until through the influence of a
healthier climate, and abundant comfort, he could be freed
from an enlarged spleen, which resulted from the frequent
attacks of fever he had suffered on his journeys.

Arriving in England after such a long sojourn in
Southern Central Africa, on December 12th, 1856, he
was received with open arms by every man in Great
Britain who was interested in Africa, or was an admirer
of physical endurance and matchless perseverance.

He closed his admirable book 'Missionary Travels in South Africa,' wherein he records his numerous adventures, the instruction he derived from his patient observations, with words which reveal his character more fully than anything the present author could write, as follows :—

I have not mentioned half the favours bestowed, but I may just add that no one has cause for more abundant gratitude to his fellow-men, and to his Maker, than I have; and may God grant that the effect on my mind be such that I may be more humbly devoted to the service of the Author of all our mercies!

The London 'Times' of the 11th of December, 1856, contained the following interesting report of Dr. Livingstone's arrival in Europe :—

The Rev. Dr. Livingstone arrived at Marseilles from Tunis on the 6th inst., and was then in good health. His left arm is, however, broken, and partly useless, it having been broken by a lion. When he was taken on board her Majesty's ship *Frolic,* on the Mozambique coast, he had great difficulty in speaking a sentence of English, having disused it so long while travelling in Africa. He had with him a native from the interior of Africa. This man, when he got to the Mauritius, was so excited with the steamers and various wonders of civilisation, that he went mad, and jumped into the sea and was drowned. Dr. Livingstone has been absent from England seventeen years. He crossed the great African continent almost in the centre, from west to east; has been where no civilised being has ever been before, and has made many notable discoveries of great value. He travelled in the twofold character of missionary and physician, having obtained a medical diploma. He is rather a short man, with a pleasing and serious countenance, which betokens the most determined resolution. He continued to wear the cap which he wore while performing his wonderful travels. On board the *Candia,* in which he voyaged from Alexandria to Tunis, he was remarkable for his modesty and unassuming manners. He never spoke of his travels, except in answer to questions. The injury to his arm was sustained in the desert while travelling with a friendly tribe of Africans. A herd of lions broke into their camp at night, and carried off some of

their cat,le. The natives, in their alarm, believed that a neighbouring
tribe had bewitched them. Livingstone taunted them with suffering
their losses through cowardice, and they then turned out to face and
hunt down the enemy. The Doctor shot a lion, which dropped wounded.
It afterwards sprang on him and caught him by the arm, and, after
wounding two natives who drew it off him, it fell down dead. The
wounded arm was not set properly, and Dr. Livingstone suffered excruciating agony in consequence.

The following sketch of the traveller as he appeared
then is so good that I transcribe it from the pages of the
'Nonconformist' journal:—

A foreign-looking person, plainly and rather carelessay dressed, of
middle height, bony frame, and Gaelic countenance, with short-cropped
hair and mustachios, and generally plain exterior, rises to address the
meeting. He appears to be about forty years of age. His face is
deeply furrowed and pretty well tanned. It indicates a man of quick
and keen discernment, strong impulses, inflexible resolution, and
habitual self-command. Unanimated, its most characteristic expression is that of severity; when excited, a varied expression of earnest
and benevolent feeling, and remarkable enjoyment of the ludicrous in
circumstances and character passes over it. The meeting rises to welcome him with deafening cheers. When he speaks, you think him at
first to be a Frenchman; but as he tells you a Scotch anecdote in true
Glasgowwegian dialect, you make up your mind that he must be, as
his face indicates, a countryman from the north. His command of his
mother-tongue being imperfect, he apologises for his broken, hesitating
speech, by informing you that he has not spoken your language for
nearly sixteen years; and then he tells you, as best a modest yet
earnest man can, concerning his travels. In doing this he leaves out
all about his personal sufferings, just remarking that he intends to
save those anecdotes for his "garrulous dotage." Much of what he says
he has already, of course, written in his journals, and of some circum-
tances he has before told at other places; but he is one from whom you
could hear the same thing more than three times. His narrative is not
very connected, and his manner is awkward, excepting once, when he
justifies his enthusiasm, and once when he graphically describes the
Mosiatunya—the great cataract of Central Africa. He ends a speech
of natural eloquence and witty simplicity by saying that he has begun

his work, and will carry it on. His broken thanks are drowned by the applause of the audience.

The 'Daily News' of a later date sums up a glowing eulogy on Livingstone's character as follows :—

Dr. Livingstone is one of the few men whose words are realities. There is a quiet, curt energy about his statements which irresistibly impresses the hearer with a conviction that he has done what he says, and that he will do it again when occasion offers. There is a transparency in the simplicity of his diction which lets us see the workings of his mind, as if by some process of intuition. . . . There is true sublimity in Dr. Livingstone's allusion to the immediate resumption of the arduous task which he has been prosecuting for sixteen years, and is about to return to after an interval of only a few months. " He saw it to be his duty to go, and he was determined to do his duty, whatever others might say about the matter.". . . It was impossible to look round upon those assemblies without feeling a thrill of exultation at the thought that, literally, the whole earth is full of our labours—that there is no region in which our industrial enterprise, our skill in arms, our benevolent eagerness to diffuse the blessings of civilisation and pure and true religion, have not been displayed.

The 'Leader' also in a similar enthusiastic strain concludes thus :—

For seventeen years, smitten by more than thirty attacks of fever, endangered by seven attempts upon his life, continually exposed to fatigue, hunger, and the chance of perishing miserably in a wilderness shut out from the knowledge of civilised men, the missionary pursued his way, an apostle and a pioneer, without fear, without egotism, without desire of reward. Such a work, accomplished by such a man, deserves all the eulogy that can be bestowed upon it, for nothing is more rare than brilliant and unsullied success.

On December 15th, 1856, the Royal Geographical Society, then under the able and graceful presidentship of Sir Roderick Murchison, testified their regard and admiration for the perseverance with which he had accom-

plished the extraordinary series of geographical explorations, with the presentation of the Patron's Gold Medal.

On the 5th o. January, 1857, at an enthusiastic meeting at the Mansion House of London, a "Livingstone
Testimonial Fund" was begun, and before the meeting
had terminated, the sum of £450 was subscribed. This
purse was subsequently increased, until it reached the
sum of one thousand guineas. Scotsmen, proud of their
countryman, formed another fund, and in Glasgow and
Edinburgh another purse of one thousand guineas was
raised. But to repeat all the encomiums lavished on the
great traveller subsequent to his return, or to enumerate
the many friendships he formed with the most loving and
generous, the noblest and best of his countrymen, would
be to extend this memoir beyond proper limits.

After a rest of nearly two years in England, he undertook a governmental expedition in 1858, to explore the
Zambezi, to extend his previous explorations into the
interior, with the view of pioneering the advent of
commerce into that part of Africa whence he had
returned in 1856. He was at this period in his forty-
sixth year. He was accompanied on this expedition
by his brother Charles Livingstone (since H.B.M. Consul
at Fernando Po, who died in the latter part of October,
1873, while on his way to England, of yellow fever).
Dr. John Kirk was the botanist of this expedition, Mr.
Francis Skead, R.N., was the surveyor, and Mr. Richard
Thornton was the geologist.

This expedition, the account of which is given in
Livingstone's book, 'The Zambezi and its Tributaries,'

lasted five years.   In the fourth year of his second period
of exploration, Mrs. Livingstone, who had followed her
husband, died, and was buried on the bank of the Zambezi,
at a place called Shupanga.

Of this brave lady and faithful wife Charles Livingstone writes :—

> Those who are not aware how this brave, good, English wife made
> a delightful home at Kolobeng, a thousand miles inland from the Cape,
> and as the daughter of Moffat, and a Christian lady exercised most
> beneficial influence over the rude tribes of the interior, may wonder
> that she should have braved the dangers and toils of this down-trodden
> land. She knew them all, and in the disinterested and dutiful attempt
> to renew her labours, was called to her rest instead. *Fiat, Domine,
> voluntas tua.*

After journeying through Southern Africa in company
with her illustrious husband over upwards of five thousand
miles, the remains of this heroic lady lie in serene solitude
by the waters of the Zambezi.   Around the grave are
palm forests and luxuriant tropical vegetation, with the
colossal crown of Morambala towering amid clouds and
blue ether, as it stands the guardian mount, over those
melancholy shades.

This East African or Zambezi Expedition was not so
fruitful in discoveries as the journey Livingstone made
while travelling alone.   But there were many most
important results obtained by it.   A port was discovered
which might easily be made available for commerce, when
it would direct itself to the Zambezi region.   The noble
River Zambezi was proved to be navigable for light
draught river steamers, as far as the Kebrabassa Rapids.
The River Shire was explored and Lakes Shirwa and

Nyassa were discovered. The Shire is capable of floating paddle-wheeled steamers, drawing three feet of water at all seasons, and Nyassa Lake, whence the Shire flows, is a capacious inland sea with many hundred miles of coast.

Livingstone's experiences on this journey are recorded in his book, published by John Murray, of Albemarle Street, London. It is replete with facts, gathered after patient investigation with African history and geography and much scientific instruction, and is an invaluable guide, for that region bordering on the Mozambique.

In 1863, a despatch was received by Dr. Livingstone from the Home Government, recalling the Expedition, and accordingly the great explorer started down the Zambezi for home.

Upon arriving at the mouth of the Zambezi, Livingstone sailed in the *Lady Nyassa* for Zanzibar; thence he left for Bombay on the 16th of April, 1864, navigating the vessel himself. This was no small feat, of crossing 2,500 miles of ocean in a small steamer, for an African explorer! The vessel was so small that no one noticed his arrival in the harbour, and it was not known that he had arrived until the next day, when he went to ask the harbour-master where his little steamer should lie in port.

It remains for the author of this memoir, as the latest friend of Livingstone, to whom were told certain facts by the traveller himself, when subsequently we met in Central Africa, to disabuse the impression, which I know to exist with many men—that Livingstone was rich.

The money which the explorer made on the sale of his

first book, 'Missionary Travels,' was sufficient to sustain him for life with a modest competence, had it been wisely put out at good interest; but the instincts and spirit of the explorer prevailed against more worldly wisdom. When he departed on his second period of exploration, under the auspices and in the pay of Government—it is true that the Government equipped a steam launch which Livingstone called the *Ma Robert*—a Makololo term for Mrs. Livingstone—and subsequently despatched another steamer, called the *Pioneer*, to him. But the *Ma Robert* was so defective in her construction, that after a very brief period of negative usefulness, she sank in the Shire river, and the *Pioneer* drew too much water for active work. The waters of the Rovuma and the Shire were too shallow for such a vessel as the *Pioneer*, and accordingly Livingstone, who had the success of the expedition nearer to his heart than his own pecuniary interests, ordered the construction of the *Lady Nyassa*, which cost him, personally, the sum of £6,000. Before she was able to prove of much service to him, the expedition was recalled. The *Lady Nyassa*, on arriving at Bombay, was sold for what she would fetch, which was only £2,000. The entire proceeds of the sale of his steamer were deposited in a banker's hands for safe keeping, but within a short time afterwards the banker became a bankrupt! Reflective readers may see much in the above to account for the peculiar spirit with which he was accredited in England at that period.

The sum Livingstone derived from the sale of 'The Zambezi and its Tributaries'—the fruits of five years' labour, did not approach to one-half the sum of £6,000, expended in the purchase of the *Lady Nyassa*.

On the 20th of July, 1864, he reached London, and again he was received with enthusiasm in his native country. Societies, deputations, and cities tendered the traveller the honours he deserved for his indomitable labours in the cause of geographical science.

Mr. and Mrs. W. F. Webb, of Newstead Abbey, prevailed upon him to accept their hospitalities. The Doctor had become acquainted with Mr. Webb in 1862, while the latter pursued with youthful ardour and a hunter's intincts the large game inhabiting South Central Africa. Both men from that period, mutually respecting each other's good qualities and virtues, became warm friends, and the friendship began in 1852 among the Bakwains of Africa, lasted until Livingstone's death in 1873.

The Doctor always remembered his friends; he never ceased to speak of those who befriended him when he returned to England from his long explorations, and among the manifold kindnesses and attentions he received none made a greater impression on his memory than those which he received from the master and mistress of Newstead Abbey.

From the month of August, 1864, to April, 1865, Livingstone resided at Newstead. It was here he wrote the second record of his travels, since which time the room he occupied has gone under the name of "Livingstone's room." The outlook from it is that of a soft velvety lawn, where the young laughing grass ever wears its spring-time colouring, of a silvery lake, whose tin-

wavelets sing eternal music to the whispering breeze ; of expanses of pasture land, invested by most lovely groupings of trees and groves. Often he must have thought as he gazed upon the scene, wearied with the strange toil of literary composition, what a wide contrast existed between that happy and healthy English paradise and the primeval solitudes and fatal atmosphere of Central Africa.

That room, which saw the good man's labours as he penned the sad litany of woes which the children of Africa suffer under, will have an attraction for many generations yet unborn.

In his Preface to his second work, Dr. Livingstone hints at undertaking a third Expedition. He says :—

The Government have supported the proposal of the Royal Geographical Society, made by my friend Sir Roderick Murchison, and have united with that body to aid me in another attempt to open Africa to civilising influences, and a valued private friend has given a thousand pounds for the same object.

I propose to go inland north of the territory which the Portuguese in Europe claim, and endeavour to commence that system on the East which has been so eminently successful on the West Coast, a system combining the repressive efforts of H.M. cruisers with lawful trade and Christian missions, the moral and material results of which have been so gratifying.

I hope to ascend the Rovuma or some other river north of Cape Delgado, and in addition to my other work shall strive, by passing along the northern end of Lake Nyassa, and round the southern end of Lake Tanganika, to ascertain the watershed of that part of Africa. In so doing, I have no wish to unsettle what, with so much toil and danger was accomplished by Speke and Grant, but rather to confirm their illustrious discoveries.

The above is what Livingstone has written, but with his own lips he supplied to me, among many other things the details of how it came about that when nearly fifty-three years old, he should undertake a third Expedition to Central Africa, which was to eclipse everything he had accomplished before.

"One morning," said Livingstone, "Sir Roderick Murchison visited me while I was stopping a day or two in London and said to me, as well as I can remember, ' My dear Livingstone, your disclosures respecting the interior of Africa have created a profound excitement in the geographical world. We (the Society) are of opinion that we ought to send another Expedition into the heart of Africa to resolve the problem of the watershed between the Nyassa and the Tanganika Lakes; for when that is settled, all questions about Central Africa will be definitely resolved. Whom could you recommend to take charge of it as a proper man?' "

Livingstone, after reflecting a short time, gave him the name of ——. Sir Roderick, when he heard of the name, was delighted; he had also thought that should Livingstone himself refuse to go, no better man could be obtained. The President of the Royal Geographical Society departed to sound the gentleman whom his friend Livingstone had recommended so strongly. When questioned as to his willingness to undertake the command of this new Expedition, this gentleman at once politely refused upon the grounds that unless he could be guaranteed a sufficient rumuneration for his services, he could not think, at his time of life, to undertake anything of the sort unless it was remunerated.

Regarding this gentleman's answer to Sir Roderick's

proposition from a practical point of view, all sane men will at once recognise the wisdom which guided him in his reply, as it is scarcely fair to expect a man of advanced years to undertake a mission of this nature without ample compensation for exchanging the conveniences of civilized life for the dangers and privations that constantly menace and surround an explorer in Central Africa.

Sir Roderick then said that the society could not guarantee any pecuniary reward, but he could promise that on his return to England from his exploration he would find himself not neglected. The gentleman, however, declined to proceed to Africa on the strength of a verbal promise of a reward.

In sore distress of mind at this refusal, the enthusiastic geographer returned to Livingstone, and after imparting to the sympathising explorer the negative results of his mission, said to Livingstone :

"Why cannot you go? Come, let me persuade you; I am sure you will not refuse an old friend."

The result of Sir Roderick's appeal was, that Livingstone consented to go as soon as possible after the publication of his book on the Zambezi. He had, however, thought that he could have enjoyed a long holiday before departing on another long journey. "Indeed," said he, "I had flattered myself that I had much prospective comfort in store for me in my old days. And pecuniary matters required looking after for the sake of my family; but since you ask me in that way, I cannot refuse you."

Sir Roderick Murchison replied, out of sincere friendship and admiration,

" Never mind about pecuniary matters, my dear Livingstone. It shall be my task to look after that; you may rest assured your interests shall not be forgotten."*

These little incidents do more than anything else towards revealing the true character of the simple-hearted David Livingstone. They will show how ready he was to sacrifice—for it has been a sacrifice indeed—himself upon the altar of friendship, and before the shrine of science. They will also show what inducements were held forth to make him commit himself at the age of fifty-three—an age when most men begin to think they have done enough for fame, science, or friendship—to this last lengthened period of exploration, which, alas! has ended so unhappily.

Another instance of his self-abnegation I can relate.

Mr. Hayward, the Queen's Counsel, was sent to him by the then Prime Minister, Earl Russell, to ask what he would like the Government to do for him—if he had any particular views as regarded himself. This referred, of course, as to what honour he coveted for himself; so that the Government of England might bestow it on him, to show how his services were appreciated. But Livingstone, ever unmindful of himself, said, " If you stop the Portuguese slave trade, you will gratify me beyond measure." Mr. Hayward asked again if anything could be done for *himself*. " No, he could not think of any-

---

* In his last letter to Sir Roderick Murchison, which I had the honour to convey to England, Livingstone reminded Sir Roderick of his promise, but Sir Roderick was dead, and all his estates and property had been bequeathed to his nephew Sir Kenneth.

thing;" and it was not until Mr. Hayward had departed, that he began to reflect on the very pointed manner the lawyer had spoken to him, and to think he had lost the opportunity to provide for his children, and to give them a proper education.

The money necessary for this Expedition was subscribed by Mr. J—— Y——, who, for the sake of his friend of college days, generously furnished him with £1,000. The Government also gave £500, while the Royal Geographical Society subscribed £500. Besides the generous sum which he placed at Doctor Livingstone's disposal, as he was about to set out on his Expedition, Mr. J——Y—— promised that whenever he lacked funds, he, Mr. Y——, would supply him to any amount, and almost *commanded* him not to refuse himself anything he wanted, but to draw at once on him. Mr. Y—— has amply fulfilled his promise; and during the great traveller's absence has supplied the father to his family. For all his kindness to himself and children, Livingstone's last words about Mr. Y—— were "May God in his infinite goodness reward him!" Amen!

Dr. Livingstone left England to set out on his last Expedition on the 14th of August, 1865, accompanied by his daughter Agnes as far as Paris. From Paris he went to Bombay, and there commenced his preparations. Thence he proceeded to Zanzibar, accompanied by two boys he had picked up in the Shire country—Chumah and Wekotani—as well as by a number of men from the Johanna Islands (one of the Comoro Isles), a Sepoy Havildar, a few enlisted Sepoys and some Wasawahili.

On the 28th of March, 1866, the great explorer and his motley followers crossed over to the mainland, from the island of Zanzibar, and at once started for the interior by way of the River Rovuma. As he journeyed on, letters came from him occasionally, informing the delighted public of his progress, and of the extremely interesting incidents which one would naturally suppose would characterise his march to the interior. But in December of the same year the leader of the Johanna men who had accompanied the Doctor arrived at Zanzibar with a tale which saddened all who heard it—that Dr. Livingstone, the great African traveller, had been murdered on the shores of Lake Nyassa, by a band of the Ma-zitus. The tale bore such an appearance of truth about it that very few people indeed had the slightest idea of doubting it.

As it may be interesting to know what Musa's tale was, the following account from the ' Times of India' will not be out of place, if published here :—

The hopes raised by the news of the rumoured safety of Dr. Livingstone have speedily been dispelled, and there can no longer be any doubt that he was killed by a savage of the Mafite tribe. The narrative of the Sepoy belonging to the Marine Battalion (21st Native Infantry) who formed one of the Doctor's escort, and who arrived from Zanzibar in the *Gazelle* on the 14th of May, turns out to be altogether inaccurate ; and, substantially, the tale told by Musa is proved correct.

The *Nadir Shah*, a vessel of war belonging to the Sultan of Zanzibar, at present used as a trader, reached Bombay on the 15th of May in cargo ; and from information we obtained on board we are enabled to give a more detailed account of the circumstances in connection with the melancholy story of the Doctor's fate than has yet been published. The *Nadir Shah* left Zanzibar on the forenoon of the 28th of March, so that the news she brings is nearly a month later than that brought by the *Gazelle*, and three days later than the last despatch received from Zanzibar by the Bombay Government.

Dr. Livingstone took his departure from Zanzibar in March, 1866, and was conveyed by her Majesty's ship *Penguin* to Mikindany, near the mouth of the Rovuma River. The expedition consisted of Dr. Livingstone and thirty-five men, ten of whom were natives of Johanna, one of the Comoro Islands, thirteen Africans, and twelve Sepoys of the Bombay Marine Battalion. It was thought by Dr. Livingstone that these Africans would be of service to him on his journey into the interior. The Africans were formerly slaves, who had been liberated and educated in the Bombay Presidency. There was no other European in the party except the Doctor himself. The beasts taken were—six camels, four buffaloes from Bombay, five asses, and two mules, and among the baggage there were forage, gunpowder, &c. The *Penguin* started from Zanzibar on the 19th of March, 1866, and the men in the Doctor's train and the beasts were taken from Zanzibar in a large dhow, which was towed by the *Penguin*. In three days the *Penguin* arrived off the Rovuma River, but, owing to the strong current, the dhow could not be got into the mouth of the stream. The expedition then made for Mikindany Bay, about thirty miles northward of Cape Delgoa, where Dr. Livingstone and his party were successfully landed on the 28th of March.

The Johanna men, who had been engaged for the Doctor's service by Mr. Sundley, the English consul at Johanna, were considered preferable for the service to Zanzibar men. On the march into the interior the Sepoys seem to have suffered much, and Dr. Livingstone thought it necessary to leave them on the route to enable them to return to Zanzibar. In returning they had but little to eat, and ran great risk of starving. One by one all the Sepoys fell ill, and the sickness that attacked the havildar was fatal, as he died of dysentery. None of the twelve Sepoys who started with the Doctor reached Nyassa, and those who survived returned to Zanzibar in August or September. In October last the Johanna men made their appearance in Zanzibar, and presented themselves before Dr. Seward, the British Consul, when for the first time the intelligence was received of the disaster which had befallen Dr. Livingstone. From the accounts of these Johanna men it would seem that the expedition reached Lake Nyassa in safety and crossed the Lake. They pushed on westward, and in the course of some time reached Goomani, a fishing village on a river. This would appear to have been on the second or third week of August last. The people of Goomani warned Dr. Livingstone that the Mafites, a wandering predatory tribe, were out on a plundering expedition, and that it would not be safe to continue the journey. But the dangers thus presented to view were not sufficient to deter a man who had braved so many before; and, treating the warnings as but of slight moment, he crossed the river in canoes the next morning, with his baggage and train of followers, in safety. Previously to this time the whole of the baggage animals had perished on the journey from the want of water; and on reaching the further side of the river the baggage had to be carried by the Doctor's men. Being a fast walker, Dr. Livingstone kept some distance in advance of the baggage-encumbered men; and Musa only, or Musa and a few others of the party, kept up with him. The march had continued some distance, when Dr. Livingstone saw three armed men ahead, and thereupon he called out to Musa, "The Mafites are out, after all," or some such words as those, and these seem to have been the last he uttered. The three Mafites were armed with bows and arrows and other weapons, and they immediately commenced hostilities. Evidently the men must have closed on the Doctor, when, finding matters desperate, he drew his revolver and shot two of his assailants; but while thus disposing of the two, the third managed to get behind Dr. Livingstone, and with one blow from an axe clove in his head. The wound was mortal, but the assassin quickly met his own doom, for a bullet from Musa's musket passed through his body, and the murderer fell dead beside his victim. Musa states that the Doctor died instantly, and that, finding the Mafites were out, he ran back to the baggage party, and told them that their master had been killed. The baggage was hastily abandoned, and the Johanna men, Musa, and the rest of the party sought safety by a hasty flight, which, according to Musa's story, they continued until sunset, when they reached a secure hiding-place in the jungle. They held a consultation, and it is alleged that Musa prevailed on them to go back to look after the body of their late master, and that on regaining the place where the murder had been perpetrated they found Dr. Livingstone's body lying there. The Doctor's watch had been carried away, together with his clothes, the only article that remained on the body being the trousers. Musa and the men who had accompanied him "scratched" a hole in the ground just deep enough to bury the body in, and there left, in a far remote and unknown spot, the remains of the self-denying and noble man who, all too soon for his country and for the cause of civilization, but not too soon for him to have earned an enduring fame, found his end at the hand of an ignoble savage. The corpses of the three Mafites were lying on the spot where they had fallen; but no attention was paid to them by Musa, who, on searching, could find no memento of his late master to bring with him to Zanzibar. In making their way to the coast great hardships were experienced by Musa and the other survivors of the party, who were in such a starving condition that they had to live upon the berries they could gather by the way, until they fell in with an Arab caravan, which entertained them kindly. They were thus enabled to reach Kilwa, in the territory of the Sultan of Zanzibar. They were here provided with clothes and necessaries, and sent on to Zanzibar, at which place they reported all the circumstances to Dr. Seward, by whom they were closely examined. Dr. Kirk, of Zanzibar, also questioned them carefully, and found that their statement of the country through which they alleged they had passed, correctly answered to the leading features of the wilds through which Dr. Livingstone had intended to track his way.

The Johanna men were taken to Johanna, and carefully interrogated by the Sultan, as well as by Mr. Sundley, and their answers tallied with Musa's narrative. The Johanna men asked Mr. Sundley to pay them the nine months' wages due to them for their services with the expedition, and, as they were entitled to what they demanded, the money was paid to them. Some of the men who went away with the expedition, and who were not accounted for as having died, were still missing.

On the 26th of December Dr. Seward left Zanzibar in Her Majesty's ship *Wasp*, and proceeded to Kilwa, but he was unable to obtain any fresh information, or to gather additional details.

Her Majesty's Consul at Zanzibar, Dr. G. E. Seward, a sincere friend of the traveller, who was thus reputed to be lost, communicated to the Foreign Office the information which he received as follows :—

Zanzibar, December 10th, 1866.

MY LORD,

I send you the saddest news. Dr. Livingstone in his despatch from Ngomano, informed your Lordship that he stood " on the threshold of the unexplored." Yet, as if that which should betide him had already thrown its shadow, he added :—" I have but little to say of the future."

My Lord, if the report of some fugitives from his party be true, this brave and good man has " crossed the threshold of the unexplored."—he has confronted the future and will never return. He was slain, so it is alleged, during a sudden and unprovoked encounter with those very Zulus of whom he says, in his despatch, that they had laid waste the country round about him, and had " swept away the food from above and in the ground." With an escort reduced to twenty, by desertion, death, and dismissals, he had traversed, as I believe, that *terra incognita* between the confluence of the Loende and Rovuma Rivers, at Ngomano, and the eastern or north-eastern littoral of Lake Nyassa; had crossed the lake at some point as yet unascertained; had reached a station named Kompoonda or Mapoonda, on its western (probably its north-western) shore, and was pushing west or north-west, into dangerous ground, when between Marenga and Mukliosowa a band of implacable savages stopped the way, a mixed horde of Zulus, or Mafite and Nyassa folk. The Nyassa folk were armed with bow and arrow, the Zulus with the traditional shield, broad-bladed spears, and axes. With Livingstone there were nine or ten muskets; his Johanna men were resting with their loads far in the rear.

The Mafite instantly came on to fight; there was no parley, no avoidance of the combat; they came on with a rush, with war cries and rattling on their shields their spears. As Livingstone and his party raised their pieces, their onset was for a moment checked, but only for a moment. Livingstone fired, and two Zulus were shot dead (his boys fired too, but their fire was harmless) ; he was in the act of reloading when three Mafite leaped upon him through the smoke. There was no resistance—there could be none—and one cruel axe-cut from behind him put him out of life. He fell, and when he fell, his terror-stricken escort fled, hunted by the Mafite. One, at least, of the fugitives escaped ; and he, the eye-witness, it is who tells the tale—Ali Musa, chief of his escort of porters.

The party had left the western shores of Nyassa about five days. They had started from Kompoonda, on the lake's borders (they left the Havildar of Sepoys there dying of dysentery; Livingstone had dismissed the other Sepoys of the Bombay 21st, at Mataka), and had rested at Marenga, where Livingstone was cautioned not to advance. The next station was Mahlivoora; they were traversing a flat country, broken by small hills, and abundantly wooded.

Indeed, the scene of the tragedy so soon to be consummated, would appear to have been an open forest glade. Livingstone, as usual, led the way, his nine or ten unpractised musketeers at his heels. Ali Musa had nearly come up with them, having left his own Johanna men resting with their loads far in the rear. Suddenly he heard Livingstone warn the boys that the Me-zitus were coming. The boys in turn beckoned Musa to press forward. Musa saw the crowd here and there between the trees.

He had just gained the party and sunk down behind a tree to deliver his own fire, when his leader fell. Musa fled for his life along the path he had come. Meeting his Johanna men, who threw down their loads, and in a body really passed Musa, his escape, and that of his party verges on the marvellous. However, at sunset, they, in great fear, left their forest refuge, and got back to the place where they hoped to find their baggage. It was gone, and then, with increasing dread, they crept to where the slain traveller lay.

Near him, in front, lay the grim Zulus who were killed under his sure aim ; here and there lay scattered some four dead fugitives of the expedition. That one blow had killed him outright, he had no other wound but this terrible gash ; it must have gone—from their description—through the neck and spine up to the throat in front, and it had nearly decapitated him. Death came mercifully in its instant suddenness, for David Livingstone was ever ready.

They found him stripped of his upper clothing, the Ma-zitus had respected him when dead. They dug, with some stakes, a shallow grave, and hid from the starlight, the stricken temple of a grand spirit— the body of an apostle, whose martyrdom should make sacred the shores of that sea which his labours made known to us, and which now, baptized with his life's blood, men should henceforth know as ' Lake Livingstone.'

The Johanna men made the most of their way back to Kompoonda or Mapoonda, not venturing near any village or station. They lost themselves in the jungle, and were fourteen days on their way. At Kompoonda they witnessed the end of the Havildar of Sepoys, Bombay 21st Native Infantry. He alone of all the Indians was faithful ; on the threshold of this Consulate at Zanzibar, he pledged himself at the moment of starting never to forsake his leader—nor did he ; to the last he struggled on, worn with dysentery, but broke down hopelessiy on the road to Marenga. A day or two later and he would have shared his leader's fate.

Insubordinate, lazy, impracticable, and useless, Livingstone had dismissed the other Sepoys at Mataka. Had they been faithful like their Havildar, I should not have had to inscribe a record of this sad happening. Their unfitness for African travel might have been predicated. At Kompoonda the Johanna men were deprived of their weapons by the Chief, who also kept the Havildar's. Here they joined an Arab slave-caravan, re-crossed the Nyassa, and made for Kilwa, the great slave outlet on the Zanzibar coast.

But here again, and where least expected, they encountered the Mafite. They had reached Keepareygree, eight days south-west of Kilwa, when the appearance of a band of these savages scattered the caravan. Abandoning ivory, slaves—their all—the Arab leaders thought but of saving their lives. The Johanna men again made their escape, and reached Kilwa, whence by the kindness of the Customs people they were at once sent on to Zanzibar. They arrived here on the 6th of December.

It will be gratifying to the many and true friends of Dr. Livingstone to learn that when, on his sad end being known, the British flag was lowered at this Consulate, the French, the American, and Hanseatic flags were at once flown half-mast high, the Consuls paying a spontaneous tribute to his memory—an example shortly followed by all the foreign vessels in the harbour. The Sultan's flag was also lowered.

I must reserve other details for a subsequent letter; but I may state that no papers, effects, or relics of Livingstone are likely to be recovered.

G. EDWARD SEWARD.

At first this sad intelligence was believed throughout Europe and America, but the keen strong sense of Sir Roderick Murchison discovered flaws in the ingenious fabrication of Musa, and by his resolute denial, and utter disbelief, which he lost no time to make public through the 'Times,' he made many converts to his view of Musa's story. Doubt grew fast in many minds, and doubt finally became conviction. But to establish conviction in the popular mind, Sir Roderick and the Society induced the Government to despatch a boat expedition to the Zambezi, whence an ascent to the

Shire and Lake Nyassa, to near the spot where the traveller was reported to be killed, was easy.

Volunteers were called for, and hundreds of resolute men offered their services at once to command the Expedition, out of whom were selected Mr. Edward Daniel Young, a warrant officer in Her Majesty's Navy, and Lieutenant Henry Faulkner of the 17th Lancers.

Mr. Young on taking command of the Search Expedition, requested that a steel boat should be given him, so constructed as to be disconnected into portable sections, whereby the difficulty of passing the Murchison Falls of the Shire might be surmounted by postage overland. This first Expedition left England on the 11th of June, 1867, to prosecute the search for Livingstone. In the following letter, Mr. Young reports how he succeeded in his enterprise.

To Sir Roderick Murchison, Bart., K.C.B., &c.

SIR,

I have the honour to lay before you a brief outline of the proceedings of the Expedition under my command, sent out to Africa by the Royal Geographical Society, for the purpose of ascertaining the truth or falsehood of the reported death of Dr. Livingstone. I am happy to inform you that our efforts have been crowned with success, and I have satisfactory evidence that Dr. Livingstone was not murdered by the Mazitu, nor by any other tribe, at the place named by the Johanna men, but had gone on in safety far beyond. I have also satisfactory evidence that the Johanna men deserted shortly after leaving Marenga, returning by the same route as they had gone.

But I must first begin the narrative from the time of our landing at the mouth of the Zambesi. Immediately on landing I succeeded in getting a negro crew to take the boats up as far as Shupanga, where I arrived on the 2nd of August. I at once engaged a fresh crew to go on to Chibisa, and the next day started for Senna. Arrived there on the 6th; found the Portuguese authorities very obliging; made what arrangements were thought necessary, and proceeded on the next day. I learned from the Portuguese that the Mazitu were in full force on the Shire, and were threatening Chibisa, so I arranged with the authorities at Senna to send on to me at Chibisa (should I require them) 100 men, fearing as the Mizitu were there, I should not be able to get the Makololo to accompany me.

We arrived at Chibisa on the 17th, and found that the reports about the Mazitu having been there were quite true, and that they had been down in force to the left bank, robbing and burning the houses, murdering some of the people they caught, and taking others prisoners. The Makololo put off in canoes from the opposite bank and shot three of them. Of course I was quite unprepared to meet the Mazitu in this part of the country.

The Makololo, as well as the people who were of the old mission party, received us gladly. I requested the Makololo to attend the next morning, which they did, when I acquainted them with the object of my mission. They agreed to accompany me on certain conditions, which I agreed to. One was that I should leave some ammunition behind with those that remained, so that should the Mazitu attempt to cross the river below the Cataracts they would be well able to encounter them. After arrangements had been completed, we started on the 19th for the Cataracts; arrived the same day, and at once began taking the boat to pieces. Hitherto all had gone on well, but no sooner had we got the boat to pieces, and everything was ready for the journey overland, than fresh reports about the Mazitu reached the Makololo, which very much daunted them, and had also a tendency to lower our spirits, for without their help we could do nothing, as it was not only their help that we required, but also that of their people, they being the chiefs of the country round about. After a good deal of persuasion the whole affair was settled to our satisfaction, and on the evening of the 23rd the Makololo appeared in force with about 150 men.

We started next morning with the boat, provisions, luggage, &c., making in all 180 loads. The men worked well, and we arrived with everything in good order at Pomfunda, above the Cataracts, in four and a half days. The heat during the journey was excessive, even for Africa. We at once commenced rebuilding the boat, and everything appeared to be going on well when fresh reports reached us about the Mazitu. We were visited by some of the Ajawa chiefs who had been driven out of their own country, and were obliged to cross the river to save themselves from being murdered. There was an encampment, close by the place where we were building the boat, of about 200 Ajawas, the sole survivors of the once powerful people under the chief Joey.

Every day fresh reports reached us, and the Makololo wanted to return home, which of course I could not consent to. At this place we first heard from a native of a white man having passed through Maponda at the south end of Lake Nyassa. He stated that he had seen him, and gave a description of his dress, &c.

Launched the boat on the 30th, and started up the river next morning. The Makololo not working well, and making every excuse, not being well, &c., thinking perhaps we would turn back. They stated that the risk was too great, that there was little chance of our ever returning, but as they had gone so far they would go on and die with us; of course all was agreed to. As we proceeded on we found vast numbers of Ajawas and Machinkas on the left bank, living in temporary huts, who had retreated before the overwhelming numbers of Mazitu. Reached the small lake Pamalombe on the evening of the 5th of September.

During our passage up the river heard several reports that a white man a twelvemonth before had stopped at Maponda for some time, having crossed from the opposite side, and that after resting there some time he had gone on in a westerly direction. I now felt almost convinced that it must have been Livingstone, but I almost feared to stop there, for I felt certain had the Makololo been satisfied that it was him they would have gone no further; for my agreement with them was, that as soon as we had satisfactory evidence that the Doctor had gone on in safety, or that he had been killed in the way described by the Johanna men, I would return with them immediately. But now, as it appeared that he had passed over the south end of Nyassa instead of the north, I wanted to find out where he had first struck the lake. The Makololo stated that they were certain that if a white man had been killed, or had died within a month's journey of where we were, we should certainly have heard of it before we got thus far.

The next morning crossed the Pamalombe, but could not find a passage in to Maponda, owing to the quantity of rushes and grass, and it blowing very hard at the time we made for the river. Here again we met great numbers of natives, who appeared very hostile. They lined the banks with their guns, and demanded that we should come into them. The Makololo appeared very much afraid, so J laid the boat to, to await the approach of two armed canoes that had shoved off from

the shore. I soon made matters right with them, and shortly after‐
wards entered Lake Nyassa, and slept the first night on the Rock
Boasuam.

Started the next morning with a fine breeze for the east side of the
lake, steering as near as possible for the Arab crossing-place, as laid
down by Livingstone. We had not run more than two hours before a
heavy gale began to blow, and for three hours we had to run along the
coast to try and find shelter, but the rocks and breakers met us at
every hand. This proved the finishing stroke to the Makololos' courage
who all laid down at the bottom of the boat to die, and although the
boat was constantly shipping heavy seas, they refused to bale out the
water. The steel boat behaved well, but was far too deep for the
stormy Lake Nyassa. At length after three hours' weary watching, we
succeeded in finding a sheltered spot where we stopped to dry our
clothes. Only one native appeared at this place, who when he saw us
first was much frightened ; but as soon as we stated we were English
he willingly came towards us. He told us an Englishman had passed
through his village a year ago, and that he had come from the
Arab settlement, and had gone south to Maponda. Started again
for the former place, but found the distance too great to reach
before dark ; put into a small sandy bay, where we found some natives,
fishing.

I must here remark that at any place, on first visiting it, no one
was allowed by me to get out of the boat, except myself, Mr. Faulkner
and the interpreter. I soon got into conversation with these men, when
they spoke of a white man who had been there, without being asked.
They stated that he had first made that place coming from Makata,
had stopped nine or ten days to rest, and then went north to the Arab
settlement to try and get them to carry him and his party across the
lake, but after waiting there some time he returned, making his way
south for Makata. They described his dress, what luggage he had,
imitated him taking sights, and sleeping under a mosquito curtain, and
stated that he had a dog with him named Chetane. They said the
head-man of the carriers was named Musa ; two of the boys spoke the
Ajawa and Mananja language, and were named Juma and Wako.
They told us what barter goods he traded with ; on being shown
an album with numbers of likenesses, they at once recognised the one
of Livingstone. That there were nine of Musa's countrymen with
him, who did not speak either the Ajawa or Mananja language. He
did not buy slaves or ivory ; he had come to see the country. Besides

numerous other things that left no doubt on my mind that it was Livingstone.

Next day we arrived at the Arab settlement, where we were received kindly, and found all that I heard before was quite correct. Livingstone waited at this place nine or ten days for the Arab boat which did not arrive, so he started south again, and they traced him as far as Maponda. I visited the house Livingstone lived in during his stay, and I purchased a few articles (all English make) that he had traded with, such as small round looking-glasses, a knife, razor, iron spoons, &c. Of course most of the calicoes, &c., were already worn out, but the chief still possessed an Indian manufactured scarf that Livingstone had presented to him on leaving. I sent two of the most trustworthy Makololo with my ever faithful interpreter (whom I brought from the Cape) on the road to Makata to see if that was the road he had come, while we again went south, making short marches inland, to try and find the route the Johanna men took in going back, as they had not visited this place or the last. We obtained other trifling articles in the shape of barter goods, and while waiting for the return of the Makololo obtained from a chief further south an English Common Prayer Book, which he stated had been left behind by the Englishman in the house he had slept at.

On the 13th the searching party returned, having gone two days' march on the road to Makata. Livingstone had come that way. They brought back some glasses, fish-hooks, &c., that he had traded with. They would have gone further, but were ill-treated by some of the natives and driven back : their reason for so doing, they said, was that the Englishman had brought fighting into the country, for the Mizitu had been killing their people ever since he left.

Sept. 14*th.*—Started for the opposite side of the lake, made for Chinsamba's. Although we started with little or no wind, it again blew a gale before we reached the opposite shore. We found that Chinsamba had been killed some time since, and nothing remained of his village. Skeletons now met our eyes in great numbers, whenever we landed along this side. Saw several natives the first day, both Ajawas and Mananja ; and those who had not seen the white man further south had heard of him, but not in a single instance was he spoken of as being dead. I wished to learn, by coming over this side, in what direction he had gone after leaving Maponda. We had not crossed long when we saw a man who had helped to carry the Englishman's luggage for two days. He described him as before. This man had been living inland some distance, but had been driven out by the Ajawa. He pointed in a north-westerly direction, and stated it was five days' journey off, which, of course, would be very much more from Marenga.

Our progress south was slow, owing to the heavy gales of wind. On our way we met several who had seen the Englishman, and more than one had helped to carry his luggage from village to village, and there was not in all their reports the slightest variation. They were not all from the same place, but they all maintained that he had gone on in a north-westerly direction towards the Loangwa. These natives were full of complaints about their neighbours, and would only have been too ready to inform against each other if Livingstone had come to an untimely end at either of their hands, and they all maintained that the Mazitu had never been in that part of the country.

Sept. 19th.—Reached Marenga. Seeing the boat approach the shore they lined the beach with their guns, &c.; but, as soon as we told them we were English, they laid their arms down and welcomed us. I at once asked to see Marenga, when I was conducted up to his house by one of his wives. Marenga rushed towards me, and, seizing me by the hand, shook it heartily, saying, "Where have you come from, and where is your brother that was here last year?" and as soon as I told him I had come to follow him, he began and told me all he knew of him. He said he had come there from Maponda, had stopped there two days; he was very kind to him, making him presents, &c., and he in return gave him what food he required. Livingstone gave him medi- cine, which was done up in doses; the papers he used formed part of a ' Nautical Almanack' for the year 1866. He lent Livingstone four canoes to take himself and luggage across the marsh, while the Johanna men carried the remainder round. He had seen him before; he said he saw him when he was up here with a boat a long time ago. He traced him a month's journey off, giving the names of the places in the same order as I had previously heard. He was quite willing to give me any guides to go to Maksuro, or where it once was; but he stated, as I had previously heard, that Maksuro had been driven out and killed by the Ajawa, and his people almost annihilated; as also had Cóómo, two days' journey beyond. Marenga stated that the Johanna men returned after being absent two days. They gave as their reason for returning that they had merely agreed with Livingstone to take his goods as far only as they liked. The head man stated that he had been in that direction before with him, and had met the Mazitu, and that they were going no further To prove their independence they passed themselves off as Arabs. Marenga gave them food, and they slept there one night, and then set out for Maponda.

Marenga is a Babisa, and rules over a populous district; he made us a present of a bullock and as much native food for our crew as we required, and he invited us to remain a long time. He has a great number of wives—I and Mr. Faulkner being introduced to forty, who were all sitting round him.

Having satisfied myself thus far, I asked him if he thought it possible that Livingstone could have died a month's journey off, and he not know it? He at once said No, and had he died three months off he should have heard of it; but as soon as I told him I had heard that the Mazitu had killed him not far distant, he laughed, and said he told me he was going the way to avoid them, and that the Mazitu had never been in that part of the country described by the Johanna men.

Marenga then sent for a man who had gone five days' journey with him, and when he returned the Johanna men had gone back. I had previously heard the same account from the same man.

The Makololo now got very impatient to return home, and nothing was talked of day or night but the Mizitu. They stated that they had fulfilled their engagement, but I very much wished to try and get to the north end of the lake. But they would not listen to it. No inducement I could offer would persuade them to go; so there was no alternative but to go round to Maponda, get what information I could, and return.

Marenga was full of complaints about his neighbours, and what he wished for more than anything else was medicine for his guns, so that if the Ajawas came to fight him his shot would kill some one every time they were fired. We, being satisfied that Livingstone had gone on in safety, started on the 20th for Maponda, calling at the several places along the coast to gain what information I could; but all I obtained only went to confirm what I had previously heard.

Arrived at Maponda on the 25th. The chief himself was not at home, having gone on a trading expedition, leaving his mother to act during his absence. Immediately on arrival I sent a messenger to acquaint her of arrival and my wish to see her. She soon came, with a train of followers, bringing us presents of native food and beer. She stated that an Englishman had been there a year before, had stopped three weeks to rest his party, and then left for Marenga, stopped there a day or two, and then left to go to the Loangwa, calling at Maksura,

Cóómo, &c. One of the boys was left behind here, being unable to travel, having very bad feet and legs, but had now quite recovered and gone with Maponda. She stated that the Englishman had left a paper with him, but that he had taken it with him on the journey. She brought some books belonging to him, one of which had his name on ("Wakitane, from Dr. Wilson, Dec., 1864," &c.), which she allowed me to take. The Johanna men returned this way, stopped one day, and proceeded on. She swore, in the presence of us all, that Maponda did not take away their guns, neither did any of the party die there. She stated that the Englishman was great friends with her son, and that if any one had molested him (even Marenga, as strong as he was) he would have gone to war with him. The old lady laughed at the idea of Livingstone having been killed by the Mazitu. Mr. Faulkner questioned her regarding the Havildar. She gave a description of a man with straight black hair, with the top of his head shaved, &c. Mr. Faulkner states it answers the description of the Indian very well. Marenga also told us the same, and I felt convinced had he died there we should have heard it from some of the numbers I questioned on the subject.

The Makololo now told me that if I intended going into the lake again, they were not going with me ; and, being entirely dependent on these men, there was no alternative but to return and to get their aid in carrying the boat back. So, having got all the news I could at Maponda, I decided on going to Makata ; but although I offered a large amount for a guide, no one would attempt to cross the river. They stated that Makata had taken to the mountains for fear of the Mazitu, and they were afraid of being cut off.

Started for the Cataracts on the 27th. Found the same state of things along the river as on coming up. Arrived at the Cataracts on the 2nd of October, and commenced taking the boat to pieces. Meanwhile we heard from Chibisa that the road was clear, and that the Mazitu had made Chore, not far from the lower Shire, their headquarters.

Oct. 8th.—Started for Chibisa with the boat, luggage, &c. ; where we arrived on the 12th. We found the boats safe, and the men left with them in very fair health. Again built the steel boat, and while there repaired the graves of the late missionaries who died there.

22nd.—Started from Chibisa.

26th.—Arrived at the Ruo, stopped and repaired the grave of the late Bishop Mackenzie. Arrived at the Kongone on the 11th of November, but on our way down we visited Senna.

H.M.S. *Racoon* arrived on the 2nd of December.
Arrived at the Cape on the evening of the 17th.
Embarked on board the mail-steamer on the 19th.

In conclusion, I must again state that this is but a brief outline of our proceedings. I should have liked to have done more by going to the north end of the lake, but was prevented by circumstances unforeseen when I left England; for, had the Mazitu not threatened Chibisa, I should have had little difficulty in getting the Makololo to accompany me. Under the circumstances, I hope that what has been done will meet with your approval, as well as that of the Royal Geographical Society.

I have the honour to be, Sir, your very obedient servant,

E. D. YOUNG.

The report proves that though Mr. Edward Young did not see Dr. Livingstone, he procured ample and satisfactory evidence that Musa's story was a tissue of the grossest falsehoods, and for his gallant service the Society tendered him unanimously their thanks.

In 1868, letters dated February 1867 from Bemba (Lake Bangweolo), were received from Dr. Livingstone by Sir Roderick Murchison, which, when read, elicited bursts of enthusiasm from Sir Samuel Baker, and the other geographical associates of the illustrious explorer. In these he stated he had been staying a long time with Mataka, a chief who rules over a division of the Ajáwa tribe.

The reasons for his long silence were that he was unable, after leaving the shores of the Nyassa, to despatch letters to England, until his arrival at Bemba in 10° 10′ S. lat. 31° 50′ long., where he found a party of Zanzibar slave-traders (See ' How I found Livingstone,' Chap. IX., Life in Unyanyembe (continued), Saturday, August 12th, 1871), one of whom was with Speke.

On the 8th July, 1868, Livingstone wrote another

letter from near Lake Bangweolo. The time between these two letters was occupied in convincing himself, by a series of journeys south-west of Lake Tanganika, that the Chambezi River, emptying into Lake Bangweolo, was the same river which flowed into Lake Moero.

On leaving the valley of the Loangwa, which he crossed west of Nyassa, on his way to the Babisa, and to Lunda, he climbed up to a plateau which had an altitude of from three thousand to six thousand feet above sea level, and which extended over an area of about three hundred and fifty miles square. This plateau was generally covered with dense or open forest, was undulating, sometimes cropping up into hills, had a rich soil, and was well watered by streams. East of the plateau were the uplands of Usango, and the west was bounded by the Kone Mountains. As he advanced north, the streams hitherto emptying themselves into the valley of the Loangwa, changed their course with a general trend towards the north-west, or towards the Chambezi, which he believed—his convictions strengthened by much travel north-west and east—to be the headwaters of the Nile. The river Chambezi henceforth became an object of great interest to him, inasmuch as it ran from a plateau to the eastward, west into Lake Bangweolo, thence to Lake Moero, under different names, and further north it was **reported** to run into Lake Ulenge, after a course of some five hundred or six hundred miles.

The above is the pith of his geographical discoveries and report on the watershed of the country between Lakes Tanganika and Nyassa, up to July, 1868.

On the 30th May, 1869, a letter was received by the British Consul at Zanzibar, from Dr. Livingstone, who was at Ujiji.

This letter complains of the disreputable conduct of the driver of certain buffaloes which were sent to Livingstone, and also requests the Consul to be good enough to send to him at Ujiji thirty pieces of sheeting, forty pieces of blue cloth, and four hundred and twenty pounds of red coral beads, besides a few pairs of shoes. He summarises the work remaining for him to accomplish west of the Tanganika, in the following words:—

As to the work to be done by me, it is only to connect the sources which I have discovered from five hundred to seven hundred miles south of Speke and Baker's with their Nile. The volume of water which flows north from lat. 12° S. is so large, I suspect that I have been working at the sources of the Congo as well as those of the Nile I have to go down the eastern line of drainage to Baker's turning-point. Tanganika, Nzige Chowambe (Baker's?) are one water, and the head of it is three hundred miles south of this. The western and central lines of drainage converge into an unvisited lake west or south-west of this. The outflow of this, whether to the Congo or the Nile, I have to ascertain. The people west of this, called Manyema, are cannibals, if Arabs speak truly. I may have to go there first, and down Tanganika, if I come out uneaten, and find my new squad from Zanzibar. I earnestly hope that you will do what you can to help me with the goods and men. £400, to be sent by Mr. Young, must surely have come to you through Fleming and Co.

Sir Roderick, remarking upon this letter after it was read to the Geographical Society, said, " If Livingstone should be supplied with carriers and provisions, he will, I doubt not, follow these waters, and thus being led on perhaps to the Congo, we may be once more subjected to a long and anxious period of suspense."

The letter of the 30th May, 1869, was the last received in Europe direct from Dr. Livingstone, until the autumn of 1872.

In his address of Nov. 8th, 1869, Sir Roderick Murchison, the ever staunch and enduring friend of Dr. Livingstone, says :—

In his wonderful labours Livingstone has not merely been the Christian Missionary and Geographical Explorer. He was also accredited as Her Majesty's Consul to all the native states in the interior. (See the 'Gazette' of March 24th, 1865, p. 1676.) Such being the public mission with which the great traveller was entrusted, let us now confidently believe that Her Majesty's Government will authorize, on his return, the grant of a suitable pension to the man whose labours have shed so much renown on Britain, and that our gracious Sovereign, who has, I know, taken the deepest interest in his career, will reward him with some appropriate token of her goodwill.

Every now and then driblets of news came from Zanzibar, but they were merely vague echoes of Arab opinions and reports, all of which, however, described him to be somewhere west of Tanganika in a state of utter destitution. Few people remained in the belief that Livingstone was alive, despite the publication of his letters of 1867–68–69; nay, the firm belief among the largest number was that the illustrious man had passed the threshold of the unexplored, that bourn whence no traveller returns.

To resolve all doubts and anxieties respecting the fate of Dr. Livingstone, Mr. James Gordon Bennett, junr. (son of the then James Gordon Bennett, sen., proprietor of the 'New York Herald' a daily newspaper published in the city of New York), commissioned the author of this memoir, then pursuing his avocations of Special War

Correspondent in Spain, to equip an expedition for the search and relief of Dr. Livingstone.

My instructions were not to regard expense, to draw whatever sums of money were necessary for the prosecution of the search, and a sufficiency for his relief, until he could communicate with his friends.

A condensed diary of my travels from the date of my instructions will serve to make this brief memoir connected.

16th October, 1869 .   Received my instructions at Paris.
16th November ,, .   Arrive at Port Saïd to witness the opening of the Suez Canal.
16th December ,, .   Arrive at Philæ, and interview Mr. Higginbotham, of Sir Samuel White Baker's Expedition.
16th January, 1870 .   Arrive at Jerusalem.
16th February ,, .   ,,   Constantinople.
16th March ,, .   ,,   the Crimea.
16th April ,, .   ,,   Bakou, on the Caspian Sea.
6th May ,, .   ,,   Teheran, Persia.
1st June ,, .   ,,   Ispahan ,,
16th June ,, .   ,,   Bushire ,,
13th July ,, .   ,,   Muscat, Arabia.
12th ,, ,, .   ,,   Bombay, India.
12th October ,, .   Leave ,, ,,
19th November ,, .   Arrive at Mauritius, Indian Ocean.
31st ,, ,, .   ,,   Mahé Seychelles.
6th January, 1871 .   ,,   Zanzibar, East Coast of Africa.
6th February ,, .   ,,   Bagamoyo—Africa.
18th ,, ,, .   First caravan departs for the interior.
21st ,, ,, .   Second ,, ,,
25th ,, ,, .   Third ,, ,,
11th March ,, .   Fourth ,, ,,
21st ,, ,, .   Fifth and last ,, ,,
23rd June ,, .   Search Expedition arrives at Unyanyembe.
4th August ,, .   ,,   fight with Mirambo, King of Uyoweh.
8th .. ..   returns to Unyanyembe.

20th September, 1871   Search Expedition Departs for Ujiji.

4th November ,,   ,,   Hears of a white man being at Ujiji.

10th   ,,   ,, .   ,,   DISCOVER LIVINGSTONE at Ujiji, on Lake Tanganika.

15th   ,,   ,, .   ,,   Livingstone and self set out to explore north end of Lake Tanganika,

11th December ,, .   Livingstone and self return to Ujiji.

27th   ,,   ,, .   Livingstone and self depart from Ujiji south to Urimba.

31st January, 1872 .   Livingstone and self arrive at Mwaru Ukonongo.

18th February ,, .   Livingstone and self arrive at Unyanyembe, having journeyed 750 miles together.

14th March   ,, .   Livingstone and self part.

7th May   ,, .   Search Expedition arrives at Zanzibar.

1st August   ,, .   Doctor Livingstone's despatches are delivered at the Foreign Office, for which Viscount Enfield gives a receipt in the name of Earl Granville.

The letter wherein the explorer relates best his annoyances, his hopes, his fears, his joys, and his sorrows, is addressed to his old friend Sir Roderick Murchison, who, a few days before the author discovered Livingstone at Ujiji, died of an attack of paralysis. Extracts only may be published here. All those who desire to penetrate to the bottom the causes which lead to his long detention, which has finally culminated in his lamented death, may read these plainly written sentences to advantage.

Unyanyembe, March 13, 1872.

MY DEAR SIR RODERICK,

    *   *   *   *   *   *   *   *

    I have written you a long account of the worry, thwarting, and baffling I have endured in trying to work my way through the cannibal

Manyuema down the central line of drainage—Webb's Lualaba; but it is not worth sending now. I got one letter from you in February, 1870, the first I received from you since one dated 13th March, 1866, but I could not doubt that you had written oftener. The loss of your letters has left me very much in the dark. I did not know that I had a penny of income till Mr. Stanley came, and brought a mail he seized for me here, after it had been fourteen months on the way, and in it I saw the Royal Geographical Society's Report stated that 3,500*l*. had been received for the East African Expedition, which I ventured to suppose means mine. [*This is an error; no such sum was ever given.—Author.*] I don't know where that money is, or if it really is for me; I wish to give my children a little, but I have to ask the Messrs. Coutts to inquire of you about it. I have been trusting to part of the price of my little steamer at Bombay, and determined, pay or no pay, to finish my work if I live. The want of letters was bad; the want of goods was worse, and the only supplies that I virtually received were part of a stock I paid for, and, with Dr. Seward, sent off from Zanzibar, in 1866, to be placed in depôt in Ujiji. They were plundered by the governor here, but I got a share; and it was a part of this share that I took the precaution to reserve at Ujiji in case of extreme need, and found on my return lately. But for this I should have been in beggary; for a lot of goods sent off by ——, through a Banian slave-trader, called Ludha Damji, were all sold off at Ujiji by the drunken half-caste tailor, Shereef, to whom they were entrusted. He must have reported that he had delivered all, for the statement was made in the House of Lords that all my wants had been supplied. He divined on the Koran, and found that I was dead, and then invested all in slaves and ivory for himself. There being no law except that of the gun or dagger, I had to wait in misery till Mr. Stanley came and proved himself truly the good Samaritan.

Another lot of goods was entrusted to Ludha again, and he to slaves again with two free head-men who were thieves. Mr. —— wrote on the 19th October, 1870, that they were all ready to leave, all impediments had been removed, and he remarked rather pleasantly " that they were not perfect, but had expressed willingness to go ;" and then they lay at Bagamoio three and a half months, and no one looked near them. Near the end of February they heard that the consul was coming, and started off two days before his arrival, not to look after them, but to look after the wild beasts along the Ujiji road, and show them to the captain of a man-of-war. Here they refused to go with Mr. Stanley to Ujiji, because of a war which did not prevent him from going, nor him and me from coming, though it is still going on. I seized what remained of the goods after the slaves had feasted sixteen months. On the 18th ultimo one of the head-men died of small-pox; the other non-perfect head-man, besides running riot on my goods, broke the lock and key of Mr. Stanley's store, and plundered his goods too.

Traders get their goods safely by the same carriers we employ; but all our slaves are deeply imbued with the idea that they are not to follow, but force me back. My expedition is looked on with disfavour by all the Banians, who are really and truly the great slave-traders of the country. But for the goods, guns, ammunition, advanced by the Banians, no Arab who travels could go inland to slave. It is by their money that the slave-trade is carried on. The wretched governor here—the same who plundered Burton and Speke pretty freely—is their trade-agent; but simple people call him the "great Sheikh Syde ben Salem," &c. All my letters disappeared here. My sketches, maps, astronomical observations, &c., sent before cholera began, were never heard of beyond this. When Shereef sold off all my stores, except a few pounds of worthless beads, a little coffee and sugar, the governor wrote to me that he had no hand in it. I never said he had. I suppose that the Banians did not sit down and instruct their slaves to rob and baffle me; a mere hint would be sufficient, and then, when they reached me, they swore that the Consul told them not to go with me—and he had paid them more than double freemen's pay. Had they been with me and mutinied, I should have blamed myself as partly the cause, from want of tact or something; but after they had been paid and fed for sixteen months, it was mortifying to find myself virtually without men. I have lost two full years of time, being burdened by one thousand eight hundred miles of extra tramp, and how much waste of money I cannot say, all through the matter of supplies and men being unwittingly committed to slave-dealing Banians and slaves. Mr. Webb sent nine packets and packages in the eleven months of his (Stanley's) trip. The sixteen months that elapsed from my last mail of November, 1870, included those eleven months, but Mr. Webb's messengers were not allowed to lie feasting at Bagamoio, in sight of the consulate, for three and a half months, as mine were. Nor were the Banian low cunning and duplicity instilled into their minds. —— may probably be able to explain it all.

* * * * * * * *

Now I am all right. I have abundant supplies of all I need to finish
my work. Some I seized from ——'s slaves, and Mr Stanley gave me
more; so I am thankful to say that I am now better off than when I
got a share of what I sent off in 1866. I feel quite exhilarated by the
prospect of starting back as soon as Mr. Stanley can send me fifty free
men from the coast. Don't imagine, from my somewhat doleful tone,
that I am trying to excite commiseration and pity. When Zanzibar
failed me so miserably, I sat down at Ujiji only till I should become
strong, and then work my way down to Mteza. I am now strong and
well and thankful, and wish only to be let alone, to finish by the rediscovery of the ancient fountains. In ——'s letter he talks hazily
about Tanganyika and my going home from being tired, and the
work being finished by another. You remember that I recommended
him for the task, and he would not accept it from you without a
good salary, and some thing to fall back on afterwards. I went unsalaried; the sole hope I had was the statement in yours of March 13,
1866 : "Do your work, and leave pecuniary matters to Young and me."
I have been tired often, and began again. I have done it all on foot,
except eight days' illness with pneumonia and the trip down Tanganyika.
I could never bear the scorn the Portuguese endure in being carried
when quite well. I am sorry to have to complain of any one; but the
loss of time, useless tramps, and waste of money, are truly no faults of
mine. If you share in ——'s idea that I must have been all this time
trying if Tanganyika communicated with Albert Nyanza, I regret the
destruction of my sketch maps and astronomical observations; but in
a former case an imperfect sketch map was made the means of fleecing
me, and in the lost maps I did my duty notwithstanding.

Tanganyika is of no importance in connection with the Nile, except
in a very remote degree. The interesting and great valley lies altogether
west of it. In that valley there are five great lakes and three large
rivers—Bangweolo, Moero, Kamolondo, Lake Lincoln and another,
which the slaves forced me to leave as the Unknown Lake. The large
rivers—Bartle Frere's, otherwise Lufira ; Webb's Lualaba—the central
line of drainage ; then Sir Paraffin Young's Lualaba,* with its name
further down Lomame—all go into the central Webb's Lualaba ; Bartle
Frere's through Lake Kamolondo ; Young's (I have been obliged to
knight him to distinguish him from our friend the man-of-war's man)
Lualaba through Lake Lincoln, and, as Lomame into Webb's, and four
or five days beyond the confluence into the Unknown Lake, which,

* Sir Paraffin Young is a facetious term applied by Dr. Livingstone to Mr
James Young of Kelley, the inventor of paraffine

from the great westing I made, some 7° W. of Ujiji, must be part of Petherick's branch. This is the interesting field. The correlation of the structure and economy of the watershed with these great lakes and lacustrine rivers is the theme of my prize. When you heard that the sources were further south than any one dreamed, in the exuberance of your kindly heart you were going to award something to B——, F——, and A——, for having dreamed about it. You had no idea that the watershed was seven hundred miles long and the fountains innumerable. I smiled, of course good naturedly, to think that you would need to divide the seven hundred miles among the three, and thereby show a great physiological discovery by your friends—the division of labour in dreaming. I am much more savage now than you, and any one who competes after I have given my own explanation will be ordered out for instant execution without benefit of clergy. I doubt if there is an Upper Nile basin. I found it a gradual slope from the sources down, and I reached the altitude ascribed to Gondokoro. Mr. Stanley will tell you about what he saw of Tanganyika. I declined to examine it in 1869 because Ujijians wished to mulct me of the few goods I had, and there was no inducement to spend all in patching up Burton's failure rather than work out the great main line of drainage from the watershed.

I earnestly hope that you will be so far recovered when this reaches you as to live in comfort, though not in the untiring activity of your earlier years. The news of our dear Lady Murchison's departure filled me with sincere sorrow. Had I known that she kindly remembered me in her prayers it would have been a source of great encouragement. I often thought that Admiral Washington and Admiral Beaufort looked down from their abodes of bliss, to which she has gone, with approbation. Sir Francis's words to the Arctic explorers, that they " were going on discovery and not on survey," have been a guide to me, and I am in hopes that, in addition to discovery, my disclosures may lead to the suppression of the East Coast Slave Trade by Banian British subjects. If the good Lord of all grants me this, I shall never grudge the toil, time, and trouble I have endured. I pray that His blessing may descend on you according to your need, and am, &c.

(Signed)　　Daviᴅ Livingstone.

P.S.—Mr. Stanley will be at the Langham Place Hotel when this reaches you ; attentions to him and James Gordon Bennett will gratify me. Agnes will keep my London box and my Journal, which I send home, sealed, by Mr. Stanley.　　　　　　　　　　　　D. L.

The account of the Search and Relief Expedition, despatched by the proprietor of the 'New York Herald,' is given in the following book, 'How I found Livingstone.' On arriving at Zanzibar from the successful search after the traveller, May 7, 1872, I despatched to Dr. Livingstone as per request a force of fifty-seven men, who were destined to convey his supplies from Unyanyembe westward until should have resolved the problem to his satisfaction whether the Lualaba was the Nile River or the Congo. The following are their names :—

1. *Chowpereh.*
2. *Sarmean.*
3. *Tabwu.*
4. *Amanvu.*
5. *Sunguru.*
6. *Msa.*
7. *Hassani.*
8. *Belali.*
9. *Khamisi.*
10. *Rojab.*
11. *Toufiki.*
12. *Twakali.*
13. *Khatib.*
14. *Shumari.*
15. *Hassani.*
16. *Tom.*
17. *Chanda.*
18. *Furjalla.*
19. *Mabruki (Burton).*
20. *Ulimengo.*
21. *Zaidi.*
22. *Maganod.*
23. *Mukudum.*
24. *Bukhet.*
25. *Baraka.*
26. *Hamadi (guide).*
27. *Makawa.*
28. *Sunguru (Stanley).*
29. *Jumah.*
30. *Sheban.*
31. *Moeni Falami.*
32. *Resasi.*
33. *Khamseen.*
34. *Mabruki (Speke).*
35. *Khamisi (Stanley).*
36. *Uredi Manwa Sera (Leader).*
37. *Majvara (Boy).*
38. *Ferousi.*
39. *Ramadan.*
40. *Ferahan.*
41. *Mdamungu.*
42. *Muriko.*
43. *Pangawassi.*
44. *Hamadi Swadi.*
45. *Khamisi.*
46. *Mabruk (Stanley).*
47. *Salina.*
48. *Carras Ferrar (Nassick Boy).*
49. *John Wainwright (Nassick Boy).*
50. *Richard Rutton (Nassick Boy).*
51. *Matthew Wellington (Nassick Boy).*
52. *Benjamin Rutton (Nassick Boy).*
53. *Jacob Wainwright (Nassick Boy).*
54. *Mvalim.*
55. *Hamadi (Stanley).*
56. *Mabruki (Unyanyembe).*
57. *Rojab the Litile.*

The people whose names are mentioned in the above list arrived at Unyanyembe about the middle of July, 1872, having conducted themselves remarkably well, and having performed their contract faithfully during the journey from Zanzibar to Unyanyembe. The leader of the men, Uledi Manwa Sera, who had accompanied Speke and Grant, and subsequently performed faithful service to the 'Herald' Expedition, was chosen by me for his good sense, and was highly recommended to Livingstone.

But there remained at Unyanyembe with Livingstone, during my journey to Zanzibar after parting from him, his own faithful souls who had followed his fortunes from March, 1866 to 1873, and had accompanied him during journeys—with extraordinary fidelity—which measured in the aggregate over eight thousand miles. As everything now connected with poor Livingstone has a melancholy interest, the names of these faithful people should not be forgotten; they are

1. Susi (chief, and confidential servant).
2. Chumah (second leader) from Nassick School.
3. Hamoydah, released from slavery on the Zambezi.
4. Edward Gardner, from Nassick School.
5. Halimah, cook, and wife of Hamoydah.

On the 2nd August, 1872 Livingstone properly equipped with an Expedition numbering about eighty souls, inclusive of his own people and the fifty-seven despatched to him by myself, with stores sufficient to last him three years, left Unyanyembe for Lunda, in a south-south-westerly direction. A glance at the map accompanying this volume will indicate the route he would naturally follow as far as Mpokwa on the borders of Ufipa. Each camping-place is plainly marked out, and located. Beyond Mpokwa is new ground to European travellers, but Arab information has enabled us to trace his subsequent footsteps through Ufipa, Uemba, or Wemba, Liemba, Marungu, and thence to Lunda and Lake Bangweolo. Which way he travelled beyond Lake Bangweolo is left to conjecture for the present.

In January, 1872, a circular was issued by the Royal Geographical Society, inviting subscriptions from the British public, in order that they might make a determined effort to FIND and RELIEVE LIVINGSTONE. This society, of which Livingstone was an associate, subscribed the sum of £500. The interest the public entertained in respect to Livingstone was signally manifested on this occasion by the munificent sums which were in a very short time subscribed.

The sums received by the society, inclusive of its own grant of £500, amounted to £4,889 1s. 5d., to which was promised an additional sum of £296 3s. 0d. The balance of a Government grant of £1,000 granted by Lord Clarendon in 1870, amounting to £557 7s. 10d., was also transferred to the Relief Fund, and a half-year's interest on £2,500 Exchequer Bills, amounting to £30 10s. 10d., swelled the total to the magnificent amount of £5,770 3s. 1d.

On the strength of this fund collected by the Geographical Society for the search and relief of their illustrious associate, an Expedition was equipped, and despatched at short notice on the 7th of February, 1872, under the com mand of Lieut. Llewellyn Dawson, Lieut. William Henn, and W. Oswell Livingstone, son of the traveller.

In the concluding chapters of 'How I found Living-stone,' I have related how this Expedition, arriving at Zanzibar after the purchase at considerable outlay of the goods necessary for the Expedition, withdrew from the mission they had undertaken to accomplish.

Out of the Relief Fund was expended for outfit, passage money, instruments, maps, presents for native chiefs, advertising, stationary, stamps, &c., sundry small charges, pay of natives employed at Zanzibar, pay of natives and goods supplied for the Native Relief Expedition, despatched by the author on his return from Livingstone; miscel-laneous expenses at Zanzibar, loss on sale of goods, on the disbanding of the Dawson Expedition; passages to Eng-land of the leaders, the sum of £2,671 15s. 11d., of which sum £2,359 6s. 6d. was made by the return of the Dawson Expedition—a dead loss to the Society's fund for the relief of Dr. Livingstone.

The balance then remaining in the hands of the Society amounted to £3,175 16s. 6d. How to employ this for the benefit of the traveller was an anxious question to the Royal Geographical Society. Some proposed that the money should be placed in the bank to draw interest, for the benefit of Livingstone's family. Others, composing the majority, proposed that a second Expedition should be equipped for the finding and relief of Livingstone, which was accordingly done, though now it appears, considering the melancholy history of this Expedition, as if it might have been the wiser course to have adopted the first suggestion. However, there is no blame attached to the trustees of the fund, for it may be assumed that they thought themselves acting for the best.

The second Relief Expedition, under the command of Lieut. Lovett Cameron, R.N., Lieut. Cecil Murphy, R.A., Dr. W. E. Dillon, R.N.—to whom was shortly attached as a junior member and assistant Robert Moffatt, nephew of Livingstone—arrived at Zanzibar, under the auspices of Sir Bartle Frere, on the 9th of February, 1873.

These young gentlemen were fully equipped with from two to four years' supplies; and it was reported by the Society to be the best equipped expedition which ever left Zanzibar for the purpose of exploration.

During the early part of April the advance caravan departed from Bagamoyo for the interior. News of its advance was received regularly, and everything promised well for a time; but in May news was received of the death of young Moffatt near a place called Simbo. (See 'How I found Livingstone,' chap. v.)

The remaining members of the Expedition arrived in Unyanyembe about the middle of September, only to hear shortly after the sad, sad account of Livingstone's death from the lips of the faithful Chumah, who, with a select party of men, had hurried forward to Unyanyembe in advance of the main portion of Livingstone's Expedition, that he might transmit the intelligence of the mournful event by first caravan proceeding to Zanzibar.

Close upon the footsteps of Chumah came the solemn funeral procession which had borne the body of the illustrious traveller many hundreds of miles, through the many tribes that dwell between Bangweolo and Unyan-yembe.

After but a short stay at Unyanyembe the Expedition continued their return march to Zanzibar under the charge of Dr. W. E. Dillon and Lieut. Cecil Murphy, while Lieut. Cameron is reported to have continued his march to Ujiji for the purpose of securing a box of papers deposited with Moeni-Kheri by Livingstone.

Soon after the return march had begun towards the coast, Dr. Dillon, rendered delirious by his sufferings from fever, and afflicted with blindness, committed suicide.

The following compose the most circumstantial details received up to the beginning of April, 1874 :—

SUEZ, SUNDAY.

The body of Dr. Livingstone, arrived per *Malwa*, left this morning for England, *viâ* the Canal. Dr. Livingstone died on the 4th of May, at Muilala, in the kingdom of Bisa, of dysentery, after five days' march through the marshy country. The body, which was escorted by Lieutenant Murphy to the coast, left Zanzibar on the 12th inst., in charge of Arthur Laing, who proceeds *viâ* Brindisi with his papers and effects. The body will go to Southampton, attended by Jacob, Dr. Livingstone's servant. The body was disemboweled and embalmed by a native, and was put on a bush to dry. Twelve days afterwards it was placed in two coffins.

The following is the copy of a telegram forwarded to the London office of the 'New York Herald':—

" The *Malwa* arrived off Suez at eleven on Saturday night, having Mr. Arthur Laing and Jacob Wainwright aboard, with the body of Dr. Livingstone. He had been ill with chronic dysentery for several months past. Although well supplied with stores and medicines, he seems to have had a presentiment that the attack would prove fatal. He rode a donkey, but was subsequently carried, and thus arrived at Muilala beyond Lake Bemba, in Bisa country, when he said, 'Build me a hut to die in.' The hut was built by his followers, who first made him a bed. He suffered greatly, groaning day and night. On the third day he said, 'I am very cold; put more grass over the hut. His followers did not speak or go near him. Kitumbo,* Chief of Bisa, sent flour and beans, and behaved well to the party. On the fourth day Livingstone became insensible, and died about midnight. Majwara, his servant, was present. His last entry in the diary was on April 27th. He spoke much and sadly of his home and family. When first seized he told his followers he intended to exchange everything for ivory, to give to them, and to push on to Ujiji and Zanzibar, and try to reach England. On the day of his death his followers consulted what to do. They determined to preserve the remains. They were afraid to inform the chief of Livingstone's death. The servants removed the body to another hut, around which they built a high fence, to insure privacy. They opened the body and removed the internals, which were placed in a tin box and buried inside the fence, under a large tree. Jacob Wainwright cut an inscription on the tree as follows: —'Dr. Livingstone died on May 4th, 1873,' and superscribed the name of the head-man, Susi. The body was preserved in salt, and dried in the sun for twelve days. Kitumbo was then informed of the death, and beat drum and fired as a token of respect, and allowed the followers to remove the body, which was placed in a coffin formed of bark, then journeyed to Unyanyembe about six months, sending an advance party with information, addressed to Livingstone's son, which met Cameron. The latter sent back bales of cloth and powder. The body arrived at Unyanyembe ten days after advance party, and rested there a fortnight. Cameron, Murphy, and Dillon together there, latter very ill—blind, and mind affected, suicided at Kasagera, buried there.

" Here Livingstone's remains were put in another bark case, smaller, done up in a bale to deceive natives, who objected to the passage of the corpse, which was thus carried to Zanzibar, Livingstone's clothing, papers, and instruments accompanying the body. When ill Livingstone prayed much. At Muilala he said 'I am going home.' Chumah remains at Zanzibar.

" Mr. Webb, American Consul at Zanzibar, is on his way home, and has letters handed to him by Murphy from Livingstone, for Stanley, which he will deliver personally only.

" Geographical news follows. After Stanley's departure the doctor left Unyanyembe, rounded the south end of Lake Tanganika, and

---

* Kitumbo is another way of spelling the Chitimbwa of Dr. Livingstone.

travelled south of Lake Bemba or Bangweolo, crossed it south to north, then along east side, returning north through Marungu to Muilala. All papers sealed and addressed to Secretary of State, are in charge of Arthur Laing, a British merchant, from Zanzibar."

Majwara, who seems according to the above report to have attended Livingstone during his last hours, is a boy about sixteen years old, and a native of Uganda. I obtained him from an Arab caravan while he was afflicted with a sore disease. He accompanied me to Ujiji, when Livingstone's medical knowledge, with the aid of some of my medicines, soon cured him.

When about to despatch the second Relief Expedition to Unyanyembe, Majwara voluntarily offered to return to Livingstone, and he was accordingly sent to him in the capacity of personal attendant, gun and over-coat bearer. It appears that the boy Majwara has faithfully performed his duties to his master, and had become a favourite, for he was the only one permitted to hear the last sighs of the dying explorer.

Livingstone's description of the place near which he breathed his last on the 4th of May, 1873, cannot be better given than in his own words in his letter to the 'Herald.'

At a spot some eighty miles S.W. of the south end of Tanganika stands the stockaded village of the chief Chitimbwa. A war had commenced between a party of Arabs numbering six hundred guns and the chief of the district situated west of Chitimbwa while I was at the south end of the lake. The Arabs hearing that an Englishman was in the country, naturally inquired where he was; and the natives, fearing that mischief was intended, denied positively that they had ever seen him. They then strongly advised me to take refuge on an inhabited island; but not explaining their reasons, I am sorry to think that I suspected them of a design to make me a prisoner, which they could easily have done by removing the canoes—the island being a mile from the land. They afterwards told me how nicely they had cheated the Arabs and saved me from harm. The end of the lake is in a deep cup-shaped cavity, with sides running sheer down at some parts 2,000 feet into the water. The rocks, of red clay schist, crop out among the sylvan vegetation, and here and there pretty cascades leap down the precipices, forming a landscape of surpassing beauty. Herds of elephants, buffaloes, and antelopes enliven the scene, and, with the stockaded villages embowered in palms along the shores of the peaceful water, realise the idea of Xenophon's Paradise. When about to leave the village of Mbette, or Pambette, down there, and climb up the steep path by which we had descended, the wife of the chief came forward and said to her husband and the crowd looking at us packing up our things, "Why do you allow this man to go away? He will certainly fall into the hands of the Mazitu (here called Batuba) and you know it and are silent." On inquiry it appeared certain that these marauders were then actually plundering the villages up above the precipices at the foot of which we sat. We waited six days, and the villagers kept watch on an ant-hill outside the stockade, all the time looking up for the enemy. When we did at last ascend we saw the well-known lines of march of the Mazitu—straight as arrows through the country, without any regard to the native paths; and in the details of their plundering, for in this case there was no bloodshed, we found that the really benevolent lady had possessed accurate information. On going thence round the end of the lake, we came to the village of Karambo, at the confluence of a large river, and the head man refused us a passage across. "Because," said he, "the Arabs have been fighting with the people west of us; and two of their people have since been killed, though only in search of ivory. You wish to go round by the west of the lake, and the people may suppose that you are Arabs; and I dare not allow you to run the risk of being killed by mistake." On seeming to disbelieve, Karambo drew his finger across his throat, and said "If at any time you discover that I have spoken falsely, I give you leave to cut my throat." That same afternoon two Arab slaves came to the village in search of ivory, and confirmed every word Karambo had spoken. Having previously been much plagued by fever, and without a particle of medicine, it may have been the irritability produced by that disease that made me so absurdly pigheaded in doubting the intentions of my really kind benefactors three several times. The same cause may be in operation when modern traveller are unable to say a civil word about the natives; cr if it must be admitted, for instance, that savages will seldom dece've you if placed on their honour, why must we turn up the whites of our eyes, and say it is an instance of the anomalous character of the Africans? Being heaps of anomalies ourselves, it would be just as easy to say that it is interesting to find other people like us. The tone which we modern travellers affect is that of infinite superiority, and it is utterly nauseous to see at every step our great and noble elevation cropping out in low cunning.

Unable to go north-west, we turned off to go due south one hundred and fifty miles or so; then proceeded west till we were past the disturbed district, and again resumed our northing. But on going some sixty miles we heard that the Arab camp was twenty miles further south, and we went to hear the news. The reception was extremely kind, for this party consisted of gentlemen from Zanzibar, and of a very different stamp from the murderers we afterwards saw in Manyuema. They were afraid that the chief with whom they had been fighting might flee southwards, and that in going that way I might fall into his hands. Being now recovered, I could readily believe them, and they being eager ivory traders, as readily believed me when I asserted that a continuance of hostilities meant shutting up the ivory market. No one would like to sell if he stood a chance of being shot. Peace, therefore, was to be made; but the process of "mixing blood," forming a matrimonial alliance with the chief's daughter, &c., &c., required three and a half months, and during long intervals of that time I remained at Chitimbwa's. The stockade was situated by a rivulet, and had a dense grove of high, damp-loving trees round a spring on one side, and open country, pretty well cultivated, on the other. It was cold, and over 4,700 feet above the sea, with a good deal of forest land and ranges of hills in the distance. The Arabs were on the west side of the stockade, and one of Chitimbwa's wives at once vacated her house on the east side for my convenience. Chitimbwa was an elderly man, with grey hair and beard, and of quiet, self-possessed manners. He had five wives, and my hut being one of the circle which their houses formed, I often sat reading or writing outside, and had a good opportunity of seeing the domestic life in this Central African harem, without appearing to be prying. The chief wife, the mother of Chitimbwa's son and heir, was somewhat aged, but was the matron in authority over the establishment. The rest were young, with fine shapes, pleasant countenances, and nothing of the West Coast African about them.

Three of them had each a child, making, with the eldest son, a family of four children to Chitimbwa. The matron seemed to reverence her husband, for when she saw him approaching she invariably went out of the way, and knelt down till he had passed. It was the time of year for planting and weeding the plantations, and the regular routine work of all the families in the town was nearly as follows: Between three and four o'clock in the morning, when the howling of the hyænas and growling of the lions or leopards told that they had spent the night fasting, the first human sounds heard were those of the good wives knocking off the red coals from the ends of the sticks in the fire, and raising up a blaze to which young and old crowded for warmth from the cold, which at this time is the most intense of the twenty-four hours. Some Bangé smoker lights his pipe, and makes the place ring with his nasty screaming, and stridulous coughing. Then the cocks begin to crow (about four A.M.), and the women call to each other to make ready to march. They go off to their gardens in companies, and keep up a brisk, loud conversation, with a view to frighten away any lion or buffalo that may not yet have retired, and for this the human voice is believed to be efficacious. The gardens, or plantations, are usually a couple of miles from the village. This is often for the purpose of securing safety for the crops from their own goats or cattle, but more frequently for the sake of the black loamy soil near the banks of rivulets. This they prefer for maize and dura (*Holcus sorghum*), while for a small species of millet, called mileza, they select a patch in the forest, which they manure by burning the branches of trees. The distances which the good wives willingly go to get the best soil adapted for different plants make their arrival just about dawn. Fire has been brought from home, and a little pot is set on with beans or pulse—something that requires long simmering; and the whole family begins to work at what seems to give them real pleasure. The husband, who had marched in front of each little squad with a spear and little axe over his shoulder, at once begins to cut off all the sprouts on the stumps left in clearing the ground. All bushes also fall to his share, and all the branches of tall trees too hard to be cut down are piled round the root to be fired when dry. He must also cut branches to make a low fence round the plantation, for few wild beasts like to cross over anything having the appearance of human workmanship. The wart-hog having a great weakness for ground-nuts, otherwise called pig-nuts (*Arachis hypogæa*), must be circumvented by a series of pitfalls, or a deep ditch, and earthern dyke all round the nut-plot. If any other animal has made free with the food of the family, papa carefully examines the trail of the intruder—makes a deep pitfall in it, covers it carefully over—and every day it is a most interesting matter to see whether the thief has been taken for the pot. The mother works away vigorously with her hoe, often adding new patches of virgin land to that already under cultivation. The children help by removing the weeds and grass which she has uprooted into heaps to be dried and burned. They seem to know and watch every plant in the field. It is all their own; no one is stinted as to the land he may cultivate; the more they plant the more they have to eat and to spare. In some parts of Africa the labour falls almost exclusively on the women, and the males are represented as atrociously cruel to them. It was not so here, nor is it so in Central Africa generally—indeed the women have often decidedly the upper hand. The clearances by law and custom were the work of the men; the weeding was the work of the whole family, and so was the reaping. The little girls were nursing baby under the shade of a watch-house perched on the tops of a number of stakes about twelve or fourteen feet high, and to this the family adjourns when the dura is in ear to scare away birds by day and antelopes by night. About eleven A.M. the sun becomes too hot for comfortable work, and all come under the shade of the lofty watch-tower, or a tree left for the purpose. Mamma serves out the pottage, now thoroughly cooked, by placing a portion into each pair of hands— it is bad manners here to receive any gift with but one hand. They eat it with keen appetites, and with so much relish that for ever afterwards they think that to eat with the hand is far nicer than with a spoon. Mamma takes and nurses baby while she eats her own share. Baby seems a general favourite, and is not exhibited till he is quite a little ball of fat. Every one then takes off beads to ornament him. He is not born with a silver spoon in his mouth, and one may see poor mothers who have no milk mix a little flour and water in the palm of the hand, and the little sisters look on with intense interest to see the little stranger making a milk-bottle of the side of the mother's hand, the crease therein just allowing enough to pass down. They are wide-awake little creatures, and I thought that my own little ones imbibed a good deal of this quality from I don't know what. I never saw such unwearied energy as they displayed the livelong day, and that too in the hot season. The meal over, the wife, and perhaps daughter, goes a little way into the forest and collects a bundle of dry wood, and, with the baby slung on her back, in a way that suggests the flattening of the noses of many Africans, the wood, on her head and the boy carrying the hoe, the party wends home. Each wife has her own granary, in which the produce of the garden is stowed. It is of the beehive shape of the huts, only the walls are about twelve feet high, and it is built on a stage about eighteen inches from the ground. It is about five feet in diameter, and roofed with wood and grass. The door is near the roof, and a ladder, made by notches being cut in a tree, is used to enable the owner to climb into it. The first thing the good wife does on coming home is to get the ladder, climb up, and bring down millet or dura grain sufficient for her family. She spreads it in the sun, and while this is drying or made crisp occurs the only idle time I have seen in the day's employment. Some rested, others dressed their husband's or neighbour's hair, others strung beads. I should have liked to have seen them take life more easily, for it is as pleasant to see the negro reclining under his palm as it is to look at the white lolling on his ottoman. But the great matter is, they enjoy their labour, and the children enjoy life as human beings ought, and have not the sap of life squeezed out of them by their own parents as is the case with nailers, glass-blowers, stockingers, fustian-cutters, brick-makers, &c., in England. At other periods of the year, when harvest is home, they enjoy more leisure and jollification with their native beer called "pombe," but in no case of free people, living in their own free land under their own free laws, are they like what slaves become.

When the grain is dry it is pounded in a large wooden mortar to separate the scales from the seed. A dexterous toss of the hand drives all the chaff to one corner of the vessel. This is lifted out, and then the dust is tossed out by another peculiar up-and-down, half horizontal motion of the vessel, difficult to describe or do, which leaves the grain quite clean. It is then ground into fine meal by a horizontal motion of the upper millstone, to which the whole weight is applied, and at each stroke the flour is shoved off the further end of the nether mill-stone. The flour finished, late in the afternoon, at the time maidens go forth to draw water, the lady poises a huge earthen pot on her head, fills it full at the rivulet, and, though containing ten or twelve gallons, balances it on her head, and, without lifting up her hands, walks jauntily home. They have meat but seldom, and make relishes for the porridge into which the flour is cooked of the leaves of certain wild and cultivated plants; or they roast some ground nuts, grind them fine, and make a curry. They seem to know that oily matter such as the nuts contain is requisite to modify their otherwise farinaceous food, and some even grind a handful of castor-oil nuts with the grain for the same purpose. The husband having employed himself in the afternoon in making mats for sleeping on, in preparing skins for clothing, or in making new handles for hoes or cutting out wooden bowls, joins the family in the evening, and all partake abundantly of the chief meal of the day before going off to sleep. They have considerable skill in agriculture, and great shrewdness in selecting the soils proper for different kinds of produce. When Bishop Mackenzie witnessed their operations in the field, he said to me, " When I was in England and spoke in public meetings about our mission, I mentioned that among other things I meant to teach them agriculture, but now I see that the Africans know a great deal more about it than I do." One of his associates, earnestly desiring to benefit the people to whom he was going, took lessons in basket-making before he left England ; but the specimens of native workmanship he met with everywhere led him to conclude that he had better say nothing about his acquisition ; in fact, he could "not hold a candle to them." The foregoing is as fair an example of the every-day life of the majority of the people in Central Africa as I can give.

The Peninsular and Oriental steamship *Malwa* arrived at Southampton on the 16th of April. As she hove to abreast of Netley Hospital she was boarded by Admiral Sir William Hall, William F. Webb, Esq., of Newstead Abbey, General Rigby, formerly Political Resident at Zanzibar, Colonel J. A. Grant, companion of Speke, the Rev. Robert Moffatt, father-in-law of Dr. Livingstone, William Oswell Livingstone, the great traveller's second son, the Rev. Horace Waller, formerly of the Zambezi Mission, and now Vicar of Leytonstone, and Arthur Laing, Esq., of Zanzibar, Mr. Fenton, representative of the 'Times,' Mr. Walter Wood, of the 'Standard,' Mr. Mackenzie, of the 'Telegraph,' and Mr. Senior, of the 'Daily News,' and other gentlemen connected with the reception of the remains of Livingstone at Southampton.

Mr. Thomas Steele Livingstone, who was a passenger on board, was soon recognised, and the Rev. Mr. Price, after seeking for Jacob Wainwright, brought him to the above-mentioned gentlemen, by whom he was warmly applauded for the fidelity which had characterised his service with the great traveller.

The information supplied by Jacob Wainwright, on being examined by me on board the *Malwa*, confirmed what was obtained from him by the 'Herald' correspondent at Suez. Beyond this he stated that Livingstone first had a relapse of dysentery at Kasera, in Ukonongo (see 'How I found Livingstone,' p. 288), while he was but twenty days from Unyanyembe, and that all the streams they journeyed across from Unyanyembe flowed westerly and northerly, which proves conclusively now that the Tanganika has no outlet in any part of the north-western, northern, eastern, or southern coasts of the lake, and that the mystery will be found to be between the north end of the island of Muzimu and the southern end of Uguhha on the western shore, which no doubt will be discovered by Lieutenant Cameron, who must have reached Ujiji in the early part of January of this year.

After the arrival of the *Malwa* in the dock, the coffin containing the mortal relics of the traveller was lifted from the mailroom of the ship and placed on board another steamer, to be conveyed to the Royal Pier, to be received ceremoniously by the Mayor and the Corporation of Southampton, and the Committee of the Royal Geographical Society; and while this was being done all hats were reverently doffed. Every flag was at half-mast. Mostly all the citizens of Southampton wore the mark of sorrow.

About eleven o'clock the procession from the Audit House, in the High Street, arrived at the Royal Pier, where the hearse, drawn by four horses, was in waiting. In a few moments the procession resumed its line of march to the South Western Station in the following order :—

The Worshipful the Mayor.

The Sheriff.

The Senior and Junior Bailiffs.

The Aldermen.

The Councillors.

The Magistrates of the Borough.

The Pier and Harbour Commissioners.

Sir F. Perkins, M.P.

THE HEARSE.

The Relatives of Dr. Livingstone.

The President and Fellows of the Royal Geographical Society.

The Clergy and Ministers of the Town.

The President of the Medical Society of Southampton.

Members of the Medical Society and of the Medical Profession generally.

The Consuls of different Nations.

The Guardians of the Southampton Incorporation

The Council of the Hartley Institution.

The Members of the Southampton School Board.

The Committee of each Literary and Philosophical Society in the Town.

The Representatives of other Public Bodies.

The Mayor, Aldermen, and the other members of the Corporation wore their official robes and insignia, but with crape on their arms. The maces and regalia were also encased in black.

The crowds were vast—people from all sections of the County of Hants had gathered in the streets on this day, to pay the only tribute in their power to all that was left of the greatest of African explorers. The manifestation of their sentiments was remarkably impressive.

On the arrival of the hearse at the station, it was placed on a truck, and a special train conveyed it to London. At Waterloo Station a hearse and mourning coaches were in readiness to take the coffin and the Committee of Arrangements to the rooms of the Royal Geographical Society, where the coffin was covered with a pall to await burial, and to be inspected by the public.

The exhibition of the respect of the good people of Southampton towards the remains of Livingstone was only what might have been expected from a people so appreciative of usefulness and virtue as the English. The worthy mayor—Edwin Jones, Esq., has faithfully demonstrated it by the large-minded hospitality with which he received the Committee of the Geographical Society and the friends of the traveller, and the perfection of the arrangements for the reception of the body.

Meanwhile an appeal has been made to the British public by Baroness Burdett-Coutts, Lord Kinnaird, Sir Bartle Frere, Hon. A. Kinnaird, W. F. Webb, Esq., Rev. Horace Waller, James Young, Esq., of Kelley, and W. C. Oswell, Esq., for means to support the family of the traveller, which no doubt will be liberally responded to.

In the following portion of a letter which Captain Webb

brought the author from Zanzibar, which was given to him by Lieutenant Murphy, Dr. Livingstone expresses his thanks to me for the promptitude and care with which I despatched to him his supplies from Zanzibar.

* Lake Bangweolo, South Central Africa.

MY DEAR STANLEY,

I wrote hurriedly to you when on the eve of starting from Unyanyembe, and the mind being occupied by all the little worries incidental to the starting of the caravan, I felt, and still feel, that I had not expressed half the gratitude that wells up in my heart for all the kind services you have rendered to me. I am also devoutly thankful to the loving Father above for helping you through all your manifold Masika (rainy season) toils, and bringing you safely to Zanzibar, with your energies unimpaired, and with a desire to exert yourself to the utmost in securing all the men and goods needed for this my concluding trip.

I am perpetually reminded that I owe a great deal to you for the drilling of the men you sent. With one exception, the party is working like a machine. I give my orders to Manwa Sera, and never need to repeat them. I parted with the Arab sent without any disagreement. He lost one of the new donkeys at Bagamoyo. He then put the two stragglers on the chain without fastening the free end, and they wisely walked off with the bridle, bits and all—then suffered a lazy Mombasian to leave the cocoa somewhere, and got five dotis at Unyanyembe. Well, no one either before or after that could get any good out of him.

Added to this, the Arab showed a disposition to get a second $500, supposing we should be one month over the year, though he could do nothing except through my native headmen. I therefore let him go, and made Manwa Sera, Chowpereh, and Susi, heads of departments at $20 if they gave satisfaction. This they have tried faithfully to do, and hitherto have been quite a contrast to Bombay, who seemed to think that you ought to please him.

Majwara has behaved perfectly—but is slow! slow!! and keeps your fine silver teapot, spoons, and knives as bright as if he were an English butler; gets a cup of coffee at five A.M. or sooner, if I don't

---

* This letter must have been written some time after Christmas of 1872.

advise him to lie down again; walks at the head of the caravan as drummer, this instrument being the African sign of peace as well as of war. He objected at first to the office, because the drum had not been bought by either you or me. Some reasons are profound—this may be one of them.

The fruits, fish, pork, biscuits, fowl have been selected far better than I could have done it. No golden syrup could be found, or you would have sent some. The tea was very nicely secured.

Your wish for joy of the plum-pudding was fulfilled, though it would have been better had we been nearer to Chambezi, where we spent Christmas, to enjoy it. I keep most of your handsome presents of champagne for a special occasion. One rifle was injured at Bagamoyo; your revolver and splendid rifle were all I could desire for efficiency. The fifteen-shooter cartridges are not satisfactory, but everything else gives so much satisfaction that I could not grumble though I were bilious. I thank you very much and very sincerely for all your kind generosity.

My reason for publishing the above is to show the reader how susceptible of gratitude was the heart of Dr. Livingstone. It is a complete and certain proof that if proper care had been taken to send him supplies Livingstone would not only have been most grateful, but would undoubtedly have been living to-day in England to express his thanks in person for the assistance he received while in Africa.

As the author of this memoir was one of the pall-bearers at the funeral of Dr. Livingstone, it is necessary that some writer unconnected with the ceremony should be left to describe what took place at Westminster Abbey, on Saturday, April 18th, 1874.

Yesterday morning, Dr. Livingstone was buried in Westminster Abbey amidst such testimonies of profound respect and mournful veneration as has seldom been shown for the fate of any since the death of the lamented Prince Consort. There was something touching in the fate of poor Livingstone. His long absence—the loss of his wife in the heart of the wilds of Africa—the rumours of his death, which were only contradicted to be again revived, the search of the gallant Stanley for him, which at length set all anxiety and misgivings at rest, and then the last news of all—the death of the great explorer. None believed in this, because none wished to do so, but kept on hoping against hope, till the terrible calamity of the fate which had overtaken the great man was found at last to be but too true. The fate of Mungo Park, of Clapperton, of Lander, in no way excited any interest in their discoveries, or more than a passing regret for their loss. Africa was then an unknown land; and, to say the truth, people cared as little about it as they knew. Lately it has been opened up to us like a region of romance, by Baker, Speke, Grant, and last, and greatest of all, the marvellous man who was to rest in England's sanctuary of sanctuaries. That the greatest of the great of this land lie beneath its sandy soil we all know, but among the mighty dead whose plain gravestones chequer its pavement, or whose monuments adorn its walls, there are none more distinguished for courage and moderation, for singleness of purpose and the simplicity of his great philanthropy, than David Livingstone. How we have all followed him in his adventures from the time that the lion first seized him thirty years ago and left such fractures in the bones of his arm as led, even after the lapse of about a year after death, to the instant identification of the body by the great surgeon who attended him when last in England! There seems to be a sort of lurking suspicion among some that the body after all may not be that of the famous geographer, and this no doubt may be accounted for by the fact that so many rumours have obtained credence as to his death. But if there is anything that was incontestably proved it is that the poor, emaciated remains which were yesterday laid under the centre of the nave of our great Abbey, were those of the most famous explorer of any time, ancient or modern. Not only has Sir William Fergusson identified what he had done to the bones of the left arm, but with the body the faithful servant, Jacob Wainwright, has brought all the diaries, the instruments, the journals, and even the poor clothes in which Livingstone breathed his last. If these are not proofs of identity, it would be hard to say what is required. They are but far too certain.

The Abbey had the usual quiet, solemn, and stately aspect, that makes, as Coleridge says, a religion in stone. The choir had a line of black cloth down it, which was met by another from the door of the

western cloisters, where the body was to be received, and in the centre
of the nave was a black aperture, amid the black cloth, of the shape of
a coffin, and just rimmed round with a broad band of white. Without
such a precaution one might have inadvertently slipped into it in the
early gloom of the morning, but as the day wore on during service the
sun came out in a flood of light, which, pouring through the stained
windows, tinted the columns and ancient monuments with all the hues
of the rainbow. The grave of Livingstone is in the very centre of the
west part of the nave. The spot is in the central line, exactly half-
way between the western doors and the choir. On the north side is
the grave of the Countess of Clanricarde, and on the other side that of
Thomas Campion, a noted watchmaker. Close by lie Major Rennell,
and Telford and Stephenson, the engineers. Like all the graves in
Westminster Abbey, it is not a deep one, for there are no vaults under
the Abbey, and the soil is so sandy that it is scarcely safe to go far down.
As it was, both sides of the grave had to be shored to prevent the sand
from slipping. These supports, however, were hidden by black cloth,
which gave, as usual, a most forbidding aspect to the large aperture
and one of most unusual depth. The central position of the grave
made the whole ceremony far more conspicuous than was the
case with the funerals of Lord Lytton or Lord Macaulay. That
of Dickens was absolutely private. Before the procession started
from the house of the Geographical Society in Saville Row, there
was a funeral service conducted by the Rev. H. W. Hamilton,
Minister of the Established Church of Scotland. The pall was
adorned with wreaths of flowers, one of them, composed of white
azaleas and delicate ferns, having been sent by her Majesty. The
service consisted of the 39th Psalm, and three other short passages
from the Bible—Mark xiii. 33–37, 1 Thessalonians, iv. 13–18, and
Rev. vii. 9–17—followed by an extempore prayer. The procession
was then formed, and passed slowly through the streets to the Abbey.
It was nearly twelve o'clock before those who were fortunate
to have tickets began to take their seats. Without a single exception, all were more or less in mourning—that is to say, some in
deep mourning, others only in ordinary black. The choir soon filled
and those beyond it made up a throng in the nave and the aisles.
But all was as silent as the grave itself; not even the usual mild
whisper of a waiting congregation went round. Earlier than all came
a group of seven ladies, some very young, and all dressed in the
deepest mourning They took their places in the seats allotted to

mourners in the southern side of the choir, just in front of the two
black velvet trestles on which the coffin was to be placed. Each lady
had with her a large chaplet of myrtles and violets or camellias and
cypresses, which were ranged in front of them, and, in spite of their
beauty, were, with their associations, a melancholy-looking row.
Towards twelve the Abbey began to fill, and there was a faint though
audible noise of the crowd which was waiting without to watch the
arrival of what was most truly a melancholy procession. Soon after
twelve o'clock such of the public as had tickets were allowed into the
building, and filled the aisles, while others who were more privileged
occupied the Sacrarium. By-and-bye all spaces were filled, and even
in the clerestory there were some lining the old monks' walk, and
looking down with a curious aspect from rather a dizzy height on to
the crowd below. At a quarter to one the bells of St. Margaret's
began to toll. The bell of the Abbey, like that of St. Paul's, never
tolls but for Royalty. The coffin was conveyed through Dean's Yard to
the entrance of the western cloisters. Thence past the time-worn fret-
work of carved mullions and pilasters, which were old and grey when
Africa was only a name, and America an unknown sound. Through
these cloisters it was reverently borne at a very slow pace.*

The pall-bearers were Mr. Henry M. Stanley, who was foremost on the
right, the Rev. Horace Waller, Vicar of Leytonstone, Dr. John Kirk,
Mr. Edward Daniel Young, who had been his companions on the
Zambezi; W. C. Oswell, Esq., Major-General Sir Thomas Steele, W.
F. Webb, Esq. (of Newstead Abbey), who had been his companions in
South Central Africa, in the region of Lake Ngami, and lastly Jacob
Wainwright, the coloured boy from Nassick School, who had been sent
by Mr. Stanley from Zanzibar to form part of the escort of the great
explorer on his last journey from Unyanyembe to Lake Bangweolo.

Among the mourners, were Thomas Steele Livingstone, William
Oswell Livingstone, Agnes Livingstone, and Mary Anna Livingstone,
the dead traveller's children; Janet and Anna Livingstone, his sisters;
Mrs. Livingstone, widow of the Rev. Charles Livingstone; Rev. Robert
Moffatt, his father-in-law, Livingstone and Bruce Moffatt, young rela-
tives of the traveller; Sir W. Fergusson, Rev. H. W. Hamilton, Dr. J.
Loudon, Mr. James Hannan, the Duke of Sutherland, Right Hon. Sir
Bartle Frere, K.C.B. (President Royal Geographical Society), Sir H. C.
Rawlinson, K.C.B. (Vice-President Geographical Society), Mr. K. R.
Murchison, General Rigby, Colonel J. A. Grant, C.B., Mr. J. Murray,

* From the " Sunday Dispatch."

Mr. J. Young, jun. (of Kelley), Vice-Admiral Baron de la Roncière le Noury (President French Geographical Society), Dr. Hooker (President Royal Society), Mr. H. W. Bates (Assistant Secretary Royal Geographical Society), Lord Houghton, the Provost of Hamilton, Mr. J. B. Braithwaite, Mr. C. R. Markham, Mr. R. H. Major (Secretaries Royal Geographical Society), Rev. Dr. Stuart, Mr. T. Nicholson, Mr. Ralston, (friends of the family), the Lord Provost of Edinburgh, Mr. Duncan M'Laren, M.P., Mr. James Cowan, M.P., Mr. Josiah Livingstone, the Lord Provost of Glasgow, Dr. Watson (Pres. Faculty Phys. Glasgow), Baillie Walls (Chief Magistrate, Glasgow), Baillie Bain, Mr. Edwin Jones (the Mayor of Southampton), Sir Frederick Perkins, Mr. A. Laing, Mr. Elliott (who brought the body from Southampton); Mr. George Sauer, Mr. Edmund Yates, and Mr. J. H. MacGahan, Correspondents of the 'New York Herald;' the Duke of Manchester, the Earl of Ducie, Lord Cottesloe, Lord Kinnaird, the Bishops of Lincoln and Sierra Leone, the Lord Mayor and City Remembrancer and twenty members of the Corporation of London ; the Mayor of Nottingham, the Provost of Dumbarton, the Provost and Town Clerk of Ayr, Lady Frere, Lady Rawlinson, Lady Strangford, Hon. Mrs. Forester, Mrs. W. F. Webb, of Newstead Abbey, Mrs. and Miss Goodlake, Sir Rutherford Alcock, Sir T. Fowell Buxton, Sir C. Nicholson, Sir C. Russell, M.P., Sir W. Thompson, Sir Harry Verney, Major-General Sir F. Goldsmid, the Right Hon. Russell Gurney, M.P., the Hon. G. C. Brodrick, Hon. A. F. Kinnaird, Count Gosloff, Chevalier Cadorna (Italian Minister), Viscount Duprat (Portuguese Consul General), Mr. Moran (United States Chargé d'Affairs), Capt. Francis R. Webb and lady, from Zanzibar U.S. Consulate, Count Munster (the German Ambassador), General Scott, Admirals Codrington, Collinson Sir W. Hall, Sherard Osborn, and Ommanney ; the Rev. Wm. Monk, who presented Dr. Livingstone in 1867 to the Vice Chancellor in the Cambridge Senate House; Colonel Ouseley, Professor Brock, and a deputation from the Anthropological Institute, and other deputations from the Royal Botanical Society of London, National Temperance League, Social Science Association, African Section of the Society of Arts, Reception Committee of Southampton Church Missionary Society, London Missionary Society, British and Foreign Anti-Slavery, East African, and other societies.

Most notable among the throng, as they carry the coffin to the grave, are the African travellers who constitute such a natural guard of honour for this dead man.   Foremost among them in right of gallant special service, and nearest to Livingstone's head, stands Stanley—sun-tanned anew from Ashantee—whose famous march of relief gives America the full right to celebrate at this moment, as we know she is doing, simultaneously with England, the obsequies of the explorer. But for Stanley, Livingstone would have died long back, without aid or news from us; but near him are Grant, the discoverer, along with Speke, of the Nyanza; Young, who was with Livingstone in old days, and who sailed the Nyassa Lake and the Shire River in quest of him; Oswell, tanned and grizzled with hunting and exploring under an African sun; and beside them Rigby, and Moffat, and Webb, the godfather of the Lualaba, and the faithful friend who buried Mrs. Livingstone in the sad day of the separation of husband and wife; Colonel Shelley, of Lake Ngami; Waller, of the Zambesi; Galton, Reade—what a band of Africani! Such a gathering of sunburnt visages and far-travelled men was never seen before; and, indeed, the list might be lengthened with the names of a hundred other famous travellers present, who listen with wistful looks round their great dead chieftain, while Tallis's hymn is being sung, after the lesson read by Canon Conway. It is a well-known hymn—one which sings of ultimate rest after wandering—the only real rest for all toils and travels. These are the words :—

" O God of Bethel, by whose hand
   Thy people still are fed,
Who through this weary pilgrimage
   Hast all our fathers led ;

" Our vows, our prayers, we now present
   Before thy throne of grace;
God of our Fathers ! be the God
   Of each succeeding race.

" Through each perplexing path of life
   Our wandering footsteps guide;
Give us each day our daily bread,
   And every want provide.

" O spread thy covering wings around
   Till all our wanderings cease,
And at our Father's loved abode
   Our souls arrive in peace ! "

After the conclusion of this hymn, in which the congregation joined with much effect, the coffin is borne down the choir into the centre of the nave, where towards its western end the grave has been prepared. Here also among the dead lying around are ancient far-travelled worthies—companionable ashes for those which are now to be consigned to the same unbroken and majestic rest. Sir John Chardin lies nigh at hand, who saw Suleiman II. crowned Monarch of Persia two hundred years gone by—a much-wandering Knight, "qui sibi nomen fecit eundo;" and Major James Rennell, who wrote on the geography of Herodotus and founded the African Society. The pall is withdrawn, and the polished oaken coffin is prepared for lowering into the dark cavity which opens so narrowly and so abruptly in the Abbey pavement, while the choir sing "Man that is born of a woman" to Croft's setting, and then the tender strains of Purcell's, "Thou knowest Lord." This is the very last that will be seen of "this our dear brother," and now indeed strong men are fain to bend their heads, and sobs, not from women only, mingle with the alternate sighing and rejoicing of the solemn music. The dizzy edges of the clerestory, eighty feet overhead, are crowded with people looking down from that perilous eminence upon the throng round the grave, and shadows are seen at many of the Abbey windows, of others peering through for a glimpse of the "last scene of all." As the precious burden descends the inscription on the plate may be seen—"David Livingstone, born at Blantyre, Lanarkshire, Scotland, 19th March, 1813, died at Ilala, Central Africa, 4th May, 1873." And then there falls the "dust to dust;" and, looking at the solemn dusky faces of the two Africans, Wainwright and little Kalulu, Mr. Stanley's boy, who are standing among the nearest, the mind reverts to that widely-different scene a year ago, when Livingstone, after much pain, which is not spared to the best and kindliest, gave up his gallant, loving, pious spirit to his Master and Maker, and when yonder negro lad read over him the very service which has now again been so grandly celebrated for him

"With pomp and rolling music, like a King."

The African—a simple-looking, quiet, honest lad—attracts many eyes as he stands by the grave; he knows alone of all present the aspect of that other burial spot, and to him more than all this one must be impressive. But he takes his wonder, like his duty, stolidly — his thoughts appear lost in his master's memory. Alas! that master did not dream in the supreme closing hour of loneliness and agony that his body would find such honour and peaceful repose at home. Of that and of all other reward, however, he never thought while he wrought patiently and constantly his appointed work for the sake of Africa—tramping, discovering, noting, hunting out the slave-hunters, and leaving himself and the results of his self-sacrifice to Heaven. And Heaven, which has given him this sweet rest in English earth, will assuredly bring forth fruits of his labour—of that we may remain well convinced; meanwhile, the work of England for Africa must henceforward begin in earnest where Livingstone left it off.

The service draws to its end with the " Forasmuch " and the following prayers, read in a clear, sustained voice of the deepest solemnity and feeling by Dean Stanley ; and then once more the organ speaks the unspeakable—as music only can—sounding forth, "I heard a voice from heaven." But the very finest musical passage of all comes last in the beautiful anthem of Handel, " His body rests in peace, but his name liveth evermore." Tenderly and meditatively the first sad dreamy sentence is set, as though it were uttered by some spirit of melody looking downward into the quiet, silent haven of the grave, where all the storms and toils of mortal life are over. Radiantly and triumphantly comes afterwards the jubilant antiphon, as though the same gentle spirit had conceived it, mindful of the sacred words, "Come ye blessed children of my Father, receive the kingdom prepared for you from the beginning of the world." Last of all, there rains down upon the lid of Livingstone's coffin a bright and fragrant shower of wreaths and fare-well-flowers from a hundred living hands; and each of those present takes a long parting glance at the great traveller's resting-place, and at the oaken coffin buried in the spring blossoms, and palms, and garlands, wherein lies " as much as could die " of the good, great-hearted, loving, fearless, and faithful David Livingstone.*

ILALA—MAY, 1873.†

The swarthy followers stood aloof,
Unled—unfathered ;
He lay beneath that grassy roof,
Fresh-gathered.

* From the ' Daily Telegraph.'   † From the ' Times

He bade them, as they passed the hut,
  To give no warning
Of their still faithful presence but
    " Good Morning."

To him, may be, through broken slee]
  And pains abated,
These words were into senses deep
    Translated.

Dear dead salutes of wife and child,
  Old kirkyard greetings;
Sunrises over hill-sides wild—
    Hearts-beatings.

Welcoming sounds of fresh-blown seas,
  Of homeward travel,
Tangles of thought's last memories
    Unravel.

*   *   *   *   *

'Neath England's fretted roof of fame—
  With flowers adorning
An open grave—comes up the same
    " Good Morning."

Morning's o'er that weird continent
  Now slowly breaking—
Europe her sullen self-restraint
    Forsaking.

Mornings of sympathy and trust
  For such as bore
Their Master's spirit's sacred crust
    To England's shore.

                        HOUGHTON

DR. LIVINGSTONE AT WORK ON HIS JOURNAL.

HOW I FOUND LIVINGSTONE.

CHAPTER. I.

INTRODUCTORY. MY INSTRUCTIONS TO FIND AND RELIEVE
LIVINGSTONE.

On the sixteenth day of October, in the year of our Lord
one thousand eight hundred and sixty-nine, I was in
Madrid, fresh from the carnage at Valencia. At 10 A.M.
Jacopo, at No.— Calle de la Cruz, handed me a telegram :
It read, "Come to Paris on important business." The
telegram was from Mr. James Gordon Bennett, jun., the
young manager of the 'New York Herald.'

Down came my pictures from the walls of my apartments on the second floor; into my trunks went my
books and souvenirs, my clothes were hastily collected,
some half washed, some from the clothes-line half dry,
and after a couple of hours of hasty hard work my
portmanteaus were strapped up and labelled "Paris."

At 3 P.M. I was on my way, and being obliged to stop
at Bayonne a few hours, did not arrive at Paris until the
following night. I went straight to the 'Grand Hotel,'
and knocked at the door of Mr. Bennett's room.

"Come in," I heard a voice say.

Entering, I found Mr. Bennett in bed.

"Who are you ?" he asked.

" My name is Stanley," I answered.

" Ah, yes! sit down; I have important business on hand for you."

After throwing over his shoulders his robe-de-chambre Mr. Bennett asked, " Where do you think Livingstone is ?"

" I really do not know, sir."

" Do you think he is alive ?"

" He may be, and he may not be," I answered.

" Well, I think he is alive, and that he can be found, and I am going to send you to find him."

" What !" said I, " do you really think I can find Dr Livingstone? Do you mean me to go to Central Africa ?"

" Yes ; I mean that you shall go, and find him wher-ever you may hear that he is, and to get what news you can of him, and perhaps "—delivering himself thought-fully and deliberately—" the old man may be in want :— take enough with you to help him should he require it. Of course you will act according to your own plans, and do what you think best—BUT FIND LIVINGSTONE !"

Said I, wondering at the cool order of sending one to Central Africa to search for a man whom I, in common with almost all other men, believed to be dead, " Have you considered seriously the great expense you are likely to incur on account of this little journey ?"

" What will it cost ?" he asked abruptly.

" Burton and Speke's journey to Central Africa cost between £3,000 and £5,000, and I fear it cannot be done under £2,500."

" Well, I will tell you what you will do. Draw a thousand pounds now; and when you have gone through that, draw another thousand, and when that is spent, draw another thousand, and when you have finished that, draw another thousand, and so on; but, FIND LIVINGSTONE."

Surprised but not confused at the order—for I knew that Mr. Bennett when once he had made up his mind was not easily drawn aside from his purpose—I yet thought, seeing it was such a gigantic scheme, that he had not quite considered in his own mind the pros and cons of the case; I said, " I have heard that should your father die you would sell the ' Herald ' and retire from business."

"Whoever told you that is wrong, for there is not money enough in New York city to buy the ' New York Herald.' My father has made it a great paper, but I mean to make it greater. I mean that it shall be a newspaper in the true sense of the word. I mean that it shall publish whatever news will be interesting to the world at no matter what cost."

" After that," said I, " I have nothing more to say. Do you mean me to go straight on to Africa to search for Dr. Livingstone ? "

" No! I wish you to go to the inauguration of the Suez Canal first, and then proceed up the Nile. I hear Baker is about starting for Upper Egypt. Find out what you can about his expedition, and as you go up describe as well as possible whatever is interesting for tourists; and then write up a guide—a practical one— for Lower Egypt; tell us about whatever is worth seeing and how to see it.

" Then you might as well go to Jerusalem; I hear Captain Warren is making some interesting discoveries there. Then visit Constantinople, and find out about that trouble between the Khedive and the Sultan.

" Then—let me see—you might as well visit the Crimea and those old battle-grounds. Then go across the Caucasus to the Caspian Sea; I hear there is a Russian expedition bound for Khiva. From thence you may get through Persia to India; you could write an interesting letter from Persepolis.

"Bagdad will be close on your way to India; suppose you go there, and write up something about the Euphrates Valley Railway. Then, when you have come to India, you can go after Livingstone. Probably you will hear by that time that Livingstone is on his way to Zanzibar; but if not, go into the interior and find him. If alive, get what news of his discoveries you can; and if you find he is dead, bring all possible proofs of his being dead. That is all. Good-night, and God be with you."

"Good-night, Sir," I said; "what it is in the power of human nature to do I will do; and on such an errand as I go upon, God will be with me."

I lodged with young Edward King, who is making such a name in New England. He was just the man who would have delighted to tell the journal he was engaged upon what young Mr. Bennett was doing, and what errand I was bound upon.

I should have liked to exchange opinions with him upon the probable results of my journey, but I dared not do so. Though oppressed with the great task before me, I had to appear as if only going to be present at the Suez Canal. Young King followed me to the express train bound for Marseilles, and at the station we parted: he to go and read the newspapers at Bowles' Reading-room— I to Central Africa and—who knows?

There is no need to recapitulate what I did before going to Central Africa.

I went up the Nile and saw Mr. Higginbotham, chief engineer in Baker's Expedition, at Philæ, and was the means of preventicg a duel between him and a mad young Frenchman, who wanted to fight Mr. Higginbotham with pistols, because that gentleman resented the idea of being taken for an Egyptian, through wearing a fez cap. I had a talk with Capt. Warren at Jerusalem, and descended one of the pits with a sergeant of engineers to see the marks of the Tyrian workmen on the foundation-stones of the Temple of Solomon. I visited the mosques of Stamboul with the Minister Resident of the United States, and the American Consul-General. I travelled over the Crimean battle-grounds with Kinglake's glorious books for reference in my hand. I dined with the widow of General Liprandi at Odessa. I saw the Arabian traveller Palgrave at Trebizond, and Baron Nicolay, the Civil Governor of the Caucasus, at Tiflis. I lived with the Russian Ambassador while at Teheran, and wherever I went through Persia I received the most hospitable welcome from the gentlemen of the Indo-European Telegraph Company; and following the examples of many illustrious men, I wrote my name upon one of the Persepolitan monuments. In the month of August, 1870, I arrived in India.

On the 12th of October I sailed on the barque 'Polly' from Bombay to Mauritius. As the 'Polly' was a slow sailer, the passage lasted thirty-seven days. On board this barque was a William Lawrence Farquhar—hailing from Leith, Scotland—in the capacity of first-mate. He was an excellent navigator, and thinking he might be useful to me, I employed him; his pay to begin from the date we should leave Zanzibar for Bagamoyo. As there was no opportunity of getting to Zanzibar direct, I took ship to Seychelles. Three or four days after arriving at Mahé, one of the Seychelles group, I was fortunate enough to get a passage for myself, William Lawrence

Farquhar, and an Arab boy from Jerusalem, who was to act as interpreter—on board an American whaling vessel, bound for Zanzibar, at which port we arrived on the 6th of January, 1871.

I have skimmed over my travels thus far, because these do not concern the reader. They led over many lands, but this book is only a narrative of my search after Livingstone, the great African traveller. It is an Icarian flight of journalism, I confess ; some even have called it Quixotic; but this is a word I can now refute, as will be seen before the reader arrives at the " Finis."

I have used the word " soldiers " in this book. The armed escort a traveller engages to accompany him into East Africa is composed of free black men, natives of Zanzibar, or freed slaves from the interior, who call themselves " askari," an Indian name which, translated, means " soldiers." They are armed and equipped like soldiers, though they engage themselves also as servants; but it would be more pretentious in me to call them servants, than to use the word " soldiers ;" and as I have been more in the habit of calling them soldiers than " my watuma " —servants—this habit has proved too much to be overcome. I have therefore allowed the word " soldiers " to appear, accompanied, however, with this apology.

But it must be remembered that I am writing a narrative of my own adventures and travels, and that until I meet Livingstone, I presume the greatest interest is attached to myself, my marches, my troubles, my thoughts, and my impressions. Yet though I may sometimes write, " my expedition," or " my caravan," it by no means follows that I arrogate to myself this right. For it must be distinctly understood that it is the " ' New York Herald ' Expedition," and that I am only charged with its command by Mr. James Gordon Bennett, the proprietor of the 'New York Herald,' as a salaried employé of that gentleman.

One thing more; I have adopted the narrative form of relating the story of the search, on account of the greater interest it appears to possess over the diary form, and I think that in this manner I avoid the great fault of repetition for v hich some travellers have been severely criticised.

CHAPTER II.

ZANZIBAR.

On the morning of the 6th January, 1871, we were sailing through the channel that separates the fruitful island of Zanzibar from Africa. The high lands of the continent loomed like a lengthening shadow in the grey of dawn. The island lay on our left, distant but a mile, coming out of its shroud of foggy folds bit by bit as the day advanced, until it finally rose clearly into view, as fair in appearance as the fairest of the gems of creation. It appeared low, but not flat ; there were gentle elevations cropping hither and yon above the languid but graceful tops of the cocoa-trees that lined the margin of the island, and there were depressions visible at agreeable intervals, to indicate where a cool gloom might be found by those who sought relief from a hot sun. With the exception of the thin line of sand, over which the sap-green water rolled itself with a constant murmur and moan, the island seemed buried under one deep stratum of verdure.

The noble bosom of the strait bore several dhows speeding in and out of the bay of Zanzibar with bellying sails. Towards the south, above the sea line of the horizon, there appeared the naked masts of several large ships, and to the east of these a dense mass of white, flat-topped houses. This was Zanzibar, the capital of the island;—which soon resolved itself into a pretty large and compact city, with all the characteristics of Arab architecture. Above some of the largest houses lining the bay front of the city streamed the blood-red banner of the Sultan, Seyd Burghash, and the flags of the American, English, North German Confederation, and French Consulates. In the harbor were thirteen large ships, four Zanzibar men-of-war, one English man-of-war—the 'Nymphe,' two American, one French, one Portuguese, two English, and two German merchantmen, besides numerous dhows hailing from Johanna and Mayotte of the Comoro Islands, dhows from Muscat and Cutch—traders between India, the Persian Gulf, and Zanzibar.

It was with the spirit of true hospitality and courtesy that Capt. Francis R. Webb, United States Consul, (formerly of the United States Navy), received me. Had this gentleman not rendered me such needful service, I must have condescended to take board and lodging at a house known as " Charley's," called after the proprietor, a Frenchman, who has won considerable local notoriety for harboring penniless itinerants, and manifesting a kindly spirit always, though hidden under such a rugged front; or I should have been obliged to pitch my double-clothed American drill tent on the sandbeach of this tropical island, which was by no means a desirable thing.

But Capt. Webb's opportune proposal to make his commodious and comfortable house my own; to enjoy myself, with the request that I would call for whatever I might require, obviated all unpleasant alternatives.

One day's life at Zanzibar made me thoroughly conscious of my ignorance respecting African people and things in general. I imagined I had read Burton and Speke through, fairly well, and that consequently I had penetrated the meaning, the full importance and grandeur, of the work I was about to be engaged upon. But my estimates, for instance, based upon book information, were simply ridiculous,—fanciful images of African attractions were soon dissipated, anticipated pleasures vanished, and all crude ideas began to resolve themselves into shape.

I strolled through the city. My general impressions are of crooked, narrow lanes, white-washed houses, mortar-plastered streets, in the clean quarter;—of seeing alcoves on each side, with deep recesses, with a fore-ground of red-turbaned Banyans, and a back-ground of flimsy cottons, prints, calicoes, domestics and what not; or of floors crowded with ivory tusks; or of dark corners with a pile of unginned and loose cotton; or of stores of crockery, nails, cheap Brummagem ware, tools, &c., in what I call the Banyan quarter;—of streets smelling very strong— in fact, exceedingly malodorous, with steaming yellow and black bodies, and woolly heads, sitting at the doors of miserable huts, chatting, laughing, bargaining, scolding, with a compound smell of hides, tar, filth, and vegetable refuse, in the negro quarter;—of streets lined with tall, solid-looking houses, flat roofed, of great carved doors with large brass knockers, with baabs sitting cross-legged watching the dark entrance to their masters' houses; of a shallow sea-inlet, with some dhows, canoes, boats, an odd steam-tub or two, leaning over on their sides in a sea of mud which the tide has just left behind it; of a place called "M'nazi-Moya," "One Cocoa-tree," whither Europeans wend on evenings with most languid steps, to inhale the sweet air that glides over the sea, while the day is dying and the red sun is sinking westward; of a few graves of dead sailors, who paid the forfeit of their lives upon arrival in this land; of a tall house wherein lives Dr. Tozer, " Missionary Bishop of Central Africa," and his school of little Africans ; and of many other things, which got together into such a tangle, that I had to go to sleep, lest I should never be able to separate the moving images, the Arab from the African ; the African from the Banyan ; the Banyan from the Hindi ; the Hindi from the European, &c.

Zanzibar is the Bagdad, the Ispahan, the Stamboul, if you like, of East Africa. It is the great mart which invites the ivory traders from the African interior. To this market come the gum-copal, the hides, the orchilla weed, the timber, and the black slaves from Africa. Bagdad had great silk bazaars, Zanzibar has her ivory bazaars ; Bagdad once traded in jewels, Zanzibar trades in gum-copal ; Stamboul imported Circassian and Georgian slaves ; Zanzibar imports black beauties from Uhiyow, Ugindo, Ugogo, Unyamwezi and Galla.

The same mode of commerce obtains here as in all Mohammedan countries—nay, the mode was in vogue long before Moses was born. The Arab never changes. He brought the custom of his forefathers with him when he came to live on this island. He is as much of an Arab here as at Muscat or Bagdad ; wherever he goes to live he carries with him his harem, his religion, his long robe, his shirt, his slippers, and his dagger. If he penetrates Africa, not all the ridicule of the negroes can make him change his modes of life. Yet the land has not become Oriental ; the Arab has not been able to change the atmosphere. The land is semi-African in aspect ; the city is but semi-Arabian.

To a new-comer into Africa, the Muscat Arabs of Zanzibar are studies. There is a certain *empressement* about them which we must admire. They are mostly all travellers. There are but few of them who have not been in many dangerous positions, as they penetrated Central Africa in search of the precious ivory; and their various experiences have given their features a certain unmistakable air of self-reliance, or of self-sufficiency; there is a calm, resolute, defiant, independent air about them, which wins unconsciously one's respect. The stories that some of these men could tell, I have often thought, would fill many a book of thrilling adventures.

For the half-castes I have great contempt. They are neither black nor white, neither good nor bad, neither to be admired nor hated. They are all things, at all times; they are always fawning on the great Arabs, and always cruel to those unfortunates brought under their yoke. If I saw a miserable, half-starved negro, I was always sure to be told he belonged to a half-caste. Cringing and hypocritical, cowardly and debased, treacherous and mean, I have always found him. He seems to be for ever ready to fall down and worship a rich Arab, but is relentless to a poor black slave. When he swears most, you may be sure he lies most, and yet this is the breed which is multiplied most at Zanzibar.

The Banyan is a born trader, the beau-ideal of a sharp money-making man. Money flows to his pockets as naturally as water down a steep. No pang of conscience will prevent him from cheating his fellow man. He excels a Jew, and his only rival in a market is a Parsee; an Arab is a babe to him. It is worth money to see him labor with all his energy, soul and body, to get advantage by the smallest fraction of a coin over a native. Possibly the native has a tusk, and it may weigh a couple of frasilahs, but, though the scales indicate the weight, and the native declares solemnly that it must be more

than two frasilahs, yet our Banyan will asseverate and
vow that the native knows nothing whatever about it,
and that the scales are wrong ; he musters up courage to
lift it—it is a mere song, not much more than a frasilah.
" Come," he will say, " close, man, take the money and
go thy way. Art thou mad ?" If the native hesitates, he
will scream in a fury; he pushes him about, spurns the
ivory with contemptuous indifference,—never was such
ado about nothing; but though he tells the astounded
native to be up and going, he never intends the ivory
shall leave his shop.

The Banyans exercise, of all other classes, most influence on the trade of Central Africa. With the exception
of a very few rich Arabs, almost all other traders are
subject to the pains and penalties which usury imposes.
A trader desirous to make a journey into the interior,
whether for slaves or ivory, gum-copal, or orchilla weed,
proposes to a Banyan to advance him $5,000, at 50, 60,
or 70 per cent. interest. The Banyan is safe enough not
to lose, whether the speculation the trader is engaged
upon pays or not. An experienced trader seldom loses,
or if he has been unfortunate, through no deed of his own,
he does not lose credit ; with the help of the Banyan, he
is easily set on his feet again.

We will suppose, for the sake of illustrating how trade
with the interior is managed, that the Arab conveys by
his caravan $5,000's worth of goods into the interior. At
Unyanyembe the goods are worth $10,000 ; at Ujiji, they
are worth $15,000 : they have trebled in price. Five
doti, or $7·50, will purchase a slave in the markets of
Ujiji that will fetch in Zanzibar $30. Ordinary men-
slaves may be purchased for $6 which would sell for $25
on the coast. We will say he purchases slaves to the full

extent of his means—after deducting $1,500 expenses of carriage to Ujiji and back—viz. $3,500, the slaves—464 in number, at $7·50 per head—would realize $13,920 at Zanzibar! Again, let us illustrate trade in ivory. A merchant takes $5,000 to Ujiji, and after deducting $1,500 for expenses to Ujiji, and back to Zanzibar, has still remaining $3,500 in cloth and beads, with which he purchases ivory. At Ujiji ivory is bought at $20 the frasilah, or 35 lbs., by which he is enabled with $3,500 to collect 175 frasilahs, which, if good ivory, is worth about $60 per frasilah at Zanzibar. The merchant thus finds that he has realized $10,500 net profit! Arab traders have often done better than this, but they almost always have come back with an enormous margin of profit.

The next people to the Banyans in power in Zanzibar are the Mohammedan Hindis. Really it has been a debateable subject in my mind whether the Hindis are not as wickedly determined to cheat in trade as the Banyans. But, if I have conceded the palm to the latter, it has been done very reluctantly. This tribe of Indians can produce scores of unconscionable rascals where they can show but one honest merchant. One of the honestest among men, white or black, red or yellow, is a Mohammedan Hindi called Tarya Topan. Among the Europeans at Zanzibar, he has become a proverb for honesty, and strict business integrity. He is enormously wealthy, owns several ships and dhows, and is a prominent man in the councils of Seyd Burghash. Tarya has many children, two or three of whom are grown-up sons, whom he has reared up even as he is himself. But Tarya is but a representative of an exceedingly small minority.

The Arabs, the Banyans, and the Mohammedan Hindis, represent the higher and the middle classes. These classes own the estates, the ships, and the trade. To these classes bow the half-caste and the negro.

The next most important people who go to make up the mixed population of this island are the negroes. They consist of the aborigines, Wasawahili, Somalis, Comorines, Wanyamwezi, and a host of tribal representatives of Inner Africa.

To a white stranger about penetrating Africa, it is a most interesting walk through the negro quarters of the Wanyamwezi and the Wasawahili. For here he begins to learn the necessity of admitting that negroes are men, like himself, though of a different colour; that they have passions and prejudices, likes and dislikes, sympathies and antipathies, tastes and feelings, in common with all human nature. The sooner he perceives this fact, and adapts himself accordingly, the easier will be his journey among the several races of the interior. The more plastic his nature, the more prosperous will be his travels.

Though I had lived some time among the negroes of our Southern States, my education was Northern, and I had met in the United States black men whom I was proud to call friends. I was thus prepared to admit any black man, possessing the attributes of true manhood or any good qualities, to my friendship, even to a brother-hood with myself; and to respect him for such, as much as if he were of my own colour and race. Neither his colour, nor any peculiarities of physiognomy should debar him with me from any rights he could fairly claim as a man. "Have these men—these black savages from pagan Africa," I asked myself, "the qualities which make man loveable among his fellows? Can these men —these barbarians—appreciate kindness or feel resent-ment like myself?" was my mental question as I travelled through their quarters and observed their actions. Need I say, that I was much comforted in observing that they were as ready to be influenced by passions, by loves and hates, as I was myself; that the keenest observation failed to detect any great difference between their nature and my own?

The negroes of the island probably number two-thirds of the entire population. They compose the working-class, whether enslaved or free. Those enslaved perform the work required on the plantations, the estates, and gardens of the landed proprietors, or perform the work of carriers, whether in the country or in the city. Outside the city they may be seen carrying huge loads on their heads, as happy as possible, not because they are kindly treated or that their work is light, but because it is their nature to be gay and light-hearted, because they have conceived neither joys nor hopes which may not be gratified at will, nor cherished any ambition beyond their reach, and therefore have not been baffled in their hopes nor known disappointment.

Within the city, negro carriers may be heard at all hours, in couples, engaged in the transportation of clove-bags, boxes of merchandise, &c., from store to " go-down " and from " go-down " to the beach, singing a kind of monotone chant for the encouragement of each other, and for the guiding of their pace as they shuffle through the streets with bare feet. You may recognise these men readily, before long, as old acquaintances, by the consistency with which they sing the tunes they have adopted. Several times during a day have I heard the same couple pass beneath the windows of the Consulate, delivering themselves of the same invariable tune and words. Some might possibly deem the songs foolish and silly, but they had a certain attraction for me, and I considered that they were as useful as anything else for the purposes they were intended.

The town of Zanzibar, situate on the south-western shore of the island, contains a population of nearly one hundred thousand inhabitants; that of the island altogether I would estimate at not more than two hundred thousand inhabitants, including all races.

The greatest number of foreign vessels trading with this port are American, principally from New York and Salem. After the American come the German, then come the French and English. They arrive loaded with American sheeting, brandy, gunpowder, muskets, beads, English cottons, brass-wire, china-ware, and other notions, and depart with ivory, gum-copal, cloves, hides, cowries, sesamum, pepper, and cocoa-nut oil.

The value of the exports from this port is estimated at $3,000,000, and the imports from all countries at $3,500,000.

The Europeans and Americans residing in the town of Zanzibar are either Government officials, independent merchants, or agents for a few great mercantile houses in Europe and America.

The climate of Zanzibar is not the most agreeable in the world. I have heard Americans and Europeans condemn it most heartily. I have also seen nearly one-half of the white colony laid up in one day from sickness. A noxious malaria is exhaled from the shallow inlet of Malagash, and the undrained filth, the garbage, offal, dead mollusks, dead pariah dogs, dead cats, all species of carrion, remains of men and beasts unburied, assist to make Zanzibar a most unhealthy city; and considering that it it ought to be most healthy, nature having pointed out to man the means, and having assisted him so far, it is most wonderful that the ruling prince does not obey the dictates of reason.

The bay of Zanzibar is in the form of a crescent, and on the south-western horn of it is built the city. On the east Zanzibar is bounded almost entirely by the Malagash Lagoon, an inlet of the sea. It penetrates to at least two hundred and fifty yards of the sea behind or south of Shangani Point. Were these two hundred and fifty yards cut through by a ten foot ditch, and the inlet deepened slightly, Zanzibar would become an island of itself, and what wonders would it not effect as to health and salubrity! I have never heard this suggestion made, but it struck me that the foreign consuls resident at Zanzibar might suggest this work to the Sultan, and so get the credit of having made it as healthy a place to live in as any near the equator. But *apropos* of this, I remember what Capt. Webb, the American Consul, told me on my first arrival, when I expressed to him my wonder at the apathy and inertness of men born with the indomitable energy which characterises Europeans and Americans, of men imbued with the progressive and stirring instincts of the white people, who yet allow themselves to dwindle into pallid phantoms of their kind, into hypochondriacal invalids, into hopeless believers in the deadliness of the climate, with hardly a trace of that daring and invincible spirit which rules the world.

" Oh," said Capt. Webb, " it is all very well for you to talk about energy and all that kind of thing, but I assure you that a residence of four or five years on this island, among such people as are here, would make you feel that it was a hopeless task to resist the influence of the example by which the most energetic spirits are subdued.

and to which they must submit in time, sooner or later. We were all terribly energetic when we first came here, and struggled bravely to make things go on as we were accustomed to have them at home, but we have found that we were knocking our heads against granite walls to no purpose whatever. These fellows—the Arabs, the Banyans, and the Hindis—you can't make them go faster by ever so much scolding and praying, and in a very short time you see the folly of fighting against the unconquerable. Be patient, and don't fret, that is my advice, or you won't live long here."

There were three or four intensely busy men, though, at Zanzibar, who were out at all hours of the day. I know one, an American; I fancy I hear the quick pit-pat of his feet on the pavement beneath the Consulate, his cheery voice ringing the salutation, " Yambo ! " to every one he met ; and he had lived at Zanzibar twelve years.

I know another, one of the sturdiest of Scotchmen, a most pleasant-mannered and unaffected man, sincere in whatever he did or said, who has lived at Zanzibar several years, subject to the infructuosities of the business he has been engaged in, as well as to the calor and ennui of the climate, who yet presents as formidable a front as ever to the apathetic native of Zanzibar. No man can charge Capt. H. C. Fraser, formerly of the Indian Navy, with being apathetic.

I might with ease give evidence of the industry of others, but they are all my friends, and they are all good. The American, English, German, and French residents have ever treated me with a courtesy and kindness I am not disposed to forget. Taken as a body, it would be hard to find a more generous or hospitable colony of white men in any part of the world.

CHAPTER III.

ORGANIZATION OF THE EXPEDITION.

I was totally ignorant of the interior, and it was difficult at first to know what I needed, in order to take an Expedition into Central Africa. Time was precious, also, and much of it could not be devoted to inquiry and investigation. In a case like this, it would have been a godsend, I thought, had either of the three gentlemen, Captains Burton, Speke, or Grant, given some information on these points; had they devoted a chapter upon, "How to get ready an Expedition for Central Africa." The purpose of this chapter, then, is to relate how I set about it, that other travellers coming after me may have the benefit of my experience.

These are some of the questions I asked myself, as I tossed on my bed at night:—

"How much money is required?"

"How many pagazis, or carriers?"

"How many soldiers?"

"How much cloth?"

"How many beads?"

"How much wire?"

"What kinds of cloth are required for the different tribes?"

Ever so many questions to myself brought me no

nearer the exact point I wished to arrive at. I scribbled over scores of sheets of paper, made estimates, drew out lists of material, calculated the cost of keeping one hundred men for one year, at so many yards of different kinds of cloth, etc. I studied Burton, Speke, and Grant in vain. A good deal of geographical, ethnological, and other information appertaining to the study of Inner Africa was obtainable, but information respecting the organization of an expedition requisite before proceeding to Africa, was not in any book. The Europeans at Zanzibar knew as little as possible about this particular point. There was not one white man at Zanzibar who could tell how many dotis a day a force of one hundred men required to buy food for one day on the road. Neither, indeed, was it their business to know. But what should I do at all, at all? This was a grand question.

I decided it were best to hunt up an Arab merchant who had been engaged in the ivory trade, or who was fresh from the interior.

Sheikh Hashid was a man of note and of wealth in Zanzibar. He had himself despatched several caravans into the interior, and was necessarily acquainted with several prominent traders who came to his house to gossip about their adventures and gains. He was also the proprietor of the large house Capt. Webb occupied; besides, he lived across the narrow street which separated his house from the Consulate. Of all men Sheikh Hashid was the man to be consulted, and he was accordingly invited to visit me at the Consulate.

From the grey-bearded and venerable-looking Sheikh, I elicited more information about African currency, the mode of procedure, the quantity and quality of stuffs I required, than I had obtained from three months' study of books upon Central Africa; and from other Arab merchants to whom the ancient Sheikh introduced me, I received most valuable suggestions and hints, which enabled me at last to organize an Expedition.

The reader must bear in mind that a traveller requires only that which is sufficient for travel and exploration; that a superfluity of goods or means will prove as fatal to him as poverty of supplies. It is on this question of quality and quantity that the traveller has first to exercise his judgment and discretion.

My informants gave me to understand that for one hundred men, 10 doti, or 40 yards of cloth per diem, would suffice for food. The proper course to pursue, I found, was to purchase 2,000 doti of American sheeting, 1,000 doti of Kaniki, and 650 doti of the coloured cloths, such as Barsati, a great favourite in Unyamwezi; Sohari, taken in Ugogo; Ismahili, Taujiri, Joho, Shash, Rehani, Jamdani or Kunguru-Cutch, blue and pink. These were deemed amply sufficient for the subsistence of one hundred men for twelve months. Two years at this rate would require 4,000 doti = 16,000 yards of American sheeting; 2,000 doti = 8,000 yards of Kaniki; 1,300 doti = 5,200 yards of mixed coloured cloths. This was definite and valuable information to me, and excepting the lack of some suggestions as to the quality of the sheeting, Kaniki, and coloured cloths, I had obtained all I desired upon this point.

Second in importance to the amount of cloth required was the quantity and quality of the beads necessary Beads, I was told, took the place of cloth currency among some tribes of the interior. One tribe preferred white to black beads, brown to yellow, red to green,

green to white, and so on. Thus, in Unyamwezi, red (sami-sami) beads would readily be taken, where all other kinds would be refused; black (bubu) beads, though currency in Ugogo, were positively worthless with all other tribes; the egg (sungomazzi) beads, though valuable in Ujiji and Uguhha, would be refused in all other countries; the white (Merikani) beads though good in Ufipa, and some parts of Usagara and Ugogo, would certainly be despised in Useguhha and Ukonongo. Such being the case, I was obliged to study closely, and calculate the probable stay of an expedition in the several countries, so as to be sure to provide a sufficiency of each kind, and guard against any great overplus. Burton and Speke, for instance, were obliged to throw away as worthless several hundred fundo of beads.

For example, supposing the several nations of Europe had each its own currency, without the means of exchange, and supposing a man was about to travel through Europe on foot, before starting he would be apt to calculate how many days it would take him to travel through France; how many through Prussia, Austria, and Russia, then to reckon the expense he would be likely to incur per day. If the expense be set down at a napoleon per day, and his journey through France would occupy thirty days, the sum required for going and returning might be properly set down at sixty napoleons, in which case, napoleons not being current money in Prussia, Austria, or Russia, it would be utterly useless for him to burden himself with the weight of a couple of thousand napoleons in gold.

My anxiety on this point was most excruciating. Over and over I studied the hard names and measures, conned again and again the polysyllables, hoping to be able to arrive some time at an intelligible definition of the terms. I revolved in my mind the words Mukunguru, Ghulabio, Sungomazzi, Kadunduguru, Mutunda, Sami-sami, Bubu, Merikani, Hafde, Lunghio-Rega, and Lakhio, until I was fairly beside myself. Finally, however, I came to the conclusion that if I reckoned my requirements at fifty khete, or five fundo per day, for two years, and if I purchased only eleven varieties, I might consider my-self safe enough. The purchase was accordingly made, and twenty-two sacks of the best species were packed and brought to Capt. Webb's house, ready for trans-portation to Bagamoyo.

After the beads came the wire question. I discovered, after considerable trouble, that Nos. 5 and 6—almost of the thickness of telegraph wire—were considered the best numbers for trading purposes. While beads stand for copper coins in Africa, cloth measures for silver; wire is reckoned as gold in the countries beyond the Tan-ga-ni-ka.* Ten frasilah, or 350 lbs., of brass-wire, my Arab adviser thought, would be ample.

Having purchased the cloth, the beads, and the wire, it was with no little pride that I surveyed the comely bales and packages lying piled up, row above row, in Capt. Webb's capacious store-room. Yet my work was not ended, it was but beginning; there were provisions, cooking-utensils, boats, rope, twine, tents, donkeys, saddles, bagging, canvas, tar, needles, tools, ammunition, guns, equipments, hatchets, medicines, bedding, presents for chiefs—in short, a thousand things not yet purchased. The ordeal of chaffering and haggling with steel-hearted

---

* It will be seen that I differ from Capt. Burton in the spelling of this word, as I deem the letter " y " superfluous.

Banyans, Hindis, Arabs, and half-castes was most trying. For instance, I purchased twenty-two donkeys at Zanzibar. $40 and $50 were asked, which I had to reduce to $15 or $20 by an infinite amount of argument worthy, I think, of a nobler cause. As was my experience with the ass-dealers so was it with the petty merchants; even a paper of pins was not purchased without a five per cent. reduction from the price demanded, involving, of course, a loss of much time and patience.

After collecting the donkeys, I discovered there were no pack-saddles to be obtained in Zanzibar. Donkeys without pack-saddles were of no use whatever. I invented a saddle to be manufactured by myself and my white man Farquhar, wholly from canvas, rope, and cotton.

Three or four frasilahs of cotton, and ten bolts of canvas were required for the saddles. A specimen saddle was made by myself in order to test its efficiency. A donkey was taken and saddled, and a load of 140 lbs. was fastened to it, and though the animal—a wild creature of Unyamwezi—struggled and reared frantically, not a particle gave way. After this experiment, Farquhar was set to work to manufacture twenty-one more after the same pattern. Woollen pads were also purchased to protect the animals from being galled. It ought to be mentioned here, perhaps, that the idea of such a saddle as I manufactured, was first derived from the Otago saddle, in use among the transport-trains of the English army in Abyssinia.

A man named John William Shaw—a native of London, England, lately third-mate of the American ship 'Nevada' —applied to me for work. Though his discharge from the 'Nevada' was rather suspicious, yet he possessed all the requirements of such a man as I needed, and was an experienced hand with the palm and needle, could cut canvas to fit anything, was a pretty good navigator, ready and willing, so far as his professions went. I saw no reason to refuse his services, and he was accordingly engaged at $300 per annum, to rank second to William L. Farquhar. Farquhar was a capital navigator and excellent mathematician; was strong, energetic, and clever.

The next thing I was engaged upon was to enlist, arm, and equip, a faithful escort of twenty men for the road. Johari, the chief dragoman of the American Consulate, informed me that he knew where certain of Speke's "Faithfuls" were yet to be found. The idea had struck me before, that if I could obtain the services of a few men acquainted with the ways of white men, and who could induce other good men to join the expedition I was organizing, I might consider myself fortunate. More especially had I thought of Seedy Mbarak Mombay, commonly called "Bombay," who though his head was "woodeny," and his hands "clumsy," was considered to be the "faithfulest" of the "Faithfuls."

With the aid of the dragoman Johari, I secured in a few hours the services of Uledi (Capt. Grant's former valet), Ulimengo, Baruti, Ambari, Mabruki (Muinyi Mabruki—Bull-headed Mabruki, Capt. Burton's former unhappy valet)—five of Speke's "Faithfuls." When I asked them if they were willing to join another white man's expedition to Ujiji, they replied very readily that they were willing to join any brother of Speke's." Dr. John Kirk, Her Majesty's Consul at Zanzibar, who was present, told them that though I was no brother of "Speke's," I spoke his language. This distinction mattered little to them, and I heard them, with great delight, declare their readiness to go anywhere with me, or do anything I wished.

Mombay, as they called him, or Bombay, as we know him, had gone to Pemba, an island lying north of Zanzibar. Uledi was sure Mombay would jump with joy at the prospect of another expedition. Johari was therefore commissioned to write to him at Pemba, to inform him of the good fortune in store for him.

On the fourth morning after the letter had been despatched, the famous Bombay made his appearance, followed in decent order and due rank by the " Faithfuls " of " Speke." I looked in vain for the " woodeny head " and " alligator teeth " with which his former master had endowed him. I saw a slender short man of fifty or thereabouts, with a grizzled head, an uncommonly high, narrow forehead, with a very large mouth, showing teeth very irregular, and wide apart. An ugly rent in the upper front row of Bombay's teeth was made with the clenched fist of Capt. Speke in Uganda when his master's patience was worn out, and prompt punishment became necessary. That Capt. Speke had spoiled him with kindness was evident, from the fact that Bombay had the audacity to stand up for a boxing-match with him. But these things I only found out, when, months afterwards, I was called upon to administer punishment to him myself. But, at his first appearance, I was favourably impressed with Bombay, though his face was rugged, his mouth large, his eyes small, and his nose flat.

" Salaam aliekum," were the words he greeted me with.

" Aliekum salaam," I replied, with all the gravity I could muster. I then informed him I required him as captain of my soldiers to Ujiji. His reply was that he was ready to do whatever I told him, go wherever I liked

—in short, be a pattern to servants, and a model to soldiers. He hoped I would give him a uniform, and a good gun, both of which were promised.

Upon inquiring for the rest of the "Faithfuls" who accompanied Speke into Egypt, I was told that at Zanzibar there were but six. Ferrajji, Maktub, Sadik, Sunguru, Manyu, Matajari, Mkata, and Almas, were dead; Uledi and Mtamani were in Unyanyembe; Hassan had gone to Kilwa, and Ferahan was supposed to be in Ujiji.

Out of the six "Faithfuls," each of whom still retained his medal for assisting in the "Discovery of the Sources of the Nile," one, poor Mabruki, had met with a sad misfortune, which I feared would incapacitate him from active usefulness.

Mabruki the "Bull-headed," owned a shamba (or a house with a garden attached to it), of which he was very proud. Close to him lived a neighbour in similar circumstances, who was a soldier of Seyd Majid, with whom Mabruki, who was of a quarrelsome disposition, had a feud, which culminated in the soldier inducing two or three of his comrades to assist him in punishing the malevolent Mabruki, and this was done in a manner that only the heart of an African could conceive. They tied the unfortunate fellow by his wrists to a branch of a tree, and after indulging their brutal appetite for revenge in torturing him, left him to hang in that position for two days, At the expiration of the second day, he was accidentally discovered in a most pitiable condition. His hands had swollen to an immense size, and the veins of one hand having been ruptured, he had lost its use. It is needless to say that, when the affair came to Seyd Majid's ears, the miscreants were severely punished. Dr. Kirk, who attended the poor fellow, succeeded in restoring one hand to something of a resemblance of its former shape, but the other hand is sadly marred, and its former usefulness gone for ever.

However, I engaged Mabruki, despite his deformed hands, his ugliness and vanity, because he was one of Speke's "Faithfuls." For if he but wagged his tongue in my service, kept his eyes open, and opened his mouth at the proper time, I assured myself I could make him useful.

Bombay, my captain of escort, succeeded in getting eighteen more free men to volunteer as "askari" (soldiers), men whom he knew would not desert, and for whom he declared himself responsible. They were an exceedingly fine-looking body of men, far more intelligent in appearance than I could ever have believed African barbarians could be. They hailed principally from Uhiyow, others from Unyamwezi, some came from Useguhha and Ugindo.

Their wages were set down at $36 each man per annum, or $3 each per month. Each soldier was provided with a flintlock musket, powder horn, bullet-pouch, knife, and hatchet, besides enough powder and ball for 200 rounds.

Bombay, in consideration of his rank, and previous faithful services to Burton, Speke and Grant, was engaged at $80 a year, half that sum in advance, a good muzzle-loading rifle, besides, a pistol, knife, and hatchet were given to him, while the other five "Faithfuls," Ambari, Mabruki, Ulimengo, Baruti, and Uledi, were engaged at $40 a year, with proper equipments as soldiers.

Having studied fairly well all the East African travellers' books regarding Eastern and Central Africa, **my** mind had conceived the difficulties which would present themselves during the prosecution of my search after Dr. Livingstone.

To obviate all of these, as well as human wit could suggest, was my constant thought and aim.

"Shall I permit myself, while looking from Ujiji over the waters of the Tanganika Lake to the other side, to be balked on the threshold of success by the insolence of a King Kannena or the caprice of a Hamed bin Sulayyam?" was a question I asked myself. To guard against such a contingency I determined to carry my own boats. "Then," I thought, "if I hear of Livingstone being on the Tanganika, I can launch my boat and proceed after him.

I procured one large boat, capable of carrying twenty persons, with stores and goods sufficient for a cruise, from the American Consul, for the sum of $80, and a smaller one from another American gentleman for $40. The latter would hold comfortably six men, with suitable stores.

I did not intend to carry the boats whole or bodily, but to strip them of their boards, and carry the timbers and thwarts only. As a substitute for the boards, I proposed to cover each boat with a double canvas skin well tarred. The work of stripping them and taking them to pieces fell to me. This little job occupied me five days. I also packed them up, for the pagazis. Each load was carefully weighed, and none exceeded 68 lbs. in weight.

John Shaw excelled himself in the workmanship displayed on the canvas boats; when finished, they fitted their frames admirably. The canvas—six bolts of English hemp, No. 3—was procured from Ludha, Damji, who furnished it from the Sultan's storeroom.

An insuperable obstacle to rapid transit in Africa is the want of carriers, and as speed was the main object of the Expedition under my command, my duty was to lessen this difficulty as much as possible. My carriers could only be engaged after arriving at Bagamoyo, on the mainland. I had over twenty good donkeys ready, and I thought a cart adapted for the footpaths of Africa might prove an advantage. Accordingly I had a cart constructed, eighteen inches wide and five feet long, supplied with two fore-wheels of a light American wagon, more for the purpose of conveying the narrow ammunition-boxes. I estimated that if a donkey could carry to Unyanyembe a load of four frasilahs, or 140 lbs., he ought to be able to draw eight frasilahs on such a cart, which would be equal to the carrying capacity of four stout pagazis or carriers. Events will prove, how my theories were borne out by practice.

When my purchases were completed, and I beheld them piled up, tier after tier, row upon row, here a mass of cooking-utensils, there bundles of rope, tents, saddles, a pile of portmanteaus and boxes, containing every imaginable thing, I confess I was rather abashed at my own temerity. Here were at least six tons of material! "How will it ever be possible," I thought, "to move all this inert mass across the wilderness stretching between the sea, and the great lakes of Africa? Bah, cast all doubts away, man, and have at them! ' Sufficient for the day is the evil thereof,' without borrowing from the morrow."

The traveller must needs make his way into the African interior after a fashion very different from that to which he has been accustomed in other countries. He requires to take with him just what a ship must have when about to sail on a long voyage. He must have his

slop chest, his little store of canned dainties, and his
medicines, besides which, he must have enough guns,
powder, and ball to be able to make a series of good
fights if necessary. He must have men to convey these
miscellaneous articles; and as a man's maximum load
does not exceed 70 lbs., to convey 11,000 lbs. requires
nearly 160 men.

Europe and the Orient, even Arabia and Turkestan,
have royal ways of travelling compared to Africa. Specie
is received in all those countries, by which a traveller
may carry his means about with him on his own person.
Eastern and Central Africa, however, demand a necklace,
instead of a cent; two yards of American sheeting,
instead of half a dollar, or a florin, and a kitindi of thick
brass-wire, in place of a gold piece.

The African traveller can hire neither wagons nor
camels, neither horses nor mules, to proceed with him into
the interior. His means of conveyance are limited to black
and naked men, who demand at least $15 a head for every
70 lbs. weight carried only as far as Unyanyembe.

One thing amongst others my predecessors omitted to
inform men bound for Africa, which is of importance,
and that is, that no traveller should ever think of coming
to Zanzibar with his money in any other shape than
gold coin. Letters of credit, circular notes, and such
civilized things I have found to be a century ahead of
Zanzibar people.

Twenty and twenty-five cents deducted out of every
dollar I drew on paper is one of the unpleasant, if not
unpleasantest things I have committed to lasting memory.
For Zanzibar is a spot far removed from all avenues of
European commerce, and coin is at a high premium.
A man may talk and entreat, but though he may have

drafts, cheques, circular notes, letters of credit, a carte-blanche to get what he wants, out of every dollar must be deducted twenty, twenty-five and thirty cents, so I was told, and so was my experience. What a pity there is no branch-bank here!

I had intended to have gone into Africa incognito. But the fact that a white man, even an American, was about to enter Africa was soon known all over Zanzibar. This fact was repeated a thousand times in the streets, proclaimed in all shop alcoves, and at the custom-house. The native bazaar laid hold of it, and agitated it day and night until my departure. The foreigners, including the Europeans, wished to know the pros and cons of my coming in and going out.

My answer to all questions, pertinent and impertinent, was, I am going to Africa. Though my card bore the words

---

HENRY M. STANLEY.

New York Herald.

---

very few, I believe, ever coupled the words ' New York Herald ' with a search after " Doctor Livingstone." It was not my fault, was it ?

Ah, me! what hard work it is to start an expedition alone! What with hurrying through the baking heat of the fierce relentless sun from shop to shop, strengthening myself with far-reaching and enduring patience for the haggling contest with the livid-faced Hindi, summoning courage and wit to brow-beat the villainous Goanese, and match the foxy Banyan, talking volumes throughout the day, correcting estimates, making up accounts, super-intending the delivery of purchased articles, measuring and weighing them, to see that everything was of full measure and weight, overseeing the white men Farquhar and Shaw, who were busy on donkey saddles, sails, tents, and boats for the Expedition, I felt, when the day was over, as though limbs and brain well deserved their rest. Such labours were mine unremittingly for a month.

Having bartered drafts on Mr. James Gordon Bennett to the amount of several thousand dollars for cloth, beads, wire, donkeys, and a thousand necessaries, having ad-vanced pay to the white men, and black escort of the Expedition, having fretted Capt. Webb and his family more than enough with the din of preparation, and filled his house with my goods, there was nothing further to do but to leave my formal adieus with the Europeans, and thank the Sultan and those gentlemen who had assisted me, before embarking for Bagamoyo.

The day before my departure from Zanzibar the American Consul, having just habited himself in his black coat, and taking with him an extra black hat, in order to be in state apparel, proceeded with me to the Sultan's palace. The prince had been generous to me; he had presented me with an Arab horse, had furnished me with letters of introduction to his agents, his chief men, and representatives in the interior, and in many other ways had shown himself well disposed towards me.

The palace is a large, roomy, lofty, square house close to the fort, built of coral, and plastered thickly with lime mortar. In appearance it is half Arabic and half Italian. The shutters are Venetian blinds painted a vivid green, and presenting a striking contrast to the whitewashed walls. Before the great, lofty, wide door were ranged in two crescents several Baluch and Persian mercenaries, armed with curved swords and targes of rhinoceros hide. Their dress consisted of a muddy-white cotton shirt, reaching to the ancles, girdled with a leather belt thickly studded with silver bosses.

As we came in sight a signal was passed to some person inside the entrance. When within twenty yards of the door, the Sultan, who was standing waiting, came down the steps, and, passing through the ranks, advanced toward us, with his right hand stretched out, and a genial smile of welcome on his face. On our side we raised our hats, and shook hands with him, after which, doing according as he bade us, we passed forward, and arrived on the highest step near the entrance door. He pointed forward; we bowed and arrived at the foot of an unpainted and narrow staircase to turn once more to the Sultan. The Consul, I perceived, was ascending sideways, a mode of progression which I saw was intended for a compromise with decency and dignity. At the top of the stairs we waited, with our faces towards the up-coming Prince. Again we were waved magnanimously forward, for before us was the reception-hall and throne-room. I noticed, as I marched forward to the furthest end, that the room was high, and painted in the Arabic style, that the carpet was thick and of Persian fabric, that the furniture consisted of a dozen gilt chairs and a chandelier

We were seated; Ludha Damji, the Banyan collector of customs, a venerable-looking old man, with a shrewd intelligent face, sat on the right of the Sultan; next to him was the great Mohammedan merchant Tarya Topan, who had come to be present at the interview, not only because he was one of the councillors of His Highness, but because he also took a lively interest in this American Expedition. Opposite to Ludha sat Capt. Webb, and next to him I was seated, opposite Tarya Topan. The Sultan sat in a gilt chair between the Americans and the councillors. Johari the dragoman stood humbly before the Sultan, expectant and ready to interpret what we had to communicate to the Prince.

The Sultan, so far as dress goes, might be taken for a Mingrelian gentleman, excepting, indeed, for the turban, whose ample folds in alternate colours of red, yellow, brown, and white, encircled his head. His long robe was of dark cloth, cinctured round the waist with his rich sword-belt, from which was suspended a gold-hilted scimitar, encased in a scabbard also enriched with gold. His legs and feet were bare, and had a ponderous look about them, since he suffered from that strange curse of Zanzibar—elephantiasis. His feet were slipped into a pair of watta (Arabic for slippers), with thick soles and a strong leathern band over the instep. His light complexion and his correct features, which are intelligent and regular, bespeak the Arab patrician. They indicate, however, nothing except his high descent and blood; no traits of character are visible unless there is just a trace of amiability, and perfect contentment with himself and all around.

Such is Prince, or Seyd Burghash, Sultan of Zanzibar and Pemba, and the East coast of Africa, from Somali Land to the Mozambique, as he appeared to me.

Coffee was served in cups supported by golden finjans, also some cocoa-nut milk, and rich sweet sherbet.

The conversation began with the question addressed to the Consul.

"Are you well?"

Consul.—"Yes, thank you. How is His Highness?"

Highness.—"Quite well!"

Highness to me.—"Are you well?"

Answer.—"Quite well, thanks!"

The Consul now introduces business; and questions about my travels follow from His Highness—

"How do you like Persia?"

"Have you seen Kerbela, Bagdad, Masr, Stamboul?"

"Have the Turks many soldiers?"

"How many has Persia?"

"Is Persia fertile?"

"How do you like Zanzibar?"

Having answered each question to his Highness' satisfaction, he handed me letters of introduction to his officers at Bagamoyo and Kaole, and a general introductory letter to all Arab merchants whom I might meet on the road, and concluded his remarks to me, with the expressed hope, that on whatever mission I was bound, I should be perfectly successful.

We bowed ourselves out of his presence in much the same manner that we had bowed ourselves in, he accompanying us to the great entrance door.

Mr. Goodhue of Salem, an American merchant long resident in Zanzibar, presented me, as I gave him my adieu, with a blooded bay horse, imported from the Cape of Good Hope, and worth, at least at Zanzibar, $500.

Feb. 4.—By the 4th of February, twenty-eight days from the date of my arrival at Zanzibar, the organization and equipment of the "'New York Herald' Expedition" was complete; tents and saddles had been manufactured, boats and sails were ready. The donkeys brayed, and the horses neighed impatiently for the road.

Etiquette demanded that I should once more present my card to the European and American Consuls at Zanzibar, and the word " farewell " was said to everybody.

On the fifth day, four dhows were anchored before the American Consulate. Into one were lifted the two horses, into two others the donkeys, into the fourth, the largest, the black escort, and bulky moneys of the Expedition.

A little before noon we set sail. The American flag, a present to the Expedition by that kind-hearted lady, Mrs. Webb, was raised to the mast-head; the Consul, his lady, and exuberant little children, Mary and Charley, were on the housetop waving the starry banner, hats, and handkerchiefs, a token of farewell to me and mine. Happy people, and good! may their course and ours be prosperous, and may God's blessing rest on us all!

CAMP AT BAGAMOYO.

CHAPTER IV.

LIFE AT BAGAMOYO.

THE isle of Zanzibar with its groves of cocoa-nut, mango, clove, and cinnamon, and its sentinel islets of Chumbi and French, with its whitewashed city and jack-fruit odor, with its harbor and ships that tread the deep, faded slowly from view, and looking westward, the African continent rose, a similar bank of green verdure to that which had just receded till it was a mere sinuous line above the horizon, looming in a northerly direction to the sublimity of a mountain chain. The distance across from Zanzibar to Bagamoyo may be about twenty-five miles, yet it took the dull and lazy dhows ten hours before they dropped anchor on the top of the coral reef plainly visible a few feet below the surface of the water, within a hundred yards of the beach.

The newly-enlisted soldiers, fond of noise and excitement, discharged repeated salvos by way of a salute to the mixed crowd of Arabs, Banyans, and Wasawahili, who stood on the beach to receive the Musungu (white man), which they did with a general stare and a chorus of " Yambo, bana ?" (how are you, master ?)

In our own land the meeting with a large crowd is rather a tedious operation, as our independent citizens insist on an interlacing of fingers, and a vigorous shaking thereof before their pride is satisfied, and the peaceful manifestation endorsed; but on this beach, well lined with spectators, a response of " Yambo, bana !" sufficed, except with one who of all there was acknowledged the greatest, and who, claiming, like all great men, individual attention, came forward to exchange another " Yambo !" on his own behalf, and to shake hands.   This personage with a long trailing turban, was Jemadar Esau, commander of the Zanzibar force of soldiers, police, or Baluch gendarmes stationed at Bagamoyo.   He had accompanied Speke and Grant a good distance into the interior, and they had rewarded him liberally.   He took upon himself the responsibility of assisting in the debarkation of the Expedition, and unworthy as was his appearance, disgraceful as he was in his filth, I here commend him for his influence over the rabble to all future East African travellers.

Foremost among those who welcomed us was a Father of the Society of St.-Esprit, who with other Jesuits, under Father Superior Horner, have established a missionary post of considerable influence and merit at Bagamoyo,

We were invited to partake of the hospitality of the Mission, to take our meals there, and, should we desire it, to pitch our camp on their grounds. But however strong the geniality of the welcome and sincere the heartiness of the invitation, I am one of those who prefer independence to dependence if it is possible. Besides, my sense of the obligation between host and guest had just had a fine edge put upon it by the delicate forbearance of my kind host at Zanzibar, who had betrayed no sign of impatience at the trouble I was only too conscious of having caused him. I therefore informed the hospitable Padre, that only for one night could I suffer myself to be enticed from my camp.

I selected a house near the western outskirts of the town, where there is a large open square through which the road from Unyanyembe enters. Had I been at Bagamoyo a month, I could not have bettered my location. My tents were pitched fronting the tembe (house) I had chosen, enclosing a small square, where business could be transacted, bales looked over, examined, and marked, free from the intrusion of curious sightseers. After driving the twenty-seven animals of the Expedition into the enclosure in the rear of the house, storing the bales of goods, and placing a cordon of soldiers round, I proceeded to the Jesuit Mission, to a late dinner, being tired and ravenous, leaving the newly-formed camp in charge of the white men and Capt. Bombay.

The Mission is distant from the town a good half mile, to the north of it; it is quite a village of itself, numbering some fifteen or sixteen houses. There are more than ten padres engaged in the establishment, and as many sisters, and all find plenty of occupation in educing from native crania the fire of intelligence. Truth compels me to state

that they are very successful, having over two hundred
pupils, boys and girls, in the Mission, and, from the oldest
to the youngest, they show the impress of the useful
education they have received.

The dinner furnished to the padres and their guest
consisted of as many plats as a first-class hotel in Paris
usually supplies, and cooked with nearly as much skill,
though the surroundings were by no means equal. I feel
assured also that the padres, besides being tasteful in
their potages and entrées, do not stultify their ideas for
lack of that element which Horace, Hafiz, and Byron have
praised so much. The champagne—think of champagne
Cliquot in East Africa!—Lafitte, La Rose, Burgundy, and
Bordeaux were of first-rate quality, and the meek and
lowly eyes of the fathers were not a little brightened
under the vinous influence. Ah! those fathers understand
life, and appreciate its duration. Their festive board
drives the African jungle fever from their doors, while it
soothes the gloom and isolation which strike one with
awe, as one emerges from the lighted room and plunges
into the depths of the darkness of an African night, enlivened only by the wearying monotone of the frogs and
crickets, and the distant ululation of the hyæna. It
requires somewhat above human effort, unaided by the
ruby liquid that cheers, to be always suave and polite
amid the dismalities of native life in Africa.

After the evening meal, which replenished my failing
strength, and for which I felt the intensest gratitude, the
most advanced of the pupils came forward, to the number
of twenty, with brass instruments, thus forming a full
band of music. It rather astonished me to hear instru-
mental sounds issue forth in harmony from such woolly-
headed youngsters; to hear well-known French music at

this isolated port, to hear negro boys, that a few months ago knew nothing beyond the traditions of their ignorant mothers, stand forth and chant Parisian songs about French valor and glory, with all the *sang-froid* of *gamins* from the purlieus of Saint-Antoine.

I had a most refreshing night's rest, and at dawn I sought out my camp, with a will to enjoy the new life now commencing. On counting the animals, two donkeys were missing; and on taking notes of my African moneys, one coil of No. 6 wire was not to be found. Everybody had evidently fallen on the ground to sleep, oblivious of the fact that on the coast there are many dishonest prowlers at night. Soldiers were despatched to search through the town and neighbourhood, and Jemadar Esau was apprised of our loss, and stimulated to discover the animals by the promise of a reward. Before night one of the missing donkeys was found outside the town nibbling at manioc-leaves, but the other animal and the coil of wire were never found.

Among my visitors this first day at Bagamoyo was Ali bin Salim, a brother of the famous Sayd bin Salim, formerly Ras Kafilah to Burton and Speke, and subsequently to Speke and Grant. His salaams were very profuse, and moreover, his brother was to be my agent in Unyamwezi, so that I did not hesitate to accept his offer of assistance. But, alas, for my white face and too trustful nature! this Ali bin Salim turned out to be a snake in the grass, a very sore thorn in my side. I was invited to his comfortable house to partake of coffee. I went there: the coffee was good though sugarless, his promises were many, but they proved valueless. Said he to me, "I am your friend; I wish to serve you; what can I do for you?" Replied I, "I am obliged to you I need a good friend who, knowing the language and customs of the Wanyamwezi, can procure me the pagazis I need and send me off quickly. Your brother is ac-quainted with the Wasungu (white men), and knows that what they promise they make good. Get me a hundred and forty pagazis and I will pay you your price." With unctuous courtesy, the reptile I was now warmly nourish-ing, said, "I do not want anything from you, my friend, for such a slight service, rest content and quiet; you shall not stop here fifteen days. To-morrow morning I will come and overhaul your bales to see what is needed." I bade him good morning, elated with the happy thought that I was soon to tread the Unyanyembe road.

The reader must be made acquainted with two good and sufficient reasons why I was to devote all my energy to lead the Expedition as quickly as possible from Bagamoyo.

First, I wished to reach Ujiji before the news reached Livingstone that I was in search of him, for my impres-sion of him was that he was a man who would try to put as much distance as possible between us, rather than make an effort to shorten it, and I should have my long journey for nothing.

Second, the Masika, or rainy season, would soon be on me, which, if it caught me at Bagamoyo, would prevent my departure until it was over, which meant a delay of forty days, and exaggerated as the rains were by all men with whom I came in contact, it rained every day for forty days without intermission. This I knew was a thing to dread; for I had my memory stored with all kinds of rainy unpleasantnesses. For instance, there was the rain of Virginia and its concomitant horrors—wetness, mildew, agues, rhuematics, and such like; then there were the English rains, a miserable drizzle causing the blue devils; then the rainy season of Abyssinia with the flood-gates of the firmament opened, and an universal down-pour of rain, enough to submerge half a continent in a few hours; lastly, there was the pelting monsoon of India, a steady shut-in-house kind of rain. To which of these rains should I compare this dreadful Masika of East Africa? Did not Burton write much about black mud in Uzaramo? Well, a country whose surface soil is called black mud in fine weather, what can it be called when forty days' rain beat on it, and feet of pagazis and donkeys make paste of it? These were natural reflections, induced by the circumstances of the hour, and I found myself much exercised in mind in consequence.

Ali bin Salim, true to his promise, visited my camp on the morrow, with a very important air, and after looking at the pile of cloth bales, informed me that I must have them covered with mat-bags. He said he would send a man to have them measured, but he enjoined me not to make any bargain for the bags, as he would make it all right.

While awaiting with commendable patience the 140 pagazis promised by Ali bin Salim we were all employed upon everything that thought could suggest needful for crossing the sickly maritime region, so that we might make the transit before the terrible fever could unnerve us, and make us joyless. A short experience at Bagamoyo showed us what we lacked, what was superfluous, and what was necessary. We were visited one night by a squall, accompanied by furious rain. I had $1,500 worth of pagazi cloth in my tent. In the morning I looked, and lo! the drilling had let in rain like a sieve, and every yard of cloth was wet. It occupied two days afterwards to dry the cloths, and fold them again. The drill-tent was condemned, and a No 5 hemp-canvas tent at once prepared. After which I felt convinced that my cloth bales, and one year's ammunition, were safe, and that I could defy the Masika.

In the hurry of departure from Zanzibar, and in my ignorance of how bales should be made, I had submitted to the better judgment and ripe experience of one Jetta, a commission merchant, to prepare my bales for carriage. Jetta did not weigh the bales as he made them up, but piled the Merikani, Kaniki, Barsati, Jamdani, Joho, Ismahili, in alternate layers, and roped the same into bales. One or two pagazis came to my camp and began to chaffer; they wished to see the bales first, before they would make a final bargain. They tried to raise them up —ugh! ugh! it was of no use, and withdrew. A fine Salter's spring balance was hung up, and a bale suspended to the hook; the finger indicated 105 lbs. or 3 frasilah, which was just 35 lbs. or one frasilah overweight. Upon putting all the bales to this test, I perceived that Jetta's guess-work, with all his experience, had caused considerable trouble to me.

The soldiers were set to work to reopen and repack, which latter task is performed in the following manner:— We cut a doti, or four yards of Merikani, ordinarily sold at Zanzibar for $2·75 the piece of thirty yards, and spread it out. We take a piece or bolt of good Merikani, and instead of the double fold given it by the Nashua and Salem mills, we fold it into three parts, by which the folds have a breadth of a foot; this piece forms the first layer, and will weigh nine pounds; the second layer consists of six pieces of Kaniki, a blue stuff similar to the blue blouse stuff of France, and the blue jeans of America, though much lighter; the third layer is formed of the second piece of Merikani, the fourth of six more pieces of Kaniki, the fifth of Merikani, the sixth of Kaniki as before, and the seventh and last of Merikani. We have thus four pieces of Merikani, which weigh 36 lbs., and 18 pieces of Kaniki weighing also 36 lbs., making a total of 72 lbs., or a little more than two frasilahs; the cloth is then folded singly over these layers, each corner tied to another. A bundle of coir-rope is then brought, and two men, provided with a wooden mallet for beating and pressing the bale, proceed to tie it up with as much nicety as sailors serve down rigging.

When complete, a bale is a solid mass three feet and a half long, a foot deep, and a foot wide. Of these bales I had to convey eighty-two to Unyanyembe, forty of which consisted solely of the Merikani and Kaniki. The other forty-two contained the Merikani and colored cloths, which latter were to serve as honga or tribute cloths, and to engage another set of pagazis from Unyanyembe to Ujiji, and from Ujiji to the regions beyond.

The fifteenth day asked of me by Ali bin Salim for the procuring of the pagazis passed by, and there was not the ghost of a pagazi in my camp. I sent Mabruki the Bull-headed to Ali bin Salim, to convey my salaams and express a hope that he had kept his word. In half an hour's time Mabruki returned with the reply of the Arab, that in a few days he would be able to collect them all; but, added Mabruki, slyly, "Bana, I don't believe him. He said aloud to himself, in my hearing, 'Why should I get the Musungu pagazis? Seyd Burghash did not send a letter to me, but to the Jemadar. Why should I trouble myself about him? Let Seyd Burghash write me a letter to that purpose, and I will procure them within two days.'"

To my mind this was a time for action: Ali bin Salim should see that it was ill trifling with a white man in earnest to start. I rode down to his house to ask him what he meant.

His reply was, Mabruki had told a lie as black as his face. He had never said anything approaching to such a thing. He was willing to become my slave—to become a pagazi himself. But here I stopped the voluble Ali, and informed him that I could not think of employing him in the capacity of a pagazi, neither could I find it in my heart to trouble Seyd Burghash to write a direct letter to him, or to require of a man who had deceived me once, as Ali bin Salim had, any service of any nature whatsoever. It would be better, therefore, if Ali bin Salim would stay away from my camp, and not enter it either in person or by proxy.

I had lost fifteen days, for Jemadar Sadur, at Kaole, had never stirred from his fortified house in that village in my service, save to pay a visit, after the receipt of the Sultan's letter. Naranji, custom-house agent at Kaole, solely under the thumb of the great Ludha Damji, had not responded to Ludha's worded request that he would procure pagazis, except with winks, nods, and promises, and it is but just stated how I fared at the hands of Ali bin Salim. In this extremity I remembered the promise made to me by the great merchant of Zanzibar—Tarya Topan—a Mohammedan Hindi—that he would furnish me with a letter to a young man named Soor Hadji Palloo, who was said to be the best man in Bagamoyo to procure a supply of pagazis.

I despatched my Arab interpreter by a dhow to Zanzibar, with a very earnest request to Capt. Webb that he would procure from Tarya Topan the introductory letter so long delayed. It was the last card in my hand.

On the third day the Arab returned, bringing with him not only the letter to Soor Hadji Palloo, but an abundance of good things from the ever-hospitable house of Mr. Webb. In a very short time after the receipt of his letter, the eminent young man Soor Hadji Palloo came to visit me, and informed me he had been requested by Tarya Topan to hire for me one hundred and forty pagazis to Unyanyembe in the shortest time possible. This he said would be very expensive, for there were scores of Arabs and Wasawahili merchants on the look out for every caravan that came in from the interior, and they paid 20 doti, or 80 yards of cloth, to each pagazi. Not willing or able to pay more, many of these merchants had been waiting as long as six months before they could get their quota. "If you," continued he, "desire to depart quickly, you must pay from 25 to 40 doti, and I can send you off before one month is ended." In reply, I said, "Here are my cloths for pagazis to the amount of $1,750, or 3,500 doti, sufficient to give one hundred and forty men 25 doti each. The most I am willing to pay is 25 doti : send one hundred and forty pagazis to Unyanyembe with my cloth and wire, and I will make your heart glad with the richest present you have ever received." With a refreshing naïveté, the "young man" said he did not want any present, he would get me my quota of pagazis, and then I could tell the "Wasungu" what a good "young man" he was, and consequently the benefit he would receive would be an increase of business. He closed his reply with the astounding remark that he had ten pagazis at his house already, and if I would be good enough to have four bales of cloth, two bags of beads, and twenty coils of wire carried to his house, the pagazis could leave Bagamoyo the next day, under charge of three soldiers.

"For," he remarked, "it is much better and cheaper to send many small caravans than one large one. Large caravans invite attack, or are delayed by avaricious chiefs upon the most trivial pretexts, while small ones pass by without notice."

The bales and beads were duly carried to Soor Hadji Palloo's house, and the day passed with me in mentally congratulating myself upon my good fortune, in complimenting the young Hindi's talents for business, the greatness and influence of Tarya Topan, and the goodness of Mr. Webb in thus hastening my departure from Bagamoyo. I mentally vowed a handsome present, and a great puff in my book, to Soor Hadji Palloo, and it was with a glad heart I prepared these soldiers for their march to Unyanyembe.

The task of preparing the first caravan for the Unyanyembe road informed me upon several things that have escaped the notice of my predecessors in East Africa, a timely knowledge of which would have been of infinite service to me at Zanzibar, in the purchase and selection of sufficient and proper cloth.

The setting out of the first caravan enlightened me also upon the subject of honga, or tribute. Tribute had to be packed by itself, all of choice cloth; for the chiefs, besides being avaricious, are also very fastidious. They will not accept the flimsy colored cloth of the pagazi, but a royal and exceedingly high-priced dabwani, Ismahili, Rehani, or a Sohari, or dotis of crimson broad cloth. The tribute for the first caravan cost $25. Having more than one hundred and forty pagazis to despatch, this tribute money would amount finally to $330 in gold, with a premium of 25c. on each dollar. Ponder on this, O traveller! I lay bare these facts for your special instruction.

But before my first caravan was destined to part company with me, Soor Hadji Palloo—worthy young man—and I, were to come to a definite understanding about money matters. The morning appointed for departure Soor Hadji Palloo came to my hut and presented his bill, with all the gravity of innocence, for supplying the pagazis with twenty-five doti each as their hire to Unyanyembe, begging immediate payment in money. Words fail to express the astonishment I naturally felt, that this sharp-looking young man should so soon have forgotten the verbal contract entered into between him and myself the morning previous, which was to the effect that out of the three thousand doti stored in my tent, and bought expressly for pagazi hire, each and every man hired for me as carriers from Bagamoyo to Unyanyembe, should be paid out of the store there in my tent. When I asked if he remembered the contract, he replied in the affirmative : his reasons for breaking it so soon were, that he wished to sell his cloths, not mine, and for his cloths he should want money, not an exchange. But I gave him to comprehend that as he was procuring pagazis for me, he was to pay my pagazis with my cloths; that all the money I expected to pay him, should be just such a sum as I thought adequate for his trouble as my agent, and that only on those terms should he act for me in this or any other matter, and that the " Musungu " was not accustomed to eat his words.

The preceding paragraph embodies many more words than are contained in it. It embodies a dialogue of an hour, an angry altercation of half-an-hour's duration, a vow taken on the part of Soor Hadji Palloo, that if I did not take his cloths he should not touch my business, many tears, entreaties woeful penitence, and much else, all of which were responded to with, "Do as I want you to do, or do nothing." Finally came relief, and a happy ending. Soor Hadji Palloo went away with a bright face, taking with him the three soldiers' posho (food), and honga (tribute) for the caravan. Well for me that it ended so, and that subsequent quarrels of a similar nature terminated so peaceably, otherwise I doubt whether my departure from Bagamoyo would have happened so early as it did. While I am on this theme, and as it really engrossed every moment of my time at Bagamoyo, I may as well be more explicit regarding Soor Hadji Palloo and his connection with my business.

Soor Hadji Palloo was a smart young man of business, energetic, quick at mental calculation, and seemed to be born for a successful salesman. His eyes were never idle; they wandered over every part of my person, over the tent. the bed, the guns, the clothes, and having swung clear round, began the silent circle over again. His fingers were never at rest, they had a fidgety, nervous action at their tips, constantly in the act of feeling something; while in the act of talking to me, he would lean over and feel the texture of the cloth of my trousers, my coat, or my shoes or socks : then he would feel his own light jamdani shirt or dabwain loin-cloth, until his eyes casually resting upon a novelty, his body would lean forward, and his arm was stretched out with the willing fingers. His jaws also were in perpetual motion, caused by vile habits he had acquired of chewing betel-nut and lime, and sometimes tobacco and lime. They gave out a sound similar to that of a young shoat, in the act of sucking. He was a pious Mohammedan, and observed the external courtesies and ceremonies of the true believers. He would affably greet me, take off his shoes, enter my tent protesting he was not fit to sit in my presence, and after being seated, would begin his ever-crooked errand. Of honesty, literal and practical honesty, this youth knew nothing; to the pure truth he was an utter stranger; the falsehoods he had uttered during his short life seemed already to have quenched the bold gaze of innocence from his eyes, to have banished the color of truthfulness from his features, to have transformed him—yet a stripling of twenty—into a most accomplished rascal, and consummate expert in dishonesty.

During the six weeks I encamped at Bagamoyo, waiting for my quota of men, this lad of twenty gave me very much trouble. He was found out half a dozen times a day in dishonesty, yet was in no way abashed by it. He would send in his account of the cloths supplied to the pagazis, stating them to be 25 paid to each; on sending a man to inquire I would find the greatest number to have been 20, and the smallest 12. Soor Hadji Palloo described the cloths to be of first-class quality, Ulyah cloths, worth in the market four times more than the ordinary quality given to the pagazis, yet a personal examination would prove them to be the flimsiest goods sold, such as American sheeting $2\frac{1}{2}$ feet broad, and worth $2·75 per 30 yards a piece at Zanzibar, or the most inferior Kaniki, which is generally sold at $9 per score. He would personally come to my camp and demand 40 lbs. of Sami-Sami, Merikani, and Bubu beads for posho, or caravan rations; an inspection of their store before departure from their first camp from Bagamoyo would show a deficiency ranging from 5 to 30 lbs. Moreover, he cheated in cash-money, such as demanding $4 for crossing the Kingani Ferry for every ten pagazis, when the fare was $2 for the same number; and an unconscionable number of pice (copper coins equal in value to ¾ of a cent) were required for posho. It was every day for four weeks that this system of roguery was carried out. Each day conceived a dozen new schemes; every instant of his time he seemed to be devising how to plunder, until I was fairly at my wits' end how to thwart him. Exposure before a crowd of his fellows brought no blush of shame to his sallow cheeks; he would listen with a mere shrug of the shoulders and that was all, which I might interpret any way it pleased me. A threat to reduce his present had no effect; a bird in the hand was certainly worth two in the bush for him, so ten dollars' worth of goods stolen and in his actual possession was of more intrinsic value than the promise of $20 in a few days, though it was that of a white man.

Readers will of course ask themselves why I did not, after the first discovery of these shameless proceedings, close my business with him, to which I make reply, that I could not do without him unless his equal were forthcoming, that I never felt so thoroughly dependent on any one man as I did upon him; without his or his duplicate's aid, I must have stayed at Bagamoyo at least six months, at the end of which time the Expedition would have become valueless, the rumour of it having been blown abroad to the four winds. It was immediate departure that was essential to my success—departure from Bagamoyo—after which it might be possible for me to control my own future in a great measure.

These troubles were the greatest that I could at this time imagine. I have already stated that I had $1,750 worth of pagazis' clothes, or 3,500 doti, stored in my tent, and above what my bales contained. Calculating one hundred and forty pagazis at 25 doti each, I supposed

I had enough, yet, though I had been trying to teach the young Hindi that the Musungu was not a fool, nor blind to his pilfering tricks, though the 3,500 doti were all spent; though I had only obtained one hundred and thirty pagazis at 25 doti each, which in the aggregate amounted to 3,200 doti: Soor Hadji Palloo's bill was $1,400 cash extra. His plea was that he had furnished Ulyah clothes for Muhongo 240 doti, equal in value to 960 of my doti, that the money was spent in ferry pice, in presents to chiefs of caravans of tents, guns, red broad cloth, in presents to people on the Mrima (coast) to induce them to hunt up pagazis. Upon this exhibition of most ruthless cheating I waxed indignant, and declared to him that if he did not run over his bill and correct it, he should go without a pice.

But before the bill could be put into proper shape, my words, threats, and promises falling heedlessly on a stony brain, a man, Kanjee by name, from the store of Tarya Topan, of Zanzibar, had to come over, when the bill was finally reduced to $738. Without any disrespect to Tarya Topan, I am unable to decide which is the most accomplished rascal, Kanjee, or young Soor Hadji Palloo; in the words of a white man who knows them both, " there is not the splitting of a straw between them." Kanjee is deep and sly, Soor Hadji Palloo is bold and incorrigible. But peace be to them both, may their shaven heads never be covered with the troublous crown I wore at Bagamoyo !

My dear friendly reader, do not think, if I speak out my mind in this or in any other chapter upon matters seemingly trivial and unimportant, that seeming such they should be left unmentioned. Every tittle related is a fact, and to know facts is to receive knowledge.

How could I ever recite my experience to you if I did not enter upon these miserable details, which sorely distract the stranger upon his first arrival? Had I been a Government official, I had but wagged my finger and my quota of pagazis had been furnished me within a week; but as an individual arriving without the graces of official recognition, armed with no Government influence, I had to be patient, bide my time, and chew the cud of irritation quietly, but the bread I ate was not all sour, as this was.

The white men, Farquhar and Shaw, were kept steadily at work upon water-proof tents of hemp canvas, for I perceived, by the premonitory showers of rain that marked the approach of the Masika that an ordinary tent of light cloth would subject myself to damp and my goods to mildew, and while there was time to rectify all errors that had crept into my plans through ignorance or over haste, I thought it was not wise to permit things to rectify themselves. Now that I have returned uninjured in health, though I have suffered the attacks of twenty-three fevers within the short space of thirteen months, I must confess I owe my life, first, to the mercy of God; secondly, to the enthusiasm for my work, which animated me from the beginning to the end; thirdly, to having never ruined my constitution by indulgence in vice and intemperance; fourthly, to the energy of my nature; fifthly, to a native hopefulness which never died; and, sixthly, to having furnished myself with a capacious water and damp proof canvas house. And here, if my experience may be of value, I would suggest that travellers, instead of submitting their better judgment to the caprices of a tent-maker, who will endeavour to pass off a handsomely made fabric of his own, which is unsuited to all climes, to use his own judgment, and get the best and strongest that money will buy. In the end it will prove the cheapest, and perhaps be the means of saving his life.

On one point I failed, and lest new and young travellers fall into the same error which marred much of my enjoyment, this paragraph is written. One must be extremely careful in his choice of weapons, whether for sport or defence. A traveller should have at least three different kinds of guns. One should be a fowling-piece, the second should be a double-barrelled rifle, No. 10 or 12, the third should be a magazine-rifle, for defence. For the fowling-piece I would suggest No. 12 bore, with barrels at least four feet in length. For the rifle for larger game, I would point out, with due deference to old sportsmen, of course, that the best guns for African game are the English Lancaster and Reilly rifles; and for a fighting weapon, I maintain that the best yet invented is the American Winchester repeating rifle, or the " sixteen-shooter " as it is called, supplied with the London Eley's ammunition. If I suggest as a fighting weapon the American Winchester, I do not mean that the traveller need take it for the purpose of offence, but as the best means of efficient defence, to save his own life against African banditti, when attacked, a thing likely to happen any time.

I met a young man soon after returning from the interior, who declared his conviction that the " Express " rifle was the most perfect weapon ever invented to destroy African game. Very possibly the young man may be right, and that the " Express " rifle is all he declares it to be, but he had never practised with it against African game, and as I had never tried it, I could not combat his assertion : but I could relate my experiences with weapons, having all the penetrating powers of the "Express," and could inform him that though the bullets penetrated through the animals, they almost always failed to bring down the game at the first fire. On the other hand, I could inform him, that during the time I travelled with Dr. Livingstone the Doctor lent me his heavy Reilly rifle with which I seldom failed to bring an animal or two home to the camp, and that I found the Fraser shell answer all purposes for which it was intended. The feats related by Capt. Speke and Sir Samuel Baker are no longer matter of wonderment to the young sportsman, when he has a Lancaster or a Reilly in his hand. After a very few trials he can imitate them, if not excel their deeds, provided he has a steady hand. And it is to forward this end that this paragraph is written. African game require "bone-crushers;" for any ordinary carbine possesses sufficient penetrative qualities, yet has not the disabling qualities which a gun must possess to be useful in the hands of an African explorer.

I had not been long at Bagamoyo before I went over to Mussoudi's camp, to visit the "Livingstone caravan" which the British Consul had despatched on the first day of November, 1870, to the relief of Livingstone. The number of packages was thirty-five, which required as many men to convey them to Unyanyembe. The men chosen to escort this caravan were composed of Johannese and Wahiyow, seven in number. Out of the seven, four were slaves. They lived in clover here— thoughtless of the errand they had been sent upon, and careless of the consequences. What these men were doing at Bagamoyo all this time I never could conceive, except indulging their own vicious propensities. It would be nonsense to say there were no pagazis, because I know there were at least fifteen caravans which had started for the interior since the Ramadan (December 15th, 1870). Yet Livingstone's caravan had arrived at this little town of Bagamoyo November 2nd, and here it had been lying until the 10th February, in all, 100 days, for lack of the limited number of thirty-five pagazis, a number that might be procured within two days through consular influence.

Bagamoyo has a most enjoyable climate. It is far preferable in every sense to that of Zanzibar. We were able to sleep in the open air, and rose refreshed and healthy each morning, to enjoy our matutinal bath in the sea; and by the time the sun had risen we were engaged in various preparations for our departure for the interior. Our days were enlivened by visits from the Arabs who were also bound for Unyanyembe; by comical scenes in the camp; sometimes by court-martials held on the refractory; by a boxing-match between Farquhar and Shaw, necessitating my prudent interference when they waxed too wroth; by a hunting excursion now and then to the Kingani plain and river; by social conversation with the old Jemadar and his band of Baluches, who were never tired of warning me that the Masika was at hand, and of advising me that my best course was to hurry on before the season for travelling expired.

Among the employés with the Expedition were two Hindi and two Goanese. They had conceived the idea that the African interior was an El Dorado, the ground of which was strewn over with ivory tusks, and they had clubbed together, while their imaginations were thus heated, to embark in a little enterprise of their own. Their names were Jako, Abdul Kader, Bunder Salaam, and Aranselar; Jako engaged in my service as carpenter and general help; Abdul Kader as a tailor, Bunder Salaam as cook, and Aranselar as chief butler.

But Aranselar, with an intuitive eye, foresaw that I was likely to prove a vigorous employer, and while there was yet time he devoted most of it to conceive how it were possible to withdraw from the engagement. He received permission upon asking for it to go to Zanzibar to visit his friends. Two days afterwards I was informed he had blown his right eye out, and received a medical confirmation of the fact, and note of the extent of the injury, from Dr. Christie, the physician to His Highness Seyd Burghash. His compatriots I imagined were about planning the same thing, but a peremptory command to abstain from such folly, issued after they had received their advance-pay, sufficed to check any sinister designs they may have formed.

A groom was caught stealing from the bales, one night, and the chase after him into the country until he vanished out of sight into the jungle, was one of the most agreeable diversions which occurred to wear away the interval employed in preparing for the march.

I had now despatched four caravans into the interior, and the fifth, which was to carry the boats and boxes, personal luggage, and a few cloth and bead loads, was ready to be led by myself. The following is the order of departure of the caravans.

1871. Feb. 6.—Expedition arrived at Bagamoyo.

1871. Feb. 18.—First caravan departs with twenty-four pagazis and three soldiers.

1871. Feb. 21.—Second caravan departs with twenty-eight pagazis, two chiefs, and two soldiers.

1871. Feb. 25,—Third caravan departs with twenty-two pagazis, ten donkeys, one white man, one cook, and three soldiers.

1871. March 11.—Fourth caravan departs with fifty-five pagazis, two chiefs, and three soldiers.

1871. March 21.—Fifth caravan departs with twenty-eight pagazis, twelve soldiers, two white men, one tailor, one cook, one interpreter, one gun-bearer, seventeen asses, two horses, and one dog.

Total number, inclusive of all souls, comprised in caravans connected with the " 'New York Herald' Expedition," 192.

PORTRAIT OF BOMBAY AND MABRUKI.

CHAPTER V.

THROUGH UKWERE, UKAMI, AND UDOE TO USEGUHHA.

Leaving Bagamoyo for the interior.—Constructing a Bridge.—Our first troubles.—Shooting Hippopotami.—A first view of the Game Land. —Anticipating trouble with the Wagogo.—The dreadful poison-flies. —Unlucky adventures while hunting.—The cunning chief of Kingaru.—Sudden death of my two horses.—A terrible experience. —The city of the "Lion Lord."

ON the 21st of March, exactly seventy-three days after my arrival at Zanzibar, the fifth caravan, led by myself, left the town of Bagamoyo for our first journey westward, with "Forward!" for its *mot du guet*. As the kirangozi unrolled the American flag, and put himself at the head of the caravan, and the pagazis, animals, soldiers, and idlers were lined for the march, we bade a long farewell to the *dolce far niente* of civilised life, to the blue ocean, and to its open road to home, to the hundreds of dusky spectators who were there to celebrate our departure with repeated salvoes of musketry.

Our caravan is composed of twenty-eight pagazis, including the kirangozi, or guide; twelve soldiers under Capt. Mbarak Bombay, in charge of seventeen donkeys and their loads; Selim, my interpreter, in charge of the donkey and cart and its load; one cook and sub, who is also to be tailor and ready hand for all, and leads the grey horse; Shaw, once mate of a ship, now transformed into rearguard and overseer for the caravan, who is mounted on a good riding-donkey, and wearing a canoe-like topee and sea-boots; and lastly, on the splendid bay horse presented to me by Mr. Goodhue, myself, called "Bana Mkuba," the "big master," by my people—the vanguard, the reporter, the thinker, and leader of the Expedition.

Altogether the Expedition numbers on the day of departure three white men, twenty-three soldiers, four supernumeraries, four chiefs, and one hundred and fifty-three pagazis, twenty-seven donkeys, and one cart, conveying cloth, beads, and wire, boat-fixings, tents, cooking utensils and dishes, medicine, powder, small shot, musket-balls, and metallic cartridges; instruments and small necessaries, such as soap, sugar, tea, coffee, Liebig's extract of meat, pemmican, candles, &c., which make a total of 153 loads. The weapons of defence which the Expedition possesses consist of one double-barrel breech-loading gun, smooth bore; one American Winchester rifle, or "sixteen-shooter;" one Henry rifle, or "sixteen-shooter;" two

Starr's breech-loaders, one Jocelyn breech-loader, one olephant rifle, carrying balls eight to the pound; two breech-loading revolvers, twenty-four muskets (flint locks) six single-barrelled pistols, one battle-axe, two swords, two daggers (Persian kummers, purchased at Shiraz by myself), one boar-spear, two American axes 4 lbs. each, twenty-four hatchets, and twenty-four butcher-knives.

The Expedition has been fitted with care; whatever it needed was not stinted; everything was provided. Nothing was done too hurriedly, yet everything was purchased, manufactured, collected, and compounded with the utmost despatch consistent with efficiency and means. Should it fail of success in its errand of rapid transit to Ujiji and back, it must simply happen from an accident which could not be controlled. So much for the *personnel* of the Expedition and its purpose, until its *point de mire* be reached.

We left Bagamoyo the attraction of all the curious, with much *éclat*, and defiled up a narrow lane shaded almost to twilight by the dense umbrage of two parallel hedges of mimosas. We were all in the highest spirits. The soldiers sang, the kirangozi lifted his voice into a loud bellowing note, and fluttered the American flag, which told all on-lookers, "Lo, a Musungu's caravan!" and my heart, I thought, palpitated much too quickly for the sober face of a leader. But I could not check it; the enthusiasm of youth still clung to me—despite my travels; my pulses bounded with the full glow of staple health; behind me were the troubles which had harassed me for over two months. With that dishonest son of a Hindi, Soor Hadji Palloo, I had said my last word; of the blatant rabble, of Arabs, Banyans, and Baluches I had taken my last look; with the Jesuits of the French Mission I had exchanged farewells, and before me beamed the sun of promise as he sped towards the Occident. Loveliness glowed around me. I saw fertile fields, riant vegetation, strange trees —I heard the cry of cricket and pee-wit, and sibilant sound of many insects, all of which seemed to tell me, "At last you are started." What could I do but lift my face toward the pure-glowing sky, and cry, "God be thanked!"

The first camp, Shamba Gonera, we arrived at in 1 hour 30 minutes, equal to 3¼ miles. This first, or "little journey," was performed very well, "considering," as the Irishman says. The boy Selim upset the cart not more than three times. Zaidi, the soldier, only once let his donkey, which carried one bag of my clothes and a box of ammunition, lie in a puddle of black water. The clothes had to be re-washed; the ammunition-box, thanks to my provision, was waterproof. Kamna perhaps knew the art of donkey-driving, but, overjoyful at the departure, had sung himself into oblivion of the difficulties with which an animal of the pure asinine breed has naturally to contend against, such as not knowing the right road, and inability to resist the temptation of straying into the depths of a manioc field; and the donkey, ignorant of the custom in vogue amongst ass-drivers of flourishing sticks before an animal's nose, and misunderstanding the direction in which he was required to go, ran off at full speed along an opposite road, until his pack got unbalanced, and he was fain to come to the earth. But these incidents were trivial, of no importance, and natural to the first "little journey" in East Africa.

The soldiers' point of character leaked out just a little. Bombay turned out to be honest and trusty, but slightly disposed to be dilatory. Uledi did more talking than work; while the runaway Ferajji and the useless-handed Mabruki Burton turned out to be true men and staunch, carrying loads the sight of which would have caused the strong-limbed hamals of Stamboul to sigh.

The saddles were excellent, surpassing expectation. The strong hemp canvas bore its one hundred and fifty-pounds' burden with the strength of bull hide, and the loading and unloading of miscellaneous baggage was performed with systematic despatch. In brief, there was nothing to regret—the success of the journey proved our departure to be anything but premature.

The next three days were employed in putting the finishing touches to our preparations for the long land journey and our precautions against the Masika, which was now ominously near, and in settling accounts.

Shamba Gonera means Gonera's Field. Gonera is a wealthy Indian widow, well disposed towards the Wasungu (whites). She exports much cloth, beads, and wire into the far interior, and imports in return much ivory. Her house is after the model of the town houses, with long sloping roof and projecting eaves, affording a cool shade, under which the pagazis love to loiter. On its southern and eastern side stretch the cultivated fields which supply Bagamoyo with the staple grain, matama, of East Africa; on the left grow Indian corn, and muhogo, a yam-like root of whitish color, called by some manioc; when dry, it is ground and compounded into cakes similar to army slapjacks. On the north, just behind the house, winds a black quagmire, a sinuous hollow, which in its deepest parts always contains water—the muddy home of the brake-and-rush-loving "kiboko" or hippopotamus. Its banks, crowded with dwarf fan-palm, tall water-reeds, acacias, and tiger-grass, afford shelter to numerous aquatic

birds, pelicans, &c. After following a course north-
easterly, it conflows with the Kingani, which, at the
distance of four miles from Gonera's country-house,
bends eastward into the sea. To the west, after a mile of
cultivation, fall and recede in succession the sea-beaches
of old in lengthy parallel waves, overgrown densely with
forest grass and marsh reeds. On the spines of these
land-swells flourish ebony, calabash, and mango.

"Sofari—sofari leo! Pakia, pakia!"—"A journey—a
journey to day! Set out!—set out!" rang the cheery
voice of the kirangozi, echoed by that of my servant,
Selim, on the morning of the fourth day, which was that
fixed for our departure in earnest. As I hurried my men
to their work, and lent a hand with energy to drop the
tents, I mentally resolved that, if my caravans ahead
should give me clear space, Unyanyembe should be our
resting-place before three months expired. By 6 A.M.
our early breakfast was despatched, and the donkeys and
pagazis were defiling from Camp Gonera. Even at this
early hour, and in this country place, there was quite a
collection of curious natives, to whom we gave the parting
"Kwaheri" with sincerity. My bay horse was found to
be invaluable for the service of a quarter-master of a
transport-train; for to such was I compelled to compare
myself. I could stay behind until the last donkey had
quitted the camp, and, by a few minutes' gallop, I could
put myself at the head, leaving Shaw to bring up the rear.

The road was a mere footpath, and led over a soil,
which, though sandy, was of surprising fertility, pro-
ducing grain and vegetables a hundredfold, the sowing
and planting of which was done in the most unskilful
manner. In their fields, at heedless labor, were men and
women in the scantiest costumes, compared to which

Adam and Eve, in their fig-tree apparel, must have been *en grande tenue*. We passed them with serious faces, while they laughed and giggled, and pointed their index fingers at this and that, which to them seemed so strange and bizarre.

In about half an hour we had left the tall matama and fields of water-melons, cucumbers, and manioc; and, crossing a reedy slough, were in an open forest of ebony and calabash. In its depths are deer in plentiful numbers, and at night it is visited by the hippopotami of the Kingani for the sake of its grass. In another hour we had emerged from the woods, and were looking down upon the broad valley of the Kingani, and a scene presented itself so utterly different from what my foolish imagination had drawn, that I felt quite relieved by the pleasing disappointment. Here was a valley stretching four miles east and west, and about eight miles north and south, left with the richest soil to its own wild growth of grass— which in civilization would have been a most valuable meadow for the rearing of cattle—invested as it was by dense forests, darkening the horizon at all points of the compass, and folded in by tree-clad ridges.

At the sound of our caravan the red antelope bounded away to our right and the left, and frogs hushed their croak. The sun shone hot, and while traversing the valley we experienced a little of its real African fervour. About half way across we came to a sluice of stagnant water which, directly in the road of the caravan, had settled down into an oozy pond. The pagazis crossed a hastily-constructed bridge, thrown up a long time ago by some Washensi Samaritans. It was an extraordinary affair; rugged tree limbs resting on very unsteady forked piles, and it had evidently tested the patience of many a loaded Mnyamwezi, as it did those porters of our caravan. Our weaker animals were unloaded, the puddle between Bagamoyo and Gonera having taught us prudence. But this did not occasion much delay; the men worked smartly under Shaw's supervision.

The turbid Kingani, famous for its hippopotami, was reached in a short time, and we began to thread the jungle along its right bank until we were halted point-blank by a narrow sluice having an immeasurable depth of black mud. The difficulty presented by this was very grave, though its breadth was barely eight feet; the donkeys, and least of all the horses, could not be made to traverse two poles like our biped carriers, neither could they be driven into the sluice, where they would quickly founder. The only available way of crossing it in safety was by means of a bridge, to endure in this conservative land for generations as the handiwork of the Wasungu. So we set to work, there being no help for it, with American axes—the first of their kind the strokes of which ever rang in this part of the world—to build a bridge. Be sure it was made quickly, for where the civilized white is found, a difficulty must vanish. The bridge was composed of six stout trees thrown across, over these were laid cross-wise fifteen pack saddles, covered again with a thick layer of grass. All the animals crossed it safely, and then for a third time that morning the process of wading was performed. The Kingani flowed northerly here, and our course lay down its right bank. A half mile in that direction through a jungle of giant reeds and extravagant climbers brought us to the ferry, where the animals had to be again unloaded—verily, I wished when I saw its deep muddy waters that I possessed the power of Moses with his magic rod, or what would have answered my purpose as well, Aladdin's ring, for then I could have found myself and party on the opposite side without further trouble; but not having either of these gifts I issued orders for an immediate crossing, for it was ill wishing sublime things before this most mundane prospect.

Kingwere, the canoe paddler, espying us from his brake covert, on the opposite side, civilly responded to our halloos, and brought his huge hollowed tree skilfully over the whirling eddies of the river to where we stood waiting for him. While one party loaded the canoe with our goods, others got ready a long rope to fasten around the animals' necks, wherewith to haul them through the river to the other bank. After seeing the work properly commenced, I sat down on a condemned canoe to amuse myself with the hippopotami by peppering their thick skulls with my No. 12 smooth-bore. The Winchester rifle (calibre 44), a present from the Hon. Edward Joy Morris—our minister at Constantinople—did no more than slightly tap them, causing about as much injury as a boy's sling; it was perfect in its accuracy of fire, for ten times in succession I struck the tops of their heads between the ears. One old fellow, with the look of a sage, was tapped close to the right ear by one of these bullets. Instead of submerging himself as others had done he coolly turned round his head as if to ask, "Why this waste of valuable cartridges on us?" The response to the mute inquiry of his sageship was an ounce-and-a-quarter bullet from the smooth-bore, which made him bellow with pain, and in a few moments he rose up again, tumbling in his death agonies. As his groans were so piteous, I refrained from a useless sacrifice of life, and left the amphibious horde in peace.

A little knowledge concerning these uncouth inmates of the African waters was gained even during the few

minutes we were delayed at the ferry. When undisturbed
by foreign sounds, they congregate in shallow water on
the sand bars, with the fore half of their bodies exposed
to the warm sunshine, and are in appearance, when thus
somnolently reposing, very like a herd of enormous swine.
When startled by the noise of an intruder, they plunge
hastily into the depths, lashing the waters into a yellowish foam, and scatter themselves below the surface, when
presently the heads of a few reappear, snorting the water
from their nostrils, to take a fresh breath and a cautious
scrutiny around them; when thus, we see but their ears,
forehead, eyes and nostrils, and as they hastily submerge
again it requires a steady wrist and a quick hand to shoot
them. I have heard several comparisons made of their
appearance while floating in this manner: some Arabs
told me before I had seen them that they looked like
dead trees carried down the river; others, who in some
country had seen hogs, thought they resembled them, but
to my mind they look more like horses when swimming—
their curved necks and pointed ears, their wide eyes and
expanded nostrils, favor greatly this comparison.

At night they seek the shore, and wander several miles
over the country, luxuriating among its rank grasses. To
within four miles of the town of Bagamoyo (the Kingani
is eight miles distant) their wide tracks are seen.
Frequently, if not disturbed by the startling human
voice, they make a raid on the rich corn-stalks of the
native cultivators, and a dozen of them will in a few
minutes make a frightful havoc in a large field of this
plant. Consequently, we were not surprised, while delayed at the ferry, to hear the owners of the corn venting
loud halloos, like the rosy-cheeked farmer boys in England
when scaring the crows away from the young wheat.

The caravan in the meanwhile had crossed safely—
bales, baggage, donkeys, and men. I had thought to
have camped on the bank, so as to amuse myself with
shooting antelope, and also for the sake of procuring
their meat, in order to save my goats, of which I had a
number constituting my live stock of provisions; but,
thanks to the awe and dread which my men entertained
of the hippopotami, I was hurried on to the outpost of
the Baluch garrison at Bagamoyo, a small village called
Kikoka, distant four miles from the river.

The western side of the river was a considerable im-
provement upon the eastern. The plain, slowly heaving
upwards, as smoothly as the beach of a watering-place,
for the distance of a mile, until it culminated in a gentle
and rounded ridge, presented none of those difficulties
which troubled us on the other side. There were none
of those cataclysms of mire and sloughs of black mud
and over-tall grasses, none of that miasmatic jungle
with its noxious emissions; it was just such a scene as
one may find before an English mansion—a noble expanse
of lawn and sward, with boscage sufficient to agreeably
diversify it. After traversing the open plain, the road
led through a grove of young ebony trees, where guinea-
fowls and a hartebeest were seen; it then wound, with
all the characteristic eccentric curves of a goat-path, up
and down a succession of land-waves crested by the dark
green foliage of the mango, and the scantier and lighter-
coloured leaves of the enormous calabash. The depressions were filled with jungle of more or less density,
while here and there opened glades, shadowed even
during noon by thin groves of towering trees. At our
approach fled in terror flocks of green pigeons, jays, ibis,
turtledoves, golden pheasants, quails and moorhens, with

crows and hawks, while now and then a solitary pelican winged its way to the distance.

Nor was this enlivening prospect without its pairs of antelope, and monkeys which hopped away like Australian kangaroos; these latter were of good size, with round bullet heads, white breasts, and long tails tufted at the end.

We arrived at Kikoka by 5 P.M., having loaded and unloaded our pack animals four times, crossing one deep puddle, a mud sluice, and a river, and performed a journey of eleven miles.

The settlement of Kikoka is a collection of straw huts, not built after any architectural style, but after a bastard form, invented by indolent settlers from the Mrima and Zanzibar for the purpose of excluding as much sunshine as possible from the eaves and interior. A sluice and some wells provide them with water, which though sweet is not particularly wholesome or appetizing, owing to the large quantities of decayed matter which is washed into it by the rains, and is then left to corrupt in it. A weak effort has been made to clear the neighbour-hood for providing a place for cultivation, but to the dire task of wood-chopping and jungle-clearing the settlers prefer occupying an open glade, which they clear of grass, so as to be able to hoe up two or three inches of soil, into which they cast their seed, confident of return.

The next day was a halt at Kikoka; the fourth caravan, consisting solely of Wanyamwezi, proving a sore obstacle to a rapid advance. Maganga, its chief, devised several methods of extorting more cloth and presents from me, he having cost already more than any three chiefs together; but his efforts were of no avail further than obtaining promises of reward if he would hurry on to Unyanyembe so that I might find my road clear.

On the 2'i th, the Wanyamwezi having started, we broke camp soon after at 7 A.M. The country was of the same nature as that lying between the Kingani and Kikoka—a park land, attractive and beautiful in every feature.

I rode in advance to secure meat should a chance present itself, but not the shadow of vert or venison did I see. Ever in our front—westerly—rolled the land-waves, now rising, now subsiding, parallel one with the other, like a ploughed field many times magnified. Each ridge had its knot of jungle or its thin combing of heavily foliaged trees, until we arrived close to Rosako, our next halting place, when the monotonous wavure of the land underwent a change, breaking into independent hummocks clad with dense jungle. On one of these, veiled by an impenetrable jungle of thorny acacia, rested Rosako, girt round by its natural fortification, neighbouring another village to the north of it similarly protected. Between them sank a valley extremely fertile and bountiful in its productions, bisected by a small stream, which serves as a drain to the valley or low hills surrounding it.

Rosako is the frontier village of Ukwere, while Kikoka is the north-western extremity of Uzaramo. We entered this village, and occupied its central portion with our tents and animals. A kitanda, or square light bedstead, without valance, fringe, or any superfluity whatever, but nevertheless quite as comfortable as with them, was brought to my tent for my use by the village chief. The animals were, immediately after being unloaded, driven out to feed, and the soldiers to a man set to work to pile the baggage up, lest the rain, which during the Masika season always appears imminent, might cause irreparable damage.

Among other experiments which I was about to try in Africa was that of a good watch-dog on any unmannerly people who would insist upon coming into my tent at untimely hours and endangering valuables. Especially did I wish to try the effect of its bark on the mighty Wagogo, who, I was told by certain Arabs, would lift the door of the tent and enter whether you wished them or not; who would chuckle at the fear they inspired, and say to you, " Hi, hi, white man, I never saw the like of you before; are there many more like you? where do you come from?" Also would they take hold of your watch and ask you with a cheerful curiosity, " What is this for, white man?" to which you of course would reply that it was to tell you the hour and minute. But the Mgogo, proud of his prowess, and more unmannerly than a brute, would answer you with a snort of insult. I thought of a watch-dog, and procured a good one at Bombay not only as a faithful companion, but to threaten the heels of just such gentry.

But soon after our arrival at Rosako it was found that the dog, whose name was " Omar," given him from his Turkish origin, was missing; he had strayed away from the soldiers during a rain-squall and had got lost. I despatched Mabruki Burton back to Kikoka to search for him. On the following morning, just as we were about to leave Rosako, the faithful fellow returned with the lost dog, having found him at Kikoka.

Previous to our departure on the morning after this, Maganga, chief of the fourth caravan, brought me the unhappy report that three of his pagazis were sick, and he would like to have some " dowa "—medicine. Though not a doctor, or in any way connected with the profession, I had a well-supplied medicine chest—without which no traveller in Africa could live—for just such a contingency as was now present. On visiting Maganga's sick men, I found one suffering from inflammation of the lungs, another from the mukunguru (African intermittent). They all imagined themselves about to die, and called loudly for " Mama!" " Mama!" though they were all grown men. It was evident that the fourth caravan could not stir that day, so leaving word with Maganga to hurry after me as soon as possible, I issued orders for the march of my own.

Excepting in the neighbourhood of the villages which we have passed there were no traces of cultivation. The country extending between the several stations is as much a wilderness as the desert of Sahara, though it possesses a far more pleasing aspect. Indeed, had the first man at the time of the Creation gazed at his world and perceived it of the beauty which belongs to this part of Africa, he would have had no cause of complaint. In the deep thickets, set like islets amid a sea of grassy verdure, he would have found shelter from the noonday heat, and a safe retirement for himself and spouse during the awesome darkness. In the morning he could have walked forth on the sloping sward, enjoyed its freshness, and performed his ablutions in one of the many small streams flowing at its foot. His garden of fruit-trees is all that is required; the noble forests, deep and cool, are round about him, and in their shade walk as many animals as one can desire. For days and days let a man walk in any direction, north, south, east, and west, and he will behold the same scene.

Earnestly as I wished to hurry on to Unyanyembe, still a heart-felt anxiety about the arrival of my goods carried by the fourth caravan, served as a drag upon me and before my caravan had marched nine miles my anxiety had risen to the highest pitch, and caused me to order a camp there and then. The place selected for it was near a long straggling sluice, having an abundance of water during the rainy season, draining as it does two extensive slopes. No sooner had we pitched our camp, built a boma of thorny acacia, and other tree branches, by stacking them round our camp, and driven our animals to grass, than we were made aware of the formidable number and variety of the insect tribe, which for a time was another source of anxiety, until a diligent examination of the several species dispelled it.

As it was a most interesting hunt which I instituted for the several specimens of the insects, I here append the record of it for what it is worth. My object in obtaining these specimens was to determine whether the genus *Glossina morsitans* of the naturalist, or the tsetse (sometimes called setse) of Livingstone, Vardon, and Cumming, said to be deadly to horses, was amongst them. Up to this date I had been nearly two months in East Africa, and had as yet seen no tsetse; and my horses, instead of becoming emaciated—for such is one of the symptoms of a tsetse bite—had considerably improved in condition. There were three different species of flies which sought shelter in my tent, which, unitedly, kept up a continual chorus of sounds—one performed the basso profondo, another a tenor, and the third a weak contralto. The first emanated from a voracious and fierce fly, an inch long, having a ventral capacity for blood quite astonishing.

This larger fly was the one chosen for the first inspection, which was of the intensest. I permitted one to alight on my flannel pyjamas, which I wore while *en déshabillé* in camp. No sooner had he alighted than his posterior was raised, his head lowered, and his weapons, consisting of four hair-like styles, unsheathed from the proboscis-like bag which concealed them, and immediately I felt pain like that caused by a dexterous lancet-cut or the probe of a fine needle. I permitted him to gorge himself, though my patience and naturalistic interest were sorely tried. I saw his abdominal parts distend with the plenitude of the repast until it had swollen to three times its former shrunken girth, when he flew away of his own accord laden with blood. On rolling up my flannel pyjamas to see the fountain whence the fly had drawn the fluid, I discovered it to be a little above the left knee, by a crimson bead resting over the incision. After wiping the blood the wound was similar to that caused by a deep thrust of a fine needle, but all pain had vanished with the departure of the fly.

Having caught a specimen of this fly, I next proceeded to institute a comparison between it and the tsetse, as described by Dr. Livingstone on pp. 56–57, ' Missionary Travels and Researches in South Africa' (Murray's edition of 1868). The points of disagreement are many, and such as to make it entirely improbable that this fly is the true tsetse, though my men unanimously stated that its bite was fatal to horses as well as to donkeys. A descriptive abstract of the tsetse would read thus : " Not much larger than a common house-fly, nearly of the same brown colour as the honey-bee. After-part of the body has yellow bars across it. It has a peculiar buzz, and its bite is death to the horse, ox, and dog. On man the bite has no effect, neither has it on wild animals. When allowed to feed on the hand, it inserts the middle prong of three portions into which the proboscis divides, it then draws the prong out a little way, and it assumes a crimson color as the mandibles come into brisk operation; a slight itching irritation follows the bite."

The fly which I had under inspection is called mabunga by the natives. It is much larger than the common house-fly, fully a third larger than the common honey-bee, and its color more distinctly marked; its head is black, with a greenish gloss to it; the after-part of the body is marked by a white line running lengthwise from its junction with the trunk, and on each side of this white line are two other lines, one of a crimson color, the other of a light brown. As for its buzz, there is no peculiarity in it, it might be mistaken for that of a honey-bee. When caught it made desperate efforts to get away, but never attempted to bite. This fly, along with a score of others, attacked my grey horse, and bit it so sorely in the legs that they appeared as if bathed in blood. Hence, I might have been a little vengeful if, with more than the zeal of an entomologist, I caused it to disclose whatever peculiarities its biting parts possessed.

In order to bring this fly as life-like as possible before my readers, I may compare its head to a most tiny miniature of an elephant's, because it has a black pro-boscis and a pair of horny antennæ, which in color and curve resemble tusks. The black proboscis, however, is simply a hollow sheath, which encloses, when not in the act of biting, four reddish and sharp lancets. Under the microscope these four lancets differ in thickness, two are very thick, the third is slender, but the fourth, of an opal color and almost transparent, is exceedingly fine. This last must be the sucker. When the fly is about to wound, the two horny antennæ are made to embrace the part, the lancets are unsheathed, and on the instant the incision is performed. This I consider to be the African " horse-fly.'

The second fly, which sang the tenor note, more nearly resembled in size and description the tsetse. It was exceedingly nimble, and it occupied three soldiers nearly an hour to capture a specimen; and, when it was finally caught, it stung most ravenously the hand, and never ceased its efforts to attack until it was pinned through. It had three or four white marks across the after-part of its body; but the biting parts of this fly consisted of two black antennæ and an opal colored style, which folded away under the neck. When about to bite, this style was shot out straight, and the antennæ embraced it closely. After death the fly lost its distinctive white marks. Only one of this species did we see at this camp.

The third fly, called "chufwa," pitched a weak alto-crescendo note, was a third larger than the house fly, and had long wings. If this insect sang the feeblest note, it certainly did the most work, and inflicted the most injury. Horses and donkeys streamed with blood, and reared and kicked through the pain. So determined was it not to be driven before it obtained its fill, that it was easily despatched; but this dreadful enemy to cattle constantly increased in numbers. The three species above named are, according to natives, fatal to cattle; and this may perhaps be the reason why such a vast expanse of first-class pasture is without domestic cattle of any kind, a few goats only being kept by the villagers. This fly I subsequently found to be the "tsetse."

On the second morning, instead of proceeding, I deemed it more prudent to await the fourth caravan. Burton experimented sufficiently for me on the promised word of the Banyans of Kaole and Zanzibar, and waited eleven months before he received the promised articles. As I did not expect to be much over that time on my errand altogether, it would be ruin, absolute and irremediable, should I be detained at Unyanyembe so long a time by my caravan. Pending its arrival, I sought the pleasures of the chase. I was but a tyro in hunting, I confess, though I had shot a little on the plains of America and Persia; yet I considered myself a fair shot, and on game ground, and within a reasonable proximity to game, I doubted not but I could bring some to camp.

After a march of a mile through the tall grass of the open, we gained the glades between the jungles. Unsuccessful here, after ever so much prying into fine hiding-places and lurking corners, I struck a trail well traversed by small antelope and hartebeest, which we followed. It led me into a jungle, and down a watercourse bisecting it; but, after following it for an hour, I lost it, and, in endeavouring to retrace it, lost my way. However, my pocket-compass stood me in good stead; and by it I steered for the open plain, in the centre of which stood the camp. But it was terribly hard work—this of plunging through an African jungle, ruinous to clothes, and trying to the cuticle. In order to travel quickly, I had donned a pair of flannel pyjamas, and my feet were encased in canvas shoes. As might be expected, before I had gone a few paces a branch of the *acacia horrida*—only one of a hundred such annoyances—caught the right leg of my pyjamas at the knee, and ripped it almost clean off; succeeding which a stumpy kolquall caught me by the shoulder, and another rip was the inevitable consequence. A few yards farther on, a prickly aloëtic plant disfigured by a wide tear the other leg of my pyjamas, and almost immediately I tripped against a convolvulus strong as ratline, and was made to measure my length on a bed of thorns. It was on all fours, like a hound on a scent, that I was compelled to travel; my solar topee getting the worse for wear every minute; my skin getting more and more wounded; my clothes at each step becoming more and more tattered. Besides these discomforts, there was a pungent, acrid plant, which, apart from its strong odorous emissions, struck me smartly on the face, leaving a burning effect similar to cayenne; and the atmosphere, pent in by the density of the jungle, was hot and stifling, and the perspiration transuded through every pore, making my flannel tatters feel as if I had been through a shower. When I had finally regained the plain, and could breathe free, I mentally vowed that the penetralia of an African jungle should not be visited by me again, save under most urgent necessity.

The second and third day passed without any news of Maganga. Accordingly, Shaw and Bombay were sent to hurry him up by all means. On the fourth morning Shaw and Bombay returned, followed by the procrastinating Maganga and his laggard people. Questions only elicited an excuse that his men had been too sick, and he had feared to tax their strength before they were quite equal to stand the fatigue. Moreover he suggested that as they would be compelled to stay one day more at the camp, I might push on to Kingaru and camp there, until his arrival. Acting upon which suggestion I broke camp and started for Kingaru, distant five miles.

On this march the land was more broken, and the caravan first encountered jungle, which gave considerable trouble to our cart. Pisolitic limestone cropped out in boulders and sheets, and we began to imagine ourselves approaching healthy highlands, and as if to give confirmation to the thought, to the north and north-west loomed the purple cones of Udoe, and topmost of all Dilima Peak, about 1,500 feet in height above the sea level. But soon after sinking into a bowl-like valley, green with tall corn, the road slightly deviated from north-west to west, the country still rolling before us in wavy undulations.

In one of the depressions between these lengthy land-swells stood the village of Kingaru, with surroundings significant in their aspect of ague and fever. Perhaps the clouds surcharged with rain, and the overhanging ridges and their dense forests dulled by the gloom, made the place more than usually disagreeable, but my first impressions of the sodden hollow, pent in by those dull woods, with the deep gully close by containing pools of stagnant water, were by no means agreeable.

Before we could arrange our camp and set the tents up, down poured the furious harbinger of the Masika season in torrents sufficient to damp the ardor and new-born love for East Africa I had lately manifested. However, despite rain, we worked on until our camp was finished and the property was safely stored from weather and thieves, and we could regard with resignation the raindrops beating the soil into mud of a very tenacious kind, and forming lakelets and rivers of our camp-ground.

Towards night, the scene having reached its acme of unpleasantness, the rain ceased, and the natives poured into camp from the villages in the woods with their vendibles. Foremost among these, as if in duty bound, came the village sultan—lord, chief, or head—bearing three measures of matama and half a measure of rice, of which he begged, with paternal smiles, my acceptance. But under his smiling mask, bleared eyes, and wrinkled front was visible the soul of trickery, which was of the cunningest kind. Responding under the same mask

adopted by this knavish elder, I said, "The chief of
Kingaru has called me a rich sultan. If I am a rich
sultan why comes not the chief with a rich present to
me, that he might get a rich return?" Said he, with
another leer of his wrinkled visage, "Kingaru is poor,
there is no matama in the village." To which I replied
that since there was no matama in the village I would
pay him half a shukka, or a yard of cloth, which would be
exactly equivalent to his present; that if he preferred to
call his small basketful a present, I should be content to
call my yard of cloth a present. With which logic he
was fain to be satisfied.

April 1st.—To-day the Expedition suffered a loss in the
death of the grey Arab horse presented by Seyd Burghash, Sultan of Zanzibar. The night previous I had
noticed that the horse was suffering. Bearing in mind
what has been so frequently asserted, namely, that no
horses' could live in the interior of Africa because of the
tsetse, I had him opened, and the stomach, which I
believed to be diseased, examined. Besides much un-
digested matama and grass there were found twenty-five
short, thick, white worms, sticking like leeches into the
coating of the stomach, while the intestines were almost
alive with the numbers of long white worms. I was
satisfied that neither man nor beast could long exist with
such a mass of corrupting life within him.

In order that the dead carcase might not taint the
valley, I had it buried deep in the ground, about a score
of yards from the encampment. From such a slight
cause ensued a tremendous uproar from Kingaru—chief
of the village—who, with his brother-chiefs of neighbouring villages, numbering in the aggregate two dozen
wattled huts, had taken counsel upon the best means of

mulcting the Musungu of a full doti or two of Merikani, and finally had arrived at the conviction that the act of burying a dead horse in their soil without "By your leave, sir," was a grievous and fineable fault. Affecting great indignation at the unpardonable omission, he, Kingaru, concluded to send to the Musungu four of his young men to say to him that "since you have buried your horse in my ground, it is well; let him remain there; but you must pay me two doti of Merikani." For reply the messengers were told to say to the chief that I would prefer talking the matter over with himself face to face, if he would condescend to visit me in my tent once again. As the village was but a stone's throw from our encampment, before many minutes had elapsed the wrinkled elder made his appearance at the door of my tent with about half the village behind him.

The following dialogue which took place will serve to illustrate the tempers of the people with whom I was about to have a year's trading intercourse :—

White Man.—" Are you the great chief of Kingaru ?"

Kingaru.—" Huh-uh.   Yes."

W. M.—" The great, great chief ?"

Kingaru.—" Huh-uh.   Yes."

W. M.—" How many soldiers have you ?"

Kingaru.—" Why ?"

W. M.—" How many fighting men have you ?"

Kingaru.—" None."

W. M.—" Oh! I thought you might have a thousand men with you, by your going to fine a strong white man, who has plenty of guns and soldiers, two doti for burying a dead horse."

Kingaru (rather perplexed).—" No ; I have no soldiers I have only a few young men."

W. M.—" Why do you come and make trouble, then ?"

Kingaru.—" It was not I; it was my brothers who said to me, ' Come here, come here, Kingaru, see what the white man has done ! Has he not taken possession of your soil, in that he has put his horse into your ground without your permission ? Come, go to him and see by what right.' Therefore have I come to ask you, who gave you permission to use my soil for a burying-ground ?"

W. M. " I want no man's permission to do what is right. My horse died ; had I left him to fester and stink in your valley, sickness would visit your village, your water would become unwholesome, and caravans would not stop here for trade ; for they would say, ' This is an unlucky spot, let us go away.' But enough said : I understand you to say that you do not want him buried in your ground ; the error I have fallen into is easily put right. This minute my soldiers shall dig him out again, and cover up the soil as it was before ; and the horse shall be left where he died." (Then shouting to Bombay.) " Ho ! Bombay, take soldiers with jembes to dig my horse out of the ground, drag him to where he died, and make everything ready for a march to-morrow morning."

Kingaru, his voice considerably higher, and his head moving to and fro with emotion, cries out, " Akuna, akuna, bana !"—" No, no, master ! Let not the white man get angry. The horse is dead, and now lies buried ; let him remain so, since he is already there, and let us be friends again."

The Sheikh of Kingaru being thus brought to his senses, we bid each other the friendly " Kwaheri," and I was left alone to ruminate over my loss. Barely half an hour had elapsed, it was 9 P.M., the camp was in a semi-doze, when I heard deep groans issuing from one of the animals. Upon inquiry as to what animal was suffering, I was surprised to hear that it was my bay horse. With a bull's-eye lantern, I visited him, and perceived that the pain was located in the stomach, but whether it was from some poisonous plant he had eaten while out grazing, or from some equine disease, I did not know. He discharged copious quantities of loose matter, but there was nothing peculiar in its color. The pain was evidently very great, for his struggles were very violent. I was up all night, hoping that it was but a temporary effect of some strange and noxious plant; but at 6 o'clock the next morning, after a short period of great agony, he also died; exactly fifteen hours after his companion. When the stomach was opened, it was found that death was caused by the internal rupture of a large cancer, which had affected the larger half of the coating of his stomach, and had extended an inch or two up the larynx. The contents of the stomach and intestines were deluged with the yellow viscous efflux from the cancer.

I was thus deprived of both my horses, and that within the short space of fifteen hours. With my limited knowledge of veterinary science, however, strengthened by the actual and positive proofs obtained by the dissection of the two stomachs, I can scarcely state that horses can live to reach Unyanyembe, or that they can travel with ease through this part of East Africa. But should I have occasion at some future day, I should not hesitate to take four horses with me, though I should certainly endeavour to ascertain previous to purchase whether they were perfectly sound and healthy, and to those travellers who cherish a good horse I would say, "Try one," and be not discouraged by my unfortunate experiences.

The 1st, 2nd, and 3rd of April passed, and nothing had

we heard or seen of the ever-lagging fourth caravan.
In the meanwhile the list of casualties was being augmented. Besides the loss of this precious time, through
the perverseness of the chief of the other caravan,
and the loss of my two horses, a pagazi carrying
boat-fixtures improved the opportunity, and deserted.
Selim was struck down with a severe attack of ague and
fever, and was soon after followed by the cook, then by
the assistant cook and tailor, Abdul Kader. Finally,
before the third day was over, Bombay had rheumatism,
Uledi (Grant's old valet) had a swollen throat, Zaidi had
the flux, Kingaru had the mukunguru ; Khamisi, a pagazi,
suffered from a weakness of the loins ; Farjalla had a
bilious fever ; and before night closed Makoviga was
very ill. Out of a force of twenty-five men one had
deserted, and ten were on the sick list, and the presentiment that the ill-looking neighbourhood of Kingaru would
prove calamitous to me was verified.

On the 4th April Maganga and his people appeared,
after being heralded by musketry-shots and horn-blowing,
the usual signs of an approaching caravan in this land.
His sick men were considerably improved, but they required one more day of rest at Kingaru. In the afternoon
he came to lay siege to my generosity, by giving details of
Soor Hadji Palloo's heartless cheats upon him ; but I
informed him, that since I had left Bagamoyo, I could no
longer be generous ; we were now in a land where cloth
was at a high premium ; that I had no more cloth than I
should need to furnish food for myself and men ; that he
and his caravan had cost me more money and trouble than
any three caravans I had, as indeed was the case. With
this counter-statement he was obliged to be content.
But I again solved his pecuniary doubts by promising

that, if he hurried his caravan on to Unyanyembe, he should have no cause of complaint.

The 5th of April saw the fourth caravan vanish for once in our front, with a fair promise that, however fast we should follow, we should not see them the hither side of Sinbamwenni.

The following morning, in order to rouse my people from the sickened torpitude they had lapsed into, I beat an exhilarating alarum on a tin pan with an iron ladle, intimating that a sofari was about to be undertaken. This had a very good effect, judging from the extraordinary alacrity with which it was responded to. Before the sun rose we started. The Kingaru villagers were out with the velocity of hawks for any rags or refuse left behind us.

The long march to Imbiki, fifteen miles, proved that our protracted stay at Kingaru had completely demoralized my soldiers and pagazis. Only a few of them had strength enough to reach Imbiki before night. The others, attending the laden donkeys, put in an appearance next morning, in a lamentable state of mind and body. Khamisi—the pagazi with the weak loins—had deserted, taking with him two goats, the property tent, and the whole of Uledi's personal wealth, consisting of his visiting dish-dasheh—a long shirt of the Arabic pattern, 10 lbs. of beads, and a few fine cloths, which Uledi, in a generous fit, had intrusted to him, while he carried the pagazi's load, 70 lbs. of Bubu beads. This defalcation was not to be overlooked, nor should Khamisi be permitted to return without an effort to apprehend him. Accordingly Uledi and Ferajji were despatched in pursuit while we rested at Imbiki, in order to give the dilapidated soldiers and animals time to recruit.

On the 8th we continued our journey, and arrived at Msuwa. This march will be remembered by our caravan as the most fatiguing of all, though the distance was but ten miles. It was one continuous jungle, except three interjacent glades of narrow limits, which gave us three breathing pauses in the dire task of jungle travelling. The odour emitted from its fell plants was so rank, so pungently acrid, and the miasma from its decayed vegetation so dense, that I expected every moment to see myself and men drop down in paroxysms of acute fever. Happily this evil was not added to that of loading and unloading the frequently falling packs. Seven soldiers to attend seventeen laden donkeys were entirely too small a number while passing through a jungle; for while the path is but a foot wide, with a wall of thorny plants and creepers bristling on each side, and projecting branches darting across it, with knots of spikey twigs stiff as spike-nails, ready to catch and hold anything above four feet in height, it is but reasonable to suppose that donkeys standing four feet high, with loads measuring across from bale to bale four feet, would come to grief. This grief was of frequent recurrence here, causing us to pause every few minutes for re-arrangements. So often had this task to be performed, that the men got perfectly discouraged, and had to be spoken to sharply before they set to work. By the time I reached Msuwa there was nobody with me and the ten donkeys I drove but Mabruk the Little, who, though generally stolid, stood to his work like a man. Bombay and Uledi were far behind, with the most jaded donkeys. Shaw was in charge of the cart, and his experiences were most bitter, as he informed me he had expended a whole vocabulary of stormy abuse known to sailors, and a new one which he had invented *ex tempore*. He did not arrive until two o'clock next morning, and was completely worn out.

Another halt was fixed at Msuwa, that we and our animals might recuperate. The chief of the village, a white man in everything but color, sent me and mine the fattest broad-tailed sheep of his flock, with five measures of matama grain. The mutton was excellent, unapproachable. For his timely and needful present I gave him two doti, and amused him with an exhibition of the wonderful mechanism of the Winchester rifle, and my breechloading revolvers.

He and his people were intelligent enough to comprehend the utility of these weapons at an emergency, and illustrated in expressive pantomime the powers they possessed against numbers of people armed only with spears and bows, by extending their arms with an imaginary gun and describing a clear circle. "Verily," said they, "the Wasungu are far wiser than the Washensi. What heads they have! What wonderful things they make! Look at their tents, their guns, their time-pieces, their clothes, and that little rolling thing (the cart) which carries more than five men,—que!"

On the 10th, recovered from the excessive strain of the last march, the caravan marched out of Msuwa, accompanied by the hospitable villagers as far as their stake defence, receiving their unanimous "Kwaheris." Outside the village the march promised to be less arduous than between Imbiki and Msuwa. After crossing a beautiful little plain intersected by a dry gully or mtoni, the route led by a few cultivated fields, where the tillers greeted us with one grand unwinking stare, as if fascinated.

Soon after we met one of those sights common in this part of the world, to wit a chain slave-gang, bound east. The slaves did not appear to be in any way down-hearted on the contrary, they seemed imbued with the philosophic jollity of the jolly servant of Martin Chuzzlewit. Were it not for their chains, it would have been difficult to discover master from slave; the physiognomic traits were alike—the mild benignity with which we were regarded was equally visible on all faces. The chains were ponderous—they might have held elephants captive; but as the slaves carried nothing but themselves, their weight could not have been insupportable.

The jungle was scant on this march, and though in some places the packs met with accidents, they were not such as seriously to retard progress. By 10 A.M. we were in camp in the midst of an imposing view of green sward and forest domed by a cloudless sky. We had again pitched our camp in the wilderness, and, as is the custom of caravans, fired two shots to warn any Washensi having grain to sell, that we were willing to trade.

Our next halting-place was Kisemo, distant but eleven miles from Msuwa, a village situated in a populous district, having in its vicinity no less than five other villages, each fortified by stakes and thorny abattis, with as much fierce independence as if their petty lords were so many Percys and Douglasses. Each topped a ridge, or a low hummock, with an assumption of defiance of the cock-on-its-own-dunghill type. Between these humble eminences and low ridges of land wind narrow vales which are favored with the cultivation of matama and Indian corn. Behind the village flows the Ungerengeri River, an impetuous stream during the Masika season, capable of overflowing its steep banks, but in the dry season it subsides into its proper status, which is that of a small stream of very clear sweet water. Its course from Kisemo is south-west, then easterly; it is the main feeder of the Kingani River.

The belles of Kisemo are noted for their vanity in brass wire, which is wound in spiral rings round their wrists and ankles, and the varieties of style which their hispid heads exhibit; while their poor lords, obliged to be contented with dingy torn clouts and split ears, show what wide sway Asmodeus holds over this terrestrial sphere—for it must have been an unhappy time when the hard-besieged husbands finally gave way before their spouses. Besides these brassy ornaments on their extremities, and the various hair-dressing styles, the women of Kisemo frequently wear lengthy necklaces, which run in rivers of colors down their bodies.

A more comical picture is seldom presented than that of one of these highly-dressed females engaged in the homely and necessary task of grinding corn for herself and family. The grinding apparatus consists of two portions: one, a thick pole of hard wood about six feet long, answering for a pestle; the other, a capacious wooden mortar, three feet in height.

While engaged in setting his tent, Shaw was obliged to move a small flat stone, to drive a peg into the ground. The village chief, who saw him do it, rushed up in a breathless fashion, and replaced the stone instantly, then stood on it in an impressive manner, indicative of the great importance attached to that stone and location. Bombay, seeing Shaw standing in silent wonder at the act, volunteered to ask the chief what was the matter. The Sheikh solemnly answered, with a finger pointing downward, " Uganga !" Whereupon I implored him to let me see what was under the stone. With a graciousness quite affecting he complied. My curiosity was

gratified with the sight of a small whittled stick, which
pinned fast to the ground an insect, the cause of a
miscarriage to a young female of the village.

During the afternoon, Uledi and Ferajji, who had
been despatched after the truant Khamisi, returned with
him and all the missing articles. Khamisi, soon after

WOMAN GRINDING CORN.

leaving the road and plunging into the jungle, where he
was mentally triumphing in his booty, was met by some
of the plundering Washensi, who are always on the *qui
vive* for stragglers, and unceremoniously taken to their
village in the woods, and bound to a tree preparatory to
being killed. Khamisi said that he asked them why
they tied him up, to which they answered, that they

were about to kill him, because he was a Mgwana, whom they were accustomed to kill as soon as they were caught. But Uledi and Ferajji shortly after coming upon the scene, both well armed, put an end to the debates upon Khamisi's fate, by claiming him as an absconding pagazi from the Musungu's camp, as well as all the articles he possessed at the time of capture. The robbers did not dispute the claim for the pagazi, goats, tent, or any other valuable found with him, but intimated that they deserved a reward for apprehending him. The demand being considered just, a reward to the extent of two doti and a fundo, or ten necklaces of beads, was given.

Khamisi, for his desertion and attempted robbery, could not be pardoned without first suffering punishment. He had asked at Bagamoyo, before enlisting in my service, an advance of $5 in money, and had received it; and a load of Bubu beads, no heavier than a pagazi's load, had been given him to carry; he had, therefore, no excuse for desertion. Lest I should overstep prudence, however, in punishing him, I convened a court of eight pagazis and four soldiers to sit in judgment, and asked them to give me their decision as to what should be done. Their unanimous verdict was that he was guilty of a crime almost unknown among the Wanyamwezi pagazis, and as it was likely to give bad repute to the Wanyamwezi carriers, they therefore sentenced him to be flogged with the "Great Master's" donkey whip, which was accordingly carried out, to poor Khamisi's crying sorrow.

On the 12th the caravan reached Mussoudi, on the Ungerengeri river. Happily for our patient donkeys this march was free from all the annoying troubles of the jungle. Happily for ourselves also, for we had no more the care of the packs and the anxiety about arriving at camp before night. The packs once put firmly on the backs of our good donkeys, they marched into camp— the road being excellent—without a single displacement or cause for one impatient word, soon after leaving Kisemo. A beautiful prospect, glorious in its wild nature, fragrant with its numerous flowers and variety of sweetly-smelling shrubs, among which I recognised the wild sage, the indigo plant, &c., terminated only at the foot of Kira Peak and sister cones, which mark the boundaries between Udoe and Ukami, yet distant twenty miles. Those distant mountains formed a not unfit background to this magnificent picture of open plain, forest patches, and sloping lawns—there was enough of picturesqueness and sublimity in the blue mountains to render it one complete whole. Suppose a Byron saw some of these scenes, he would be inclined to poetize in this manner:

> Morn dawns, and with it stern Udoè's hills,
> Dark Urruguru's rocks, and Kira's peak,
> Robed half in mist, bedewed with various rills,
> Arrayed in many a dun and purple streak.

When drawing near the valley of Ungerengeri, granite knobs and protuberances of dazzling quartz showed their heads above the reddish soil. Descending the ridge where these rocks were prominent, we found ourselves in the sable loam deposit of the Ungerengeri, and in the midst of teeming fields of sugar-cane and matama, Indian corn, muhogo, and gardens of curry, egg, and cucumber plants. On the banks of the Ungerengeri flourished the banana, and overtopping it by seventy feet and more, shot up the stately mparamusi, the rival in beauty of the Persian chenar and Abyssinian plane. Its trunk is straight and comely enough for the mainmast of a first-class frigate, while its expanding crown of leafage is distinguished from all others by its density and vivid greenness. There were a score of varieties of the larger kind of trees, whose far-extending branches embraced across the narrow but swift river. The depressions of the valley and the immediate neighbourhood of the river were choked with young forests of tiger-grass and stiff reeds.

Mussoudi is situated on a higher elevation than the average level of the village, and consequently looks down upon its neighbours, which number a hundred and more. It is the western extremity of Ukwere. On the western bank of the Ungerengeri the territory of the Wakami commences. We had to halt one day at Mussoudi because the poverty of the people prevented us from procuring the needful amount of grain. The cause of this scantiness in such a fertile and populous valley was, that the numerous caravans which had preceded us had drawn heavily for their stores for the upmarches.

On the 14th we crossed the Ungerengeri, which here flows southerly to the southern extremity of the valley, where it bends easterly as far as Kisemo. After crossing the river here, fordable at all times and only twenty yards in breadth, we had another mile of the valley with its excessively moist soil and rank growth of grass. It then ascended into a higher elevation, and led through a forest of mparamusi, tamarind, tamarisk, acacia, and the blooming mimosa. This ascent was continued for two hours, when we stood upon the spine of the largest ridge, where we could obtain free views of the wooded plain below and the distant ridges of Kisemo, which we had but lately left. A descent of a few hundred feet terminated in a deep but dry mtoni with a sandy bed, on the other side of which we had to regain the elevation we had lost, and a similar country opened into view until we found a newly-made boma with well-built huts of grass near a pool of water, which we at once occupied as a halting-place for the night. The cart gave us considerable trouble; not even our strongest donkey, though it carried with ease on its back 196 lbs., could draw the cart with a load of only 225 lbs. weight.

Early on the morning of the 15th we broke camp and started for Mikeseh. By 8.30 A.M. we were ascending the southern face of the Kira Peak. When we had gained the height of two hundred feet above the level of the surrounding country, we were gratified with a magnificent view of a land whose soil knows no Sabbath.

After travelling the spine of a ridge abutting against the southern slope of Kira we again descended into the little valley of Kiwrima, the first settlement we meet in Udoe, where there is always an abundant supply of water. Two miles west of Kiwrima is Mikiseh.

On the 16th we reached Ulagalla after a few hours' march. Ulagalla is the name of a district, or a portion of a district, lying between the mountains of Uruguru, which bound it southerly, and the mountains of Udoe, lying northerly and parallel with them, and but ten miles apart. The principal part of the basin thus formed is called Ulagalla.

Muhalleh is the next settlement, and here we found ourselves in the territory of the Waseguhha. On this march we were hemmed in by mountains—on our left by those of Uruguru, on our right by those of Udoe and Useguhha—a most agreeable and welcome change to us after the long miles of monotonous level we had hitherto seen. When tired of looking into the depths of the forest that still ran on either side of the road, we had but to look up to the mountain's base, to note its strange trees,

its plants and vari-colored flowers, we had but to raise
our heads to vary this pleasant occupation by observing
the lengthy and sinuous spine of the mountains, and
mentally report upon their outline, their spurs, their projections and ravines, their bulging rocks and deep clefts,
and, above all, the dark green woods clothing them from
summit to base. And when our attention was not required for the mundane task of regarding the donkeys'
packs, or the pace of the cautious-stepping pagazis, it was
gratifying to watch the vapours play about the mountain
summits — to see them fold into fleecy crowns and
fantastic clusters, dissolve, gather together into a pall
that threatened rain, and sail away again before the
brightening sun.

At Muhalleh was the fourth caravan under Maganga
with three more sick men, who turned with eager eyes
to myself, " the dispenser of medicine," as I approached.
Salvos of small arms greeted me, and a present of rice
and ears of Indian corn for roasting were awaiting my
acceptance ; but, as I told Maganga, I would have preferred to hear that his party were eight or ten marches
ahead. At this camp, also, we met Salim bin Rashid,
bound eastward, with a hugh caravan carrying three
hundred ivory tusks. This good Arab, besides welcoming the new comer with a present of rice, gave me news
of Livingstone. He had met the old traveller at Ujiji,
had lived in the next hut to him for two weeks, described
him as looking old, with long grey moustaches and beard,
just recovered from severe illness, looking very wan ; when
fully recovered Livingstone intended to visit a country
called Manyema by way of Marungu.

The valley of the Ungerengeri with Muhalleh exhibits
wonderful fertility. Its crops of matama were of the

tallest, and its Indian corn would rival the best crops ever seen in the Arkansas bottoms. The numerous mountain-fed streams rendered the great depth of loam very sloppy, in consequence of which several accidents occurred before we reached the camp, such as wetting cloth, mildewing tea, watering sugar, and rusting tools; but prompt attention to these necessary things saved us from considerable loss.

There was a slight difference noticed in the demeanour and bearing of the Waseguhha compared with the Wadoe, Wakami, and Wakwere heretofore seen. There was none of that civility we had been until now pleased to note: their express desire to barter was accompanied with insolent hints that we ought to take their produce at their own prices. If we remonstrated they became angry; retorting fiercely, impatient of opposition, they flew into a passion, and were glib in threats. This strange conduct, so opposite to that of the calm and gentle Wakwere, may be excellently illustrated by comparing the manner of the hot-headed Greek with that of the cool and collected German. Necessity compelled us to purchase eatables of them, and, to the credit of the country and its productions, be it said, their honey had the peculiar flavour of that of famed Hymettus.

Following the latitudinal valley of the Ungerengeri, within two hours on the following morning we passed close under the wall of the capital of Useguhha—Simbamwenni. The first view of the walled town at the western foot of the Uruguru mountains, with its fine valley abundantly beautiful, watered by two rivers, and several pellucid streams of water distilled by the dew and cloud-enriched heights around, was one that we did not anticipate to meet in Eastern Africa. In Mazanderan,

Persia, such a scene would have answered our expectations, but here it was totally unexpected. The town may contain a population of 3,000, having about 1,000 houses; being so densely crowded, perhaps 5,000 would more closely approximate. The houses in the town are eminently African, but of the best type of construction. The fortifications are on an Arabic Persic model—combining Arab neatness with Persian plan. Through a ride of 950 miles in Persia I never met a town outside of the great cities better fortified than Simbamwenni. In Persia the fortifications were of mud, even those of Kasvin, Teheran, Ispahan, and Shiraz; those of Simbamwenni are of stone, pierced with two rows of loopholes for musketry. The area of the town is about half a square mile, its plan being quadrangular. Well-built towers of stone guard each corner; four gates, one facing each cardinal point, and set half way between the several towers, permit ingress and egress for its inhabitants. The gates are closed with solid square doors made of African teak, and carved with the infinitesimally fine and complicated devices of the Arabs, from which I suspect that the doors were made either at Zanzibar or on the coast, and conveyed to Simbamwenni plank by plank; yet as there is much communication between Bagamoyo and Simbamwenni, it is just possible that native artisans are the authors of this ornate workmanship, as several doors chiselled and carved in the same manner, though not quite so elaborately, were visible in the largest houses. The palace of the Sultan is after the style of those on the coast, with long sloping roof, wide eaves, and veranda in front.

The Sultana is the eldest daughter of the famous Kisabengo, a name infamous throughout the neighbouring countries of Udoe, Ukami, Ukwere, Kingaru, Ukwenni, and Kiranga-Wanna, for his kidnapping propensities. Kisabengo was another Theodore on a small scale. Sprung from humble ancestry, he acquired distinction for his personal strength, his powers of harangue, and his amusing and versatile address, by which he gained great ascendency over fugitive slaves, and was chosen a leader among them. Fleeing from justice, which awaited him at the hands of the Zanzibar Sultan, he arrived in Ukami, which extended at that time from Ukwere to Usagara, and here he commenced a career of conquest, the result of which was the cession by the Wakami of an immense tract of fertile country, in the valley of the Ungerengeri. On its most desirable site, with the river flowing close under the walls, he built his capital, and called it Simbamwenni, which means "The Lion," or the strongest, City. In old age the successful robber and kidnapper changed his name of Kisabengo, which had gained such a notoriety, to Simbamwenni, after his town; and when dying, after desiring that his eldest daughter should succeed him, he bestowed the name of the town upon her also, which name of Simbamwenni the Sultana now retains and is known by.

While crossing a rapid stream, which, as I said before flowed close to the walls, the inhabitants of Simbamwenni had a fine chance of gratifying their curiosity of seeing the "Great Musungu," whose several caravans had preceded him, and who unpardonably, because unlicensed, had spread a report of his great wealth and power. I was thus the object of a universal stare. At one time on the banks there were considerably over a thousand natives going through the several tenses and moods of the verb "to stare," or exhibiting every phase of the substantive, viz.—the stare peremptory, insolent, sly, cunning, modest, and casual. The warriors of the Sultana, holding in one hand the spear, the bow, and sheaf or musket, embraced with the other their respective friends, like so many models of Nisus and Euryalus, Theseus and Pirithous, Damon and Pythias, or Achilles and Patroclus, to whom they confidentially related their divers opinions upon my dress and color. The words " Musungu kuba " had as much charm for these people as the music of the Pied Piper had for the rats of Hamelin, since they served to draw from within the walls across their stream so large a portion of the population ; and when I continued the journey to the Ungerengeri, distant four miles, I feared that the Hamelin catastrophe might have to be repeated before I could rid myself of them. But fortunately for my piece of mind, they finally proved vincible under the hot sun, and the distance we had to go to camp.

As we were obliged to overhaul the luggage, and repair saddles, as well as to doctor a few of the animals, whose backs had by this time become very sore, I determined to halt here two days. Provisions were very plentiful also at Simbamwenni, though comparatively dear.

On the second day I was, for the first time, made aware that my acclimatization in the ague-breeding swamps of Arkansas was powerless against the mukunguru of East Africa. The premonitory symptoms of the African type were felt in my system at 10 A.M. First, general lassitude prevailed, with a disposition to drowsiness ; secondly, came the spinal ache which, commencing from the loins, ascended the vertebræ, and extended around the ribs, until it reached the shoulders, where it settled into a weary pain ; thirdly, came a chilliness over the whole body, which was quickly followed by a heavy head, swimming eyes, and throbbing temples, with vague vision, which distorted and transformed all objects of sight. This lasted until 10 P.M., and the mukunguru left me, much prostrated in strength.

The remedy, applied for three mornings in succession after the attack, was such as my experience in Arkansas had taught me was the most powerful corrective, viz., a quantum of fifteen grains of quinine, taken in three doses of five grains each, every other hour from dawn to meridian—the first dose to be taken immediately after the first effect of the purging medicine taken at bed-time the night previous. I may add that this treatment was perfectly successful in my case, and in all others which occurred in my camp. After the mukunguru had declared itself, there was no fear, with such a treatment of it, of a second attack, until at least some days afterwards.

On the third day the camp was visited by the ambassadors of Her Highness the Sultana of Simbamwenni, whc came as her representatives to receive the tribute which she regards herself as powerful enough to enforce. But they, as well as Madame Simbamwenni, were informed, that as we knew it was their custom to charge owners of caravans but one tribute, and as they remembered the Musungu (Farquhar) had paid already, it was not fair that I should have to pay again. The ambassadors replied with a " Ngema " (very well), and promised to carry my answer back to their mistress. Though it was by no means " very well " in fact, as it will be seen in a subsequent chapter how the female Simbamwenni took advantage of an adverse fortune which befell me to pay herself. With this I close the chapter of incidents experienced during our transit across the maritime region.

PORTRAIT OF SHAW AND FARQUHAR

CHAPTER VI.

TO UGOGO.

A valley of despond, and hot-bed of malaria.—Myriads of vermin.—
The Makata swamp.—A sorrowful experience catching a deserter.—
A far-embracing prospect.—Illness of William Farquhar.—Lake
Ugombo.—A land of promise.—The great Kisesa.—The plague of
earwigs.

THE distance from Bagamoyo to Simbamwenni we found
to be 119 miles, and was accomplished in fourteen marches.
But these marches, owing to difficulties arising from the
Masika season, and more especially to the lagging of the
fourth caravan under Maganga, extended to twenty-nine

days, thus rendering our progress very slow indeed—but
a little more than four miles a-day. I infer, from what I
have seen of the travelling, that had I not been encumbered by the sick Wanyamwezi porters, I could have accomplished the distance in sixteen days. For it was not
the donkeys that proved recreant to my confidence; they,
poor animals, carrying a weight of 150 lbs. each, arrived
at Simbamwenni in first-rate order; but it was Maganga,
composed of greed and laziness, and his weakly-bodied
tribe, who were ever falling sick. In dry weather the
number of marches might have been much reduced. Of
the half-dozen of Arabs or so who preceded this Expedition along this route, two accomplished the entire distance in eight days. From the brief descriptions given
of the country, as it day by day expanded to our view,
enough may be gleaned to give readers a fair idea of it.
The elevation of Simbamwenni cannot be much over 1,000
feet above the level, the rise of the land having been
gradual. It being the rainy season, about which so many
ominous statements were doled out to us by those ignorant
of the character of the country, we naturally saw it under
its worst aspect; but, even in this adverse phase of it,
with all its depth of black mud, its excessive dew,
its dripping and chill grass, its density of rank jungle,
and its fevers, I look back upon the scene with
pleasure, for the wealth and prosperity it promises to
some civilized nation, which in some future time will
come and take possession of it. A railroad from Bagamoyo to Simbamwenni might be constructed with as much
ease and rapidity as, and at far less cost than the Union
Pacific Railway, whose rapid strides day by day towards
completion the world heard of and admired. A residence
in this part of Africa, after a thorough system of drainage

had been carried out, would not be attended with any more discomfort than generally follows upon the occupation of new land. The temperature at this season during the day never exceeded 85° Fahrenheit. The nights were pleasant—too cold without a pair of blankets for covering; and, as far as Simbamwenni, they were without that pest which is so dreadful on the Nebraska and Kansas prairies, the mosquito. The only annoyances I know of that would tell hard on the settler is the determined ferocity of the mabungu, or horse-fly, the chufwa, &c., already described, which, until the dense forests and jungles were cleared, would be certain to render the keeping of domestic cattle unremunerative.

Contrary to expectation the Expedition was not able to start at the end of two days; the third and the fourth days were passed miserably enough in the desponding valley of Ungerengeri. This river, small as it is in the dry seasons, becomes of considerable volume and power during the Masika, as we experienced to our sorrow. It serves as a drain to a score of peaks and two long ranges of mountains; winding along their base, it is the recipient of the cascades seen flashing during the few intervals of sunlight, of all the nullahs and ravines which render the lengthy frontage of the mountain slopes so rugged and irregular, until it glides into the valley of Simbamwenni a formidable body of water, opposing a serious obstacle to caravans without means to build bridges; added to which was an incessant downfall of rain—such a rain as shuts people in-doors and renders them miserable and unamiable—a real London rain—an eternal drizzle accompanied with mist and fog. When the sun shone it appeared but a pale image of itself, and old pagazis, wise in their traditions as old whaling captains, shook their heads ominously at the dull spectre, and declared it was doubtful if the rain would cease for three weeks yet.

The site of the caravan camp on the hither side of the Ungerengeri was a hot-bed of malaria, unpleasant to witness—an abomination to memory. The filth of generations of pagazis had gathered innumerable hosts of creeping things. Armies of black, white, and red ants infest the stricken soil ; centipedes, like worms, of every hue, clamber over shrubs and plants ; hanging to the undergrowth are the honey-combed nests of yellow-headed wasps with stings as harmful as scorpions; enormous beetles, as large as full-grown mice, roll dunghills over the ground ; of all sorts, shapes, sizes, and hues are the myriad-fold vermin with which the ground teems ; in short, the richest entomological collection could not vie in variety and numbers with the species which the four walls of my tent enclosed from morning until night.

On the fifth morning, or the 23rd April, the rain gave us a few hours' respite, during which we managed to wade through the Stygian quagmire reeking with noisomeness to the inundated river-bank. The soldiers commenced at 5 A.M. to convey the baggage across from bank to bank over a bridge which was the most rustic of the rustic kind. Only an ignorant African would have been satisfied with its small utility as a means to cross a deep and rapid body of water. Even for light-footed Wanyamwezi pagazis it was anything but comfortable to traverse. Only a professional tight-rope performer could have carried a load across with ease. To travel over an African bridge requires, first, a long leap from land to the limb of a tree (which may or may not be covered by water), followed by a long jump ashore. With 70 lbs. weight on his back, the carrier finds it difficult enough. Sometimes he is assisted by ropes extemporized from the long convolvuli which hang from almost every tree, but not always, these being deemed superfluities by the Washensi.

Fortunately the baggage was transferred without a single accident, and though the torrent was strong, the donkeys were dragged through the flood by vigorous efforts and much objurgation without a casualty. This performance of crossing the Ungerengeri occupied fully five hours, though energy, abuse, and fury enough were expended for an army.

Reloading and wringing our clothes dry, we set out from the horrible neighbourhood of the river, with its reek and filth, in a northerly direction, following a road which led up to easy and level ground. Two obtruding hills were thus avoided on our left, and after passing them we had shut out the view of the hateful valley.

I always found myself more comfortable and light-hearted while travelling than when chafing and fretting in camp at delays which no effort could avoid, and consequently I fear that some things, while on a march, may be tinted somewhat stronger than their appearance or merit may properly warrant. But I thought that the view opening before us was much more agreeable than the valley of Simbamwenni with all its indescribable fertility. It was a series of glades opening one after another between forest clumps of young trees, hemmed in distantly by isolated peaks and scattered mountains. Now and again, as we crested low eminences we caught sight of the blue Usagara mountains, bounding the horizon westerly and northerly, and looked down upon a vast expanse of plain which lay between.

At the foot of the lengthy slope, well-watered by bubbling springs and mountain rills, we found a comfortable
khambi with well-made huts, which the natives call Simbo.
It lies just two hours or five miles north-west of the Ungerengeri crossing. The ground is rocky, composed principally of quartzose detritus swept down by the constant
streams.   In the neighbourhood of these grow bamboo,
the thickest of which was about two and a half
inches in diameter; the " myombo," a very shapely
tree, with a clean trunk like an ash, the " imbite,"
with large, fleshy leaves like the " mtamba," sycamore,
plum-tree, the " ugaza," ortamarisk, and the " mgungu,"
a tree containing several wide branches with small
leaves clustered together in a clump, and the silk-cotton
tree.

Though there are no villages or settlements in view of
Simbo Khambi, there are several clustered within the
mountain folds, inhabited by Waseguhha somewhat prone
to dishonest acts and murder.

The long broad plain visible from the eminences crossed
between the Ungerengeri and Simbo was now before us,
and became known to sorrowful memory subsequently, as
the Makata Valley.   The initial march was from Simbo,
its terminus at Rehenneko, at the base of the Usagara
mountains, six marches distant.   The valley commences
with broad undulations, covered with young forests of
bamboo, which grow thickly along the streams, the dwarf
fan-palm, the stately Palmyra, and the mgungu.   These
undulations soon become broken by gullies containing
water, nourishing dense crops of cane reeds and broad-
bladed grass, and, emerging from this district, wide
savannahs covered with tall grass open into view, with

an isolated tree here and there agreeably breaking the monotony of the scene. The Makata is a wilderness containing but one village of the Waseguhha throughout its broad expanse. Venison, consequently, abounds within the forest clumps, and the kudu, hartebeest, antelope, and zebra may be seen at early dawn emerging into the open savannahs to feed. At night, the cyn-hyæna prowls about with its hideous clamour seeking for sleeping prey, man or beast.

The slushy mire of the savannahs rendered marching a work of great difficulty; its tenacious hold of the feet told terribly on men and animals. A ten-mile march required ten hours, we were therefore compelled to camp in the middle of this wilderness, and construct a new khambi, a measure which was afterwards adopted by half a dozen caravans.

The cart did not arrive until nearly midnight, and with it, besides three or four broken-down pagazis, came Bombay with the dolorous tale, that having put his load —consisting of the property tent, one large American axe, his two uniform coats, his shirts, beads and cloth, powder, pistol, and hatchet—on the ground, to go and assist the cart out of a quagmire, he had returned to the place where he had left it and could not find it, that he believed that some thieving Washensi, who always lurk in the rear of caravans to pick up stragglers, had decamped with it. Which dismal tale told me at black midnight was not received at all graciously, but rather with most wrathful words, all of which the penitent captain received as his proper due. Working myself into a fury, I enumerated his sins to him; he had lost a goat at Muhalleh, he had permitted Khamisi to desert with valuable property at Imbiki; he had frequently shown culpable negligence in not looking after the donkeys, permitting them to be tied up at night without seeing that they had water, and in the mornings, when about to march, he preferred to sleep until 7 o'clock, rather than wake up early and saddle the donkeys, that we might start at 6 o'clock; he had shown of late great love for the fire, cowering like a bloodless man before it, torpid and apathetic; he had now lost the property-tent in the middle of the Masika season, by which carelessness the cloth bales would rot and become valueless; he had lost the axe which I should want at Ujiji to construct my boat; and finally, he had lost a pistol and hatchet, and a flaskful of the best powder. Considering all these things, how utterly incompetent he was to be captain, I would degrade him from his office and appoint Mabruki Burton instead. Uledi, also, following the example of Bombay, instead of being second captain, should give no orders to any soldiers in future, but should himself obey those given by Mabruki—the said Mabruki being worth a dozen Bombays, and two dozen Uledis; and so he was dismissed with orders to return at daylight to find the tent, axe, pistol, powder, and hatchet.

The next morning the caravan, thoroughly fatigued with the last day's exertions, was obliged to halt. Bombay was despatched after the lost goods; Kingaru, Mabruki the Great, and Mabruki the Little were despatched to bring back three doti-worth of grain, on which we were to subsist in the wilderness.

Three days passed away and we were still at camp, awaiting, with what patience we possessed, the return of the soldiers. In the meantime provisions ran very low, no game could be procured, the birds were so wild. Two days' shooting procured but two potfuls of birds, consisting of grouse, quail, and pigeons. Bombay returned unsuccessfully from his search after the missing property, and suffered deep disgrace.

On the fourth day I despatched Shaw with two more soldiers, to see what had become of Kingaru and the two Mabrukis. Towards night he returned completely prostrated, with a violent attack of the mukunguru, or ague; but bringing the missing soldiers, who were thus left to report for themselves.

With most thankful hearts did we quit our camp, where so much anxiety of mind and fretfulness had been suffered, not heeding a furious rain, which, after drenching us all night, might have somewhat damped our ardor for the march under other circumstances. The road for the first mile led over reddish ground, and was drained by gentle slopes falling east and west; but, leaving the cover of the friendly woods, on whose eastern margin we had been delayed so long, we emerged into one of the savannahs, whose soil during the rain is as soft as slush and tenacious as thick mortar, where we were all threatened with the fate of the famous Arkansas traveller, who had sunk so low in one of the many quagmires in Arkansas county, that nothing but his tall "stove-pipe" hat was left visible.

Shaw was sick, and the whole duty of driving the foundering caravan devolved upon myself. The Wanyamwezi donkeys stuck in the mire as if they were rooted to it. As fast as one was flogged from his stubborn position, prone to the depths fell another, giving me a Sisyphean labour, which was maddening under pelting rain, assisted by such men as Bombay and Uledi, who could not for a whole skin's sake stomach the storm and mire. Two hours of such a task enabled me to drag my

caravan over a savannah one mile and a half broad ; and
barely had I finished congratulating myself over my
success before I was halted by a deep ditch, which, filled
with rain-water from the inundated savannahs, had become a considerable stream, breast-deep, flowing swiftly
into the Makata. Donkeys had to be unloaded, led
through a torrent, and loaded again on the other bank—
an operation which consumed a full hour.

Presently, after straggling through a wood clump,
barring our progress was another stream, swollen into
a river. The bridge being swept away, we were obliged
to swim and float our baggage over, which delayed us
two hours more. Leaving this second river-bank, we
splashed, waded, occasionally half-swimming, and reeled
through mire, water-dripping grass and matama stalks,
along the left bank of the Makata proper, until farther
progress was effectually prevented for that day by a deep
bend of the river, which we should be obliged to cross the
next day.

Though but six miles were traversed during that miserable day, the march occupied ten hours.

Half dead with fatigue, I yet could feel thankful that
it was not accompanied by fever, which it seemed a
miracle to avoid ; for if ever a district was cursed with
the ague, the Makata wilderness ranks foremost of those
afflicted. Surely the sight of the dripping woods en-
veloped in opaque mist, of the inundated country with
lengthy swathes of tiger-grass laid low by the turbid
flood, of mounds of decaying trees and canes, of the
swollen river and the weeping sky, was enough to en-
gender the mukunguru! The well-used khambi, and
the heaps of filth surrounding it, were enough to create
a cholera !

DISCOMFORTS OF AFRICAN TRAVEL.—THE MAKATA SWAMP.

The Makata, a river whose breadth during the dry season is but forty feet, in the Masika season assumes the breadth, depth, and force of an important river. Should it happen to be an unusually rainy season, it inundates the great plain which stretches on either side, and converts it into a great lake. It is the main feeder of the Wami river, which empties into the sea between the ports of Saadani and Whinde. About ten miles north-east of the Makata crossing, the Great Makata, the Little Makata, a nameless creek, and the Rudewa river unite; and the river thus formed becomes known as the Wami. Throughout Usagara the Wami is known as the Mukondokwa. Three of these streams take their rise from the crescent-like Usagara range, which bounds the Makata plain south and south-westerly; while the Rudewa rises in the northern horn of the same range.

So swift was the flow of the Makata, and so much did its unsteady bridge, half buried in the water, imperil the safety of the property, that its transfer from bank to bank occupied fully five hours. No sooner had we landed every article on the other side, undamaged by the water, than the rain poured down in torrents that drenched them all, as if they had been dragged through the river. To proceed through the swamp which an hour's rain had formed was utterly out of the question. We were accordingly compelled to camp in a place where every hour furnished its quota of annoyance. One of the Wangwana soldiers engaged at Bagamoyo, named Kingaru, improved an opportunity to desert with another Mgwana's kit. My two detectives, Uledi (Grant's valet), and Sarmean, were immediately despatched in pursuit, both being armed with American breech-loaders. They went about their

task with an adroitness and celerity which augured well
for their success. In an hour they returned with the
runaway, having found him hidden in the house of a
Mseguhha chief called Kigondo, who lived about a mile
from the eastern bank of the river, and who had accompanied Uledi and Sarmean to receive his reward, and
render an account of the incident.

Kigondo said, when he had been seated, "I saw this
man carrying a bundle, and running hard, by which I
knew that he was deserting you. We (my wife and I)
were sitting in our little watch-hut, watching our corn;
and, as the road runs close by, this man was obliged to
come close to us. We called to him when he was near,
saying, 'Master, where are you going so fast? Are you
deserting the Musungu, for we know you belong to him,
since you bought from us yesterday two doti worth of
meat?' 'Yes,' said he, 'I am running away; I want to
get to Simbamwenni. If you will take me there, I will
give you a doti.' We said to him then, 'Come into our
house, and we will talk it over quietly. When he was in
our house in an inner room, we locked him up, and went
out again to the watch; but leaving word with the
women to look out for him. We knew that, if you
wanted him, you would send askari (soldiers) after him.
We had but lit our pipes when we saw two men armed
with short guns, and having no loads, coming along the
road, looking now and then on the ground, as if they
were looking at footmarks. We knew them to be the
men we were expecting; so we hailed them, and said,
'Masters, what are ye looking for?' They said, 'We are
looking for a man who has deserted our master. Here
are his footsteps. If you have been long in your hut you
must have seen him. Can you tell us where he is?' We

said, 'Yes; he is in our house. If you will come with us, we will give him up to you; but your master must give us something for catching him.'"

As Kigondo had promised to deliver Kingaru up, there remained nothing further to do for Uledi and Sarmean but to take charge of their prisoner, and bring him and his captors to my camp on the western bank of the Makata. Kingaru received two dozen lashes, and was chained; his captor a doti, besides five khete of red coral beads for his wife.

That down-pour of rain which visited us the day we crossed the Makata proved the last of the Masika season. As the first rainfall which we had experienced occurred on the 23rd March, and the last on the 30th April, its duration was thirty-nine days. The seers of Bagamoyo had delivered their vaticinations concerning this same Masika with solemnity. "For forty days," said they, "rain would fall incessantly;" whereas we had but experienced eighteen days' rain. Nevertheless, we were glad that it was over, for we were tired of stopping day after day to dry the bales and grease the tools and ironware, and of seeing all things of cloth and leather rot visibly before our eyes.

The 1st of May found us struggling through the mire and water of the Makata with a caravan bodily sick, from the exertion and fatigue of crossing so many rivers and wading through marshes. Shaw was still suffering from his first mukunguru; Zaidi, a soldier, was critically ill with the small-pox; the kichuma-chuma, "little irons," had hold of Bombay across the chest, rendering him the most useless of the unserviceables; Mabruk Saleem, a youth of lusty frame, following the example of Bombay, laid himself down on the marshy ground, professing his total inability to breast the Makata swamp; Abdul Kader, the Hindi tailor and adventurer—the weakliest of mortal bodies—was ever ailing for lack of "force," as he expressed it in French, i.e. "strength," ever indisposed to work, shiftless, mock-sick, but ever hungry. "Oh! God," was the cry of my tired soul, "were all the men of my Expedition like this man I should be compelled to return. Solomon was wise perhaps from inspiration, perhaps from observation; I was becoming wise by experience, and I was compelled to observe that when mud and wet sapped the physical energy of the lazily-inclined, a dog-whip became their backs, restoring them to a sound—sometimes to an extravagant activity.

For thirty miles from our camp was the Makata plain an extensive swamp. The water was on an average one foot in depth; in some places we plunged into holes three, four, and even five feet deep. Plash, splash, plash, splash, were the only sounds we heard from the commencement of the march until we found the bomas occupying the only dry spots along the line of march. This kind of work continued for two days, until we came in sight of the Rudewa river, another powerful stream with banks brimful of rushing rain-water. Crossing a branch of the Rudewa, and emerging from the dank reedy grass crowding the western bank, the view consisted of an immense sheet of water topped by clumps of grass tufts and foliage of thinly scattered trees, bounded ten or twelve miles off by the eastern front of the Usagara mountain range. The *acme* of discomfort and vexation was realized on the five-mile march from the Rudewa branch. As myself and the Wangwana appeared with the loaded donkeys, the pagazis were observed huddled on a mound. When asked if the mound was the camp,

they replied " N." Why, then, **do** you stop here ?"—
"Ugh! water plenty!!" One drew a line across his
loins to indicate the depth of water before us, another
drew a line across his chest, another across his throat,
another held his hand over his head, by which he meant
that we should have to swim. Swim five miles through a
reedy marsh! It was impossible; it was also impossible
that such varied accounts could all be correct. Without
hesitation, therefore, I ordered the Wangwana to proceed
with the animals. After three hours of splashing through
four feet of water we reached dry land, and had traversed
the swamp of Makata. But not without the swamp with
its horrors having left a durable impression upon our
minds; no one was disposed to forget its fatigues, nor
the nausea of travel which it almost engendered. Subsequently, we had to remember its passage still more
vividly, and to regret that we had undertaken the journey
during the Masika season, when the animals died from
this date by twos and threes, almost every day, until but
five sickly worn-out beasts remained; when the Wangwana, soldiers, and pagazis sickened of diseases innumerable; when I myself was finally compelled to lie a-bed
with an attack of acute dysentery which brought me to
the verge of the grave. I suffered more, perhaps, than I
might have done had I taken the proper medicine, but
my over-confidence in that compound, called "Collis
Brown's Chlorodyne," delayed the cure which ultimately
resulted from a judicious use of Dover's powder. In no
one single case of diarrhœa or acute dysentery had this
"Chlorodyne," about which so much has been said and
written, any effect of lessening the attack whatever,
though I used three bottles. To the dysentery contracted during the transit of the Makata swamp, only

two fell victims, and those were a pagazi and my poor little dog "Omar," my companion from India.

The only tree of any prominence in the Makata valley was the Palmyra palm (*Borassus flabelliformis*), and this grew in some places in numbers sufficient to be called a grove; the fruit was not ripe while we passed, otherwise we might have enjoyed it as a novelty. The other vegetation consisted of the several species of thorn bush, and the graceful parachute-topped and ever-green mimosa.

The 4th of May we were ascending a gentle slope towards the important village of Rehenneko, the first village near to which we encamped in Usagara. It lay at the foot of the mountain, and its plenitude and mountain air promised us comfort and health. It was a square, compact village, surrounded by a thick wall of mud, enclosing cone-topped huts, roofed with bamboo and holcus-stalks; and contained a population of about a thousand souls. It has several wealthy and populous neighbours, whose inhabitants are independent enough in their manner, but not unpleasantly so. The streams are of the purest water, fresh, and pellucid as crystal, bubbling over round pebbles and clean gravel, with a music delightful to hear to the traveller in search of such a sweetly potable element.

The bamboo grows to serviceable size in the neighbourhood of Rehenneko, strong enough for tent and banghy poles; and in numbers sufficient to supply an army The mountain slopes are densely wooded with trees that might supply very good timber for building purposes.

We rested four days at this pleasant spot, to recruit ourselves, and to allow the sick and feeble time to recover a little before testing their ability in the ascent of the Usagara mountains.

The 8th of May saw us with our terribly jaded men and animals winding up the steep slopes of the first line of hills; gaining the summit of which we obtained a view remarkably grand, which exhibited as in a master picture the broad valley of the Makata, with its swift streams like so many cords of silver, as the sunshine played on the unshadowed reaches of water, with its thousands of graceful palms adding not a little to the charm of the scene, with the great wall of the Uruguru and Uswapanga mountains dimly blue, but sublime in their loftiness and immensity—forming a fit background to such an extensive, far-embracing prospect.

Turning our faces west, we found ourselves in a mountain world, fold rising above fold, peak behind peak, cone jostling cone; away to the north, to the west, to the south, the mountain tops rolled like so many vitrified waves; not one adust or arid spot was visible in all this scene. The diorama had no sudden changes or striking contrasts, for a universal forest of green trees clothed every peak, cone, and summit.

To the men this first day's march through the mountain region of Usagara was an agreeable interlude after the successive journey over the flats and heavy undulations of the maritime region, but to the loaded and enfeebled animals it was most trying. We were minus two by the time we had arrived at our camp, but seven miles from Rehenneko, our first instalment of the debt we owed to Makata. Water, sweet and clear, was abundant in the deep hollows of the mountains, flowing sometimes over beds of solid granite, sometimes over a rich red sandstone, whose soft substance was soon penetrated by the aqueous element, and whose particles were swept away constantly to enrich the valley below; and in other ravines it dashed, and roared miniature thunder, as it leaped over granite boulders and quartz rock.

The 9th of May, after another such an up-and-down course, ascending hills and descending into the twilight depths of deepening valleys, we came suddenly upon the Mukondokwa, and its narrow pent-up valley crowded with rank reedy grass, cane, and thorny bushes; and rugged tamarisk which grappled for existence with monster convolvuli, winding their coils around their trunks with such tenacity and strength, that the tamarisk seemed grown but for their support.

The valley was barely a quarter of a mile broad in some places—at others it widened to about a mile. The hills on either side shot up into precipitous slopes, clothed with mimosa, acacia, and tamarisk, enclosing a river and valley whose curves and folds were as various as a serpent's.

Shortly after debouching into the Mukondokwa valley, we struck the road traversed by Captains Burton and Speke in 1857, between Mbumi and Kadetamare (the latter place should be called Misonghi, Kadetamare being but the name of a chief). After following the left bank of the Mukondokwa, during which our route diverged to every point from south-east to west, north and north-east, for about an hour, we came to the ford. Beyond the ford, a short half-hour's march, we came to Kiora.

At this filthy village of Kiora, which was well-grounded with goat-dung, and peopled with a wonderful number of children for a hamlet that did not number twenty families, with a hot sun pouring on the limited open space, with a fury that exceeded 128° Fahrenheit; which swarmed with flies and insects of known and unknown species; I found, as I had been previously informed, the third caravan, which had started out of Bagamoyo so well fitted and supplied. The leader, who was no other than the white man Farquhar, was sick-a-bed with swollen legs (Bright's disease), unable to move.

As he heard my voice, Farquhar staggered out of his tent, so changed from my spruce mate who started from Bagamoyo, that I hardly knew him at first. His legs were ponderous, elephantine, since his leg-illness was of elephantiasis, or dropsy. His face was of a deathly pallor, for he had not been out of his tent for two weeks.

A breezy hill, overlooking the village of Kiora, was chosen by me for my camping-ground, and as soon as the tents were pitched, the animals attended to, and a boma made of thorn bushes, Farquhar was carried up by four men into my tent. Upon being questioned as to the cause of his illness, he said he did not know what had caused it. He had no pain, he thought, anywhere. I asked, "Do you not sometimes feel pain on the right side?"—"Yes, I think I do; but I don't know."—"Nor over the left nipple sometimes—a quick throbbing, with a shortness of breath?"—"Yes, I think I have. I know I breathe quick sometimes." He said his only trouble was in the legs, which were swollen to an immense size. Though he had a sound appetite, he yet felt weak in the legs.

From the scant information of the disease and its peculiarities, as given by Farquhar himself, I could only make out, by studying a little medical book I had with me, that "a swelling of the legs, and sometimes of the body, might result from either heart, liver, or kidney disease." But I did not know to what to ascribe the disease, unless it was to elephantiasis—a disease most common in Zanzibar; nor did I know how to treat it in a man who could not tell me whether he felt pain in his head or in his back, in his feet or in his chest.

It was therefore fortunate for me that I overtook him at Kiora; though he was about to prove a sore incumbrance to me, for he was not able to walk, and the donkey-carriage, after the rough experience of the Makata valley, was failing. I could not possibly leave him at Kiora, death would soon overtake him there; but how long I could convey a man in such a state, through a country devoid of carriage, was a question to be resolved by circumstances.

On the 11th of May, the third and fifth caravans, now united, followed up the right bank of the Mukondokwa, through fields of holcus, the great Mukondokwa ranges rising in higher altitude as we proceeded west, and enfolding us in the narrow river valley round about. We left Muniyi Usagara on our right, and soon after found hill-spurs athwart our road, which we were obliged to ascend and descend.

A march of eight miles from the ford of Misonghi brought us to another ford of the Mukondokwa, where we bid a long adieu to Burton's road, which led up to the Goma pass and up the steep slopes of Rubeho. Our road left the right bank and followed the left over a country quite the reverse of the Mukondokwa Valley, enclosed between mountain ranges. Fertile soils and spontaneous vegetation, reeking with miasma and overpowering from their odour, we had exchanged for a drouthy wilderness of aloetic and cactaceous plants, where the kolquall and several thorn bushes grew paramount.

Instead of the tree-clad heights, slopes and valleys, instead of cultivated fields, we saw now the confines of an uninhabited wilderness. The hill-tops were bared of their bosky crowns, and revealed their rocky natures bleached white by rain and sun. Nguru Peak, the loftiest of the Usagara cones, stood right shoulderwards of us as we ascended the long slope of dun-grey soil which rose beyond the brown Mukondokwa on the left.

At the distance of two miles from the last ford, we found a neat khambi, situated close to the river, where it first broke into a furious rapid.

The next morning the caravan was preparing for the march, when I was informed that the " Bana Mdogo "— little master—Shaw, had not yet arrived with the cart, and the men in charge of it. Late the previous night I had despatched one donkey for Shaw, who had said he was too ill to walk, and another for the load that was on the cart; and had retired satisfied that they would soon arrive. My conclusion, when I learned in the morning that the people had not yet come in, was that Shaw was not aware that for five days we should have to march through a wilderness totally uninhabited. I therefore despatched Chowpereh, a Mgwana soldier, with the following note to him:—" *You will, upon receipt of this order, pitch the cart into the nearest ravine, gully, or river, as well as all the extra pack saddles; and come at once, for God's sake, for we must not starve here!*"

One, two, three, and four hours were passed by me in the utmost impatience, waiting, but in vain, for Shaw. Having a long march before us, I could wait no longer, but went to meet his party myself. About a quarter of a mile from the ford I met the van of the laggards—stout, burly Chowpereh—and, O cartmakers, listen! he carried the cart on his head—wheels, shafts, body, axle, and all complete; he having found that carrying it was much

easier than drawing it. The sight was such a damper to
my regard for it as an experiment, that the cart was
wheeled into the depths of the tall reeds, and there left.
The central figure was Shaw himself, riding at a gait
which seemed to leave it doubtful on my mind whether
he or his animal felt most sleepy. Upon expostulating
with him for keeping the caravan so long waiting when
there was a march on hand, in a most peculiar voice—
which he always assumed when disposed to be ugly-
tempered—he said he had done the best he could; but as
I had seen the solemn pace at which he rode, I felt
dubious about his best endeavours; and of course there
was a little scene, but the young European mtongi of an
East African expedition must needs sup with the fellows
he has chosen.

We arrived at Madete at 4 P.M., minus two donkeys,
which had stretched their weary limbs in death. We
had crossed the Mukondokwa about 3 P.M., and after
taking its bearings and course, I made sure that its rise
took place near a group of mountains about forty miles
north by west of Nguru Peak. Our road led W.N.W.,
and at this place finally diverged from the river.

On the 14th, after a march of seven miles over hills
whose sandstone and granite formation cropped visibly
here and there above the surface, whose stony and dry
aspect seemed reflected in every bush and plant, and
having gained an altitude of about eight hundred feet
above the flow of the Mukondokwa, we sighted the Lake
of Ugombo—a grey sheet of water lying directly at the
foot of the hill, from whose summit we gazed at the
scene. The view was neither beautiful nor pretty, but
what I should call refreshing; it afforded a pleasant
relief to the eyes fatigued from dwelling on the bleak

country around. Besides, the immediate neighbourhood of the lake was too tame to call forth any enthusiasm ; there were no grandly swelling mountains, no smiling landscapes—nothing but a dun-brown peak, about one thousand feet high above the surface of the lake at its western extremity, from which the lake derived its name, Ugombo; nothing but a low dun-brown irregular range, running parallel with its northern shore at the distance of a mile; nothing but a low plain stretching from its western shore far away towards the Mpwapwa Mountains and Marenga Mkali, then apparent to us from our coign of vantage, from which extensive scene of dun-brownness we were glad to rest our eyes on the quiet grey water beneath.

Descending from the summit of the range, which bounded the lake east for about four hundred feet, we travelled along the northern shore. The time occupied in the journey from the eastern to the western extremity was exactly one hour and thirty minutes.

As this side represents its greatest length, I conclude that the lake is three miles long by two miles greatest breadth. The immediate shores of the lake on all sides, for at least fifty feet from the water's edge, is one impassable morass nourishing rank reeds and rushes, where the hippopotamus' ponderous form has crushed into watery trails the soft composition of the morass as he passes from the lake on his nocturnal excursions; the lesser animals, such as the " mbogo " (buffalo), the " punda-terra " (zebra), the " twiga " (giraffe), the boar, the kudu, the hyrax or coney, and the antelope, come here also to quench their thirst by night. The surface of the lake swarms with an astonishing variety of water-fowl, such as black swan, duck, ibis sacra, cranes, pelicans ; and soaring above on the look-out for their prey are fish-eagles, and hawks, while the neighbourhood is resonant with the loud chirps of the guinea-fowls calling for their young, with the harsh cry of the toucan, the cooing of the pigeon, and the " tu-whit, tu-whoo " of the owl. From the long grass in its vicinity also issue the grating and loud cry of the florican, woodcock, and grouse.

Being obliged to halt here two days, owing to the desertion of the Hindi cooper Jako with one of my best carbines, I improved the opportunity of exploring the northern and southern shores of the lake. At the rocky foot of a low, humpy hill on the northern side, about fifteen feet above the present surface of the water I detected in most distinct and definite lines the agency of waves. From its base could be traced clear to the edge of the dank morass tiny lines of comminuted shell as plainly marked as the small particles which lie in rows on a beech after a receding tide. There is no doubt that the wave-marks on the sandstone might have been traced much higher by one skilled in geology; it was only its elementary character that was visible to me. Nor do I entertain the least doubt, after a two days' exploration of the neighbourhood, especially of the low plain at the western end, that this Lake of Ugombo is but the tail of what was once a large body of water equal in extent to the Tanganika; and, after ascending half way up Ugombo Peak, this opinion was confirmed when I saw the long-depressed line of plain at its base stretching towards the Mpwapwa Mountains thirty miles off, and thence round to Marenga Mkali, and covering all that extensive surface of forty miles in breadth, and an unknown length. A depth of twelve feet more, I thought, as I gazed upon it, would give the lake a length of thirty miles, and a breadth of ten. A depth of thirty feet would increase its length over a hundred miles, and give it a breadth of fifty, for such was the level nature of the plain that stretched west of Ugombo, and north o. Marenga Mkali. Besides the water of the lake partook slightly of the bitter nature of the Matamombo creek, distant fifteen miles, and in a still lesser degree of that of Marenga Mkali, forty miles off.

Towards the end of the first day of our halt the Hindi cooper Jako arrived in camp, alleging as an excuse, that feeling fatigued he had fallen asleep in some bushes a few feet from the roadside. Having been the cause of our detention in the hungry wilderness of Ugombo, I was not in a frame of mind to forgive him; so, to prevent any future truant tricks on his part, I was under the necessity of including him with the chained gangs of runaways.

Two more of our donkeys died, and to prevent any of the valuable baggage being left behind, I was obliged to send Farquhar off on my own riding-ass to the village of Mpwapwa, thirty miles off, under charge of Mabruki Burton.

To save the Expedition from ruin, I was reluctantly compelled to come to the conclusion that it were better for me, for him, and all concerned, that he be left with some kind chief of a village, with a six months' supply of cloth and beads, until he got well, than that he make his own recovery impossible.

The 16th of May saw us journeying over the plain which lies between Ugombo and Mpwapwa, skirting close, at intervals, a low range of trap-rock, out of which had become displaced by some violent agency several immense boulders. On its slopes grew the kolquall to a size which I had not seen in Abyssinia. In the plain grew baobab, and immense tamarind, and a variety of thorn.

Within five hours from Ugombo the mountain range deflected towards the north-east, while we continued on a north-westerly course, heading for the lofty mountain-line of the Mpwapwa. To our left towered to the blue clouds the gigantic Rubeho. The adoption of this new road to Unyanyembe by which we were travelling was now explained—we were enabled to avoid the passes and stiff steeps of Rubeho, and had nothing worse, to encounter than a broad smooth plain, which sloped gently to Ugogo.

After a march of fifteen miles we camped at a dry mtoni, called Matamombo, celebrated for its pools of bitter water of the colour of ochre. Monkeys and rhinoceroses, besides kudus, steinboks, and antelopes, were numerous in the vicinity. At this camp my little dog "Omar" died of inflammation of the bowels, almost on the threshold of the country—Ugogo—where his faithful watchfulness would have been invaluable to me.

The next day's march was also fifteen miles in length, through one interminable jungle of thorn-bushes. Within two miles of the camp, the road led up a small river bed, broad as an avenue, clear to the khambi of Mpwapwa, which was situated close to a number of streams of the purest water.

The following morning found us much fatigued after the long marches from Ugombo, and generally disposed to take advantage of the precious luxuries Mpwapwa offered to caravans fresh from the fly-plagued lands of the Waseguhha and Wadoe. Sheikh Thani—clever but innocently-speaking old Arab—was encamped under the grateful umbrage of a huge Mtamba sycamore, and had been regaling himself with fresh milk, luscious mutton, and rich bullock humps, ever since his arrival here, two days before; and, as he informed me, it did not suit his views to quit such a happy abundance so soon for the saline nitrous water of Marenga Mkali, with its several terekezas, and manifold disagreeables. "No!" said he to me, emphatically, "better stop here two or three days, give your tired animals some rest; collect all the pagazis you can, fill your inside with fresh milk, sweet potatoes, beef, mutton, ghee, honey, beans, matama, maweri, and nuts;—then, Inshallah! we shall go together through Ugogo without stopping anywhere." As the advice tallied accurately with my own desires and keen appetite for the good things he named, he had not long to wait for my assent to his counsel. "Ugogo," continued he, "is rich with milk and honey—rich in flour, beans, and almost every eatable thing; and, Inshallah! before another week is gone we shall be in Ugogo!"

I had heard from passing caravans so many extremely favourable reports respecting Ugogo and its productions that it appeared to me a very Land of Promise, and I was most anxious to refresh my jaded stomach with some of the precious esculents raised in Ugogo; but when I heard that Mpwapwa also furnished some of those delicate eatables, and good things, most of the morning hours were spent in inducing the slow-witted people to part with them; and when, finally, eggs, milk, honey, mutton, ghee, ground matama and beans had been collected in sufficient quantities to produce a respectable meal, my keenest attention and best culinary talents were occupied for a couple of hours in converting this crude supply into a breakfast which should be accepted by and befit a stomach at once fastidious and famished, such as mine was. The subsequent healthy digestion of it proved my endeavours to have been eminently successful. At the termination of this eventful day, the following remark was jotted down in my diary: "Thank God! After fifty-seven days of living upon matama porridge and tough goat, I have enjoyed with unctuous satisfaction a real breakfast and dinner."

It was in one of the many small villages which are situated upon the slopes of the Mpwapwa that a refuge and a home for Farquhar was found until he should be enabled by restored health to start to join us at Unyanyembe.

Food was plentiful and of sufficient variety to suit the most fastidious—cheap also, much cheaper than we had experienced for many a day. Leucole, the chief of the village, with whom arrangements for Farquhar's protection and comfort were made, was a little old man of mild eye and very pleasing face, and on being informed that it was intended to leave the Musungu entirely under his charge, suggested that some man should be left to wait on him, and interpret his wishes to his people.

As Jako was the only one who could speak English, except Bombay and Selim, Jako was appointed, and the chief Leucole was satisfied. Six months' provisions of white. beads, Merikani and Kaniki cloth, together with two doti of handsome cloth to serve as a present to Leucole after his recovery, were taken to Farquhar by Bombay, together with a Starr's carbine, 300 rounds of cartridge, a set of cooking pots, and 3 lbs. of tea.

Abdullah bin Nasib, who was found encamped here with five hundred pagazis, and a train of Arab and Wasawahili satellites, who revolved around his importance, treated me in somewhat the same manner that Hamed bin Sulayman treated Speke at Kasenge. Followed by his satellites, he came (a tall nervous-looking man, of fifty or

thereabouts) to see me in my camp, and asked me if I
wished to purchase donkeys. As all my animals were
either sick or moribund, I replied very readily in the
affirmative, upon which he graciously said he would sell
me as many as I wanted, and for payment I could give
him a draft on Zanzibar. I thought him a very considerate and kind person, fully justifying the encomiums
lavished on him in Burton's 'Lake Regions of Central
Africa,' and accordingly I treated him with the consideration due to so great and good a man. The morrow
came, and with it went Abdullah bin Nasib, or "Kisesa,"
as he is called by the Wanyamwezi, with all his pagazis,
his train of followers, and each and every one of his
donkeys, towards Bagamoyo, without so much as giving
a "Kwaheri," or good-bye.

At this place there are generally to be found from ten
to thirty pagazis awaiting up-caravans. I was fortunate
enough to secure twelve good people, who, upon my
arrival at Unyanyembe, without an exception, voluntarily engaged themselves as carriers to Ujiji. With the
formidable marches of Marenga Mkali in front, I felt
thankful for this happy windfall, which resolved the
difficulties I had been anticipating; for I had but ten
donkeys left, and four of these were so enfeebled that
they were worthless as baggage animals.

Mpwapwa—so called by the Arabs, who have managed
to corrupt almost every native word—is called "Mbamb-
wa" by the Wasagara. It is a mountain range rising
over 6,000 feet above the sea, bounding on the north the
extensive plain which commences at Ugombo lake, and on
the east that part of the plain which is called Marenga
Mkali, which stretches away beyond the borders of
Uhumba. Opposite Mpwapwa, at the distance of thirty

miles or so, rises the Anak peak of Rubeho, with several
other ambitious and tall brethren cresting long lines of
rectilinear scarps, which ascend from the plain of
Ugombo and Marenga Mkali as regularly as if they had
been chiselled out by the hands of generations of masons
and stonecutters.

Upon looking at Mpwapwa's greenly-tinted slopes, dark
with many a densely-foliaged tree; its many rills flowing
sweet and clear, nourishing besides thick patches of gum
and thorn bush, giant sycamore and parachute-topped
mimosa, and permitting my imagination to picture sweet
views behind the tall cones above, I was tempted to brave
the fatigue of an ascent to the summit. Nor was my love
for the picturesque disappointed. One sweep of the eyes
embraced hundreds of square miles of plain and mountain,
from Ugombo Peak away to distant Ugogo, and from
Rubeho and Ugogo to the dim and purple pasture lands
of the wild, untamable Wahumba. The plain of Ugombo
and its neighbour of Marenga Mkali, apparently level as
a sea, was dotted here and there with " hillocks dropt in
Nature's careless haste," which appeared like islands amid
the dun and green expanse. Where the jungle was dense
the color was green, alternating with dark brown; where
the plain appeared denuded of bush and brake it had a
whity-brown appearance, on which the passing clouds
now and again cast their deep shadows. Altogether this
side of the picture was not inviting; it exhibited too
plainly the true wilderness in its sternest aspect; but
perhaps the knowledge that in the bosom of the vast
plain before me there was not one drop of water but was
bitter as nitre, and undrinkable as urine, prejudiced me
against it. The hunter might consider it a paradise, for
in its depths were all kinds of game to attract his keenest

instincts; but to the mere traveller it had a stern out-look. Nearer, however, to the base of the Mpwapwa the aspect of the plain altered. At first the jungle thinned, openings in the wood appeared, then wide and naked clearings, then extensive fields of the hardy holcus, Indian corn, and maweri or bajri, with here and there a square tembe or village. Still nearer ran thin lines of fresh young grass, great trees surrounded a patch of alluvial meadow. A broad river-bed, containing several rivulets of water, ran through the thirsty fields, convey-ing the vivifying element which in this part of Usagara was so scarce and precious. Down to the river-bed sloped the Mpwapwa, roughened in some places by great boulders of basalt, or by rock masses, which had parted from a precipitous scarp, where clung the kolquall with a sure hold, drawing nourishment where every other green thing failed; clad in others by the hardy mimosa, which rose like a sloping bank of green verdure almost to the summit. And, happy sight to me so long a stranger to it, there were hundreds of cattle grazing, imparting a pleasing animation to the solitude of the deep folds of the mountain range.

But the fairest view was obtained by looking north-ward towards the dense group of mountains which buttressed the front range, facing towards Rubeho. It was the home of the winds, which starting here and sweeping down the precipitous slopes and solitary peaks on the western side, and gathering strength as they rushed through the prairie-like Marenga Mkali, howled through Ugogo and Unyamwezi with the force of a storm. It was also the home of the dews, where sprang the clear springs which cheered by their music the bosky dells below, and enriched the populous district of Mpwapwa.

One felt better, stronger, on this breezy height, drinking in the pure air and feasting the eyes on such a varied landscape as it presented, on spreading plateaus green as lawns, on smooth rounded tops, on mountain vales containing recesses which might charm a hermit's soul, on deep and awful ravines where reigned a twilight gloom, on fractured and riven precipices, on huge fantastically-worn boulders which overtopped them, on picturesque tracts which embraced all that was wild, and all that was poetical in Nature.

Mpwapwa, though the traveller from the coast will feel grateful for the milk it furnished after being so long deprived of it, will be kept in mind as a most remarkable place for earwigs. In my tent they might be counted by thousands; in my slung cot they were by hundreds; on my clothes they were by fifties; on my neck and head they were by scores. The several plagues of locusts, fleas, and lice sink into utter insignificance compared with this fearful one of earwigs. It is true they did not bite, and they did not irritate the cuticle, but what their presence and numbers suggested was something so horrible that it drove one nearly insane to think of it. Who will come to East Africa without reading the experiences of Burton and Speke? Who is he that having read them will not remember with horror the dreadful account given by Speke of his encounters with these pests? My intense nervous watchfulness alone, I believe, saved me from a like calamity.

Second to the earwigs in importance and in numbers were the white ants, whose powers of destructiveness were simply awful. Mats, cloth, portmanteaus, clothes, in short, every article I possessed, seemed on the verge of destruction, and, as I witnessed their voracity, I felt anxious lest my tent should be devoured while I slept. This was the first khambi since leaving the coast where their presence became a matter of anxiety; at all other camping places hitherto the red and black ants had usurped our attention, but at Mpwapwa the red species were not seen, while the black were also very scarce.

After a three days' halt at Mpwapwa I decided on a march to Marenga Mkali, which should be uninterrupted until we reached Mvumi in Ugogo, where I should be inducted into the art of paying tribute to the Wagogo chiefs. The first march to Kisokweh was purposely made short, being barely four miles, in order to enable Sheikh Thani, Sheikh Hamed, and five or six Wasawahili caravans to come up with me at Chunyo on the confines of Marenga Mkali.

OUR CAMP AT CHUNYO

CHAPTER VII.

THROUGH MARENGA MKALI, UGOGO, AND UYANZI, TO UNYANYEMBE.

Mortality amongst the baggage animals.—The contumacious Wagogo.
—Mobs of Mænads.—Tribute paying.—Necessity of prudence.—
Oration of the guide.—The genuine "Ugogians."—Vituperative
power.—A surprised chief.—The famous Mizanza.—Killing hyænas.
—The Greeks and Romans of Africa.—A critical moment.—The
"elephant's back."—The wilderness of Ukimbu.—End of the first
stage of the search.—Arrival at Unyanyembe.

THE 22nd of May saw Thani and Hamed's caravans united
with my own at Chunyo, three and a half hours' march
from Mpwapwa. The road from the latter place ran along

the skirts of the Mpwapwa range; at three or four places it crossed outlying spurs that stood isolated from the main body of the range. The last of these hill spurs, joined by an elevated cross ridge to the Mpwapwa, shelters the tembe of Chunyo, situated on the western face, from the stormy gusts that come roaring down the steep slopes. The water of Chunyo is eminently bad, in fact it is its saline-nitrous nature which has given the name Marenga Mkali—bitter water—to the wilderness which separates Usagara from Ugogo. Though extremely offensive to the palate, Arabs and the natives drink it without fear, and without any bad results; but they are careful to withhold their baggage animals from the pits. Being ignorant of its nature, and not exactly understanding what precise location was meant by Marenga Mkali, I permitted the donkeys to be taken to water, as usual after a march; and the consequence was calamitous in the extreme. What the fearful swamp of Makata had spared, the waters of Marenga Mkali destroyed. In less than five days after our departure from Chunyo or Marenga Mkali, five out of the nine donkeys left to me at the time—the five healthiest animals—fell victims.

We formed quite an imposing caravan as we emerged from inhospitable Chunyo, in number amounting to about four hundred souls. We were strong in guns, flags, horns, sounding drums and noise. To Sheikh Hamed, by permission of Sheikh Thani, and myself was allotted the task of guiding and leading this great caravan through dreaded Ugogo; which was a most unhappy selection, as will be seen hereafter.

Marenga Mkali, over thirty miles across, was at last before us. This distance had to be traversed within thirty-six hours, so that the fatigue of the ordinary march would be more than doubled by this. From Chunyo to Ugogo not one drop of water was to be found. As a large caravan, say over two hundred souls, seldom travels over one and three-quarter miles per hour, a march of thirty miles would require seventeen hours of endurance without water and but little rest. East Africa generally possessing unlimited quantities of water, caravans have not been compelled for lack of the element to have recourse to the mushok of India and the khirbeh of Egypt. Being able to cross the waterless districts by a couple of long marches, they content themselves for the time with a small gourdful, and with keeping their imaginations dwelling upon the copious quantities they will drink upon arrival at the watering-place.

The march through this waterless district was most monotonous, and a dangerous fever attacked me, which seemed to eat into my very vitals. The wonders of Africa that bodied themselves forth in the shape of flocks of zebras, giraffes, elands, or antelopes, galloping over the jungleless plain, had no charm for me; nor could they serve to draw my attention from the severe fit of sickness which possessed me. Towards the end of the first march I was not able to sit upon the donkey's back; nor would it do, when but a third of the way across the wilderness, to halt until the next day; soldiers were therefore detailed to carry me in a hammock, and, when the terekeza was performed in the afternoon, I lay in a lethargic state, unconscious of all things. With the night passed the fever, and, at 3 o'clock in the morning, when the march was resumed, I was booted and spurred, and the recognized mtongi of my caravan once more. At 8 A.M. we had performed the thirty-two miles. The wilderness of Marenga Mkali had been passed and we had entered Ugogo, which was at once a dreaded land to my caravan, and a Land of Promise to myself.

The transition from the wilderness into this Promised Land was very gradual and easy. Very slowly the jungle thinned, the cleared land was a long time appearing, and when it had finally appeared, there were no signs of cultivation until we could clearly make out the herbage and vegetation on some hill slopes to our right running parallel with our route, then we saw timber on the hills, and broad acreage under cultivation—and, lo! as we ascended a wave of reddish earth covered with tall weeds and cane, but a few feet from us, and directly across our path, were the fields of matama and grain we had been looking for, and Ugogo had been entered an hour before.

The view was not such as I expected. I had imagined a plateau several hundred feet higher than Marenga Mkali, and an expansive view which should reveal Ugogo and its characteristics at once. But instead, while travelling from the tall weeds which covered the clearing which had preceded the cultivated parts, we had entered into the depths of the taller matama stalks, and, excepting some distant hills near Mvumi, where the Great Sultan lived—the first of the tribe to whom we should pay tribute —the view was extremely limited.

However, in the neighbourhood of the first village a glimpse at some of the peculiar features of Ugogo was obtained, and there was a vast plain—now flat, now heaving upwards, here level as a table, there tilted up into rugged knolls bristling with scores of rough boulders of immense size, which lay piled one above another as if the children of a Titanic race had been playing at house-building. Indeed, these piles of rounded, angular, and riven rock formed miniature hills of themselves, and appeared as if each body had been ejected upwards by some violent agency beneath. There was one of these in particular, near Mvumi, which was so large, and being slightly obscured from view by the outspreading branches of a gigantic baobab, bore such a strong resemblance to a square tower of massive dimensions, that for a long time I cherished the idea that I had discovered something most interesting which had strangely escaped the notice of my predecessors in East Africa. A nearer view dispelled the illusion, and proved it to be a huge cube of rock, measuring about forty feet each way. The baobabs were also particularly conspicuous on this scene, no other kind of tree being visible in the cultivated parts. These had probably been left for two reasons: first, want of proper axes for felling trees of such enormous growth; secondly, because during a famine the fruit of the baobab furnishes a flour which, in the absence of anything better, is said to be eatable and nourishing.

The first words I heard in Ugogo were from a Wagogo elder, of sturdy form, who in an indolent way tended the flocks, but showed a marked interest in the stranger clad in white flannels, with a Hawkes' patent cork solar topee on his head, a most unusual thing in Ugogo, who came walking past him, and there were "Yambo, Musungu, Yambo, bana, bana," delivered with a voice loud enough to make itself heard a full mile away. No sooner had the greeting been delivered than the word "Musungu" seemed to electrify his entire village; and the people of other villages, situated at intervals near the road, noting the excitement that reigned at the first, also participated in the general frenzy which seemed suddenly to have possessed them. I consider my progress from the first village to Mvumi to have been most triumphant; for I was accompanied by a furious mob of men, women, and children, all almost as naked as Mother Eve when the world first dawned upon her in the garden of Eden, fighting, quarrelling, jostling, staggering against each other for the best view of the white man, the like of whom was now seen for the first time in this part of Ugogo. The cries of admiration, such as " Hi-le !" which broke often and in confused uproar upon my ear, were not gratefully accepted, inasmuch as I deemed many of them impertinent. A respectful silence and more reserved behaviour would have won my esteem; but, ye powers, who cause etiquette to be observed in Usungu,* respectful silence, reserved behaviour, and esteem are terms unknown in savage Ugogo. Hitherto I had compared myself to a merchant of Bagdad travelling among the Kurds of Kurdistan, selling his wares of Damascus silk, kefiyehs, &c.; but now I was compelled to lower my standard, and thought myself not much better than a monkey in a zoological collection. One of my soldiers requested them to lessen their vociferous noise; but the evil-minded race ordered him to shut up, as a thing unworthy to speak to the Wagogo ! When I imploringly turned to the Arabs for counsel in this strait, old Sheikh Thani, always worldly wise, said, " Heed them not; they are dogs who bite besides barking."

At 9 A.M. we were in our boma, near Mvumi village; but here also crowds of Wagogo came to catch a glimpse of the Musungu, whose presence was soon made known throughout the district of Mvumi. But two hours later I was oblivious of their endeavours to see me; for, despite repeated doses of quinine, the mukunguru had sure hold of me.

The next day was a march of eight miles, from East

* White man's land.

Mvumi to West Mvumi, where lived the Sultan of the district. The quantity and variety of provisions which arrived at our boma did not belie the reports respecting the productions of Ugogo. Milk, sour and sweet, honey, beans, matama, maweri, Indian corn, ghee, pea-nuts, and a species of bean-nut very like a large pistachio or an almond, water-melons, pumpkins, mush-melons, and cucumbers were brought, and readily exchanged for Merikani, Kaniki, and for the white Merikani beads and Sami-Sami, or Sam-Sam. The trade and barter which progressed in the camp from morning till night reminded me of the customs existing among the Gallas and Abyssinians. Eastward, caravans were obliged to despatch men with cloth, to purchase from the villagers. This was unnecessary in Ugogo, where the people voluntarily brought every vendible they possessed to the camp. The smallest breadth of white or blue cloth became saleable and useful in purchasing provisions—even a loin-cloth worn threadbare.

The day after our march was a halt. We had fixed this day for bearing the tribute to the Great Sultan of Mvumi. Prudent and cautious Sheikh Thani early began this important duty, the omission of which would have been a signal for war. Hamed and Thani sent two faithful slaves, well up to the eccentricities of the Wagogo sultans—well spoken, having glib tongues and the real instinct for trade as carried on amongst Orientals. They bore six doti of cloths, viz., one doti of Dabwani Ulyah contributed by myself, also one doti of Barsati from me, two doti Merikani Satine from Sheikh Thani, and two doti of Kaniki from Sheikh Hamed, as a first instalment of the tribute. The slaves were absent a full hour, but having wasted their powers of pleading, in vain, they returned with the demand for more, which Sheikh Thani communicated to me in this wise :

"Auf! this Sultan is a very bad man—a very bad man indeed ; he says, the Musungu is a great man, I call him a sultan ; the Musungu is very rich, for he has several caravans already gone past ; the Musungu must pay forty doti, and the Arabs must pay twelve doti each, for they have rich caravans. It is of no use for you to tell me you are all one caravan, otherwise why so many flags and tents ? Go and bring me sixty doti, with less I will not be satisfied."

I suggested to Sheikh Thani, upon hearing this exorbitant demand, that had I twenty Wasungu* armed with Winchester repeating rifles, the Sultan might be obliged to pay tribute to me ; but Thani prayed and begged me to be cautious lest angry words might irritate the Sultan and cause him to demand a double tribute, as he was quite capable of doing so ; " and if you preferred war," said he, " your pagazis would all desert, and leave you and your cloth to the small mercy of the Wagogo." But I hastened to allay his fears by telling Bombay, in his presence, that I had foreseen such demands on the part of the Wagogo, and that having set aside one hundred and twenty doti of honga cloths, I should not consider myself a sufferer if the Sultan demanded and I paid forty cloths to him ; that he must therefore open the honga bale, and permit Sheikh Thani to extract such cloths as the Sultan might like.

Sheikh Thani, having put on the cap of consideration and joined heads with Hamed and the faithful serviles, thought if I paid twelve doti, out of which three should be of Ulyah† quality, that the Sultan might possibly condescend to accept our tribute ; supposing he was per-

---

* White men.   † Best, or superior.

suaded by the oratorical words of the "Faithfuls," that the Musungu* had nothing with him but the mashiwa (boat), which would be of no use to him, come what might,—with which prudent suggestion the Musungu concurred, seeing its wisdom.

The slaves departed, bearing this time from our boma thirty doti, with our best wishes for their success. In an hour they returned with empty hands, but yet unsuccessful. The Sultan demanded six doti of Merikani, and a fundo of bubu, from the Musungu ; and from the Arabs and other caravans, twelve doti more. For the third time the slaves departed for the Sultan's tembe, carrying with them six doti Merikani and a fundo of bubu from myself, and ten doti from the Arabs. Again they returned to us with the Sultan's words, "That, as the doti of the Musungu were short measure, and the cloths of the Arabs of miserable quality, the Musungu must send three doti full measure, and the Arabs five doti of Kaniki." My three doti were at once measured out with the longest fore-arm—according to Kigogo measure—and sent off by Bombay ; but the Arabs, almost in despair, declared they would be ruined if they gave way to such demands, and out of the five doti demanded sent only two, with a pleading to the Sultan that he would consider what was paid as just and fair Muhongo, and not ask any more. But the Sultan of Mvumi was by no means disposed to consider any such proposition, but declared he must have three doti, and these to be two of Ulyah cloth, and one Kitambi Barsati, which, as he was determined to obtain, were sent to him heavy with the deep maledictions of Sheikh Hamed and the despairing sighs of Sheikh Thani.

* White man.

Altogether the sultanship of a district in Ugogo must be very remunerative, besides being a delightful sinecure, so long as the Sultan has to deal with timid Arab merchants who fear to exhibit anything approaching to independence and self-reliance, lest they might be mulcted in cloth. In one day from one camp the sultan received forty-seven doti, consisting of Merikani, Kaniki, Barsati, and Dabwani, equal to $35·25, besides seven doti of superior cloths, consisting of Rehani, Sohari, and Daobwani Ulyah, and one fundo of Bubu, equal to $14·00, making a total of $49·25—a most handsome revenue for a Mgogo chief.

On the 27th May we gladly shook the dust of Mvumi from our feet, and continued on our route—ever westward. Five of my donkeys had died the night before, from the effects of the water of Marenga Mkali. Before leaving the camp of Mvumi, I went to look at their carcases; but found them to have been clean picked by the hyænas, and the bones taken possession of by an army of white-necked crows.

As we passed the numerous villages, and perceived the entire face of the land to be one vast field of grain, and counted the people halted by scores on the roadside to feast their eyes with a greedy stare on the Musungu, I no longer wondered at the extortionate demands of the Wagogo. For it was manifest that they had but to stretch out their hands to possess whatever the wealth of a caravan consisted of; and I began to think better of the people who, knowing well their strength, did not use it— of people who were intellectual enough to comprehend that their interest lay in permitting the caravans to pass on without attempting any outrage.

Between Mvumi and the next Sultan's district, that of

Matamburu, I counted no less than twenty-five villages
scattered over the clayey, colored plain. Despite the
inhospitable nature of the plain, it was better cultivated
than any part of any other country we had seen since
leaving Bagamoyo.

When we had at last arrived at our boma of Matamburu, the same groups of curious people, the same eager
looks, the same exclamations of surprise, the same peals
of laughter at something they deemed ludicrous in the
Musungu's dress or manner, awaited us, as at Mvumi.
The Arabs being "Wakonongo" travellers, whom they
saw every day, enjoyed a complete immunity from the
vexations which we had to endure.

The Sultan of Matamburu, a man of herculean form,
and massive head well set on shoulders that might vie
with those of Milo, proved to be a very reasonable person.
Not quite so powerful as the Sultan of Mvumi, he yet
owned a fair share of Ugogo and about forty villages, and
could, if he chose, have oppressed the mercantile souls of
my Arab companions, in the same way as he of Mvumi.
Four doti of cloth were taken to him as a preliminary
offering to his greatness, which he said he would accept,
if the Arabs and Musungu would send him four more.
As his demands were so reasonable, this little affair was
soon terminated to everybody's satisfaction; and soon
after, the kirangozi of Sheikh Hamed sounded the signal
for the morrow's march.

At the orders of the same Sheikh, the kirangozi stood
up to speak before the assembled caravans. "Words,
words, from the Bana," he shouted. "Give ear, kirangozis! Listen, children of Unyamwezi! The journey is
for to-morrow! The road is crooked and bad, bad! The
jungle is there, and many Wagogo lie hidden within it!

Wagogo spear the pagazis, and cut the throats of those who carry mutumba (bales) and ushanga (beads)! The Wagogo have been to our camp, they have seen your bales; to-night they seek the jungle: to-morrow watch well, O Wanyamwezi! Keep close together, lag not behind! Kirangozis walk slow, that the weak, the sick, and the young may keep up with the strong! Take two rests on the journey! These are the words of the Bana (master). Do you hear them, Wanyamwezi? (A loud shout in the affirmative from all.) Do you understand them well? (another chorus); then Bas;" having said which, the eloquent kirangozi retired into the dark night, and his straw hut.

The march to Bihawana, our next camp, was rugged and long, through a continuous jungle of gums and thorns, up steep hills and finally over a fervid plain, while the sun waxed hotter and hotter as it drew near the meridian, until it seemed to scorch all vitality from inanimate nature, while the view was one white blaze, unbearable to the pained sight, which sought relief from the glare in vain. Several sandy watercourses, on which were impressed many a trail of elephants, were also passed on this march. The slope of these stream-beds trended south-east and south.

In the middle of this scorching plain stood the villages of Bihawana, almost undistinguishable, from the extreme lowness of the huts, which did not reach the height of the tall bleached grass which stood smoking in the untempered heat.

Our camp was in a large boma, about a quarter of a mile from the Sultan's tembe. Soon after arriving at the camp, I was visited by three Wagogo, who asked me if I had seen a Mgogo on the road with a woman and child.

I was about to answer, very innocently, " Yes," when
Mabruki—cautious and watchful always for the interests
of the master—requested me not to answer, as the
Wagogo, as customary, would charge me with having done
away with them, and would require their price from me.
Indignant at the imposition they were about to practise
upon me, I was about to raise my whip to flog them out
of the camp, when again Mabruki, with a roaring voice,
bade me beware, for every blow would cost me three or
four doti of cloth. As I did not care to gratify my anger
at such an expense, I was compelled to swallow my
wrath, and consequently the Wagogo escaped chastise-
ment.

We halted for one day at this place, which was a great
relief to me, as I was suffering severely from intermittent
fever, which lasted in this case two weeks, and entirely
prevented my posting my diary in full, as was my custom
every evening after a march.

The Sultan of Bihawana, though his subjects were evil-
disposed, and ready-handed at theft and murder, contented
himself with three doti as honga. From this chief I
received news of my fourth caravan, which had distinguished itself in a fight with some outlawed subjects of
his; my soldiers had killed two who had attempted, after
waylaying a couple of my pagazis, to carry away a bale of
cloth and a bag of beads; coming up in time, the soldiers
decisively frustrated the attempt. The Sultan thought
that if all caravans were as well guarded as mine were,
there would be less depredations committed on them
while on the road; with which I heartily agreed.

The next sultan's tembe through whose territory we
marched, this being on the 30th May, was at Kididimo,
but four miles from Bihawna. The road led through a

flat elongated plain, lying between two lengthy hilly ridges, thickly dotted with the giant forms of the baobab. Kididimo is exceedingly bleak in aspect. Even the faces of the Wagogo seemed to have contracted a bleak hue from the general bleakness around. The water of the pits obtained in the neighbourhood had an execrable flavor, and two donkeys sickened and died in less than an hour from its effects. Man suffered nausea and a general irritability of the system, and accordingly revenged himself by cursing the country and its imbecile ruler most heartily. The climax came, however, when Bombay reported, after an attempt to settle the Muhongo, that the chief's head had grown big since he heard that the Musungu had come, and that its "bigness" could not be reduced unless he could extract ten doti as tribute. Though the demand was large, I was not in a humour— being feeble, and almost nerveless, from repeated attacks of the Mukunguru—to dispute the sum: consequently it was paid without many words. But the Arabs continued the whole afternoon negotiating, and at the end had to pay eight doti each.

Between Kididimo and Nyambwa, the district of the Sultan Pembera Pereh, was a broad and lengthy forest and jungle inhabited by the elephant, rhinoceros, zebra, deer, antelope, and giraffe. Starting at dawn of the 31st, we entered the jungle, whose dark lines and bosky banks were clearly visible from our bower at Kididimo; and, travelling for two hours, halted for rest and breakfast, at pools of sweet water surrounded by tracts of vivid green verdure, which were a great resort for the wild animals of the jungle, whose tracks were numerous and recent. A narrow nullah, shaded deeply with foliage, afforded excellent retreats from the glaring sunshine. At meridian, our thirst quenched, our hunger satisfied, our gourds refilled, we set out from the shade into the heated blaze of hot noon. The path serpentined in and out of jungle, and thin forest, into open tracts of grass bleached white as stubble, into thickets of gums and thorns, which emitted an odour as rank as a stable; through clumps of wide-spreading mimosa and colonies of baobab, through a country teeming with noble game, which, though we saw them frequently, were yet as safe from our rifles as if we had been on the Indian Ocean. A terekeza, such as we were now making, admits of no delay. Water we had left behind at noon: until noon of the next day not a drop was to be obtained; and unless we marched fast and long on this day, raging thirst would demoralize everybody. So for six long weary hours we toiled bravely; and at sunset we camped, and still a march of two hours, to be done before the sun was an hour high, intervened between us and our camp at Nyambwa. That night the men bivouacked under the trees, surrounded by many miles of dense forest, enjoying the cool night unprotected by hat or tent, while I groaned and tossed throughout the night in a paroxysm of fever.

The morn came; and, while it was yet young, the long caravan, or string of caravans, was under way. It was the same forest, admitting, on the narrow line which we threaded, but one man at a time. Its view was as limited. To our right and left the forest was dark and deep. Above was a riband of glassy sky flecked by the floating nimbus. We heard nothing save a few stray notes from a flying bird, or the din of the caravans as the men sang, or hummed, or conversed, or shouted, as the thought struck them that we were nearing water. One of my pagazis, wearied and sick, fell, and never rose again. The last of the caravan passed him before he died.

At 7 A.M. we were encamped at Nyambwa, drinking the excellent water found here with the avidity of thirsty camels. Extensive fields of grain had heralded the neighbourhood of the villages, at the sight of which we were conscious that the caravan was quickening its pace, as approaching its halting-place. As the Wasungu drew within the populated area, crowds of Wagogo used their utmost haste to see them before they passed by. Young and old of both genders pressed about us in a multitude—a very howling mob. This excessive demonstrativeness elicited from my sailor overseer the characteristic remark, "Well, I declare, these must be the genuine Ugogians, for they stare! stare—there is no end to their staring. I'm almost tempted to slap 'em in the face!" In fact, the conduct of the Wagogo of Nyambwa was an exaggeration of the general conduct of Wagogo. Hitherto, those we had met had contented themselves with staring and shouting; but these outstepped all bounds, and my growing anger at their excessive insolence vented itself in gripping the rowdiest of them by the neck, and before he could recover from his astonishment administering a sound thrashing with my dog-whip, which he little relished. This proceeding educed from the tribe of starers all their native power of vituperation and abuse, in expressing which they were peculiar. Approaching in manner to angry tom-cats, they jerked their words with something of a splitting hiss and a half bark. The ejaculation, as near as I can spell it phonetically, was "hahcht" uttered in a shrill crescendo tone. They paced backwards and forwards, asking themselves, "Are the Wagogo to be beaten like slaves by this Musungu?

A Mgogo is a Mgwana (a free man); he is not used to be beaten,—hahcht." But whenever I made motion, flourishing my whip, towards them, these mighty braggarts found it convenient to move to respectable distances from the irritated Musungu.

Perceiving that a little manliness and show of power was something which the Wagogo long needed, and that in this instance it relieved me from annoyance, I had recourse to my whip, whose long lash cracked like a pistol shot, whenever they overstepped moderation. So long as they continued to confine their obtrusiveness to staring, and communicating to each other their opinions respecting my complexion, and dress, and accoutrements, I philosophically resigned myself in silence for their amusement; but when they pressed on me, barely allowing me to proceed, a few vigorous and rapid slashes right and left with my serviceable thong, soon cleared the track.

Pembera Pereh is a queer old man, very small, and would be very insignificant were he not the greatest sultan in Ugogo ; and enjoying a sort of dimediate power over many other tribes. Though such an important chief, he is the meanest dressed of his subjects,—is always filthy,—ever greasy—eternally foul about the mouth ; but these are mere eccentricities : as a wise judge, he is without parallel, always has a dodge ever ready for the abstraction of cloth from the spiritless Arab merchants, who trade with Unyanyembe every year ; and disposes with ease of a judicial case which would overtask ordinary men.

Sheikh Hamed, who was elected guider of the united caravans now travelling through Ugogo, was of such a fragile and small make, that he might be taken for an imitation of his famous prototype "Dapper." Being of such dimensions, what he lacked for weight and size he made up by activity. No sooner had he arrived in camp than his trim dapper form was seen frisking about from side to side of the great boma, fidgeting, arranging, disturbing everything and everybody. He permitted no bales or packs to be intermingled, or to come into too close proximity to his own; he had a favourite mode of stacking his goods, which he would see carried out; he had a special eye for the best place for his tent, and no one else must trespass on that ground. One would imagine that walking ten or fifteen miles a day, he would leave such trivialities to his servants, but no, nothing could be right unless he had personally superintended it; in which work he was tireless and knew no fatigue.

Another not uncommon peculiarity pertained to Sheikh Hamed; as he was not a rich man, he laboured hard to make the most of every shukka and doti expended, and each fresh expenditure seemed to gnaw his very vitals: he was ready to weep, as he himself expressed it, at the high prices of Ugogo, and the extortionate demands of its sultans. For this reason, being the leader of the caravans, so far as he was able we were very sure not to be delayed in Ugogo, where food was so dear.

The day we arrived at Nyambwa will be remembered by Hamed as long as he lives, for the trouble and vexation which he suffered. His misfortunes arose from the fact that, being too busily engaged in fidgeting about the camp, he permitted his donkeys to stray into the matama fields of Pembera Pereh, the Sultan. For hours he and his servants sought for the stray donkeys, returning towards evening utterly unsuccessful, Hamed bewailing, as only an Oriental can do, when hard fate visits him

with its inflictions, the loss of a hundred dollars' worth of
Muscat donkeys. Sheikh Thani, older, more experienced,
and wiser, suggested to him that he should notify the
Sultan of his loss. Acting upon the sagacious advice,
Hamed sent an embassy of two slaves, and the information they brought back was, that Pembera Pereh's
servants had found the two donkeys eating the unripened
matama, and that unless the Arab who owned them
would pay nine doti of first-class cloths, he, Pembera
Pereh, would surely keep them to remunerate him for
the matama they had eaten. Hamed was in despair.
Nine doti of first-class cloths, worth $25 in Unyanyembe,
for half a shukka's worth of grain, was, as he thought, an
absurd demand ; but then if he did not pay it, what
would become of the hundred dollars' worth of donkeys ?
He proceeded to the Sultan to show him the absurdity of
the damage claim, and to endeavour to make him accept
one shukka, which would be more than double the worth
of what grain the donkeys had consumed. But the Sultan
was sitting on pombe ; he was drunk, which I believe to
be his normal state—too drunk to attend to business,
consequently his deputy, a renegade Mnyamwezi, gave
ear to the business. With most of the Wagogo chiefs
lives a Mnyamwezi, as their right-hand man, prime
minister, counsellor, executioner, ready man at all things
save the general good ; a sort of harlequin Unyamwezi,
who is such an intriguing, restless, unsatisfied person,
that as soon as one hears that this kind of man forms one
of and the chief of a Mgogo sultan's council, one feels
very much tempted to do damage to his person. Most of
the extortions practised upon the Arabs are suggested by
these crafty renegades. Sheikh Hamed found that the
Mnyamwezi was far more obdurate than the Sultan—

nothing under nine doti first-class cloths would redeem the donkeys. The business that day remained unsettled, and the night following was, as one may imagine, a very sleepless one to Hamed. As it turned out, however, the loss of the donkeys, the after heavy fine, and the sleepless night, proved to be blessings in disguise; for, towards midnight, a robber Mgogo visited his camp, and while attempting to steal a bale of cloth, was detected in the act by the wide-awake and irritated Arab, and was made to vanish instantly with a bullet whistling in close proximity to his ear.

From each of the principals of the caravans, the Mnyamwezi had received as tribute for his drunken master fifteen doti, and from the other six caravans six doti each, altogether fifty-one doti, yet on the next morning when we took the road he was not a whit disposed to deduct a single cloth from the fine imposed on Hamed, and the unfortunate Sheikh was therefore obliged to liquidate the claim, or leave his donkeys behind.

After travelling through the corn-fields of Pembera Pereh we emerged upon a broad flat plain, as level as the still surface of a pond, whence the salt of the Wagogo is obtained. From Kanyenyi on the southern road, to beyond the confines of Uhumba and Ubanarama, this saline field extends, containing many large ponds of salt bitter water whose low banks are covered with an effervescence partaking of the nature of nitrate. Subsequently, two days afterwards, having ascended the elevated ridge which separates Ugogo from Uyanzi, I obtained a view of this immense saline plain, embracing over a hundred square miles. I may have been deceived, but I imagined I saw large expanses of greyish-blue water, which causes me to believe that this salina is but a corner of a great salt lake. The Wahumba, who are numerous, from Nyambwa to the Uyanzi border, informed my soldiers that there was a "Maji Kuba" away to the north.

Mizanza, our next camp after Nyambwa, is situated in a grove of palms, about thirteen miles from the latter place. Soon after arriving I had to bury myself under blankets, plagued with the same intermittent fever which first attacked me during the transit of Marenga Mkali. Feeling certain that one day's halt, which would enable me to take regular doses of the invaluable sulphate of quinine, would cure me, I requested Sheikh Thani to tell Hamed to halt on the morrow, as I should be utterly unable to continue thus long, under repeated attacks of a virulent disease which was fast reducing me into a mere frame of skin and bone. Hamed, in a hurry to arrive at Unyanyembe in order to dispose of his cloth before other caravans appeared in the market, replied at first that he would not, that he could not, stop for the Musungu. Upon Thani's reporting his answer to me, I requested him to inform Hamed that, as the Musungu did not wish to detain him, or any other caravan, it was his express wish that Hamed would march and leave him, as he was quite strong enough in guns to march through Ugogo alone. Whatever cause modified the Sheikh's resolution and his anxiety to depart, Hamed's horn signal for the march was not heard that night, and on the morrow he had not gone.

Early in the morning I commenced on my quinine doses; at 6 A.M. I took a second dose; before noon I had taken four more—altogether, fifty measured grains—the effect of which was manifest in the copious perspiration which drenched flannels, linen, and blankets. After noon I arose, devoutly thankful that the disease which had clung to me for the last fourteen days had at last succumbed to quinine.

On this day the lofty tent, and the American flag which ever flew from the centre pole, attracted the Sultan of Mizanza towards it, and was the cause of a visit with which he honored me. As he was notorious among the Arabs for having assisted Manwa Sera in his war against Sheikh Sny bin Amer, high eulogies upon whom have been written by Burton, and subsequently by Speke, and as he was the second most powerful chief in Ugogo, of course he was quite a curiosity to me. As the tent-door was uplifted that he might enter, the ancient gentleman was so struck with astonishment at the lofty apex, and internal arrangements, that the greasy Barsati cloth which formed his sole and only protection against the chills of night and the heat of noon, in a fit of abstraction was permitted to fall down to his feet, exposing to the Musungu's unhallowed gaze the sad and aged wreck of what must once have been a towering form. His son, a youth of about fifteen, attentive to the infirmities of his father, hastened with filial duty to remind him of his condition, upon which, with an idiotic titter at the incident, he resumed his scanty apparel and sat down to wonder and gibber out his admiration at the tent and the strange things which formed the Musungu's personal baggage and furniture. After gazing in stupid wonder at the table, on which was placed some crockery and the few books I carried with me; at the slung hammock, which he believed was suspended by some magical contrivance; at the portmanteaus which contained my stock of clothes, he ejaculated, " Hi-le! the Musungu is a great sultan, who has come from his country to see Ugogo." He then noticed me, and was again wonder-struck at my pale complexion and straight hair, and the question now propounded was, "How on earth was I white when the sun had burned his people's skins into blackness?" Whereupon he was shown my cork topee, which he tried on his woolly head, much to his own and to our amusement. The guns were next shown to him; the wonderful repeating rifle of the Winchester Company, which was fired thirteen times in rapid succession to demonstrate its remarkable murderous powers. If he was astonished before he was a thousand times more so now, and expressed his belief that the Wagogo could not stand before the Musungu in battle, for wherever a Mgogo was seen such a gun would surely kill him. Then the other fire-arms were brought forth, each with its peculiar mechanism explained, until, in a burst of enthusiasm at my riches and power, he said he would send me a sheep or goat, and that he would be my brother. I thanked him for the honor, and promised to accept whatever he was pleased to send me. At the instigation of Sheikh Thani, who acted as interpreter, who said that Wagogo chiefs must not depart with empty hands, I cut off a shukka of Kaniki and presented it to him, which, after being examined and measured, was refused upon the ground that, the Musungu being a great sultan should not demean himself so much as to give him only a shukka. This, after the twelve doti received as muhongo from the caravans, I thought, was rather sore; but as he was about to present me with a sheep or goat another shukka would not matter much.

Shortly after he departed, and true to his promise, I received a large, fine sheep, with a broad tail, heavy with fat; but with the words, "That being now his brother, I must send him three doti of good cloth." As the price of a sheep is but a doti and a half, I refused the sheep and the fraternal honor, upon the ground that the gifts were all on one side; and that, as I had paid muhongo, and given him a doti of Kaniki as a present, I could not afford to part with any more cloth without an adequate return.

During the afternoon one more of my donkeys died, and at night the hyænas came in great numbers to feast upon the carcase. Ulimengo, the chasseur, and best shot of my Wangwana, stole out and succeeded in shooting two, which turned out to be some of the largest of their kind. One of them measured six feet from the tip of the nose to the extremity of the tail, and three feet around the girth.

On the 4th June we struck camp, and after travelling westward for about three miles, passing several ponds of salt water, we headed north by west, skirting the range of low hills which separates Ugogo from Uyanzi.

After a three hours' march, we halted for a short time at Little Mukondoku, to settle tribute with the brother of him who rules at Mukondoku Proper. Three doti satisfied the Sultan, whose district contains but two villages, mostly occupied by pastoral Wahumba and renegade Wahehe. The Wahumba live in plastered (cow-dung) cone huts, shaped like the tartar tents of Turkestân.

The Wahumba, so far as I have seen them, are a fine and well-formed race. The men are positively handsome, tall, with small heads, the posterior parts of which project considerably. One will look in vain for a thick lip or a flat nose amongst them; on the contrary, the mouth is exceedingly well cut, delicately small; the nose is that of the Greeks, and so universal was the peculiar feature, that I at once named them the Greeks of Africa. Their lower limbs have not the heaviness of the Wagogo and other tribes, but are long and shapely, clean as those of an antelope. Their necks are long and slender, on which their small heads are poised most gracefully. Athletes from their youth, shepherd bred, and intermarrying among themselves, thus keeping the race pure, any of them would form a fit subject for the sculptor who would wish to immortalize in marble an Antinous, a Hylas, a Daphnis, or an Apollo. The women are as beautiful as the men are handsome. They have clear ebon skins, not coal-black, but of an inky hue. Their ornaments consist of spiral rings of brass pendent from the ears, brass ring collars about the necks, and a spiral cincture of brass wire about their loins for the purpose of retaining their calf and goat skins, which are folded about their bodies, and, depending from the shoulder, shade one half of the bosom, and fall to the knees.

The Wahehe may be styled the Romans of Africa.

Resuming our march, after a halt of an hour, in four hours more we arrived at Mukondoku Proper. This extremity of Ugogo is most populous. The villages which surround the central tembe, where the Sultan Swaruru lives, amount to thirty-six. The people who flocked from these to see the wonderful men whose faces were white, who wore the most wonderful things on their persons, and possessed the most wonderful weapons; guns which "bum-bummed" as fast as you could count on your fingers, formed such a mob of howling savages, that I for an instant thought there was something besides mere curiosity which caused such commotion, and attracted such numbers to the roadside. Halting, I asked what was the matter, and what they wanted, and why they made such noise? One burly rascal, taking my words for a declaration of hostilities, promptly drew his bow, but as prompt as he had fixed his arrow my faithful Winchester with thirteen shots in the magazine was ready and at the shoulder, and but waited to see the arrow fly to pour the leaden messengers of death into the crowd. But the crowd vanished as quickly as they had come, leaving the burly Thersites, and two or three irresolute fellows of his tribe, standing within pistol range of my levelled rifle. Such a sudden dispersion of the mob which, but a moment before, was overwhelming in numbers, caused me to lower my rifle, and to indulge in a hearty laugh at the disgraceful flight of the men-destroyers. The Arabs, who were as much alarmed at their boisterous obtrusiveness, now came up to patch a truce, in which they succeeded to everybody's satisfaction. A few words of explanation, and the mob came back in greater numbers than before; and the Thersites who had been the cause of the momentary disturbance was obliged to retire abashed before the pressure of public opinion. A chief now came up, whom I afterwards learned was the second man to Swaruru, and lectured the people upon their treatment of the "White Stranger."

"Know ye not, Wagogo," shouted he, "that this Musungu is a sultan (mtemi—a most high title). He has not come to Ugogo like the Wakonongo (Arabs), to trade in ivory, but to see us, and give presents. Why do you molest him and his people? Let them pass in peace. If you wish to see him, draw near, but do not mock him. The first of you who creates a disturbance, let him beware; our great mtemi shall know how you treat his friends." This little bit of oratorical effort on the part

of the chief was translated to me there and then by the
old Sheikh Thani; which having understood, I bade the
Sheikh inform the chief that, after I had rested, I should
like him to visit me in my tent.

Having arrived at the khambi, which always surrounds
some great baobab in Ugogo, at the distance of about half
a mile from the tembe of the Sultan, the Wagogo pressed
in such great numbers to the camp that Sheikh Thani
resolved to make an effort to stop or mitigate the nuisance.
Dressing himself in his best clothes, he went to appeal to
the Sultan for protection against his people. The Sultan
was very much inebriated, and was pleased to say, " What
is it you want, you thief? You have come to steal my
ivory or my cloth. Go away, thief!" But the sensible
chief, whose voice had just been heard reproaching the
people for their treatment of the Wasungu, beckoned to
Sheikh Thani to come out of the tembe, and then proceeded
with him towards the khambi.

The camp was in a great uproar; the curious Wagogo
monopolized almost every foot of ground; there was no
room to turn anywhere. The Wanyamwezi were quarreling with the Wagogo, the Wasawahili servants were
clamoring loud that the Wagogo pressed down their
tents, and that the property of the masters was in
danger; while I, busy on my diary within my tent, cared
not how great was the noise and confusion outside as long
as it confined itself to the Wagogo, Wanyamwezi, and
Wangwana.

The presence of the chief in the camp was followed by
such a deep silence that I was prevailed upon to go
outside to see what had caused it. The chief's words
were few, and to the point. He said, " To your tembes,
Wagogo—to your tembes! Why do you come to trouble

the Wakonongo? What have you to do with them? To your tembes: go! Each Mgogo found in the khambi without meal, without cattle to sell, shall pay to the mtemi cloth or cows. Away with you!" Saying which, he snatched up a stick and drove the hundreds out of the khambi, who were as obedient to him as so many children. During the two days we halted at Mukondoku we saw no more of the mob, and there was peace.

The muhongo of the Sultan Swaruru was settled with few words. The chief who acted for the Sultan as his prime minister having been "made glad" with a doti of Rehani Ulyah from me, accepted the usual tribute of six doti, only one of which was of first-class cloth.

There remained but one more sultan to whom muhongo must be paid after Mukondoku, and this was the Sultan of Kiwyeh, whose reputation was so bad that owners of property who had control over their pagazis seldom passed by Kiwyeh, preferring the hardships of long marches through the wilderness to the rudeness and exorbitant demands of the chief of Kiwyeh. But the pagazis, on whom no burden or responsibility fell save that of carrying their loads, who could use their legs and show clean heels in the case of a hostile outbreak, preferred the march to Kiwyeh to enduring thirst and the fatigue of a terekeza. Often the preference of the pagazis won the day, when their employers were timid, irresolute men, like Sheikh Hamed.

The 7th of June was the day fixed for our departure from Mukondoku, so the day before, the Arabs came to my tent to counsel with me as to the route we should adopt. On calling together the kirangozis of the respective caravans and veteran Wanyamwezi pagazis, we learned there were three roads leading from Mukondoku to Uyanzi. The first was the southern road, and the one generally adopted, for the reasons already stated, and led by Kiwyeh. To this Hamed raised objections. "The Sultan was bad," he said; "he sometimes charged a caravan twenty doti; our caravan would have to pay about sixty doti. The Kiwyeh road would not do at all. Besides," he added, "we have to make a terekeza to reach Kiwyeh, and then we will not reach it before the day after to-morrow." The second was the central road. We should arrive at Munieka on the morrow; the day after would be a terekeza from Mabunguru Nullah to a camp near Unyambogi; two hours the next day would bring us to Kiti, where there was plenty of water and food. As neither of the kirangozis or Arabs knew this road, and its description came from one of my ancient pagazis, Hamed said he did not like to trust the guidance of such a large caravan in the hands of an old Mnyamwezi, and would therefore prefer to hear about the third road, before rendering his decision. The third road was the northern. It led past numerous villages of the Wagogo for the first two hours; then we should strike a jungle; and a three hours' march would then bring us to Simbo, where there was water, but no village. Starting early next morning, we would travel six hours when we would arrive at a pool of water. Here taking a short rest, an afternoon march of five hours would bring us within three hours of another village. As this last road was known to many, Hamed said, "Sheikh Thani, tell the Sahib that I think this is the best road." Sheikh Thani was told, after he had informed me that, as I had marched with them through Ugogo, if they decided upon going by Simbo, my caravan would follow.

Immediately after the discussion among the principals

respecting the merits of the several routes, arose a discussion among the pagazis which resulted in an obstinate clamor against the Simbo road, for its long terekeza and scant prospects of water, the dislike to the Simbo road communicated itself to all the caravans, and soon it was magnified by reports of a wilderness reaching from Simbo to Kusuri, where there was neither food nor water to be obtained. Hamed's pagazis, and those of the Arab servants, rose in a body and declared they could not go on that march, and if Hamed insisted upon adopting it they would put their packs down and leave him to carry them himself.

Hamed Kimiani, as he was styled by the Arabs, rushed up to Sheikh Thani, and declared that he must take the Kiwyeh road, otherwise his pagazis would all desert. Thani replied that all the roads were the same to him, that wherever Hamed chose to go, he would follow. They then came to my tent, and informed me of the determination at which the Wanyamwezi had arrived. Calling my veteran Mnyamwezi, who had given me the favourable report once more to my tent, I bade him give a correct account of the Kiti road. It was so favourable that my reply to Hamed was, that I was the master of my caravan, that it was to go wherever I told the kirangozi, not where the pagazis chose; that when I told them to halt they must halt, and when I commanded a march, a march should be made; and that as I fed them well and did not overwork them, I should like to see the pagazi or soldier that disobeyed me. "You made up your mind just now that you would take the Simbo road, and we were agreed upon it, now your pagazis say they will take the Kiwyeh road, or desert. Go on the Kiwyeh road and pay twenty doti muhongo. I and my caravan to-morrow morning will take the Kiti road, and when you find me in Unyanyembe one day ahead of you, you will be sorry you did not take the same road."

This resolution of mine had the effect of again changing the current of Hamed's thoughts, for he instantly said, "That is the best road after all, and as the Sahib is determined to go on it, and we have all travelled together through the bad land of the Wagogo, Inshallah! let us all go the same way," and Thani—good old man—not objecting, and Hamed having decided, they both joyfully went out of the tent to communicate the news.

On the 7th the caravans—apparently unanimous that the Kiti road was to be taken—were led as usual by Hamed's kirangozi. We had barely gone a mile before I perceived that we had left the Simbo road, had taken the direction of Kiti, and, by a cunning detour, were now fast approaching the defile of the mountain ridge before us, which admitted access to the higher plateau of Kiwyeh. Instantly halting my caravan, I summoned the veteran who had travelled by Kiti, and asked him whether we were not going towards Kiwyeh. He replied that we were. Calling my pagazis together, I bade Bombay tell them that the Musungu never changed his mind; that as I had said my caravan should march by Kiti, to Kiti it must go whether the Arabs followed or not. I then ordered the veteran to take up his load and show the kirangozi the proper road to Kiti. The Wanyamwezi pagazis put down their bales, and then there was every indication of a mutiny. The Wangwana soldiers were next ordered to load their guns and to flank the caravan, and shoot the first pagazis who made an attempt to run away. Dismounting, I seized my whip, and, advancing towards the first pagazi who had put down his load, I motioned to him to take up his load and march. It was unnecessary to proceed further; without an exception, all marched away obediently after the kirangozi. I was about bidding farewell to Thani and Hamed, when Thani said, "Stop a bit, Sahib; I have had enough of this child's play; I come with you," and his caravan was turned after mine. Hamed's caravan was by this time close to the defile, and he himself was a full mile behind it, weeping like a child at what he was pleased to call our desertion of him. Pitying his strait—for he was almost beside himself as thoughts of Kiwyeh's sultan, his extortion and rudeness, swept across his mind—I advised him to run after his caravan, and tell it, as all the rest had taken the other road, to think of the Sultan of Kiwyeh. Before reaching the Kiti defile I was aware that Hamed's caravan was following us.

The ascent of the ridge was rugged and steep, thorns of the prickliest nature punished us severely, the *acacia horrida* was here more horrid than usual, the gums stretched out their branches, and entangled the loads, the mimosa with its umbrella-like top served to shade us from the sun, but impeded a rapid advance. Steep outcrops of syenite and granite, worn smooth by many feet, had to be climbed over, rugged terraces of earth and rock had to be ascended, and distant shots resounding through the forest added to the alarm and general discontent, and had I not been immediately behind my caravan, watchful of every manœuvre, my Wanyamwezi had deserted to a man.

Though the height we ascended was barely 800 feet above the salina we had just left, the ascent occupied two hours.

Having surmounted the plateau and the worst difficulties, we had a fair road comparatively, which ran through jungle, forest, and small open tracts, which in three hours more brought us to Munieka, a small village, surrounded by a clearing richly cultivated by a colony of subjects of Swaruru of Mukondoku.

By the time we had arrived at camp everybody had recovered his good humor and content except Hamed. Thani's men happened to set his tent too close to Hamed's tree, around which his bales were stacked. Whether the little Sheikh imagined honest old Thani capable of stealing one is not known, but it is certain that he stormed and raved about the near neighbourhood of his best friend's tent, until Thani ordered its removal a hundred yards off. This proceeding even, it seems, did not satisfy Hamed, for it was quite midnight—as Thani said—when Hamed came, and kissing his hands and feet, on his knees implored forgiveness, which of course Thani, being the soul of good-nature, and as large-hearted as any man, willingly gave. Hamed was not satisfied, however, until, with the aid of his slaves, he had transported his friend's tent to where it had at first been pitched.

The water at Munieka was obtained from a deep depression in a hump of syenite, and was as clear as crystal, and cold as ice-water—a luxury we had not experienced since leaving Simbamwenni.

We were now on the borders of Uyanzi, or, as it is better known, "Magunda Mkali"—the Hot-ground, or Hot-field. We had passed the village populated by Wagogo, and were about to shake the dust of Ugogo from our feet. We had entered Ugogo full of hopes, believing it a most pleasant land--a land flowing with milk and honey. We had been grievously disappointed; it proved to be a land of gall and bitterness, full of trouble and vexation of spirit, where danger was imminent at every step—where we were exposed to the caprice of inebriated sultans. Is it a wonder, then, that all felt happy at such a moment? With the prospect before us of what was believed by many to be a real wilderness, our ardor was not abated, but was rather strengthened. The wilderness in Africa proves to be, in many instances, more friendly than the populated country.

The kirangozi blew his kudu horn much more merrily on this morning than he was accustomed to do while in Ugogo. We were about to enter Magunda Mkali. At 9 A.M., three hours after leaving Munieka, and two hours since we had left the extreme limits of Ugogo, we were halted at Mabunguru Nullah. The Nullah runs southwesterly after leaving its source in the chain of hills dividing Ugogo from Magunda Mkali. During the rainy season it must be nearly impassable, owing to the excessive slope of its bed. Traces of the force of the torrent are seen in the syenite and basalt boulders which encumber the course. Their rugged angles are worn smooth, and deep basins are excavated where the bed is of the rock, which in the dry season serve as reservoirs. Though the water contained in them has a slimy and greenish appearance, and is well populated with frogs, it is by no means unpalatable.

At noon we resumed our march, the Wanyamwezi cheering, shouting, and singing, the Wangwana soldiers, servants, and pagazis vieing with them in volume of voice and noise—making the dim forest through which we were now passing resonant with their voices.

The scenery was much more picturesque than any we had yet seen since leaving Bagamoyo. The ground rose into grander waves—hills cropped out here and there—great castles of syenite appeared, giving a strange and weird appearance to the forest. From a distance it would almost seem as if we were approaching a bit of England as it must have appeared during feudalism ; the rocks assumed such strange fantastic shapes. Now they were round boulders raised one above another, apparently susceptible to every breath of wind; anon, they towered like blunt-pointed obelisks, taller than the tallest trees ; again they assumed the shape of mighty waves, vitrified; here, they were a small heap of fractured and riven rock; there, they rose to the grandeur of hills.

By 5 P.M. we had travelled twenty miles, and the signal was sounded for a halt. At 1 A.M., the moon being up, Hamed's horn and voice were heard throughout the silent camp awaking his pagazis for the march. Evidently Sheikh Hamed was gone stark mad, otherwise why should he be so frantic for the march at such an early hour? The dew was falling heavily, and chilled one like frost; and an ominous murmur of deep discontent responded to the early call on all sides. Presuming, however, that he had obtained better information than we had, Sheikh Thani and I resolved to be governed as the events proved him to be right or wrong.

As all were discontented, this night march was performed in deep silence. The thermometer was at 53°, we being about 4,500 feet above the level of the sea. The pagazis, almost naked, walked quickly in order to keep warm, and by so doing many a sore foot was made by stumbling against obtrusive roots and rocks, and treading on thorns. At 3 A.M. we arrived at the village of Unyam-bogi, where we threw ourselves down to rest and sleep until dawn should reveal what else was in store for the hard-dealt-with caravans.

It was broad daylight when I awoke; the sun was flaring his hot beams in my face. Sheikh Thani came soon after to inform me that Hamed had gone to Kiti two hours since; but he, when asked to accompany him, positively refused, exclaiming against it as folly, and utterly unnecessary, when my advice was asked by Thani. I voted the whole thing as sheer nonsense; and, in turn, asked him what a terekeza was for? Was it not an afternoon march to enable caravans to reach water and food? Thani replied that it was. I then asked him if there was no water or food to be obtained in Unyambogi. Thani replied that he had not taken pains to inquire, but was told by the villagers that there was an abundance of matamia, hindi, maweri, sheep, goats, and chickens in their village at cheap prices, such as were not known in Ugogo.

"Well, then," said I, "if Hamed wants to be a fool, and kill his pagazis, why should we? I have as much cause for haste as Sheikh Hamed; but Unyanyembe is far yet, and I am not going to endanger my property by playing the madman."

As Thani had reported, we found an abundance of provisions at the village, and good sweet water from some pits close by. A sheep cost one shukka; six chickens were also purchased at that price; six measures of matama, maweri, or hindi, were procurable for the same sum; in short, we were coming, at last, into the land of plenty.

On the 10th June we arrived at Kiti after a journey of
four hours and a half, where we found the irrepressible
Hamed halted in sore trouble. He who would be a Cæsar,
proved to be an irresolute Antony. He had to sorrow
over the death of a favourite slave girl, the loss of five
dish-dashes (Arab shirts), silvered-sleeve and gold-em-
broidered jackets, with which he had thought to enter
Unyanyembe in state, as became a merchant of his
standing, which had disappeared with three absconding
servants, besides copper trays, rice, and pilau dishes, and
two bales of cloth with runaway Wangwana pagazis.
Selim, my Arab servant, asked him, "What are you
doing here, Sheikh Hamed? I thought you were well on
the road to Unyanyembe." Said he, "Could I leave Thani,
my friend, behind?"

Kiti abounded in cattle and grain, and we were able to
obtain food at easy rates. The Wakimbu, emigrants from
Ukimbu, near Urori, are a quiet race, preferring the
peaceful arts of agriculture to war; of tending their
flocks to conquest. At the least rumor of war they
remove their property and family, and emigrate to the
distant wilderness, where they begin to clear the land,
and to hunt the elephant for his ivory. Yet we found
them to be a fine race, and well armed, and seemingly
capable, by their numbers and arms, to compete with any
tribe. But here, as elsewhere, disunion makes them weak.
They are mere small colonies, each colony ruled by its
own chief; whereas, were they united, they might make
a very respectable front before an enemy.

Our next destination was Msalalo, distant fifteen miles
from Kiti. Hamed, after vainly searching for his runaways and the valuable property he had lost, followed us,

and tried once more, when he saw us encamped at Msalalo, to pass us; but his pagazis failed him, the march having been so long.

Welled Ngaraiso was reached on the 15th, after a three and a half hours' march. It is a flourishing little place, where provisions were almost twice as cheap as they were at Unyambogi. Two hours' march south is Jiweh la Mkoa, on the old road, towards which the road which we have been travelling since leaving Bagamoyo was now rapidly leading.

Unyanyembe being near, the pagazis and soldiers having behaved excellently during the lengthy marches we had lately made, I purchased a bullock for three doti, and had it slaughtered for their special benefit. I also gave each a khete of red beads to indulge his appetite for whatever little luxury the country afforded. Milk and honey were plentiful, and three frasilah of sweet potatoes were bought for a shukka, equal to about 40 cents of our money.

The 13th June brought us to the last village of Magunda Mkali, in the district of Jiweh la Singa, after a short march of eight miles and three-quarters. Kusuri— so called by the Arabs—is called Konsuli by the Wakimbu who inhabit it. This is, however, but one instance out of many where the Arabs have misnamed or corrupted the native names of villages and districts.

Between Ngaraiso and Kusuri we passed the village of Kirurumo, now a thriving place, with many a thriving village near it. As we passed it, the people came out to greet the Musungu, whose advent had been so long neralded by his loud-mouthed caravans, and whose soldiers had helped them win the day in a battle against their fractious brothers of Jiweh la Mkoa.

A little further on we came across a large khambi, oc·
cupied by Sultan bin Mohammed, an Omani Arab of high
descent, who, as soon as he was notified of my approach,
came out to welcome me, and invite me to his khambi.
As his harem lodged in his tent, of course I was not
invited thither; but a carpet outside was ready for his
visitor. After the usual questions had been asked about
my health, the news of the road, the latest from Zanzibar
and Oman, he asked me if I had much cloth with me.
This was a question often asked by owners of down
caravans, and the reason of it is that the Arabs, in their
anxiety to make as much as possible of their cloth at the
ivory ports on the Tanganika and elsewhere, are liable to
forget that they should retain a portion for the down
marches. As, indeed, I had but a bale left of the quantity
of cloth retained for provisioning my party on the road,
when outfitting my caravans on the coast, I could un-
blushingly reply in the negative.

I halted a day at Kusuri to give my caravan a rest,
after its long series of marches, before venturing on the
two days' march through the uninhabited wilderness that
separates the district of Jiweh la Singa Uyanzi from the
district of Tura in Unyanyembe. Hamed preceded,
promising to give Sayd bin Salim notice of my coming,
and to request him to provide a tembe for me.

On the 15th, having ascertained that Sheikh Thani
would be detained several days at Kusuri, owing to the
excessive number of his people who were laid up with
that dreadful plague of East Africa, the small-pox, I bade
him farewell, and my caravan struck out of Kusuri once
more for the wilderness and the jungle. A little before
noon we halted at the Khambi of Mgongo Tembo, or the

Elephant's Back—so called from a wave of rock whose back, stained into dark brownness by atmospheric influences, is supposed by the natives to resemble the blue-brown back of this monster of the forest. My caravan had quite an argument with me here, as to whether we should make the terekeza on this day or on the next. The majority was of the opinion that the next day would be the best for a terekeza; but I, being the " bana," consulting my own interests, insisted, not without a flourish or two of my whip, that the terekeza should be made on this day.

Mgongo Tembo, when Burton and Speke passed by, was a promising settlement, cultivating many a fair acre of ground. But two years ago war broke out, for some bold act of its people upon caravans, and the Arabs came from Unyanyembe with their Wangwana servants, attacked them, burnt the villages, and laid waste the work of years. Since that time Mgongo Tembo has been but blackened wrecks of houses, and the fields a sprouting jungle.

A cluster of date palm-trees, overtopping a dense grove close to the mtoni of Mgongo Tembo, revived my recollections of Egypt. The banks of the stream, with their verdant foliage, presented a strange contrast to the brown and dry appearance of the jungle which lay on either side.

At 1 P.M. we resumed our loads and walking staffs, and in a short time were *en route* for the Ngwhalah Mtoni, distant eight and three-quarter miles from the khambi. The sun was hot; like a globe of living, seething flame, it flared its heat full on our heads; then as it descended towards the west, scorched the air before it was inhaled by the lungs which craved it. Gourds of water were emptied speedily to quench the fierce heat that burned the throat and lungs. One pagazi, stricken heavily with the small-pox, succumbed, and threw himself down on the roadside to die. We never saw him afterwards, for the progress of a caravan on a terekeza, is something like that of a ship in a hurricane. The caravan must proceed —woe befall him who lags behind, for hunger and thirst will overtake him—so must a ship drive before the fierce gale to escape foundering—woe befall him who falls overboard !

An abundance of water, good, sweet, and cool, was found in the bed of the mtoni in deep stony reservoirs. Here also the traces of furious torrents were clearly visible as at Mabunguru.

The Nghwhalah commences in Ubanarama to the north —a country famous for its fine breed of donkeys—and after running south, south-south-west, crosses the Unyanyembe road, from which point it has more of a westerly turn.

On the 16th we arrived at Madedita, so called from a village which was, but is now no more. Madedita is twelve and a half miles from the Nghwhalah Mtoni. A pool of good water a few hundred yards from the roadside is the only supply caravans can obtain, nearer than Tura in Unyamwezi. The tsetse or chufwa-fly, as called by the Wasawahili, stung us dreadfully, which is a sign that large game visit the pool sometimes, but must not be mistaken for an indication that there is any in the immediate neighbourhood of the water. A single pool so often frequented by passing caravans, which must of necessity halt here, could not be often visited by the animals of the forest, who are shy in this part of Africa of the haunts of man.

At dawn the next day we were on the road striding at a quicker pace than on most days, since we were about to quit Magunda Mkali for the more populated and better land of Unyamwezi. The forest held its own for a wearisomely long time, but at the end of two hours it thinned, then dwarfed into low jungle, and finally vanished altogether, and we had arrived on the soil of Unyamwezi, with a broad plain, swelling, subsiding, and receding in lengthy and grand undulations in our front to one indefinite horizontal line which purpled in the far distance. The view consisted of fields of grain ripening, which followed the contour of the plain, and which rustled merrily before the morning breeze that came laden with the chills of Usagara.

At 8 A.M. we had arrived at the frontier village of Unyamwezi, Eastern Tura, which we invaded without any regard to the disposition of the few inhabitants who lived there. Here we found Nondo, a runaway of Speke's, one of those who had sided with Baraka against Bombay, who, desiring to engage himself with me, was engaging enough to furnish honey and sherbet to his former companions, and lastly to the pagazis. It was only a short breathing pause we made here, having another hour's march to reach Central Tura.

The road from Eastern Tura led through vast fields of millet, Indian corn, holcus sorghum, maweri, or panicum, or bajri, as called by the Arabs; gardens of sweet potatoes, large tracts of cucumbers, water-melons, mush-melons, and pea-nuts which grew in the deep furrows between the ridges of the holcus.

Some broad-leafed plantain plants were also seen in the neighbourhood of the villages, which as we advanced became very numerous. The villages of the Wakimbu are like those of the Wagogo, square, flat-roofed, enclosing an open area, which is sometimes divided into three or four parts by fences or matama stalks.

At central Tura, where we encamped, we had evidence enough of the rascality of the Wakimbu of Tura. Hamed, who, despite his efforts to reach Unyanyembe in time to sell his cloths before other Arabs came with cloth supplies, was unable to compel his pagazis to the double march every day, was also encamped at Central Tura, together with the Arab servants who preferred Hamed's imbecile haste to Thani's cautious advance. Our first night in Unyamwezi was very exciting indeed. The Musungu's camp was visited by two crawling thieves, but they were soon made aware by the portentous click of a trigger that the white man's camp was well guarded.

Hamed's camp was next visited; but here also the restlessness of the owner frustrated their attempts, for he was pacing backwards and forwards through his camp, with a loaded gun in his hand; and the thieves were obliged to relinquish the chance of stealing any of his bales. From Hamed's they proceeded to Hassan's camp (one of the Arab servants), where they were successful enough to reach and lay hold of a couple of bales; but, unfortunately, they made a noise, which awoke the vigilant and quick-eared slave, who snatched his loaded musket, and in a moment had shot one of them through the heart. Such were our experiences of the Wakimbu of Tura.

On the 18th the three caravans, Hamed's Hassan's,

and my own, left Tura by a road which zig-zagged towards all points through the tall matama fields. In an hour's time we had passed Tura Perro, or Western Tura, and had entered the forest again, whence the Wakimbu of Tura obtain their honey, and where they excavate deep traps for the elephants with which the forest is said to abound. An hour's march from Western Tura brought us to a ziwa, or pond. There were two, situated in the midst of a small open mbuga, or plain, which, even at this late season, was yet soft from the water which overflows it during the rainy season. After resting three hours, we started on the terekeza, or afternoon march.

It was one and the same forest that we had entered soon after leaving Western Tura, that we travelled through until we reached the Kwala Mtoni, or, as Burton has misnamed it on his map, "Kwale." The water of this mtoni is contained in large ponds, or deep depressions in the wide and crooked gully of Kwala. In these ponds a species of mud-fish was found, off one of which I made a meal, by no means to be despised by one who had not tasted fish since leaving Bagamoyo. Probably, if I had my choice, being, when occasion demands it, rather fastidious in my tastes, I would not select the mud-fish.

From Tura to the Kwala Mtoni is seventeen and a half miles, a distance which, however easy it may be traversed once a fortnight, assumes a prodigious length when one has to travel it almost every other day, at least, so my pagazis, soldiers, and followers found it, and their murmurs were very loud when I ordered the signal to be sounded on the march. Abdul Kader, the tailor who had attached himself to me, as a man ready-handed at all things, from mending a pair of pants, making a delicate *entremets*, or shooting an elephant, but whom the interior proved to be the weakliest of the weakly, unfit for anything except eating and drinking—almost succumbed on this march.

Long ago the little stock of goods which Abdul had brought from Zanzibar folded in a pocket-handkerchief, and with which he was about to buy ivory and slaves, and make his fortune in the famed land of Unyamwezi, had disappeared with the great eminent hopes he had built on them, like those of Alnaschar the unfortunate owner of crockery in the Arabian tale. He came to me as we prepared for the march, with a most dolorous tale about his approaching death, which he felt in his bones, and weary back: his legs would barely hold him up; in short, he had utterly collapsed—would I take mercy on him, and let him depart? The cause of this extraordinary request, so unlike the spirit with which he had left Zanzibar, eager to possess the ivory and slaves of Un-yamwezi, was that on the last long march, two of my donkeys being dead, I had ordered that the two saddles which they had carried should be Abdul Kader's load to Unyanyembe. The weight of the saddles was 16 lbs., as the spring balance-scale indicated, yet Abdul Kader became weary of life, as he counted the long marches that intervened between the mtoni and Unyanyembe. On the ground he fell prone, to kiss my feet, begging me in the name of God to permit him to depart.

As I had had some experience of Hindoos, Malabarese, and coolies in Abyssinia, I knew exactly how to deal with a case like this. Unhesitatingly I granted the request as soon as asked, for as much tired as Abdul Kader said he was of life, I was with Abdul Kader's worthlessness. But the Hindi did not want to be left in the jungle, he said, but after arriving in Unyanyembe. "Oh," said I, "then you must reach Unyanyembe first; in the meanwhile you will carry those saddles there for the food which you must eat."

As the march to Rubuga was eighteen and three-quarter miles, the pagazis walked fast and long without resting.

Rubuga, in the days of Burton, according to his book, was a prosperous district. Even when we passed, the evidences of wealth and prosperity which it possessed formerly, were plain enough in the wide extent of its grain fields, which stretched to the right and left of the Unyanyembe road for many a mile. But they were only evidences of what once were numerous villages, a well-cultivated and populous district, rich in herds of cattle and stores of grain. All the villages are burnt down, the people have been driven north three or four days from Rubuga, the cattle were taken by force, the grain fields were left standing, to be overgrown with jungle and rank weeds. We passed village after village that had been burnt, and were mere blackened heaps of charred timber and smoked clay; field after field of grain ripe years ago was yet standing in the midst of a crop of gums and thorns, mimosa and kolquall.

We arrived at the village, occupied by about sixty Wangwana, who have settled here to make a living by buying and selling ivory. Food is provided for them in the deserted fields of the people of Rubuga. We were very tired and heated from the long march, but the pagazis had all arrived by 3 P.M.

At the Wangwana village we met Amer bin Sultan, the very type of an old Arab sheikh, such as we read of in books, with a snowy beard, and a clean reverend face, who was returning to Zanzibar after a ten years' residence in Unyanyembe. He presented me with a goat, and a goat-skin full of rice; a most acceptable gift in a place where a goat costs five cloths.

After a day's halt at Rubuga, during which I despatched soldiers to notify Sheikh Sayd bin Salim and Sheikh bin Nasib, the two chief dignitaries of Unyanyembe, of my coming, on the 21st of June we resumed the march for Kigwa, distant five hours. The road ran through another forest similar to that which separated Tura from Rubuga, the country rapidly sloping as we proceeded westward. Kigwa we found to have been visited by the same vengeance which rendered Rubuga such a waste.

The next day, after a three and a half hours' rapid march, we crossed the mtoni—which was no mtoni— separating Kigwa from Unyanyembe district, and after a short halt to quench our thirst, in three and a half hours more arrived at Shiza. It was a most delightful march, though a long one, for its picturesqueness of scenery which every few minutes was revealed, and the proofs we everywhere saw of the peaceable and industrious disposition of the people. A short half hour from Shiza we beheld the undulating plain wherein the Arabs have chosen to situate the central depôt which commands such a wide and extensive field of trade. The lowing of cattle and the bleating of the goats and sheep were everywhere heard, giving the country a happy, pastoral aspect.

The Sultan of Shiza desired me to celebrate my arrival

in Unyanyembe, with a five-gallon jar of pombe, which he brought for that purpose.

As the pombe was but stale ale in taste, and milk and water in color, after drinking a small glassful I passed it to the delighted soldiers and pagazis. At my request the Sultan brought a fine fat bullock, for which he accepted four and a half doti of Merikani. The bullock was immediately slaughtered and served out to the caravan as a farewell feast.

No one slept much that night, and long before the dawn the fires were lit, and great steaks were broiling, that their stomachs might rejoice before parting with the Musungu, whose bounty they had so often tasted. Six rounds of powder were served to each soldier and pagazi who owned a gun, to fire away when we should be near the Arab houses. The meanest **pa**gazi had his best cloth about his loins, and some **were** exceedingly brave in gorgeous Ulyah "Coombeesa Poonga" and crimson "Jawah," the glossy "Rehani," and the neat "Dabwani." The soldiers were mustered in new tarbooshes, and the long white shirts of the Mrima and the Island. For this was the great and happy day which had been on our tongues ever since quitting the coast, for which we had made those noted marches latterly—one hundred and seventy-eight and a half miles in sixteen days, including pauses—something over eleven miles a day!

The signal sounded and the caravan was joyfully off with banners flying, and trumpets and horns blaring. A short two and a half hours' march brought us within sight of Kwikuru, which is about two miles south of Tabora, the main Arab town; on the outside of which we saw a long line of men in clean shirts, whereat we opened our **s**harged batteries, and fired a volley of small arms such as Kwikuru seldom heard before. The pagazis closed up and adopted the swagger of veterans : the soldiers blazed away uninterruptedly, while I, seeing that the Arabs were advancing towards me, left the ranks, and held out my hand, which was immediately grasped by Sheikh Sayd bin Salim, and then by about two dozen people, and thus our *entrée* into Unyanyembe was effected.

VIEW IN FRONT OF MY TEMBE.

CHAPTER VIII.

MY LIFE AND TROUBLES DURING MY RESIDENCE IN UNYA-
NYEMBE. I BECOME ENGAGED IN A WAR.

I RECEIVED a noiseless ovation as I walked side by side
with the governor, Sayd bin Salim, towards his tembe in
Kwikuru, or the capital. The Wanyamwezi pagazis were
out by hundreds, the warriors of Mkasiwa, the sultan,
hovered around their chief, the children were seen between
the legs of their parents, even infants, a few months old,
slung over their mothers' backs, all paid the tribute due
to my color, with one grand concentrated stare. The
only persons who talked with me were the Arabs, and
aged Mkasiwa, ruler of Unyanyembe.

Sayd bin Salim's house was at the north-western corner
of the inclosure, a stockaded boma of Kwikuru. We had
tea made in a silver tea-pot, and a bountiful supply of
" dampers " were smoking under a silver cover; and to
this repast I was invited. When a man has walked eight
miles or so without any breakfast, and a hot tropical sun
has been shining on him for three or four hours, he is apt
to do justice to a meal, especially if his appetite is
healthy. I think I astonished the governor by the
dexterous way in which I managed to consume eleven
cups of his aromatic concoction of an Assam herb, and
the easy effortless style with which I demolished his high
tower of " slap-jacks," that but a minute or so smoked
hotly under their silver cover.

For the meal, I thanked the Sheikh, as only an earnest
and sincerely hungry man, now satisfied, could thank
him. Even if I had not spoken, my gratified looks had
well informed him, under what obligations I had been
laid to him.

Out came my pipe and tobacco-pouch.

" My friendly Sheikh, wilt thou smoke ? "

" No, thanks ! Arabs never smoke."

" Oh, if you don't, perhaps you would not object to me
smoking, in order to assist digestion ? "

" Ngema—good—go on, master." Then began the
questions, the gossipy, curious, serious, light questions :

" How came the master ? "

" By the Mpwapwa road."

" It is good. Was the Makata bad ?

" Very bad."

" What news from Zanzibar ? "

" Good ; Syed Toorkee has possession of Muscat, and
Azim bin Ghis was slain in the streets."

" Is this true, Wallahi ? " (by God.)

" It is true."

" Heh-heh-h ! This is news ! "—stroking his beard.

" Have you heard, master, of Suleiman bin Ali ? "

" Yes, the Bombay governor sent him to Zanzibar, in a man-of-war, and Suleiman bin Ali now lies in the gurayza (fort)."

" Heh, that is very good."

" Did you have to pay much tribute to the Wagogo ? "

" Eight times ; Hamed Kimiani wished me to go by Kiwyeh, but I declined, and struck through the forest to Munieka. Hamed and Thani thought it better to follow me, than brave Kiwyeh by themselves."

" Where is that Hajji Abdullah (Captain Burton) that came here, and Spiki ? " (Speke.)

" Hajji Abdullah ! What Hajji Abdullah ? Ah ! Sheikh Burton we call him. Oh, he is a great man now ; a balyuz (a consul) at El Scham " (Damascus.)

" Heh-heh ; balyuz ! Heh, at El Scham ! Is not that near Betlem el Kuds ? " (Jerusalem.)

" Yes, about four days. Spiki is dead. He shot himself by accident."

" Ah, ah, Wallah (by God), but this is bad news. Spiki dead ? Mash-Allah ! Ough, he was a good man—a good man ! Dead ! "

" But where is this Kazeh, Sheikh Sayd ? "

" Kazeh ? Kazeh ? I never heard the name before."

" But you were with Burton, and Speke, at Kazeh ; you lived there several months, when you were all stopping in Unyanyembe ; it must be close here somewhere. Where did Hajji Abdullah and Spiki live when they were in Unyanyembe ? Was it not in Musa Mzuri's house ? "

"That was in Tabora."

"Well, then, where is Kazeh? I have never seen the man yet who could tell me where that place is, and yet the three white men have that word down, as the name of the place they lived at when you were with them. You must know where it is."

"Wallahi, bana, I never heard the name; but stop, Kazeh, in Kinyamwezi, means 'kingdom.' Perhaps they gave that name to the place they stopped at. But then, I used to call the first house Sny bin Amer's house, and Speke lived at Musa Mzuri's house, but both houses, as well as all the rest, are in Tabora."

"Thank you, sheikh. I should like to go and look after my people; they must all be wanting food."

"I shall go with you to show you your house. The tembe is in Kwihara, only an hour's walk from Tabora."

On leaving Kwikuru we crossed a low ridge, and soon saw Kwihara lying between two low ranges of hills, the northernmost of which was terminated westward by the round fortress-like hill of Zimbili. There was a cold glare of intense sunshine over the valley, probably the effect of an universal bleakness or an autumnal ripeness of the grass, unrelieved by any depth of color to vary the universal sameness. The hills were bleached, or seemed to be, under that dazzling sunshine, and clearest atmosphere. The corn had long been cut, and there lay the stubble, and fields,—a browny-white expanse; the houses were of mud, and their flat roofs were of mud, and the mud was of a browny-whiteness; the huts were thatched, and the stockades around them of barked timber, and these were of a browny whiteness. The cold, fierce, sickly wind from the mountains of Usagara sent a deadly chill to our very marrows, yet the intense sunshiny glare never changed, a black cow or two, or a tall tree here and there, caught the eye for a moment, but they never made one forget that the first impression of Kwihara was as of a picture without color, or of food without taste; and if one looked up, there was a sky of a pale blue, spotless, and of an awful serenity.

As I approached the tembe of Sayd bin Salim, Sheikh bin Nasib and other great Arabs joined us. Before the great door of the tembe the men had stacked the bales, and piled the boxes, and were using their tongues at a furious rate, relating to the chiefs and soldiers of the first, second, and fourth caravans the many events which had befallen them, and which seemed to them the only things worth relating. Outside of their own limited circles they evidently cared for nothing. Then the several chiefs of the other caravans had in turn to relate their experiences of the road; and the noise of tongues was loud and furious. But as we approached, all this loud-sounding gabble ceased, and my caravan chiefs and guides rushed to me to hail me as " master," and to salute me as their friend. One fellow, faithful Baruti, threw himself at my feet, the others fired their guns and acted like madmen suddenly become frenzied, and a general cry of " welcome " was heard on all sides.

" Walk in, master, this is your house, now; here are your men's quarters; here you will receive the great Arabs, here is the cook-house; here is the store-house; here is the prison for the refractory; here are your white man's apartments; and these are your own: see, here is the bedroom, here is the gun-room, bath-room, &c.;" so Sheikh Sayd talked, as he showed me the several places.

On my honor, it was a most comfortable place, this, in Central Africa. One could almost wax poetic, but we will keep such ambitious ideas for a future day. Just now, however, we must have the goods stored, and the little army of carriers paid off and disbanded.

Bombay was ordered to unlock the strong store-room, to pile the bales in regular tiers, the beads in rows one above another, and the wire in a separate place. The boats, canvas, &c., were to be placed high above reach of white ants, and the boxes of ammunition and powder kegs were to be stored in the gun-room, out of reach of danger. Then a bale of cloth was opened, and each carrier was rewarded according to his merits, that each of them might proceed home to his friends and neighbours, and tell them how much better the white man behaved than the Arabs.

The reports of the leaders of the first, second, and fourth caravans were then received, their separate stores inspected, and the details and events of their marches heard. The first caravan had been engaged in a war at Kirurumo, and had come out of the fight successful, and had reached Unyanyembe without loss of anything. The second had shot a thief in the forest between Pembera Pereh and Kididimo; the fourth had lost a bale in the jungle of Marenga Mkali, and the porter who carried it had received a "very sore head" from a knob stick wielded by one of the thieves, who prowl about the jungle near the frontier of Ugogo. I was delighted to find that their misfortunes were no more, and each leader was then and there rewarded with one handsome cloth, and five doti of Merikani.

Just as I began to feel hungry again, came several slaves in succession, bearing trays full of good things from the Arabs; first an enormous dish of rice, with a bowlful of curried chicken, another with a dozen huge wheaten cakes, another with a plateful of smoking hot crullers, another with papaws, another with pomegranates and lemons; after these came men driving five fat hump‐backed oxen, eight sheep, and ten goats, and another man came with a dozen chickens, and a dozen fresh eggs. This was real, practical, noble courtesy, munificent hospitality, which quite took my gratitude by storm.

My people, now reduced to twenty-five, were as delighted at the prodigal plenitude visible on my tables and in my yard, as I was myself. And as I saw their eyes light up at the unctuous anticipations presented to them by their riotous fancies, I ordered a bullock to be slaughtered and distributed.

The second day of the arrival of the Expedition in the country which I now looked upon as classic ground, since Capts. Burton, Speke, and Grant years ago had visited it, and described it, came the Arab magnates from Tabora to congratulate me.

Tabora* is the principal Arab settlement in Central Africa. It contains over a thousand huts and tembes, and one may safely estimate the population, Arabs, Wangwana, and natives, at five thousand people. Between Tabora and the next settlement, Kwihara, rise two rugged hill ridges, separated from each other by a low saddle, over the top of which Tabora is always visible from Kwihara.

They were a fine, handsome body of men, these Arabs. They mostly hailed from Oman: others were Wasawahili; and each of my visitors had quite a retinue with him. At Tabora they live quite luxuriously. The plain on which the settlement is situated is exceedingly fertile, though naked of trees; the rich pasturage it furnishes permits them to keep large herds of cattle and goats, from which they have an ample supply of milk, cream, butter, and

* There is no such recognised place as Kazeh.

ghee. Rice is grown everywhere; sweet potatoes, yams,
muhogo, holcus sorghum, maize, or Indian corn, sesame,
millet, field-peas, or vetches, called choroko, are cheap,
and always procurable. Around their tembes the Arabs
cultivate a little wheat for their own purposes, and have
planted orange, lemon, papaw, and mangoes, which thrive
here fairly well. Onions and garlic, chilies, cucumbers,
tomatoes, and brinjalls, may be procured by the white
visitor from the more important Arabs, who are undoubted
epicureans in their way. Their slaves convey to them
from the coast, once a year at least, their stores of tea,
coffee, sugar, spices, jellies, curries, wine, brandy, biscuits,
sardines, salmon, and such fine cloths and articles as they
require for their own personal use. Almost every Arab
of any eminence is able to show a wealth of Persian
carpets, and most luxurious bedding, complete tea and
coffee-services, and magnificently carved dishes of tinned
copper and brass lavers. Several of them sport gold
watches and chains, mostly all a watch and chain of some
kind. And, as in Persia, Afghanistan, and Turkey, the
harems form an essential feature of every Arab's household; the sensualism of the Mohammedans is as prominent
here as in the Orient.

The Arabs who now stood before the front door of my
tembe were the donors of the good things received the
day before. As in duty bound, of course, I greeted
Sheikh Sayd first, then Sheikh bin Nasib, his Highness
of Zanzibar's consul at Karagwa, then I greeted the
noblest Trojan amongst the Arab population, noblest in
bearing, noblest in courage and manly worth—Sheikh
Khamis bin Abdullah; then young Amram bin Mussoud,
who is now making war on the king of Urori and his
fractious people; then handsome, courageous Soud, the

son of Sayd bin Majid; then dandified Thani bin
Abdullah; then Mussoud bin Abdullah and his cousin
Abdullah bin Mussoud, who own the houses where formerly
lived Burton and Speke; then old Suliman Dowa, Sayd
bin Sayf, and the old Hetman of Tabora—Sheikh Sultan
bin Ali.

As the visit of these magnates, under whose loving
protection white travellers must needs submit themselves,
was only a formal one, such as Arab etiquette, ever of
the stateliest and truest, impelled them to, it is unnecessary to relate the discourse on my health, and their
wealth, my thanks, and their professions of loyalty, and
attachment to me. After having expended our mutual
stock of congratulations and nonsense, they departed,
having stated their wish that I should visit them at
Tabora and partake of a feast which they were about to
prepare for me.

Three days afterwards I sallied out of my tembe,
escorted by eighteen bravely dressed men of my escort,
to pay Tabora a visit. On surmounting the saddle over
which the road from the valley of Kwihara leads to
Tabora, the plain on which the Arab settlement is
situated lay before us, one expanse of dun pasture land,
stretching from the base of the hill on our left as far as the
banks of the northern Gombe, which a few miles beyond
Tabora heave into purple-coloured hills and blue cones.

Within three-quarters of an hour we were seated on
the mud veranda of the tembe of Sultan bin Ali, who,
because of his age, his wealth, and position—being a
colonel in Seyd Burghash's unlovely army—is looked
upon by his countrymen, high and low, as referee and
counsellor. His boma or enclosure contains quite a
village of hive-shaped huts and square tembes. From

here, after being presented with a cup of Mocha coffee, and some sherbet, we directed our steps towards Khamis bin Abdullah's house, who had, in anticipation of my coming, prepared a feast to which he had invited his friends and neighbours. The group of stately Arabs in their long white dresses, and jaunty caps, also of a snowy white, who stood ready to welcome me to Tabora, produced quite an effect on my mind. I was in time for a council of war they were holding—and I was requested to attend.

Khamis bin Abdullah, a bold and brave man, ever ready to stand up for the privileges of the Arabs, and their rights to pass through any countries for legitimate trade, is the man who, in Speke's 'Journal of the Discovery of the Source of the Nile,' is reported to have shot Maula, an old chief who sided with Manwa Sera during the wars of 1860; and who subsequently, after chasing his relentless enemy for five years through Ugogo and Unyamwezi as far as Ukonongo, had the satisfaction of beheading him, was now urging the Arabs to assert their rights against a chief called Mirambo of Uyoweh, in a crisis which was advancing.

This Mirambo of Uyoweh, it seems, had for the last few years been in a state of chronic discontent with the policies of the neighbouring chiefs. Formerly a pagazi for an Arab, he had now assumed regal power, with the usual knack of unconscionable rascals who care not by what means they step into power. When the chief of Uyoweh died, Mirambo, who was head of a gang of robbers infesting the forests of Wilyankuru, suddenly entered Uyoweh, and constituted himself lord paramount by force. Some feats of enterprise, which he performed to the enrichment of all those who recognised his authority, established him firmly in his position. This was but a beginning; he carried war through Ugara to Ukonongo, through Usagozi to the borders of Uvinza, and after destroying the populations over three degrees of latitude, he conceived a grievance against Mkasiwa, and against the Arabs, because they would not sustain him in his ambitious projects against their ally and friend, with whom they were living in peace.

The first outrage which this audacious man committed against the Arabs was the halting of an Ujiji-bound caravan, and the demand for five kegs of gunpowder, five guns, and five bales of cloth. This extraordinary demand, after expending more than a day in fierce controversy, was paid; but the Arabs, if they were surprised at the exorbitant black-mail demanded of them, were more than ever surprised when they were told to return the way they came; and that no Arab caravan should pass through his country to Ujiji except over his dead body.

On the return of the unfortunate Arabs to Unyanyembe, they reported the facts to Sheikh Sayd bin Salim, the governor of the Arab colony. This old man, being averse to war, of course tried every means to induce Mirambo as of old to be satisfied with presents; but Mirambo this time was obdurate, and sternly determined on war unless the Arabs aided him in the warfare he was about to wage against old Mkasiwa, sultan of the Wanyamwezi of Unyanyembe.

" This is the status of affairs," said Khamis bin Abdullah. " Mirambo says: that for years he has been engaged in war against the neighbouring Washensi and has come out of it victorious; he says this is a great year with him; that he is going to fight the Arabs, and the Wanyamwezi of Unyanyembe, and that he shall not stop until every Arab is driven from Unyanyembe, and he rules over this country in place of Mkasiwa. Children of Oman, shall it be so? Speak, Salim, son of Sayf, shall we go to meet this Mshensi (pagan) or shall we return to our island?"

A murmur of approbation followed the speech of Khamis bin Abdullah, the majority of those present being young men eager to punish the audacious Mirambo. Salim, the son of Sayf, an old patriarch, slow of speech, tried to appease the passions of the young men, scions of the aristocracy of Muscat and Muttrah, and Bedaweens of the Desert, but Khamis's bold words had made too deep an impression on their minds.

Soud, the handsome Arab whom I have noticed already as the son of Sayd the son of Majid, spoke: "My father used to tell me that he remembered the days when the Arabs could go through the country from Bagamoyo to Ujiji, and from Kilwa to Lunda, and from Usenga to Uganda armed with canes. Those days are gone by. We have stood the insolence of the Wagogo long enough. Swaruru of Usui just takes from us whatever he wants; and now, here is Mirambo, who says, after taking more than five bales of cloth as tribute from one man, that no Arab caravan shall go to Ujiji, but over his body. Are we prepared to give up the ivory of Ujiji, of Urundi, of Karagwah, of Uganda, because of this one man? I say war—war until we have got his beard under our feet— war until the whole of Uyoweh and Wilyankuru is destroyed—war until we can again travel through any part of the country with only our walking canes in our hands!"

The universal assent that followed Soud's speech proved

beyond a doubt that we were about to have a war. I thought of Livingstone. What if he were marching to Unyanyembe directly into the war country?

Having found from the Arabs that they intended to finish the war quickly—at most within fifteen days, as Uyoweh was only four marches distant—I volunteered to accompany them, take my loaded caravan with me as far as Mfuto, and there leave it in charge of a few guards, and with the rest march on with the Arab army. And my hope was, that it might be possible, after the defeat of Mirambo, and his forest banditti—the Ruga-Ruga—to take my Expedition direct to Ujiji by the road now closed. The Arabs were sanguine of victory, and I partook of their enthusiasm.

The council of war broke up. A great dishful of rice and curry, in which almonds, citron, raisins, and currants were plentifully mixed, was brought in, and it was wonderful how soon we forgot our warlike fervor after our attention had been drawn to this royal dish. I, of course, not being a Mohammedan, had a dish of my own, of a similar composition, strengthened by platters containing roast chicken, and kabobs, crullers, cakes, sweetbread, fruit, glasses of sherbet and lemonade, dishes of gum-drops and Muscat sweetmeats, dry raisins, prunes, and nuts. Certainly Khamis bin Abdullah proved to me that if he had a warlike soul in him, he could also attend to the cultivated tastes acquired under the shade of the mangoes on his father's estates in Zanzibar—the island.

After gorging ourselves on these uncommon dainties some of the chief Arabs escorted me to other tembes of Tabora. When we went to visit Mussoud bin Abdullah, he showed me the very ground where Burton and Speke's house stood—now pulled down and replaced by his office—Sny bin Amer's house was also torn down, and the fashionable tembe of Unyanyembe, now in vogue, built over it,—finely-carved rafters—hugh carved doors, brass knockers, and lofty airy rooms—a house built for defence and comfort.

The finest house in Unyanyembe belongs to Amram bin Mussoud, who paid sixty frasilah of ivory—over $3,000—for it. Very fair houses can be purchased for from twenty to thirty frasilah of ivory. Amram's house is called the "Two Seas"—"Baherein." It is one hundred feet in length, and twenty feet high, with walls four feet thick, neatly plastered over with mud mortar. The great door is a marvel of carving-work for Unyanyembe artisans. Each rafter within is also carved with fine designs. Before the front of the house is a young plantation of pomegranate trees, which flourish here as if they were indigenous to the soil. A shadoof, such as may be seen on the Nile, serves to draw water to irrigate the gardens.

Towards evening we walked back to our own finely situated tembe in Kwihara, well satisfied with what we had seen at Tabora. My men drove a couple of oxen, and carried three sacks of native rice—a most superior kind—the day's presents of hospitality from Khamis bin Abdullah.

In Unyanyembe I found the Livingstone caravan, which started off in a fright from Bagamoyo upon the rumour that the English Consul was coming. As all the caravans were now halted at Unyanyembe because of the now approaching war, I suggested to Sayd bin Salim, that it were better that the men of the Livingstone caravan should live with mine in my tembe, that I might watch over the white man's goods. Sayd bin Salim agreed with me, and the men and goods were at once brought to my tembe.

One day Asmani, who was now chief of Livingstone's caravan, the other having died of small-pox, two or three days before, brought out a tent to the veranda where I was sitting writing, and shewed me a packet of letters, which to my surprise was marked:—

<blockquote>
"To Dr. Livingstone,
<blockquote>
"Ujiji,
</blockquote>
"November 1st, 1870.
<blockquote>
"Registered letters."
</blockquote>
</blockquote>

From November 1st, 1870, to February 10, 1871, just one hundred days, at Bagamoyo! A miserable small caravan of thirty-three men halting one hundred days at Bagamoyo, only twenty-five miles by water from Zanzibar! Poor Livingstone! Who knows but he may be suffering for want of these very supplies that were detained so long near the sea. The caravan arrived in Unyanyembe some time about the middle of May. About the latter part of May the first disturbances took place. Had this caravan arrived here in the middle of March, or even the middle of April, they might have travelled on to Ujiji without trouble.

On the 7th of July, about 2 P.M., I was sitting on the burzani as usual; I felt listless and languid, and a drowsiness came over me; I did not fall asleep, but the power of my limbs seemed to fail me. Yet the brain was busy; all my life seemed passing in review before me; when these retrospective scenes became serious, I looked serious; when they were sorrowful, I wept hysterically; when they were joyous, I laughed loudly. Reminiscences of

yet a young life's battles and hard struggles came surging
into the mind in quick succession : events of boyhood, of
youth, and manhood ; perils, travels, scenes, joys, and
sorrows ; loves and hates ; friendships and indifferences.
My mind followed the various and rapid transition of my
life's passages ; it drew the lengthy, erratic, sinuous lines
of travel my footsteps had passed over.   If I had drawn
them on the sandy floor, what enigmatical problems they
had been to those around me, and what plain, readable,
intelligent histories they had been to me !

The loveliest feature of all to me was the form of a
noble, and true man, who called me son.   Of my life in
the great pine forests of Arkansas, and in Missouri, I
retained the most vivid impressions.   The dreaming days
I passed under the sighing pines on the Ouachita's shores ;
the new clearing, the block-house, our faithful black
servant, the forest deer, and the exuberant life I led, were
all well remembered.   And I remembered how one day,
after we had come to live near the Mississipi, I floated
down, down, hundreds of miles, with a wild fraternity of
knurly giants, the boatmen of the Mississipi, and how a
dear old man welcomed me back, as if from the grave.   I
remembered also my travels on foot through sunny Spain,
and France, with numberless adventures in Asia Minor,
among Kurdish nomads.   I remembered the battle-fields
of America and the stormy scenes of rampant war.   I remembered gold mines, and broad prairies, Indian councils,
and much experience in the new western lands.   I remembered the shock it gave me to hear after my return
from a barbarous country of the calamity that had overtaken the fond man whom I called father, and the hot
fitful life that followed it.   Stop ! * * * * * *

Dear me ; is it the 21st of July ? Yes, Shaw informed

me that it was the 21st of July after I recovered from my terrible attack of fever; the true date was the 14th of July, but I was not aware that I had jumped a week, until I met Dr. Livingstone. We two together examined the 'Nautical Almanack,' which I brought with me. We found that the Doctor was three weeks out of his reckoning, and to my great surprise I was also one week out, or one week ahead of the actual date. The mistake was made by my being informed that I had been two weeks sick, and as the day I recovered my senses was Friday, and Shaw and the people were morally sure that I was in bed two weeks, I dated it on my Diary the 21st of July. However, on the tenth day after the first of my illness, I was in excellent trim again, only, however, to see and attend to Shaw, who was in turn taken sick. By the 22nd July Shaw was recovered, then Selim was prostrated, and groaned in his delirium for four days, but by the 28th we were all recovered, and were beginning to brighten up at the prospect of a diversion in the shape of a march upon Mirambo's stronghold.

The morning of the 29th I had fifty men loaded with bales, beads, and wire, for Ujiji. When they were mustered for the march outside the tembe, the only man absent was Bombay. While men were sent to search for him, others departed to get one more look, and one more embrace with their black Delilahs. Bombay was found some time about 2 P.M., his face faithfully depicting the contending passions under which he was labouring— sorrow at parting from the fleshpots of Unyanyembe— regret at parting from his Dulcinea of Tabora—to be bereft of all enjoyment now, nothing but marches—hard, long marches—to go to the war—to be killed, perhaps. Oh! Inspired by such feelings, no wonder Bombay was inclined to be pugnacious when I ordered him to his place, and I was in a shocking bad temper for having been kept waiting from 8 A.M. to 2 P.M. for him. There was simply a word and a savage look, and my cane was flying around Bombay's shoulders, as if he were to be annihilated. I fancy that the eager fury of my onslaught broke his stubbornness more than anything else; for before I had struck him a dozen times he was crying for "pardon." At that word I ceased belaboring him, for this was the first time he had ever uttered that word. Bombay was conquered at last.

"March!" and the guide led off, followed in solemn order by forty-nine of his fellows, every man carrying a heavy load of African moneys, besides his gun, hatchet, and stock of ammunition, and his ugali-pot. We presented quite an imposing sight while thus marching on in silence and order, with our flags flying, and the red blanket robes of the men streaming behind them as the furious north-easter blew right on our flank.

The men seemed to feel they were worth seeing, for I noticed that several assumed a more martial tread as they felt their royal Joho cloth tugging at their necks, as it was swept streaming behind by the wind. Maganga, a tall Mnyamwezi, stalked along like a very Goliah about to give battle alone, to Mirambo and his thousand warriors. Frisky Khamisi paced on under his load, imitating a lion: and there was the rude jester—the incorrigible Ulimengo —with a stealthy pace like a cat. But their silence could not last long. Their vanity was so much gratified, the red cloaks danced so incessantly before their eyes, that it would have been a wonder if they could have maintained such serious gravity or discontent one half hour longer.

Ulimengo was the first who broke it. He had constituted himself the kirangozi or guide, and was the standard-bearer, bearing the American flag, which the men thought would certainly strike terror into the hearts of the enemy. Growing confident first, then valorous, then exultant, he suddenly faced the army he was leading, and shouted

                    "Hoy !   Hoy !
        Chorus.—Hoy !   Hoy !
                    Hoy !   Hoy !
        Chorus.—Hoy !   Hoy !
                    Hoy !   Hoy !
        Chorus.—Hoy !   Hoy !
                    Where are ye going ?
        Chorus.—Going to war.
                    Against whom ?
        Chorus.—Against Mirambo.
                    Who is your master ?
        Chorus.—The White Man.
                    Ough !   Ough !
        Chorus.—Ough !   Ough !
                    Hyah !   Hyah !
        Chorus.—Hyah .   Hyah !"

This was the ridiculous song they kept up all day without intermission.

We camped the first day at Bomboma's village, situated a mile to the south-west of the natural hill fortress of Zimbili. Bombay was quite recovered from his thrashing, and had banished the sullen thoughts that had aroused my ire, and the men having behaved themselves so well, a five-gallon pot of pombe was brought to further nourish the valour, which they one and all thought they possessed.

The second day we arrived at Masangi. I was visited soon afterwards by Soud, the son of Sayd bin Majid, who told me the Arabs were waiting for me ; that they would not march from Mfuto until I had arrived.

Eastern Mfuto, after a six hours' march, was reached on the third day from Unyanyembe. Shaw gave in, laid down in the road, and declared he was dying. This news was brought to me about 4 P.M. by one of the last stragglers. I was bound to despatch men to carry him to me, into my camp, though every man was well tired after the long march. A reward stimulated half-a-dozen to venture into the forest just at dusk to find Shaw, who was supposed to be at least three hours away from camp.

About two o'clock in the morning my men returned, having carried Shaw on their backs the entire distance. I was roused up, and had him conveyed to my tent. I examined him, and I assured myself he was not suffering from fever of any kind; and in reply to my inquiries as to how he felt, he said he could neither walk nor ride, that he felt such extreme weakness and lassitude that he was incapable of moving further. After administering a glass of port wine to him in a bowlful of sago gruel, we both fell asleep.

We arrived early the following morning at Mfuto, the rendezvous of the Arab army. A halt was ordered the next day, in order to make ourselves strong by eating the beeves, which we freely slaughtered.

The personnel of our army was as follows:—

Sheikh Sayd bin Salim . . . . . . 25 half caste
   „   Khamis bin Abdullah . . . . . 250 slaves
   „   Thani bin Abdullah . . . . . 80 „
   „   Mussoud bin Abdullah . . . . 75 „
   „   Abdullah bin Mussoud . . . . 80 „
   „   Ali bin Sayd bin Nasib . . . . 250 ,
   „   Nasir bin Mussoud . . . . . 50 „
   „   Hamed Kimiami . . . . . . 70 „
   „   Sheikh Hamdam . . . . . . 30 „
   „   Sayd bin Habib . . . . . . 50 „

Sheikh Salim bin Sayf	100	slaves
„ Sunguru	25	„
„ Sarboko	25	„
„ Soud bin Sayd bin Majid	50	„
„ Mohammed bin Mussoud	30	„
„ Sayd bin Hamed	90	„
„ The 'Herald' Expedition	50	soldiers
„ Mkasiwa's Wanyamwezi	800	„
„ Half-castes and Wangwana . . .	125	„
„ Independent chiefs and their followers	300	„

These made a total of 2,255, according to numbers given me by Thani bin Abdullah, and corroborated by a Baluch in the pay of Sheikh bin Nasib. Of these men 1,500 were armed with guns—flint-lock muskets, German and French double-barrels, some English Enfields, and American Springfields—besides these muskets, they were mostly armed with spears and long knives for the purpose of decapitating, and inflicting vengeful gashes in the dead bodies. Powder and ball were plentiful: some men were served a hundred rounds each, my people received each man sixty rounds.

As we filed out of the stronghold of Mfuto, with waving banners denoting the various commanders, with booming horns, and the roar of fifty bass drums, called gomas—with blessings showered on us by the mollahs, and happiest predications from the soothsayers, astrologers, and the diviners of the Korân—who could have foretold that this grand force, before a week passed over its head, would be hurrying into that same stronghold of Mfuto, with each man's heart in his mouth from fear?

The date of our leaving Mfuto for battle with Mirambo was the 3rd of August. All my goods were stored in Mfuto, ready for the march to Ujiji, should we be victorious over the African chief, but at least for safety, whatever befel us.

Long before we reached Umanda, I was in my hammock in the paroxysms of a fierce attack of intermittent fever, which did not leave me until late that night.

At Umanda, six hours from Mfuto, our warriors bedaubed themselves with the medicine which the wise men had manufactured for them—a compound of matama flour mixed with the juices of a herb whose virtues were only known to the Waganga of the Wanyamwezi.

At 6 A.M. on the 4th of August we were once more prepared for the road, but before we were marched out of the village, the " manneno," or speech, was delivered by the orator of the Wanyamwezi :

" Words! words! words! Listen, sons of Mkasiwa, children of Unyamwezi! the journey is before you, the thieves of the forest are waiting; yes, they are thieves, they cut up your caravans, they steal your ivory, they murder your women. Behold, the Arabs are with you, El Wali of the Arab sultan, and the white man are with you. Go, the son of Mkasiwa is with you; fight, kill, take slaves, take cloth, take cattle, kill, eat, and fill yourselves! Go!"

A loud, wild shout followed this bold harangue, the gates of the village were thrown open, and blue, red, and white-robed soldiers were bounding upward like so many gymnasts, firing their guns incessantly, in order to encourage themselves with noise, or to strike terror into the hearts of those who awaited us within the strong enclosure of Zimbizo, Sultan Kolongo's place.

As Zimbizo was distant only five hours from Umanda, at 11 A.M. we came in view of it. We halted on the verge of the cultivated area around it and its neighbours within the shadow of the forest. Strict orders had been given by the several chiefs to their respective commands not to fire, until they were within shooting distance of the boma.

Khamis bin Abdullah crept through the forest to the west of the village. The Wanyamwezi took their position before the main gateway, aided by the forces of Soud the son of Sayd on the right, and the son of Habib on the left, Abdullah, Mussoud, myself, and others made ready to attack the eastern gates, which arrangement effectually shut them in, with the exception of the northern side.

Suddenly, a volley opened on us, as we emerged from the forest along the Unyanyembe road, in the direction they had been anticipating the sight of an enemy, and immediately the attacking forces began their firing in most splendid style. There were some ludicrous scenes of men pretending to fire, then jumping off to one side, then forward, then backward, with the agility of hopping frogs, but the battle was none the less in earnest. The breech-loaders of my men swallowed my metallic cartridges much faster than I liked to see ; but happily there was a lull in the firing, and we were rushing into the village from the west, the south, the north, through the gates and over the tall palings that surrounded the village, like so many Merry Andrews ; and the poor villagers were flying from the enclosure towards the mountains, through the northern gate, pursued by the fleetest runners of our force, and pelted in the back by bullets from breech-loaders and shot-guns.

The village was strongly defended, and not more than twenty dead bodies were found in it, the strong thick wooden paling having afforded excellent protection against our bullets.

From Zimbizo, after having left a sufficient force within, we sallied out, and in an hour had cleared the neighbourhood of the enemy, having captured two other villages, which we committed to the flames, after gutting them of all valuables. A few tusks of ivory, and about fifty slaves, besides an abundance of grain, composed the "loot," which fell to the lot of the Arabs.

On the 5th, a detachment of Arabs and slaves, seven hundred strong, scoured the surrounding country, and carried fire and devastation up to the boma of Wilyankuru.

On the 6th, Soud bin Sayd and about twenty other young Arabs led a force of five hundred men against Wilyankuru itself, where it was supposed Mirambo was living. Another party went out towards the low wooded hills, a short distance north of Zimbizo, near which place they surprised a youthful forest thief asleep, whose head they stretched backwards, and cut it off as though he were a goat or a sheep. Another party sallied out southward, and defeated a party of Mirambo's "bush-whackers," news of which came to our ears at noon.

In the morning I had gone to Sayd bin Salim's tembe, to represent to him how necessary it was to burn the long grass in the forest of Zimbizo, lest it might hide any of the enemy; but soon afterwards I had been struck down with another attack of intermittent fever, and was obliged to turn in and cover myself with blankets to produce perspiration; but not, however, till I had ordered Shaw and Bombay not to permit any of my men to leave the camp. But I was told soon afterwards by Selim that more than one half had gone to the attack on Wilyankuru with Soud bin Sayd.

About 6 P.M. the entire camp of Zimbizo was electrified with the news that all the Arabs who had accompanied

Soud bin Sayd had been killed; and that more than one-half of his party had been slain. Some of my own men returned, and from them I learned that Uledi, Grant's former valet, Mabruki Khatálabu (Killer of his father), Mabruki (the Little), Baruti of Useguhha, and Ferahan had been killed. I learned also that they had succeeded in capturing Wilyankuru in a very short time, that Mirambo and his son were there, that as they succeeded in effecting an entrance, Mirambo had collected his men, and after leaving the village, had formed an ambush in the grass, on each side of the road, between Wilyankuru and Zimbizo, and that as the attacking party were returning home laden with over a hundred tusks of ivory, and sixty bales of cloth, and two or three hundred slaves, Mirambo's men suddenly rose up on each side of them, and stabbed them with their spears. The brave Soud had fired his double-barrelled gun and shot two men, and was in the act of loading again when a spear was launched, which penetrated through and through him: all the other Arabs shared the same fate. This sudden attack from an enemy they believed to be conquered so demoralized the party that, dropping their spoil, each man took to his heels, and after making a wide detour through the woods, returned to Zimbizo to repeat the dolorous tale.

The effect of this defeat is indescribable. It was impossible to sleep, from the shrieks of the women whose husbands had fallen. All night they howled their lamentations, and sometimes might be heard the groans of the wounded who had contrived to crawl through the grass unperceived by the enemy. Fugitives were continually coming in throughout the night, but none of my men who were reported to be dead, were ever heard of again,

The 7th was a day of distrust, sorrow, and retreat; the Arabs accused one another for urging war without expending all peaceful means first. There were stormy councils of war held, wherein were some who proposed to return at once to Unyanyembe, and keep within their own houses; and Khamis bin Abdullah raved, like an insulted monarch, against the abject cowardice of his compatriots. These stormy meetings and propositions to retreat were soon known throughout the camp, and assisted more than anything else to demoralize completely the combined forces of Wanyamwezi and slaves. I sent Bombay to Sayd bin Salim to advise him not to think of retreat, as it would only be inviting Mirambo to carry the war to Unyanyembe.

After despatching Bombay with this message, I fell asleep, but about 1.30 P.M. I was awakened by Selim saying, "Master, get up, they are all running away, and Khamis bin Abdullah is himself going."

With the aid of Selim I dressed myself, and staggered towards the door. My first view was of Thani bin Abdullah being dragged away, who, when he caught sight of me, shouted out "Bana—quick—Mirambo is coming." He was then turning to run, and putting on his jacket, with his eyes almost starting out of their sockets with terror. Khamis bin Abdullah was also about departing, he being the last Arab to leave. Two of my men were following him; these Selim was ordered to force back with a revolver. Shaw was saddling his donkey with my own saddle, preparatory to giving me the slip, and leaving me in the lurch to the tender mercies of Mirambo. There were only Bombay, Mabruki Speke, Chanda who was coolly eating his dinner, Mabruk Unyanyembe, Mtamani, Juma, and Sarmean—only seven out of fifty. All the others had deserted, and were by this time far away, except Uledi (Manwa Sera) and Zaidi, whom Selim brought back at the point of a loaded revolver. Selim was then told to saddle my donkey, and Bombay to assist Shaw to saddle his own. In a few moments we were on the road, the men ever looking back for the coming enemy; they belabored the donkeys to some purpose, for they went at a hard trot, which caused me intense pain. I would gladly have lain down to die, but life was sweet, and I had not yet given up all hope of being able to preserve it to the full and final accomplishment of my mission. My mind was actively at work planning and contriving during the long lonely hours of night, which we employed to reach Mfuto, whither I found the Arabs had retreated. In the night Shaw tumbled off his donkey, and would not rise, though implored to do so. As I did not despair myself, so I did not intend that Shaw should despair. He was lifted on his animal, and a man was placed on each side of him to assist him; thus we rode through the darkness. At midnight we reached Mfuto safely, and were at once admitted into the village, from which we had issued so valiantly, but to which we were now returned so ignominiously.

I found all my men had arrived here before dark. Ulimengo, the bold guide who had exulted in his weapons and in our numbers, and was so sanguine of victory, had performed the eleven hours' march in six hours; sturdy Chowpereh, whom I regarded as the faithfullest of my people, had arrived only half an hour later than Ulimengo; and frisky Khamisi, the dandy—the orator—the rampant demagogue—yes—he had come third; and Speke's "Faithfuls" had proved as cowardly as any poor "nigger" of them all. Only Selim was faithful.

I asked Selim, " Why did you not also run away, and leave your master to die ?"

" Oh, sir," said the Arab boy, naïvely, " I was afraid you would whip me."

GROUP OF WANYAMWEZI.

CHAPTER IX.

MY LIFE AND TROUBLES IN UNYANYEMBE—(*continued*).

IT never occurred to the Arab magnates that I had
cause of complaint against them, or that I had a right
to feel aggrieved at their conduct, for the base desertion
of an ally, who had, as a duty to friendship, taken
up arms for their sake. Their "salaams" the next
morning after the retreat, were given as if nothing
had transpired to mar the good feeling that had existed
between us.

They were hardly seated, however, before I began to
inform them that as the war was only between them and

Mirambo, and that as I was afraid, if they were accustomed to run away after every little check, that the war might last a much longer time than I could afford to lose; and that as they had deserted their wounded on the field, and left their sick friends to take care of themselves, they must not consider me in the light of an ally any more. "I am satisfied," said I, "having seen your mode of fighting, that the war will not be ended in so short a time as you think it will. It took you five years, I hear, to conquer and kill Manwa Sera, you will certainly not conquer Mirambo in less than a year.* I am a white man, accustomed to wars after a different style, I know something about fighting, but I never saw people run away from an encampment like ours at Zimbizo for such slight cause as you had. By running away, you have invited Mirambo to follow you to Unyanyembe; you may be sure he will come."

The Arabs protested one after another that they had not intended to have left me, but the Wanyamwezi of Mkasiwa had shouted out that the "Musungu" was gone, and the cry had caused a panic among their people, which it was impossible to allay.

Later that day the Arabs continued their retreat to Tabora, which is twenty-two miles distant from Mfuto. I determined to proceed more leisurely, and on the second day after the flight from Zimbizo, the Expedition, with all the stores and baggage, marched back to Masangi, and on the third day to Kwihara.

The following extracts from my Diary will serve to show better than anything else, my feelings and thoughts about this time, after our disgraceful retreat:

Kwihara. Friday, 11th August, 1871.—Arrived to-day

* The same war is still raging, April, 1874.

from Zimbili, village of Bomboma's. I am quite disappointed and almost disheartened. But I have one consolation, I have done my duty by the Arabs, a duty I thought I owed to the kindness they received me with, now, however, the duty is discharged, and I am free to pursue my own course. I feel happy, for some reasons, that the duty has been paid at such a slight sacrifice. Of course if I had lost my life in this enterprise, I should have been justly punished. But apart from my duty to the consideration with which the Arabs had received me, was the necessity of trying every method of reaching Livingstone. This road which the war with Mirambo has closed, is only a month's march from this place, and if the road could be opened with my aid, sooner than without it, why should I refuse my aid? The attempt has been made for the second time to Ujiji—both have failed. I am going to try another route; to attempt to go by the north would be folly. Mirambo's mother and people, and the Wasui, are between me and Ujiji, without including the Watuta, who are his allies, and robbers. The southern route seems to be the most practicable one. Very few people know anything of the country south; those whom I have questioned concerning it speak of "want of water" and robber Wazavira, as serious obstacles; they also say that the settlements are few and far between.

But before I can venture to try this new route, I have to employ a new set of men, as those whom I took to Mfuto consider their engagements at an end, and the fact of five of their number being killed rather damps their ardor for travelling. It is useless to hope that Wanyamwezi can be engaged, because it is against their custom to go with caravans, as carriers, during war time. My position is most serious. I have a good excuse for returning to the coast, but my conscience will not permit me to do so, after so much money has been expended, and so much confidence has been placed in me. In fact, I feel I must die sooner than return.

Saturday, August 12th.—My men, as I supposed they would, have gone; they said that I engaged them to go to Ujiji by Mirambo's road. I have only thirteen left. With this small body of men, whither can I go? I have over one hundred loads in the storeroom. Livingstone's caravan is also here ; his goods consist of seventeen bales of cloth, twelve boxes, and six bags of beads. His men are luxuriating upon the best the country affords.

If Livingstone is at Ujiji, he is now locked up with small means of escape. I may consider myself also locked up at Unyamyembe, and I suppose cannot go to Ujiji until this war with Mirambo is settled. Livingstone cannot get his goods, for they are here with mine. He cannot return to Zanzibar, and the road to the Nile is blocked up. He might, if he has men and stores, possibly reach Baker by travelling northwards, through Urundi, thence through Ruanda, Karagwah, Uganda, Unyoro, and Ubari to Gondokoro. Pagazis he cannot obtain, for the sources whence a supply might be obtained are closed. It is an erroneous supposition to think that Livingstone, any more than any other energetic man of his calibre, can travel through Africa without some sort of an escort, and a durable supply of marketable cloth and beads.

I was told to-day by a man that when Livingstone was coming from Nyassa Lake towards the Tanganika (the very time that people thought him murdered) he was met by Sayd bin Omar's caravan, which was bound for Ulamba. He was travelling with Mohammed bin Gharib. This

Arab, who was coming from Urungu, met Livingstone at
Chi-cumbi's, or Kwa-chi-kumbi's, country, and travelled
with him afterwards, I hear, to Manyuema or Manyema.
Manyuema is forty marches from the north of Nyassa.
Livingstone was walking; he was dressed in American
sheeting. He had lost all his cloth in Lake Liemba
while crossing it in a boat. He had three canoes with
him; in one he put his cloth, another he loaded with his
boxes and some of his men, into the third he went himself
with two servants and two fishermen. The boat with his
cloth was upset. On leaving Nyassa, Livingstone went to
Ubisa, thence to Uemba, thence to Urungu. Livingstone
wore a cap. He had a breech-loading double-barreled
rifle with him, which fired fulminating balls. He was
also armed with two revolvers. The Wahiyow with
Livingstone told this man that their master had many
men with him at first, but that several had deserted
him.

August 13th.—A caravan came in to-day from the sea-
coast. They reported that William L. Farquhar, whom I
left sick at Mpwapwa, Usagara, and his cook, were dead.
Farquhar, I was told, died a few days after I had entered
Ugogo, his cook died a few weeks later. My first impulse
was for revenge. I believed that Leukole had played me
false, and had poisoned him, or that he had been murdered in some other manner; but a personal interview
with the Msawahili who brought the news informing me
that Farquhar had succumbed to his dreadful illness has
done away with that suspicion. So far as I could understand him, Farquhar had in the morning declared himself
well enough to proceed, but in attempting to rise, had
fallen backward and died. I was also told that the
Wasagara, possessing some superstitious notions respecting

the dead, had ordered Jako to take the body out for burial, that Jako, not being able to carry it, had dragged the body to the jungle, and there left it naked without the slightest covering of earth, or anything else.

"There is one of us gone, Shaw, my boy! Who will be the next?" I remarked that night to my companion.

August 14th.—Wrote some letters to Zanzibar. Shaw was taken very ill last night.

August 19th. Saturday.—My soldiers are employed stringing beads. Shaw is still a-bed. We hear that Mirambo is coming to Unyanyembe. A detachment of Arabs and their slaves have started this morning to possess themselves of the powder left there by the redoubtable Sheikh Sayd bin Salim, the commander-in-chief of the Arab settlements.

August 21st. Monday.—Shaw still sick. One hundred fundo of beads have been strung. The Arabs are preparing for another sally against Mirambo. The advance of Mirambo upon Unyanyembe was denied by Sayd bin Salim, this morning.

August 22nd.—We were stringing beads this morning, when, about 10 A.M., we heard a continued firing from the direction of Tabora. Rushing out from our work to the front door facing Tabora, we heard considerable volleying, and scattered firing, plainly; and ascending to the top of my tembe, I saw with my glasses the smoke of the guns. Some of my men who were sent on to ascertain the cause came running back with the information that Mirambo had attacked Tabora with over two thousand men, and that a force of over one thousand Watuta, who had allied themselves with him for the sake of plunder, had come suddenly upon Tabora, attacking from opposite directions.

Later in the day, or about noon, watching the low

saddle over which we could see Tabora, we saw it crowded with fugitives from that settlement, who were rushing to our settlement at Kwihara for protection. From these people we heard the sad information that the noble Khamis bin Abdullah, his little protégé, Khamis, Mohammed bin Abdullah, Ibrahim bin Rashid, and Sayf, the son of Ali, the son of Sheikh, the son of Nasib, had been slain.

When I inquired into the details of the attack, and the manner of the death of these Arabs, I was told that after the first firing which warned the inhabitants of Tabora that the enemy was upon them, Khamis bin Abdullah and some of the principal Arabs who happened to be with him had ascended to the roof of his tembe, and with his spy-glass he had looked towards the direction of the firing. To his great astonishment he saw the plain around Tabora filled with approaching savages, and about two miles off, near Kazima, a tent pitched, which he knew to belong to Mirambo, from its having been presented to that chief by the Arabs of Tabora when they were on good terms with him.

Khamis bin Abdullah descended to his house saying, "Let us go to meet him. Arm yourselves, my friends, and come with me." His friends advised him strongly not to go out of his tembe; for so long as each Arab kept to his tembe they were more than a match for the Ruga-Ruga and the Watuta together. But Khamis broke out impatiently with, "Would you advise us to stop in our tembes, for fear of this Mshensi (pagan)? Who goes with me?" His little protégé, Khamis, son of a dead friend, asked to be allowed to be his gun-bearer; Mohammed bin Abdulluh, Ibrahim bin Rashid, and Sayf, the son of Ali, young Arabs of good families, who were proud to live with the noble Khamis, also offered to go with him. After hastily arming eighty of his slaves, contrary to the advice of his prudent friends, he sallied out, and was soon face to face with his cunning and determined enemy Mirambo. This chief, upon seeing the Arabs advance towards him, gave orders to retreat slowly. Khamis, deceived by this, rushed on with his friends after them. Suddenly Mirambo ordered his men to advance upon them in a body, and at the sight of the precipitate rush upon their party, Khamis's slaves incontinently took to their heels, never even deigning to cast a glance behind them, leaving their master to the fate which was now overtaking him. The savages surrounded the five Arabs, and though several of them fell before the Arabs' fire, continued to shoot at the little party, until Khamis bin Abdullah received a bullet in the leg, which brought him to his knees, and, for the first time, to the knowledge that his slaves had deserted him. Though wounded, the brave man continued shooting, but he soon afterwards received a bullet through the heart. Little Khamis, upon seeing his adopted father's fall, exclaimed: " My father Khamis is dead, I will die with him," and continued fighting until he received, shortly after, his death wound. In a few minutes there was not one Arab left alive.

Late at night some more particulars arrived of this tragic scene. I was told by people who saw the bodies, that the body of Khamis bin Abdullah, who was a fine noble, brave, portly man, was found with the skin of his forehead, the beard and skin of the lower part of his face, the fore part of the nose, the fat over the stomach and abdomen, and, lastly, a bit from each heel, cut off, by the savage allies of Mirambo. And in the same condition were found the bodies of his adopted son and fallen friends. The flesh and skin thus taken from the bodies was taken, of course, by the waganga or medicine men, to make what they deem to be the most powerful potion of all to enable men to be strong against their enemies. This potion is mixed up with their ugali and rice, and is taken in this manner with the most perfect confidence in its efficacy, as an invulnerable protection against bullets and missiles of all descriptions.

It was a most sorry scene to witness from our excited settlement at Kwihara, almost the whole of Tabora in flames, and to see the hundreds of people crowding into Kwihara.

Perceiving that my people were willing to stand by me, I made preparations for defence by boring loopholes for muskets into the stout clay walls of my tembe. They were made so quickly, and seemed so admirably adapted for the efficient defence of the tembe, that my men got quite brave, and Wangwana refugees with guns in their hands, driven out of Tabora, asked to be admitted into our tembe to assist in its defence. Livingstone's men were also collected, and invited to help defend their master's goods against Mirambo's supposed attack. By night I had one hundred and fifty armed men in my courtyard, stationed at every possible point where an attack might be expected. To-morrow Mirambo has threatened that he will come to Kwihara. I hope he will come, and if he comes within range of an American rifle, I shall see what virtue lies in American lead.

August 23rd.—We have passed a very anxious day in the valley of Kwihara. Our eyes were constantly directed towards unfortunate Tabora. It has been said that three tembes only have stood the brunt of the attack. Abid bin Suliman's house has been destroyed, and over two hundred tusks of ivory that belonged to him have become the property of the African Bonaparte. My tembe is in as efficient a state of defence as its style and means of defence will allow. Rifle-pits surround the house outside, and all native huts that obstructed the view have been torn down, and all trees and shrubs which might serve as a shelter for any one of the enemy have been cut. Provisions and water enough for six days have been brought. I have ammunition enough to last two weeks. The walls are three feet thick, and there are apartments within apartments, so that a desperate body of men could fight until the last room had been taken.

The Arabs, my neighbours, endeavour to seem brave, but it is evident they are about despairing; I have heard it rumoured that the Arabs of Kwihara, if Tabora is taken, will start *en masse* for the coast, and give the country up to Mirambo. If such are their intentions, and they are really carried into effect, I shall be in a pretty mess. However, if they do leave me, Mirambo will not reap any benefit from my stores, nor from Livingstone's either, for I shall burn the whole house, and everything in it.

August 24th.—The American flag is still waving above my house, and the Arabs are still in Unyanyembe.

About 10 A.M., a messenger came from Tabora, asking us if we were not going to assist them against Mirambo. I felt very much like going out to help them; but after debating long upon the pros and cons of it,—asking myself, Was it prudent? Ought I to go? What will become of the people if I were killed? Will they not desert me again? What was the fate of Khamis bin Abdullah?—I sent word that I would not go; that they ought to feel perfectly at home in their tembes against such a force as Mirambo had, that I should be glad if they could induce him to come to Kwihara, in which case I would try and pick him off.

They say that Mirambo, and his principal officer, carry umbrellas over their heads, that he himself has long hair like a Mnyamwezi pagazi, and a beard. If he comes, all the men carrying umbrellas will have bullets rained on them in the hope that one lucky bullet may hit him. According to popular ideas, I should make a silver bullet, but I have no silver with me. I might make a gold one.

About noon I went over to see Sheikh bin Nasib, leaving about 100 men inside the house to guard it while I was absent. This old fellow is quite a philosopher in his way. I should call him a professor of minor philosophy. He is generally so sententious—fond of aphorisms, and a very deliberate character. I was astonished to find him so despairing. His aphorisms have deserted him, his philosophy has not been able to stand against disaster. He listened to me, more like a moribund, than one possessing all the means of defence and offence.

I loaded his two-pounder with ball, and grape, and small slugs of iron, and advised him not to fire it until Mirambo's people were at his gates.

About 4 P.M. I heard that Mirambo had deported himself to Kazima, a place north-west of Tabora a couple of miles.

August 26th.—The Arabs sallied out this morning to attack Kazima, but refrained, because Mirambo asked for a day's grace, to eat the beef he had stolen from them. He has asked them impudently to come to-morrow morning, at which time he says he will give them plenty of fighting.

Kwihara is once more restored to a peaceful aspect, and fugitives no longer throng its narrow limits in fear and despair.

August 27th.—Mirambo retreated during the night; and when the Arabs went in force to attack his village of Kazima, they found it vacant.

The Arabs hold councils of war now-a-days—battle meetings, of which they seem to be very fond, but extremely slow to act upon. They were about to make friends with the northern Watuta, but Mirambo was ahead of them. They had talked of invading Mirambo's territory the second time, but Mirambo invaded Unyanyembe with fire and sword, bringing death to many a household, and he has slain the noblest of them all.

The Arabs spend their hours in talking and arguing, while the Ujiji and Karagwah roads are more firmly closed than ever. Indeed many of the influential Arabs are talking of returning to Zanzibar; saying, "Unyanyembe is ruined."

Meanwhile, with poor success, however, perceiving the impossibility of procuring Wanyamwezi pagazis, I am hiring the Wangwana renegades living in Unyanyembe to proceed with me to Ujiji, at treble prices. Each man is offered 30 doti, ordinary hire of a carrier being only from 5 to 10 doti to Ujiji. I want fifty men. I intend to leave about sixty or seventy loads here under charge of a guard. I shall leave all personal baggage behind, except one small portmanteau.

August 28th.—No news to-day of Mirambo. Shaw is getting strong again.

Sheikh bin Nasib called on me to-day, but, except on minor philosophy, he had nothing to say.

I have determined, after a study of the country, to

lead a flying caravan to Ujiji, by a southern road through northern Ukonongo and Ukawendi. Sheikh bin Nasib has been informed to-night of this determination.

August 29th.—Shaw got up to-day for a little work. Alas! all my fine-spun plans of proceeding by boat over the Victoria N'Yanza, thence down the Nile, have been totally demolished, I fear, through this war with Mirambo —this black Bonaparte. Two months have been wasted here already. The Arabs take such a long time to come to a conclusion. Advice is plentiful, and words are as numerous as the blades of grass in our valley; all that is wanting is decision. The Arabs' hope and stay is dead—Khamis bin Abdullah is no more. Where are the other warriors of whom the Wangwana and Wanyamwezi bards sing? Where is mighty Kisesa—great Abdullah bin Nasib? Where is Sayd, the son of Majid? Kisesa is in Zanzibar, and Sayd, the son of Majid, is in Ujiji, as yet ignorant that his son has fallen in the forest of Wilyankuru.

Shaw is improving fast. I am unsuccessful as yet in procuring soldiers. I almost despair of ever being able to move from here. It is such a drowsy, sleepy, slow, dreaming country. Arabs, Wangwana, Wanyamwezi, are all alike—all careless how time flies. Their to-morrow means sometimes within a month. To me it is simply maddening.

August 30th.—Shaw will not work. I cannot get him to stir himself. I have petted him and coaxed him; I have even cooked little luxuries for him myself. And, while I am straining every nerve to get ready for Ujiji, Shaw is satisfied with looking on listlessly. What a change from the ready-handed bold man he was at Zanzibar!

I sat down by his side to-day with my palm and needle in order to encourage him, and to-day, for the first time,

I told him of the real nature of my mission. I told him that I did not care about the geography of the country half as much as I cared about FINDING LIVINGSTONE! I told him, for the first time, "Now, my dear Shaw, you think probably that I have been sent here to find the depth of the Tanganika. Not a bit of it, man; I was told to find Livingstone. It is to find Livingstone I am here. It is to find Livingstone I am going. Don't you see, old fellow, the importance of the mission; don't you see what reward you will get from Mr. Bennett, if you will help me? I am sure, if ever you come to New York, you will never be in want of a fifty-dollar bill. So shake yourself; jump about; look lively. Say you will not die; that is half the battle. Snap your fingers at the fever. I will guarantee the fever won't kill you. I have medicine enough for a regiment here!"

His eyes lit up a little, but the light that shone in them shortly faded, and died. I was quite disheartened. I made some strong punch, to put fire in his veins, that I might see life in him. I put sugar, and eggs, and seasoned it with lemon and spice. "Drink, Shaw," said I, " and forget your infirmities. You are not sick, dear fellow; it is only *ennui* you are feeling. Look at Selim there. Now, I will bet any amount, that he will not die; that I will carry him home safe to his friends! I will carry you home also, if you will let me!"

September 1st.—According to Thani bin Abdullah whom I visited to-day, at his tembe in Maroro, Mirambo lost two hundred men in the attack upon Tabora, while the Arabs' losses were, five Arabs, thirteen freemen and eight slaves, besides three tembes, and over one hundred small huts burned, two hundred and eighty ivory tusks, and sixty cows and bullocks captured.

September 3rd.—Received a packet of letters and news-papers from Capt. Webb, at Zanzibar. What a good thing it is that one's friends, even in far America, think of the absent one in Africa! They tell me, that no one dreams of my being in Africa yet!

I applied to Sheikh bin Nasib to-day to permit Livingstone's caravan to go under my charge to Ujiji, but he would not listen to it. He says he feels certain I am going to my death.

September 4th.—Shaw is quite well to-day, he says. Selim is down with the fever. My force is gradually increasing, though some of my old soldiers are falling off. Umgareza is blind; Baruti has the small-pox very badly; Sadala has the intermittent.

September 5th.—Baruti died this morning. He was one of my best soldiers; and was one of those men who accompanied Speke to Egypt. Baruti is number seven of those who have died since leaving Zanzibar.

To-day my ears have been poisoned with the reports of the Arabs, about the state of the country I am about to travel through. "The roads are bad; they are all stopped; the Ruga-Ruga are out in the forests; the Wakonongo are coming from the south to help Mirambo; the Washensi are at war, one tribe against another." My men are getting dispirited, they have imbibed the fears of the Arabs and the Wanyamwezi. Bombay begins to feel that I had better go back to the coast, and try again some other time.

We buried Baruti under the shade of the banyan-tree, a few yards west of my tembe. The grave was made four and a half feet deep and three feet wide. At the bottom on one side a narrow trench was excavated, into which the body was rolled on his side, with his face turned towards Mecca. The body was dressed in a doti and a half of new American sheeting. After it was placed properly in its narrow bed, a sloping roof of sticks, covered over with matting and old canvas, was made, to prevent the earth from falling over the body. The grave was then filled, the soldiers laughing merrily. On the top of the grave was planted a small shrub, and into a small hole made with the hand, was poured water lest he might feel thirsty—they said—on his way to Paradise; water was then sprinkled all over the grave, and the gourd broken. This ceremony being ended, the men recited the Arabic Fat-hah, after which they left the grave of their dead comrade to think no more of him.

September 7th.—An Arab named Mohammed presented me to-day with a little boy-slave, called " Ndugu M'hali " (my brother's wealth). As I did not like the name, I called the chiefs of my caravan together, and asked them to give him a better name. One suggested " Simba " (a lion), another said he thought "Ngombe" (a cow) would suit the boy-child, another thought he ought to be called " Mirambo," which raised a loud laugh. Bombay thought "Bombay Mdogo" would suit my black-skinned infant very well. Ulimengo, however, after looking at his quick eyes, and noting his celerity of movement, pronounced the name Ka-lu-lu as the best for him, "because," said he, "just look at his eyes, so bright! look at his form, so slim! watch his movements, how quick! Yes, Kalulu is his name." "Yes, bana," said the others, " let it be Kalulu."

"Kalulu" is a Kisawahili term for the young of the blue-buck (*perpusilla*) antelope.

"Well, then," said I, water being brought in a huge tin pan, Selim, who was willing to stand godfather, holding him over the water, "let his name henceforth be Kalulu, and let no man take it from him," and thus it was that the little black boy of Mohammed's came to be called Kalulu.

The Expedition is increasing in numbers.

We had quite an alarm before dark. Much firing was heard at Tabora, which led us to anticipate an attack on Kwihara. It turned out, however, to be a salute fired in honor of the arrival of Sultan Kitambi to pay a visit to Mkasiwa, Sultan of Unyanyembe.

September 8th.—Towards night Sheikh bin Nasib received a letter from an Arab at Mfuto, reporting that an attack was made on that place by Mirambo and his Watuta allies. It also warned him to bid the people of Kwihara hold themselves in readiness, because if Mirambo succeeded in storming Mfuto, he would march direct on Kwihara.

September 9th.—Mirambo was defeated with severe loss yesterday, in his attack upon Mfuto. He was successful in an assault he made upon a small Wanyamwezi village, but when he attempted to storm Mfuto, he was repulsed with severe loss, losing three of his principal men. Upon withdrawing his forces from the attack, the inhabitants sallied out, and followed him to the forest of Umanda, where he was again utterly routed, himself ingloriously flying from the field.

The heads of his chief men slain in the attack were brought to Kwikuru, the boma of Mkasiwa.

September 14th.—The Arab boy Selim is delirious from constant fever. Shaw is sick again. These two occupy most of my time. I am turned into a regular nurse, for I have no one to assist me in attending upon them. If I try to instruct Abdul Kader in the art of being useful, his head is so befogged with the villainous fumes of Unyam-wezi tobacco, that he wanders bewildered about, breaking dishes, and upsetting cooked dainties, until I get so exasperated that my peace of mind is broken completely for a full hour. If I ask Ferajji, my now formally constituted cook, to assist, his thick wooden head fails to receive an idea, and I am thus obliged to play the part of *chef de cuisine.*

September 15*th.*—The third month of my residence in Unyanyembe is almost finished, and I am still here, but I hope to be gone before the 23rd inst.

All last night, until nine A.M. this morning, my soldiers danced and sang to the manes of their dead comrades, whose bones now bleach in the forests of Wilyankuru. Two or three huge pots of pombe failed to satisfy the raging thirst which the vigorous exercise they were engaged in, created. So, early this morning, I was called upon to contribute a shukka for another potful of the potent liquor.

To-day I was busy selecting the loads for each soldier and pagazi. In order to lighten their labor as much as possible, I reduced each load from 70lbs. to 50lbs., by which I hope to be enabled to make some long marches. I have been able to engage ten pagazis during the last two or three days.

I have two or three men still very sick, and it is almost useless to expect that they will be able to carry anything, but I am in hopes that other men may be engaged to take their places before the actual day of departure, which now seems to be drawing near rapidly.

September 16*th.*—We have almost finished our work— on the fifth day from this—God willing—we shall march. I engaged two more pagazis besides two guides, named Asmani and Mabruki. If vastness of the human form could terrify any one, certainly Asmani's appearance is well calculated to produce that effect. He stands considerably over six feet without shoes, and has shoulders broad enough for two ordinary men.

To-morrow I mean to give the people a farewell feast, to celebrate our departure from this forbidding and unhappy country.

September 17*th.*—The banquet is ended. I slaughtered two bullocks, and had a barbacue; three sheep, two goats, and fifteen chickens, 120lbs. of rice, twenty large loaves of bread made of Indian corn-flour, one hundred eggs, 10lbs. of butter, and five gallons of sweet-milk, were the contents of which the banquet was formed. The men invited their friends and neighbours, and about one hundred women and children partook of it.

After the banquet was ended, the pombe, or native beer, was brought in in five gallon pots, and the people commenced their dance, which continues even now as I write.

September 19*th.*—I had a slight attack of fever to-day, which has postponed our departure. Selim and Shaw are both recovered.

About 8 P.M. Sheik bin Nasib came to me imploring me not to go away to-morrow, because I was so sick. Thani Sakhburi suggested to me that I might stay another month. In answer, I told them that white men are not accustomed to break their words. I had said I would go, and I intended to go.

Sheikh bin Nasib gave up all hope of inducing me to remain another day, and he has gone away, with a promise to write to Seyd Burghash to tell him how obstinate I am, and that I am determined to be killed. This was a parting shot.

About 10 P.M. the fever had gone. All were asleep in the tembe but myself, and an unutterable loneliness came on me as I reflected on my position, and my intentions, and felt the utter lack of sympathy with me in all around. It requires more nerve than I possess, to dispel all the dark presentiments that come upon the mind. But probably what I call presentiments are simply the impress on the mind of the warnings which these false-hearted Arabs have repeated so often. This melancholy and loneliness I feel, may probably have their origin from the same cause. The single candle, which barely lights up the dark shade that fills the corners of my room, is but a poor incentive to cheerfulness. I feel as though I were imprisoned between stone walls. But why should I feel as if baited by these stupid, slow-witted Arabs and their warnings and croakings? I fancy a suspicion haunts my mind, as I write, that there lies some motive behind all this. I wonder if these Arabs tell me all these things to keep me here, in the hope that I might be induced another time to assist them in their war with Mirambo! If they think so, they are much mistaken, for I have taken a solemn, enduring oath, an oath to be kept while the least hope of life remains in me, not to be tempted to break the resolution I have formed, never to give up the search, until I find Livingstone alive, or find his dead body; and never to return home without the strongest possible proofs that he is alive, or that he is dead. No living man, or living men, shall stop me, only death can prevent me. But death—not even this; I shall not die, I will not die, I cannot die! And something tells me, I do not know what it is—perhaps it is the ever-living hopefulness of my own nature, perhaps it is the natural presumption born out of an abundant and glowing vitality, or the outcome of an overweening confidence in oneself—anyhow and everyhow, something tells me to-night I shall find him, and—write it larger—FIND HIM! FIND HIM! Even the words are inspiring. I feel more happy. Have I uttered a prayer? I shall sleep calmly to-night.

I have felt myself compelled to copy out of my Diary the above notes, as they explain, written as they are on the spot, the vicissitudes of my "Life at Unyanyembe." To me they appear to explain far better than any amount of descriptive writing, even of the most graphic, the nature of the life I led. There they are, unexaggerated, in their literality, precisely as I conceived them at the time they happened. They speak of fevers without number to myself and men, they relate our dangers, and little joys, our annoyances and our pleasures, as they occurred.

CHAPTER X.

TO MRERA, UKONONGO.

Departure from Unyanyembe.—The expedition reorganized.—Bombay.
—Mr. Shaw returns sick to Unyanyembe.—A noble forest.—The
fever described.—Happiness of the camp.—A park-land.—Herds of
game and noble sport.—A mutiny.—Punishment of the ringleaders.
Elephants.—Arrival at Mrera

The 20th of September had arrived. This was the day
I had decided to cut loose from those who tormented me
with their doubts, their fears, and beliefs, and commence
the march to Ujiji by a southern route. I was very
weak from the fever that had attacked me the day before,
and it was a most injudicious act to commence a march
under such circumstances. But I had boasted to Sheikh
bin Nasib that a white man never breaks his word, and
my reputation as a white man would have been ruined
had I stayed behind, or postponed the march, in consequence of feebleness.

I mustered the entire caravan outside the tembe, our
flags and streamers were unfurled, the men had their
loads resting on the walls, there was considerable shouting, and laughing, and negroidal fanfaronnade. The
Arabs had collected from curiosity's sake to see us off—
all except Sheikh bin Nasib, whom I had offended by my

asinine opposition to his wishes. The old Sheikh took to his bed, but sent his son to bear me a last morsel of philosophic sentimentality, which I was to treasure up as the last words of the patriarchal Sheikh, the son of Nasib, the son of Ali, the son of Sayf. Poor Sheikh! if thou hadst only known what was at the bottom of this stubbornness—this ass-like determination to proceed the wrong way—what wouldst thou then have said, O Sheikh? But the Sheikh comforted himself with the thought that I might know what I was about better than he did, which is most likely, only neither he nor any other Arab will ever know exactly the motive that induced me to march at all westward—when the road to the east was ever so much easier.

My braves whom I had enlisted for a rapid march somewhere, out of Unyanyembe, were named as follows :—

1. John William Shaw, London, England.
2. Selim Heshmy, Arab.
3. Seedy Mbarak Mombay, Zanzibar.
4. Mabruki Speke, ditto.
5. Ulimengo, ditto.
6. Ambari, ditto.
7. Uledi, ditto.
8. Asmani, ditto.
9. Sarmean, ditto.
10. Kamna, ditto.
11. Zaidi, ditto.
12. Khamisi, ditto.
13. Chowpereh, Bagamoyo
14. Kingaru, ditto.
15. Belali, ditto.
16. Ferous, Unyanyembe.
17. Rojab, Bagamoyo.
18. Mabruk Unyanyembe, Unyanyembe.
19. Mtamani, ditto.
20. Chanda, Maroro.
21. Sadala, Zanzibar.
22. Kombo, ditto.
23. Saburi the Great, Marorc.
24. Saburi the Little, ditto.
25. Marora, ditto.
26. Ferajji (the cook), Zanzibar.
27. Mabruk Saleem, Zanzibar.
28. Baraka, ditto.
29. Ibrahim, Maroro.
30. Mabruk Ferous, ditto.
31. Baruti, Bagamoyo.
32. Umgareza, Zanzibar.
33. Hamadi (the guide), ditto.
34. Asmani,   ditto   ditto.
35. Mabruk,   ditto   ditto.

36. Hamdallah (the guide), Tabora.
37. Jumah, Zanzibar.
38. Maganga, Mkwenkwe.
39. Muccadum, Tabora.
40. Dasturi, ditto.
41. Tumayona, Ujiji.
42. Mparamoto, Ujiji.
43. Wakiri, ditto.
44. Mufu, ditto.

45. Mpepo, ditto.
46. Kapingu, Ujiji.
47. Mashishanga, ditto.
48. Muheruka, ditto.
49. Missossi, ditto.
50. Tufum Byah, ditto.
51. Majwara (boy), Uganda.
52. Belali (boy), Uemba.
53. Kalulu (boy), Lunda.
54. Abdul Kader (tailor), Malabar.

These are the men and boys whom I had chosen to be my companions on the apparently useless mission of seeking for the lost traveller, David Livingstone. The goods with which I had burdened them, consisted of 1,000 doti, or 4,000 yds. of cloth, six bags of beads, four loads of ammunition, one tent, one bed and clothes, one box of medicine, sextant and books, two loads of tea, coffee, and sugar, one load of flour and candles, one load of canned meats, sardines, and miscellaneous necessaries, and one load of cooking utensils.

The men were all in their places except Bombay. Bombay had gone; he could not be found. I despatched a man to hunt him up. He was found weeping in the arms of his Delilah.

"Why did you go away, Bombay, when you knew I intended to go, and was waiting?"

"Oh, master, I was saying good-bye to my missis."

"Oh, indeed?"

"Yes, master; you no do it, when you go away?"

"Silence, sir."

"Oh! all right."

"What is the matter with you, Bombay?"

"Oh, nuffin."

As I saw he was in a humour to pick a quarrel with

me before those Arabs who had congregated outside of my tembe to witness my departure, and as I was not in a humour to be balked by anything that might turn up, the consequence was, that I was obliged to thrash Bombay, an operation which soon cooled his hot choler, but brought down on my head a loud chorus of remonstrances from my pretended Arab friends—"Now, master, don't, don't—stop it, master: the poor man knows better than you what he and you may expect on the road you are now taking."

If anything was better calculated to put me in a rage than Bombay's insolence before a crowd it was this gratuitous interference with what I considered my own especial business; but I restrained myself, though I told them, in a loud voice, that I did not choose to be interfered with, unless they wished to quarrel with me.

"No, no, bana," they all exclaimed; "we do not wish to quarrel with you. In the name of God! go on your way in peace."

"Fare you well, then," said I, shaking hands with them.

"Farewell, master, farewell. We wish you, we are sure, all success, and God be with you, and guide you!"

"March!"

A parting salute was fired; the flags were raised up by the guides, each pagazi rushed for his load, and in a short time, with songs and shouts, the head of the Expedition had filed round the western end of my tembe along the road to Ugunda.

"Now, Mr. Shaw, I am waiting, sir. Mount your donkey, if you cannot walk."

"Please, Mr. Stanley, I am afraid I cannot go."

"Why?"

" I don't know, I am sure. I feel very weak."

" So am I weak. It was but late last night, as you know, that the fever left me. Don't back out before these Arabs; remember you are a white man. Here, Selim, Mabruki, Bombay, help Mr. Shaw on his donkey, and walk by him."

" Oh, bana, bana," said the Arabs, " don't take him. Do you not see he is sick?"

" You keep away; nothing will prevent me from taking him. He shall go."

" Go on, Bombay."

The last of my party had gone. The tembe, so lately a busy scene, had already assumed a naked, desolate appearance. I turned towards the Arabs, lifted my hat, and said again, "Farewell," then faced about for the south, followed by my four young gun-bearers, Selim, Kalulu, Majwara, and Belali.

After half an hour's march the scenery became more animated. Shaw began to be amused. Bombay had forgotten our quarrel, and assured me, if I could pass Mirambo's country, I should " catch the Tanganika; " Mabruki Burton also believed we should. Selim was glad to leave Unyanyembe, where he had suffered so much from fever; and there was a something in the bold aspect of the hills which cropped upward above fair valleys, that enlivened and encouraged me to proceed.

In an hour and a half, we arrived at our camp in the Kinyamwezi village of Mkwenkwe, the birthplace of our famous chanter Maganga.

My tent was pitched, the goods were stored in one of the tembes; but one-half the men had returned to Kwihara, to take one more embrace of their wives and concubines.

Towards night I was attacked once again with the intermittent fever. Before morning it had departed, leaving me terribly prostrated with weakness. I had heard the men conversing with each other over their camp-fires upon the probable prospects of the next day. It was a question with them whether I should continue the march. Mostly all were of opinion that, since the master was sick, there would be no march. A superlative obstinacy, however, impelled me on, merely to spite their supine souls; but when I sallied out of my tent to call them to get ready, I found that at least twenty were missing; and Livingstone's letter-carrier, "Kaif-Halek" —or, How-do-ye-do?—had not arrived with Dr. Livingstone's letter-bag.

Selecting twenty of the strongest and faithfulest men I despatched them back to Unyanyembe in search of the missing men; and Selim was sent to Sheikh bin Nasib to borrow, or buy, a long slave-chain.

Towards night my twenty detectives returned with nine of the missing men. The Wajiji had deserted in a body, and they could not be found. Selim also returned with a strong chain, capable of imprisoning within the collars attached to it at least ten men. Kaif-Halek also appeared with the letter-bag which he was to convey to Livingstone under my escort. The men were then addressed, and the slave-chain exhibited to them. I told them that I was the first white man who had taken a slave-chain with him on his travels; but, as they were all so frightened of accompanying me, I was obliged to make use of it, as it was the only means of keeping them together. The good need never fear being chained by me —only the deserters, the thieves, who received their hire and presents, guns and ammunition, and then ran away.

I would not put any one this time in chains; but whoever
deserted after this day, I should halt, and not continue the
march till I found him, after which he should march to
Ujiji with the slave-chain round his neck. "Do you
hear?"—"Yes," was the answer. "Do you understand?"
—"Yes."

We broke up camp at 6 P.M., and took the road for
Inesuka, at which place we arrived at 8 P.M.

When we were about commencing the march the next
morning, it was discovered that two more had deserted.
Baraka and Bombay were at once despatched to Unyanyembe to bring back the two missing men—Asmani and
Kingaru—with orders not to return without them. This
was the third time that the latter had deserted, as the
reader may remember. While the pursuit was being
effected we halted at the village of Inesuka, more for the
sake of Shaw than any one else.

In the evening the incorrigible deserters were brought
back, and, as I had threatened, were well flogged and
chained, to secure them against further temptation. Bombay and Baraka had a picturesque story to relate of the
capture; and, as I was in an exceedingly good humor,
their services were rewarded with a fine cloth each.

On the following morning another carrier had absconded,
taking with him his hire of fifteen new cloths and a gun;
but to halt anywhere near Unyanyembe any longer was a
danger that could be avoided only by travelling without
stoppages towards the southern jungle-lands. It will be
remembered I had in my train the redoubtable Abdul
Kader, the tailor, he who had started from Bagamoyo with
such bright anticipations of the wealth of ivory to be obtained in the great interior of Africa. On this morning,
daunted by the reports of the dangers ahead, Abdul

Kader craved to be discharged. He vowed he was sick, and unable to proceed any further. As I was pretty well tired of him, I paid him off in cloth, and permitted him to go.

About half way to Kasegera Mabruk Saleem was suddenly taken sick. I treated him with a grain of calomel, and a couple of ounces of brandy. As he was unable to walk, I furnished him with a donkey. Another man named Zaidi was ill with a rheumatic fever; and Shaw tumbled twice off the animal he was riding, and required an infinite amount of coaxing to mount again. Verily, my expedition was pursued by adverse fortunes, and it seemed as if the Fates had determined upon our return. It really appeared as if everything was going to wreck and ruin. If I were only fifteen days from Unyanyembe, thought I, I should be saved!

Kasegera was a scene of rejoicing the afternoon and evening of our arrival. Absentees had just returned from the coast, and the youths were brave in their gaudy bedizenment, their new barsatis, their soharis, and long cloths of bright new kaniki, with which they had adorned themselves behind some bush before they had suddenly appeared dressed in all this finery. The women " Hi-hi'ed " like mænads, and the " Lu-lu-lu'ing " was loud, frequent, and fervent the whole of that afternoon. Sylph-like damsels looked up to the youthful heroes with intensest admiration on their features; old women coddled and fondled them; staff-using, stooping-backed patriarchs blessed them. This is fame in Unyamwezi! All the fortunate youths had to use their tongues until the wee hours of next morning had arrived, relating all the wonders they had seen near the Great Sea, and in the

"Unguja," the island of Zanzibar; of how they saw great white men's ships, and numbers of white men, of their perils and trials during their journey through the land of the fierce Wagogo, and divers other facts, with which the reader and I are by this time well acquainted.

On the 24th we struck camp, and marched through a forest of imbiti wood in a S.S.W. direction, and in about three hours came to Kigandu.

On arriving before this village, which is governed by a daughter of Mkasiwa, we were informed we could not enter unless we paid toll. As we would not pay toll, we were compelled to camp in a ruined, rat-infested boma, situated a mile to the left of Kigandu, being well scolded by the cowardly natives for deserting Mkasiwa in his hour of extremity. We were accused of running away from the war.

Almost on the threshold of our camp Shaw, in endeavouring to dismount, lost his stirrups, and fell prone on his face. The foolish fellow actually laid on the ground in the hot sun a full hour; and when I coldly asked him if he did not feel rather uncomfortable, he sat up, and wept like a child.

"Do you wish to go back, Mr. Shaw?"

"If you please. I do not believe I can go any farther; and if you would only be kind enough, I should like to return very much."

"Well, Mr. Shaw, I have come to the conclusion that it is best you should return. My patience is worn out. I have endeavoured faithfully to lift you above these petty miseries which you nourish so devotedly. You are simply suffering from hypochondria. You imagine yourself sick, and nothing, evidently, will persuade you that you are

not. Mark my words—to return to Unyanyembe, is to
DIE! Should you happen to fall sick in Kwihara who
knows how to administer medicine to you? Supposing you
are delirious, how can any of the soldiers know what you
want, or what is beneficial and necessary for you? Once
again, I repeat, if you return, you DIE!"

"Ah, dear me; I wish I had never ventured to come!
I thought life in Africa was so different from this. I
would rather go back if you will permit me."

The next day was a halt, and arrangements were made
for the transportation of Shaw back to Kwihara. A strong
litter was made, and four stout pagazis were hired at
Kigandu to carry him. Bread was baked, a canteen was
filled with cold tea, and a leg of a kid was roasted for his
sustenance while on the road.

The night before we parted we spent together. Shaw
played some tunes on an accordion which I had purchased
for him at Zanzibar; but, though it was only a miserable
ten-dollar affair, I thought the homely tunes evoked from
the instrument that night were divine melodies. The last
tune played before retiring was " Home, sweet Home."

The morning of the 27th we were all up early. There
was considerable vis in our movements. A long, long
march lay before us that day; but then I was to leave
behind all the sick and ailing. Only those who were
healthy, and could march fast and long, were to accompany
me. Mabruk Saleem I left in charge of a native doctor,
who was to medicate him for a gift of cloth which I gave
him in advance.

The horn sounded to get ready. Shaw was lifted in
his litter on the shoulders of his carriers. My men formed
two ranks; the flags were lifted; and between these two

living rows, and under those bright streamers, which were to float over the waters of the Tanganika before he should see them again, Shaw was borne away towards the north; while we filed off to the south, with quicker and more elastic steps, as if we felt an incubus had been taken from us.

We ascended a ridge bristling with syenite boulders of massive size, appearing above a forest of dwarf trees. The view which we saw was similar to that we had often seen elsewhere. An illimitable forest stretching in grand waves far beyond the ken of vision—ridges, forest-clad, rising gently one above another until they receded in the dim purple-blue distance — with a warm haze floating above them, which, though clear enough in our neighbourhood, became impenetrably blue in the far distance. Woods, woods, woods, leafy branches, foliage globes, or parachutes, green, brown, or sere in color, forests one above another, rising, falling, and receding—a very leafy ocean. The horizon, at all points, presents the same view, there may be an indistinct outline of a hill far away, or here and there a tall tree higher than the rest conspicuous in its outlines against the translucent sky—with this exception it is the same—the same clear sky dropping into the depths of the forest, the same outlines, the same forest, the same horizon, day after day, week after week; we hurry to the summit of a ridge, expectant of a change, but the wearied eyes, after wandering over the vast expanse, return to the immediate surroundings, satiated with the ever-sameness of such scenes. Carlyle, somewhere in his writings, says, that though the Vatican is great, it is but the chip of an eggshell compared to the star-fretted dome where Arcturus and Orion glance for ever ; and I say that, though the

grove of Central Park, New York, is grand compared to
the thin groves seen in other great cities, that though the
Windsor and the New Forests may be very fine and noble
in England, yet they are but fagots of sticks compared
to these eternal forests of Unyamwezi.

We marched three hours, and then halted for refresh-
ments. I perceived that the people were very tired, not
yet inured to a series of long marches, or rather, not in
proper trim for earnest, hard work after our long rest in
Kwihara. When we resumed our march again there
were several manifestations of bad temper and weariness,
But a few good-natured remarks about their laziness put
them on their mettle, and we reached Ugunda at 2 p.m.
after another four hours' spurt.

Ugunda is a very large village in the district of
Ugunda, which adjoins the southern frontier of Unyanyembe. The village probably numbers four hundred
families, or two thousand souls. It is well protected by
a tall and strong palisade of three-inch timber. Stages
have been erected at intervals above the palisades with
miniature embrasures in the timber, for the muskets of
the sharpshooters, who take refuge within these box-
like stages to pick out the chiefs of an attacking force.
An inner ditch, with the sand or soil thrown up three
or four feet high against the palings, serves as protection
for the main body of the defenders, who kneel in the
ditch, and are thus enabled to withstand a very large
force. For a mile or two outside the village all obstructions are cleared, and the besieged are thus warned by
sharp-eyed watchers to be prepared for the defence
before the enemy approaches within musket range.
Mirambo withdrew his force of robbers from before this

strongly-defended village after two or three ineffectual attempts to storm it, and the Wagunda have been congratulating themselves ever since, upon having driven away the boldest marauder that Unyamwezi has seen for generations.

The Wagunda have about three thousand acres under cultivation around their principal village, and this area suffices to produce sufficient grain not only for their own consumption, but also for the many caravans which pass by this way for Ufipa and Marungu.

However brave the Wagunda may be within the strong enclosure with which they have surrounded their principal village, they are not exempt from the feeling of insecurity which fills the soul of a Mnyamwezi during war-time. At this place the caravans are accustomed to recruit their numbers from the swarms of pagazis who volunteer to accompany them to the distant ivory regions south; but I could not induce a soul to follow me, so great was their fear of Mirambo and his Ruga-Ruga. They were also full of rumors of wars ahead. It was asserted that Mbogo was advancing towards Ugunda with a thousand Wakonongo, that the Wazavira had attacked a caravan four months previously, that Simba was scouring the country with a band of ferocious mercenaries, and much more of the same nature and to the same intent.

On the 28th we arrived at a small snug village embosomed within the forest called Benta, three hours and a quarter from Ugunda. The road led through the cornfields of the Wagunda, and then entered the clearings around the villages of Kisari, within one of which we found the proprietor of a caravan who was drumming up carriers for Ufipa. He had been halted here two

months, and he made strenuous exertions to induce my
men to join his caravan, a proceeding that did not tend
to promote harmony between us. A few days afterwards
I found, on my return, that he had given up the idea of
proceeding south. Leaving Kisari, we marched through
a thin jungle of black jack, over sun-cracked ground
with here and there a dried-up pool, the bottom of which
was well tramped by elephant and rhinoceros. Buffalo
and zebra tracks were now frequent, and we were buoyed
up with the hope that before long we should meet
game.

Benta was well supplied with Indian corn and a grain
which the natives called choroko, which I take to be
vetches. I purchased a large supply of choroko for my
own personal use, as I found it to be a most healthy
food. The corn was stored on the flat roofs of the tembes
in huge boxes made out of the bark of the mtundu-tree.
The largest box I have ever seen in Africa was seen here.
It might be taken for a Titan's hat-box; it was seven
feet in diameter, and ten feet in height.

On the 29th, after travelling in a S.W. by S. direction,
we reached Kikuru. The march lasted for five hours
over sun-cracked plains, growing the black jack, and
ebony, and dwarf shrubs, above which numerous ant-hills
of light chalky-coloured earth appeared like sand dunes.

The mukunguru, a Kisawahili term for fever, is frequent in this region of extensive forests and flat plains,
owing to the imperfect drainage provided by nature for
them. In the dry season there is nothing very offensive
in the view of the country. The burnt grass gives rather
a sombre aspect to the country, covered with the hard-
baked tracks of animals which haunt these plains during
the latter part of the rainy season. In the forest

numbers of trees lie about in the last stages of decay,
and working away with might and main on the prostrate trunks may be seen numberless insects of various
species. Impalpably, however, the poison of the dead
and decaying vegetation is inhaled into the system with
a result sometimes as fatal as that which is said to arise
from the vicinity of the Upas-tree.

The first evil results experienced from the presence
of malaria are confined bowels and an oppressive languor,
excessive drowsiness, and a constant disposition to yawn.
The tongue assumes a yellowish, sickly hue, colored
almost to blackness; even the teeth become yellow, and
are coated with an offensive matter. The eyes of the
patient sparkle lustrously, and become suffused with
water. These are sure symptoms of the incipient fever
which shortly will rage through the system.

Sometimes this fever is preceded by a violent shaking
fit, during which period blankets may be heaped on the
patient's form, with but little amelioration of the deadly
chill he feels. It is then succeeded by an unusuall,
severe headache, with excessive pains about the loins
and spinal column, which presently will spread over the
shoulder-blades, and, running up the neck, find a final
lodgment in the back and front of the head. Usually,
however, the fever is not preceded by a chill, but after
languor and torpitude have seized him, with excessive
heat and throbbing temples, the loin and spinal column
ache, and raging thirst soon possesses him. The brain
becomes crowded with strange fancies, which sometimes
assume most hideous shapes. Before the darkened vision
of the suffering man, float in a seething atmosphere,
figures of created and uncreated reptiles, which are
metamorphosed every instant into stranger shapes and

designs, growing every moment more confused, more complicated, more hideous and terrible. Unable to bear longer the distracting scene, he makes an effort and opens his eyes, and dissolves the delirious dream, only, however, to glide again unconsciously into another dream-land where another unreal inferno is dioramically revealed, and new agonies suffered. Oh! the many many hours that I have groaned under the terrible incubi which the fits of real delirium evoke. Oh! the racking anguish of body that a traveller in Africa must undergo! Oh! the spite, the fretfulness, the vexation which the horrible phantasmagoria of diabolisms induce! The utmost patience fails to appease, the most industrious attendance fails to gratify, the deepest humility displeases. During these terrible transitions, which induce fierce distraction, Job himself would become irritable, insanely furious, and choleric. A man in such a state regards himself as the focus of all miseries. When recovered, he feels chastened, becomes urbane and ludicrously amiable, he conjures up fictitious delights from all things which, but yesterday, possessed for him such awful portentous aspects. His men he regards with love and friendship; whatever is trite he views with ecstasy. Nature appears charming; in the dead woods and monotonous forest his mind becomes overwhelmed with delight. I speak for myself, as a careful analysation of the attack, in all its severe, plaintive, and silly phases, appeared to me. I used to amuse myself with taking notes of the humorous and the terrible, the fantastic and exaggerated pictures that were presented to me—even while suffering the paroxysms induced by fever.

We arrived at a large pool, known as the Ziwani, after a four hours' march in a S.S.W. direction, the 1st of October. We discovered an old half-burnt khambi, sheltered by a magnificent mkuyu (sycamore), the giant of the forests of Unyamwezi, which after an hour we transformed into a splendid camp.

If I recollect rightly, the stem of the tree measured thirty-eight feet in circumference. It is the finest tree of its kind I have seen in Africa. A regiment might

GIGANTIC SYCAMORE, AND CAMP BENEATH IT.

with perfect ease have reposed under this enormous dome of foliage during a noon halt. The diameter of the shadow it cast on the ground was one hundred and twenty feet. The healthful vigor that I was enjoying about this time enabled me to regard my surroundings admiringly. A feeling of comfort and perfect content-

ment took possession of me, such as I knew not while
fretting at Unyanyembe, wearing my life away in
inactivity. I talked with my people as to my friends
and equals. We argued with each other about our
prospects in quite a companionable, sociable vein.

When daylight was dying, and the sun was sinking
down rapidly over the western horizon, vividly paint-
ing the sky with the colors of gold and silver, saffron,
and opal, when its rays and gorgeous tints were reflected
upon the tops of the everlasting forest, with the quiet
and holy calm of heaven resting upon all around, and
infusing even into the untutored minds of those about me
the exquisite enjoyments of such a life as we were now
leading in the depths of a great expanse of forest, the
only and sole human occupants of it—this was the time,
after our day's work was ended, and the camp was in a
state of perfect security, when we all would produce our
pipes, and could best enjoy the labors which we had
performed, and the contentment which follows a work
well done.

Outside nothing is heard beyond the cry of a stray
florican, or guinea-fowl, which has lost her mate, or the
hoarse croaking of the frogs in the pool hard by, or the
song of the crickets which seems to lull the day to rest;
inside our camp are heard the gurgles of the gourd pipes
as the men inhale the blue ether, which I also love. I
am contented and happy, stretched on my carpet under
the dome of living foliage, smoking my short meerschaum,
indulging in thoughts—despite the beauty of the still
grey light of the sky, and of the air of serenity which
prevails around—of home and friends in distant America,
and these thoughts soon change to my work—yet in-
complete to the man who to me is yet a myth, who, for

all I knew, may be dead, or may be near or far from me tramping through just such a forest, whose tops I see bound the view outside my camp. We are both on the same soil, perhaps in the same forest—who knows?—yet is he to me so far removed that he might as well be in his own little cottage of Ulva. Though I am even now ignorant of his very existence, yet I feel a certain complacency, a certain satisfaction which would be difficult to describe. Why is man so feeble, and weak, that he must tramp, tramp hundreds of miles to satisfy the doubts his impatient and uncurbed mind feels? Why cannot my form accompany the bold flights of my mind and satisfy the craving I feel to resolve the vexed question that ever rises to my lips—"Is he alive?" O soul of mine, be patient, thou hast a felicitous tranquillity, which other men might envy thee! Sufficient for the hour is the consciousness thou hast that thy mission is a holy one! Onward, and be hopeful!

Monday, the 2nd of October, found us traversing the forest and plain that extends from the Ziwani to Manyara, which occupied us six and a half hours. The sun was intensely hot; but the mtundu and miombo trees grew at intervals, just enough to admit free growth to each tree, while the blended foliage formed a grateful shade. The path was clear and easy, the tamped and firm red soil offered no obstructions. The only provocation we suffered was from the attacks of the tsetse, or panga (sword) fly, which swarmed here. We knew we were approaching an extensive habitat of game, and we were constantly on the alert for any specimens that might be inhabiting these forests.

While we were striding onward, at the rate of nearly three miles an hour, the caravan I perceived sheered off from the road, resuming it about fifty yards ahead of something on the road, to which the attention of the men was directed. On coming up, I found the object to be the dead body of a man, who had fallen a victim to that fearful scourge of Africa, the small-pox. He was one of Oseto's gang of marauders, or guerillas, in the service of Mkasiwa of Unyanyembe, who were hunting these forests for the guerillas of Mirambo. They had been returning from Ukonongo from a raid they had instituted against the Sultan of Mbogo, and they had left their comrade to perish in the road. He had apparently been only one day dead.

Apropos of this, it was a frequent thing with us to discover a skeleton or a skull on the roadside. Almost every day we saw one, sometimes two, of these relics of dead, and forgotten humanity.

Shortly after this we emerged from the forest, and entered a mbuga, or plain, in which we saw a couple of giraffes, whose long necks were seen towering above a bush they had been nibbling at. This sight was greeted with a shout; for we now knew we had entered the game country, and that near the Gombe creek, or river, where we intended to halt, we should see plenty of these animals.

A walk of three hours over this hot plain brought us to the cultivated fields of Manyara. Arriving before the village-gate, we were forbidden to enter, as the country was throughout in a state of war, and it behoved them to be very careful of admitting any party, lest the villagers might be compromised. We were, however, directed to a khambi to the right of the village, near some pools of clear water, where we discovered some half dozen ruined huts, which looked very uncomfortable to tired people.

After we had built our camp, the kirangozi was furnished with some cloths to purchase food from the village for the transit of a wilderness in front of us, which was said to extend nine marches, or 135 miles. He was informed that the Mtemi had strictly prohibited his people from selling any grain whatever.

This evidently was a case wherein the exercise of a little diplomacy could only be effective; because it would detain us several days here, if we were compelled to send men back to Kikuru for provisions. Opening a bale of choice goods, I selected two royal cloths, and told Bombay to carry them to him, with the compliments and friendship of the white man. The Sultan sulkily refused them, and bade him return to the white man and tell him not to bother him. Entreaties were of no avail, he would not relent; and the men, in exceedingly bad temper, and hungry, were obliged to go to bed supperless. The words of Njara, a slave-trader, and parasite of the great Sheikh bin Nasib, recurred to me. "Ah, master, master, you will find the people will be too much for you, and that you will have to return. The Wa-manyara are bad, the Wakonongo are very bad, the Wazavira are the worst of all. You have come to this country at a bad time. It is war everywhere." And, indeed, judging from the tenor of the conversations around our camp-fires, it seemed but too evident. There was every prospect of a general decamp of all my people. However, I told them not to be discouraged; that I would get food for them in the morning.

The bale of choice cloths was opened again next morning, and four royal cloths were this time selected, and two dotis of Merikani, and Bombay was again despatched, burdened with compliments, and polite words.

It was necessary to be very politic with a man who was so surly, and too powerful to make an enemy of. What if he made up his mind to imitate the redoubtable Mirambo, King of Uyoweh! The effect of my munificent liberality was soon seen in the abundance of provender which came to my camp. Before an hour went by, there came boxes full of choroko, beans, rice, matama or dourra, and Indian corn, carried on the heads of a dozen villagers, and shortly after the Mtemi himself came, followed by about thirty musketeers and twenty spearmen, to visit the first white man ever seen on this road. Behind these warriors came a liberal gift, fully equal in value to that sent to him, of several large gourds of honey, fowls, goats, and enough vetches and beans to supply my men with four days' food.

I met the chief at the gate of my camp, and bowing profoundly, invited him to my tent, which I had arranged as well as my circumstances would permit, for this reception. My Persian carpet and bear skin were spread out, and a broad piece of bran-new crimson cloth covered my kitanda, or bedstead.

The chief, a tall robust man, and his chieftains, were invited to seat themselves. They cast a look of such gratified surprise at myself, at my face, my clothes, and guns, as is almost impossible to describe. They looked at me intently for a few seconds, and then at each other, which ended in an uncontrollable burst of laughter, and repeated snappings of the fingers. They spoke the Kinyamwezi language, and my interpreter Maganga was requested to inform the chief of the great delight I felt in seeing them. After a short period expended in interchanging compliments, and a competitive excellence at laughing at one another, their chief desired me to show him my guns. The "sixteen-shooter," the Winchester rifle, elicited a thousand flattering observations from the excited man; and the tiny deadly revolvers, whose beauty and workmanship they thought were superhuman, evoked such gratified eloquence that I was fain to try something else. The double-barrelled guns fired with heavy charges of power, caused them to jump up in affected alarm, and then to subside into their seats convulsed with laughter. As the enthusiasm of my guests increased, they seized each other's index fingers, screwed them, and pulled at them until I feared they would end in their dislocation. After having explained to them the difference between white men and Arabs, I pulled out my medicine chest, which evoked another burst of rapturous sighs at the cunning neatness of the array of vials. He asked what they meant.

"Dowa," I replied sententiously, a word which may be interpreted—medicine.

"Oh-h, oh-h," they murmured admiringly. I succeeded, before long, in winning unqualified admiration, and my superiority, compared to the best of the Arabs they had seen, was but too evident. "Dowa, dowa," they added.

"Here," said I, uncorking a vial of medicinal brandy, "is the Kisungu pombe" (white man's beer); "take a spoonful and try it," at the same time handing it.

"Hacht, hacht, oh, hacht,! what! eh! what strong beer the white men have! Oh, how my throat burns!"

"Ah, but it is good," said I, "a little of it makes men feel strong, and good; but too much of it makes men bad, and they die."

"Let me have some," said one of the chiefs; "and me," "and me," "and me," as soon as each had tasted.

"I next produced a bottle of concentrated ammonia, which as I explained was for snake bites, and head-aches; the Sultan immediately complained he had a head-ache, and must have a little. Telling him to close his eyes, I suddenly uncorked the bottle, and presented it to His Majesty's nose. The effect was magical, for he fell back as if shot, and such contortions as his features underwent are indescribable. His chiefs roared with laughter, and clapped their hands, pinched each other, snapped their fingers, and committed many other ludicrous things. I verily believe if such a scene were presented on any stage in the world the effect of it would be visible instantaneously on the audience; that had they seen it as I saw it, they would have laughed themselves to hysteria and madness. Finally the Sultan recovered himself, great tears rolling down his cheeks, and his features quivering with laughter, then he slowly uttered the word "kali,"—hot, strong, quick, or ardent medicine. He required no more, but the other chiefs pushed forward to get one wee sniff, which they no sooner had, than all went into paroxysms of uncontrollable laughter. The entire morning was passed in this state visit, to the mutual satisfaction of all concerned. "Oh," said the Sultan at parting, "these white men know everything, the Arabs are dirt compared to them!"

That night Hamdallah, one of the guides, deserted, carrying with him his hire (27 doti), and a gun. It was useless to follow him in the morning, as it would have detained me many more days than I could afford; but I mentally vowed that Mr. Hamdallah should work out those 27 doti of cloths before I reached the coast.

Wednesday, October 4th, saw us travelling to the Gombe River, which is 4 h. 15 m. march from Manyara.

We had barely left the waving cornfields of my friend Ma-manyara before we came in sight of a herd of noble zebra; two hours afterwards we had entered a grand and noble expanse of park land, whose glorious magnificence and vastness of prospect, with a far-stretching carpet or verdure darkly flecked here and there by miniature clumps of jungle, with spreading trees growing here and there, was certainly one of the finest scenes to be seen in Africa. Added to which, as I surmounted one of the numerous small knolls, I saw herds after herds of buffalo and zebra, giraffe and antelope, which sent the blood coursing through my veins in the excitement of the moment, as when I first landed on African soil. We crept along the plain noiselessly to our camp on the banks of the sluggish waters of the Gombe.

Here at last was the hunter's Paradise! How petty and insignificant appeared my hunts after small antelope and wild boar, what a foolish waste of energies those long walks through damp grasses and through thorny jungles! Did I not well remember my first bitter experience in African jungles when in the maritime region! But this —where is the nobleman's park that can match this scene? Here is a soft, velvety expanse of young grass, grateful shade under those spreading clumps; herds of large and varied game browsing within easy rifle range. Surely I must feel amply compensated now for the long southern détour I have made, when such a prospect as this opens to the view! No thorny jungles and rank smelling swamps are here to daunt the hunter, and to sicken his aspirations after true sport! No hunter could aspire after a nobler field to display his prowess.

Having settled the position of the camp, which over-looked one of the pools found in the depression of the

Gombe creek, I took my double-barrelled smooth-bore, and sauntered off to the park-land. Emerging from behind a clump, three fine plump spring-bok were seen browsing on the young grass just within one hundred yards. I knelt down and fired; one unfortunate antelope bounded upward instinctively, and fell dead. Its companions sprang high into the air, taking leaps about twelve feet in length, as if they were quadrupeds practising gymnastics, and away they vanished, rising up like India-rubber balls, until a knoll hid them from view. My success was hailed with loud shouts by the soldiers, who came running out from the camp as soon as they heard the reverberation of the gun, and my gun-bearer had his knife at the beast's throat, uttering a fervent " Bismillah !" as he almost severed the head from the body.

Hunters were now directed to proceed east and north to procure meat, because in each caravan it generally happens that there are fundi, whose special trade it is to hunt for meat for the camp. Some of these are experts in stalking, but often find themselves in dangerous positions, owing to the near approach necessary, before they can fire their most inaccurate weapons with any certainty.

After luncheon, consisting of spring-bok steak, hot corn-cake, and a cup of delicious Mocha coffee, I strolled towards the south-west, accompanied by Kalulu and Majwara, two boy gun-bearers. The tiny perpusilla started up like rabbits from me as I stole along through the underbrush; the honey-bird hopped from tree to tree chirping its call, as if it thought I was seeking the little sweet treasure, the hiding-place of which it only knew; but no! I neither desired perpusilla nor the honey. I was on the search for something great this day. Keen-eyed fish-eagles and bustards poised on trees above the sinuous Gombe thought, and probably with good reason, that I was after them; judging by the ready flight with which both species disappeared as they sighted my approach. Ah, no! nothing but hartebeest, zebra, giraffe, eland, and buffalo this day! After following the Gombe's course for about a mile, delighting my eyes with long looks at the broad and lenghty reaches of water to which I was so long a stranger, I came upon a scene which delighted the innermost recesses of my soul; five, six, seven, eight, ten zebras switching their beautiful striped bodies, and biting one another, within about one hundred and fifty yards. The scene was so pretty, so romantic, never did I so thoroughly realize that I was in Central Africa. I felt momentarily proud that I owned such a vast domain, inhabited with such noble beasts. Here I possessed, within reach of a leaden ball, any one I chose of the beautiful animals, the pride of the African forests! It was at my option to shoot any of them! Mine they were without money or without price; yet, knowing this, twice I dropped my rifle, loth to wound the royal beasts, but—crack! and a royal one was on his back battling the air with his legs. Ah, it was such a pity! but, hasten, draw the keen sharp-edged knife across the beautiful stripes which fold around the throat; and—what an ugly gash! it is done, and I have a superb animal at my feet. Hurrah! I shall taste of Ukonongo zebra to-night.

I thought a spring-bok and zebra enough for one day's sport, especially after a long march. The Gombe, a long stretch of deep water, winding in and out of green groves, calm, placid, with lotus leaves lightly resting on its surface, all pretty, picturesque, peaceful as a summer's dream, looked very inviting for a bath. I sought out the most shady spot under a wide-spreading mimosa, from which the ground sloped smooth as a lawn, to the still, clear water. I ventured to undress, and had already stepped in to my ancles in the water, and had brought my hands together for a glorious dive, when my attention was attracted by an enormously long body which shot into view, occupying the spot beneath the surface that I was about to explore by a " header." Great heavens, it was a crocodile ! I sprang backward instinctively, and this proved my salvation, for the monster turned away with the most disappointed look, and I was left to congratulate myself upon my narrow escape from his jaws, and to register a vow never to be tempted again by the treacherous calm of an African river.

As soon as I had dressed I turned away from the now repulsive aspect of the stream. In strolling through the jungle, towards my camp, I detected the forms of two natives looking sharply about them, and, after bidding my young attendants to preserve perfect quiet, I crept on towards them, and, by the aid of a thick clump of under-bush, managed to arrive within a few feet of the natives undetected. Their mere presence in the immense forest, unexplained, was a cause of uneasiness in the then disturbed state of the country, and my intention was to show myself suddenly to them, and note its effect, which, if it betokened anything hostile to the Expedition, could without difficulty be settled at once, with the aid of my double-barrelled smooth-bore.

As I arrived on one side of this bush, the two suspicious-looking natives arrived on the other side, and we were separated by only a few feet. I made a bound, and we were face to face. The natives cast a glance at the sudden figure of a white man, and seemed petrified for a

moment, but then, recovering themselves, they shrieked
out, "Bana, bana, you don't know us. We are Wakonongo,
who came to your camp to accompany you to Mrera, and
we are looking for honey."

"Oh, to be sure, you are the Wakonongo. Yes—Yes.
Ah, it is all right now, I thought you might be Ruga-Ruga."

So the two parties, instead of being on hostile terms
with each other, burst out laughing. The Wakonongo
enjoyed it very much, and laughed heartily as they
proceeded on their way to search for the wild honey.
On a piece of bark they carried a little fire with which
they smoked the bees out from their nest in the great
mtundu-trees.

The adventures of the day were over; the azure of the
sky had changed to a dead grey; the moon was appearing
just over the trees; the water of the Gombe was like a
silver belt; hoarse frogs bellowed their notes loudly by
the margin of the creek; the fish-eagles uttered their
dirge-like cries as they were perched high on the tallest
tree; elands snorted their warning to the herds in the
forest; stealthy forms of the carnivora stole through the
dark woods outside of our camp. Within the high inclosure of bush and thorn, which we had raised around
our camp, all was jollity, laughter, and radiant, genial
comfort. Around every camp-fire dark forms of men
were seen squatted: one man gnawed at a luscious bone;
another sucked the rich marrow in a zebra's leg-bone;
another turned the stick, garnished with huge kabobs, to
the bright blaze; another held a large rib over a flame;
there were others busy stirring industriously great black
potfuls of ugali, and watching anxiously the meat simmering, and the soup bubbling, while the fire-light flickered
and danced bravely, and cast a bright glow over the

naked forms of the men, and gave a crimson tinge to the tall tent that rose in the centre of the camp, like a temple sacred to some mysterious god; the fires cast their reflections upon the massive arms of the trees, as they branched over our camp, and, in the dark gloom of their foliage, the most fantastic shadows were visible. Altogether it was a wild, romantic, and impressive scene. But little recked my men for shadows and moonlight, for crimson tints, and temple-like tents—they were all busy relating their various experiences, and gorging themselves with the rich meats our guns had obtained for us. One was telling how he had stalked a wild boar, and the furious onset the wounded animal made on him, causing him to drop his gun, and climb a tree, and the terrible grunt of the beast he well remembered, and the whole welkin rang with the peals of laughter which his mimic powers evoked. Another had shot a buffalo-calf, and another had bagged a hartebeest; the Wakonongo related their laughable rencontre with me in the woods, and were lavish in their description of the stores of honey to be found in the woods; and all this time Selim and his youthful subs were trying their sharp teeth on the meat of a young pig which one of the hunters had shot, but which nobody else would eat, because of the Mohammedan aversion to pig, which they had acquired during their transformation from negro savagery to the useful docility of the Zanzibar freed-man.

We halted the two following days, and made frequent raids on the herds of this fine country. The first day I was fairly successful again in the sport. I bagged a couple of antelopes, a kudu (*A. strepsiceros*) with fine twisting horns, and a pallah-buck (*A. melampus*), a reddish-brown animal, standing about three and a half feet, with broad posteriors. I might have succeeded in getting dozens of animals had I any of those accurate, heavy rifles manufactured by Lancaster, Reilly, or Blissett, whose every shot tells. But my weapons, save my light smooth-bore, were unfit for African game. My weapons were more for men. With the Winchester rifle, and the Starr's carbine, I was able to hit anything within two hundred yards, but the animals, though wounded, invariably managed to escape the knife, until I was disgusted with the pea-bullets. What is wanted for this country is a heavy bore—No. 10 or 12 is the real bone-crusher—that will drop every animal shot, in its tracks, by which all fatigue and disappointment are avoided. Several times during these two days was I disappointed after most laborious stalking and creeping along the ground. Once I came suddenly upon an eland while I had a Winchester rifle in my hand—the eland and myself mutually as-tonished—at not more than twenty-five yards apart. I fired at its chest, and bullet, true to its aim, sped far into the internal parts, and the blood spouted from the wound: in a few minutes he was far away, and I was too much disappointed to follow him. All love of the chase seemed to be dying away before these several mishaps. What were two antelopes for one day's sport to the thousands that browsed over the plain?

The animals taken to camp during our three days' sport were two buffaloes, two wild boar, three hartebeest, one zebra, and one pallah; besides which, were shot eight guinea-fowls, three florican, two fish-eagles, one pelican, and one of the men caught a couple of large silurus fish. In the meantime the people had cut, sliced, and dried this bounteous store of meat for our transit through the long wilderness before us.

Saturday the 7th day of October, we broke up camp, to the great regret of the meat-loving, gormandizing Wangwana. They delegated Bombay early in the morning to speak to me, and entreat of me to stop one day longer. It was ever the case; they had always an unconquerable aversion to work, when in presence of meat. Bombay was well scolded for bearing any such request to me after two days' rest, during which time they had been filled to repletion with meat. And Bombay was by no means in the best of humour; flesh-pots full of meat were more to his taste than a constant tramping, and its consequent fatigues. I saw his face settle into sulky ugliness, and his great nether lip hanging down limp, which meant as if expressed in so many words, " Well, get them to move yourself, you wicked hard man! I shall not help you."

An ominous silence followed my order to the kirangozi to sound the horn, and the usual singing and chanting were not heard. The men turned sullenly to their bales, and Asmani, the gigantic guide, our fundi, was heard grumblingly to say he was sorry he had engaged to guide me to the Tanganika. However, they started, though reluctantly. I stayed behind with my gunbearers, to drive the stragglers on. In about half an hour I sighted the caravan at a dead stop, with the bales thrown on the ground, and the men standing in groups conversing angrily and excitedly.

Taking my double-barrelled gun from Selim's shoulder, I selected a dozen charges of buck-shot, and slipping two of them into the barrels, and adjusting my revolvers in order for handy work, I walked on towards them. I noticed that the men seized their guns, as I advanced. When within thirty yards of the groups, I discovered the heads of two men appear above an anthill on my left, with the barrels of their guns carelessly pointed toward the road.

I halted, threw the barrel of my gun into the hollow of the left hand, and then, taking a deliberate aim at them, threatened to blow their heads off if they did not come forward to talk to me. These two men were, gigantic Asmani and his sworn companion Mabruki, the guides of Sheikh bin Nasib. As it was dangerous not to comply with such an order, they presently came, but, keeping my eye on Asmani, I saw him move his fingers to the trigger of his gun, and bring his gun to a " ready." Again I lifted my gun, and threatened him with instant death, if he did not drop his gun.

Asmani came on in a sidelong way with a smirking smile on his face, but in his eyes shone the lurid light of murder, as plainly as ever it shone in a villain's eyes. Mabruki sneaked to my rear, deliberately putting powder in the pan of his musket, but sweeping the gun sharply round, I planted the muzzle of it at about two feet from his wicked-looking face, and ordered him to drop his gun instantly. He let it fall from his hand quickly, and giving him a vigorous poke in the breast with my gun, which sent him reeling away a few feet from me, I faced round to Asmani, and ordered him to put his gun down, accompanying it with a nervous move-ment of my gun, pressing gently on the trigger at the same time. Never was a man nearer his death than was Asmani during those few moments. I was reluctant to shed his blood, and I was willing to try all possible means to avoid doing so; but if I did not succeed in cowing this ruffian, authority was at an end. The truth was, they feared to proceed further on the road, and the only possible way of inducing them to move was by an overpowering force, and exercise of my power and will in this instance, even though he might pay the penalty of his disobedience with death. As I was beginning to feel that Asmani had passed his last moment on earth, as he was lifting his gun to his shoulder, a form came up from behind him, and swept his gun aside with an impatient, nervous movement, and I heard Mabruki Burton say in horror-struck accents:

"Man, how dare you point your gun at the master?" Mabruki then threw himself at my feet, and endeavoured to kiss them and entreated me not to punish him. "It was all over now," he said; "there would be no more quarreling, they would all go as far as the Tanganika, without any more noise; and Inshallah!" said he, "we shall find the old Musungu * at Ujiji."

"Speak, men, freedmen, shall we not?—shall we not go to the Tanganika without any more trouble? tell the master with one voice."

"Ay Wallah! Ay Wallah! Bana yango! Hamuna manneno mgini!" which literally translated means, "Yes by God! Yes by God! my master! There are no other words," said each man loudly.

"Ask the master's pardon, man, or go thy way," said Mabruki peremptorily, to Asmani: which Asmani did, to the gratification of us all.

It remained for me only to extend a general pardon to all except to Bombay and Ambari, the instigators of the mutiny, which was now happily quelled. For Bombay could have by a word, as my captain, nipped all manifestation of bad temper at the outset, had he been so disposed. But no, Bombay was more averse to marching

* Livingstone.

than the cowardliest of his fellows, not because he was cowardly, but because he loved indolence.

Again the word was given to march, and each man, with astonishing alacrity, seized his load, and filed off quickly out of sight.

While on this subject, I may as well give here a sketch of each of the principal men whose names must often appear in the following chapters. According to rank, they consist of Bombay, Mabruki Burton, Asmani the guide, Chowpereh, Ulimengo, Khamisi, Ambari, Jumah, Ferajji the cook, Maganga the Mnyamwezi, Selim the Arab boy, and youthful Kalulu a gunbearer.

Bombay has received an excellent charater from Burton and Speke. "Incarnation of honesty" Burton grandly terms him. The truth is, Bombay was neither very honest nor very dishonest, i.e., he did not venture to steal much. He sometimes contrived cunningly, as he distributed the meat, to hide a very large share for his own use. This peccadillo of his did not disturb me much; he deserved as captain a larger share than the others. He required to be closely watched, and when aware that this was the case, he seldom ventured to appropriate more cloth than I would have freely given him, had he asked for it. As a personal servant, or valet, he would have been unexceptionable, but as a captain or jemadar over his fellows, he was out of his proper sphere. It was too much brain-work, and was too productive of anxiety to keep him in order. At times he was helplessly imbecile in his movements, forgot every order the moment it was given him, consistently broke or lost some valuable article, was fond of argument, and addicted to bluster. He thinks Hajji Abdullah one of the wickedest white men born, because he saw him pick up men's skulls and put them in sacks, as if he was about to prepare a horrible medicine with them. He wanted to know whether his former master had written down all he himself did, and when told that Burton had not said anything, in his books upon the Lake Regions, upon collecting skulls at Kilwa, thought I would be doing a good work if I published this important fact.* Bombay intends to make a pilgrimage to visit Speke's grave some day.

Mabruki, "Ras-bukra Mabruki," Bull-headed Mabruki, as Burton calls him, is a sadly abused man in my opinion. Mabruki, though stupid, is faithful. He is entirely out of his element as valet, he might as well be *clerk*. As a watchman he is invaluable, as a second captain or fundi, whose duty it is to bring up stragglers, he is superexcellent. He is ugly and vain, but he is no coward.

Asmani the guide is a large fellow, standing over six feet, with the neck and shoulders of a Hercules. Besides being guide, he is a fundi, sometimes called Fundi Asmani, or hunter. A very superstitious man, who takes great care of his gun, and talismanic plaited cord, which he has dipped in the blood of all the animals he has ever shot. He is afraid of lions, and will never venture out where lions are known to be. All other animals he regards as game, and is indefatigable in their pursuit. He is seldom seen without an apologetic or a treacherous smile on his face. He could draw a knife across a man's throat and still smile.

Chowpereh is a sturdy short man of thirty or there-

---

* I find upon returning to England, that Capt. Burton has informed the world of this "wicked and abominable deed," in his book upon Zanzibar, and that the interesting collection may be seen at the Royal College of Surgeons, London.

abouts ; very good-natured, and humorous. When Chowpereh speaks in his dry Mark Twain style, the whole
camp laughs. I never quarrel with Chowpereh, never
did quarrel with him. A kind word given to Chowpereh
is sure to be reciprocated with a good deed. He is the
strongest, the healthiest, the amiablest, the faithfulest of
all. He is the embodiment of a good follower.

Khamisi is a neat, cleanly boy of twenty, or thereabouts, active, loud-voiced, a boaster, and the cowardliest
of the cowardly. He will steal at every opportunity.
He clings to his gun most affectionately ; is always excessively anxious if a screw gets loose, or if a flint will
not strike fire, yet I doubt that he would be able to fire
his gun at an enemy from excessive trembling. Khamisi
would rather trust his safety to his feet, which are small,
and well shaped.

Ambari is a man of about forty. He is one of the
" Faithfuls " of Speke, and one of my Faithfuls. He
would not run away from me except when in the presence
of an enemy, and imminent personal danger. He is
clever in his way, but is not sufficiently clever to enact
the part of captain—could take charge of a small party,
and give a very good account of them. Is lazy, and an
admirer of good living—abhors marching, unless he has
nothing to carry but his gun.

Jumah is the best abused man of the party, because he
has old-womanish ways with him, yet in his old-womanish
ways he is disposed to do the best he can for me, though
he will not carry a pound in weight without groaning
terribly at his hard fate. To me he is sentimental and
pathetic ; to the unimportant members of the caravan he
is stern and uncompromising. But the truth is, that I
could well dispense with Jumah's presence : he was one

of the incorrigible *inutiles*, eating far more than he was worth; besides being an excessively grumbling and querulous fool.

Ulimengo, a strong stalwart fellow of thirty, was the maddest and most hare-brained of my party. Though an arrant coward, he was a consummate boaster. But though a devotee of pleasure and fun, he was not averse from work. With one hundred men such as **he**, I could travel through Africa provided there was no fighting to do. It will be remembered that he was the martial coryphæus who led my little army to war against Mirambo, chanting the battle-song of the Wangwana; and that I stated, that when the retreat was determined upon, he was the first of my party to reach the stronghold of Mfuto. He is a swift runner, and a fair hunter. I have been indebted to him on several occasions for a welcome addition to my larder.

Ferajji, a former dish-washer to Speke, was my cook. He was promoted to this office upon the defection of Bunder Salaam, and the extreme non-fitness of Abdul Kader. For cleaning dishes, the first corn-cob, green twig, a bunch of leaves or grass, answered Ferajji's purposes in the absence of a cloth. If I ordered a plate, and I pointed out a black, greasy, sooty thumbmark to him, a rub of a finger Ferajji thought sufficient to remove all objections. If I hinted that a spoon was rather dirty, Ferajji fancied that with a little saliva, and a rub of his loin cloth, the most fastidious ought to be satisfied. Every pound of meat, and every three spoonfuls of musk or porridge I ate in Africa, contained at least ten grains of sand. Ferajji was considerably exercised at a threat I made to him that on arrival at Zanzibar, I would get the great English doctor there to open my stomach, and count

every grain of sand found in it, for each grain of which
Ferajji should be charged one dollar. The consciousness
that my stomach must contain a large number, for which
the forfeits would be heavy, made him feel very sad at
times. Otherwise, Ferajji was a good cook, most industrious, if not accomplished. He could produce a cup
of tea, and three or four hot pancakes, within ten minutes
after a halt was ordered, for which I was most grateful,
as I was almost always hungry after a long march.
Ferajji sided with Baraka against Bombay in Unyoro,
and when Speke took Bombay's side of the question,
Ferajji, out of love for Baraka, left Speke's service, and so
forfeited his pay.

Maganga was a Mnyamwezi, a native of Mkwenkwe, a
strong, faithful servant, an excellent pagazi, with an irre-
proachable temper. He it was who at all times, on the
march, started the wildly exuberant song of the Wanyamwezi porters, which, no matter how hot the sun, or
how long the march, was sure to produce gaiety and
animation among the people. At such times all hands
sang, sang with voices that could be heard miles away,
which made the great forests ring with the sounds, which
startled every animal big or little, for miles around. On
approaching a village the temper of whose people might
be hostile to us, Maganga would commence his song, with
the entire party joining in the chorus, by which mode we
knew whether the natives were disposed to be friendly or
hostile. If hostile, or timid, the gates would at once be
closed, and dark faces would scowl at us from the interior;
if friendly, they rushed outside of their gates to welcome
us, or to exchange friendly remarks.

An important member of the Expedition was Selim, the
young Arab. Without some one who spoke good Arabic,

I could not have obtained the friendship of the chief Arabs in Unyanyembe; neither could I have well communicated with them, for though I understood Arabic, I could not speak it.

I have already related how Kalulu came to be in my service, and how he came to bear his present name. I soon found how apt and quick he was to learn, in consequence of which, he was promoted to the rank of personal attendant. Even Selim could not vie with Kalulu in promptness and celerity, or in guessing my wants at the table. His little black eyes were constantly roving over the dishes, studying out the problem of what was further necessary, or had become unnecessary.

We arrived at the Ziwani, in about 4 h. 30 m. from the time of our quitting the scene which had well-nigh witnessed a sanguinary conflict. The Ziwani, or pool, contained no water, not a drop, until the parched tongues of my people warned them that they must proceed and excavate for water. This excavation was performed (by means of strong hard sticks sharply pointed) in the dry hard-caked bottom. After digging to a depth of six feet their labours were rewarded with the sight of a few drops of muddy liquid percolating through the sides, which were eagerly swallowed to relieve their raging thirst. Some voluntarily started with buckets, gourds, and canteens south to a deserted clearing called the "Tongoni" in Ukamba, and in about three hours returned with a plentiful supply for immediate use, of good and clear water.

In 1 h. 30 m. we arrived at this Tongoni, or deserted clearing of the Wakamba. Here were three or four villages burnt, and an extensive clearing desolate, the work of the Wa-Ruga-Ruga of Mirambo. Those of the inhabitants who were left, after the spoliation and complete destruction of the flourishing settlement, emigrated westerly to Ugara. A large herd of buffalo now slake their thirst at the pool which supplied the villages of Ukamba with water.

Great masses of iron hæmatite cropped up above the surfaces in these forests. Wild fruit began to be abundant; the wood-apple and tamarind and a small plum-like fruit, furnished us with many an agreeable repast.

The honey-bird is very frequent in these forests of Ukonongo. Its cry is a loud, quick chirrup. The Wakonongo understand how to avail themselves of its guidance to the sweet treasure of honey which the wild bees have stored in the cleft of some great tree. Daily, the Wakonongo who had joined our caravan brought me immense cakes of honey-comb, containing delicious white and red honey. The red honey-comb generally contains large numbers of dead bees, but our exceedingly gluttonous people thought little of these. They not only ate the honey-bees, but they also ate a good deal of the wax.

As soon as the honey-bird descries the traveller, he immediately utters a series of wild, excited cries, hops about from twig to twig, and from branch to branch, then hops to another tree, incessantly repeating his chirruping call. The native, understanding the nature of the little bird, unhesitatingly follows him; but perhaps his steps are too slow for the impatient caller, upon which he flies back, urging him louder, more impatient cries, to hasten, and then darts swiftly forward, as if he would show how quickly he could go to the honey-store, until at last the treasure is reached, the native has applied fire to the bees' nest, and secured the honey, while the little bird preens himself, and chirrups in triumphant notes, as if he were informing the biped that without his aid he never could have found the honey.

Buffalo gnats and tsetse were very troublesome on this march, owing to the numerous herds of game in the vicinity.

On the 9th of October we made a long march in a southerly direction, and formed our camp in the centre of a splendid grove of trees. The water was very scarce on the road. The Wamrima and Wanyamwezi are not long able to withstand thirst. When water is plentiful they slake their thirst at every stream and pool; when it is scarce, as it is here and in the deserts of Marenga and Magunda Mkali, long afternoon-marches are made; the men previously, however, filling their gourds, so as to enable them to reach the water early next morning. Selim was never able to endure thirst. It mattered not how much of the precious liquid he carried, he generally drank it all before reaching camp, and he consequently suffered during the night. Besides this, he endangered his life by quaffing from every muddy pool; and on this day he began to complain that he discharged blood, which I took to be an incipient stage of dysentery.

During these marches, ever since quitting Ugunda, a favourite topic at the camp-fires were the Wa-Ruga-Ruga, and their atrocities, and a possible encounter that we might have with these bold rovers of the forest. I verily believe that a sudden onset of half a dozen of Mirambo's people would have set the whole caravan a-running.

We reached Marefu the next day, after a short three hours' march. We there found an embassy sent by the

Arabs of Unyanyembe, to the Southern Watuta, bearing presents of several bales, in charge of Hassan the
Mseguhha.   This valiant leader and diplomatist had halted
here some ten days because of wars and rumours of wars
in his front.   It was said that Mbogo, Sultan of Mbogo
in Ukonongo, was at war with the brother of Manwa
Sera, and as Mbogo was a large district of Ukonongo,
only two days' march from Marefu, fear of being
involved in it was deterring old Hassan from proceeding.   He advised me also not to proceed, as it was
impossible to be able to do so without being embroiled in
the conflict.   I informed him that I intended to proceed
on my way, and take my chances, and graciously offered
him my escort as far as the frontier of Ufipa, from which
he could easily and safely continue on his way to the
Watuta, but he declined it.

We had now been travelling fourteen days in a south-
westerly direction, having made a little more than one
degree of latitude.   I had intended to have gone a little
further south, because it was such a good road, also since
by going further south we should have labored under no
fear of meeting Mirambo ; but the report of this war in
our front, only two days off, compelled me, in the interest
of the Expedition, to strike across towards the Tanganika,
on a west-by-north course through the forest, travelling,
when it was advantageous, along elephant tracks and local
paths.   This new plan was adopted after consulting with
Asmani, the guide.   We were now in Ukonongo, having
entered this district when we crossed the Gombe creek.

The next day after arriving at Marefu we plunged
westward, in view of the villagers, and the Arab ambassador, who kept repeating until the last moment that we
should " certainly catch it."

We marched eight hours through a forest, where the forest peach, or the "mbembu," is abundant. The tree that bears this fruit is very like a pear-tree, and is very productive. I saw one tree, upon which I estimated there were at least six or seven bushels. I ate numbers of the peaches on this day. So long as this fruit can be produced, a traveller in these regions need not fear starvation.

At the base of a graceful hilly cone we found a village called Utende, the inhabitants of which were in a state of great alarm, as we suddenly appeared on the ridge above them. Diplomacy urged me to send forward a present of one doti to the Sultan, who, however, would not accept it, because he happened to be drunk with pombe, and was therefore disposed to be insolent. Upon being informed that he would refuse any present, unless he received four more cloths, I immediately ordered a strong boma to be constructed on the summits of a little hill, near enough to a plentiful supply of water, and quietly again packed up the present in the bale. I occupied a strategically chosen position, as I could have swept the face of the hill, and the entire space between its base and the village of Watende. Watchmen were kept on the look-out all night; but we were fortunately not troubled until the morning; when a delegation of the principal men came to ask if I intended to depart without having made a present to the chief. I replied to them that I did not intend passing through any country without making friends with the chief; and if their chief would accept a good cloth from me, I would freely give it to him. Though they demurred at the amount of the present at first, the difference between us was finally ended by my adding a fundo of red beads—sami-sami—for the chief's wife.

From the hill and ridge of Utende sloped a forest for miles and miles westerly, which was terminated by a grand and smooth-topped ridge rising 500 or 600 feet above the plain.

A four hours' march, on the 12th of October, brought us to a nullah similar to the Gombe, which, during the wet season, flows to the Gombe River, and thence into the Malagarazi River.

A little before camping we saw a herd of nimba, or pallah; I had the good fortune to shoot one, which was a welcome addition to our fast diminishing store of dried meats, prepared in our camp on the Gombe. By the quantity of bois de vaches, we judged buffaloes were plentiful here, as well as elephant and rhinoceros. The feathered species were well represented by ibis, fish-eagles, pelicans, storks, cranes, several snowy spoon-bills, and flamingoes.

From the nullah, or mtoni, we proceeded to Mwaru, the principal village of the district of Mwaru, the chief of which is Ka-mirambo. Our march lay over desolated clearings once occupied by Ka-mirambo's people, but who were driven away by Mkasiwa some ten years ago, during his warfare against Manwa Sera. Niongo, the brother of the latter, now waging war against Mbogo, had passed through Mwaru the day before we arrived, after being defeated by his enemy.

The hilly ridge that bounded the westward horizon, visible from Utende, was surmounted on this day. The western slope trends south-west, and is drained by the River Mrera, which empties into the Malagarazi River.

We perceived the influence of the Tanganika, even here, though we were yet twelve or fifteen marches from the lake. The jungles increased in density, and the grasses became enormously tall; these points reminded us of the maritime districts of Ukwere and Ukami.

We heard from a caravan at this place, just come from Ufipa, that a white man was reported to be in "Urua," whom I supposed to mean Livingstone.

Upon leaving Mwaru we entered the district of Mrera, a chief who once possessed great power and influence over this region. Wars, however, have limited his possessions to three or four villages snugly embosomed within a jungle, whose outer rim is so dense that it serves like a stone wall to repel invaders. There were nine bleached skulls, stuck on the top of as many poles, before the principal gate of entrance, which told us of existing feuds between the Wakonongo and the Wazavira. This latter tribe dwelt in a country a few marches west of us; whose territory we should have to avoid, unless we sought another opportunity to distinguish ourselves in battle with the natives. The Wazavira, we were told by the Wakonongo of Mrera, were enemies to all Wangwana.

In a narrow strip of marsh between Mwaru and Mrera, we saw a small herd of wild elephants. It was the first time I had ever seen these animals in their native wildness, and my first impressions of them I shall not readily forget. I am induced to think that the elephant deserves the title of "king of beasts." His huge form, the lordly way in which he stares at an intruder on his domain, and his whole appearance indicative of conscious might, afford good grounds for his claim to that title. This herd, as we passed it at the distance of a mile, stopped to survey the caravan as it passed: and, after having satisfied their curiosity, the elephants trooped into the forest which bounded the marshy plain southward, as if caravans were every-day things to them, whilst they—the free and unconquerable lords of the forest and the marsh —had nothing in common with the cowardly bipeds, who never found courage to face them in fair combat. The destruction which a herd makes in a forest is simply tremendous. When the trees are young whole swathes may be found uprooted and prostrate, which mark the track of the elephants as they "trampled their path through wood and brake."

The boy Selim was so ill at this place that I was compelled to halt the caravan for him for two days. He seemed to be affected with a disease in the limbs, which caused him to sprawl, and tremble most painfully, besides suffering from an attack of acute dysentery. But constant attendance and care soon brought him round again; and on the third day he was able to endure the fatigue of riding.

I was able to shoot several animals during our stay at Mrera. The forest outside of the cultivation teems with noble animals. Zebra, giraffe, elephant, and rhinoceros are most common; ptarmigan and guinea-fowl were also plentiful.

The warriors of Mrera are almost all armed with muskets, of which they take great care. They were very importunate in their demands for flints, bullets, and powder, which I always made it a point to refuse, lest at any moment a fracas occurring they might use the ammunition thus supplied to my own disadvantage. The men of this village were an idle set, doing little but hunting, gaping, gossiping, and playing like great boys.

During the interval of my stay at Mrera I employed

a large portion of my time in mending my shoes, and patching up the great rents in my clothes, which the thorn species, during the late marches, had almost destroyed. Westward, beyond Mrera, was a wilderness, the transit of which we were warned would occupy nine days; hence arose the necessity to purchase a large supply of grain, which, ere attempting the great uninhabited void in our front, was to be ground and sifted.

VIEW IN UVINZA.

CHAPTER XI.

THROUGH UKAWENDI, UVINZA, AND UHHA, TO UJIJI.

Happy auspices.—Ant-hills.—The water-shed of the Tanganika Lion.—
The king of Kasera.—The home of the lion and the leopard.—
A donkey frightens a leopard.—Sublime scenes in Kawendi.—
Starvation imminent.—Amenities of travel in Africa.—Black-
mailers.—The stormy children of Uhha.—News of a white man.—
Energetic marches—Mionvu, chief of tribute-takers.—An escape at
midnight.—Toiling through the jungles.—The Lake Mountains.—
First view of the Tanganika.—Arrival at Ujiji.—The happy meeting
with Livingstone.

WE bade farewell to Mrera on the 17th of October, to
continue our route north-westward. All the men and I
were firm friends now; all squabbling had long ceased.
Bombay and I had forgotten our quarrel; the kirangozi

and myself were ready to embrace, so loving and affectionate were the terms upon which we stood towards one another.   Confidence returned to all hearts—for now, as Mabruk Unyanyembe said, "we could smell the fish of the Tanganika."   Unyanyembe, with all its disquietude, was far behind. We could snap our fingers at that terrible Mirambo and his unscrupulous followers, and by-and-by, perhaps, we may be able to laugh at the timid seer who always prophesied portentous events—Sheikh, the son of Nasib. We laughed joyously, as we glided in Indian file through the young forest jungle beyond the clearing of Mrera, and boasted of our prowess.   Oh! we were truly brave that morning!

Emerging from the jungle, we entered a thin forest, where numerous ant-hills were seen like so many sand-dunes. I imagine that these ant-hills were formed during a remarkably wet season, when, possibly, the forest-clad plain was inundated. I have seen the ants at work by thousands, engaged in the work of erecting their hills in other districts suffering from inundation. What a wonderful system of cells these tiny insects construct! A perfect labyrinth—cell within cell, room within room, hall within hall—an exhibition of engineering talents and high architectural capacity—a model city, cunningly contrived for safety and comfort!

Emerging after a short hour's march out of the forest, we welcome the sight of a murmuring translucent stream, swiftly flowing towards the north-west, which we regard with the pleasure which only men who have for a long time sickened themselves with that potable liquid of the foulest kind, found in salinas, mbugas, pools, and puddle-holes, can realize. Beyond this stream rises a rugged and steep ridge, from the summit of which our eyes are gladdened with scenes that are romantic, animated and picturesque. They form an unusual feast to eyes sated with looking into the depths of forests, at towering stems of trees, and at tufted crowns of foliage. We have now before us scores of cones, dotting the surface of a plain which extends across Southern Ukonongo to the territory of the Wafipa, and which reaches as far as the Rikwa Plain. The immense prospect before which we are suddenly ushered is most varied ; exclusive of conical hills and ambitious flat-topped and isolated mountains, we are in view of the watersheds of the Rungwa River, which empties into the Tanganika south of where we stand, and of the Malagarazi River, which the Tanganika receives, a degree or so north of this position. A single but lengthy latitudinal ridge serves as a dividing line to the watershed of the Rungwa and Malagarazi ; and a score of miles or so further west of this ridge rises another, which runs north and south.

We camped on this day in the jungle, close to a narrow ravine with a marshy bottom, through the oozy, miry contents of which the waters from the watershed of the Rungwa slowly trickled southward towards the Rikwa Plain. This was only one of many ravines, however, some of which were several hundred yards broad, others were but a few yards in width, the bottoms of which were most dangerous quagmires, overgrown with dense tall reeds and papyrus. Over the surface of these great depths of mud were seen hundreds of thin threads of slimy ochre-colored water, which swarmed with animalculæ. By-and-by, a few miles south of the base of this ridge (which I call Kasera, from the country which it cuts in halves), these several ravines converge and debouch into the broad,

marchy, oozy, spongy "river" of Usense, which trends in
a south-easterly direction; after which, gathering the
contents of the watercourses from the north and north-
east into its own broader channel, it soon becomes a
stream of some breadth and consequence, and meets a
river flowing from the east, from the direction of Urori,
with which it conflows in the Rikwa Plain, and empties
about sixty rectilineal miles further west into the Tanganika Lake. The Rungwa River, I am informed, is considered as a boundary line between the country of Usowa
on the north, and Ufipa on the south.

We had barely completed the construction of our camp
defences when some of the men were heard challenging a
small party of natives which advanced towards our camp,
headed by a man who, from his garb and head-dress, we
knew was from Zanzibar. After interchanging the customary salutations, I was informed that this party was an
embassy from Simba ("Lion"), who ruled over Kasera, in
Southern Unyamwezi. Simba, I was told, was the son of
Mkasiwa, King of Unyanyembe, and was carrying on war
with the Wazavira, of whom I was warned to beware. He
had heard such reports of my greatness that he was sorry
I did not take his road to Ukawendi, that he might have
had the opportunity of seeing me, and making friends
with me; but in the absence of a personal visit Simba
had sent this embassy to overtake me, in the hope that I
would present him with a token of my friendship in the
shape of cloth. Though I was rather taken aback by the
demand, still it was politic in me to make this powerful
chief my friend, lest on my return from the search after
Livingstone he and I might fall out. And since it was
incumbent on me to make a present, for the sake of peace,

it was necessary to exhibit my desire for peace by giving —if I gave at all—a royal present. The ambassador conveyed from me to Simba, or the "Lion" of Kasera, two gorgeous cloths, and two other doti consisting of Merikani and Kaniki; and, if I might believe the ambassador, I had made Simba a friend for ever.

On the 18th of October, breaking camp at the usual hour, we continued our march north-westward by a road which zig-zagged along the base of the Kasera mountains, and which took us into all kinds of difficulties. We traversed at least a dozen marshy ravines, the depth of mire and water in which caused the utmost anxiety. I sunk up to my neck in deep holes in the Stygian ooze caused by elephants, and had to tramp through the oozy beds of the Rungwa sources with my clothes wet and black with mud and slime. Decency forbade that I should strip; and the hot sun would also blister my body. Moreover, these morasses were too frequent to lose time in undressing and dressing, and, as each man was weighted with his own proper load, it would have been cruel to compel the men to bear me across. Nothing remained, therefore, but to march on, all encumbered as I was with my clothing and accoutrements, into these several marshy watercourses, with all the philosophical stoicism that my nature could muster for such emergencies. But it was very uncomfortable, to say the least of it.

We soon entered the territory of the dreaded Wazavira, but no enemy was in sight. Simba, in his wars, had made clean work of the northern part of Uzavira, and we encountered nothing worse than a view of the desolated country, which must have been once—judging from the

number of burnt huts and débris of ruined villages—
extremely populous. A young jungle was sprouting up
vigorously in their fields, and was rapidly becoming the
home of wild denizens of the forest. In one of the
deserted and ruined villages, I found quarters for the
Expedition, which were by no means uncomfortable. I
shot three brace of guinea-fowl in the neighborhood of
Misonghi, the deserted village we occupied, and Ulimengo, one of my hunters, bagged an antelope, called
the "mbawala," for whose meat some of the Wanyamwezi
have a superstitious aversion. I take this species of
antelope, which stands about three and a half feet high,
of a reddish hide, head long, horns short, to be the
"Nzoe" antelope discovered by Speke in Uganda, and
whose Latin designation is, according to Dr. Sclater,
"Tragelaphus Spekii." It has a short bushy tail, and
long hair along the spine.

A long march in a west-by-north direction, lasting
six hours, through a forest where the sable antelope
was seen, and which was otherwise prolific with game,
brought us to a stream which ran by the base of a lofty
conical hill, on whose slopes flourished quite a forest of
feathery bamboo.

On the 20th, leaving our camp, which lay between the
stream and the conical hill above mentioned, and surmounting a low ridge which sloped from the base of the
hill-cone, we were greeted with another picturesque view,
of cones and scarped mountains, which heaved upward in
all directions. A march of nearly five hours through
this picturesque country brought us to the Mpokwa
River, one of the tributaries of the Rungwa, and to a
village lately deserted by the Wazavira. The huts were

almost all intact, precisely as they were left by their former inhabitants. In the gardens were yet found vegetables, which, after living so long on meat, were most grateful to us. On the branches of trees still rested the Lares and Penates of the Wazavira, in the shape of large and exceedingly well-made earthen pots.

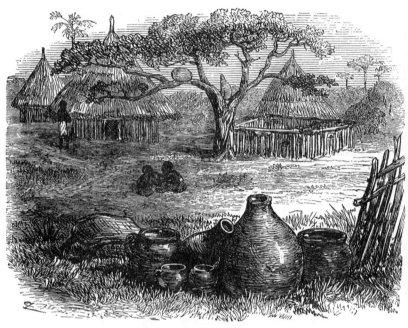

VILLAGE IN UZAVIRA—NATIVE POTTERY.

In the neighboring river one of my men succeeded, in a few minutes, in catching sixty fish of the silurus species by the hand alone. A number of birds hovered about the stream, such as the white-headed fish-eagle and the black kingfisher, enormous snowy spoonbills, ibis, martins,

&c. This river issued from a mountain clump eight miles
or so north of the village of Mpokwa, and comes flowing
down a narrow thread of water, sinuously winding amongst
tall reeds and dense brakes on either side—the home of
hundreds of antelopes and buffaloes. South of Mpokwa,
the valley broadens, and the mountains deflect eastward
and westward, and beyond this point commences the
plain known as the Rikwa, which, during the Masika is
inundated, but which, in the dry season, presents the
same bleached aspect that plains in Africa generally do
when the grass has ripened.

Travelling up along the right bank of the Mpokwa,
on the 21st we came to the head of the stream, and
the sources of the Mpokwa, issuing out of deep defiles
enclosed by lofty ranges. The mbawala and the buffalo
were plentiful.

On the 22nd, after a march of four hours and a half,
we came to the beautiful stream of Mtambu—the water
of which was sweet, and clear as crystal, and flowed
northward. We saw for the first time the home of the
lion and the leopard. Hear what Freiligrath says of the
place :

> Where the thorny brake and thicket
>   Densely fill the interspace
> Of the trees, through whose thick branches
>   Never sunshine lights the place,
> There the lion dwells, a monarch,
>   Mightiest among the brutes ;
> There his right to reign supremest
>   Never one his claim disputes.
> There he layeth down to slumber,
>   Having slain and ta'en his fill ;
> There he roameth, there he croucheth,
>   As it suits his lordly will.

We camped but a few yards from just such a place as the poet describes. The herd-keeper who attended the goats and donkeys, soon after our arrival in camp, drove the animals to water, and in order to obtain it they travelled through a tunnel in the brake, caused by elephants and rhinoceros. They had barely entered the dark cavernous passage, when a black-spotted leopard sprang, and fastened its fangs in the neck of one of the donkeys, causing it, from the pain, to bray hideously. Its companions set up such a frightful chorus, and so lashed their heels in the air at the feline marauder, that the leopard bounded away through the brake, as if in sheer dismay at the noisy cries which the attack had provoked. The donkey's neck exhibited some frightful wounds, but the animal was not dangerously hurt.

Thinking that possibly I might meet with an adventure with a lion or a leopard in that dark belt of tall trees, under whose impenetrable shade grew the dense thicket that formed such admirable coverts for the carnivorous species, I took a stroll along the awesome place with the gunbearer, Kalulu, carrying an extra gun, and a further supply of ammunition. We crept cautiously along, looking keenly into the deep dark dens, the entrances of which were revealed to us, as we journeyed, expectant every moment to behold the reputed monarch of the brake and thicket, bound forward to meet us, and I took a special delight in picturing, in my imagination, the splendor and majesty of the wrathful brute, as he might stand before me. I peered closely into every dark opening, hoping to see the deadly glitter of the great angry eyes, and the glowering menacing front of the lion as he would regard me. But, alas! after an hour's search for adventure, I had encountered nothing, and I accordingly waxed courageous, and crept into one of these leafy, thorny caverns, and found myself shortly standing under a canopy of foliage that was held above my head fully a hundred feet by the shapely and towering stems of the royal mvule. Who can imagine the position? A smooth lawn-like glade; a dense and awful growth of impenetrable jungle around us; those stately natural pillars—a glorious phalanx of royal trees, bearing at such sublime heights vivid green masses of foliage, through which no single sun-ray penetrated, while at our feet babbled the primeval brook, over smooth pebbles, in soft tones befitting the sacred quiet of the scene! Who could have desecrated this solemn, holy harmony of nature? But just as I was thinking it impossible that any man could be tempted to disturb the serene solitude of the place, I saw a monkey perched high on a branch over my head, contemplating, with something of an awe-struck look, the strange intruders beneath. Well, I could not help it, I laughed—laughed loud and long, until I was hushed by the chaos of cries and strange noises which seemed to respond to my laughing. A troop of monkeys, hidden in the leafy depths above, had been rudely awakened, and, startled by the noise I made, were hurrying away from the scene with a dreadful clamor of cries and shrieks.

Emerging again into the broad sunlight, I strolled further in search of something to shoot. Presently, I saw, feeding quietly in the forest which bounded the valley of the Mtambu on the left, a huge, reddish-colored wild boar, armed with most horrid tusks. Leaving Kalulu crouched down behind a tree, and my solar helmet behind another close by—that I might more safely stalk the animal—I advanced towards him some forty yards, and after taking a deliberate aim, fired at his fore shoulder. As if nothing had hurt him whatever, the animal made a furious bound, and then stood with his bristles erected, and tufted tail, curved over the back—a most formidable brute in appearance. While he was thus listening, and searching the neighbourhood with his keen, small eyes, I planted another shot in his chest, which ploughed its way through his body. Instead of falling, however, as I expected he would, he charged furiously in the direction the bullet had come, and as he rushed past me, another ball was fired, which went right through him; but still he kept on, until, within six or seven yards from the trees behind which Kalulu was crouching down on one side, and the helmet was resting behind another, he suddenly halted, and then dropped. But as I was about to advance on him with my knife to cut his throat, he suddenly started up; his eyes had caught sight of the little boy Kalulu, and were then, almost immediately afterwards, attracted by the sight of the snowy helmet. These strange objects on either side of him proved too much for the boar, for, with a terrific grunt, he darted on one side into a thick brake, from which it was impossible to oust him, and as it was now getting late, and the camp was about three miles away, I was reluctantly obliged to return without the meat.

On our way to camp we were accompanied by a large animal which persistently followed us on our left. It was too dark to see plainly, but a large form was visible, if not very clearly defined. It must have been a lion, unless it was the ghost of the dead boar.

That night, about 11 P.M., we were startled by the roar

of a lion, in close proximity to the camp. Soon it was
joined by another, and another still, and the novelty of
the thing kept me awake. I peered through the gate of
the camp, and endeavoured to sight a rifle—my little
Winchester, in the accuracy of which I had perfect confidence; but, alas! for the cartridges, they might have
been as well filled with sawdust for all the benefit I
derived from them. Disgusted with the miserable ammunition, I left the lions alone, and turned in, with their
roaring as a lullaby.

That terrestrial paradise for the hunter, the valley of
the pellucid Mtambu, was deserted by us the next morning for the settlement commonly known to the Wakawendi as Imrera's, with as much unconcern as though it
were a howling desert. The village near which we
encamped was called Itaga, in the district of Rusawa.
As soon as we had crossed the River Mtambu we had
entered Ukawendi, commonly called "Kawendi" by the
natives of the country.

The district of Rusawa is thickly populated. The
people are quiet and well-disposed to strangers, though
few ever come to this region from afar. One or two
Wasawahili traders visit it every year or so from Pumburu and Usowa; but very little ivory being obtained from
the people, the long distance between the settlements
serves to deter the regular trader from venturing hither.

If caravans arrive here, the objective point to them is
the district of Pumburu, situated south-westerly one
day's good marching, or, say, thirty statute miles from
Imrera; or they make for Usowa, on the Tanganika, viâ
Pumburu, Katuma, Uyombeh, and Ugarawah. Usowa is
quite an important district on the Tanganika, populous

and flourishing. This was the road we had intended to adopt after leaving Imrera, but the reports received at the latter place forbade such a venture. For Mapunda, the Sultan of Usowa, though a great friend to Arab traders, was at war with the colony of the Wazavira, who we must remember were driven from Mpokwa and vicinity in Utanda, and who were said to have settled between Pumburu and Usowa.

It remained for us, like wise, prudent men, having charge of a large and valuable Expedition on our hands, to decide what to do, and what route to adopt, now that we had approached much nearer to Ujiji than we were to Unyanyembe. I suggested that we should make direct for the Tanganika by compass, trusting to no road or guide, but to march direct west until we came to the Tanganika, and then follow the lake shore on foot until we came to Ujiji. For it ever haunted my mind, that, if Dr. Livingstone should hear of my coming, which he might possibly do if I travelled along any known road, he would leave, and that my search for him would consequently be a "stern chase." But my principal men thought it better that we should now boldly turn our faces north, and march for the Malagarazi, which was said to be a large river flowing from the east to the Tanganika. But none of my men knew the road to the Malagarazi, neither could guides be hired from Sultan Imrera. We were, however, informed that the Malagarazi was but two days' march from Imrera. I thought it safe, in such a case, to provision my men with three days' rations.

The village of Itaga is situated in a deep mountain hollow, finely overlooking a large extent of cultivation. The people grow sweet potatoes, manioc—out of which tapioca is made—beans, and the holcus. Not one chicken was to be purchased for love or money, and, besides grain, only a lean, scraggy specimen of a goat, a long time ago imported from Uvinza, was procurable.

October the 25th will be remembered by me as a day of great troubles ; in fact, a series of troubles began from this date. We struck an easterly road in order to obtain a passage to the lofty plateau which bounded the valley of Imrera on the west and on the north. We camped, after a two and a half hours' march, at its foot. The defile promised a feasible means of ascent to the summit of the plateau, which rose upward in a series of scarps a thousand feet above the valley of Imrera.

While ascending that lofty arc of mountains which bounded westerly and northerly the basin of Imrera, extensive prospects southward and eastward were revealed. The character of the scenery at Ukawendi is always animated and picturesque, but never sublime. The folds of this ridge contained several ruins of bomas, which seemed to have been erected during war time.

The mbembu fruit was plentiful along this march, and every few minutes I could see from the rear one or two of the men hastening to secure a treasure of it which they discovered on the ground.

A little before reaching the camp I had a shot at a leopard, but failed to bring him down as he bounded away. At night the lions roared as at the Mtambu River.

A lengthy march under the deep twilight shadows of a great forest, which protected us from the hot sunbeams, brought us, on the next day, to a camp newly constructed by a party of Arabs from Ujiji, who had advanced thus far on their road to Unyanyembe, but, alarmed at the reports of the war between Mirambo and the Arabs, had returned. Our route was along the right bank of the Rugufu, a broad sluggish stream, well choked with the matete reeds and the papyrus. The tracks and the bois de vaches of buffaloes were numerous, and there were several indications of rhinoceros being near. In a deep clump of timber near this river we discovered a colony of bearded and leonine-looking monkeys.

As we were about leaving our camp on the morning of the 28th a herd of buffalo walked deliberately into view. Silence was quickly restored, but not before the animals, to their great surprise, had discovered the danger which confronted them. We commenced stalking them, but we soon heard the thundering sound of their gallop, after which it becomes a useless task to follow them, with a long march in a wilderness before one.

The road led on this day over immense sheets of sandstone and iron ore. The water was abominable, and scarce, and famine began to stare us in the face. We travelled for six hours, and had yet seen no sign of cultivation anywhere. According to my map we were yet two long marches from the Malagarazi—if Captain Burton had correctly laid down the position of the river; according to the natives' account, we should have arrived at the Malagarazi on this day.

On the 29th we left our camp, and after a few minutes, we were in view of the sublimest, but ruggedest scenes we had yet beheld in Africa. The country was cut up in all directions by deep, wild, and narrow ravines trending in all directions, but generally toward the north-west, while on either side rose enormous square masses of naked rock (sandstone), sometimes towering, and rounded, sometimes pyramidal, sometimes in truncated cones, sometimes in circular ridges, with sharp, rugged, naked backs, with

but little vegetation anywhere visible, except it obtained
a precarious tenure in the fissured crown of some gigantic
hill-top, whither some soil had fallen, or at the base of
the reddish ochre scarps which everywhere lifted their
fronts to our view.

A long series of descents down rocky gullies, wherein
we were environed by threatening masses of disintegrated
rock, brought us to a dry, stony ravine, with mountain
heights looming above us a thousand feet high. This
ravine we followed, winding around in all directions, but
which gradually widened, however, into a broad plain,
with a western trend. The road, leaving this, struck
across a low ridge to the north ; and we were in view of
deserted settlements where the villages were built on
frowning castellated masses of rock. Near an upright
mass of rock over seventy feet high, and about fifty yards
in diameter, which dwarfed the gigantic sycamore close to
it, we made our camp, after five hours and thirty minutes'
continuous and rapid marching.

The people were very hungry; they had eaten every
scrap of meat, and every grain they possessed, twenty
hours before, and there was no immediate prospect of
food. I had but a pound and a half of flour left, and this
would not have sufficed to begin to feed a force of over
forty-five people ; but I had something like thirty pounds
of tea, and twenty pounds of sugar left, and I at once, as
soon as we arrived at camp, ordered every kettle to be
filled and placed on the fire, and then made tea for all,
giving each man a quart of a hot, grateful beverage, well
sweetened. Parties stole out also into the depths of the
jungle to search for wild fruit, and soon returned laden
with baskets of the wood-peach and tamarind fruit, which
though it did not satisfy, relieved them. That night,

before going to sleep, the Wangwana set up a loud prayer to " Allah " to give them food.

We rose betimes in the morning, determined to travel on until food could be procured, or we dropped down from sheer fatigue and weakness. Rhinoceros' tracks abounded, and buffalo seemed to be plentiful, but we never beheld a living thing. We crossed scores of short steeps, and descended as often into the depths of dry, stony gullies, and then finally entered a valley, bounded on one side by a triangular mountain with perpendicular sides, and on the other by a bold group, a triplet of hills. While marching down this valley—which soon changed its dry, bleached aspect to a vivid green—we saw a forest in the distance, and shortly found ourselves in corn-fields. Looking keenly around for a village, we descried it on the summit of the lofty triangular hill on our right. A loud exultant shout was raised at the discovery. The men threw down their packs, and began to clamour for food. Volunteers were asked to come forward to take cloth, and scale the heights to obtain it from the village, at any price. While three or four sallied off we rested on the ground, quite worn out.

In about an hour the foraging party returned with the glorious tidings that food was plentiful ; that the village we saw was called, " Welled Nzogera's "—the son of Nzogera—by which, of course, we knew that we were in Uvinza, Nzogera being the principal chief in Uvinza. We were further informed that Nzogera, the father, was at war with Lokanda-Mira, about some salt-pans in the valley of the Malagarazi, and that it would be difficult to go to Ujiji by the usual road, owing to this war ; but, for a consideration, the son of Nzogera was willing to supply us with guides, who would take us safely, by a northern road, to Ujiji.

Everything auguring well for our prospects, we encamped to enjoy the good cheer, for which our troubles and privations, during the transit of the Ukawendi forests and jungles, had well prepared us.

I am now going to extract from my Diary of the march, as, without its aid, I deem it impossible to relate fully our various experiences, so as to show them properly as they occurred to us; and as these extracts were written and recorded at the close of each day, they possess more interest, in my opinion, than a cold relation of facts, now toned down in memory.

October 31st. Tuesday.—Our road led E.N.E. for a considerable time after leaving the base of the triangular mountain whereon the son of Nzogera has established his stronghold, in order to avoid a deep and impassable portion of marsh, that stood between us and the direct route to the Malagarazi River. The valley sloped rapidly to this marsh, which received in its broad bosom the drainage of three extensive ranges. Soon we turned our faces northwest, and prepared to cross the marsh; and the guides informed us, as we halted on its eastern bank, of a terrible catastrophe which occurred a few yards above where we were preparing to cross. They told of an Arab and his caravan, consisting of thirty-five slaves, who had suddenly sunk out of sight, and who were never more heard of. This marsh, as it appeared to us, presented a breadth of some hundreds of yards, on which grew a close network of grass, with much decayed matter mixed up with it. In the centre of this, and underneath it, ran a broad, deep, and rapid stream. As the guides proceeded across, the men stole after them with cautious footsteps. As they arrived near the centre we began to see this unstable grassy bridge, so curiously provided by nature for us, move up and down in heavy languid undulations, like the swell of the sea after a storm. Where the two asses of the Expedition moved, the grassy waves rose a foot high; but suddenly one unfortunate animal plunged his feet through, and as he was unable to rise, he soon made a deep hollow, which was rapidly filling with water. With the aid of ten men, however, we were enabled to lift him bodily up and land him on a firmer part, and guiding them both across rapidly, the entire caravan crossed without accident.

On arriving at the other side, we struck off to the north, and found ourselves in a delightful country, in every way suitable for agriculturists. Great rocks rose here and there, but in their fissures rose stately trees, under whose umbrage nestled the villages of the people. We found the various village elders greedy for cloth, but the presence of the younger son of Nzogera's men restrained their propensity for extortion. Goats and sheep were remarkably cheap, and in good condition; and, consequently, to celebrate our arrival near the Malagarazi, a flock of eight goats was slaughtered, and distributed to the men.

November 1st.—Striking north-west, after leaving our camp, and descending the slope of a mountain, we soon beheld the anxiously looked-for Malagarazi, a narrow but deep stream, flowing through a valley pent in by lofty mountains. Fish-eating birds lined the trees on its banks; villages were thickly scattered about. Food was abundant and cheap.

After travelling along the left bank of the river a few miles, we arrived at the settlements recognizing Kiala as their ruler. I had anticipated we should be able at once to cross the river, but difficulties arose. We were told to camp, before any negotiations could be entered into. When we demurred, we were informed we might cross the river if we wished, but we should not be assisted by any Mvinza.

Being compelled to halt for this day, the tent was pitched in the middle of one of the villages, and the bales were stored in one of the huts, with four soldiers to guard them. After despatching an embassy to Kiala, eldest son of the great chief Nzogera, to request permission to cross the river as a peaceable caravan, Kiala sent word that the white man should cross his river after the payment of fifty-six cloths! Fifty-six cloths signified a bale nearly! Here was another opportunity for diplomacy. Bombay and Asmani were empowered to treat with Kiala about the honga, but it was not to exceed twenty-five doti. At 6 A.M., having spoken for seven hours, the two men returned, with the demand for thirteen doti for Nzogera, and ten doti for Kiala. Poor Bombay was hoarse, but Asmani still smiled; and I relented, congratulating myself that the preposterous demand, which was simply robbery, was no worse.

Three hours later another demand was made. Kiala had been visited by a couple of chiefs from his father; and the chiefs being told that a white man was at the ferry, put in a claim for a couple of guns and a keg of gunpowder. But here my patience was exhausted, and I declared that they should have to take them by force, for I would never consent to be robbed and despoiled after any such fashion.

Until 11 P.M., Bombay and Asmani were negotiating about this extra demand, arguing, quarreling, threatening, until Bombay declared they would talk him mad if it lasted much longer. I told Bombay to take two cloths, one for each chief, and, if they did not consider it enough, then I should fight. The present was taken, and the negotiations were terminated at midnight.

November 2nd.—Ihata Island, one and a half hour west of Kiala's. We arrived before the Island of Ihata, on the left bank of the Malagarazi, at 5 P.M.; the morning having been wasted in puerile talk with the owner of the canoes at the ferry. The final demand for ferriage across was eight yards of cloth and four fundo* of sami-sami, or red beads; which was at once paid. Four men, with their loads, were permitted to cross in the small, unshapely, and cranky canoes. When the boatmen had discharged their canoes of their passengers and cargoes, they were ordered to halt on the other side, and, to my astonishment, another demand was made. The ferrymen had found that two fundo of these were of short measure, and two fundo more must be paid, otherwise the contract for ferrying us across would be considered null and void. So two fundo more were added, but not without demur and much "talk," which in these lands is necessary.

Three times the canoes went backwards and forwards, when, lo! another demand was made, with the usual clamour and fierce wordy dispute; this time for five khete † for the man who guided us to the ferry, a shukka of cloth for a babbler, who had attached himself to the old-womanish Jumah, who did nothing but babble and increase the clamòr. These demands were also settled.

About sunset we endeavoured to cross the donkeys. "Simba," a fine wild Kinyamwezi donkey, went in first, with a rope attached to his neck. He had arrived at the middle of the stream when we saw him begin to struggle

---

* 4 fundo = 40 necklaces; 1 fundo being 10 necklaces.

† Necklaces.

—a crocodile had seized him by the throat. The poor animal's struggles were terrific. Chowpereh was dragging on the rope with all his might, but to no use, for the donkey sank, and we saw no more of him. The depth of the river at this place was about fifteen feet. We had seen the light-brown heads, the glittering eyes, and the ridgy backs, hovering about the vicinity, but we had never thought that the reptiles would advance so near such an exciting scene as the vicinity of the ferry presented during the crossing. Saddened a little by this loss, we resumed our work, and by 7 P.M. we were all across, excepting Bombay and the only donkey now left, which was to be brought across in the morning, when the crocodiles should have deserted the river.

November 3rd.—What contention have we not been a witness to these last three days! What anxiety have we not suffered ever since our arrival in Uvinza! The Wavinza are worse than the Wagogo, and their greed is more insatiable. We got the donkey across with the aid of a mganga, or medicine man, who spat some chewed leaves of a tree which grows close to the stream over him. He informed me he could cross the river at any time, day or night, after rubbing his body with these chewed leaves, which he believed to be a most potent medicine.

About 10 A.M. appeared from the direction of Ujiji a caravan of eighty Waguhha, a tribe which occupies a tract of country on the south-western side of the Lake Tanganika. We asked the news, and were told a white man had just arrived at Ujiji from Manyuema. This news startled us all.

"A white man?" we asked.

"Yes, a white man," they replied.

"How is he dressed?"

" Like the master," they answered, referring to me.

" Is he young, or old ?"

" He is old. He has white hair on his face, and is sick."

" Where has he come from ?"

" From a very far country away beyond Uguhha, called Manyuema."

" Indeed! and is he stopping at Ujiji now ?"

" Yes, we saw him about eight days ago."

" Do you think he will stop there until we see him ?"

" *Sigue* " (don't know).

" Was he ever at Ujiji before ?"

" Yes, he went away a long time ago."

Hurrah! This is Livingstone! He must be Living-stone ! He *can* be no other ; but still ;—he may be some one else—some one from the West Coast—or perhaps he is Baker ! No ; Baker has no white hair on his face. But we must now march quick, lest he hears we are coming, and runs away.

I addressed my men, and asked them if they were willing to march to Ujiji without a single halt, and then promised them, if they acceded to my wishes, two doti each man. All answered in the affirmative, almost as much rejoiced as I was myself. But I was madly rejoiced ; intensely eager to resolve the burning question, "Is it Dr. David Livingstone ?" God grant me patience, but I do wish there was a railroad, or, at least, horses in this country.

We set out at once from the banks of the Malagarazi, accompanied by two guides furnished us by Usenge, the old man of the ferry, who, now that we had crossed, showed himself more amiably disposed to us. We arrived at the village of **Isinga,** Sultan Katalambula, after a little over an hour's march across a saline plain, but which as we advanced into the interior became fertile and productive.

November 4th.—Started early with great caution, maintaining deep silence. The guides were sent forward, one two hundred yards ahead of the other, that we might be warned in time. The first part of the march was through a thin jungle of dwarf trees, which got thinner and thinner until finally it vanished altogether, and we had entered Uhha—a plain country. Villages were visible by the score among the tall bleached stalks of dourra and maize. Sometimes three, sometimes five, ten, or twenty beehive-shaped huts formed a village. The Wahha were evidently living in perfect security, for not one village amongst them all was surrounded with the customary defence of an African village. A narrow dry ditch formed the only boundary between Uhha and Uvinza. On entering Uhha, all danger from Makumbi vanished.

We halted at Kawanga, the chief of which lost no time in making us understand that he was the great Mutware of Kimenyi under the king, and that he was the tribute gatherer for his Kiha majesty. He declared that he was the only one in Kimenyi—an eastern division of Uhha— who could demand tribute; and that it would be very satisfactory to him, and a saving of trouble to ourselves, if we settled his claim of twelve doti of good cloths at once. We did not think it the best way of proceeding, knowing as we did the character of the native African ; so we at once proceeded to diminish this demand ; but, after six hours' hot argument, the Mutware only reduced it by two. This claim was then settled, upon the understanding that we should be allowed to travel through Uhha as far as the Rusugi River without being further mulcted.

November 5th.—Leaving Kawanga early in the morning and continuing our march over the boundless plains, which were bleached white by the hot equatorial sun, we were marching westward full of pleasant anticipations that we were nearing the end of our troubles, joyfully congratulating ourselves that within five days we should see that which I had come so far from civilisation, and through so many difficulties, to see, and were about passing a cluster of villages, with all the confidence which men possess against whom no one had further claim or a word to say, when I noticed two men darting from a group of natives who were watching us, and running towards the head of the Expedition, with the object, evidently, of preventing further progress.

The caravan stopped, and I walked forward to ascertain the cause from the two natives. I was greeted politely by the two Wahha with the usual "Yambos," and was then asked,

"Why does the white man pass by the village of the King of Uhha without salutation and a gift? Does not the white man know there lives a king in Uhha, to whom the Wangwana and Arabs pay something for right of passage?"

"Why, we paid last night to the chief of Kawanga, who informed us that he was the man deputed by the King of Uhha to collect the toll."

"How much did you pay?"

"Ten doti of good cloth."

"Are you sure?"

"Quite sure. If you ask him, he will tell you so."

"Well," said one of the Wahha, a fine, handsome, intelligent-looking youth, "it is our duty to the king to halt you here until we find out the truth of this. Will you walk to our village, and rest yourselves under the shade of our trees until we can send messengers to Kawanga?"

"No; the sun is but an hour high, and we have far to travel; but, in order to show you we do not seek to pass through your country without doing that which is right, we will rest where we now stand, and we will send with your messengers two of our soldiers, who will show you the man to whom we paid the cloth."

The messengers departed; but, in the meantime, the handsome youth, who turned out to be the nephew of the King, whispered some order to a lad, who immediately hastened away, with the speed of an antelope, to the cluster of villages which we had just passed. The result of this errand, as we saw in a short time, was the approach of a body of warriors, about fifty in number, headed by a tall, fine-looking man, who was dressed in a crimson robe called Joho, two ends of which were tied in a knot over the left shoulder; a new piece of American sheeting was folded like a turban around his head, and a large curved piece of polished ivory was suspended to his neck. He and his people were all armed with spears, and bows and arrows, and their advance was marked with a deliberation that showed they felt confidence in any issue that might transpire.

We were halted on the eastern side of the Pombwe stream, near the village of Lukomo, in Kimenyi, Uhha.

The gorgeously-dressed chief was a remarkable man in appearance. His face was oval in form, high cheek-bones, eyes deeply sunk, a prominent and bold forehead, a fine nose, and a well-cut mouth; he was tall in figure, and perfectly symmetrical.

When near to us, he hailed me with the words,

"Yambo, bana?—How do you do, master?" in quite a cordial tone.

I replied cordially also, "Yambo, mutware?—How do you do, chief?"

We, myself and men, interchanged "Yambos" with his warriors; and there was nothing in our first introduction to indicate that the meeting was of a hostile character.

The chief seated himself, his haunches resting on his heels, laying down his bow and arrows by his side; his men did likewise.

I seated myself on a bale, and each of my men sat down on their loads, forming quite a semicircle. The Wahha slightly outnumbered my party; but, while they were only armed with bows and arrows, spears, and knob-sticks, we were armed with rifles, muskets, revolvers, pistols, and hatchets.

All were seated, and deep silence was maintained by the assembly. The great plains around us were as still in this bright noon as if they were deserted of all living creatures. Then the chief spoke:

"I am Mionvu, the great Mutware of Kimenyi, and am next to the King, who lives yonder," pointing to a large village near some naked hills about ten miles to the north. "I have come to talk with the white man. It has always been the custom of the Arabs and the Wangwana to make a present to the King when they pass through his country. Does not the white man mean to pay the King's dues? Why does the white man halt in the road? Why will he not enter the village of Lukomo, where there is food and shade—where we can discuss this thing quietly? Does the white man mean to fight? I know well he is stronger than we are. His men have guns, and the Wahha have

but bows and arrows, and spears; but Uhha is large, and
our villages are many. Let him look about him everywhere—all is Uhha, and our country extends much further
than he can see or walk in a day. The King of Uhha is
strong; yet he wishes friendship only with the white man.
Will the white man have war or peace?"

A deep murmur of assent followed this speech of Mionvu
from his people, and disapprobation, blended with a certain uneasiness, from my men. When about replying, the
words of General Sherman, which I heard him utter to
the chiefs of the Arapahoes and Cheyennes at North
Platte, in 1867, came to my mind; and something of
their spirit I embodied in my reply to Mionvu, Mutware
of Kimenyi.

"Mionvu, the great Mutware, asks me if I have come
for war. When did Mionvu ever hear of white men
warring against black men? Mionvu must understand
that the white men are different from the black. White
men do not leave their country to fight the black people,
neither do they come here to buy ivory or slaves. They
come to make friends with black people; they come to
search for rivers, and lakes, and mountains; they come to
discover what countries, what peoples, what rivers, what
lakes, what forests, what plains, what mountains and hills
are in your country; to know the different animals that
are in the land of the black people, that, when they go
back, they may tell the white kings, and men, and children, what they have seen and heard in the land so far
from them. The white people are different from the Arabs
and Wangwana; the white people know everything, and
are very strong. When they fight, the Arabs and the
Wangwana run away. We have great guns which thunder,
and when they shoot the earth trembles; we have guns

which carry bullets further than you can see: even with these little things" (pointing to my revolvers) " I could kill ten men quicker than you could count. We are stronger than the Wahha. Mionvu has spoken the truth, yet we do not wish to fight. I could kill Mionvu now, yet I talk to him as to a friend. I wish to be a friend to Mionvu, and to all black people. Will Mionvu say what I can do for him?"

As these words were translated to him—imperfectly, I suppose, but still, intelligibly—the face of the Wahha showed how well they appreciated them. Once or twice I thought I detected something like fear, but my asser- tions that I desired peace and friendship with them soon obliterated all such feelings.

Mionvu replied:

" The white man tells me he is friendly. Why does he not come to our village? Why does he stop on the road? The sun is hot. Mionvu will not speak here any more. If the white man is a friend he will come to the village."

" We must stop now. It is noon. You have broken our march. We will go and camp in your village," I said, at the same time rising and pointing to the men to take up their loads.

We were compelled to camp; there was no help for it; the messengers had not returned from Kawanga. Having arrived in his village, Mionvu had cast himself at full length under the scanty shade afforded by a few trees within the boma. About 2 P.M. the messengers returned, saying it was true the chief of Kawanga had taken ten cloths; not, however for the King of Uhha, but for himself!

Mionvu, who evidently was keen-witted, and knew perfectly what he was about, now roused himself, and began to make miniature faggots of thin canes, ten in each faggot, and shortly he presented ten of these small bundles, which together contained one hundred, to me, saying each stick represented a cloth, and the amount of the "honga" required by the King of Uhha was ONE HUNDRED CLOTHS !—nearly two bales !

Recovering from our astonishment, which was almost indescribable, we offered TEN.

"Ten! to the King of Uhha! Impossible. You do not stir from Lukomo until you pay us one hundred!" exclaimed Mionvu, in a significant manner.

I returned no answer, but went to my hut, which Mionvu had cleared for my use, and Bombay, Asmani, Mabruki, and Chowpereh were invited to come to me for consultation. Upon my asking them if we could not fight our way through Uhha, they became terror-stricken, and Bombay, in imploring accents, asked me to think well what I was about to do, because it was useless to enter on a war with the Wahha. "Uhha is all a plain country; we cannot hide anywhere. Every village will rise all about us, and how can forty-five men fight thousands of people? They would kill us all in a few minutes, and how would you ever reach Ujiji if you died? Think of it, my dear master, and do not throw your life away for a few rags of cloth."

Well, but, Bombay, this is robbery. Shall we submit to be robbed? Shall we give this fellow everything he asks? He might as well ask me for all the cloth, and all my guns, without letting him see that we can fight. I can kill Mionvu and his principal men myself, and you can slay all those howlers out there without much trouble. If Mionvu and his principal were dead we should not be troubled much, and we could strike south to the Malagarazi, and go west to Ujiji."

"No, no, dear master, don't think of it for a moment. If we went near the Malagarazi we should come across Lokanda-Mira."

"Well, then, we will go north."

"Up that way Uhha extends far; and beyond Uhha are the Watuta."

"Well, then, say what we shall do. We must do something; but we must not be robbed."

"Pay Mionvu what he asks, and let us go away from here. This is the last place we shall have to pay. And in four days we shall be in Ujiji."

"Did Mionvu tell you that this is the last time we would have to pay?"

"He did, indeed."

"What do you say, Asmani? Shall we fight or pay?"

Asmani's face wore the usual smile, but he replied, "I am afraid we must pay. This is positively the last time."

"And you, Chowpereh?"

"Pay, bana; it is better to get along quietly in this country. If we were strong enough they would pay us. Ah, if we had only two hundred guns, how these Wahha would run!"

"What do you say, Mabruki?"

"Ah, master, dear master; it is very hard, and these people are great robbers. I would like to chop their heads off, all; so I would. But you had better pay. This is the last time; and what are one hundred cloths to you?"

"Well, then, Bombay and Asmani, go to Mionvu, and offer him twenty. If he will not take twenty, give him thirty. If he refuses thirty, give him forty; then go up to eighty, slowly. Make plenty of talk; not one doti more. I swear to you I will shoot Mionvu if he demands more than eighty. Go, and remember to be wise."

I will cut the matter short. At 9 P.M. sixty-four doti were handed over to Mionvu, for the King of Uhha; six doti for himself, and five doti for his sub; altogether seventy-five doti—a bale and a quarter! No sooner had we paid than they began to fight amongst themselves over the booty, and I was in hopes that the factions would proceed to battle, that I might have good excuse for leaving them, and plunging south to the jungle that I believed existed there, by which means, under its friendly cover, we might strike west. But no, it was only a verbose war, which portended nothing more than a noisy clamor.

November 6th.—At dawn we were on the road, very silent and sad. Our stock of cloth was much diminished; we had nine bales left, sufficient to have taken us to the Atlantic Ocean—aided by the beads, which were yet untouched—if we practised economy. If I met many more like Mionvu I had not enough to take me to Ujiji, and, though we were said to be so near, Livingstone seemed to me to be just as far as ever.

We crossed the Pombwe, and then struck across a slowly-undulating plain rising gradually to mountains on our right, and on our left sinking towards the valley of the Malagarazi, which river was about twenty miles away. Villages rose to our view everywhere. Food was cheap, milk was plentiful, and the butter good.

After a four hours' march, we crossed the Kanengi River, and entered the boma of Kahirigi, inhabited by several Watusi and Wahha. Here, we were told, lived the King of Uhha's brother. This announcement was anything but welcome, and I began to suspect I had fallen into another hornets' nest. We had not rested two hours before two Wangwana entered my tent, who were slaves of Thani bin Abdullah, our dandified friend of Unyanyembe. These men came, on the part of the king's brother, to claim the HONGA! The king's brother demanded thirty doti! Half a bale! Merciful Providence! What shall I do?

We had been told by Mionvu that the honga of Uhha was settled—and now here is another demand from the King's brother! It is the second time the lie has been told, and we have twice been deceived. We shall be deceived no more.

These two men informed us there were five more chiefs, living but two hours from each other, who would exact tribute, or black-mail, like those we had seen. Knowing this much, I felt a certain calm. It was far better to know the worst at once. Five more chiefs with their demands would assuredly ruin us. In view of which, what is to be done? How am I to reach Livingstone, without being beggared?

Dismissing the men, I called Bombay, and told him to assist Asmani in settling the honga—"as cheaply as possible." I then lit my pipe, put on the cap of consideration, and began to think. Within half an hour, I had made a plan, which was to be attempted to be put in execution that very night.

I summoned the two slaves of Thani bin Abdullah, after the honga had been settled to everybody's satisfaction—though the profoundest casuistries and diplomatic arguments failed to reduce it lower than twenty-six doti—and began asking them about the possibility of evading the tribute-taking Wahha ahead.

This rather astonished them at first, and they declared it to be impossible; but, finally, after being pressed, they replied, that one of their number should guide us at midnight, or a little after, into the jungle which grew on the frontiers of Uhha and Uvinza. By keeping a direct west course through this jungle until we came to Uka-ranga we might be enabled—we were told—to travel through Uhha without further trouble. If I were willing to pay the guide twelve doti, and if I were able to impose silence on my people while passing through the sleeping village, the guide was positive I could reach Ujiji without paying another doti. It is needless to add, that I accepted the proffered assistance at such a price with joy.

But there was much to be done. Provisions were to be purchased, sufficient to last four days, for the tramp through the jungle, and men were at once sent with cloth to purchase grain at any price. Fortune favoured us, for before 8 P.M. we had enough for six days.

November 7th.—I did not go to sleep at all last night, but a little after midnight, as the moon was beginning to show itself, by gangs of four, the men stole quietly out of the village; and by 3 A.M. the entire Expedition was outside the boma, and not the slightest alarm had been made. After a signal to the new guide, the Expedition began to move in a southern direction along the right bank of the Kanengi River. After an hour's march in this direction, we struck west, across the grassy plain, and maintained it, despite the obstacles we encountered, which were sore enough to naked men. The bright moon lighted our path: dark clouds now and then cast immense long shadows over the deserted and silent plains, and the moonbeans were almost obscured, and at such times our position seemed awful—

> Till the moon,
> Rising in clouded majesty, at length,
> Apparent queen, unveiled her peerless light,
> And o'er the dark her silver mantle threw.

Bravely toiled the men, without murmur, though their legs were bleeding from the cruel grass. "Ambrosial morn" at last appeared, with all its beautiful and lovely features. Heaven was born anew to us, with comforting omens and cheery promise. The men, though fatigued at the unusual travel, sped forward with quicker pace as daylight broke, until, at 8 A.M., we sighted the swift Rusugi River, when a halt was ordered in a clump of jungle near it, for breakfast and rest. Both banks of the river were alive with buffalo, eland, and antelope, but, though the sight was very tempting, we did not fire, because we dared not. The report of a gun would have alarmed the whole country. I preferred my coffee, and the contentment which my mind experienced at our success.

An hour after we had rested, some natives, carrying salt from the Malagarazi, were seen coming up the right bank of the river. When abreast of our hiding-place, they detected us, and dropping their salt-bags, they took to their heels at once, shouting out as they ran, to alarm some villages that appeared about four miles north of us. The men were immediately ordered to take up their loads, and in a few minutes we had crossed the Rusugi, and were making direct for a bamboo jungle that appeared in our front. On, on, we kept steadily until, at 1 P.M., we sighted the little lake of Musunya, as wearied as possible with our nine hours' march.

Lake Musunya is one of the many circular basins found in this part of Uhha. There was quite a group of them. The more correct term of these lakes would be immense pools. In the Masika season, Lake Musunya must extend to three or four miles in length by two in breadth. It swarms with hippopotami, and its shores abound with noble game.

We were very quiet, as may be imagined, in our bivouac; neither tent nor hut was raised, nor was fire kindled, so that, in case of pursuit, we could move off without delay. I kept my Winchester rifle (the gift of my friend Mr. Morris, and a rare gift it was for such a crisis) with its magazine full, and two hundred cartridges in a bag slung over my shoulders. Each soldier's gun was also ready and loaded, and we retired to sleep our fatigues off with a feeling of perfect security.

November 8th.—Long before dawn appeared, we were on the march, and, as daylight broke, we emerged from the bamboo jungle, and struck across the naked plain of Uhha, once more passing several large pools by the way —far-embracing prospects of undulating country, with here and there a characteristic clump of trees relieving the general nudity of the whole. Hour after hour we toiled on, across the rolling land waves, the sun shining with all its wonted African fervor, but with its heat slightly tempered by the welcome breezes, which came laden with the fragrance of young grass, and perfume of strange flowers of various hues, that flecked the otherwise pale-green sheet which extended so far around us.

We arrived at the Rugufu River—not the Ukawendi Rugufu, but the northern stream of that name, a tributary of the Malagarazi. It was a broad shallow stream, and sluggish, with an almost imperceptible flow south-west. While we halted in the deep shade afforded by a dense clump of jungle, close to the right bank, resting awhile before continuing our journey. I distinctly heard a sound as of distant thunder in the west. Upon asking if it were thunder, I was told it was Kabogo.

"Kabogo? what is that?"

"It is a great mountain on the other side of the Tanganika, full of deep holes, into which the water rolls; and when there is wind on the Tanganika, there is a sound like mvuha (thunder). Many boats have been lost there, and it is a custom with Arabs and natives to throw cloth—Merikani and Kaniki—and especially white (Merikani) beads, to appease the mulungu (god) of the lake. Those who throw beads generally get past without trouble, but those who do not throw beads into the lake get lost, and are drowned. Oh, it is a dreadful place!" This story was told me by the ever-smiling guide Asmani, and was corroborated by other former mariners of the lake whom I had with me.

At the least, this place where we halted for dinner, on the banks of the Rugufu River, is eighteen and a half hours, or forty-six miles, from Ujiji; and, as Kabogo is said to be near Uguhha, it must be over sixty miles from Ujiji; therefore the sound of the thundering surf, which is said to roll into the caves of Kabogo, was heard by us at a distance of over one hundred miles away from them.

Continuing our journey for three hours longer, through thin forests, over extensive beds of primitive rock, among fields of large boulders thickly strewn about, passing by numerous herds of buffalo, giraffe, and zebra, over a quaking quagmire which resembled peat, we arrived at the small stream of Sunuzzi, to a camping place only a mile removed from a large settlement of Wahha. But we were buried in the depths of a great forest—no road was in the vicinity, no noise was made, deep silence was preserved ; nor were fires lit. We might therefore rest tranquilly secure, certain that we should not be disturbed. To-morrow morning the kirangozi has promised we shall be out of Uhha, and if we travel on to Niamtaga, in Ukaranga, the same day, the next day would see us in Ujiji.

Patience, my soul! A few hours more, then the end of all this will be known! I shall be face to face with that "white man with the white hairs on his face, whoever he is!"

November 9th.—Two hours before dawn we left our camp on the Sunuzzi River, and struck through the forest in a north-by-west direction, having muzzled our goats previously, lest, by their bleating, they might betray us. This was a mistake which might have ended tragically, for just as the eastern sky began to assume a pale greyish tint, we emerged from the jungle on the high road. The guide thought we had passed Uhha, and set up a shout which was echoed by every member of the caravan, and marched onward with new vigor and increased energy, when plump we came to the outskirts of a village, the inhabitants of which were beginning to stir. Silence was called for at once, and the Expedition halted immediately. I walked forward to the front to advise with the guide. He did not know what to do. There was no time to consider, so I ordered the goats to be slaughtered and left on the road, and the guide to push on boldly through the village. The chickens also had their throats cut; after which the Expedition resumed the march quickly and silently, led by the guide, who had orders to plunge into the jungle south of the road. I stayed until the last man had disappeared; then, after preparing my Winchester, brought up the rear, followed by my gunbearers with their stock of amunition. As we were about disappearing beyond the last hut, a man darted out of his hut, and uttered an exclamation of alarm, and loud voices were heard as if in dispute. But in a short time we were in the depths of the jungle, hurrying away from the road in a southern direction, and edging slightly westward. Once I thought we were pursued, and I halted behind a tree to check our foes if they persisted in following us; but a few minutes proved to me that we were not pursued. After half-an-hour's march we again turned our faces westward. It was broad daylight now, and our eyes were delighted with most picturesque and sequestered little valleys, where wild fruit-trees grew, and rare flowers blossomed, and tiny brooks tumbled over polished pebbles —where all was bright and beautiful—until, finally, wading through one pretty pure streamlet, whose soft murmurs we took for a gentle welcome, we passed the boundary of wicked Uhha, and had entered Ukaranga!— an event that was hailed with extravagant shouts of joy.

Presently we found the smooth road, and we trod gaily with elastic steps, with limbs quickened for the march which we all knew to be drawing near its end. What cared we now for the difficulties we had encountered—for the rough and cruel forests, for the thorny thickets and hurtful grass, for the jangle of all savagedom, of which we had been the joyless audience! To-morrow! Ay, the great day draws nigh, and we may well laugh and sing while in this triumphant mood. We have been sorely tried; we have been angry with each other when vexed by troubles, but we forget all these now, and there is no face but is radiant with the happiness we have all deserved.

We made a short halt at noon, for rest and refreshment. I was shown the hills from which the Tanganika could be seen, which bounded the valley of the Liuche on the east. I could not contain myself at the sight of them. Even with this short halt I was restless and unsatisfied. We resumed the march again. I spurred my men forward with the promise that to-morrow should see their reward.

We were in sight of the villages of the Wakaranga; the people caught sight of us, and manifested considerable excitement. I sent men ahead to reassure them, and they came forward to greet us. This was so new and welcome to us, so different from the turbulent Wavinza and the black-mailers of Uhha, that we were melted. But we had no time to loiter by the way to indulge our joy. I was impelled onward by my almost uncontrollable feelings. I wished to resolve my doubts and fears. Was HE still there? Had HE heard of my coming? Would HE fly?

How beautiful Ukaranga appears! The green hills are crowned by clusters of straw-thatched cones. The hills rise and fall; here denuded and cultivated, there in pasturage, here timbered, yonder swarming with huts. The country has somewhat the aspect of Maryland.

We cross the Mkuti, a glorious little river! We ascend the opposite bank, and stride through the forest like men who have done a deed of which they may be proud. We have already travelled nine hours, and the sun is sinking rapidly towards the west; yet, apparently, we are not fatigued.

We reach the outskirts of Niamtaga, and we hear drums beat. The people are flying into the woods; they desert their villages, for they take us to be Ruga-Ruga—

the forest thieves of Mirambo, who, after conquering the Arabs of Unyanyembe, are coming to fight the Arabs oᴸ Ujiji. Even the King flies from his village, and every man, woman, and child, terror-stricken, follows him. We enter into it and quietly take possession. Finally, the word is bruited about that we are Wangwana, from Unyanyembe.

"Well, then, is Mirambo dead?" they ask.

"No," we answer.

"Well, how did you come to Ukaranga?'

"By way of Ukonongo, Ukawendi, and Uhha."

"Oh—hi-le!" Then they laugh heartily at their fright, and begin to make excuses. The King is introduced to me, and he says he had only gone to the woods in order to attack us again—he meant to have come back and killed us all, if we had been Ruga-Ruga. But then we know the poor King was terribly frightened, and would never have dared to return, had we been Ruga-Ruga—not he. We are not, however, in a mood to quarrel with him about an idiomatic phrase peculiar to him, but rather take him by the hand and shake it well, and say we are so very glad to see him. And he shares in our pleasure, and immdiately three of the fattest sheep, pots of beer, flour, and honey are brought to us as a gift, and I make him happier still with two of the finest cloths I have in my bales; and thus a friendly pact is entered into between us.

While I write my Diary of this day's proceedings, I tell my servant to lay out my new flannel suit, to oil my boots, to chalk my helmet, and fold a new puggaree around it, that I may make as presentable an appearance as possible before the white man with the grey beard, and before the Arabs of Ujiji; for the clothes I have worn through jungle and forest are in tatters. Good-night; only let one day come again, and we shall see what we shall see.

November 10th. Friday.—The 236th day from Bagamoyo on the Sea, and the 51st day from Unyanyembe. General direction to Ujiji, west-by-south. Time of march, six hours.

It is a happy, glorious morning. The air is fresh and cool. The sky lovingly smiles on the earth and her children. The deep woods are crowned in bright vernal leafage; the water of the Mkuti, rushing under the emerald shade afforded by the bearded banks, seems to challenge us for the race to Ujiji, with its continuous brawl.

We are all outside the village cane fence, every man of us looking as spruce, as neat, and happy as when we embarked on the dhows at Zanzibar, which seems to us to have been ages ago—we have witnessed and experienced so much.

" Forward ! "

" Ay Wallah, ay Wallah, bana yango ! " and the light-hearted braves stride away at a rate which must soon bring us within view of Ujiji. We ascend a hill over-grown with bamboo, descend into a ravine through which dashes an impetuous little torrent, ascend another short hill, then, along a smooth footpath running across the slope of a long ridge, we push on as only eager, light-hearted men can do.

In two hours I am warned to prepare for a view of the Tanganika, for, from the top of a steep mountain the kirangozi says I can see it. I almost vent the feeling of my heart in cries. But wait, we must behold it first. And we press forward and up the hill breathlessly, lest the grand scene hasten away. We are at last on the summit. Ah! not yet can it be seen. A little further on —just yonder, oh! there it is—a silvery gleam. I merely catch sight of it between the trees, and—but here it is at last! True—THE TANGANIKA! and there are the blue-black mountains of Ugoma and Ukaramba. An immense broad sheet, a burnished bed of silver—lucid canopy of blue above—lofty mountains are its valances, palm forests form its fringes! The Tanganika!—Hurrah! and the men respond to the exultant cry of the Anglo-Saxon with the lungs of Stentors, and the great forests and the hills seem to share in our triumph.

"Was this the place where Burton and Speke stood, Bombay, when they saw the lake first?"

"I don't remember, master; it was somewhere about here, I think."

"Poor fellows! The one was half-paralyzed, the other half-blind," said Sir Roderick Murchison, when he described Burton and Speke's arrival in view of the Tanganika.

And I? Well, I am so happy that, were I quite paralyzed and blinded, I think that at this supreme moment I could take up my bed and walk, and all blindness would cease at once. Fortunately, however, I am quite well; I have not suffered a day's sickness since the day I left Unyanyembe. How much would Shaw be willing to give to be in my place now? Who is happiest —he, revelling in the luxuries of Unyanyembe, or I, standing on the summit of this mountain, looking down with glad eyes and proud heart on the Tanganika?

We are descending the western slope of the mountain, with the valley of the Liuche before us. Something like an hour before noon we have gained the thick matete brake, which grows on both banks of the river; we wade through the clear stream, arrive on the other side, emerge out of the brake, and the gardens of the Wajiji are around us—a perfect marvel of vegetable wealth. Details escape my hasty and partial observation. I am almost overpowered with my own emotions. I notice the graceful palms, neat plots, green with vegetable plants, and small villages surrounded with frail fences of the matete-cane.

We push on rapidly, lest the news of our coming might reach the people of Ujiji before we come in sight, and are ready for them. We halt at a little brook, then ascend the long slope of a naked ridge, the very last of the myriads we have crossed. This alone prevents us from seeing the lake in all its vastness. We arrive at the summit, travel across and arrive at its western rim, and—pause, reader—the port of Ujiji is below us, embowered in the palms, only five hundred yards from us!

At this grand moment we do not think of the hundreds of miles we have marched, or of the hundreds of hills that we have ascended and descended, or of the many forests we have traversed, or of the jungles and thickets that annoyed us, or of the fervid salt plains that blistered our feet, or of the hot suns that scorched us, nor of the dangers and difficulties, now happily surmounted!

At last the sublime hour has arrived;—our dreams, our hopes, and anticipations are now about to be realised! Our hearts and our feelings are with our eyes, as we peer into the palms and try to make out in which hut or house lives the "white man with the grey beard" we heard about when we were at the Malagarazi.

"Unfurl the flags, and load your guns!"

"We will, master, we will, master!" respond the men eagerly.

" One, two, three,—fire !"

A volley from nearly fifty guns roars like a salute from a battery of artillery : we shall note its effect presently on the peaceful-looking village below.

"Now, kirangozi, hold the white man's flag up high, and let the Zanzibar flag bring up the rear. And you men keep close together, and keep firing until we halt in the market-place, or before the white man's house. You have said to me often that you could smell the fish of the Tanganika—I can smell the fish of the Tanganika now. There are fish, and beer, and a long rest waiting for you. MARCH !"

Before we had gone a hundred yards our repeated volleys had the effect desired. We had awakened Ujiji to the knowledge that a caravan was coming, and the people were witnessed rushing up in hundreds to meet us. The mere sight of the flags informed every one immediately that we were a caravan, but the American flag borne aloft by gigantic Asmani, whose face was one vast smile on this day, rather staggered them at first. However, many of the people who now approached us, remembered the flag. They had seen it float above the American Consulate, and from the mast-head of many a ship in the harbor of Zanzibar, and they were soon heard welcoming the beautiful flag with cries of " Bindera Kisungu !"—a white man's flag ! " Bindera Merikani !" —the American flag !

Then we were surrounded by them : by Wajiji, Wanyamwezi, Wangwana, Warundi, Waguhha, Wamanyuema, and Arabs, and were almost deafened with the shouts of " Yambo, yambo, bana ! Yambo, bana ! Yambo, bana !" To all and each of my men the welcome was given.

We were now about three hundred yards from the

village of Ujiji, and the crowds are dense about me.
Suddenly I hear a voice on my right say,

"Good morning, sir!"

Startled at hearing this greeting in the midst of such
a crowd of black people, I turn sharply around in search
of the man, and see him at my side, with the blackest of
faces, but animated and joyous—a man dressed in a long
white shirt, with a turban of American sheeting around
his woolly head, and I ask:

"Who the mischief are you?"

"I am Susi, the servant of Dr. Livingstone," said he,
smiling, and showing a gleaming row of teeth.

"What! Is Dr. Livingstone here?"

"Yes, sir."

"In this village?"

"Yes, sir."

"Are you sure?"

"Sure, sure, sir. Why, I leave him just now."

"Good morning, sir," said another voice.

"Hallo," said I, "is this another one?"

"Yes, sir."

"Well, what is your name?"

"My name is Chumah, sir."

"What! are you Chumah, the friend of Wekotani?"

"Yes, sir."

"And is the Doctor well?"

"Not very well, sir."

"Where has he been so long?"

"In Manyuema."

"Now, you Susi, run, and tell the Doctor I am
coming."

"Yes, sir," and off he darted like a madman.

But by this time we were within two hundred yards

of the village, and the multitude was getting denser, and almost preventing our march. Flags and streamers were out; Arabs and Wangwana were pushing their way through the natives in order to greet us, for according to their account, we belonged to them. But the great wonder of all was, "How did you come from Unyanyembe?"

Soon Susi came running back, and asked me my name; he had told the Doctor I was coming, but the Doctor was too surprised to believe him, and when the Doctor asked him my name, Susi was rather staggered.

But, during Susi's absence, the news had been conveyed to the Doctor that it was surely a white man that was coming, whose guns were firing, and whose flag could be seen; and the great Arab magnates of Ujiji—Mohammed bin Sali, Sayd bin Majid, Abid bin Suliman, Mohammed bin Gharib, and others—had gathered together before the Doctor's house, and the Doctor had come out from his veranda to discuss the matter and await my arrival.

In the meantime, the head of the Expedition had halted, and the kirangozi was out of the ranks, holding his flag aloft, and Selim said to me, "I see the Doctor, sir. Oh, what an old man! He has got a white beard." And I——what would I not have given for a bit of friendly wilderness, where, unseen, I might vent my joy in some mad freak, such as idiotically biting my hand, turning a somersault, or slashing at trees, in order to allay those exciting feelings that were well-nigh uncontrollable. My heart beats fast, but I must not let my face betray my emotions, lest it shall detract from the dignity of a white man appearing under such extraordinary circumstances.

So I did that which I thought was most dignified. I pushed back the crowds, and, passing from the rear,

"DR. LIVINGSTONE, I PRESUME."

walked down a living avenue of people, until I came in front of the semicircle of Arabs, before which stood the " white man with the grey beard."

As I advanced slowly towards him I noticed he was pale, that he looked wearied and wan, that he had grey whiskers and moustache, that he wore a bluish cloth cap with a faded gold band on a red ground round it, and that he had on a red-sleeved waistcoat, and a pair of grey tweed trousers.

I would have run to him, only I was a coward in the presence of such a mob—would have embraced him, but that I did not know how he would receive me; so I did what moral cowardice and false pride suggested was the best thing—walked deliberately to him, took off my hat, and said :

" DR. LIVINGSTONE, I PRESUME ?"

" YES," said he, with a kind, cordial smile, lifting his cap slightly.

I replaced my hat on my head, and he replaced his cap, and we both grasped hands. I then said aloud :

" I thank God, Doctor, I have been permitted to see you."

He answered, " I feel thankful that I am here to welcome you."

I turned to the Arabs, took off my hat to them in response to the saluting chorus of " Yambos " I received, and the Doctor introduced them to me by name. Then, oblivious of the crowds, oblivious of the men who shared with me my dangers, we—Livingstone and I—turned our faces towards his house. He pointed to the veranda, or rather, mud platform, under the broad overhanging eaves; he pointed to his own particular seat, which I saw his age and experience in Africa had suggested, namely, a straw mat, with a goatskin over it, and another skin nailed against the wall to protect his back from contact with the cold mud. I protested against taking this seat, which so much more befitted him than I, but the Doctor would not yield: I must take it.

We were seated—the Doctor and I—with our backs to the wall. The Arabs took seats on our left. More than a thousand natives were in our front, filling the whole square densely, indulging their curiosity, and discussing the fact of two white men meeting at Ujiji—one just come from Manyuema, in the west, the other from Unyanyembe, in the east.

Conversation began. What about? I declare I have forgotten. Oh! we mutually asked questions of one another, such as:

"How did you come here?" and "Where have you been all this long time?—the world has believed you to be dead." Yes, that was the way it began: but whatever the Doctor informed me, and that which I communicated to him, I cannot correctly report, for I found myself gazing at him, conning the wonderful figure and face of the man at whose side I now sat in Central Africa. Every hair of his head and beard, every wrinkle of his face, the wanness of his features, and the slightly wearied look he wore, were all imparting intelligence to me—the knowledge I craved for so much ever since I heard the words, "Take what you want, but find Livingstone." What I saw was deeply interesting intelligence to me, and unvarnished truth. I was listening and reading at the same time .What did these dumb witnesses relate to me?

Oh, reader, had you been at my side on this day in Ujiji, how eloquently could be told the nature of this man's work! Had you been there but to see and hear!

His lips gave me the details; lips that never lie.   I cannot repeat what he said ; I was too much engrossed to take my note-book out, and begin to stenograph his story.   He had so much to say that he began at the end, seemingly oblivious of the fact that five or six years had to be accounted for.   But his account was oozing out; it was growing fast into grand proportions—into a most marvellous history of deeds.

The Arabs rose up, with a delicacy I approved, as if they intuitively knew that we ought to be left to ourselves.

I sent Bombay with them to give them the news they also wanted so much to know about the affairs at Unyanyembe.   Sayd bin Majid was the father of the gallant young man whom I saw at Masangi, and who fought with me at Zimbizo, and who soon afterwards was killed by Mirambo's Ruga-Ruga in the forest of Wilyankuru ; and, knowing that I had been there, he earnestly desired to hear the tale of the fight; but they had all friends at Unyanyembe, and it was but natural that they should be anxious to hear of what concerned them.

After giving orders to Bombay and Asmani for the provisioning of the men of the Expedition, I called "Kaif-Halek," or "How-do-ye-do," and introduced him to Dr. Livingstone as one of the soldiers in charge of certain goods left at Unyanyembe, whom I had compelled to accompany me to Ujiji, that he might deliver in person to his master the letter-bag with which he had been in-trusted.   This was that famous letter-bag marked "Nov. 1st, 1870," which was now delivered into the Doctor's hands 365 days after it left Zanzibar !   How long, I wonder, had it remained at Unyanyembe had I not been despatched into Central Africa in search of the great traveller ?

The Doctor kept the letter-bag on his knee, then, presently, opened it, looked at the letters contained there, and read one or two of his children's letters, his face in the meanwhile lighting up.

He asked me to tell him the news. "No, Doctor," said I, "read your letters first, which I am sure you must be impatient to read."

"Ah," said he, "I have waited years for letters, and I have been taught patience. I can surely afford to wait a few hours longer. No, tell me the general news: how is the world getting along?

"You probably know much already. Do you know that the Suez Canal is a fact—is opened, and a regular trade carried on between Europe and India through it?"

"I did not hear about the opening of it. Well, that is grand news! What else?"

Shortly I found myself enacting the part of an annual periodical to him. There was no need of exaggeration—of any penny-a-line news, or of any sensationalism. The world had witnessed and experienced much the last few years. The Pacific Railroad had been completed; Grant had been elected President of the United States; Egypt had been flooded with savans: the Cretan rebellion had terminated; a Spanish revolution had driven Isabella from the throne of Spain, and a Regent had been appointed: General Prim was assassinated; a Castelar had electrified Europe with his advanced ideas upon the liberty of worship; Prussia had humbled Denmark, and annexed Schleswig-Holstein, and her armies were now around Paris; the "Man of Destiny" was a prisoner at Wilhelm-shöhe; the Queen of Fashion and the Empress of the French was a fugitive; and the child born in the purple had lost for ever the Imperial crown intended for his head the Napoleon dynasty was extinguished by the Prussians, Bismarck and Von Moltke; and France, the proud empire, was humbled to the dust.

What could a man have exaggerated of these facts? What a budget of news it was to one who had emerged from the depths of the primeval forests of Manyuema! The reflection of the dazzling light of civilisation was cast on him while Livingstone was thus listening in wonder to one of the most exciting pages of history ever repeated. How the puny deeds of barbarism paled before these! Who could tell under what new phases of uneasy life Europe was labouring even then, while we, two of her lonely children, rehearsed the tale of her late woes and glories? More worthily, perhaps, had the tongue of a lyric Demodocus recounted them; but, in the absence of the poet, the newspaper correspondent performed his part as well and truthfully as he could.

Not long after the Arabs had departed, a dishful of hot hashed-meat cakes was sent to us by Sayd bin Majid, and a curried chicken was received from Mohammed bin Sali, and Moeni Kheri sent a dishful of stewed goat-meat and rice; and thus presents of food came in succession, and as fast as they were brought we set to. I had a healthy, stubborn digestion—the exercise I had taken had put it in prime order; but Livingstone—he had been complaining that he had no appetite, that his stomach refused everything but a cup of tea now and then—he ate also— ate like a vigorous, hungry man; and, as he vied with me in demolishing the pancakes, he kept repeating, "You have brought me new life. You have brought me new life."

"Oh, by George!" I said, "I have forgotten something Hasten, Selim, and bring that bottle; you know which and bring me the silver goblets. I brought this bottle on purpose for this event, which I hoped would come to pass, though often it seemed useless to expect it."

Selim knew where the bottle was, and he soon returned with it—a bottle of Sillery champagne; and, handing the Doctor a silver goblet brimful of the exhilarating wine, and pouring a small quantity into my own, I said,

"Dr. Livingstone, to your very good health, sir."

"And to yours!" he responded, smilingly.

And the champagne I had treasured for this happy meeting was drunk with hearty good wishes to each other.

But we kept on talking and talking, and prepared food was being brought to us all that afternoon; and we kept on eating each time it was brought, until I had eaten even to repletion, and the Doctor was obliged to confess that he had eaten enough. Still, Halimah, the female cook of the Doctor's establishment, was in a state of the greatest excitement. She had been protruding her head out of the cookhouse to make sure that there were really two white men sitting down in the veranda, when there used to be only one, who would not, because he could not, eat anything; and she had been considerably exercised in her mind about this fact. She was afraid the Doctor did not properly appreciate her culinary abilities; but now she was amazed at the extraordinary quantity of food eaten, and she was in a state of delightful excitement. We could hear her tongue rolling off a tremendous volume of clatter to the wondering crowds who halted before the kitchen to hear the current of news with which she edified them. Poor, faithful soul! While we listened to the noise of her furious gossip, the Doctor related her faithful services, and the terrible anxiety she evinced when the guns first announced the arrival of another white man in Ujiji; how she had been flying about in a state of the utmost excitement, from the kitchen into his presence, and out again into the square, asking all sorts of questions; how she was in despair at the scantiness of the general larder and treasury of the strange household; how she was anxious to make up for their poverty by a grand appearance—to make up a sort of Barmecide feast to welcome the white man. "Why," said she, "is he not one of us? Does he not bring plenty of cloth and beads? Talk about the Arabs! Who are they that they should be compared to white men? Arabs, indeed!"

The Doctor and I conversed upon many things, especially upon his own immediate troubles, and his disappointments, upon his arrival in Ujiji, when told that all his goods had been sold, and he was reduced to poverty. He had but twenty cloths or so left of the stock he had deposited with the man called Sherif, the half-caste drunken tailor, who was sent by the Consul in charge of the goods. Besides which he had been suffering from an attack of dysentery, and his condition was most deplorable. He was but little improved on this day, though he had eaten well, and already began to feel stronger and better.

This day, like all others, though big with happiness to me, at last was fading away. While sitting with our faces looking to the east, as Livingstone had been sitting for days preceding my arrival, we noted the dark shadows which crept up above the grove of palms beyond the village, and above the rampart of mountains which we had crossed that day, now looming through the fast approaching darkness; and we listened, with our hearts full of gratitude to the Great Giver of Good and Dispenser of all Happiness, to the sonorous thunder of the surf of the Tanganika, and to the chorus which the night insects sang. Hours passed, and we were still sitting there with our minds busy upon the day's remarkable events, when I remembered that the traveller had not yet read his letters.

"Doctor," I said, "you had better read your letters. I will not keep you up any longer."

"Yes," he answered," it is getting late; and I will go and read my friends' letters. Good-night, and God bless you."

"Good-night, my dear Doctor; and let me hope that your news will be such as you desire."

I have now related, by means of my Diary, "How I found Livingstone," as recorded on the evening of that great day. I have been averse to reduce it by process of excision and suppression, into a mere cold narrative, because, by so doing, I would be unable to record what feelings swayed each member of the Expedition as well as myself, during the days preceding the discovery of the lost traveller, and more especially the day it was the good fortune of both Livingstone and myself to clasp each other's hands in the strong friendship which was born in that hour we thus strangely met. The aged traveller, though cruelly belied, contrary to all previous expectation, received me as a friend; and the cordial warmth with which he accepted my greeting; the courtesy with which he tendered to me a shelter in his own house; the simple candour of his conversation; graced by unusual modesty of manner, and meekness of spirit, wrought in me such a violent reaction in his favor, that when the parting " good-night " was uttered, I felt a momentary vague fear lest the fulness of joy which I experienced that evening would be diminished by some envious fate, before the morrow's sun should rise above Ujiji.

CHAPTER XII.

INTERCOURSE WITH LIVINGSTONE AT UJIJI—LIVINGSTONE'S
OWN STORY OF HIS JOURNEYS, HIS TROUBLES, AND DIS-
APPOINTMENTS.

" If there is love between us, inconceivably delicious, and profitable
will our intercourse be; if not, your time is lost, and you will only
annoy me. I shall seem to you stupid, and the reputation I have false.
All my good is magnetic, and I educate not by lessons, but by going
about my business."—Emerson's *Representative Men.*

I WOKE up early next morning with a sudden start. The
room was strange! It was a house, and not my tent!
Ah, yes! I recollected I had discovered Livingstone,
and I was in his house. I listened, that the knowledge
dawning on me might be confirmed by the sound of his
voice. I heard nothing but the sullen roar of the
surf.

I lay quietly in bed. Bed! Yes, it was a primitive
four-poster, with the leaves of the palm-tree spread upon
it instead of down, and horsehair and my bearskin spread
over this serving me in place of linen. I began to put

myself under a rigid mental cross-examination, and to an analyzation of my position.

"What was I sent for?"

"To find Livingstone."

"Have you found him?"

"Yes, of course; am I not in his house? Whose compass is that hanging on a peg there? Whose clothes, whose boots, are those? Who reads those newspapers, those 'Saturday Reviews' and numbers of 'Punch' lying on the floor?"

"Well, what are you going to do now?"

"I shall tell him this morning who sent me, and what brought me here. I will then ask him to write a letter to Mr. Bennett, and to give what news he can spare. I did not come here to rob him of his news. Sufficient for me is it that I have found him. It is a complete success so far. But it will be a greater one if he gives me letters for Mr. Bennett, and an acknowledgment that he has seen me."

"Do you think he will do so?"

"Why not? I have come here to do him a service. He has no goods. I have. He has no men with him. I have. If I do a friendly part by him, will he not do a friendly part by me? What says the poet?—

> Nor hope to find
> A friend, but who has found a friend in thee.
> All like the purchase; few the price will pay:
> And this makes friends such *wonders* here below.

I have paid the purchase, by coming so far to do him a service. But I think, from what I have seen of him last night, that he is not such a niggard and misanthrope as I was led to believe. He exhibited considerable emotion, despite the monosyllabic greeting, when he shook my hand. If he were a man to feel annoyance at any person coming after him, he would not have received me as he did, nor would he ask me to live with him, but he would have surlily refused to see me, and told me to mind my own business. Neither does he mind my nationality; for 'here,' said he, 'Americans and Englishmen are the same people. We speak the same language and have the same ideas.' Just so, Doctor; I agree with you. Here at least, Americans and Englishmen shall be brothers, and whatever I can do for you, you may command me freely."

I dressed myself quietly, intending to take a stroll along the Tanganika before the Doctor should rise; opened the door, which creaked horribly on its hinges, and walked out to the veranda.

"Halloa, Doctor!—you up already? I hope you have slept well?"

"Good-morning, Mr. Stanley! I am glad to see you. I hope you rested well. I sat up late reading my letters. You have brought me good and bad news. But sit down." He made a place for me by his side. "Yes, many of my friends are dead. My eldest son has met with a sad accident—that is, my boy Tom; my second son, Oswell, is at college studying medicine, and is doing well I am told. Agnes, my eldest daughter, has been enjoying herself in a yacht, with 'Sir Paraffine' Young and his family. Sir Roderick, also, is well, and expresses a hope that he will soon see me. You have brought me quite a budget."

The man was not an apparition, then, and yesterday's scenes were not the result of a dream! and I gazed on him intently, for thus I was assured he had not run away, which was the great fear that constantly haunted me as I was journeying to Ujiji.

"Now, Doctor," said I, "you are, probably, wondering why I came here?"

"It is true," said he; "I have been wondering. I thought you, at first, an emissary of the French Government, in the place of Lieutenant Le Saint, who died a few miles above Gondokoro. I heard you had boats, plenty of men, and stores, and I really believed you were some French officer, until I saw the American flag; and, to tell you the truth, I was rather glad it was so, because I could not have talked to him in French; and if he did not know English, we had been a pretty pair of white men in Ujiji! I did not like to ask you yesterday, because I thought it was none of my business."

"Well," said I, laughing, "for your sake I am glad that I am an American, and not a Frenchman, and that we can understand each other perfectly without an interpreter. I see that the Arabs are wondering that you, an Englishman, and I, an American, understand each other. We must take care not to tell them that the English and Americans have fought, and that there are 'Alabama' claims left unsettled, and that we have such people as Fenians in America, who hate you. But, seriously, Doctor—now don't be frightened when I tell you that I have come after—you!"

"After me?"

"Yes."

"How?"

"Well. You have heard of the 'New York Herald?'"

"Oh—who has not heard of that newspaper?"

"Without his father's knowledge or consent, Mr. James Gordon Bennett, son of Mr. James Gordon Bennett, the proprietor of the 'Herald,' has commissioned me to find you—to get whatever news of your discoveries you like to give—and to assist you, if I can, with means."

"Young Mr. Bennett told you to come after me, to find me out, and help me! It is no wonder, then, you praised Mr. Bennett so much last night."

"I know him—I am proud to say—to be just what I say he is. He is an ardent, generous, and true man."

"Well, indeed! I am very much obliged to him; and it makes me feel proud to think that you Americans think so much of me. You have just come in the proper time; for I was beginning to think that I should have to beg from the Arabs. Even they are in want of cloth, and there are but few beads in Ujiji. That fellow Sherif has robbed me of all. I wish I could embody my thanks to Mr. Bennett in suitable words; but if I fail to do so, do not, I beg of you, believe me the less grateful."

"And now, Doctor, having disposed of this little affair, Ferajji shall bring breakfast; if you have no objection."

"You have given me an appetite," he said. "Halimah is my cook, but she never can tell the difference between tea and coffee.

Ferajji, the cook, was ready as usual with excellent tea, and a dish of smoking cakes; "dampers," as the Doctor called them. I never did care much for this kind of a cake fried in a pan, but they were necessary to the Doctor, who had nearly lost all his teeth from the hard fare of Lunda. He had been compelled to subsist on green ears of Indian corn; there was no meat in that district; and the effort to gnaw at the corn ears had loosened all his teeth. I preferred the corn scones of

Virginia, which, to my mind, were the nearest approach to palatable bread obtainable in Central Africa.

The Doctor said he had thought me a most luxurious and rich man, when he saw my great bath-tub carried on the shoulders of one of my men; but he thought me still more luxurious this morning, when my knives and forks, and plates, and cups, saucers, silver spoons, and silver tea-pot were brought forth shining and bright, spread on a rich Persian carpet, and observed that I was well attended to by my yellow and ebon Mercuries.

This was the beginning of our life at Ujiji. I knew him not as a friend before my arrival. He was only an object to me—a great item for a daily newspaper, as much as other subjects in which the voracious news-loving public delight in. I had gone over battlefields, witnessed revolutions, civil wars, rebellions, émeutes and massacres; stood close to the condemned murderer to record his last struggles and last sighs; but never had I been called to record anything that moved me so much as this man's woes and sufferings, his privations and disappointments, which now were poured into my ear. Verily did I begin to perceive that " the Gods above do with just eyes survey the affairs of men." I began to recognize the hand of an overruling and kindly Providence.

The following are singular facts worthy for reflection. I was commissioned for the duty of discovering Living-stone sometime in October, 1869. Mr. Bennett was ready with the money, and I was ready for the journey. But, observe, reader, that I did not proceed directly upon the search mission. I had many tasks to fulfil before pro-ceeding with it, and many thousand miles to travel over. Supposing that I had gone direct to Zanzibar from Paris, seven or eight months afterwards, perhaps, I should have found myself at Ujiji, but Livingstone would not have been found there then; he was on the Lualaba; and I should have had to follow him on his devious tracks through the primeval forests of Manyuema, and up along the crooked course of the Lualaba for hundreds of miles. The time taken by me in travelling up the Nile, back to Jerusalem, then to Constantinople, Southern Russia, the Caucasus, and Persia, was employed by Livingstone in fruitful discoveries west of the Tanganika. Again, consider that I arrived at Unyanyembe in the latter part of June, and that owing to a war I was delayed three months at Unyanyembe, leading a fretful, peevish and impatient life. But while I was thus fretting myself, and being delayed by a series of accidents, Livingstone was being forced back to Ujiji in the same month. It took him from June to October to march to Ujiji. Now, in September, I broke loose from the thraldom which accident had imposed on me, and hurried southward to Ukonongo, then westward to Kawendi, then northward to Uvinza, then westward to Ujiji, only about three weeks after the Doctor's arrival, to find him resting under the veranda of his house with his face turned eastward, the direction from which I was coming. Had I gone direct from Paris on the search I might have lost him; had I been enabled to have gone direct to Ujiji from Unyanyembe I might have lost him.

The days came and went peacefully and happily, under the palms of Ujiji. My companion was improving in health and spirits. Life had been brought back to him; his fading vitality was restored, his enthusiasm for his work was growing up again into a height that was compelling him to desire to be up and doing. But what could he do, with five men and fifteen or twenty cloths?

"Have you seen the northern head of the Tanganika, Doctor?" I asked one day.

"No; I did try to go there, but the Wajiji were doing their best to fleece me, as they did both Burton and Speke, and I had not a great deal of cloth. If I had gone to the head of the Tanganika, I could not have gone to Manyuema. The central line of drainage was the most important, and that is the Lualaba. Before this line the question whether there is a connection between the Tanganika and the Albert N'Yanza sinks into insignificance. The great line of drainage is the river flowing from latitude 11° south, which I followed for over seven degrees northward. The Chambezi, the name given to its most southern extremity, drains a large tract of country south of the southernmost source of the Tanganika; it must, therefore, be the most important. I have not the least doubt, myself, but that this lake is the Upper Tanganika, and the Albert N'Yanza of Baker is the Lower Tanganika, which are connected by a river flowing from the upper to the lower. This is my belief, based upon reports of the Arabs, and a test I made of the flow with water-plants. But I really never gave it much thought."

"Well, if I were you, Doctor, before leaving Ujiji, I should explore it, and resolve the doubts upon the subject; lest, after you leave here, you should not return by this way. The Royal Geographical Society attach much importance to this supposed connection, and declare you are the only man who can settle it. If I can be of any service to you, you may command me. Though I did not come to Africa as an explorer, I have a good deal of curiosity upon the subject, and should be willing to accompany you. I have with me about twenty men who understand rowing we have plenty of guns, cloth, and beads; and if we can get a canoe from the Arabs we can manage the thing easily."

"Oh, we can get a canoe from Sayd bin Majid. This man has been very kind to me, and if ever there was an Arab gentleman, he is one."

"Then it is settled, is it, that we go?"

"I am ready, whenever you are."

"I am at your command. Don't you hear my men call you the 'Great Master,' and me the 'Little Master?' It would never do for the 'Little Master' to command."

By this time Livingstone was becoming known to me. I defy any one to be in his society long without thoroughly fathoming him, for in him there is no guile, and what is apparent on the surface is the thing that is in him. I simply write down my own opinion of the man as I have seen him, not as he represents himself; as I know him to be, not as I have heard of him. I lived with him from the 10th November, 1871, to the 14th March, 1872; witnessed his conduct in the camp, and on the march, and my feelings for him are those of unqualified admiration. The camp is the best place to discover a man's weaknesses, where, if he is flighty or wrong-headed, he is sure to develop his hobbies and weak side. I think it possible, however, that Livingstone, with an unsuitable companion, might feel annoyance. I know I should do so very readily, if a man's character was of that oblique nature that it was an impossibility to travel in his company. I have seen men, in whose company I felt nothing but a thraldom, which it was a duty to my own self-respect to cast off as soon as possible; a feeling of utter incompatibility, with whose nature mine could never assimilate. But Livingstone's was a character that I venerated, that called forth all my enthusiasm, that evoked nothing but sincerest admiration.

Dr. Livingstone is about sixty years old, though after he was restored to health he appeared more like a man who had not passed his fiftieth year. His hair has a brownish colour yet, but is here and there streaked with grey lines over the temples; his whiskers and moustache are very grey. He shaves his chin daily. His eyes, which are hazel, are remarkably bright; he has a sight keen as a hawk's. His teeth alone indicate the weakness of age; the hard fare of Lunda has made havoc in their lines. His form, which soon assumed a stoutish appearance, is a little over the ordinary height with the slightest possible bow in the shoulders. When walking he has a firm but heavy tread, like that of an overworked or fatigued man. He is accustomed to wear a naval cap with a semicircular peak, by which he has been identified throughout Africa. His dress, when first I saw him, exhibited traces of patching and repairing, but was scrupulously clean.

I was led to believe that Livingstone possessed a splenetic, misanthropic temper; some have said that he is garrulous, that he is demented; that he has utterly changed from the David Livingstone whom people knew as the reverend missionary; that he takes no notes or observations but such as those which no other person could read but himself; and it was reported, before I proceeded to Central Africa, that he was married to an African princess.

I respectfully beg to differ with all and each of the above statements. I grant he is not an angel, but he approaches to that being as near as the nature of a living man will allow. I never saw any spleen or misanthropy in him as for being garrulous, Dr. Livingstone is quite

the reverse: he is reserved, if anything; and to the man
who says Dr. Livingstone is changed, all I can say is,
that he never could have known him, for it is notorious
that the Doctor has a fund of quiet humor, which he
exhibits at all times whenever he is among friends. I
must also beg leave to correct the gentleman who informed me that Livingstone takes no notes or observations. The huge Letts's Diary which I carried home to
his daughter is full of notes, and there are no less than a
score of sheets within it filled with observations which he
took during the last trip he made to Manyuema alone;
and in the middle of the book there is sheet after sheet,
column after column, carefully written, of figures alone.
A large letter which I received from him has been sent to
Sir Thomas MacLear, and this contains nothing but
observations. During the four months I was with him, I
noticed him every evening making most careful notes; and
a large tin box that he has with him contains numbers of
field note-books, the contents of which I dare say will
see the light some time. His maps also evince great care
and industry. As to the report of his African marriage,
it is unnecessary to say more than that it is untrue, and it
is utterly beneath a gentleman to hint at such a thing in
connection with the name of David Livingstone.

There is a good-natured *abandon* about Livingstone
which was not lost on me. Whenever he began to laugh,
there was a contagion about it, that compelled me to
imitate him. It was such a laugh as Herr Teufelsdröckh's
—a laugh of the whole man from head to heel. If he
told a story, he related it in such a way as to convince
one of its truthfulness; his face was so lit up by the sly
fun it contained, that I was sure the story was worth
relating, and worth listening to.

The wan features which had shocked me at first meeting, the heavy step which told of age and hard travel, the grey beard and bowed shoulders, belied the man. Underneath that well-worn exterior lay an endless fund of high spirits and inexhaustible humor; that rugged frame of his enclosed a young and most exuberant soul. Every day I heard innumerable jokes and pleasant anecdotes; interesting hunting stories, in which his friends Oswell, Webb, Vardon, and Gorden Cumming were almost always the chief actors. I was not sure, at first, but this joviality, humor, and abundant animal spirits were the result of a joyous hysteria; but as I found they continued while I was with him, I am obliged to think them natural.

Another thing which specially attracted my attention was his wonderfully retentive memory. If we remember the many years he has spent in Africa, deprived of books, we may well think it an uncommon memory that can recite whole poems from Byron, Burns, Tennyson, Long-fellow, Whittier, and Lowell. The reason of this may be found, perhaps, in the fact, that he has lived all his life almost, we may say, within himself. Zimmerman, a great student of human nature, says on this subject: "The unencumbered mind recalls all that it has read, all that pleased the eye, and delighted the ear; and reflecting on every idea which either observation, or experience, or discourse has produced, gains new information by every reflection. The intellect contemplates all the former scenes of life; views by anticipation those that are yet to come; and blends all ideas of past and future in the actual enjoyment of the present moment." He has lived in a world which revolved inwardly, out of which he seldom awoke except to attend to the immediate practical necessities of himself and people; then relapsed again into the same happy inner world, which he must have peopled with his own friends, relations, acquaintances, familiar readings, ideas, and associations; so that wherever he might be, or by whatsoever he was surrounded, his own world always possessed more attractions to his cultured mind than were yielded by external circumstances.

The study of Dr. Livingstone would not be complete if we did not take the religious side of his character into consideration. His religion is not of the theoretical kind, but it is a constant, earnest, sincere practice. It is neither demonstrative nor loud, but manifests itself in a quiet, practical way, and is always at work. It is not aggressive, which sometimes is troublesome, if not impertinent. In him, religion exhibits its loveliest features; it governs his conduct not only towards his servants, but towards the natives, the bigoted Mohammedans, and all who come in contact with him. Without it, Livingstone, with his ardent temperament, his enthusiasm, his high spirit and courage, must have become uncompanionable, and a hard master. Religion has tamed him, and made him a Christian gentleman: the crude and wilful have been refined and subdued; religion has made him the most companionable of men and indulgent of masters—a man whose society is pleasurable.

In Livingstone I have seen many amiable traits. His gentleness never forsakes him; his hopefulness never deserts him. No harassing anxieties, distraction of mind, long separation from home and kindred, can make him complain. He thinks "all will come out right at last;" he has such faith in the goodness of Providence. The sport of adverse circumstances, the plaything of the miserable beings sent to him from Zanzibar—he has been baffled and worried, even almost to the grave, yet he will not desert the charge imposed upon him by his friend, Sir Roderick Murchison. To the stern dictates of duty, alone, has he sacrificed his home and ease, the pleasures, refinements, and luxuries of civilized life. His is the Spartan heroism, the inflexibility of the Roman, the enduring resolution of the Anglo-Saxon—never to relinquish his work, though his heart yearns for home; never to surrender his obligations until he can write Finis to his work.

But you may take any point in Dr. Livingstone's character, and analyse it carefully, and I would challenge any man to find a fault in it. He is sensitive, I know; but so is any man of a high mind and generous nature. He is sensitive on the point of being doubted or being criticised. An extreme love of truth is one of his strongest characteristics, which proves him to be a man of strictest principles, and conscientious scruples; being such, he is naturally sensitive, and shrinks from any attacks on the integrity of his observations, and the accuracy of his reports. He is conscious of having laboured in the course of geography and science with zeal and industry, to have been painstaking, and as exact as circumstances would allow. Ordinary critics seldom take into consideration circumstances, but, utterly regardless of the labor expended in obtaining the least amount of geographical information in a new land, environed by inconceivable dangers and difficulties, such as Central Africa presents, they seem to take delight in rending to tatters, and reducing to nil, the fruits of long years of labor, by sharply-pointed shafts of ridicule and sneers.

Livingstone no doubt may be mistaken in some of his

conclusions about certain points in the geography of Central Africa, but he is not so dogmatic and positive a man as to refuse conviction. He certainly demands, when arguments in contra are used in opposition to him, higher authority than abstract theory. His whole life is a testimony against its unreliability, and his entire labor of years were in vain if theory can be taken in evidence against personal observation and patient investigation.

The reluctance he manifests to entertain suppositions, possibilities regarding the nature, form, configuration of concrete immutable matter like the earth, arises from the fact, that a man who commits himself to theories about such an untheoretical subject as Central Africa is deterred from bestirring himself to prove them by the test of exploration. His opinion of such a man is, that he unfits himself for his duty, that he is very likely to become a slave to theory—a voluptuous fancy, which would master him.

It is his firm belief that a man who rests his sole knowledge of the geography of Africa on theory, deserves to be discredited. It has been the fear of being discredited and criticised and so made to appear before the world as a man who spent so many valuable years in Africa for the sake of burdening the geographical mind with theory that has detained him so long in Africa, doing his utmost to test the value of the main theory which clung to him, and would cling to him until he proved or disproved it.

This main theory is his belief that in the broad and mighty Lualaba he has discovered the head waters of the Nile. His grounds for believing this are of such nature and weight as to compel him to despise the warning that years are advancing on him, and his former iron constitution is failing. He believes his speculations on this point will be verified; he believes he is strong enough to pursue his explorations until he can return to his country, with the announcement that the Lualaba is none other than the Nile.

On discovering that the insignificant stream called the Chambezi, which rises between 10° S. and 12° S., flowed westerly, and then northerly through several lakes, now under the names of the Chambezi, then as the Luapula, and then as the Lualaba, and that it still continued its flow towards the north for over 7°, Livingstone became firmly of the opinion that the river whose current he followed was the Egyptian Nile. Failing at lat, 4° S. to pursue his explorations further without additional supplies, he determined to return to Ujiji to obtain them.

And now, having obtained them, he intends to return to the point where he left off work. He means to follow that great river until it is firmly established what name shall eventually be given the noble water-way whose course he has followed through so many sick toilings and difficulties. To all entreaties to come home, to all the glowing temptations which home and innumerable friends offer, he returns the determined answer :—

" No; not until my work is ended."

I have often heard our servants discuss our respective merits. " Your master," say my servants to Livingstone's, " is a good man—a very good man; he does not beat you, for he has a kind heart; but ours—oh ! he is sharp—hot as fire "—" mkali sana, kana moto." From being hated and thwarted in every possible way by the Arabs and half-castes upon first arrival in Ujiji, he has, through his uniform kindness and mild, pleasant temper, won all hearts. I observed that universal respect was paid to him. Even the Mohammedans never passed his house without calling to pay their compliments, and to say, "The blessing of God rest on you." Each Sunday morning he gathers his little flock around him, and reads prayers and a chapter from the Bible, in a natural, unaffected, and sincere tone; and afterwards delivers a short address in the Kisawahili language, about the subject read to them, which is listened to with interest and attention.

There is another point in Livingstone's character about which readers of his books, and students of his travels, would like to know, and that is his ability to withstand the dreadful climate of Central Africa, and the consistent energy with which he follows up his explorations. His consistent energy is native to him and to his race. He is a very fine example of the perseverance, doggedness, and tenacity which characterise the Anglo-Saxon spirit; but his ability to withstand the climate is due not only to the happy constitution with which he was born, but to the strictly temperate life he has ever led. A drunkard and a man of vicious habits could never have withstood the climate of Central Africa.

The second day after my arrival in Ujiji I asked the Doctor if he did not feel a desire, sometimes, to visit his country, and take a little rest after his six years' explorations; and the answer he gave me fully reveals the man. Said he :

"I should like very much to go home and see my children once again, but I cannot bring my heart to abandon the task I have undertaken, when it is so nearly completed. It only requires six or seven months more to trace the true source that I have discovered with

Petherick's branch of the White Nile, or with the Albert N'Yanza of Sir Samuel Baker, which is the lake called by the natives ' Chowambe.' Why should I go home before my task is ended, to have to come back again to do what I can very well do now ? "

"And why ? " I asked, " did you come so far back without finishing the task which you say you have got to do ? "

" Simply because I was forced. My men would not budge a step forward. They mutinied, and formed a secret resolution—if I still insisted upon going on—to raise a disturbance in the country, and after they had effected it to abandon me; in which case I should have been killed. It was dangerous to go any further. I had explored six hundred miles of the watershed, had traced all the principal streams which discharge their waters into the central line of drainage, but when about starting to explore the last hundred miles the hearts of my people failed them, and they set about frustrating me in every possible way. Now, having returned seven hundred miles to get a new supply of stores, and another escort, I find myself destitute of even the means to live but for a few weeks, and sick in mind and body."

Here I may pause to ask any brave man how he would have comported himself in such a crisis. Many would have been in exceeding hurry to get home to tell the news of the continued explorations and discoveries, and to relieve the anxiety of the sorrowing family and friends awaiting their return. Enough surely had been accomplished towards the solution of the problem that had exercised the minds of his scientific associates of the Royal Geograpical Society. It was no negative exploration, it was hard, earnest labor of years, self abnegation, enduring patience, and exalted fortitude, such as ordinary men fail to exhibit.

Suppose Livingstone had hurried to the coast after he had discovered Lake Bangweolo, to tell the news to the geographical world ; then had returned to discover Moéro, and run away again ; then went back once more only to discover Kamolondo, and to race back again. This would not be in accordance with Livingstone's character. He must not only discover the Chambezi, Lake Bangweolo, Luapula River, Lake Moero, Lualaba River, and Lake Kamolondo, but he must still tirelessly urge his steps forward to put the final completion to the grand lacustrine river system. Had he followed the example of ordinary explorers, he would have been running backwards and forwards to tell the news, instead of exploring ; and he might have been able to write a volume upon the discovery of each lake, and earn much money thereby. They are no few months' explorations that form the contents of his books. His 'Missionary Travels' embraces a period of sixteen years ; his book on the Zambezi, five years ; and if the great traveller lives to come home, his third book, the grandest of all, must contain the records of eight or nine years.

It is a principle with Livingstone to do well what he undertakes to do ; and in the consciousness that he is doing it, despite the yearning for his home which is sometimes overpowering, he finds, to a certain extent, contentment, if not happiness. To men differently constituted, a long residence amongst the savages of Africa would be contemplated with horror, yet Livingstone's mind can find pleasure and food for philosophic studies. The wonders of primeval nature, the great forests and sublime mountains, the perennial streams and sources of the great lakes, the marvels of the earth, the splendors of the tropic sky by day and by night—all terrestrial and celestial phenomena are manna to a man of such self-abnegation and devoted philanthropic spirit. He can be charmed with the primitive simplicity of Ethiop's dusky children, with whom he has spent so many years of his life; he has a sturdy faith in their capabilities; sees virtue in them where others see nothing but savagery; and wherever he has gone among them, he has sought to elevate a people that were apparently forgotten of God and Christian man.

One night I took out my note-book, and prepared to take down from his own lips what he had to say about his travels; and unhesitatingly he related his experiences, of which the following is a summary:

Dr. David Livingstone left the Island of Zanzibar in March, 1866. On the 7th of the following month he departed from Mikindany Bay for the interior, with an expedition consisting of twelve Sepoys from Bombay, nine men from Johanna, of the Comoro Islands, seven liberated slaves, and two Zambezi men, taking them as an experiment; six camels, three buffaloes, two mules, and three donkeys. He had thus thirty men with him, twelve of whom, viz., the Sepoys, were to act as guards for the Expedition. They were mostly armed with the Enfield rifles presented to the Doctor by the Bombay Government. The baggage of the expedition consisted of ten bales of cloth and two bags of beads, which were to serve as the currency by which they would be enabled to purchase the necessaries of life in the countries the Doctor intended to visit. Besides the cumbrous moneys, they carried several boxes of instruments, such as chronometers, air thermometers, sextant, and artificial horizon,

boxes containing clothes, medicines, and personal necessaries. The expedition travelled up the left bank of the
Rovuma River, a rout as full of difficulties as any that
could be chosen. For miles Livingstone and his party
had to cut their way with their axes through the dense
and almost impenetrable jungles which lined the river's
banks. The road was a mere footpath, leading in the
most erratic fashion into and through the dense vegetation, seeking the easiest outlet from it without any regard
to the course it ran. The pagazis were able to proceed
easily enough; but the camels, on account of their
enormous height, could not advance a step without the
axes of the party clearing the way. These tools of
foresters were almost always required; but the advance
of the expedition was often retarded by the unwillingness
of the Sepoys and Johanna men to work.

Soon after the departure of the expedition from the
coast, the murmurings and complaints of these men
began, and upon every occasion and at every opportunity
they evinced a decided hostility to an advance. In order
to prevent the progress of the Doctor, and in hopes that
it would compel him to return to the coast, these men so
cruelly treated the animals that before long there was
not one left alive. But as this scheme failed, they set
about instigating the natives against the white men,
whom they accused most wantonly of strange practices.
As this plan was most likely to succeed, and as it was
dangerous to have such men with him, the Doctor arrived
at the conclusion that it was best to discharge them, and
accordingly sent the Sepoys back to the coast; but not
without having first furnished them with the means of
subsistence on their journey to the coast. These men
were such a disreputable set that the natives spoke of

them as the Doctor's slaves. One of their worst sins was the custom of giving their guns and ammunition to carry to the first woman or boy they met, whom they impressed for that purpose by such threats or promises as they were totally unable to perform, and unwarranted in making. An hour's marching was sufficient to fatigue them, after which they lay down on the road to bewail their hard fate, and concoct new schemes to frustrate their leader's purposes. Towards night they generally made their appearance at the camping-ground with the looks of half-dead men. Such men naturally made but a poor escort; for, had the party been attacked by a wandering tribe of natives of any strength, the Doctor could have made no defence, and no other alternative would have been left to him but to surrender and be ruined.

The Doctor and his little party arrived on the 18th July, 1866, at a village belonging to a chief of the Wahiyou, situate eight days' march south of the Rovuma, and overlooking the watershed of the Lake Nyassa. The territory lying between the Rovuma River and this Wahiyou village was an uninhabited wilderness, during the transit of which Livingstone and his expedition suffered considerably from hunger and desertion of men.

Early in August, 1866, the Doctor came to the country of Mponda, a chief who dwelt near the Lake Nyassa. On the road thither, two of the liberated slaves deserted him. Here also, Wekotani, a protégé of the Doctor, insisted upon his discharge, alleging as an excuse —an excuse which the Doctor subsequently found to be untrue—that he had found his brother. He also stated that his family lived on the east side of the Nyassa Lake. He further stated that Mponda's favourite wife was his sister. Perceiving that Wekotani was unwilling to go with him further, the Doctor took him to Mponda, who now saw and heard of him for the first time, and, having furnished the ungrateful boy with enough cloth and beads to keep him until his "big brother" should call for him, left him with the chief, after first assuring himself that he would receive honorable treatment from him. The Doctor also gave Wekotanti writing-paper—as he could read and write, being accomplishments acquired at Bombay, where he had been put to school—so that, should he at any time feel disposed, he might write to his English friends, or to himself. The Doctor further enjoined him not to join in any of the slave raids usually made by his countrymen, the men of Nyassa, on their neighbours. Upon finding that his application for a discharge was successful, Wekotani endeavoured to induce Chumah, another protégé of the Doctor's, and a companion, or chum, of Wekotani, to leave the Doctor's service and proceed with him, promising, as a bribe, a wife and plenty of pombe from his "big brother." Chumah, upon referring the matter to the Doctor, was advised not to go, as he (the Doctor) strongly suspected that Wekotani wanted only to make him his slave. Chumah wisely withdrew from his tempter. From Mponda's, the Doctor proceeded to the heel of the Nyassa, to the village of a Babisa chief, who required medicine for a skin disease. With his usual kindness, he stayed at this chief's village to treat his malady.

While here, a half-caste Arab arrived from the western shore of the lake, and reported that he had been plundered by a band of Mazitu, at a place which the Doctor and Musa, chief of the Johanna men, were very well aware was at least 150 miles north-north-west of where they were then stopping. Musa, however, for his own reasons

—which will appear presently—eagerly listened to the Arab's tale, and gave full credence to it. Having well digested its horrible details, he came to the Doctor to give him the full benefit of what he had heard with such willing ears. The traveller patiently listened to the narrative, which lost nothing of its portentous significance through Musa's relation, and then asked Musa if he believed it. "Yes," answered Musa, readily; "he tell me true, true. I ask him good, and he tell me true, true." The Doctor, however, said he did not believe it, for the Mazitu would not have been satisfied with merely plundering a man, they would have murdered him; but suggested, in order to allay the fears of his Moslem subordinate, that they should both proceed to the chief with whom they were staying, who, being a sensible man, would be able to advise them as to the probability or improbability of the tale being correct. Together, they proceeded to the Babisa chief, who, when he had heard the Arab's story, unhesitatingly denounced the Arab as a liar, and his story without the least foundation in fact; giving as a reason that, if the Mazitu had been lately in that vicinity, he should have heard of it soon enough.

But Musa broke out with "No, no, Doctor; no, no, no; I no want to go to Mazitu. I no want Mazitu to kill me. I want to see my father, my mother, my child, in Johanna. I want no Mazitu." These are Musa's words *ipsissima verba*.

To which the Doctor replied, " I don't want the Mazitu to kill me either; but, as you are afraid of them, I promise to go straight west until we get far past the beat of the Mazitu."

Musa was not satisfied, but kept moaning and sorrowing, saying, "If we had two hundred guns with us I would go; but our small party of men they will attack by night, and kill all."

The Doctor repeated his promise, "But I will not go near them; I will go west."

As soon as he turned his face westward, Musa and the Johanna men ran away in a body.

The Doctor says, in commenting upon Musa's conduct, that he felt strongly tempted to shoot Musa and another ringleader, but was, nevertheless, glad that he did not soil his hands with their vile blood. A day or two afterwards, another of his men—Simon Price by name—came to the Doctor with the same tale about the Mazitu, but, compelled by the scant number of his people to repress all such tendencies to desertion and faint-heartedness, the Docter silenced him at once, and sternly forbade him to utter the name of the Mazitu any more.

Had the natives not assisted him, he must have despaired of ever being able to penetrate the wild and unexplored interior which he was now about to tread. "Fortunately," as the Doctor says with unction, "I was in a country now, after leaving the shores of Nyassa, which the foot of the slave-trader has not trod; it was a new and virgin land, and of course, as I have always found in such cases, the natives were really good and hospitable, and for very small portions of cloth my baggage was conveyed from village to village by them." In many other ways the traveller, in his extremity, was kindly treated by the yet unsophisticated and innocent natives.

On leaving this hospitable region in the early part of December, 1866, the Doctor entered a country where the Mazitu had exercised their customary marauding propensities. The land was swept clean of provisions and cattle, and the people had emigrated to other countries, beyond the bounds of those ferocious plunderers. Again the Expedition was besieged by pinching hunger from which they suffered; they had recourse to the wild fruits which some parts of the country furnished. At intervals the condition of the hard-pressed band was made worse by the heartless desertion of some of its members, who more than once departed with the Doctor's personal kit, changes of clothes, linen, &c. With more or less misfortunes constantly dogging his footsteps, he traversed in safety the countries of the Babisa, Bobemba, Barungu, Ba-ulungu, and Lunda.

In the country of Lunda lives the famous Cazembe, who was first made known to Europeans by Dr. Lacerda, the Portuguese traveller. Cazembe is a most intelligent prince; he is a tall, stalwart man, who wears a peculiar kind of dress, made of crimson print, in the form of a prodigious kilt. In this state dress, King Cazembe received Dr. Livingstone, surrounded by his chiefs and body-guards. A chief, who had been deputed by the King and elders to discover all about the white man, then stood up before the assembly, and in a loud voice gave the result of the inquiry he had instituted. He had heard that the white man had come to look for waters, for rivers, and seas; though he could not understand what the white man could want with such things, he had no doubt that the object was good. Then Cazembe asked what the Doctor proposed doing, and where he thought of going. The Doctor replied that he had thought of proceeding south, as he had heard of lakes and rivers being in that direction. Cazembe asked, " What can you want to go there for? The water is close here. There is plenty of large water in this neighbourhood." Before breaking up the assembly, Cazembe gave orders to let the white man go where he would through his country undisturbed and unmolested. He was the first Englishman he had seen, he said, and he liked him.

Shortly after his introduction to the King, the Queen entered the large house, surrounded by a body-guard of Amazons with spears. She was a fine, tall, handsome young woman, and evidently thought she was about to make an impression upon the rustic white man, for she had clothed herself after a most royal fashion, and was armed with a ponderous spear. But her appearance—so different from what the Doctor had imagined—caused him to laugh, which entirely spoiled the effect intended; for the laugh of the Doctor was so contagious, that she herself was the first to imitate it, and the Amazons, courtier-like, followed suit. Much disconcerted by this, the Queen ran back, followed by her obedient damsels—a retreat most undignified and unqueenlike, compared with her majestic advent into the Doctor's presence. But Livingstone will have much to say about his reception at this court, and about this interesting King and Queen; and who can so well relate the scenes he witnessed, and which belong exclusively to him, as he himself?

Soon after his arrival in the country of Lunda, or Londa, and before he had entered the district ruled over by Cazembe, he had crossed a river called the Chambezi, which was quite an important stream. The similarity of the name with that large and noble river south, which will be for ever connected with his name, misled Livingstone at that time, and he, accordingly, did not pay to it the attention it deserved, believing that the Chambezi was but the head-waters of the Zambezi, and consequently had no bearing or connection with the sources of the river of

Egypt, of which he was in search. His fault was in relying too implicitly upon the correctness of Portuguese information. This error it cost him many months of tedious labour and travel to rectify.

From the beginning of 1867—the time of his arrival at Cazembe's—till the middle of March, 1869—the time of his arrival at Ujiji—he was mostly engaged in correcting the errors and misrepresentations of the Portuguese travellers. The Portuguese, in speaking of the River Chambezi, invariably spoke of it as " our own Zambezi,"— that is, the Zambezi which flows through the Portuguese possessions of the Mozambique. " In going to Cazembe from Nyassa," said they, " you will cross our own Zambezi." Such positive and reiterated information— given not only orally, but in their books and maps—was naturally confusing. When the Doctor perceived that what he saw and what they described were at variance, out of a sincere wish to be correct, and lest he might have been mistaken himself, he started to retravel the ground he had travelled before. Over and over again he traversed the several countries watered by the several rivers of the complicated water system, like an uneasy spirit. Over and over again he asked the same questions from the different peoples he met, until he was obliged to desist, lest they might say, " The man is mad; he has got water on the brain !"

But his travels and tedious labours in Lunda and the adjacent countries have established beyond doubt—first, that the Chambezi is a totally distinct river from the Zambezi of the Portuguese; and, secondly, that the Chambezi, starting from about latitude 11° south, is no other than the most southerly feeder of the great Nile; thus giving that famous river a length of over

2,000 miles of direct latitude; making it, second to the Mississippi, the longest river in the world. The real and true name of the Zambezi is Dombazi. When Lacerda and his Portuguese successors, coming to Cazembe, crossed the Chambezi, and heard its name, they very naturally set it down as "our own Zambezi," and, without further inquiry, sketched it as running in that direction.

During his researches in that region, so pregnant in discoveries, Livingstone came to a lake lying north-east of Cazembe, which the natives call Liemba, from the country of that name which bordered it on the east and south. In tracing the lake north, he found it to be none other than the Tanganika, or the south-eastern extremity of it, which looks, on the Doctor's map, very much like an outline of Italy. The latitude of the southern end of this great body of water is about 8° 42' south, which thus gives it a length, from north to south, of 360 geographical miles. From the southern extremity of the Tanganika he crossed Marungu, and came in sight of Lake Moero. Tracing this lake, which is about sixty miles in length, to its southern head, he found a river, called the Luapula, entering it from that direction. Following the Luapula south, he found it issue from the large lake of Bangweolo, which is nearly as large in superficial area as the Tanganika. In exploring for the waters which discharged themselves into the lake, he found that by far the most important of these feeders was the Chambezi; so that he had thus traced the Chambezi from its source to Lake Bangweolo, and the issue from its northern head, under the name of Luapula, and found it enter Lake Moero. Again he returned to Cazembe's, well satisfied that the river running north through three degrees of latitude could not be the river running south under the name of Zambezi, though there might be a remarkable resemblance in their names.

At Cazembe's he found an old white-bearded half-caste named Mohammed bin Sali, who was kept as a kind of prisoner at large by the King because of certain suspicious circumstances attending his advent and stay in the country. Through Livingstone's influence Mohammed bin Sali obtained his release. On the road to Ujiji he had bitter cause to regret having exerted himself in the half-caste's behalf. He turned out to be a most ungrateful wretch, who poisoned the minds of the Doctor's few followers, and ingratiated himself with them by selling the favours of his concubines to them, by which he reduced them to a kind of bondage under him. The Doctor was deserted by all but two, even faithful Susi and Chumah deserted him for the service of Mohammed bin Sali. But they soon repented, and returned to their allegiance. From the day he had the vile old man in his company manifold and bitter misfortunes followed the Doctor up to his arrival at Ujiji in March, 1869.

From the date of his arrival until the end of June, 1869, he remained at Ujiji, whence he dated those letters which, though the outside world still doubted his being alive, satisfied the minds of the Royal Geographical people, and his intimate friends, that he still existed, and that Musa'a tale was the false though ingenious fabrication of a cowardly deserter. It was during this time that the thought occurred to him of sailing around the Lake Tanganika, but the Arabs and natives were so bent upon fleecing him that, had he undertaken it, the remainder or his goods would not have enabled him to explore the **central line of drainage**, the initial point of which he found far south of Cazembe's in about latitude 11°, in the river called Chambezi.

In the days when tired Captain Burton was resting in Ujiji, after his march from the coast near Zanzibar, the land to which Livingstone, on his departure from Ujiji, bent his steps was unknown to the Arabs save by vague report. Messrs. Burton and Speke never heard of it, it seems. Speke, who was the geographer of Burton's Expedition, heard of a place called Urua, which he placed on his map, according to the general direction indicated by the Arabs; but the most enterprising of the Arabs, in their search after ivory, only touched the frontiers of Rua, as the natives and Livingstone call it; for Rua is an immense country, with a length of six degrees of latitude, and as yet an undefined breadth from east to west.

At the end of June, 1869, Livingstone quitted Ujiji and crossed over to Uguhha, on the western shore, for his last and greatest series of explorations; the result of which was the further discovery of a lake of considerable magnitude connected with Moero by the large river called the Lualaba, and which was a continuation of the chain of lakes he had previously discovered.

From the port of Uguhha he set off, in company with a body of traders, in an almost direct westerly course, for the country of Urua. Fifteen days' march brought them to Bambarre, the first important ivory depôt in Manyema, or, as the natives pronounce it, Manyuema. For nearly six months he was detained at Bambarre from ulcers in the feet, which discharged bloody ichor as soon as he set them on the ground. When recovered, he set off in a northerly direction, and after several days came to a broad lacustrine river, called the Lualaba, flowing northward and westward, and in some places southward, in a most confusing way. The river was from one to three miles broad. By exceeding pertinacity he contrived to follow its erratic course, until he saw the Lualaba enter the narrow, long lake of Kamolondo, in about latitude 6° 30′. Retracing this to the south, he came to the point where he had seen the Luapula enter Lake Moero.

One feels quite enthusiastic when listening to Livingstone's description of the beauties of Moero scenery. Pent in on all sides by high mountains, clothed to the edges with the rich vegetation of the tropics, the Moero discharges its superfluous waters through a deep rent in the bosom of the mountains. The impetuous and grand river roars through the chasm with the thunder of a cataract, but soon after leaving its confined and deep bed it expands into the calm and broad Lualaba, stretching over miles of ground. After making great bends west and south-west, and then curving northward, it enters Kamolondo. By the natives it is called the Lualaba, but the Doctor, in order to distinguish it from other rivers of the same name, has given it the name of "Webb's River," after Mr. Webb, the wealthy proprietor of Newstead Abbey, whom the Doctor distinguishes as one of his oldest and most consistent friends. Away to the south-west from Kamolondo is another large lake, which discharges its waters by the important River Loeki, or Lomami, into the great Lualaba. To this lake, known as Chebungc by the natives, Dr. Livingstone has given the name of "Lincoln," to be hereafter distinguished on maps and in books as Lake Lincoln, in memory of Abraham Lincoln, our murdered President. This was done from the vivid impression produced on his mind by hearing a portion of his inauguration speech read from an English pulpit, which related to the causes that induced him to issue his

Emancipation Proclamation, by which memorable deed 4,000,000 of slaves were for ever freed. To the memory of the man whose labours on behalf of the negro race deserves the commendation of all good men, Livingstone has contributed a monument more durable than brass or stone.

Entering Webb's River from the south-south-west, a little north of Kamolondo, is a large river called Lufira, but the streams that discharge themselves from the water-shed into the Lualaba are so numerous that the Doctor's map would not contain them, so he has left all out except the most important. Continuing his way north, tracing the Lualaba through its manifold and crooked curves as far as latitude 4° south, he came to where he heard of another lake to the north, into which it ran. But here you may come to a dead halt, and read what lies beyond this spot thus . . . . . This was the furthermost point, whence he was compelled to return on the weary road to Ujiji, a distance of 700 miles.

In this brief sketch of Dr. Livingstone's wonderful travels it is to be hoped the most superficial reader, as well as the student of geography, comprehends this grand system of lakes connected together by Webb's River. To assist him, let him glance at the map accompanying this book. He will then have a fair idea of what Dr. Livingstone has been doing during these long years, and what additions he has made to the study of African geography. That this river, distinguished under several titles, flowing from one lake into another in a northerly direction, with all its great crooked bends and sinuosities, is the Nile—the true Nile —the Doctor has not the least doubt. For a long time he entertained great scepticism, because of its deep bends

and curves west, and south-west even ; but having traced
it from its head waters, the Chambezi, through 7° of
latitude—that is, from 11° S. to lat. 4° N.—he has been
compelled to come to the conclusion that it can be no
other river than the Nile. He had thought it was the
Congo ; but has discovered the sources of the Congo to
be the Kassai and the Kwango, two rivers which rise on
the western side of the Nile watershed, in about the
latitude of Bangweolo ; and he was told of another river
called the Lubilash, which rose from the north, and ran
west. But the Lualaba, the Doctor thinks, cannot be the
Congo, from its great size and body, and from its steady
and continued flow northward through a broad and extensive valley, bounded by enormous mountains westerly
and easterly. The altitude of the most northerly point
to which the Doctor traced the wonderful river was a
little in excess of 2,000 feet ; so that, though Baker makes
out his lake to be 2,700 feet above the sea, yet the Bahr
Ghazal, through which Petherick's branch of the White
Nile issues into the Nile, is but 2,000 feet ; in which
case there is a possibility that the Lualaba may be none
other than Petherick's branch.

It is well known that trading stations for ivory have
been established for about 500 miles up Petherick's
branch. We must remember this fact when told that
Gondokoro, in lat. 4° N., is 2,000 feet above the sea, and
lat. 4° S., where the halt was made, is only a little over
2,000 feet above the sea. That the two rivers said to be
2,000 feet above the sea, separated from each other by 8°
of latitude, are one and the same river, may among some
men be regarded as a startling statement. But we must
restrain mere expressions of surprise, and take into consideration that this mighty and broad Lualaba is a lacus-

trine river broader than the Mississippi; that at intervals the body of water forms extensive lakes; then, contracting into a broad river, it again forms a lake, and so on, to lat. 4°; and even beyond this point the Doctor hears of a large lake again north.

We must wait also until the altitudes of the two rivers, the Lualaba, where the Doctor halted, and the southern point on the Bahr Ghazal, where Petherick has been, are known with perfect accuracy.

Now, for the sake of argument, suppose we give this nameless lake a length of 6° of latitude, as it may be the one discovered by Piaggia, the Italian traveller, from which Petherick's branch of the White Nile issues out through reedy marshes, into the Bahr Ghazal, thence into the White Nile, south of Gondokoro. By this method we can suppose the rivers one; for if the lake extends over so many degrees of latitude, the necessity of explaining the differences of altitude that must naturally exist between two points of a river 8° of latitude apart, would be obviated.

Also, Livingstone's instruments for observation and taking altitudes may have been in error; and this is very likely to have been the case, subjected as they have been to rough handling during nearly six years of travel. Despite the apparent difficulty of the altitude, there is another strong reason for believing Webb's River, or the Lualaba, to be the Nile. The watershed of this river, 600 miles of which Livingstone has travelled, is drained from a valley which lies north and south between lofty eastern and western ranges.

This valley, or line of drainage, while it does not receive the Kassai and the Kwango, receives rivers flowing from a great distance west, for instance, the important tributaries Lufira and Lomami, and large rivers from the east, such as the Lindi and Luamo; and, while the most intelligent Portuguese travellers and traders state that the Kassai, the Kwango, and Lubilash are the head waters of the Congo River, no one has yet started the supposition that the grand river flowing north, and known by the natives as the Lualaba, is the Congo.

This river may be the Congo, or, perhaps, the Niger. If the Lualaba is only 2,000 feet above the sea, and the Albert N'Yanza 2,700 feet, the Lualaba cannot enter that lake. If the Bahr Ghazal does not extend by an arm for eight degrees above Gondokoro, then the Lualaba cannot be the Nile. But it would be premature to dogmatise on the subject. Livingstone will clear up the point himself; and if he finds it to be the Congo, will be the first to admit his error.

Livingstone admits the Nile sources have not been found, though he has traced the Lualaba through seven degress of latitude flowing north; and, though he has not a particle of doubt of its being the Nile, not yet can the Nile question be said to be resolved and ended. For two reasons:

1. He has heard of the existence of four fountains, two of which gave birth to a river flowing north, Webb's River, or the Lualaba, and to a river flowing south, which is the Zambezi. He has repeatedly heard of these fountains from the natives. Several times he has been within 100 and 200 miles from them, but something always interposed to prevent his going to see them. According to those who have seen them, they rise on either side of a mound or level, which contains no stones. Some have called it an ant-hill. One of these fountains is said to be so large that a man, standing on one side,

cannot be seen from the other. These fountains must be discovered, and their position taken. The Doctor does not suppose them to be south of the feeders of Lake Bangweolo. In his letter to the 'Herald' he says: "These four full-grown gushing fountains, rising so near each other, and giving origin to four large rivers, answer in a certain degree to the description given of the unfathomable fountains of the Nile, by the secretary of Minerva, in the city of Sais, in Egypt, to the father of all travellers—Herodotus."

For the information of such readers as may not have the original at hand, I append the following from Cary's translation of Herodotus:—

With respect to the sources of the Nile, no man of all the Egyptians, Libyans, or Grecians, with whom I have conversed, ever pretended to know anything, except the registrar of Minerva's treasury at Sais, in Egypt. He, indeed, seemed to be trifling with me when he said he knew perfectly well; yet his account was as follows: "That there are two mountains, rising into a sharp peak, situated between the city of Syene, in Thebais, and Elephantine. The names of these mountains are, the one Crophi, the other Mophi; that the sources of the Nile, which are bottomless, flow from between these mountains and that half of the water flows over Egypt and to the north, the other half over Ethiopia and the south. That the fountains of the Nile are bottomless, he said, Psammitichus, king of Egypt, proved by experiment: for, having caused a line to be twisted many thousand fathoms in length, he let it down, but could not find a bottom." Such, then, was the opinion the registrar gave, if, indeed, he spoke the real truth; *proving*, in my opinion, that there are strong whirlpools and an eddy here, so that the water beating against the rocks, a sounding-line, when let down, cannot reach the bottom. I was unable to learn anything more from any one else. But thus much I learnt by carrying my researches as far as possible, having gone and made my own observations as far as Elephantine, and beyond that obtaining information from hearsay. As one ascends the river, above the city of Elephantine, the country is steep; here, therefore, it is necessary to attach a rope on both sides of a boat, as one does with an ox in a plough, and so proceed; but if the rope should happen to break, the boat is carried away by the force of the stream. This kind of country lasts for a four-days' passage, and the Nile here winds as much as the Mæander. There are twelve schœni, which it is necessary to sail through in this manner; and after that you will come to a level plain, where the Nile flows round an island; its name is Tachompso. Ethiopians inhabit the country immediately above Elephantine, and one half of the island; the other half is inhabited by Egyptians. Near to this island lies a vast lake, on the borders of which Ethiopian nomades dwell. After sailing through this lake you will come to the channel of the Nile, which flows into it: then you will have to land and travel forty days by the side of the river, for sharp rocks rise in the Nile, and there are many sunken ones, through which it is not possible to navigate a boat. Having passed this country in the forty days, you must go on board another boat, and sail for twelve days; and then you will arrive at a large city, called Meroe: this city is said to be the capital of all Ethiopia. The inhabitants worship no other gods than Jupiter and Bacchus; but these they honour with great magnificence. They have also an oracle of Jupiter; and they make war whenever that god bids them by an oracular warning, and against whatever country he bids them. Sailing from this city, you will arrive at the country of the Automoli, in a space of time equal to that which you took in coming from Elephantine to the capital of the Ethiopians. These Automoli are called by the name of Asmak, which, in the language of Greece, signifies "those that stand at the left hand of the king." These, to the number of two hundred and forty thousand of the Egyptian war-tribe, revolted to the Ethiopians on the following occasion. In the reign of King Psammitichus garrisons were stationed at Elephantine against the Ethiopians, and another at the Pelusian Daphnæ against the Arabians and Syrians, and another at Marea against Libya; and even in my time garrisons of the Persians are stationed in the same places as they were in the time of Psammitichus, for they maintain guards at Elephantine and Daphnæ. Now, these Egyptians, after they had been on duty three years, were not relieved; therefore, having consulted together and come to an unanimous resolution, they all revolted from Psammitichus, and went to Ethiopia. Psammitichus, hearing of this, pursued them; and when he overtook them he entreated them by many arguments, and adjured them not to forsake the gods of their fathers, and their

children and wives But one of them is reported to have uncovered
and to have said, "that wheresoever these were
there they should find both children and wives." These men, when
they arrived in Ethiopia, offered their services to the king of the
Ethiopians, who made them the following recompense. There were
certain Ethiopians disaffected towards him; these he bade them expel,
and take possession of their land. By the settlement of these men
among the Ethiopians, the Ethiopians became more civilized, and
learned the manners of the Egyptians.

Now, for a voyage and land journey of four months, the Nile is
known, in addition to the part of the stream that is in Egypt; for,
upon computation, so many months are known to be spent by a person
who travels from Elephantine to the Automoli. This river flows from
the west and the setting of the sun; but beyond this no one is able
to speak with certainty, for the rest of the country is desert by reason
of the excessive heat. But I have heard the following account from
certain Cyrenæans, who say that they went to the oracle of Ammon,
and had a conversation with Etearchus, King of the Ammonians, and
that, among other subjects, they happened to discourse about the Nile
—that nobody knew its sources; whereupon Etearchus said that
certain Nasamonians once came to him—this nation is Lybian, and
inhabits the Syrtis, and the country for no great distance eastward of
the Syrtis—and that when these Nasamonians arrived, and were asked
if they could give any further information touching the deserts of
Libya, they answered, that there were some daring youths amongst
them, sons of powerful men; and that they, having reached man's
estate, formed many other extravagant plans, and, moreover, chose five
of their number by lot to explore the deserts of Libya, to see if they
could make any further discovery than those who had penetrated the
farthest. (For, as respects the parts of Libya along the Northern
Sea, beginning from Egypt to the promontory of Solois, where is the
extremity of Libya, Libyans and various nations of Libyans reach
all along it, except those parts which are occupied by Grecians and
Phœnicians; but as respects the parts above the sea, and those nations
which reach down to the sea, in the upper parts Libya is infested by
wild beasts; and all beyond that is sand, dreadfully short of water,
and utterly desolate.) *They further related,* "that when the young
men deputed by their companions set out, well furnished with water
and provisions, they passed first through the inhabited country; and

having traversed this, they came to the region infested by wild beasts; and after this they crossed the desert, making their way towards the west; and when they had traversed much sandy ground, during a journey of many days, they at length saw some trees growing in a plain; and that they approached and began to gather the fruit that grew on the trees; and while they were gathering, some diminutive men, less than men of middle stature, came up, and having seized them carried them away; and that the Nasamonians did not at all understand their language, nor those who carried them off the language of the Nasamonians. However, they conducted them through vast morasses, and when they had passed these, they came to a city in which all the inhabitants were of the same size as their conductors, and black in colour: and by the city flowed a great river, running from the west to the east, and that crocodiles were seen in it." Thus far I have set forth the account of Etearchus the Ammonian; to which may be added, as the Cyrenæans assured me, "that he said the Nasamonians all returned safe to their own country, and that the men whom they came to were all necromancers." Etearchus also conjectured that this river, which flows by their city, is the Nile; and reason so evinces: for the Nile flows from Libya, and intersects it in the middle; and (as I conjecture, inferring things unknown from things known) it sets out from a point corresponding with the Ister. For the Ister, beginning from the Celts, and the city of Pyrene, divides Europe in its course; but the Celts are beyond the pillars of Hercules, and border on the territories of the Cynesians, who lie in the extremity of Europe to the westward; and the Ister terminates by flowing through all Europe into the Euxine Sea, where a Milesian colony is settled in Istria. Now the Ister, as it flows through a well-peopled country, is generally known; but no one is able to speak about the sources of the Nile, because Libya, through which it flows, is uninhabited and desolate. Respecting this stream, therefore, as far as I was able to reach by inquiry, I have already spoken. It however discharges itself into Egypt; and Egypt lies, as near as may be, opposite to the mountains of Cilicia; from whence to Sinope, on the Euxine Sea, is a five days' journey in a straight line to an active man; and Sinope is opposite to the Ister, where it discharges itself into the sea. So I think that the Nile, traversing the whole of Libya, may be properly compared with the Ister. Such, then, is the account that I am able to give respecting the Nile.

2. Webb's River must be traced to its connection with some portion of the old Nile.

When these two things have been accomplished, then, and not till then, can the mystery of the Nile be explained. The two countries through which the marvellous lacustrine river, the Lualaba, flows, with its manifold lakes and broad expanse of water, are Rua (the Uruwwa of Speke) and Manyuema. For the first time Europe is made aware that between the Tanganika and the known sources of the Congo there exist teeming millions of the negro race, who never saw, or heard of the white people who make such a noisy and busy stir outside of Africa. Upon the minds of those who had the good fortune to see the first specimen of these remarkable white races in Dr. Livingstone, he seems to have made a favourable impression, though, through misunderstanding his object, and coupling him with the Arabs, who make horrible work there, his life was sought after more than once. These two extensive countries, Rua and Manyuema, are populated by true heathens, governed, not as the sovereignties of Karagwah, Urundi, and Uganda, by despotic kings, but each village by its own sultan or lord. Thirty miles outside of their own immediate settlements, the most intelligent of these small chiefs seem to know nothing. Thirty miles from the Lualaba, there were but few people who had ever heard of the great river. Such ignorance among the natives of their own country naturally increased the labours of Livingstone. Compared with these, all tribes and nations in Africa with whom Livingstone came in contact may be deemed civilized, yet, in the arts of home manufacture, these wild people of Manyuema were far superior to any he had seen. Where other tribes and nations contented themselves with hides and skins, of animals thrown negligently over their shoulders, the people of Manyuema manufactured a cloth from fine grass, which may favorably compare with the finest grass cloth of India. They also know the art of dying them in various colours—black, yellow, and purple. The Wangwana, or freed-men of Zanzibar, struck with the beauty of the fabric, eagerly exchange their cotton cloths for fine grass cloth; and on almost every black man from Manyuema I have seen this native cloth converted into elegantly made damirs (Arabic)—short jackets. These countries are also very rich in ivory. The fever for going to Manyuema to exchange tawdry beads for its precious tusks is of the same kind as that which impelled men to go to the gulches and placers of California, Colorado, Montana, and Idaho; after nuggets to Australia, and diamonds to Cape Colony. Manyuema is at present the El Dorado of the Arab and the Wamrima tribes. It is only about four years since that the first Arab returned from Manyuema, with such wealth of ivory, and reports about the fabulous quantities found there, that ever since the old beaten tracks of Karagwah, Uganda, Ufipa, and Marungu have been comparatively deserted. The people of Manyuema, ignorant of the value of the precious article, reared their huts upon ivory stanchions. Ivory pillars were common sights in Manyuema, and, hearing of these, one can no longer wonder at the ivory palace of Solomon. For generations they have used ivory tusks as door-posts and supports to the eaves, until they had become perfectly rotten and worthless. But the advent of the Arabs soon taught them the value of the article. It has now risen considerably in price, though still fabulously cheap. At Zanzibar the value of ivory per frasilah of 35 lbs. weight is from $50 to $60, according to its quality. In Unyanyembe it is about $1·10 per pound, but in Manyuema it may be purchased for from half a cent to 1¼ cent's worth of copper per pound of ivory. The Arabs, however, have the knack of spoiling markets by their rapacity and cruelty. With muskets, a small party of Arabs is invincible against such people as those of Manyuema, who, until lately, never heard the sound of a gun. The discharge of a musket inspires mortal terror in them, and it is almost impossible to induce them to face the muzzle of a gun. They believe that the Arabs have stolen the lightning, and that against such people the bow and arrow can have little effect. They are by no means devoid of courage, and they have often declared that, were it not for the guns, not one Arab would leave the country alive; this tends to prove that they would willingly engage in fight with the strangers who had made themselves so detestable, were it not that the startling explosion of gunpowder inspires them with terror.

Into what country soever the Arabs enter, they contrive to render their name and race abominated. But the mainspring of it all is not the Arab's nature, color, or name, but simply the slave-trade. So long as the slave-trade is permitted to be kept up at Zanzibar, so long will these otherwise enterprising people, the Arabs, kindle against them the hatred of the natives throughout Africa.

On the main line of travel from Zanzibar into the interior of Africa these acts of cruelty are unknown, for the very good reason that the natives having been armed with guns, and taught how to use those weapons, are by no means loth to do so whenever an opportunity presents itself. When, too late, they have perceived their folly in selling guns to the natives, the Arabs now begin to vow vengeance on the person who will in future sell a gun to a native. But they are all guilty of the same mistake, and it is strange they did not perceive that it was folly when they were doing so.

In former days the Arab, when protected by his slave escort, armed with guns, could travel through Useguhha, Urori, Ukonongo, Ufipa, Karagwah, Unyoro, and Uganda, with only a stick in his hand; now, however, it is impossible for him or any one else to do so. Every step he takes, armed or unarmed, is fraught with danger. The Waseguhha, near the coast, detain him, and demand the tribute, or give him the option of war; entering Ugogo, he is subjected every day to the same oppressive demand, or to the fearful alternative. The Wanyamwezi also show their readiness to take the same advantage; the road to Karagwah is besieged with difficulties; the terrible Mirambo stands in the way, defeats their combined forces with ease, and makes raids even to the doors of their houses in Unyanyembe; and should they succeed in passing Mirambo, a chief—Swaruru—stands before them who demands tribute by the bale, and against whom it is useless to contend.

These remarks have reference to the slave-trade inaugurated in Manyuema by the Arabs. Harassed on the road between Zanzibar and Unyanyembe by minatory natives, who with bloody hands are ready to avenge the slightest affront, the Arabs have refrained from kidnapping between the Tanganika and the sea; but in Manyuema, where the natives are timid, irresolute, and divided into small weak tribes, they recover their audacity, and exercise their kidnapping propensities unchecked.

The accounts which the Doctor brings from that new region are most deplorable. He was an unwilling spectator of a horrible deed—a massacre committed on the inhabitants of a populous district who had assembled in the market-place on the banks of the Lualaba, as they had been accustomed to do for ages. It seems that the Wamanyuema are very fond of marketing, believing it to be the *summum bonum* of human enjoyment. They find endless pleasure in chaffering with might and main for the least mite of their currency—the last bead; and when they gain the point to which their peculiar talents are devoted, they feel intensely happy. The women are excessively fond of this marketing, and, as they are very beautiful, the market place must possess considerable attractions for the male sex. It was on such a day amidst such a scene, that Tagamoyo, a half-caste Arab, with his armed slave escort, commenced an indiscriminate massacre by firing volley after volley into the dense mass of human beings. It is supposed that there were about 2,000 present, and at the first sound of the firing these poor people all made a rush for their canoes. In the fearful hurry to avoid being shot, the canoes were paddled away by the first fortunate few who got possession of them; those that were not so fortunate sprang into the deep waters of the Lualaba, and though many of them became an easy prey to the voracious crocodiles which swarmed to the scene, the majority received their deaths from the bullets of the merciless Tagamoyo and his villanous band. The Doctor believes, as do the Arabs themselves, that about 400 people, mostly women and children, lost their lives, while many more were made slaves. This outrage is only one of many such he has unwillingly witnessed, and he is utterly unable to describe the feelings of loathing he feels for the inhuman perpetrators.

Slaves from Manyuema command a higher price than those of any other country, because of their fine forms and general docility. The women, the Doctor saia repeatedly, are remarkably pretty creatuies, and have nothing, except the hair, in common with the negroes of the West Coast. They are of very light color, have fine noses, well-cut and not over-full lips, while the prognathous jaw is uncommon. These women are eagerly sought after as wives by the half-castes of the East Coast, and even the pure Omani Arabs do not disdain to take them in marriage.

To the north of Manyuema, Livingstone came to the light-complexioned race, of the color of Portuguese, or our own Louisiana quadroons, who are very fine people, and singularly remarkable for commercial " 'cuteness " and sagacity. The women are expert divers for oysters, which are found in great abundance in the Lualaba.

Rua, at a place called Katanga, is rich in copper. The copper-mines of this place have been worked for ages. In the bed of a stream, gold has been found, washed down in pencil-shaped pieces or in particles as large as split peas. Two Arabs have gone thither to prospect for this metal ; but, as they are ignorant of the art of gulch-mining, it is scarcely possible that they will succeed. From these highly-important and interesting discoveries, Dr. Livingstone was turned back, when almost on the threshold of success, by the positive refusal of his men to accompany him further. They were afraid to go on unless accompanied by a large force of men ; and, as these were not procurable in Manyuema, the Doctor reluctantly turned his face towards Ujiji.

It was a long and weary road back. The journey had now no interest for him. He had travelled the road before when going westward, full of high hopes and aspirations, impatient to reach the goal which promised him rest from his labors—now, returning unsuccessful, baffled, and thwarted, when almost in sight of the end, and having to travel the same path back on foot, with disappointed expectations and defeated hopes preying on his mind, no wonder that the old brave spirit almost succumbed, and the strong constitution almost went to wreck.

Livingstone arrived at Ujiji, October 16th, almost at death's door. On the way he had been trying to cheer himself up, since he had found it impossible to contend against the obstinacy of his men, with, "It won't take long; five or six months more; it matters not since it cannot be helped. I have got my goods in Ujiji, and can hire other people, and make a new start again." These are the words and hopes by which he tried to delude himself into the idea that all would be right yet; but imagine the shock he must have suffered, when he found that the man to whom was entrusted his goods for safe keeping had sold every bale for ivory.

The evening of the day Livingstone had returned to Ujiji, Susi and Chuma, two of his most faithful men, were seen crying bitterly. The Doctor asked of them what ailed them, and was then informed, for the first time, of the evil tidings that awaited him.

Said they, "All our things are sold, sir; Sherif has sold everything for ivory."

Later in the evening, Sherif came to see him, and shamelessly offered his hand, but Livingstone repulsed him, saying he could not shake hands with a thief. As an excuse, Sherif said he had divined on the Korân, and that this had told him the Hakim (Arabic for Doctor) was dead.

Livingstone was now destitute; he had just enough

to keep him and his men alive for about a month, when he would be forced to beg from the Arabs.

The Doctor further stated, that when Speke gives the altitude of the Tanganika at only 1,800 feet above the sea, Speke must have fallen into that error by a frequent writing of the Anno Domini, a mere slip of the pen; for the altitude, as he makes it out, is 2,800 feet by boiling point, and a little over 3,000 feet by barometer.

The Doctor's complaints were many because slaves were sent to him, in charge of goods, after he had so often implored the people at Zanzibar to send him freemen. A very little effort on the part of those entrusted with the despatch of supplies to him might have enabled them to procure good and faithful freemen; but if they contented themselves, upon the receipt of a letter from Dr. Livingstone, with sending to Ludha Damji for men, it is no longer a matter of wonder that dishonest and incapable slaves were sent forward. It is no new fact that the Doctor has discovered when he states that a negro freeman is a hundred times more capable and trustworthy than a slave. Centuries ago Eumæus, the herdsman, said to Ulysses:

> Jove fixed it certain, that whatever day
> Makes man a slave, takes half his worth away.

We passed several happy days at Ujiji, and it was time we were now preparing for our cruise on the Tanganika. Livingstone was improving every day under the different diet which my cook furnished him. I could give him no such suppers as that which Jupiter and Mercury received at the cottage of Baucis and Philemon. We had no berries of chaste Minerva, pickled cherries, endive, radishes, dried figs, dates, fragrant apples, and grapes; but we had cheese, and butter which I made myself, new-laid eggs, chickens, roast mutton, fish from the lake, rich curds and cream, wine from the Guinea-palm, egg-plants, cucumbers, sweet potatoes, pea-nuts, and beans, white honey from Ukaranga, luscious singwe—a plum-like fruit—from the forests of Ujiji, and corn scones and dampers, in place of wheaten bread.

During the noontide heats we sat under our veranda discussing our various projects, and in the early morning and evening we sought the shores of the lake—promenading up and down the beach to breathe the cool breezes which ruffled the surface of the water, and rolled the unquiet surf far up on the smooth and whitened shore.

It was the dry season, and we had most lovely weather; the temperature never was over 80° in the shade.

The market-place overlooking the broad silver water afforded us amusement and instruction. Representatives of most of the tribes dwelling near the lake were daily found there. There were the agricultural and pastoral Wajiji, with their flocks and herds; there were the fishermen from Ukaranga and Kaole, from beyond Bangwe, and even from Urundi, with their whitebait, which they called *dogara*, the silurus, the perch, and other fish; there were the palm-oil merchants, principally from Ujiji and Urundi, with great five-gallon pots full of reddish oil, of the consistency of butter; there were the salt merchants from the salt-plains of Uvinza and Uhha; there were the ivory merchants from Uvira and Usowa; there were the canoe-makers from Ugoma and Urundi; there were the cheap-Jack pedlers from Zanzibar, selling flimsy prints, and brokers exchanging blue

mutunda beads for sami-sami, and sungomazzi, and sofi,
The sofi beads are like pieces of thick clay-pipe stem
about half an inch long, and are in great demand here.
Here were found Waguhha, Wamanyuema, Wagoma,
Wavira, Wasige, Warundi, Wajiji, Waha, Wavinza,
Wasowa, Wangwana, Wakawendi, Arabs, and Wasawahili, engaged in noisy chaffer and barter. Bare-
headed, and almost barebodied, the youths made love to
the dark-skinned and woolly-headed Phyllises, who knew
not how to blush at the ardent gaze of love, as their
white sisters; old matrons gossiped, as the old women do
everywhere; the children played, and laughed, and
struggled, as children of our own lands; and the old
men, leaning on their spears or bows, were just as
garrulous in the Place de Ujiji as aged elders in other
climes.

VIEW ON LAKE TANGANIKA.

CHAPTER XIII.

OUR CRUISE ON THE LAKE TANGANIKA—EXPLORATION OF
THE NORTH-END OF THE LAKE—THE RUSIZI IS DISCOVERED
TO ENTER INTO THE LAKE—RETURN TO UJIJI.

"I distinctly deny that 'any misleading by my instructions from
the Royal Geographical Society as to the position of the White Nile'
made me unconscious of the vast importance of ascertaining the direction of the Rusizi River. The fact is, we did our best to reach it, and
we failed."—Burton's *Zanzibar*.

"The universal testimony of the natives to the Rusizi River being an
influent is the most conclusive argument that it does run out of the
lake."—Speke.

"I therefore claim for Lake Tanganika the honour of being the
SOUTHERNMOST RESERVOIR OF THE NILE, until some more positive
evidence, by actual observation, shall otherwise determine it."—
Findlay, R.G.S.

HAD Livingstone and myself, after making up our minds

to visit the northern head of the Lake Tanganika, been compelled by the absurd demands or fears of a crew of Wajiji to return to Unyanyembe without having resolved the problem of the Rusizi River, we had surely deserved to be greeted by everybody at home with a universal giggling and cackling. But Capt. Burton's failure to settle it, by engaging Wajiji, and that ridiculous savage chief Kannena, had warned us of the negative assistance we could expect from such people for the solution of a geographical problem. We had enough good sailors with us, who were entirely under our commands. Could we but procure the loan of a canoe, we thought all might be well.

Upon application to Sayd bin Majid, he at once generously permitted us to use his canoe for any service for which we might require it. After engaging two Wajiji guides at two doti each, we prepared to sail from the port of Ujiji, in about a week or so after my entrance into Ujiji.

I have already stated how it was that the Doctor and I undertook the exploration of the northern half of the Tanganika and the River Rusizi, about which so much had been said and written.

Before embarking on this enterprise, Dr. Livingstone had not definitely made up his mind which course he should take, as his position was truly deplorable. His servants consisted of Susi, Chumah, Hamoydah, Gardner, and Halimah, the female cook and wife of Hamoydah; to these was added Kaif-Halek, the man whom I compelled to follow me from Unyanyembe to deliver the Livingstone letters to his master.

Whither could Dr. Livingstone march with these few men, and the few table-cloths and beads that remained

to him from the store squandered by the imbecile Sherif?
This was a puzzling question. Had Dr. Livingstone
been in good health, his usual hardihood and indomitable
spirit had answered it in a summary way. He might
have borrowed some cloth from Sayd bin Majid at an
exorbitant price, sufficient to bring him to Unyanyembe
and the sea-coast. But how long would he have been
compelled to sit down at Ujiji, waiting and waiting for
the goods that were said to be at Unyanyembe, a prey to
high expectations, hoping day after day that the war
would end—hoping week after week to hear that his
goods were coming? Who knows how long his weak
health had borne up against the several disappointments
to which he would be subjected?

Though it was with all due deference to Dr. Livingstone's vast experience as a traveller, I made bold to
suggest the following courses to him, either of which he
could adopt:

1st. To go home, and take the rest he so well deserved
and, as he appeared then, to be so much in need of.

2nd. To proceed to Unyanyembe, receive his goods,
and enlist pagazis sufficient to enable him to travel
anywhere, either to Manyuema or Rua, and settle the
Nile problem, which he said he was in a fair way of
doing.

3rd. To proceed to Unyanyembe, receive his caravan,
enlist men, and try to join Sir Samuel Baker, either
by going to Muanza, and sailing through Ukerewe or
Victoria N'Yanza in my boats—which I should put up
—to Mtesa's palace at Uganda, thus passing by Mirambo
and Swaruru of Usui, who would rob him if he took the
usual caravan road to Uganda; thence from Mtesa to
Kamrasi, King of Unyoro, where he would of course hear

of the great white man who was said to be with a large
force of men at Gondokoro.

4th. To proceed to Unyanyembe, receive his caravan,
enlist men, and return to Ujiji, and back to Manyuema by
way of Uguhha.

5th. To proceed by way of the Rusizi through Ruanda,
and so on to Itara, Unyoro, and Baker.

For either course, whichever he thought most ex-
pedient, I and my men would assist him as escort and
carriers, to the best of our ability. If he should elect
to go home, I informed him I should be proud to escort
him, and consider myself subject to his commands—
travelling only when he desired, and camping only when
he gave the word.

6th. The last course which I suggested to him, was
to permit me to escort him to Unyanyembe, where he
could receive his own goods, and where I could deliver
up to him a large supply of first-class cloth and beads,
guns and ammunition, cooking utensils, clothing, boats,
tents, &c., and where he could rest in a comfortable
house, while I would hurry down to the coast, organise a
new expedition composed of fifty or sixty faithful men,
well armed, by whom I could send an additional supply
of needful luxuries in the shape of creature comforts.

After long consideration, he resolved to adopt the
last course, as it appeared to him to be the most feasible
one, and the best, though he did not hesitate to comment
upon the unaccountable apathy of his agent at Zanzibar,
which had caused him so much trouble and vexation, and
weary marching of hundreds of miles.

Our ship—though nothing more than a cranky canoe
hollowed out of a noble mvule tree of Ugoma—was an
African Argo, bound on a nobler enterprise than its

famous Grecian prototype. We were bound upon no
mercenary errand, after no Golden Fleece, but perhaps
to discover a highway for commerce which should bring
the ships of the Nile up to Ujiji, Usowa, and far Marungu.
We did not know what we might discover on our voyage
to the northern head of the Tanganika; we supposed
that we should find the Rusizi to be an effluent of the
Tanganika, flowing down to the Albert or the Victoria
N'Yanza. We were told by natives and Arabs that the
Rusizi ran out of the lake.

Sayd bin Majid had stated that his canoe would carry
twenty-five men, and 3,500 lbs. of ivory. Acting upon
this information, we embarked twenty-five men, several
of whom had stored away bags of salt for the purposes of
trade with the natives; but upon pushing off from the
shore near Ujiji, we discovered the boat was too heavily
laden, and was down to the gunwale. Returning in-shore,
we disembarked six men, and unloaded the bags of salt,
which left us with sixteen rowers, Selim, Ferajji the cook,
and the two Wajiji guides.

Having thus properly trimmed our boat we again
pushed off, and steered her head for Bangwe Island,
which was distant four or five miles from the Bunder of
Ujiji. While passing this island the guides informed us
that the Arabs and Wajiji took shelter on it during an
incursion of the Watuta—which took place some years
ago—when they came and invaded Ujiji, and massacred
several of the inhabitants. Those who took refuge on
the island were the only persons who escaped the fire and
sword with which the Watuta had visited Ujiji.

After passing the island and following the various
bends and indentations of the shore, we came in sight of
the magnificent bay of Kigoma, which strikes one at once

as being an excellent harbor from the variable winds which blow over the Tanganika. About 10 A.M. we drew in towards the village of Kigoma, as the east wind was then rising, and threatened to drive us to sea. With those travelling parties who are not in much hurry Kigoma is always the first port for canoes bound north from Ujiji. The next morning at dawn we struck tent, stowed baggage, cooked, and drank coffee, and set off northward again.

The lake was quite calm; its waters, of a dark-green color, reflected the serene blue sky above. The hippopotami came up to breathe in alarmingly close proximity to our canoe, and then plunged their heads again, as if they were playing hide-and-seek with us. Arriving opposite the high wooded hills of Bemba, and being a mile from shore, we thought it a good opportunity to sound the depth of the water, whose color seemed to indicate great depth. We found thirty-five fathoms at this place.

Our canoeing of this day was made close in-shore, with a range of hills, beautifully wooded and clothed with green grass, sloping abruptly, almost precipitously, into the depths of the fresh-water sea, towering immediately above us, and as we rounded the several capes or points, roused high expectations of some new wonder, or some exquisite picture being revealed as the deep folds disclosed themselves to us. Nor were we disappointed. The wooded hills, with a wealth of boscage of beautiful trees, many of which were in bloom, and crowned with floral glory, exhaling an indescribably sweet fragrance, lifting their heads in varied contour—one pyramidal, another a truncated cone; one table-topped, another ridgy, like the steep roof of a church; one a glorious heave with an even outline, another jagged and savage—interested us considerably; and the pretty pictures, exquisitely pretty, at the head of the several bays, evoked many an exclamation of admiration. It was the most natural thing in the world that I should feel deepest admiration for these successive pictures of quiet scenic beauty, but the Doctor had quite as much to say about them as I had myself, though, as one might imagine, satiated with pictures of this kind far more beautiful—far more wonderful—he should long ago have expended all his powers of admiring scenes in nature.

From Bagamoyo to Ujiji I had seen nothing to compare to them—none of these fishing settlements under the shade of a grove of palms and plantains, banians and mimosa, with cassava gardens to the right and left of palmy forests, and patches of luxuriant grain looking down upon a quiet bay, whose calm waters at the early morn reflected the beauties of the hills which sheltered them from the rough and boisterous tempests that so often blew without.

The fishermen evidently think themselves comfortably situated. The lake affords them all the fish they require, more than enough to eat, and the industrious a great deal to sell. The steep slopes of the hills, cultivated by the housewives, contribute plenty of grain, such as dourra and Indian corn, besides cassava, ground-nuts or peanuts, and sweet potatoes. The palm trees afford oil, and the plantains an abundance of delicious fruit. The ravines and deep gullies supply them with the tall shapely trees from which they cut out their canoes. Nature has supplied them bountifully with all that a man's heart or stomach can desire. It is while looking at what seems both externally and internally complete and perfect happiness that the thought occurs—how must these people sigh, when driven across the dreary wilderness that intervenes between the lake country and the sea-coast, for such homes as these!—those unfortunates who, bought by the Arabs for a couple of doti, are taken away to Zanzibar to pick cloves, or do hamal work!

As we drew near Niasanga, our second camp, the comparison between the noble array of picturesque hills and receding coves, with their pastoral and agricultural scenes, and the shores of old Pontus, was very great. A few minutes before we hauled our canoe ashore, two little incidents occurred. I shot an enormous dog-faced monkey, which measured from nose to end of tail 4 feet 9 inches; the face was 8½ inches long, its body weighed about 100 lbs. It had no mane or tuft at end of tail, but the body was covered with long wiry hair. Numbers of these specimens were seen, as well as of the active cat-headed and long-tailed smaller ones. The other was the sight of a large lizard, about 2 ft. 6 in. long, which waddled into cover before we had well noticed it. The Doctor thought it to be the *Monitor terrestris*.

We encamped under a banian tree; our surroundings were the now light-grey waters of the Tanganika, an amphitheatral range of hills, and the village of Niasanga, situated at the mouth of the rivulet Niasanga, with its grove of palms, thicket of plantains, and plots of grain and cassava fields. Near our tent were about half-a-dozen canoes, large and small, belonging to the villagers. Our tent door fronted the glorious expanse of fresh water, inviting the breeze, and the views of distant Ugoma and Ukaramba, and the Island of Muzimu, whose ridges appeared of a deep-blue color. At our feet were the clean and well-washed pebbles, borne upward into tiny lines and heaps by the restless surf. A search amongst these would reveal to us the material of the mountain heaps which rose behind and on our right and left; there was schist, conglomerate sandstone, a hard white clay, an ochreish clay containing much iron, polished quartz, &c. Looking out of our tent, we could see a line on each side of us of thick tall reeds, which form something like a hedge between the beach and the cultivated area around Niasanga. Among birds seen here, the most noted were the merry wagtails, which are regarded as good omens and messengers of peace by the natives, and any harm done unto them is quickly resented, and is fineable. Except to the mischievously inclined, they offer no inducement to commit violence. On landing, they flew to meet us, balancing themselves in the air in front, within easy reach of our hands. The other birds were crows, turtle-doves, fish-hawks, kingfishers, ibis nigra and ibis religiosa, flocks of whydah birds, geese, darters, paddy birds, kites, and eagles.

At this place the Doctor suffered from dysentery—it is his only weak point, he says; and, as I afterwards found, it is a frequent complaint with him. Whatever disturbed his mind, or any irregularity in eating, was sure to end in an attack of dysentery, which had lately become of a chronic character.

The third day of our journey on the Tanganika brought us to Zassi River and village, after a four hours' pull. Along the line of road the mountains rose 2,000 and 2,500 feet above the waters of the lake. I imagined the scenery getting more picturesque and animated at every step, and thought it by far lovelier than anything seen near Lake George or on the Hudson. The cosy nooks at the head of the many small bays constitute most admirable

pictures, filled in as they are with the ever-beautiful
feathery palms and broad green plantain fronds. These
nooks have all been taken possession of by fishermen,
and their conically beehive-shaped huts always peep from
under the frondage. The shores are thus extremely
populous; every terrace, small plateau, and bit of level
ground is occupied.

Zassi is easily known by a group of conical hills which
rise near by, and are called Kirassa. Opposite to these,
at the distance of about a mile from shore, we sounded,
and obtained 35 fathoms, as on the previous day. Getting
out a mile further, I let go the whole length of my line,
115 fathoms, and obtained no bottom. In drawing it up
again the line parted, and I lost the lead, with three-
fourths of the line. The Doctor stated, apropos of this,
that he had sounded opposite the lofty Kabogo, south of
Ujiji, and obtained the great depth of 300 fathoms. He
also lost his lead and 100 fathoms of his line, but he had
nearly 900 fathoms left, and this was in the canoes. We
hope to use this long sounding line in going across from
the eastern to the western shore.

On the fourth day we arrived at Nyabigma, a sandy
island in Urundi. We had passed the boundary line
between Ujiji and Urundi half-an-hour before arriving at
Nyabigma. The Mshala River is considered by both
nations to be the proper divisional line; though there
are parties of Warundi who have emigrated beyond
the frontier into Ujiji; for instance, the Mutware and
villagers of populous Kagunga, distant an hour north
from Zassi. There are also several small parties of
Wajiji, who have taken advantage of the fine lands in
the deltas of the Kasokwe, Namusinga, and Luaba
Rivers, the two first of which enter the Tanganika

in this bay, near the head of which Nyabigma is situated.

From Nyabigma, a pretty good view of the deep curve in the great mountain range which stretches from Cape Kazinga and terminates at Cape Kasofu, may be obtained —a distance of twenty or twenty-five miles. It is a most imposing scene, this great humpy, ridgy, and irregular line of mountains. Deep ravines and chasms afford outlets to the numerous streams and rivers which take their rise in the background; the pale fleecy ether almost always shrouds its summit. From its base extends a broad alluvial plain, rich beyond description, teeming with palms and plantains, and umbrageous trees. Villages are seen in clusters everywhere. Into this alluvial plain run the Luaba, or Ruaba River, on the north side of Cape Kitunda, and the Kasokwe, Namusinga, and Mshala Rivers, on the south side of the cape. All the deltas of rivers emptying into the Tanganika are hedged in on all sides with a thick growth of matete, a gigantic species of grass, and papyrus. In some deltas, as that of Luaba and Kasokwe, morasses have been formed, in which the matete and papyrus jungle is impenetrable. In the depths of them are quiet and deep pools, frequented by various aquatic birds, such as geese, ducks, snipes, widgeons, kingfishers and ibis, cranes and storks, and pelicans. To reach their haunts is, however, a work of great difficulty to the sportsman in quest of game; a work often attended with great danger, from the treacherous nature of these morasses, as well as from the dreadful attacks of fever which, in these regions, invariably follow wet feet and wet clothes.

At Nyabigma we prepared, by distributing ten rounds of ammunition to each of our men, for a tussle with the

Warundi of two stages ahead, should they invite it by a too forward exhibition of their prejudice to strangers.

At dawn of the fifth day we quitted the haven of Nyabigma Island, and in less than an hour had arrived off Cape Kitunda. This cape is a low platform of conglomerate sandstone, extending for about eight miles from the base of the great mountain curve which gives birth to the Luaba and its sister streams. Crossing the deep bay, at the head of which is the delta of the Luaba, we came to Cape Kasofu. Villages are numerous in this vicinity. From hence we obtained a view of a series of points or capes, Kigongo, Katunga, and Buguluka, all of which we passed before coming to a halt at the pretty position of Mukungu.

At Mukungu, where we stopped on the fifth day, we were asked for honga, or tribute. The cloth and beads upon which we subsisted during our lake voyage were mine, but the Doctor, being the elder of the two, more experienced, and the "big man" of the party, had the charge of satisfying all such demands. Many and many a time had I gone through the tedious and soul-wearying task of settling the honga, and I was quite curious to see how the great traveller would perform the work.

The Mateko (a man inferior to a Mutware) of Mukungu asked for two and a half doti. This was the extent of the demand, which he made known to us a little after dark. The Doctor asked if nothing had been brought to us. He was answered, "No, it was too late to get anything now; but, if we paid the honga, the Mateko would be ready to give us something when we came back.' Livingstone, upon hearing this, smiled, and the Mateko being then and there in front of him, he said to him. 'Well, if you can't get us anything now, and intend to

give something when we return, we had better keep the
honga until then." The Mateko was rather taken aback
at this, and demurred to any such proposition. Seeing
that he was dissatisfied, we urged him to bring one sheep
—one little sheep—for our stomachs were nearly empty,
having been waiting more than half a day for it. The
appeal was successful, for the old man hastened, and
brought us a lamb and a three-gallon pot of sweet but
strong zogga, or palm toddy, and in return the Doctor
gave him two and a half doti of cloth. The lamb was
killed, and, our digestions being good, its flesh agreed
with us; but, alas, for the effects of zogga, or palm toddy!
Susi, the invaluable adjunct of Dr. Livingstone, and
Bombay, the headman of my caravan, were the two
charged with watching the canoe; but, having imbibed
too freely of this intoxicating toddy, they slept heavily,
and in the morning the Doctor and I had to regret the
loss of several valuable and indispensable things; among
which may be mentioned the Doctor's 900-fathom sounding-
line, 500 rounds of pin, rim, and central-fire cartridges for
my arms, and ninety musket bullets, also belonging to
me. Besides these, which were indispensable in hostile
Warundi, a large bag of flour and the Doctor's entire
stock of white sugar were stolen. This was the third
time that my reliance in Bombay's trustworthiness resulted
in a great loss to me, and for the ninety-ninth time I had
to regret bitterly having placed such entire confidence in
Speke's loud commendation of him. It was only the
natural cowardice of ignorant thieves that prevented the
savages from taking the boat and its entire contents,
together with Bombay and Susi as slaves. I can well
imagine the joyful surprise which must have been called
forth at the sight and exquisite taste of the Doctor's

sugar, and the wonder with which they must have regarded the strange ammunition of the Wasungu. It is to be sincerely hoped that they did not hurt themselves with the explosive bullets and rim cartridges through any ignorance of the nature of the deadly contents; in which case the box and its contents would prove a very Pandora's casket.

Much grieved at our loss, we set off on the sixth day at the usual hour on our watery journey. We coasted close to the several low headlands formed by the rivers Kigwena, Kikuma, and Kisunwe; and when any bay promised to be interesting, steered the canoe according to its indentations. While travelling on the water— each day brought forth similar scenes—on our right rose the mountains of Urundi, now and then disclosing the ravines through which the several rivers and streams issued into the great lake; at their base were the alluvial plains, where flourished the oil-palm and grateful plantain, while scores of villages were grouped under their shade. Now and then we passed long narrow strips of pebbly or sandy beach, whereon markets were improvised for selling fish, and the staple products of the respective communities. Then we passed broad swampy morasses, formed by the numerous streams which the mountains discharged, where the matete and papyrus flourished. Now the mountains approached to the water, their sides descending abruptly to the water's edge; then they receded into deep folds, at the base of which was sure to be seen an alluvial plain from one to eight miles broad. Almost constantly we observed canoes being punted vigorously close to the surf, in fearless defiance of a catastrophe, such as a capsize and gobbling-up by voracious crocodiles.

Sometimes we sighted a canoe a short distance ahead of us; whereupon our men, with song and chorus, would exert themselves to the utmost to overtake it. Upon observing our efforts, the natives would bend themselves to their tasks, and paddling standing and stark naked, give us ample opportunities for studying at our leisure comparative anatomy. Or we saw a group of fishermen lazily reclining *in puris naturalibus* on the beach, regarding with curious eye the canoes as they passed their neighbourhood; then we passed a flotilla of canoes, their owners sitting quietly in their huts, busily plying the rod and hook, or casting their nets, or a couple of men arranging their long drag nets close in shore for a haul; or children sporting fearlessly in the water, with their mothers looking on approvingly from under the shade of a tree, from which I infer that there are not many crocodiles in the lake, except in the neighbourhood of the large rivers.

After passing the low headland of Kisunwe, formed by the Kisunwe River, we came in view of Murembwe Cape, distant about four or five miles : the intervening ground being low land, a sandy and pebbly beach. Close to the beach are scores of villages, while the crowded shore indicates the populousness of the place beyond. About half way between Cape Kisunwe and Murembwe, is a cluster of villages called Bikari, which has a mutware who is in the habit of taking honga. As we were rendered unable to cope for any length of time with any mischievously inclined community, all villages having a bad reputation with the Wajiji were avoided by us. But even the Wajiji guides were sometimes mistaken, and led us more than once into dangerous places. The guides evidently had no objections to halt at Bikari, as it was the second camp from Mukungu; because with them a halt in the cool shade of plaintains was infinitely preferable to sitting like carved pieces of wood in a cranky canoe. But before they stated their objections and preferences, the Bikari people called to us in a loud voice to come ashore, threatening us with the vengeance of the great Wami if we did not halt. As the voices were anything but siren-like, we obstinately refused to accede to the request. Finding threats of no avail, they had recourse to stones, and, accordingly, flung them at us in a most hearty manner. As one came within a foot of my arm, I suggested that a bullet be sent in return in close proximity to their feet; but Livingstone, though he said nothing, yet showed plainly enough that he did not quite approve of this. As these demonstrations of hostility were anything but welcome, and as we saw signs of it almost every time we came opposite a village, we kept on our way until we came to Murembwe Point, which, being a delta of a river of the same name, was well protected by a breadth of thorny jungle, spiky cane, and a thick growth of reed and papyrus, from which the boldest Mrundi might well shrink, especially if he called to mind that beyond this inhospitable swamp were the guns of the strangers his like had so rudely challenged. We drew our canoe ashore here, and, on a limited area of clean sand, Ferajji, our rough-and-ready cook, lit his fire, and manufactured for us a supply of most delicious Mocha coffee. Despite the dangers which still beset us, we were quite happy, and seasoned our meal with a little moral philosophy, which lifted us unconsciously into infinitely superior beings to the pagans by whom we were surrounded—upon whom we now looked down, under the influence of Mocha coffee and moral philosophy, with calm contempt, not unmixed with a certain amount of compassion. The Doctor related some experiences he had had among people of similar disposition, but did not fail to ascribe them, with the wisdom of a man of ripe experiences, to the unwise conduct of the Arabs and half-castes; in this opinion I unreservedly concur.

From Murembwe Point, having finished our coffee and ended our discourse on ethics, we proceeded on our voyage, steering for Cape Sentakeyi, which, though it was eight or ten miles away, we hoped to make before dark. The Wangwana pulled with right good will, but ten hours went by, and night was drawing near, and we were still far from Sentakeyi. As it was a fine moonlight night, and we were fully alive to the dangerous position in which we might find ourselves, they consented to pull an hour or two more. About 1 P.M., we pulled in shore for a deserted spot—a clean shelf of sand, about thirty feet long by ten deep, from which a clay bank rose about ten or twelve feet above, while on each side there were masses of disintegrated rock. Here we thought, that by preserving some degree of silence, we might escape observation, and consequent annoyance, for a few hours, when, being rested, we might continue our journey. Our kettle was boiling for tea, and the men had built a little fire for themselves, and had filled their black earthen pot with water for porridge, when our look-outs perceived dark forms creeping towards our bivouac. Being hailed, they at once came forward, and saluted us with the native " Wake." Our guides explained that we were Wangwana, and intended to camp until morning, when, if they had anything to sell, we should be glad to trade with them. They said they were rejoiced to hear this, and after they had exchanged a few words more—during which time we observed that they were taking mental notes of the camp—they went away. Upon leaving, they promised to return in the morning with food, and make friends with us. While drinking our tea, the look-outs warned us of the approach of a second party, which went through the same process of saluting and observing as the first had done. These also went away, over-exuberant, as I thought, and were shortly succeeded by a third party, who came and went as the others had. From all this we inferred that the news was spreading rapidly through the villages about, and we had noticed two canoes passing backwards and forwards with rather more haste than we deemed usual or necessary. We had good cause to be suspicious; it is not customary for people (at least, between Ujiji and Zanzibar) to be about visiting and saluting after dark, under any pretence; it is not permitted to persons to prowl about camp after dark without being shot at; and this going backward and forward, this ostentatious exuberance of joy at the arrival of a small party of Wangwana, which in many parts of Urundi would be regarded as a very common event, was altogether very suspicious. While the Doctor and I were arriving at the conclusion that these movements were preliminary to or significant of hostility, a fourth body, very boisterous and loud, came and visited us. Our supper had been by this time despatched, and we thought it high time to act. The fourth party having gone with extravagant manifest-ations of delight, the men were hurried into the canoe, and, when all were seated, and the look-outs embarked, we quietly pushed off, but not a moment too soon. As the canoe was gliding from the darkened light that surrounded us, I called the Doctor's attention to several dark forms; some of whom were crouching behind the rocks on our right, and others scrambling over them to obtain good or better positions; at the same time people were approaching from the left of our position, in the same suspicious way; and directly a voice hailed us from the top of the clay bank overhanging the sandy shelf where we had lately been resting. "Neatly done,' cried the Doctor, as we were shooting through the water, leaving the discomfited would-be robbers behind us. Here, again, my hand was stayed from planting a couple of good shots, as a warning to them in future from molesting strangers, by the mere presence of the Doctor, who, as I thought, if it were actually necessary, would not hesitate to give the word.

After pulling six hours more, during which we had rounded Cape Sentakeyi, we stopped at the small fishing village of Mugeyo, where we were permitted to sleep unmolested. At dawn we continued our journey, and about 8 A.M. arrived at the village of the friendly Mutware of Magala. We had pulled for eighteen hours at a stretch, which, at the rate of two miles and a half per hour, would make forty-five miles. Taking bearings from our camp at Cape Magala, one of the most prominent points in travelling north from Ujiji, we found that the large island of Muzimu, which had been in sight ever since rounding Cape Bangwe, near Ujiji Bunder, bore about south-south-west, and that the western shore had considerably approached to the eastern; the breadth of the lake being at this point about eight or ten miles. We had a good view of the western highlands, which seemed to be of an average height, about 3,000 feet above the lake. Luhanga Peak, rising a little to the north of west from Magala, might be about 500 feet higher; and Sumburizi, a little north of Luhanga, where lived Mruta, Sultan of Uvira, the country opposite to this part of Urundi, about 300 feet higher than the neighbouring heights. Northward from Magala Cape the lake streamed away between two chains of mountains; both meeting in a point about thirty miles north of us.

The Warundi of Magala were very civil, and profound starers. They flocked around the tent door, and most pertinaciously gazed on us, as if we were subjects of most intense interest, but liable to sudden and eternal departure. The Mutware came to see us late in the afternoon, dressed with great pomp. He turned out to be a boy whom I had noticed in the crowd of gazers for his good looks and fine teeth, which he showed, being addicted to laughing continually. There was no mistaking him, though he was now decorated with many ivory ornaments, with necklaces, and with heavy brass bracelets and iron wire anklets. Our admiration of him was reciprocated; and, in return for our two doti of cloth and a fundo of samsam, he gave a fine fat and broad-tailed sheep, and a pot of milk. In our condition both were extremely acceptable.

At Magala we heard of a war raging between Mukamba, for whose country we were bound, and Warumashanya, a Sultan of an adjoining district; and we were advised that, unless we intended to assist one of these chiefs against the other, it would be better for us to return. But, as we had started to solve the problem of the Rusizi River, such considerations had no weight with us.

On the eighth morning from leaving Ujiji we bade farewell to the hospitable people of Magala, and set off for Mukamba's country, which was in view. Soon after passing the boundary between Urundi proper, and what is known as Usige, a storm from the south-west arose; and the fearful yawing of our canoe into the wave trough warned us from proceeding further; so we turned her head for Kisuka village, about four miles north, where Mugere, in Usige, begins.

At Kisuka a Mgwana living with Mukamba came to see us, and gave us details of the war between Mukamba and Warumashanya, from which it seemed that these two chiefs were continually at loggerheads. It is a tame way of fighting, after all. One chief makes a raid into the other's country, and succeeds in making off with a herd of cattle, killing one or two men who have been surprised. Weeks, or perhaps months elapse before the other retaliates, and effects a capture in a similar way, and then a balance is struck in which neither is the gainer. Seldom do they attack each other with courage and hearty goodwill, the constitution of the African being decidedly against any such energetic warfare.

This Mgwana, further, upon being questioned, gave us information far more interesting, viz., about the Rusizi. He told us positively, with the air of a man who knew all about it, and as if anybody who doubted him might well be set down as an egregious ass, that the Rusizi River flowed out of the lake, away to Suna's (Mtesa's) country. "Where else could it flow to?" he asked. The Doctor was inclined to believe it, or, perhaps he was more inclined to let it rest as stated until our own eyes should confirm it. I was more inclined to doubt, as I told the Doctor; first, it was too good to be true; second, the fellow was too enthusiastic upon a subject that could not possibly interest him. His "Barikallahs" and "Inshallahs" were far too fervid; his answers too much in accordance with our wishes. The Doctor laid great stress on the report of a Mgwana he met far south, who stated that the grandfather or father of Rumanika, present King of Karagwah, had thought of excavating the bed of the Kitangule River, in order that his canoes might go to Ujiji to open a trade. From this, I imagine, coinciding as it did with his often-expressed and present firm belief that the waters of the Tanganika had an outlet somewhere, the Doctor was partial to the report of the Mgwana; but as we proceed we shall see how all this will end.

On the ninth morning from Ujiji, about two hours after sunrise, we passed the broad delta of the Mugere, a river which gives its name also to the district on the eastern shore ruled over by Mukamba. We had come directly opposite the most southern of its three mouths, when we found quite a difference in the colour of the water. An almost straight line, drawn east and west from the mouth would serve well to mark off the difference that existed between the waters. On the south side was pure water of a light green, on the north side it was muddy, and the current could be distinctly seen flowing north. Soon after passing the first mouth we came to a second, and then a third mouth, each only a few yards broad, but each discharging sufficient water to permit our following the line of the currents several rods north beyond the respective mouths.

Beyond the third mouth of the Mugere a bend disclosed itself, with groups of villages beyond on its bank. These were Mukamba's, and in one of them lived Mukamba, the chief. The natives had yet never seen a white man, and, of course, as soon as we landed we were surrounded by a large concourse, all armed with long spears—the only weapon visible amongst them save a club-stick, and here and there a hatchet.

We were shown into a hut, which the Doctor and I shared between us. What followed on that day I have but a dim recollection, having been struck down by fever —the first since leaving Unyanyembe. I dimly recollect trying to make out what age Mukamba might be, and noting that he was good-looking withal, and kindly-disposed towards us. And during the intervals of agony and unconsciousness, I saw, or fancied I saw, Livingstone's form moving towards me, and felt, or fancied I felt, Livingstone's hand tenderly feeling my hot head and limbs. I had suffered several fevers between Bagamoyo and Unyanyembe, without anything or anybody to relieve me of the tedious racking headache and pain, or to illumine the dark and gloomy prospect which must necessarily surround the bedside of the sick and solitary traveller. But though this fever, having enjoyed immunity from it for three months, was more severe than usual, I did not much regret its occurrence, since I became the recipient of the very tender and fatherly kindness of the good man whose companion I now found myself.

The next morning, having recovered slightly from the fever, when Mukamba came with a present of an ox, a sheep, and a goat, I was able to attend to the answers which he gave to the questions about the Rusizi River and the head of the lake. The ever cheerful and enthusiastic Mgwana was there also, and he was not a whit abashed, when, through him, the chief told us that the Rusizi, joined by the Ruanda, or Luanda, at a distance of two days' journey by water, or one day by land from the head of the lake, flowed INTO the lake.

Thus our hopes, excited somewhat by the positive and repeated assurances that the river flowed out away towards Karagwah, collapsed as speedily as they were raised.

We paid Mukamba the honga, consisting of nine doti and nine fundo of samsam, lunghio, muzurio n'zige. The printed handkerchiefs, which I had in abundance at Unyanyembe, would have gone well here. After receiving his present, the chief introduced his son, a tall youth of eighteen or thereabouts, to the Doctor, as a would-be son of the Doctor; but, with a good-natured laugh, the Doctor scouted all such relationship with him, as it was instituted only for the purpose of drawing more cloth out of him. Mukamba took it in good part, and did not insist on getting more.

Our second evening at Mukamba's, Susi, the Doctor's servant, got gloriously drunk, through the chief's liberal and profuse gifts of pombe. Just at dawn next morning I was awakened by hearing several sharp, crack-like sounds. I listened, and I found the noise was in our hut. It was caused by the Doctor, who, towards midnight, had felt some one come and lie down by his side on the same bed, and, thinking it was me, he had kindly made room, and laid down on the edge of the bed. But in the morning, feeling rather cold, he had been thoroughly awakened, and, on rising on his elbow to see who his bed-fellow was, he discovered, to his great astonishment, that it was no other than his black servant, Susi, who taking possession of his blankets, and folding them about himself most selfishly, was occupying almost the whole bed. The Doctor, with that gentleness characteristic of him, instead of taking a rod, had contented himself with slapping Susi on the back, saying, " Get up, Susi, will you? You are in my bed. How dare you, sir, get drunk in this way, after I have told you so often not to. Get up. You won't? Take that, and that, and that." Still Susi slept and grunted; so the slapping continued, until even Susi's thick hide began to feel it, and he was thoroughly awakened to the sense of his want of devotion and sympathy for his master in the usurping of even his master's bed. Susi looked very much crestfallen after this *exposé* of his infirmity before the " little master," as I was called.

SUSI THE SERVANT OF LIVINGSTONE.

The next day at dusk—Mukamba having come to bid us good-bye, and requested that as soon as we reached his brother Ruhinga, whose country was at the head of the lake, we would send our canoe back for him, and that in the meanwhile we should leave two of our men with him, with their guns, to help defend him in case Warumashanya should attack him as soon as we were gone—we embarked and pulled across. In nine hours we had arrived at the head of the lake in Mugihewa, the country of Ruhinga, Mukamba's elder brother. In looking back to where we had come from we perceived that we had made a diagonal cut across from south-east to north-west, instead of having made a direct east and west course; or, in other words, from Mugere—which was at least ten miles from the northernmost point of the eastern shore—we had come to Mugihewa, situated at the northernmost point of the western shore. Had we continued along the eastern shore, and so round the northern side of the lake, we should have passed by Mukanigi, the country of Warumashanya, and Usumbura of Simveh, his ally and friend. But by making a diagonal course, as just described, we had arrived at the extreme head of the lake without any difficulty.

The country in which we now found ourselves, Mugihewa, is situated in the delta of the Rusizi River. It is an extremely flat country, the highest part of which is not ten feet above the lake, with numerous depressions in it overgrown with the rankest of matete-grass and the tallest of papyrus, and pond-like hollows, filled with stagnant water, which emit malaria wholesale. Large herds of cattle are reared on it; for where the ground is not covered with marshy plants it produces rich, sweet grass. The sheep and goats, especially the former, are always in good condition; and though they are not to be compared with English or American sheep, they are the finest I have seen in Africa. Numerous villages are seen on this land because the intervening spaces are not occupied with the rank and luxuriant jungle common in other parts of Africa. Were it not for the Euphorbia kolquall of Abyssinia—which some chief has caused to be planted as a defence round the villages—one might see from one end of Mugihewa to the other. The waters along the head of the lake, from the western to the eastern shores, swarm with crocodiles. From the banks, I counted ten heads of crocodiles, and the Rusizi, we were told, was full of them.

Ruhinga, who came to see us soon after we had taken up our quarters in his village, was a most amiable man, who always contrived to see something that excited his risibility; though older by five or six years perhaps—he said he was a hundred years old—than Mukamba, he was not half no dignified, nor regarded with so much admiration by his people as his younger brother. Ruhinga had a better knowledge, however, of the country than Mukamba, and an admirable memory, and was able to impart his knowledge of the country intelligently. After he had done the honours as chief to us—presented us with an ox and a sheep, milk and honey—we were not backward in endeavouring to elicit as much information as possible out of him.

The summary of the information derived from Ruhinga may be stated as follows:

The country bordering the head of the lake from Urundi proper, on the eastern shore, to Uvira on the western, is divided into the following districts: 1st. Mugere, governed by Mukamba, through which issued into the lake the small rivers of Mugere and Mpanda. 2nd. Mukanigi, governed by Warumashanya, which occupied the whole of the north-eastern head of the lake, through which issued into the lake the small rivers of Karindwa and Mugera wa Kanigi. 3rd. On the eastern half of the district, at the head of the lake, was Usumbura, governed by Simveh, ally and friend of Warumashanya, extending to the eastern bank of the Rusizi. 4th. Com-

mencing from the western bank of the Rusizi, to the
extreme north-western head of the lake, was Mugihewa—
Ruhinga's country. 5th. From Uvira on the west,
running north past Mugihewa, and overlapping it on the
north side as far as the hills of Chamati, was Ruwenga,
also a country governed by Mukamba. Beyond Ruwenga,
from the hills of Chamati to the Ruanda River, was the
country of Chamati. West of Ruwenga, comprising all
the mountains for two days' journey in that direction,
was Uashi. These are the smaller sub-divisions of what
is commonly known as Ruwenga and Usige. Ruwenga
comprises the countries of Ruwenga and Mugihewa;
Usige, the countries of Usumbura, Mukanigi, and Mugere.
But all these countries are only part and parcel of Urundi,
which comprises all that country bordering the lake from
Mshala River, on the eastern shore, to Uvira, on the
western, extending over ten days' journey direct north
from the head of the lake, and one month in a north-
eastern direction to Murukuko, the capital of Mwezi,
Sultan of all Urundi. Direct north of Urundi is Ruanda;
also a very large country.

The Rusizi River—according to Ruhinga—rose near a
lake called Kivo, which he said is as long as from Mugihawa to Mugere, and as broad as from Mugihawa to
Warumashanya's country, or, say eighteen miles in length
by about eight in breadth. The lake is surrounded by
mountains on the western and northern sides: on the
south-western side of one of these mountains issues the
Rusizi—at first a small rapid stream; but as it proceeds
towards the lake it receives the rivers Kagunissi, Kaburan,
Mohira, Nyamagana, Nyakagunda, Ruviro, Rofubu, Ka-
vimvira, Myove, Ruhuha, Mukindu, Sange, Rubirizi,
Kiriba, and, lastly, the Ruanda River, which seems to be

the largest of them all. Kivo Lake is so called from the country in which it is situated. On one side is Mutumbi (probably the Utumbi of Speke and Baker), on the west is Ruanda; on the east is Urundi. The name of the chief of Kivo is Kwansibura.

After so many minute details about the River Rusizi, it only remained for us to see it. On the second morning of our arrival at Mugihewa we mustered ten strong paddlers, and set out to explore the head of the lake and the mouth of the Rusizi. We found that the northern head of the lake was indented with seven broad bays, each from one and a half to three miles broad; that long broad spits of sand, overgrown with matete, separated each bay from the other. The first, starting from west to east, at the broadest part, to the extreme southern point of Mugihewa, was about three miles broad, and served as a line of demarcation between Mukamba's district of Ruwenga and Mugihewa of Ruhinga; it was also two miles deep. The second bay was a mile from the southern extremity of Mugihewa to Ruhinga's village at the head of the bay, and it was a mile across to another spit of sand which was terminated by a small island. The third bay stretched for nearly a mile to a long spit, at the end of which was another island, one and a quarter mile in length, and was the western side of the fourth bay, at the head of which was the delta of the Rusizi. This fourth bay, at its base, was about three miles in depth, and penetrated half a mile further inland than any other. Soundings indicated six feet deep, and the same depth was kept to within a few hundred yards of the principal mouth of the Rusizi. The current was very sluggish; not more than a mile an hour. Though we constantly kept our binocular searching for the river, we

could not see the main channel until within 200 yards of
it, and then only by watching by what outlet the fishing
canoes came out. The bay at this point had narrowed
from two miles to about 200 yards in breadth. Inviting
a canoe to show us the way, a small flotilla of canoes
preceded us, from the sheer curiosity of their owners.
We followed, and in a few minutes were ascending the
stream, which was very rapid, though but about ten
yards wide, and very shallow; not more than two feet
deep. We ascended about half a mile, the current being
very strong, from six to eight miles an hour, and quite
far enough to observe the nature of the stream at its
embouchure. We could see that it widened and spread
out in a myriad of channels, rushing by isolated clumps
of sedge and matete grass; and that it had the appearance of a swamp. We had ascended the central, or main
channel. The western channel was about eight yards
broad. We observed, after we had returned to the bay,
that the easternmost channel was about six yards broad,
and about ten feet deep, but very sluggish. We had
thus examined each of its three mouths, and settled all
doubts as to the Rusizi being an effluent or influent. It
was not necessary to ascend higher, there being nothing
about the river itself to repay exploration of it.

The question, " Was the Rusizi an effluent or an influent ?" was answered for ever. There was now no doubt
any more on that point. In size it was not to be compared with the Malagarazi River, neither is it, or can it
be, navigable for anything but the smallest canoes. The
only thing remarkable about it is that it abounds in
crocodiles, but not one hippopotamus was seen; which
may be taken as another evidence of its shallowness. The
bays to the east of the Rusizi are of the same conforma-

tion as those on the west. Carefully judging from the width of the several bays from point to point, and of the several spits which separate them, the breadth of the lake may be said to be about twelve or fourteen miles. Had we contented ourselves with simply looking at the conformation, and the meeting of the eastern and western ranges, we should have said that the lake ended in a point, as Captain Speke has sketched it on his map. But its exploration dissolved that idea. Chamati Hill is the extreme northern termination of the western range, and seems, upon a superficial examination, to abut against the Ramata mountains of the eastern range, which are opposite Chamati; but a valley about a mile in breadth separates the two ranges, and through this valley the Rusizi flows towards the lake.* Though Chamati terminates the western range, the eastern range continues for miles beyond, north-westerly. After its issue from this broad gorge, the Rusizi runs seemingly in a broad and mighty stream, through a wide alluvial plain, its own formation, in a hundred channels, until, approaching the lake, it flows into it by three channels only, as above described.

I should not omit to state here, that though the Doctor and I have had to contend against the strong current of the Rusizi River, as it flowed swift and strong INTO the Tanganika, the Doctor still adheres to the conviction that, whatever part the Rusizi plays, there must be an outlet to the Tanganika somewhere, from the fact that all fresh-water lakes have outlets. The Doctor

---

* After the patient investigation of the North end of the Lake, and satisfying ourselves by personal observation that the Rusizi ran into the Lake, the native rumor which Sir Samuel Baker brought home that the Tanganika and the Albert N'Yanza have a water connection still finds many believers!

is able to state his opinions and reasons far better than
I can find for him; and, lest I misconstrue the subject,
I shall leave it until he has an opportunity to explain
them himself; which his great knowledge of Africa will
enable him to do with advantage.

One thing is evident to me, and I believe to the Doctor,
that Sir Samuel Baker will have to curtail the Albert
N'Yanza by one, if not two degrees of latitude. That
well-known traveller has drawn his lake far into the
territory of the Warundi, while Ruanda has been placed
on the eastern side; whereas a large portion of it, if not
all, should be placed north of what he has designated on
his map as Usige. The information of such an intelligent
man as Ruhinga is not to be despised; for, if Lake Albert
came within a hundred miles of the Tanganika, he would
surely have heard of its existence, even if he had not seen
it himself. Originally he came from Mutumbi, and he
has travelled from that country into Mugihewa, the
district he now governs. He has seen Mwezi, the great
King of Urundi, and describes him as a man about forty
years old, and as a very good man.

Our work was now done; there was nothing more to
detain us at Mugihewa. Ruhinga had been exceedingly
kind, and given us one ox after another to butcher and
eat. Mukamba had done the same. Their women had
supplied us with an abundance of milk and butter, and
we had now bounteous supplies of both.

The Doctor had taken a series of observations for
latitude and longitude; and Mugihewa was made out to
be in 3° 19' S. latitude.

On the 7th December, early in the morning, we left
Mugihewa, and rowing past the southern extremity of the
Katangara Islands, we approached the highlands of Uashi,

near the boundary line between Mukamba's country and Uvira. The boundary line is supposed to be a wide ravine, in the depths of which is a grove of tall, beautiful, and straight-stemmed trees, out of which the natives make their canoes.

Passing Kanyamabengu River, which issues into the lake close to the market-ground of Kirabula, the extreme point of Burton and Speke's explorations of the Tanganika, we steered south along the western shore of the lake for half an hour longer to Kavimba, where we halted to cook breakfast.

The village where lived Mruta, the King of Uvira, was in sight of our encampment, and as we observed parties of men ascending and descending the mountains much more often than we thought augured good to ourselves, we determined to continue on our course south. Besides, there was a party of disconsolate-looking Wajiji here, who had been plundered only a few days before our arrival, for attempting, as the Wavira believed, to evade the honga payment. Such facts as these, and our knowledge of the general state of insecurity in the country, resulting from the many wars in which the districts of the Tanganika were engaged, determined us not to halt at Kavimba.

We embarked quickly in our boat before the Wavira had collected themselves, and headed south against a strong gale, which came driving down on us from the south-west. After a hard pull of about two hours in the teeth of the storm, which was rapidly rising, we pointed the head of the boat into a little quiet cove, almost hidden in tall reeds, and disembarked for the night.

Cognizant of the dangers which surrounded us, knowing that savage and implacable man was the worst enemy we had to fear, we employed our utmost energies in the construction of a stout fence of thorn bushes, and then sat down to supper after our work was done, and turned in to sleep ; but not before we had posted watchmen to guard our canoe, lest the daring thieves of Uvira might abstract it, in which case we should have been in a pretty plight, and in most unenviable distress.

At daybreak, leaving Kukumba Point after our humble breakfast of coffee, cheese, and dourra cakes was despatched, we steered south once more. Our fires had attracted the notice of the sharp-eyed and suspicious fishermen of Kukumba; but our precautions and the vigilant watch we had set before retiring, had proved an effectual safeguard against the Kivira thieves.

The western shores of the lake as we proceeded were loftier, and more bold than the wooded heights of Urundi and bearded knolls of Ujiji. A back ridge—the vanguard of the mountains which rise beyond—disclosed itself between the serrated tops of the front line of mountains, which rose to a height of from 2,500 to 3,000 feet above the lake. Within the folds of the front line of mountains rise isolated hills of considerable magnitude, precipitous and abrupt, but scenically very picturesque. The greater part of these hills have the rounded and smooth top, or are tabularly summited. The ridge enfolding these hills shoots out, at intervals, promontorial projections of gradual sloping outlines, which on the map I have designated capes, or points. When rounding these points, up went our compasses for the taking of bearings, and observing the directions of all prominent objects of interest. Often these capes are formed by the alluvial plains, through which we may be sure a river will be found flowing. These **pretty alluvial plains**, enfolded on the south, the west, and the north by a grand mountain arc, present most luxurious and enchanting scenery. The vegetation seems to be of spontaneous growth. Groups of the Elæis Guineansis palm embowering some dun-brown village; an array of majestic, superb growth of mvule trees; a broad extent covered with vivid green sorghum stalks; parachute-like tops of mimosa; a line of white sand, on which native canoes are drawn far above the reach of the plangent, uneasy surf; fishermen idly reclining in the shade of a tree;—these are the scenes which reveal themselves to us as we voyage in our canoe on the Tanganika. When wearied with the romance of wild tropic scenes such as these, we have but to lift our eyes to the great mountain tops looming darkly and grandly on our right; to watch the light pencilling of the cirrus, brushing their summits, as it is drifted toward the north by the rising wind: to watch the changing forms which the clouds assume, from the fleecy horizontal bars of the cirrus, to the denser, gloomier cumulus, prognosticator of storm and rain, which soon settles into a portentous group—Alps above Alps, one above another—and we know the storm which was brewing is at hand, and that it is time to seek shelter.

Passing Muikamba, we saw several groves of the tall mvule tree. As far as Bemba the Wabembe occupy the mountain summits, while the Wavira cultivate the alluvial plains along the base and lower slopes of the mountain. At Bemba we halted to take in pieces of pipe-clay, in accordance with the superstition of the Wajiji, who thought us certain of safe passage and good fortune if we complied with the ancient custom.

Passing Ngovi, we came to a deep bend, which curved off to Cape Kabogi at the distance of ten miles. About two-thirds of the way we arrived at a group of islets, three in number, all very steep and rocky; the largest about 300 feet in length at the base, and about 200 feet in breadth. Here we made preparations to halt for the night. The inhabitants of the island were a gorgeously-feathered old cock, which was kept as a propitiatory offering to the spirit of the island, a sickly yellow-looking thrush, a hammer-headed stork, and two fish-hawks, who, finding we had taken possession of what had been religiously reserved for them, took flight to the most western island, where from their perches they continued to eye us most solemnly.

As these islands were with difficulty pronounced by us as Kavunvweh, the Doctor, seeing that they were the only objects we were likely to discover, named them the " ' New York Herald ' Islets;" and, in confirmation of the new designation given them, shook hands with me upon it. Careful dead-reckoning settled them to be in lat. 3° 41' S.

The summit of the largest island was well adapted to take bearings, and we improved the opportunity, as most extensive views of the broad and lengthy lake and surrounding lines of imposing mountains were attainable. The Ramata Hills were clearly visible, and bore N.N.E. from it; Katanga Cape, S.E. by S.; Sentakeyi, E.S.E.; Magala, E. by N.; south-western point of Muzimu bore S., northern point of Muzimu island, S.S.E.

At dawn on the 9th December we prepared to resume our voyage. Once or twice in the night we had been visited by fishermen, but our anxious watchfulness prevented any marauding. It seemed to me, however, that the people of the opposite shore, who were our visitors, were eagerly watching an opportunity to pounce upon our canoe, or take us bodily for a prey; and our men were considerably affected by these thoughts, if we may judge from the hearty good-will with which they rowed away from our late encampment.

Arriving at Cape Kabogi, we came to the territory of the Wasansi. We knew we were abreast of a different tribe by the greeting "Moholo," which a group of fishermen gave us; as that of the Wavira was "Wake," like that of Urundi, Usige, and Uhha.

We soon sighted Cape Luvumba—a sloping projection of a mountain ridge which shot far into the lake. As a storm was brewing, we steered for a snug little cove that appeared before a village; and, drawing our canoe from the water, began to set the tent, and make other preparations for passing the night.

As the natives appeared quiet and civil enough, we saw no reason to suspect that they entertained any hostility to Arabs and Wangwana. Accordingly we had our breakfast cooked, and as usual laid down for an afternoon nap. I soon fell asleep, and was dreaming away in my tent, in happy oblivion of the strife and contention that had risen since I had gone to sleep, when I heard a voice hailing me with, "Master, master! get up, quick. Here is a fight going to begin!" I sprang up, and snatching my revolver belt from the gun-stand, walked outside. Surely, there appeared to be considerable animus between the several factions; between a noisy, vindictive-looking set of natives of the one part, and our people of the other part. Seven or eight of our people had taken refuge behind the canoe, and had their loaded guns half pointing at the passionate mob, which was momentarily increasing in numbers, but I could not see the Doctor anywhere.

"Where is the Doctor?" I asked.

"He has gone over that hill, sir, with his compass," said Selim.

"Anybody with him?"

"Susi and Chumah."

"You, Bombay, send two men off to warn the Doctor, and tell him to hurry up here."

But just at this period the Doctor and his two men appeared on the brow of the hill, looking down in a most complacent manner upon the serio-comic scene that the little basin wherein we were encamped presented. For, indeed, despite the serious aspect of it, there was much that was comical blended with it—in a naked young man who—perfectly drunk, barely able to stand on his feet— was beating the ground with his only loin-cloth, screaming and storming away like a madman; declaring by this, and by that, in his own choice language, that no Mgwana or Arab should halt one moment on the sacred soil of Usansi. His father, the Sultan, was as inebriated as himself, though not quite so violent in his behaviour.

In the meantime the Doctor arrived upon the scene, and Selim had slipped my Winchester rifle, with the magazine full of cartridges, into my hand. The Doctor calmly asked what was the matter, and was answered by the Wajiji guides that the people wished us to leave, as they were on hostile terms with the Arabs, because the eldest son of the Sultan of Muzimu, the large island nearly opposite, had been beaten to death by a Baluch, named Khamis, at Ujiji, because the young fellow had dared look into his harem, and ever since peace had been broken between the Wasansi and Arabs.

After consulting with the guides, the Doctor and I came to the conclusion that it were better that we should endeavour to pacify the Sultan by a present, rather than take offence at a drunken boy's extravagant freak. In his insane fury he had attempted **to** slash at one of my men with a billhook he carried. This had been taken as a declaration of hostilities, and the soldiers were ready enough to engage in war; but there was no necessity to commence fighting with a drunken mob, who could have been cleared off the ground with our revolvers alone had we desired it.

The Doctor, baring his arm, said to them that he was not a Mgwana, or an Arab; but a white man; that Arabs and Wangwana had no such color as we had. We were white men, different people altogether from those whom they were accustomed to see: that no black men had ever suffered injury from white men. This seemed to produce great effect, for after a little gentle persuasion the drunken youth, and his no less inebriate sire, were induced to sit down to talk quietly. In their conversation with us, they frequently referred to Mombo, the son of Kisesa, Sultan of Muzimu, who was brutally murdered. "Yes, brutally murdered!" they exclaimed several times, in their own tongue; illustrating, by a faithful pantomime, how the unfortunate youth had died.

Livingstone continued talking with them in a mild, paternal way, and their loud protestations against Arab cruelty were about to subside, when the old Sultan suddenly rose up and began to pace about in an excited manner, and in one of his perambulations deliberately slashed his leg with the sharp blade of his spear, and then exclaimed that the Wangwana had wounded him!

At this cry one half of the mob hastily took to flight, but one old woman, who carried a strong staff with a carved lizard's body on its top, commenced to abuse **the** chief with all the power of her voluble tongue, charging him with a desire to have them all killed, and other women joined in with her in advising him to be quiet, and accept the present we were willing to give.

But it is evident that there was little needed to cause all men present in that little hollow to begin a most sanguinary strife. The gentle, patient bearing of the Doctor had more effect than anything else in making all forbear bloodshed, while there was left the least chance of an amicable settlement, and in the end it prevailed. The Sultan and his son were both sent on their way rejoicing.

While the Doctor conversed with them, and endeavoured to calm their fierce passions, I had the tent struck, and the canoes launched, and the baggage stowed, and when the negotiations had concluded amicably, I begged the Doctor to jump into the boat, as this apparent peace was simply a lull before a storm; besides, said I, there are two or three cowardly creatures in the boat, who, in case of another disturbance, would not scruple to leave both of us here.

From Cape Luvumba, about 4.30 P.M. we commenced pulling across; at 8 P.M. we were abreast of Cape Panza, the northern extremity of the island of Muzimu; at 6 A.M. we were southward of Bikari, and pulling for Mukungu, in Urundi, at which place we arrived at 10 A.M., having been seventeen hours and a half in crossing the lake, which, computing at two miles an hour, may be said to be thirty-five miles direct breadth, and a little more than forty-three miles from Cape Luvumba.

On the 11th of December, after seven hours' pulling, we arrived at picturesque Zassi again; on the 12th, at the pretty cove of Niasanga; and at 11 A.M. we had rounded past Bangwe, and Ujiji was before us.

We entered the port very quietly, without the usual firing of guns, as we were short of powder and ball. As we landed, our soldiers and the Arab magnates came to the water's edge to greet us.

Mabruki had a rich budget to relate to us, of what had occurred during our absence. This faithful man, left behind in charge of Livingstone's house, had done most excellently. Kalulu had scalded himself, and had a frightful raw sore on his chest in consequence. Mabruki had locked up Marora in chains for wounding one of the asses. Bilali, the stuttering coward, a bully of women, had caused a tumult in the market-place, and had been sharply belaboured with the stick by Mabruki. And, above all most welcome, was a letter I received from the American Consul at Zanzibar, dated June 11th, containing telegrams from Paris as late as April 22nd of the same year! Poor Livingstone exclaimed, "And I have none. What a pleasant thing it is to have a real and good friend!"

Our voyage on the Tanganika had lasted twenty-eight days, during which time we had traversed over 300 miles of water.

OUR HOUSE IN UJIJI.

CHAPTER XIV.

OUR JOURNEY FROM UJIJI TO UNYANYEMBE.

WE felt quite at home when we sat down on our black
bear-skin, gay Persian carpet and clean new mats, to rest
with our backs to the wall, sipping our tea with the air
of comfortable men, and chat over the incidents of the
" picnic," as Livingstone persisted in calling our journey
to the Rusizi. It seemed as if old times, which we loved
to recall, had come back again, though our house was
humble enough in its aspect, and our servants were only
naked barbarians; but it was near this house that I had
met him—Livingstone—after that eventful march from

Unyanyembe; it was on this same veranda that I listened
to that wonderful story of his about those far, enchanting
regions west of the Lake Tanganika; it was in this same
spot that I first became acquainted with him; and ever
since my admiration has been growing for him, and I feel
elated when he informs me that he must go to Unyanyembe under my escort, and at my expense. The old mud
walls and the bare rafters, and the ancient thatched roof,
and this queer-looking old veranda, will have an historical
interest for me while I live, and so, while I can, I have
taken pains and immortalized the humble old building by
a sketch.

I have just said that my admiration for Livingstone
has been growing. This is true. The man that I was
about to interview so calmly and complacently, as I would
interview any prominent man with the view of specially
delineating his nature, or detailing his opinions, has
conquered me. I had intended to interview him, report
in detail what he said, picture his life and his figure,
then bow him my " *au revoir*," and march back. That
he was specially disagreeable and brusque in his manner,
which would make me quarrel with him immediately, was
firmly fixed in my mind.

But Livingstone — true, noble Christian, generous-
hearted, frank man—acted like a hero, invited me to
his house, said he was glad to see me, and got well on
purpose to prove the truth of his statement, " You have
brought new life unto me;" and when I fell sick with
the remittent fever, hovering between life and death, he
attended me like a father, and we have now been together
for more than a month.

Can you wonder, then, that I like this man, whose face
is the reflex of his nature, whose heart is essentially all

goodness, whose aims are so high, that I break out impetuously sometimes: "But your family, Doctor, they would like to see you, oh! so much. Let me tempt you to come home with me. I promise to carry you every foot of the way to the coast. You shall have the finest donkey to ride that is in Unyanyembe. Your wants— you have but to hint them, and they shall be satisfied. Let the sources of the Nile go—do you come home and rest; then, after a year's rest, and restored health, you can return and finish what you have to do."

But ever the answer was, "No, I should like to see my family very much indeed. My children's letters affect me intensely; but I must not go home; I must finish my task. It is only the want of supplies that has detained me. I should have finished the discovery of the Nile by this, by tracing it to its connection with either Baker's Lake, or Petherick's branch of the Nile. If I had only gone one month further, I could have said, 'the work is done.'"

Some of these men who had turned the Doctor back from his interesting discoveries were yet in Ujiji, and had the Government Enfield rifles in their hands, which they intended to retain until their wages had been paid to them; but as they had received $60 advance each at Zanzibar from the English Consul, with the understanding entered into by contract that they should follow their master wherever he required them to go; and as they had not only not gone where they were required to proceed with him, but had baffled and thwarted him, it was preposterous that a few men should triumph over the Doctor, by keeping the arms given to him by the Bombay Government. I had listened to the Arab sheikhs, friends of the Doctor, advising them in mild tones to give them up; I had witnessed the mutineer's stubbornness; and it was then, on the burzani of Sayd bin Majid's house, that I took advantage to open my mind on the subject, not only for the benefit of the stubborn slaves, but also for the benefit of the Arabs; and to tell them that it was well that I had found Livingstone alive, for if they had but injured a hair of his head, I should have gone back to the coast, to return with a party which would enable me to avenge him. I had been waiting to see Livingstone's guns returned to him every day, hoping that I should not have to use force; but when a month or more had elapsed, and still the arms had not been returned, I applied for permission to take them, which was granted. Susi, the gallant servant of Dr. Livingstone, was immediately despatched with about a dozen armed men to recover them, and in a few minutes we had possession of them without further trouble.

The Doctor had resolved to accompany me to Unyanyembe, in order to meet his stores, which had been forwarded from Zanzibar, November 1st, 1870. As I had charge of the escort, it was my duty to study well the several routes to Unyanyembe from Ujiji. I was sufficiently aware of the difficulties and the responsibilities attached to me while escorting such a man. Besides, my own personal feelings were involved in the case. If Livingstone came to any harm through any indiscretion of mine while he was with me, it would immediately be said, "Ah! had he not accompanied Stanley, he would have been alive now."

I took out my chart—the one I had made myself—in which I had perfect faith, and I sketched out a route which would enable us to reach Unyanyembe without paying a single cloth as tribute, and without encountering any worse thing than a jungle, by which we could avoid all the Wavinza and the plundering Wahha. This peaceable, secure route led by water, south, along the coast of Ukaranga and Ukawendi, to Cape Tongwe. Arriving at Cape Tongwe, I should be opposite the village of Itaga, Sultan Imrera, in the district of Rusawa of Ukawendi; after which we should strike my old road, which I had traversed from Unyanyembe, when bound for Ujiji. I explained it to the Doctor, and he instantly recognised its feasibility and security; and if I struck Imrera, as I proposed to do, it would demonstrate whether my chart was correct or not.

We arrived at Ujiji from our tour of discovery, north of the Tanganika, December 13th; and from this date the Doctor commenced writing his letters to his numerous friends, and to copy into his mammoth Letts's Diary, from his field books, the valuable information he had acquired during his years of travel south and west of the Tanganika. I sketched him while sitting in his shirt-sleeves in the veranda, with his Letts's Diary on his knee; and the likeness on the frontispiece is an admirable portrait of him, because the artist who has assisted me, has with an intuitive eye, seen the defects in my own sketch; and by this I am enabled to restore him to the reader's view exactly as I saw him—as he pondered on what he had witnessed during his long marches.

Soon after my arrival at Ujiji, he had rushed to his paper, and indited a letter to James Gordon Bennett, Esq., wherein he recorded his thanks; and after he had finished it, I asked him to add the word "Junior" to it, as it was young Mr. Bennett to whom he was indebted. I thought the letter admirable, and requested the Doctor not to add another word to it. The feelings of his heart had found expression in the grateful words he had written; and if I judged Mr. Bennett rightly, I knew he would be satisfied with it. For it was not the geographical news he cared so much about, as the grand fact of Livingstone's being alive or dead.

In this latter part of December he was writing letters to his children, to Sir Roderick Murchison, and to Lord Granville. He had intended to have written to the Earl of Clarendon, but it was my sad task to inform him of the death of that distinguished nobleman.

In the meantime I was preparing the Expedition for its return march to Unyanyembe, apportioning the bales and luggage, the Doctor's large tin boxes, and my own among my own men; for I had resolved upon permitting the Doctor's men to march as passengers, because they had so nobly performed their duty to their master.

Sayd bin Majid had left, December 12, for Mirambo's country, to give the black Bonaparte battle for the murder of his son Soud in the forests of Wilyankuru; and he had taken with him 300 stout fellows, armed with guns, from Ujiji. The stout-hearted old chief was burning with rage and resentment, and a fine warlike figure he made with his 7-foot gun. Before we had departed for the Rusizi, I had wished him *bon voyage*, and expressed a hope that he would rid the Central African world of the tyrant Mirambo.

On the 20th of December the rainy season was ushered in with heavy rain, thunder, lightning, and hail; the thermometer falling to 66° Fahrenheit. The evening of this day I was attacked with urticaria, or " nettle rash," for the third time since arriving in Africa, and I suffered a woeful sickness; and it was the forerunner of an attack of remittent fever, which lasted four days. This is the malignant type, which has proved fatal to so many African travellers on the Zambezi, the White Nile, the Congo, and the Niger. The head throbs, the pulses bound, the heart struggles painfully, while the sufferer's thoughts are in a strange world, such only as a sick man's fancy can create. This was the fourth attack of fever since the day I met Livingstone. The excitement of the march, and the high hope which my mind constantly nourished, had kept my body almost invincible against an attack of fever while advancing towards Ujiji; but two weeks after the great event had transpired my energies were relaxed, my mind was perfectly tranquil, and I became a victim.

Christmas came, and the Doctor and I had resolved upon the blessed and time-honored day being kept as we keep it in Anglo-Saxon lands, with a feast such as Ujiji could furnish us. The fever had quite gone from me the night before, and on Christmas morning, though exceedingly weak, I was up and dressed, and lecturing Ferajji, the cook, upon the importance of this day to white men, and endeavouring to instil into the mind of the sleek and pampered animal some cunning secrets of the culinary art. Fat broad-tailed sheep, goats, zogga and pombe, eggs, fresh milk, plantains, singwe, fine corn-flour, fish, onions, sweet potatoes, &c., &c., were procured in the Ujiji market, and from good old Moeni Kheri. But, alas! for my weakness. Ferajji spoiled the roast, and our custard was burned—the dinner was a failure. That the fat-brained rascal escaped a thrashing was due only to my inability to lift my hands for punishment; but my looks were dreadful and alarming, and capable of annihilating any one except Ferajji. The stupid, hard-headed cook only chuckled, and I believe he had the subsequent gratification of eating the pies, custards, and roast that his carelessness had spoiled for European palates.

Sayd bin Majid, previous to his departure, had left orders that we should be permitted to use his canoe for our homeward trip, and Moeni Kheri kindly lent his huge vessel for the same purpose. The Expedition, now augmented by the Doctor and his five servants, and their luggage, necessitated the employment of another canoe. We had our flocks of milch-goats and provision of fat sheep for the jungle of Ukawendi, the transit of which I was about to attempt. Good Halimah, Livingstone's cook, had made ready a sackful of fine flour, such as she only could prepare in her fond devotion for her master. Hamoydah, her husband, also had freely given his assistance and attention to this important article of food. I purchased a donkey for the Doctor, the only one available in Ujiji, lest the Doctor might happen to suffer on the long march from his ancient enemy. In short, we were luxuriously furnished with food, sheep, goats, cheese, cloth, donkeys, and canoes, sufficient to convey us a long distance; we needed nothing more.

The 27th of December has arrived; it is the day of our departure from Ujiji. I was probably about to give an eternal farewell to the port whose name will for ever be sacred in my memory. The canoes—great lumbering hollow trees—are laden with good things; the rowers are in their places; the flag of England is hoisted at the stern of the Doctor's canoe; the flag of America waves and rustles joyously above mine; and I cannot look at them without feeling a certain pride that the two Anglo-Saxon nations are represented this day on this great inland sea, in the face of wild nature and barbarism.

We are escorted to our boats by the great Arab merchants, by the admiring children of Unyamwezi, by the freemen of Zanzibar, by wondering Waguhha and Wajiji, by fierce Warundi, who are on this day quiet, even sorrowful, that the white men are going—" Whither ?" they all ask.

At 8 A.M. we start, freely distributing our farewells as the Arabs and quidnuncs wave their hands. On the part of one or two of them there was an attempt to say something sentimental and affecting, especially by the convicted sinner Mohammed bin Sali; but though outwardly I manifested no disapprobation of his words, or of the emphatic way in which he shook my hand, I was not sorry to see the last of him, after his treachery to Livingstone in 1869. I was earnestly requested to convey to Unyanyembe " Mengi salaams " to everybody, but had I done so, as he evidently desired me to do, I would not have been surprised at being regarded by all as hopelessly imbecile.

We pushed off from the clayey bank at the foot of the market-place, while the land party, unencumbered with luggage, under the leadership of gigantic Asmani and Bombay, commenced their journey southward along the shores of the lake. We had arranged to meet them at the mouth of every river to transport them across from bank to bank.

The Doctor being in Sayd bin Majid's boat, which was a third or so shorter than the one under my command, took the lead, with the British flag, held aloft by a bamboo, streaming behind like a crimson meteor. My boat—manned by Wajiji sailors, whom we had engaged to take the canoes back from Tongwe Cape to Ujiji Bunder—came astern, and had a much taller flagstaff, on which was hoisted the ever-beautiful Stars and Stripes. Its extreme height drew from the Doctor — whose patriotism and loyalty had been excited—the remark that he would cut down the tallest palmyra for his flagstaff, as it was not fitting that the British flag should be so much lower than that of the United States.

Our soldiers were not a whit behind us in lightheartedness at the thought of going to Unyanyembe. They struck up the exhilarating song of the Zanzibar boatmen, with the ecstatic chorus—

> Kinan de re re Kitunga,

rowing away like madmen, until they were compelled to rest from sheer exhaustion, while the perspiration exuded from the pores of their bodies in streams. When refreshed, they bent back to their oars, raising the song of the Mrima—

> O mama, re de mi Ky,

which soon impelled them to an extravagant effort again, It was by this series of ferocious spurts, racing, shouting, singing, perspiring, laughing, groaning, and puffing, that our people vented their joyous feelings, as the thought filled their minds that we were homeward bound, and that by the route I had adopted between us and Unyanyembe there was not the least danger.

> We have given the Waha, the slip! ha, ha!
> The Wavinza will trouble us no more! ho! ho!
> Mionvu can get no more cloth from us! hy, hy!
> And Kiala will see us no more—never more! he, he!

they shouted with wild bursts of laughter, seconded by tremendous and rapid strokes with their oars, which caused the stiff old canoes to quiver from stem to stern.

Our party ashore seemed to partake of our excitement, and joined in the wild refrain of the mad African song. We watched them urging their steps forward to keep pace with us, as we rounded the capes and points, and rowed across the bays whose margins were sedge, and rush, and reed; the tiny and agile Kalulu, little Bilali, and Majwara were seen racing the herds of goats, sheep, and donkeys which belonged to the caravan, and the animals even seemed to share the general joy.

Nature, also—proud, wild nature—with the lofty azure dome upheaved into infinity—with her breadth and depth of vivid greenness and enormous vastness on our left—with her immense sheet of bright, glancing water—with her awful and intense serenity—she partook of and added to our joy.

About 10 A.M. we arrived at Kirindo's, an old chief, noted for his singular kindness to Dr. Livingstone, while he bore animosity to the Arabs. To the Arabs this was unaccountable—to the Doctor it was plain: he had but spoken kind and sincere words, while all the Arabs spoke to him as if he were not even a man, least of all a chief.

Kirindo's place is at the mouth of the Liuche, which is very wide; the river oozes out through a forest of æschinomenæ (pith tree). This was a rendezvous agreed upon between shore and lake parties, that the canoes might all cross to the other side, distant a mile and a half. The mouth of the Liuche forms the Bay of Ukaranga, so named because on the other side, whither we were about to cross our party, was situated the village of Ukaranga, a few hundred yards from the lake. All the baggage was taken out of the largest canoe, and stowed snugly in the smaller one, and a few select oarsmen having taken seats, pushed off with the Doctor on board, who was to superintend pitching the encampment at Ukaranga; while I remained behind to bind the fractious and ill-natured donkeys, and stow them away in the bottom of the large canoe, that no danger of upsetting might be incurred, and a consequent gobbling-up by hungry crocodiles, which were all about us waiting their opportunity. The flock of goats were then embarked, and as many of our people as could be got in. About thirty still remained behind with myself, for whom my canoe was to return.

We all arrived safe at Ukaranga, though we got dangerously near a herd of hippopotami. The crossing of the wide mouth (the Liuche being then in flood) was effected in about four hours.

The next day, in the same order as on our departure from Ujiji, we pursued our way south, the lake party keeping as closely as possible to the shore, yet, when feasible, wind and weather permitting, we struck off boldly across the numerous small bays which indent the shores of the Tanganika. The shores were beautifully green, the effect of the late rains; the waters of the lake were a faithful reflex of the blue firmament above. The hippopotami were plentiful. Those noticed on this day were colored with reddish rings round the base of their ears and on the neck. One monster, coming up rather late, was surprised by the canoe making full for him, and in great fright took a tremendous dive which showed the whole length of his body. Half way between the mouth of the Malagarazi and that of the Liuche we

saw a camp on shore—that of Mohammed bin Gharib, a
Msawahili, who figured often in Livingstone's verbal
narrative to me of his adventures and travels as one of
the kindest and best of the Moslems in Central Africa.
He appeared to me a kindly disposed man, with a face
seldom seen, having the stamp of an unusual characteristic on it—that of sincerity.

The vegetation of the shores as we proceeded was truly
tropical, each curve revealed new beauties. With the
soft chalky stone, of which most of the cliffs and bluffs
are made, seen as we neared the mouth of the Malagarazi,
the surf has played strange freaks.

We arrived at the mouth of the Malagarazi about
2 P.M., having rowed eighteen miles from Ukaranga.
The shore party arrived, very much fatigued, about
5 P.M.

The next day was employed in crossing the caravan
across the broad mouth of the Malagarazi to our camp,
a couple of miles north of the river. This is a river
which a civilised community would find of immense
advantage for shortening the distance between the
Tanganika and the coast. Nearly one hundred miles
might be performed by this river, which is deep enough
at all seasons to allow navigation as far as Kiala, in
Uvinza, whence a straight road might be easily made to
Unyanyembe. Missionaries also might reap the same
benefit from it for conversion-tours to Uvinza, Uhha, and
Ugala. Pursuing our way on the 30th, and rounding
the picturesque capes of Kagongo, Mviga and Kivoe, we
came, after about three hours' rowing, in sight of villages
at the mouth of the swift and turbid Rugufu. Here we
had again to transport the caravan over the crocodile-in-
fested mouth of the river.

On the morning of the 31st we sent a canoe with men to search for food in the two or three villages that were visible on the other side. Four doti purchased just sufficient for four days for our caravan of forty-eight persons. We then got under weigh, having informed the kirangozi that Urimba was our destination, and bidding him keep as closely as possible to the lake shore, where it was practicable, but if not, to make the best he could of it. From the débouchement of the Rugufu, the head-waters of which we had crossed on our random route to Ujiji, to Urimba, a distance of six days by water, there are no villages, and consequently no food. The shore party, however, before leaving Ujiji, had eight days' rations, and on this morning four days', distributed to each person, and therefore was in no danger of starvation should the mountain headlands, now unfolding, abrupt and steep, one after another, prevent them from communicating with us. It must be understood that such a journey as this had never been attempted before by any Arab or Msawahili, and every step taken was in sheer ignorance of where the road would lead the men ashore. Rounding Kivoe's steep promontory, whose bearded ridge and rugged slope, wooded down to the water's edge, whose exquisite coves and quiet recesses, might well have evoked a poetical effusion to one so inclined, we dared the chopping waves of Kivoe's bay, and stood direct for the next cape, Mizohazy, behind which, owing to wind and wave, we were compelled to halt for the night.

After Mizohazy is the bold cape of Kabogo—not the terrible Kabogo around whose name mystery has been woven by the superstitious natives—not the Kabogo whose sullen thunder and awful roar were heard when crossing the Rugufu on our flight from the Wahha—but

a point in Ukaranga, on whose hard and uninviting rocks
many a canoe has been wrecked. We passed close to its
forbidding walls, thankful for the calm of the Tanganika.
Near Kabogo are some very fine mvule trees, well adapted
for canoe building, and there are no loud-mouthed natives
about to haggle for the privilege of cutting them.

Along the water's edge, and about three feet above it,
was observed very clearly on the smooth face of the
rocky slopes of Kabogo the high-water mark of the lake.
This went to show that the Tanganika, during the rainy
season, rises about three feet above its dry season level,
and that, during the latter season, evaporation reduces it
to its normal level. The number of rivers which we
passed on this journey enabled me to observe whether, as
I was told, there was any current setting north. It was
apparent to me that, while the south-west, south, or
south-east winds blew, the brown flood of the rivers swept
north; but it happened that, while passing, once or twice,
the mouths of rivers, after a puff from the north-west and
north, that the muddied waters were seen southward of
the mouths, from which I conclude that there is no
current in the Tanganika except such as is caused by the
fickle wind.

Finding a snug nook of a bay at a place called Sigunga,
we put in for lunch. An island at the mouth of the bay
suggested to our minds that this was a beautiful spot for
a mission station; the grandly sloping hills in the background, with an undulating shelf of land well-wooded
between them and the bay, added to the attractions of
such a spot. The island, capable of containing quite a
large village, and perfectly defensible, might, for prudence'
sake, contain the mission and its congregation; the land-
locked bay would protect their fishery and trade vessels;

the fertile ground between the hills and the bay would more than sustain a hundred times the number of the population of the island. Wood for building their canoes and houses is close at hand; the neighbouring country would afford game in abundance; and the docile and civil people of Ukaranga but wait religious shepherds.

From beautiful Sigunga, after a brief halt, we set off, and, after three hours, arrived at the mouth of the River Uwelasia. Hippopotami and crocodiles being numerous, we amused ourselves by shooting at them, having also a hope of attracting the attention of our shore party, the sound of whose guns we had not heard since leaving the Rugufu.

On the 3rd of January we left Uwelasia, and, passing by Cape Herembe, were in the bay of Tongwe. This bay is about twenty-five miles broad, and stretches from Cape Herembe to Cape Tongwe. Finding themselves so near their destination, Urimba being but six miles from Herembe Point, the men of both boats bent them-selves to their oars, and, with shouts, songs, and laughter, encouraged each other to do their utmost. The flags of the two great Anglo-Saxon nations rippled and played in the soft breeze, sometimes drawing near caressingly to-gether, again bending away, like two lovers coy to unite. The tight little boat of the Doctor would keep ahead, and the crimson and crossed flag of England would wave before me, and it seemed to say to the beautiful laggard astern, " Come on, come on; England leads the way." But was it not England's place to be in the front here? She won the right to it by discovering the Tanganika; America came but second.

Urimba, though a large district of Kawendi, has a village of the same name peopled by refugees from

Yombeh, who found the delta of the Loajeri, though the unhealthiest of spots—equal to that of the Rusizi—far preferable to the neighbourhood of Sultan Pumburu, of Southern Kawendi. A good chase by the victors seems to have given a shock to their systems, for they are very timid and distrustful of strangers, and would by no means permit us to enter their village, of which, to say the truth, I was very glad, after a glance at the reeking corruption on which they were encamped. In the immediate neighbourhood—nay, for a couple of miles on either side—I should suppose that to a white man it were death to sleep a single night. Leading the way south of the village, I found a fit camping-place at the extreme south-east corner of Tongwe Bay, about a mile and a half due west of the lofty peak of Kivanga, or Kakungu. By an observation taken by the Doctor, we found ourselves to be in latitude 5° 54′ south.

None of the natives had heard of our shore party, and, as the delta of the Loajeri and Mogambazi extended for about fifteen miles, and withal was the most impassable of places, being perfectly flat, overgrown with the tallest of matete, eschinomenæ, and thorny bush, and flooded with water, it was useless to fatigue our men searching for the shore party in such an inhospitable country. No provisions were procurable, for the villages were in a state of semi-starvation, the inhabitants living from hand to mouth on what reluctant Fortune threw into their nets.

The second day of our arrival at Urimba I struck off into the interior with my gun-bearer, Kalulu, carrying the Doctor's splendid double-barreled rifle (a Reilly, No. 12), on the search for venison. After walking about a mile I came to a herd of zebras. By creeping on all-fours I managed to come within one hundred yards of them; but I was in a bad spot—low prickly shrubs; and tsetse flies alighting on the rifle-sight, biting my nose, and dashing into my eyes, completely disconcerted me; and, to add to my discontent, my efforts to disengage myself from the thorns, alarmed the zebras, which all stood facing the suspicious object in the bush. I fired at the breast of one, but, as might be expected, missed. The zebras galloped away to about three hundred yards off, and I dashed into the open, and, hastily cocking the left-hand trigger, aimed at a proud fellow trotting royally before his fellows, and by good chance sent a bullet through his heart. A fortunate shot also brought down a huge goose, which had a sharp horny spur on the fore part of each wing. This supply of meat materially contributed towards the provisioning of the party for the transit of the unknown land that lay between us and Mrera, in Rusawa, Kawendi.

It was not until the third day of our arrival at our camp at Urimba that our shore party arrived. They had perceived our immense flag hoisted on a twenty-feet long bamboo above the tallest tree near our camp as they surmounted the sharp lofty ridge behind Nerembe, fifteen miles off, and had at first taken it for a huge bird; but there were sharp eyes in the crowd, and, guided by it, they came to camp, greeted as only lost and found men are greeted.

I suffered from another attack of fever at this camp, brought on by the neighbourhood of the vile delta, the look of which sickened the very heart in me.

On the 7th of January we struck camp, and turned our faces eastward, and for me, home! Yet regretfully! There had been enough happiness and pleasure, and pleasantest of social companionship found on the shores of the lake for me. I had seen enough lovely scenes which, siren-like, invited one to quiet rest; gentle scenes, where there was neither jar nor tumult, neither strife nor defeat, neither hope nor disappointment, but rest—a drowsy, indolent, yet pleasant rest. And only a few drawbacks to these. There was fever; there were no books, no newspapers, no wife of my own race and blood, no theatres, no hotels, no restaurants, no East River oysters, no mince-pies, neither buckwheat cakes, nor anything much that was good for a cultivated palate to love. So, in turning to say farewell to the then placid lake and the great blue mountains, that grew bluer as they receded on either hand, I had the courage to utter that awful word tearlessly, and without one sigh.

Our road led up through the valley of the Loajeri, after leaving its delta, a valley growing ever narrower, until it narrowed into a ravine choked by the now roaring, bellowing river, whose resistless rush seemed to affect the very air we breathed. It was getting oppressive, this narrowing ravine, and opportunely the road breasted a knoll, then a terrace, then a hill, and lastly a mountain, where we halted to encamp. As we prepared to select a camping-place, the Doctor silently pointed forward, and suddenly a dead silence reigned everywhere. The quinine which I had taken in the morning seemed to affect me in every crevice of my brain; but a bitter evil remained, and, though I trembled under the heavy weight of the Reilly rifle, I crept forward to where the Doctor was pointing. I found myself looking down a steep ravine, on the other bank of which a fine buffalo cow was scrambling upward. She had just reached the summit, and was turning round to survey her enemy, when I succeeded in planting a shot just behind the shoulder-blade, and close to the spine, evoking from her a deep bellow of pain. "She is shot! she is shot!" exclaimed the Doctor; "that is a sure sign you have hit her." And the men even raised a shout at the prospect of meat. A second, planted in her spine, brought her to her knees, and a third ended her. We thus had another supply of provisions, which, cut up and dried over a fire, as the Wangwana are accustomed to do, would carry them far over the unpeopled wilderness before us. For the Doctor and myself, we had the tongue, the hump, and a few choice pieces salted down, and in a few days had prime corned beef. It is not inapt to state that the rifle had more commendations bestowed on it than the hunter by the Wangwana.

The next day we continued the march eastward, under the guidance of our kirangozi; but it was evident, by the road he led us, that he knew nothing of the country, though, through his volubility, he had led us to believe that he knew all about Ngondo, Yombeh, and Pumburu's districts. When recalled from the head of the caravan, we were about to descend into the rapid Loajeri, and beyond it were three ranges of impassable mountains, which we were to cross in a north-easterly direction, quite out of our road. After consulting with the Doctor, I put myself at the head of the caravan, and following the spine of the ridge, struck off due east, regardless of how the road ran. At intervals a travelled road crossed our path, and, after following it a while, we came to the ford of the Loajeri. The Loajeri rises south and south-east of Kakungu Peak. We made the best we could of the road after crossing the river, until we reached the main path that runs from Karah to Ngondo and Pumburu, in Southern Kawendi.

On the 9th, soon after leaving camp, we left the travelled path, and made for a gap in the arc of hills before us, as Pumburu was at war with the people of Manya Msonge, a district of northern Kawendi. The country teemed with game, the buffaloes and zebras were plentiful. Among the conspicuous trees were the hyphene and borassus palm trees, and a tree bearing a fruit about the size of a 600-pounder cannon-ball, called by some natives "mabyah,"* according to the Doctor, the seeds of which are roasted and eaten. They are not to be recommended as food to Europeans.

On the 10th, putting myself at the head of my men, with my compass in hand, I led the way east for three hours. A beautiful park-land was revealed to us; but the grass was very tall, and the rainy season, which had commenced in earnest, made my work excessively disagreeable. Through this tall grass, which was as high as my throat, I had to force my way, compass in hand, to lead the Expedition, as there was not the least sign of a road, and we were now in an untravelled country. We made our camp on a beautiful little stream flowing north; one of the feeders of the Rugufu River.

The 11th still saw me plunging through the grass, which showered drops of rain on me every time I made a step forward. In two hours we crossed a small stream, with slippery syenitic rocks in its bed, showing the action of furious torrents. Mushrooms were in abundance, and very large. In crossing, an old pagazi of Unyamwezi, weather-beaten, uttered, in a deplorable tone, "My kibuyu is dead;" by which he meant that he had slipped, and in falling had broken his gourd, which in Kisawahili is "kibuyu."

* In the Kisawahili tongue, "mabyah," "mbyah," byah," mean bad, unpleasant.

On the eastern bank we halted for lunch, and, after an hour and a half's march, arrived at another stream, which I took to be the Mtambu, at first from the similarity of the land, though my map informed me that it was impossible. The scenery around was very similar, and to the north we had cited a similar tabular hill to the "Magdala" Mount I had discovered north of Imrera, while going to the Malagarazi. Though we had only travelled three and a half hours the Doctor was very tired as the country was exceedingly rough.

The next day, crossing several ranges, with glorious scenes of surpassing beauty everywhere around us, we came in view of a mighty and swift torrent, whose bed was sunk deep between enormous lofty walls of sandstone rock, where it roared and brawled with the noise of a little Niagara.

Having seen our camp prepared on a picturesque knoll, I thought I would endeavour to procure some meat, which this interesting region seemed to promise. I sallied out with my little Winchester along the banks of the river eastward. I travelled for an hour or two, the prospect getting more picturesque and lovely, and then went up a ravine which looked very promising. Unsuccessful, I strode up the bank, and my astonishment may be conceived when I found myself directly in front of an elephant, who had his large broad ears held out like studding sails —the colossal monster, the incarnation of might of the African world. Methought when I saw his trunk stretched forward, like a warning finger, that I heard a voice say, " *Siste*, Venator!" But whether it did not proceed from my imagination or—No; I believe it proceeded from Kalulu, who must have shouted, " Tembo, tembo! bana yango!" "Lo! an elephant! an elephant, my master!"

For the young rascal had fled as soon as he had witnessed the awful colossus in such close vicinage. Recovering from my astonishment, I thought it prudent to retire also —especially with a pea-shooter loaded with treacherous sawdust cartridges in my hand. As I looked behind, I saw him waving his trunk, which I understood to mean, " Good-bye, young fellow ; it is lucky for you you went in time, for I was going to pound you to a jelly."

As I was congratulating myself, a wasp darted fiercely at me and planted its sting in my neck, and for that afternoon my anticipated pleasures were dispelled. Arriving at camp I found the men grumbling ; their provisions were ended, and there was no prospect for three days, at least, of procuring any. With the improvidence usual with the gluttons, they had eaten their rations of grain, all their store of zebra and dried buffalo meat, and were now crying out that they were famished.

The tracks of animals were numerous, but it being the rainy season the game was scattered everywhere ; whereas, had we travelled during the dry season through these forests our larders might have been supplied fresh each day.

Some time about 6 P.M., as the Doctor and I were taking our tea outside the tent, a herd of elephants, twelve in number, passed about 800 yards off. Our fundi, Asmani and Mabruki Kisesa, were immediately despatched in pursuit. I would have gone myself with the heavy Reilly rifle, only I was too much fatigued. We soon heard their guns firing, and hoped they were successful, as a plentiful supply of meat might then have been procured, while we ourselves would have secured one of the elephant's feet for a nice delicate roast; but within an hour they returned unsuccessful, having only drawn blood, some of which they exhibited to us on a leaf.

It requires a very good rifle to kill an African elephant. A No. 8 bore with a Frazer's shell, planted in the temple, I believe, would drop an elephant each shot. Faulkner makes some extraordinary statements, about walking up in front of an elephant and planting a bullet in his forehead, killing him instantly. The tale, however, is so incredible that I would prefer not to believe it; especially when he states that the imprint of the muzzle of his rifle was on the elephant's trunk. African travellers—especially those with a taste for the chase—are too fond of relating that which borders on the incredible for ordinary men to believe them. Such stories must be taken with a large grain of salt, for the sake of the amusement they afford to readers at home. In future, whenever I hear a man state how he broke the back of an antelope at 600 yards, I shall incline to believe a cipher had been added by a slip of the pen, or attribute it to a typographical error, for this is almost an impossible feat in an African forest. It may be done once, but it could never be done twice running. An antelope makes a very small target at 600 yards distance; but, then, all these stories belong by right divine to the chasseur who travels to Africa for the sake only of sport.

On the 13th we continued our march across several ridges; and the series of ascents and descents revealed to us valleys and mountains never before explored streams; rushing northward, swollen by the rains, and grand primeval forests, in whose twilight shade no white man ever walked before.

On the 14th the same scenes were witnessed—an unbroken series of longitudinal ridges, parallel one with another and with Lake Tanganika. Eastward the faces of these ridges present abrupt scarps and terraces, rising

from deep valleys, while the western declivities have
gradual slopes. These are the peculiar features of
Ukawendi, the eastern watershed of the Tanganika.

In one of these valleys on this day we came across a
colony of reddish-bearded monkeys, whose howls, or
bellowing, rang amongst the cliffs as they discovered the
caravan. I was not able to approach them, for they
scrambled up trees and barked their defiance at me, then
bounded to the ground as I still persisted in advancing;
and they would have soon drawn me in pursuit if I had
not suddenly remembered that my absence was halting
the Expedition.

About noon we sighted our Magdala — the grand
towering mount whose upright frowning mass had
attracted our eyes, as it lifted itself from above the plain
in all its grandeur, when we were hurrying along the
great ridge of Rusawa towards the "Crocodile" River.
We recognised the old, mystic beauty of the tree-clad
plain around it. Then it was bleached, and a filmy haze
covered it lovingly; now it was vivid greenness. Every
vegetable, plant, herb and tree, had sprung into quick life
—the effect of the rains. Rivers that ran not in those
hot summer days now fumed and rushed impetuously
between thick belts of mighty timber, brawling hoarsely
in the glades. We crossed many of these streams, all of
which are feeders of the Rugufu.

Beautiful, bewitching Ukawendi! By what shall I
gauge the loveliness of the wild, free, luxuriant, spontaneous nature within its boundaries? By anything in
Europe? No. By anything in Asia? Where? India,
perhaps. Yes; or say Mingrelia and Imeritia. For
there we have foaming rivers; we have picturesque
hillocks; we have bold hills, ambitious mountains, and

broad forests, with lofty solemn rows of trees, with clean straight stems, through which you can see far, lengthy vistas, as you see here. Only in Ukawendi you can almost behold the growth of vegetation; the earth is so generous, nature so kind and loving, that without entertaining any aspiration for a residence, or a wish to breathe the baleful atmosphere longer than is absolutely necessary, one feels insensibly drawn towards it, as the thought creeps into his mind, that though all is foul beneath the captivating, glamorous beauty of the land, the foulness might be removed by civilized people, and the whole region made as healthy as it is productive. Even while staggering under the pressure of the awful sickness, with mind getting more and more embittered, brain sometimes reeling with the shock of the constantly recurring fevers—though I knew how the malaria, rising out of that very fairness, was slowly undermining my constitution, and insidiously sapping the powers of mind and body—I regarded the alluring face of the land with a fatuous love, and felt a certain sadness steal over me as each day I was withdrawing myself from it, and felt disposed to quarrel with the fate that seemed to eject me out of Ukawendi.

On the ninth day of our march from the shores of the Tanganika we again perceived our "Magdala Mount," rising like a dark cloud to the north-east, by which I knew that we were approaching Imrera, and that our Icarian attempt to cross the uninhabited jungle of Ukawendi would soon be crowned with success. Against the collective counsel of the guides, and hypothetical suggestions of the tired and hungry souls of our Expedition, I persisted in being guided only by the compass and my chart. The guides strenuously strove to induce me to alter my course and strike in a south-west direction, which, had I listened to them, would have undoubtedly taken me to South-western Ukonongo, or North-eastern Ufipa. The veteran and experienced soldiers asked mournfully if I were determined to kill them with famine, as the road I should have taken was north-east; but I preferred putting my trust in the compass. No sun shone upon us as we threaded our way through the primeval forest, by clumps of jungle, across streams, up steep ridges, and down into deep valleys. A thick haze covered the forests; rain often pelted us; the firmament was an unfathomable depth of grey vapour. The Doctor had perfect confidence in me, and I held on my way.

As soon as we arrived at our camp the men scattered themselves through the forest to search for food. A grove of singwe trees was found close by. Mushrooms grew in abundance, and these sufficed to appease the gnawing hunger from which the people suffered. Had it not been such rainy weather I should have been enabled to procure game for the camp; but the fatigue which I suffered, and the fever which enervated me, utterly prevented me from moving out of the camp after we once came to a halt. The fear of lions, which were numerous in our vicinity, whose terrible roaring was heard by day and by night, daunted the hunters so much, that though I offered five doti of cloth for every animal brought to camp, none dared penetrate the gloomy glades, or awesome belts of timber, outside the friendly defence of the camp.

The morning of the tenth day I assured the people that we were close to food; cheered the most amiable of them with promise of abundant provender, and hushed the most truculent knaves with a warning not to tempt my patience too much, lest we came to angry blows; and then struck away east by north through the forest, with the almost exhausted Expedition dragging itself weakly and painfully behind me. It was a most desperate position certainly, and I pitied the poor people far more than they pitied themselves; and though I fumed and stormed in their presence when they were disposed to lie down and give up, never was a man further from doing them injury. I was too proud of them; but under the circumstances it was dangerous—nay, suicidal—to appear doubtful or dubious of the road. The mere fact that I still held on my way according to the Doctor's little pearly monitor (the compass) had a grand moral effect on them, and though they demurred in plaintive terms and with pinched faces, they followed my footsteps with a trustfulness which quite affected me.

For long miles we trudged over smooth sloping sward, with a vision of forest and park-land beauty on our right and left, and in front of us such as is rarely seen. At a pace that soon left the main body of the Expedition far behind, I strode on with a few gallant fellows, who, despite their heavy loads, kept pace with me. After a couple of hours we were ascending the easy slope of a ridge, which promised to decide in a few minutes the truth or the inaccuracy of my chart. Presently we arrived at the eastern edge of the ridge, and about five miles away, and 1,000 feet below the high plateau on which we stood, we distinguished the valley of Imrera!

By noon we were in our old camp. The natives gathered round, bringing supplies of food, and to congratulate us upon having gone to Ujiji and returned. But it was long before the last member of the Expedition arrived. The Doctor's feet were very sore, and bleeding from the weary march. His shoes were in a very worn-out state, and he had so cut and slashed them with a knife to ease his blistered feet, that any man of our force would have refused them as a gift, no matter how ambitious he might be to encase his feet à la Wasungu.

Asmani, the guide, was very much taken aback when he discovered that the tiny compass knew the way better than he did, and he declared it as his solemn opinion that it could not lie. He suffered much in reputation from having contested the palm with the "little thing," and ever afterwards his boasted knowledge of the country was considerably doubted.

After halting a day to recruit ourselves, we continued our journey on the 18th January, 1872, towards Unyanyembe. A few miles beyond Imrera, Asmani lost the road again, and I was obliged to show it to him, by which I gained additional honor and credit as a leader and guide. My shoes were very bad, and it was difficult to decide whose were the worst in condition, the Doctor's or mine. A great change had come upon the face of the land since I had passed northward en route to Ujiji. The wild grapes now hung in clusters along the road; the corn ears were advanced enough to pluck and roast for food; the various plants shed their flowers; and the deep woods and grasses of the country were greener than ever.

On the 19th we arrived at Mpokwa's deserted village. The Doctor's feet were very much chafed and sore by the marching. He had walked on foot all the way from Urimba, though he owned a donkey; while I, considerably to my shame be it said, had ridden occasionally to husband my strength, that I might be enabled to hunt after arrival at camp.

Two huts were cleared for our use, but, just as we had made ourselves comfortable, our sharp-eyed fellows had discovered several herds of game in the plain west of Mpokwa. Hastily devouring a morsel of corn-bread with coffee, I hastened away, with Bilali for a gun-bearer, taking with me the famous Reilly rifle of the Doctor and a supply of Fraser's shells. After plunging through a deep stream, and getting wet again, and pushing my way through a dense brake, I arrived at a thin belt of forest, through which I was obliged to crawl, and, in half an hour, I had arrived within one hundred and forty yards of a group of zebras, which were play-fully biting each other under the shade of a large tree. Suddenly rising up, I attracted their attention; but the true old rifle was at my shoulder, and "crack—crack" went both barrels, and two fine zebras, a male and female, fell dead under the tree where they had stood. In a few seconds their throats were cut, and after giving the signal of my success, I was soon surrounded by a dozen of my men, who gave utterance to their delight by fulsome compliments to the merits of the rifle, though very few to me. When I returned to camp with the meat I received the congratulations of the Doctor, which I valued far higher, as he knew from long experience what shooting was.

When the eatable portions of the two zebras were hung to the scale, we found, according to the Doctor's own figures, that we had 719 lbs. of good meat, which, divided among forty-four men, gave a little over 16 lbs. to each person. Bombay, especially, was very happy, as he had dreamed a dream wherein I figured prominently as shooting animals down right and left; and, when he had seen me depart with that wonderful Reilly rifle, he had not entertained a doubt of my success, and, accordingly, had commanded the men to be ready to go after me, as soon as they should hear the reports of the gun.

The following is quoted from my Diary:

January 20*th*, 1872.—To-day was a halt. On going out for a hunt I saw a herd of eleven giraffes. After crossing Mpokwa stream I succeeded in getting within one hundred and fifty yards of one of them, and fired at it; but, though it was wounded, I did not succeed in dropping it, though I desired the skin of one of them very much.

In the afternoon I went out to the east of the village, and came to a herd of six giraffes. I wounded one of them, but it got off, despite my efforts.

What remarkable creatures they are! How beautiful their large limpid eyes! I could have declared on oath that both shots had been a success, but they sheered off with the stately movements of a clipper about to tack. When they ran they had an ungainly, dislocated motion, somewhat like the contortions of an Indian nautch or a Theban *danseuse*—a dreamy, undulating movement, which even the tail, with its long fringe of black hair, seemed to partake of.

The Doctor, who knew how to console an ardent but disappointed young hunter, attributed my non-success to shooting with leaden balls, which were too soft to penetrate the thick hide of the giraffes, and advised me to melt my zinc canteens with which to harden the lead. It was not the first time that I had cause to think the Doctor an admirable travelling companion;

none knew so well how to console one for bad luck—
none knew so well how to elevate one in his own mind.
If I killed a zebra, did not his friend Oswell—the South
African hunter—and himself long ago come to the
conclusion that zebra meat was the finest in Africa?
If I shot a buffalo cow, she was sure to be the best of
her kind, and her horns were worth while carrying
home as specimens; and was she not fat? If I returned
without anything, the game was very wild, or the
people had made a noise, and the game had been
frightened; and who could stalk animals already alarmed?
Indeed, he was a most considerate companion, and, knowing
him to be literally truthful, I was proud of his praise
when successful, and when I failed I was easily consoled.

Ibrahim, the old pagazi whose feelings had been so
lacerated in Ukawendi, when his ancient kibuyu broke,
before leaving Ujiji invested his cloth in a slave from
Manyuema, who bore the name of "Ulimengo," which
signifies the "World." As we approached Mpokwa,
Ulimengo absconded with all his master's property, consisting of a few cloths and a bag of salt, which he had
thought of taking to Unyanyembe for trade. Ibrahim was
inconsolable, and he kept lamenting his loss daily in such
lugubrious tones that the people, instead of sympathizing,
laughed at him. I asked him why he purchased such a
slave, and, while he was with him, why he did not feed
him? Replied he, tartly, "Was he not my slave? Was
not the cloth with which I bought him mine? If the
cloth was my own, could I not purchase what I liked?
Why do you talk so?"

Ibrahim's heart was made glad this evening by the
return of Ulimengo with the salt and the cloth, and the
one-eyed old man danced with his great joy, and came in

all haste to impart to me the glad news. "Lo, the 'World' has come back. Sure. My salt and my cloth are with him also. Sure." To which I replied, that he had better feed him in future, as slaves required food as well as their masters.

From 10 P.M. to midnight the Doctor was employed in taking observations from the star Canopus, the result of which was that he ascertained Mpokwa, district of Utanda, Ukonongo, to be in S. latitude 6° 18' 40". On comparing it with its position as laid down in my map by dead reckoning, I found we differed by three miles; I having laid it down at 6° 15' south latitude.

The day following was a halt. The Doctor's feet were so inflamed and sore that he could not bear his shoes on. My heels were also raw, and I viciously cut large circles out of my shoes to enable me to move about.

Having converted my zinc canteens into bullets, and provided myself with a butcher and gun-bearer, I set out for the lovely park-land and plain west of Mpokwa stream, with the laudable resolution to obtain something; and seeing nothing in the plain, I crossed over a ridge, and came to a broad basin covered with tall grass, with clumps here and there of hyphene palm, with a stray mimosa or so scattered about. Nibbling off the branches of the latter, I saw a group of giraffes, and then began stalking them through the grass, taking advantage of the tall grass-grown ant-hills that I might approach the wary beasts before their great eyes could discover me. I contrived to come within 175 yards, by means of one of these curious hummocks; but beyond it no man could crawl without being observed—the grass was so thin and short. I took a long breath, wiped my perspiring brow, and sat down for a while; my black assistants also, like myself, were almost breathless with the exertion, and the high expectations roused by the near presence of the royal beasts. I toyed lovingly with the heavy Reilly, saw to my cartridges, and then stood up and turned, with my rifle ready; took one good, long, steady aim; then lowered it again to arrange the sights, lifted it up once more—dropped it. A giraffe half turned his body; for the last time I lifted it, took one quick sight at the region of the heart, and fired. He staggered, reeled, then made a short gallop; but the blood was spouting from the wound in a thick stream, and before he had gone 200 yards he came to a dead halt, with his ears drawn back, and allowed me to come within twenty yards of him, when, receiving a zinc bullet through the head, he fell dead.

"*Allah ho, akhbar!*" cried Khamisi, my butcher, fervently. "This is meat, master!"

I was rather saddened than otherwise at seeing the noble animal stretched before me. If I could have given him his life back I think I should have done so. I thought it a great pity that such splendid animals, so well adapted for the service of man in Africa, could not be converted to some other use than that of food. Horses, mules, and donkeys died in these sickly regions; but what a blessing for Africa would it be if we could tame the giraffes and zebras for the use of explorers and traders! Mounted on a zebra, a man would be enabled to reach Ujiji in one month from Bagamoyo; whereas it took me over seven months to travel that distance!

The dead giraffe measured 16 feet 9 inches from his right fore-hoof to the top of his head, and was one of the largest size, though some have been found to measure over 17 feet. He was spotted all over with large black, nearly round, patches.

I left Khamisi in charge of the dead beast, while I returned to camp to send off men to cut it up, and convey the meat to our village. But Khamisi climbed a tree for fear of the lions, and the vultures settled on it, so that when the men arrived on the spot, the eyes, the tongue, and a great part of the posteriors were eaten up. What remained weighed as follows, when brought in and hung to the scales :—

1 hind leg	134 lbs.
1 „	136 „
1 fore leg	160 „
1 „	160 „
Ribs	158 „
Neck	74 „
Rump	87 „
Breast	46 „
Liver	20 „
Lungs	12 „
Heart	6 „
Total weight of eatable portions . .	993 lbs.

Skin and head, 181 lbs.

The three days following I suffered from a severe attack of fever, and was unable to stir from bed. I applied my usual remedies for it, which consisted of colocynth and quinine; but experience has shown me that an excessive use of the same cathartic weakens its effect, and that it would be well for travellers to take with them different medicines to cause proper action in the liver, such as colocynth, calomel, resin of jalap, Epsom salts; and that no quinine should be taken until such medicines shall have prepared the system for its reception.

The Doctor's prescription for fever consists of 3 grains

of resin of jalap, and 2 grains of calomel, with tincture of cardamoms put in just enough to prevent irritation of the stomach—made into the form of a pill—which is to be taken as soon as one begins to feel the excessive languor and weariness which is the sure forerunner of the African type of fever. An hour or two later a cup of coffee, unsugared and without milk, ought to be taken, to cause a quicker action. The Doctor also thinks that quinine should be taken with the pill; but my experience— though it weighs nothing against what he has endured— has proved to me that quinine is useless until after the medicine has taken effect. My stomach could never bear quinine unless subsequent to the cathartic. A well-known missionary at Constantinople recommends travellers to take 3 grains of tartar-emetic for the ejection of the bilious matter in the stomach; but the reverend doctor possibly forgets that much more of the system is disorganized than the stomach; and though in one or two cases of a slight attack, this remedy may have proved successful, it is altogether too violent for an enfeebled man in Africa. I have treated myself faithfully after this method three or four times; but I could not conscientiously recommend it. For cases of urticaria, I could recommend taking 3 grains of tartar-emetic; but then a stomach-pump would answer the purpose as well.

On the 27th we set out for Misonghi. About half-way I saw the head of the Expedition on the run, and the motive seemed to be communicated quickly, man after man, to those behind, until my donkey commenced to kick, and lash behind with his heels. In a second, I was made aware of the cause of this excitement, by a cloud of wild bees buzzing about my head, three or four of which settled on my face, and stung me frightfully. We raced madly for about half a mile, behaving in as wild a manner as the poor bestung animals.

As this was an unusually long march, I doubted if the Doctor could march it, because his feet were so sore, so I determined to send four men back with the kitanda; but the stout old hero refused to be carried, and walked all the way to camp after a march of eighteen miles. He had been stung dreadfully in the head and in the face; the bees had settled in handfuls in his hair; but, after partaking of a cup of warm tea and some food, he was as cheerful as if he had never travelled a mile.

At Mrera, Central Ukonongo, we halted a day to grind grain, and to prepare the provision we should need during the transit of the wilderness between Mrera and Manyara.

On the 31st of January, at Mwaru, Sultan Ka-mirambo, we met a caravan under the leadership of a slave of Sayd bin Habib, who came to visit us in our camp, which was hidden in a thick clump of jungle. After he was seated, and had taken his coffee, I asked,

"What is thy news, my friend, that thou hast brought from Unyanyembe?"

"My news is good, master."

"How goes the war?"

"Ah, Mirambo is where? He eats the hides even. He is famished. Sayd bin Habib, my master, hath possession of Kirira. The Arabs are thundering at the gates of Wilyankuru. Sayd bin Majid, who came from Ujiji to Usagozi in twenty days, hath taken and slain 'Moto' (Fire), the King. Simba of Kasera hath taken up arms for the defence of his father, Mkasiwa of Unyanyembe. The chief of Ugunda hath sent five hundred men to the field. Ough—Mirambo is where ? In a month he will be dead of hunger."

" Great and good news truly, my friend."

" Yes—in the name of God."

" And whither art thou bound with thy caravan ?"

" Sayd, the son of Majid, who came from Ujiji, hath told us of the road that the white man took, that he had arrived at Ujiji safely, and that he was on his way back to Unyanyembe. So we have thought that if the white man could go there, we could also. Lo, the Arabs come by the hundred by the white man's road, to get the ivory from Ujiji.

" I am that white man."

" You ?"

" Yes."

" Why it was reported that you were dead—that you fought with the Wazavira."

" Ah, my friend, these are the words of Njara, the son of Khamis. See " (pointing to Livingstone), " this is the white man, my father,* whom I saw at Ujiji. He is going with me to Unyanyembe to get his cloth, after which he will return to the great waters."

" Wonderful !—thou sayest truly."

" What has thou to tell me of the white man at Unyanyembe ?"

" Which white man ?"

" The white man I left in the house of Sayd, the son of Salim—my house—at Kwihara."

" He is dead."

" Dead !"

" True."

* It is a courteous custom in Africa to address elderly people as " Baba," (Father).

" You do not mean to say the white man is dead ?"

" True—he is dead."

" How long ago ?"

" Many months now."

" What did he die of ?"

" Homa (fever)."

" Any more of my people dead ?"

" I know not."

" Enough." I looked sympathetically at the Doctor, and he replied,

"I told you so. When you described him to me as a drunken man, I knew he could not live. Men who have been habitual drunkards cannot live in this country, any more than men who have become slaves to other vices. I attribute the deaths that occurred in my expedition on the Zambezi to much the same cause."

" Ah, Doctor, there are two of us gone. I shall be the third, if this fever lasts much longer."

' Oh no, not at all. If you would have died from fever, you would have died at Ujiji when you had that severe attack of remittent. Don't think of it. Your fever now is only the result of exposure to wet. I never travel during the wet season. This time I have travelled because I was anxious, and I did not wish to detain you at Ujiji."

" Well, there is nothing like a good friend at one's back in this country to encourage him, and keep his spirits up. Poor Shaw! I am sorry—very sorry for him. How many times have I not endeavoured to cheer him up! But there was no life in him. And among the last words I said to him, before parting, were, ' Remember, if you return to Unyanyembe, you DIE ! ' "

We also obtained news from the chief of Sayd bin Habib's caravan that several packets of letters and news-

papers, and boxes, had arrived for me from Zanzibar by
my messengers and Arabs; that Selim, the son of Sheikh
Hashid of Zanzibar, was amongst the latest arrivals in
Unyanyembe. The Doctor also reminded me with the
utmost good-nature that, according to his accounts, he
had a stock of jellies and crackers, soups, fish, and potted
ham, besides cheese, awaiting him in Unyanyembe, and
that he would be delighted to share his good things;
whereupon I was greatly cheered, and, during the
repeated attacks of fever I suffered about this time, my
imagination loved to dwell upon the luxuries at Unyanyembe. I pictured myself devouring the hams and
crackers and jellies like a madman. I lived on my raving
fancies. My poor vexed brain rioted on such homely
things as wheaten bread and butter, hams, bacon, caviare,
and I would have thought no price too high to pay for
them. Though so far away and out of the pale of
Europe and America, it was a pleasure to me, during the
athumia or despondency into which I was plunged by
ever recurring fevers, to dwell upon them. I wondered
that people who had access to such luxuries should ever
get sick, and become tired of life. I thought that if a
wheaten loaf with a nice pat of fresh butter were
presented to me, I would be able, though dying, to spring
up and dance a wild fandango.

Though we lacked the good things of this life above
named, we possessed salted giraffe and pickled zebra
tongues; we had ugali made by Halimah herself; we had
sweet potatoes, tea, coffee, dampers, or slap-jacks; but I
was tired of them. My enfeebled stomach, harrowed and
irritated with medicinal compounds, with ipecac, colocynth, tartar-emetic, quinine, and such things, protested
against the coarse food. "Oh, for a wheaten loaf!" my

soul cried in agony. "Five hundred dollars for one loaf of bread!"

The Doctor, somehow or another, despite the incessant rain, the dew, fog, and drizzle, the marching, and sore feet, ate like a hero, and I manfully, sternly, resolved to imitate the persevering attention he paid to the welfare of his gastric powers; but I miserably failed.

Dr. Livingstone possesses all the attainments of a traveller. His knowledge is great about everything concerning Africa—the rocks, the trees, the fruits, and their virtues, are known to him. He is also full of philosophic reflections upon ethnological matter. With camp-craft, with its cunning devices, he is *au fait.* His bed is luxurious as a spring mattress. Each night he has it made under his own supervision. First, he has two straight poles cut, three or four inches in diameter; which are laid parallel one with another, at the distance of two feet; across these poles are laid short sticks, saplings, three feet long, and over them is laid a thick pile of grass; then comes a piece of waterproof canvas and blankets--and thus a bed has been improvised fit for a king.

It was at Livingstone's instigation I purchased milch goats, by which, since leaving Ujiji, we have had a supply of fresh milk for our tea and coffee three times a day. Apropos of this, we are great drinkers of these welcome stimulants; we seldom halt drinking until we have each had six or seven cups. We have also been able to provide ourselves with music, which, though harsh, is better than none. I mean the musical screech of parrots from Manyuema.

Half-way between Mwaru—Kamirambo's village—and the deserted Tongoni of Ukamba, I carved the Doctor's initials and my own on a large tree, with the date February 2nd. I have been twice guilty of this in Africa: once when we were famishing in Southern Uvinza I inscribed the date, my initials, and the word "Starving" in large letters on the trunk of a sycamore.

In passing through the forest of Ukamba, we saw the bleached skull of an unfortunate victim to the privations of travel. Referring to it, the Doctor remarked that he could never pass through an African forest, with its solemn stillness and serenity, without wishing to be buried quietly under the dead leaves, where he would be sure to rest undisturbed. In England there was no elbow-room, the graves were often desecrated; and ever since he had buried his wife in the woods of Shupanga he had sighed for just such a spot, where his weary bones would receive the eternal rest they coveted.

The same evening, when the tent door was down, and the interior was made cheerful by the light of a paraffin candle, the Doctor related to me some incidents respecting the career and the death of his eldest son, Robert. Readers of Livingstone's first book, 'South Africa,' without which no boy should be, will probably recollect the dying Sebituane's regard for the little boy "Robert." Mrs. Livingstone and family were taken to the Cape of Good Hope, and thence sent to England, where Robert was put in the charge of a tutor; but wearied of inactivity, when he was about eighteen, he left Scotland and came to Natal, whence he endeavoured to reach his father. Unsuccessful in his attempt, he took ship and sailed for New York, and enlisted in the Northern Army, in a New Hampshire regiment of Volunteers, discarding his own name of Robert Moffatt Livingstone, and taking that of Rupert Vincent, that his tutor, who seems to have been ignorant of his duties to the youth, might not find him. From one of the battles before Richmond, he was conveyed to a North Carolina hospital, where he died from his wounds.

On the 7th of February we arrived at the Gombe, and camped near one of its largest lakes. This lake is probably several miles in length, and swarms with hippopotami and crocodiles.

From this camp I despatched Ferajji, the cook, and Chowpereh to Unyanyembe, to bring the letters and medicines that were sent to me from Zanzibar, and meet us at Ugunda, while the next day we moved to our old quarters on the Gombe, where we were first introduced to the real hunter's paradise in Central Africa. The rain had scattered the greater number of the herds, but there was plenty of game in the vicinity. Soon after breakfast I took Khamisi and Kalulu with me for a hunt. After a long walk we arrived near a thin jungle, where I discovered the tracks of several animals—boar, antelope, elephant, rhinoceros, hippopotamus, and an unusual number of imprints of the lion's paw. Suddenly I heard Khamisi say, "Master, master! here is a 'simba!' (lion);" and he came up to me trembling with excitement and fear—for the young fellow was an arrant coward—to point out the head of a beast, which could be seen just above the tall grass, looking steadily towards us. It immediately afterwards bounded from side to side, but the grass was so high that it was impossible to tell exactly what it was. Taking advantage of a tree in my front, I crept quietly onwards, intending to rest the heavy rifle against it, as I was so weak from the effects of several fevers that I felt myself utterly incapable of supporting my rifle for a steady aim. But my surprise was great

when I cautiously laid it against the tree, and then
directed its muzzle to the spot where I had seen him
stand. Looking further away—to where the grass was
thin and scant—I saw the animal bound along at a great
rate, and that it was a lion: the noble monarch of the
forest was in full flight! From that moment I ceased to
regard him as the "mightiest among the brutes;" or his
roar as anything more fearful in broad daylight than a
sucking dove's.

The next day was also a halt, and unable to contain my
longing for the chase, where there used to be such a
concourse of game of all kinds, soon after morning coffee,
and after despatching a couple of men with presents to
my friend Ma-manyara, of ammonia-bottle memory, I
sauntered out once more for the park. Not five hundred
yards from the camp, myself and men were suddenly
halted by hearing in our immediate vicinity, probably
within fifty yards or so, a chorus of roars, issuing from a
triplet of lions. Instinctively my fingers raised the two
hammers, as I expected a general onset on me; for though
one lion might fly, it was hardly credible that three
should. While looking keenly about I detected, within
easy rifle-shot, a fine hartebeest, trembling and cowering
behind a tree, as if it expected the fangs of the lion in its
neck. Though it had its back turned to me, I thought a
bullet might plough its way to a vital part, and without a
moment's hesitation I aimed and fired. The animal gave
a tremendous jump, as if it intended to take a flying leap
through the tree; but recovering itself it dashed through
the underbrush in a different direction from that in which
I supposed the lions to be, and I never saw it again,
though I knew I had struck it from the bloody trail it
left; neither did I see nor hear anything more of the lions.

I searched far and wide over the park-land for prey of some kind, but was compelled to return unsuccessful to camp.

Disgusted with my failure, we started a little after noon for Manyara, at which place we were hospitably greeted by my friend, who had sent men to tell me that his white brother must not halt in the woods but must come to his village. We received a present of honey and food from the chief, which was most welcome to us in our condition. Here was an instance of that friendly disposition among Central African chiefs when they have not been spoiled by the Arabs, which Dr. Livingstone found among the Babisa and Ba-ulungu, and in Manyuema. I received the same friendly recognition from all the chiefs, from Imrera, in Ukawendi, to Unyanyembe, as I did from Ma-manyara.

On the 14th we arrived at Ugunda, and soon after we had established ourselves comfortably in a hut which the chief lent us for our use, in came Ferajji and Chowpereh, bringing with them Sarmean and Uledi Manwa Sera, who, it will be recollected, were the two soldiers sent to Zanzibar with letters and who should Sarmean have in charge but the deserter Hamdallah, who decamped at Manyara, as we were going to Ujiji. This fellow, it seems, had halted at Kigandu, and had informed the chief and the doctor of the village that he had been sent by the white man to take back the cloth left there for the cure of Mabruk Saleem ; and the simple chief had commanded it to be given up to him upon his mere word, in consequence of which the sick man had died.

Upon Sarmean's arrival in Unyanyembe from Zanzibar, about fifty days after the Expedition had departed for Ujiji, the news he received was that the white man (Shaw) was dead ; and that a man called Hamdallah, who

had engaged himself as one of my guides, but who had
shortly after returned, was at Unyanyembe. He had
left him unmolested until the appearance of Ferajji
and his companion, when they at once, in a body, made
a descent on his hut and secured him. With the zeal
which always distinguished him in my service, Sarmean
had procured a forked pole, between the prongs of
which the neck of the absconder was placed; and a cross
stick, firmly lashed, effectually prevented him from
relieving himself of the incumbrance attached to him so
deftly.

There were no less than seven packets of letters and
newspapers from Zanzibar, which had been collecting
during my absence from Unyanyembe. These had been
intrusted at various times to the chiefs of caravans, who
had faithfully delivered them at my tembe, according to
their promise to the Consul. There was one packet for
me, which contained two or three letters for Dr. Livingstone, to whom, of course, they were at once transferred,
with my congratulations. In the same packet there was
also a letter to me from the British Consul at Zanzibar
requesting me to take charge of Livingstone's goods and
do the best I could to forward them on to him, dated 25th
September, 1871, five days after I left Unyanyembe on my
apparently hopeless task.

"Well, Doctor," said I to Livingstone, "the English
Consul requests me to do all I can to push forward your
goods to you. I am sorry that I did not get the authority
sooner, for I should have attempted it; but in the absence
of these instructions I have done the best I could by
pushing you towards the goods. The mountain has not
been able to advance towards Mohammed, but Mohammed
has been compelled to advance towards the mountain."

But Dr. Livingstone was too deeply engrossed in his own letters from home, which were just a year old.

I received good and bad news from New York, but the good news was subsequent, and wiped out all feelings that might have been evoked had I received the bad only. But the newspapers, nearly a hundred of them, New York, Boston, and London journals, were full of most wonderful news. The Paris Commune was in arms against the National Assembly; the Tuileries, the Louvre, and the ancient city Lutetia Parisiorum had been set in flames by the blackguards of Saint-Antoine! French troops massacring and murdering men, women, and children; rampant diabolism, and incarnate revenge were at work in the most beautiful city in the world! Fair women converted into demons, and dragged by ruffianly soldiery through the streets to universal execration and pitiless death; children of tender age pinned to the earth and bayoneted; men innocent or not, shot, cut, stabbed, slashed, destroyed —a whole city given up to the *summa injuria* of an infuriate, reckless, and brutal army! Oh France! Oh Frenchmen! Such things are unknown even in the heart of barbarous Central Africa. We spurned the newspapers with our feet; and for relief to sickened hearts gazed on the comic side of our world, as illustrated in the innocent pages of ' Punch.' Poor ' Punch !' good-hearted, kindly-natured ' Punch !' a traveller's benison on thee! Thy jokes were as physic; thy innocent satire was provocative of hysteric mirth.

Our doors were crowded with curious natives, who looked with indescribable wonder at the enormous sheets. I heard them repeat the words, " Khabari Kisungu "— white man's news—often, and heard them discussing the nature of such a quantity of news, and expressing their belief that the "Wasungu" were "mbyah sana," and very "mkali;" by which they meant to say that the white men were very wicked, and very smart and clever though the term wicked is often employed to express high admiration.

On the fourth day from Ugunda, or the 18th of February, and the fifty-third day from Ujiji, we made our appearance with flags flying and guns firing in the valley of Kwihara, and when the Doctor and myself passed through the portals of my old quarters I formally welcomed him to Unyanyembe and to my house.

Since the day I had left the Arabs, sick and weary almost with my life, but, nevertheless, imbued with the high hope that my mission would succeed, 131 days had elapsed—with what vicissitudes of fortune the reader well knows—during which time I had journeyed over 1,200 miles.

The myth after which I travelled through the wilderness proved to be a fact; and never was the fact more apparent than when the Living Man walked with me arm in arm to my old room, and I said to him, "Doctor, we are at last HOME!"

MAKING THE MOST OF A HALT.

CHAPTER XV.

HOMEWARD BOUND.—LIVINGSTONE'S LAST WORDS!—
THE FINAL FAREWELL!

UNYANYEMBE was now to me a terrestrial Paradise.
Livingstone was no less happy; he was in comfortable
quarters, which were a palace compared to his hut in
Ujiji. Our store-rooms were full of the good things
of this life, besides cloth, beads, wire, and the thousand
and one impedimenta and paraphernalia of travel with
which I had loaded over one hundred and fifty men at
Bagamoyo. I had seventy-four loads of miscellaneous
things, the most valuable of which were now to be turned

over to Livingstone, for his march back to the sources of the Nile.

It was a great day with us when, with hammer and chisel, I broke open the Doctor's boxes, that we might feast our famished stomachs on the luxuries which were to redeem us from the effect of the cacotrophic dourra and maize food we had been subjected to in the wilderness. I conscientiously believed that a diet on potted ham, crackers, and jellies would make me as invincible as Talus, and that I only required a stout flail to be able to drive the mighty Wagogo into the regions of annihiliation, should they dare even to wink in a manner I disapproved.

The first box opened contained three tins of biscuits, six tins of potted hams—tiny things, not much larger than thimbles, which, when opened, proved to be nothing more than a table spoonful of minced meat plentifully seasoned with pepper: the Doctor's stores fell five hundred degrees below zero in my estimation. Next were brought out five pots of jam, one of which was opened—this was also a delusion. The stone jars weighed a pound, and in each was found a little over a tea-spoonful of jam. Verily, we began to think our hopes and expectations had been raised to too high a pitch. Three bottles of curry were next produced—but who cares for curry? Another box was opened, and out tumbled a fat dumpy Dutch cheese, hard as a brick, but sound and good; though it is bad for the liver in Unyamwezi. Then another cheese was seen, but this was all eaten up—it was hollow and a fraud. The third box contained nothing but two sugar loaves; the fourth, candles; the fifth, bottles of salt, Harvey, Worcester, and Reading sauces, essence of anchovies, pepper, and mustard. Bless me! what food were these for the revivifying of a moribund such as I was! The sixth box contained four shirts, two pairs of stout shoes, some stockings and shoe-strings, which delighted the Doctor so much when he tried them on that he exclaimed, " Richard is himself again !" " That man," said I, " whoever he is, is a friend, indeed." " Yes, that is my friend Waller."

The five other boxes contained potted meat and soups; but the twelfth, containing one dozen bottles of medicinal brandy, was gone; and a strict cross-examination of Asmani, the head man of Livingstone's caravan, elicited the fact, that not only was one case of brandy missing, but also two bales of cloth and four bags of the most valuable beads in Africa—sami-sami—which are as gold with the natives.

I was grievously disappointed after the stores had been examined; everything proved to be deceptions in my jaundiced eyes. Out of the tins of biscuits when opened, there was only one sound box; the whole of which would not make one full meal. The soups—who cared for meat soups in Africa? Are there no bullocks, and sheep, and goats in the land, from which far better soup can be made than any that was ever potted? Peas, or any other kind of vegetable soup, would have been a luxury; but chicken and game soups !—what nonsense !

I then overhauled my own stores. I found some fine old brandy and one bottle of champagne still left; though it was evident, in looking at the cloth bales, that dishonesty had been at work; and some person happened to suggest Asmani—the head man sent by **Dr.** Kirk in charge of Livingstone's goods—as the guilty party. Upon his treasures being examined, I found eight or ten colored cloths, with the mark of my own agent at Zanzibar on them. As he was unable to give a clear account of how they came in his box, they were at once confiscated, and distributed among the most deserving of the Doctor's people. Some of the watchmen also accused him of having entered into my store-room, and of having abstracted two or three gorah of domestics from my bales, and of having, some days afterwards, snatched the keys from the hands of one of my men, and broken them, lest other people might enter, and find evidences of his guilt. As Asmani was proved to be another of the "moral idiots," Livingstone discharged him on the spot. Had we not arrived so soon at Unyanyembe, it is probable that the entire stock sent from Zanzibar had in time disappeared.

Unyanyembe being rich in fruits, grain, and cattle, we determined to have our Christmas dinner over again in style, and, being fortunately in pretty good health, I was enabled to superintend its preparation. Never was such prodigality seen in a tembe of Unyamwezi as was seen in ours, nor were ever such delicacies provided.

There were but few Arabs in Unyanyembe when we arrived, as they were investing the stronghold of Mirambo. About a week after our return, "the little mannikin," Sheikh Sayd bin Salim—El Wali—who was the commander-in-chief of their forces, came to Kwihara from the front. But the little Sheikh was in no great hurry to greet the man he had wronged so much. As soon as we heard of his arrival we took the opportunity to send men immediately after the goods which were forwarded to the Wali's care soon after Livingstone's departure for Mikindany Bay. The first time we sent men for them the governor declared himself too sick to attend to such matters, but the second day they were surrendered, with a request that the Doctor would not be very angry at their condition, as the white ants had destroyed everything.

The stores this man had detained at Unyanyembe were in a most sorry state. The expenses were prepaid for their carriage to Ujiji, but the goods had been purposely detained at this place by Sayd bin Salim since 1867 that he might satisfy his appetite for liquor, and probably fall heir to two valuable guns that were known to be with them. The white ants had not only eaten up bodily the box in which the guns were packed, but they had also eaten the gunstocks. The barrels were corroded, and the locks were quite destroyed. The brandy bottles, most singular to relate, had also fallen a prey to the voracious and irresistible destroyers— the white ants—and, by some unaccountable means, they had imbibed the potent Hennessy, and replaced the corks with corn-cobs. The medicines had also vanished, and the zinc pots in which they had been snugly packed up were destroyed by corrosion. Two bottles of brandy and one small zinc case of medicines only were saved out of the otherwise utter wreck.

I also begged the Doctor to send to Sheikh Sayd, and ask him if he had received the two letters despatched by him upon his first arrival at Ujiji for Dr. Kirk and Lord Clarendon; and if he had forwarded them to the coast, as he was desired to do. The reply to the messengers was in the affirmative; and, subsequently, I obtained the same answer in the presence of the Doctor,

On the 22nd of February, the pouring rain, which had dogged us the entire distance from Ujiji, ceased, and we had now beautiful weather; and while I prepared for the homeward march, the Doctor was busy writing his letters, and entering his notes into his journal, which I was to take to his family. When not thus employed, we paid visits to the Arabs at Tabora, by whom we were both received with that bounteous hospitality for which they are celebrated.

Among the goods turned over by me to Dr. Livingstone, while assorting such cloths as I wished to retain for my homeward trip, were—

	Doti.		Yards.
First-class American sheeting . . .	285	=	1140
„ Kaniki (blue stuff) . . .	16	=	64
Medium „ (blue stuff) . . .	60	=	240
„ Dabwani cloth	41	=	164
Barsati cloths	28	=	112
Printed handkerchiefs . .	70	=	280
Medium Rehani cloth	127	=	508
„ Ismahili „	20	=	80
„ Sohari „	20	=	80
4 pieces fine Kunguru (red check) .	22	=	88
4 gorah Rehani	8	=	32
Total number of cloths . 697	697	=	2788

Besides :—

Cloth, 2788 yards.
Assorted beads, 16 sacks, weight = 992 lbs.
Brass wire, Nos. 5 and 6, 10 fraslilah = 350 lbs.
1 canvas tent, waterproof.
1 air-bed.
1 boat (canvas).
1 bag of tools, carpenters.
1 rip saw.
2 barrels of tar.

12 sheets of ship's copper = 60 lbs.
Clothes.
1 Jocelyn breech-loader (metallic cartridge).
1 Starr's   „   „   „
1 Henry (16-shooter)   „   „
1 revolver.
200 rounds revolver ammunition.
2000   „   Jocelyn and Starr's ammunition.
1500   „   Henry rifle ammunition.
     Cooking utensils, medicine chest, books, sextant, canvas
       bags, &c., &c., &c.

The above made a total of about forty loads. Many
things in the list would have brought fancy prices in
Unyanyembe, especially the carbines and ammunition, the
saw, carpenter's tools, the beads, and wire. Out of the
thirty-three loads which were stored for him in my tembe
—the stock sent to Livingstone, Nov. 1, 1870—but few of
them would be available for his return trip to Rua and
Manyuema. The 696 doti of cloth which were left to him
formed the only marketable articles of value he possessed ;
and in Manyuema, where the natives manufactured their
own cloth, such an article would be considered a drug ;
while my beads and wire, with economy, would suffice to
keep him and his men over two years in those regions.
His own cloth, and what I gave him, made in the aggregate 1,393 doti, which, at 2 doti per day for food, were
sufficient to keep him and sixty men 696 days. He had
thus four years' supplies. The only articles he lacked to
make a new and completely fitted-up expedition were the
following, a list of which he and I drew up :—

    A few tins of American wheat-flour.
      „   „   soda crackers.
      „   „   preserved fruits.
      „   „   sardines.

A few tins of salmon,
10 lbs. Hyson tea.
Some sewing thread and needles.
1 dozen official envelopes.
'Nautical Almanac' for 1872 and 1873.
1 blank journal.
1 chronometer, stopped.
1 chain for refractory people.

With the articles just named he would have a total of
seventy loads, but without carriers they were an incumbrance to him ; for, with only the nine men which he now
had, he could go nowhere with such a splendid assortment
of goods. I was therefore commissioned to enlist,—as
soon as I reached Zanzibar,—fifty freemen, arm them
with a gun and hatchet each man, besides accoutrements,
and to purchase two thousand bullets, one thousand flints,
and ten kegs of gunpowder. The men were to act as
carriers, to follow wherever Livingstone might desire to
go. For, without men, he was simply tantalized with the
aspirations roused in him by the knowledge that he had
abundance of means, which were irrealizable without
carriers. All the wealth of London and New York piled
before him were totally unavailable to him without the
means of locomotion. No Mnyamwezi engages himself as
carrier during war-time. You who have read the diary of
my 'Life in Unyanyembe' know what stubborn Conser-
vatives the Wanyamwezi are. A duty lay yet before me
which I owed to my illustrious companion, and that was
to hurry to the coast as if on a matter of life and death—
act for him in the matter of enlisting men as if he were
there himself—to work for him with the same zeal as I
would for myself—not to halt or rest until his desires
should be gratified, And this I vowed to do; but it was

a death-blow to my project of going down the Nile, and getting news of Sir S. Baker.

The Doctor's task of writing his letters was ended. He delivered into my hand twenty letters for Great Britain, six for Bombay, two for New York, and one for Zanzibar. The two letters for New York were for James Gordon Bennett, junior, as he alone, not his father, was responsible for the Expedition sent under my command. I beg the reader's pardon for republishing one of these letters here, as its spirit and style indicate the man, the mere knowledge of whose life or death was worth a costly Expedition:

UJIJI, ON TANGANIKA, EAST AFRICA,
November, 1871.

JAMES GORDON BENNETT, Jr., Esq.

MY DEAR SIR,—It is in general somewhat difficult to write to one we have never seen—it feels so much like addressing an abstract idea —but the presence of your representative, Mr. H. M. Stanley, in this distant region takes away the strangeness I should otherwise have felt, and in writing to thank you for the extreme kindness that prompted you to send him, I feel quite at home.

If I explain the forlorn condition in which he found me you will easily perceive that I have good reason to use very strong expressions of gratitude. I came to Ujiji off a tramp of between four hundred and five hundred miles, beneath a blazing vertical sun, having been baffled, worried, defeated and forced to return, when almost in sight of the end of the geographical part of my mission, by a number of half-caste Moslem slaves sent to me from Zanzibar, instead of men. The sore heart made still sorer by the woeful sights I had seen of man's inhumanity to man racked and told on the bodily frame, and depressed it beyond measure. I thought that I was dying on my feet. It is not too much to say that almost every step of the weary sultry way was in pain, and I reached Ujiji a mere ruckle of bones.

There I found that some five hundred pounds' sterling worth of goods which I had ordered from Zanzibar had unaccountably been entrusted to a drunken half-caste Moslem tailor, who, after squandering them for sixteen months on the way to Ujiji, finished up by selling off all that remained for slaves and ivory for himself. He had "divined" on the Koran and found that I was dead. He had also written to the Governor of Unyanyembe that he had sent slaves after me to Manyuema, who returned and reported my decease, and begged permission to sell off the few goods that his drunken appetite had spared.

He, however, knew perfectly well, from men who had seen me, that I was alive, and waiting for the goods and men; but as for morality, he is evidently an idiot, and there being no law here except that of the dagger or musket, I had to sit down in great weakness, destitute of everything save a few barter cloths and beads, which I had taken the precaution to leave here in case of extreme need.

The near prospect of beggary among Ujijians made me miserable.

I could not despair, because I laughed so much at a friend who, on reaching the mouth of the Zambezi, said that he was tempted to despair on breaking the photograph of his wife. We could have no success after that. Afterward the idea of despair had to me such a strong smack of the ludicrous that it was out of the question.

Well, when I had got to about the lowest verge, vague rumors of an English visitor reached me. I thought of myself as the man who went down from Jerusalem to Jericho; but neither priest, Levite, nor Samaritan could possibly pass my way. Yet the good Samaritan was close at hand, and one of my people rushed up at the top of his speed, and, in great excitement, gasped out, "An Englishman coming! I see him!" and off he darted to meet him.

An American flag, the first ever seen in these parts, at the head of a caravan, told me the nationality of the stranger.

I am as cold and non-demonstrative as we islanders are usually reputed to be; but your kindness made my frame thrill. It was, indeed, overwhelming, and I said in my soul, "Let the richest blessings descend from the Highest on you and yours!"

The news Mr. Stanley had to tell was thrilling. The mighty political changes on the Continent; the success of the Atlantic cables; the election of General Grant, and many other topics riveted my attention for days together, and had an immediate and beneficial effect on my health. I had been without news from home for years save what I could glean from a few 'Saturday Reviews' and 'Punch' of 1868. The appetite revived, and in a week I began to feel strong again.

Mr. Stanley brought a most kind and encouraging despatch from Lord Clarendon (whose loss I sincerely deplore), the first I have received from the Foreign Office since 1866, and information that the British Government had kindly sent a thousand pounds sterling to my aid. Up to his arrival I was not aware of any pecuniary aid. I came unsalaried, but this want is now happily repaired, and I am anxious that you and all my friends should know that, though uncheered by letter, I have stuck to the task which my friend Sir Roderick Murchison set me with " John Bullish " tenacity, believing that all would come right at last.

The watershed of South Central Africa is over seven hundred miles in length. The fountains thereon are almost innumerable—that is, it would take a man's lifetime to count them. From the watershed they converge into four large rivers, and these again into two mighty streams in the great Nile valley, which begins in ten degrees to twelve degrees south latitude. It was long ere light dawned on the ancient problem and gave me a clear idea of the drainage. I had to feel my way, and every step of the way, and was, generally, groping in the dark—for who cared where the rivers ran? " We drank our fill and let the rest run by."

The Portuguese who visited Cazembe asked for slaves and ivory, and heard of nothing else. I asked about the waters, questioned and cross-questioned, until I was almost afraid of being set down as afflicted with hydrocephalus.

My last work, in which I have been greatly hindered from want of suitable attendants, was following the central line of drainage down through the country of the cannibals, called Manyuema, or, shortly Manyema. This line of drainage has four large lakes in it. The fourth I was near when obliged to turn. It is from one to three miles broad, and never can be reached at any point, or at any time of the year. Two western drains, the Lufira, or Bartle Frere's River, flow into it at Lake Kamolondo. Then the great River Lomame flows through Lake Lincoln into it too, and seems to form the western arm of the Nile, on which Petherick traded.

Now, I knew about six hundred miles of the watershed, and unfortunately the seventh hundred is the most interesting of the whole; for in it, if I am not mistaken, four fountains arise from an earthen mound, and the last of the four becomes, at no great distance off, a large river.

Two of these run north to Egypt, Lufira and Lomame, an 1 two run south into inner Ethiopia, as the Leambaye, or Upper Zambezi, and the Kaful.

Are not these the sources of the Nile mentioned by the Secretary of Minerva, in the city of Sais, to Herodotus ?

I have heard of them so often, and at great distances off, that I cannot doubt their existence, and in spite of the sore longing for home that seizes me every time I think of my family, I wish to finish up by their rediscovery.

Five hundred pounds sterling worth of goods have again unaccountably been entrusted to slaves, and have been over a year on the way, instead of four months. I must go where they lie at your expense, ere I can put the natural completion to my work.

And if my disclosures regarding the terrible Ujijian slavery should lead to the suppression of the East Coast slave trade, I shall regard that as a greater matter by far than the discovery of all the Nile sources together. Now that you have done with domestic slavery for ever, lend us your powerful aid toward this great object. This fine country is blighted, as with a curse from above, in order that the slavery privileges of the petty Sultan of Zanzibar may not be infringed, and the rights of the Crown of Portugal, which are mythical, should be kept in abeyance till some future time when Africa will become another India to Portuguese slave-traders.

I conclude by again thanking you most cordially for your great generosity, and am,

Gratefully yours,

DAVID LIVINGSTONE.

To the above letter I have nothing to add—it speaks for itself; but I then thought it was the best evidence of my success. For my own part, I cared not one jot or tittle about his discoveries, except so far as it concerned the newspaper which commissioned me for the "search." It is true I felt curious as to the result of his travels; but, since he confessed that he had not completed what he had begun, I felt considerable delicacy to ask for more than he could afford to give. His discoveries were the fruits of his own labours—to him they belonged—by their publication he hoped to obtain his reward, which he desired to settle on his children. Yet Livingstone had a higher and nobler ambition than the mere pecuniary sum he would receive: he followed the dictates of duty. Never was such a willing slave to that abstract virtue. His inclinations impelled him home, the fascinations of which it required the sternest resolves to resist. With every foot of new ground he travelled over he forged a chain of sympathy which should hereafter bind the Christian nations in bonds of love and charity to the Heathen of the African tropics. If he were able to complete this chain of love—by actual discovery and description of them to embody such peoples and nations as still live in darkness, so as to attract the good and charitable of his own land to bestir themselves for their redemption and salvation—this, Livingstone would consider an ample reward.

" A delirious and fatuous enterprise, a Quixotic scheme!" some will say. Not it, my friends; for as sure as the sun shines on both Christian and Infidel, civilised and Pagan, the day of enlightenment will come; and, though Livingstone, the Apostle of Africa, may not behold it himself, nor we younger men, not yet our children, the Hereafter will see it, and posterity will recognise the daring pioneer of its civilization.

The following items are extracted in their entirety from my Diary:

March 12*th.*—The Arabs have sent me as many as forty-five letters to carry to the coast. I am turned courier in my latter days; but the reason is that no regularly organized caravans are permitted to leave Unyanyembe now, because of the war with Mirambo.

What if I had stayed all this time at Unyanyembe waiting for the war to end! It is my opinion that the Arabs will not be able to conquer Mirambo under nine months yet.

To-night the natives have gathered themselves together to give me a farewell dance in front of my house. I find them to be the pagazis of Singiri, chief of Mtesa's caravan. My men joined in, and, captivated by the music despite myself, I also struck in, and performed the "light fantastic," to the intense admiration of my braves, who were delighted to see their master unbend a little from his usual stiffness.

It is a wild dance altogether. The music is lively, and evoked from the sonorous sound of four drums, which are arranged before the bodies of four men, who stand in the centre of the weird circle. Bombay, as ever comical, never so much at home as when in the dance of the Mrima, has my water-bucket on his head ; Chowpereh— the sturdy, the nimble, sure-footed Chowpereh—has an axe in his hand, and wears a goatskin on his head ; Baraka has my bearskin, and handles a spear ; Mabruki, the "Bull-headed," has entered into the spirit of the thing, and steps up and down like a solemn elephant ; Ulimengo has a gun, and is a fierce Drawcansir, and you would imagine he was about to do battle to a hundred thousand, so ferocious is he in appearance ; Khamisi and Kamna are before the drummers, back to back, kicking up ambitiously at the stars ; Asmani,—the embodiment of giant strength, —a towering Titan,—has also a gun, with which he is dealing blows in the air, as if he were Thor, slaying myriads with his hammer. The scruples and passions of us all are in abeyance ; we are contending demons under the heavenly light of the stars, enacting only the part of a weird drama, quickened into action and movement by the appalling energy and thunder of the drums.

The warlike music is ended, and another is started. The choragus has fallen on his knees, and dips his head two or three times in an excavation in the ground, and a choir, also on their knees, repeat in dolorous tones the last words of a slow and solemn refrain. The words are literally translated :—

Choragus.   Oh-oh-oh! the white man is going home!

Choir.   Oh-oh·oh! going home!
            Going home, oh-oh-oh!

Choragus.   To the happy island on the sea,
            Where the beads are plenty, oh-oh-oh!

Choir.   Oh-oh-oh! where the beads are plenty,
            Oh-oh-oh!

Choragus.   While Singiri has kept us, oh, very long
            From our homes very long, oh-oh-oh!

Choir.   From our homes, oh-oh-oh!
            Oh-oh-oh!

Choragus.   And we have had no food for very long—
            We are half-starved, oh, for so long!
            Bana Singiri!

Choir.   For so very long, oh-oh-oh!
            Bana Singiri-Singiri!
            Singiri! oh, Singiri

Choragus.   Mirambo has gone to war
            To fight against the Arabs;
            The Arabs and Wangwana
            Have gone to fight Mirambo!

Choir.   Oh-oh-oh! to fight Mirambo!
            Oh, Mirambo! Mirambo
            Oh, to fight Mirambo!

Choragus. But the white man will make us glad,
        He is going home! For he is going home,
        And he will make us glad! Sh-sh-sh!

Choir.   The white man will make us glad! Sh-sh-sh
        Sh——sh-h-h——sh-h-h-h-h-h!
        Um-m—mu—um-m-m—sh!

This is the singular farewell which I received from the Wanyamwezi of Singiri, and for its remarkable epic beauty (?), rhythmic excellence (?), and impassioned force (?), I have immortalised it in the pages of this book, as one of the most wonderful productions of the chorus-loving children of Unyamwezi.

March 13th.—The last day of my stay with Livingstone has come and gone, and the last night we shall be together is present, and I cannot evade the morrow! I feel as though I would rebel against the fate which drives me away from him. The minutes beat fast, and grow into hours.

Our door is closed, and we are both of us busy with our own thoughts. What his thoughts are I know not. Mine are sad. My days seem to have been spent in an Elysian field; otherwise, why should I so keenly regret the near approach of the parting hour? Have I not been battered by successive fevers, prostrate with agony day after day lately? Have I not raved and stormed in madness? Have I not clenched my fists in fury, and fought with the wild strength of despair when in delirium? Yet, I regret to surrender the pleasure I have felt in this man's society, though so dearly purchased.

I cannot resist the sure advance of time, which flies this night as if it mocked me, and gloated on the misery it created! Be it so!

How many times have I not suffered the pang of parting with friends! I wished to linger longer, but the inevitable would come—Fate sundered us. This is the same regretful feeling, only it is more poignant, and the farewell may be for ever! FOR EVER? And "FOR EVER," echo the reverberations of a woful whisper.

I have noted down all he has said to-night; but the reader shall not share it with me. It is mine!

I am as jealous as he is himself of his Journal; and I have written in German text, and in round hand, on either side of it, on the waterproof canvas cover, "POSITIVELY NOT TO BE OPENED;" to which he has affixed his signature. I have stenographed every word he has said to me respecting the equable distribution of certain curiosities among his friends and children, and his last wish about "his" dear old friend, Sir Roderick Murchison, because he has been getting anxious about him ever since we received the newspapers at Ugunda, when we read that the old man was suffering from a paralytic stroke. I must be sure to send him the news, as soon as I get to Aden; and I have promised that he will receive the message from me quicker than anything was ever received in Central Africa.

" To-morrow night, Doctor, you will be alone!"

" Yes; the house will look as though a death had taken place. You had better stop until the rains, which are now near, are over."

"I would to God I could, my dear Doctor; but every day I stop here, now that there is no necessity for me to stay longer, keeps you from your work and home."

"I know; but consider your health—you are not fit to travel. What is it? Only a few weeks longer. You will travel to the coast just as quickly when the rains are over as you will by going now. The plains will be inundated between here and the coast."

"You think so; but I will reach the coast in forty days; if not in forty, I will in fifty—certain. The thought that I am doing you an important service will spur me on."

March 14th.—At dawn we were up, the bales and baggage were taken outside of the building, and the men prepared themselves for the first march towards home.

We had a sad breakfast together. I could not eat, my heart was too full; neither did my companion seem to have an appetite. We found something to do which kept us longer together. At 8 o'clock I was not gone, and I had thought to have been off at 5 A.M.

"Doctor," said I, "I will leave two men with you, who will stop to-day and to-morrow with you, for it may be that you have forgotten something in the hurry of my departure. I will halt a day at Tura, on the frontier of Unyamwezi, for your last word, and your last wish; and now we must part—there is no help for it. Good-bye."

"Oh, I am coming with you a little way. I must see you off on the road."

"Thank you. Now, my men, Home! Kirangozi, lift the flag, and MARCH!"

The house looked desolate—it faded from our view. Old times, and the memories of my aspirations and kindling hopes, came strong on me. The old hills round about, that I once thought tame and uninteresting, had become invested with histories and reminiscences for me. On that burzani I have sat hour after hour, dreaming, and hoping, and sighing. On that col I stood, watching the battle and the destruction of Tabora. Under that roof I have sickened and been delirious, and cried out like a child at the fate that threatened my mission. Under that banian tree lay my dead comrade—poor Shaw; I would have given a fortune to have had him by my side at this time. From that house I started on my journey to Ujiji; to it I returned as to a friend, with a newer and dearer companion; and now I leave all. Already it all appears like a strange dream.

We walked side by side; the men lifted their voices into a song. I took long looks at Livingstone, to impress his features thoroughly on my memory.

"The thing is, Doctor, so far as I can understand it, you do not intend to return home until you have satisfied yourself about the 'Sources of the Nile.' When you have satisfied yourself, you will come home and satisfy others. Is it not so?"

"That is it, exactly. When your men come back, I shall immediately start for Ufipa; then, crossing the Rungwa River, I shall strike south, and round the extremity of the Tanganika. Then, a south-east course will take me to Chicumbi's, on the Luapula. On crossing the Luapula, I shall go direct west to the copper-mines of Katanga. Eight days south of Katanga, the natives declare the fountains to be. When I have found them, I shall return by Katanga to the underground houses of Rua. From the caverns, ten days north-east will take me to Lake Kamolondo. I shall be able to travel from the lake, in your boat, up the River Lufira, to Lake Lincoln. Then, coming down again, I can proceed north, by the Lualaba, to the fourth lake—which, I think, will explain the whole problem; and I will probably find that it is either Chowambe (Baker's lake), or Piaggia's lake."

"And how long do you think this little journey will take you?"

"A year and a half, at the furthest, from the day I leave Unyanyembe."

"Suppose you say two years; contingencies might arise, you know. It will be well for me to hire these new men for two years; the day of their engagement to begin from their arrival at Unyanyembe."

"Yes, that will do excellently well."

"Now, my dear Doctor, the best friends must part. You have come far enough; let me beg of you to turn back."

"Well, I will say this to you: you have done what few men could do—far better than some great travellers I know. And I am grateful to you for what you have done for me. God guide you safe home, and bless you, my friend."

"And may God bring you safe back to us all, my dear friend. FAREWELL!"

"FAREWELL!"

We wrung each other's hands, and I had to tear myself away before I unmanned myself; but Susi, and Chumah, and Hamoydah—the Doctor's faithful fellows—they must all shake and kiss my hands before I could quite turn away. I betrayed myself!

"Good-bye, Doctor—dear friend!"

"Good-bye!"

The FAREWELL between Livingstone and myself had been spoken. We were parted, he to whatever fate Destiny had yet in store for him, to battling against difficulties, to many, many days of marching through wildernesses, with little or nothing much to sustain him save his own high spirit, and enduring faith in God—"who would bring all things right at last;" and I to that which Destiny may have in store for me.

But though I may live half a century longer, I shall never forget that parting scene in Central Africa. I shall never cease to think of the sad tones of that sorrowful word Farewell, how they permeated through every core of my heart, how they clouded my eyes, and made me wish unutterable things which could never be.

An audacious desire to steal one embrace from the dear old man came over me, and almost unmanned me. I felt tempted to stop with him and assist him, on his long return march to the fountain region, but these things were not to be, any more than many other impulsive wishes, and despite the intensified emotions which filled both of us, save by silent tears, and a tremulous parting word, we did not betray our stoicism of manhood and race.

I assumed a gruff voice, and ordered the Expedition to march, and I resolutely turned my face toward the eastern sky. But ever and anon my eyes would seek that deserted figure of an old man in grey clothes, who with bended head and slow steps was returning to his solitude, the very picture of melancholy, and each time I saw him— as the plain was wide and clear of obstructions—I felt my eyes stream, and my heart swell with a vague, indefinable feeling of foreboding and sorrow.

I thought of his lonely figure sitting day after day on the burzani of his house, by which all caravans from the coast would have to pass, and of the many, many times he would ask the new-comers whether they had passed any men coming along the road for him, and I thought as each day passed, and his stores and letters had not arrived now he would grieve at the lengthening delay. I then felt strong again, as I felt that so long as I should be doing service for Livingstone, I was not quite parted from him, and by doing the work effectively and speedily the bond of friendship between us would be strengthened. Such thoughts spurred me to the resolution to march so quickly for the coast, that Arabs in after time should marvel at the speed with which the white man's caravan travelled from Unyanyembe to Zanzibar.

I took one more look at him; he was standing near the gate of Kwikuru with his servants near him. I waved a handkerchief to him, as a final token of farewell, and he responded to it by lifting his cap. It was the last opportunity, for we soon surmounted the crest of a land-wave, and began the descent into the depression on the other side, and I *never* saw him more.

God grant, dear reader, that if ever you take to travelling in Central Africa, you find as good and true a man, for your companion, as I found in noble David Livingstone. For four months and four days he and I occupied the same house, or, the same tent, and I never had one feeling of resentment against him, nor did he show any against me, and the longer I lived with him the more did my admiration and reverence for him increase.

What were Livingstone's thoughts during the time which elapsed between my departure for the coast, and the arrival of his supplies, may be gathered from a letter which he wrote on the 2nd of July to Mr. John F. Webb, American Consul at Zanzibar.

I have been waiting up here like Simeon Stylites on his pillar, and counting every day, and conjecturing each step taken by our friend towards the coast, wishing and praying that no sickness might lay him up, no accident befall him, and no unlooked-for combinations of circum‧

stances render his kind intentions vain or fruitless. Mr. Stanley had got over the tendency to the continued form of fever which is the most dangerous, and was troubled only with the intermittent form, which is comparatively safe, or I would not have allowed him, but would have accompanied him to Zanzibar. I did not tell himself so; nor did I say what I thought, that he really did a very plucky thing in going through the Mirambo war in spite of the remonstrances of all the Arabs, and from Ujiji guiding me back to Unyanyembe. The war, as it is called, is still going on. The danger lay not so much in the actual fighting as in the universal lawlessness the war engendered.

I am not going to inflict on the reader a repetition of our march back, except to record certain incidents which occurred to us as we journeyed to the coast.

March 17th.—We came to the Kwalah River. The first rain of the Masika season fell on this day; I shall be mildewed before I reach the coast. Last year's Masika began at Bagamoyo, March 23rd, and ended 30th April.

The next day I halted the Expedition at Western Tura, on the Unyamwezi frontier, and on the 20th arrived at Eastern Tura; when, soon after, we heard a loud report of a gun, and Susi and Hamoydah, the Doctor's servants, with Uredi, and another of my men, appeared with a letter for " Sir Thomas MacLear, Observatory, Cape of Good Hope," and one for myself, which read as follows :—

KWIHARA, March 15, 1872.

.DEAR STANLEY,

If you can telegraph on your arrival in London, be particular, please, to say how Sir Roderick is. You put the matter exactly yesterday, when you said that I was "not yet satisfied about the Sources; but as soon as I shall be satisfied, I shall return and give satisfactory reasons fit for other people." This is just as it stands.

I wish I could give you a better word than the Scotch one to "put a stout heart to a stey brae"—(a steep ascent)—for you will do that ; and I am thankful that, before going away, the fever had changed into the

Intermittent, or safe form. I would not have let you go, but with great concern, had you still been troubled with the continued type. I feel comfortable in commending you to the guardianship of the good Lord and Father of all.

I am gratefully yours,
DAVID LIVINGSTONE.

I have worked as hard as I could copying observations made in one line of march from Kabuire, back again to Cazembe, and on to Lake Bangweolo, and am quite tired out. My large figures fill six sheets of foolscap, and many a day will elapse ere I take to copying again. I did my duty when ill at Ujiji in 1869, and am not to blame, though they grope a little in the dark at home. Some Arab letters have come, and I forward them to you. D. L.

March 16, 1872.

P.S.—I have written a note this morning to Mr. Murray, 50, Albemarle Street, the publisher, to help you, if necessary, in sending the Journal by book post, or otherwise, to Agnes. If you call on him you will find him a frank gentleman. A pleasant journey to you.

DAVID LIVINGSTONE.

To HENRY M. STANLEY, Esq.,
 Wherever he may be found.

Several Wangwana arrived at Tura to join our returning Expedition, as they were afraid to pass through Ugogo by themselves; others were reported coming; but as all were sufficiently warned at Unyanyembe that the departure of the caravan would take place positively on the 14th, I was not disposed to wait longer.

As we were leaving Tura, on the 21st, Susi and Hamoydah were sent back to the Doctor, with last words from me, while we continued our march to Nghwhalah River.

Two days afterwards we arrived before the village of

Ngaraisa, into which the head of the caravan attempted to enter, but the angry Wakimbu forcibly ejected them.

On the 24th, we encamped in the jungle, in what is called the " tongoni," or clearing.

This region was at one period in a most flourishing state; the soil is exceedingly fertile; the timber is large, and would be valuable near the coast; and, what is highly appreciated in Africa, there is an abundance of water. We camped near a smooth, broad hump of syenite, at one end of which rose, upright and grand, a massive square rock, which towered above several small trees in the vicinity; at the other end stood up another singular rock, which was loosened at the base.

The members of the Expedition made use of the great sheet of rock to grind their grain; a common proceeding in these lands where villages are not near, or when the people are hostile.

On the 27th of March we entered Kiwyeh. At dawn, when leaving Mdaburu River, the solemn warning had been given that we were about entering Ugogo; and as we left Kaniyaga village, with trumpet-like blasts of the guide's horn, we filed into the depths of an expanse of rustling Indian corn. The ears were ripe enough for parching and roasting, and thus was one anxiety dispelled by its appearance; for generally, in early March, caravans suffer from famine, which overtakes both natives and strangers.

We soon entered the gum-tree districts, and we knew we were in Ugogo. The forests of this country are chiefly composed of the gum and thorn species—mimosa and tamarisk, with often a variety of wild fruit trees. The grapes were plentiful, though they were not quite ripe; and there was also a round, reddish fruit with the sweetness of the Sultana grape, with leaves like a goose-berry-bush. There was another about the size of an apricot, which was excessively bitter.

Emerging from the entangled thorn jungle, the extensive settlements of Kiwyoh came into view; and to the east of the chief's village we found a camping place under the shade of a group of colossal baobab.

We had barely encamped when we heard the booming, bellowing war horns sounding everywhere, and we espied messengers darting swiftly in every direction giving the alarm of war. When first informed that the horns were calling the people to arm themselves, and prepare for war, I half suspected that an attack was about to be made on the Expedition; but the words "Urugu, warugu"— (thief! thieves!)—bandied about, declared the cause. Mukondoku, the chief of the populous district two days to the north-east, where we experienced some excitement when westward-bound, was marching to attack the young Mtemi, Kiwyeh, and Kiwyeh's soldiers were called to the fight. The men rushed to their villages, and in a short time we saw them arrayed in full fighting costume. Feathers of the ostrich and the eagle waved over their fronts, or the mane of the zebra surrounded their heads; their knees and ankles were hung with little bells; joho robes floated behind, from their necks; spears, assegais, knob-sticks, and bows were flourished over their heads, or held in their right hands, as if ready for hurling. On each flank of a large body which issued from the principal village, and which came at a uniform swinging double-quick, the ankle and knee bells all chiming in admirable unison, were a cloud of skirmishers, consisting of the most enthusiastic, who exercised themselves in mimic war as they sped along. Column after column, companies, and groups from every village hurried on past our camp until, probably, there were nearly a thousand soldiers gone to the war. This scene gave me a better idea than anything else of the weakness of even the largest caravans which travelled between Zanzibar and Unyanyembe.

At night the warriors returned from the forest; the alarm proved to be without foundation. At first it was generally reported that the invaders were Wahehe, or the Wadirigo, as that tribe are scornfully called from their thieving propensities. The Wahehe frequently make a foray upon the fat cattle of Ugogo. They travel from their own country in the south-east, and advance through the jungle, and when about to approach the herds, stoop down, covering their bodies with their shields of bull-hide. Having arrived between the cattle and the herdsmen, they suddenly rise up and begin to switch the cattle heartily, and, having started them off into the jungle in the care of men already detailed for the work, they turn about, and plant their shields before them, to fight the aroused shepherds.

On the 30th we arrived at Khonze, which is remarkable for the mighty globes of foliage which the giant syca-mores and baobabs put forth above the plain. The chief of Khonze boasts of four tembes, out of which he could muster in the aggregate fifty armed men; yet this fellow, instigated by the Wanyamwezi residents, prepared to resist our advance, because I only sent him three doti—twelve yards of cloth—as honga.

We were halted, waiting the return of a few friendly Wagogo travellers who had joined us, and who were asked to assist Bombay in the negotiation of the tribute, when the Wagogo returned to us at breathless speed, and shouted out to me, "Why do you halt here? Do you wish to die? These pagans will not take the tribute, but they boast that they will eat up all your cloth."

The renegade Wanyamwezi who had married into Wagogo families were always our bane in this country. As the chief of Khonze came up I ordered the men to load their guns, and I loaded my own ostentatiously in his presence, and then strode up to him, and asked if he had come to take the cloth by force, or if he were going to accept quietly what I would give him. As the Mnyamwezi who caused this show of hostilities was beginning to speak, I caught him by the throat, and threatened to make his nose flatter if he attempted to speak again in my presence, and to shoot him first, if we should be forced to fight. The rascal was then pushed away into the rear. The chief, who was highly amused with this proceeding, laughed loudly at the discomfiture of the parasite, and in a short time he and I had settled the tribute to our mutual satisfaction, and we parted great friends. The Expedition arrived at Sanza that night.

On the 31st we came to Kanyenyi, to the great Mtemi —Magomba's—whose son and heir is Mtundu M'gondeh. As we passed by the tembe of the great Sultan, the msagira, or chief counsellor, a pleasant grey-haired man, was at work making a thorn fence around a patch of young corn. He greeted the caravan with a sonorous " Yambo," and, putting himself at its head, he led the way to our camp. When introduced to me he was very cordial in his manner. He was offered a kiti—stool—and began to talk very affably. He remembered my predecessors, Burton, Speke, and Grant, very well; declared me to be much younger than any of them; and, recol-

lecting that one of the white men used to drink asses'
milk (Burton?), offered to procure me some. The way I
drank it seemed to give him very great satisfaction.

His son, Unamapokera, was a tall man of thirty or
thereabouts, and he conceived a great friendship for me,
and promised that the tribute should be very light, and
that he would send a man to show me the way to Myumi,

UNAMAPOKERA.

which was a village on the frontier of Kanyenyi, by
which I would be enabled to avoid the rapacious Kisewah,
who was in the habit of enforcing large tribute from
caravans.

With the aid of Unamapokera and his father, we contrived to be mulcted very lightly, for we only paid ten doti, while Burton was compelled to pay sixty doti or two hundred and forty yards of cloth.

On the 1st of April, rising early, we reached Myumi after a four hours' march; then plunged into the jungle, and, about 2 P.M., arrived at a large ziwa, or pond, situate in the middle of a jungle; and on the next day, at 10 A.M., reached the fields of Mapanga. We were passing the village of Mapanga to a resting-place beyond the village, where we might breakfast and settle the honga, when a lad rushed forward to meet us, and asked us where we were going. Having received a reply that we were going to a camping-place, he hastened on ahead, and presently we heard him talking to some men in a field on our right.

In the meantime, we had found a comfortable shady place, and had come to a halt; the men were reclining on the ground, or standing up near their respective loads; Bombay was about opening a bale, when we heard a great rush of men, and loud shouts, and, immediately after, out rushed from the jungle near by a body of forty or fifty armed men, who held their spears above their heads, or were about to draw their bows, with a chief at their head, all uttering such howls of rage as only savages can, which sounded like a long-drawn "Hhaat-uh—Hhaat—uhh-uhh," which meant, unmistakably, "You will, will you? No, you will not!"—at once determined, defiant, and menacing.

I had suspected that the voices I heard boded no good to us, and I had accordingly prepared my weapons and cartridges. Verily, what a fine chance for adventure this was! One spear flung at us, or one shot fired into this minatory mob of savages, and the opposing bands had been plunged into a fatal conflict! There would have been no order of battle, no pomp of war, but a murderous strife, a quick firing of breech-loaders, and volleys from flint-lock muskets, mixed with the flying of spears and twanging of bows, the cowardly running away at once, pursued by yelping savages; and who knows how it all would have terminated? Forty spears against forty guns —but how many guns would not have decamped? Perhaps all, and I should have been left with my boy gun-bearers to have my jugular deliberately severed, or to be decapitated, leaving my head to adorn a tall pole in the centre of a Kigogo village, like poor Monsieur Maizan's at Dege la Mhora, in Uzaramo. Happy end of an Expedition! And the Doctor's Journal lost for ever—the fruits of six years' labor!

But in this land it will not do to fight unless driven to the very last extremity. No belligerent Mungo Park can be successful in Ugogo unless he has a sufficient force of men with him. With five hundred Europeans one could traverse Africa from north to south, by tact, and the moral effect that such a force would inspire. Very little fighting would be required.

Without rising from the bale on which I was seated, I requested the kirangozi to demand an explanation of their furious hubbub and threatening aspect;—if they were come to rob us.

"No," said the chief; "we do not want to stop the road, or to rob you; but we want the tribute."

"But don't you see us halted, and the bale opened to send it to you? We have come so far from your village that after the tribute is settled we can proceed on our way, as the day is yet young."

The chief burst into a loud laugh, and was joined by

ourselves. He evidently felt ashamed of his conduct for he voluntarily offered the explanation, that as he and his men were cutting wood to make a new fence for his village, a lad came up to him, and said that a caravan of Wang-wana were about passing through the country without stopping to explain who they were. We were soon very good friends. He begged of me to make rain for him, as his crops were suffering, and no rain had fallen for months. I told him that though white people were very great and clever people, much superior to the Arabs, yet we could not make rain. Though very much disappointed, he did not doubt my statement, and after receiving his honga, which was very light, he permitted us to go on our way, and even accompanied us some distance to show us the road.

At 3 P.M. we entered a thorny jungle; and by 5 P.M. we had arrived at Muhalata, a district lorded over by the chief Nyamzaga. A Mgogo, of whom I made a friend, proved very stanch. He belonged to Mulowa, a country to the S.S.E., and south of Kulabi; and was active in promoting my interests by settling the tribute, with the assistance of Bombay, for me. When, on the next day, we passed through Kulabi on our way to Mvumi, and the Wagogo were about to stop us for the honga, he took upon himself the task of relieving us from further toll, by stating we were from Ugogo or Kanyenyi. The chief simply nodded his head, and we passed on. It seems that the Wagogo do not exact blackmail of those caravans who intend only to trade in their own country, or have no intention of passing beyond their own frontier.

Leaving Kulabi, we traversed a naked, red, loamy plain, over which the wind from the heights of Usagara, now rising a bluish-black jumble of mountains in our front, howled most fearfully. With clear, keen, incisive force, the terrible blasts seemed to penetrate through and through our bodies, as though we were but filmy gauze. Manfully battling against this mighty "peppo"—storm— we passed through Mukamwa's, and crossing a broad sandy bed of a stream, we entered the territory of Mvumi, the last tribute-levying chief of Ugogo.

The 4th of April, after sending Bombay and my friendly Mgogo with eight doti, or thirty-two yards of cloth, as a farewell tribute to the Sultan, we struck off through the jungle, and in five hours we were on the borders of the wilderness of "Marenga Mkali"—the "hard," bitter or brackish, water.

From our camp I despatched three men to Zanzibar with letters to the American Consul, and telegraphic despatches for the 'Herald,' with a request to the Consul that he would send the men back with a small case or two containing such luxuries as hungry, worn-out, and mildewed men would appreciate. The three messengers were charged not to halt for anything—rain or no rain, river or inundation—as if they did not hurry up we should catch them before they reached the coast. With a fervent " Inshallah, bana," they departed.

On the 5th, with a loud, vigorous, cheery "Hurrah!" we plunged into the depths of the wilderness, which, with its eternal silence and solitude, was far preferable to the jarring, inharmonious discord of the villages of the Wagogo. For nine hours we held on our way, starting with noisy shouts the fierce rhinoceros, the timid quagga, and the herds of antelopes which crowd the jungles of this broad salina. On the 7th, amid a pelting rain, we entered Mpwapwa, where my Scotch assistant, Farquhar, died.

We had performed the extraordinary march of 338

English statute miles from the 14th of March to the 7th of April, or within twenty-four days, inclusive of halts, which was a little over fourteen miles a day.

Leukole, the chief of Mpwapwa, with whom I left Farquhar, gave the following account of the death of the latter :—

" The white man seemed to be improving after you left him, until the fifth day, when, while attempting to rise and walk out of his tent, he fell back ; from that minute he got worse and worse, and in the afternoon he died, like one going to sleep. His legs and abdomen had swollen considerably, and something, I think, broke within him when he fell, for he cried out like a man who was very much hurt, and his servant said, ' The master says he is dying.'

" We had him carried out under a large tree, and after covering him with leaves, there left him. His servant took possession of his things, his rifle, clothes, and blanket, and moved off to the tembe of a Mnyamwezi, near Kisokweh, where he lived for three months, when he also died. Before he died he sold his master's rifle to an Arab going to Unyanyembe for ten doti (forty yards of cloth). That is all I know about it."

He subsequently showed me the hollow into which the dead body of Farquhar was thrown, but I could not find a vestige of his bones, though we looked sharply about that we might make a decent grave for them. Before we left Unyanyembe fifty men were employed two days carrying rocks, with which I built up a solid enduring pile around Shaw's grave, eight feet long and five feet broad, which Dr. Livingstone said would last hundreds of years, as the grave of the first white man who died in Unyamwezi. But though we could not discover any remains of the unfortunate Farquhar, we collected a large quantity of stones, and managed to raise a mound near the banks of the stream to commemorate the spot where his body was laid.

It was not until we had entered the valley of the Mukondokwa River that we experienced anything like privation or hardship from the Masika. Here the torrents thundered and roared; the river was a mighty brown flood, sweeping downward with an almost resistless flow. The banks were brimful, and broad nullahs were full of water, and the fields were inundated, and still the rain came surging down in a shower, that warned us of what we might expect during our transit of the seacoast region. Still we urged our steps onward like men to whom every moment was precious—as if a deluge was overtaking us. Three times we crossed this awful flood at the fords by means of ropes tied to trees from bank to bank, and arrived at Kadetamare on the 11th, a most miserable, most woe-begone set of human beings; and camped on a hill opposite Mount Kibwe, which rose on the right of the river—one of the tallest peaks of the range.

On the 12th of April, after six hours of the weariest march I had ever undergone, we arrived at the mouth of the Mukondokwa Pass, out of which the river debouches into the Plain of Makata. We knew that it was an unusual season, for the condition of the country, though bad enough the year before, was as nothing compared to this year. Close to the edge of the foaming, angry flood lay our route, dipping down frequently into deep ditches, wherein we found ourselves sometimes up to the waist in water, and sometimes up to the throat. Urgent necessity impelled us onward, lest we might have to camp at one of these villages until the end of the monsoon rains; so we kept on, over marshy bottoms, up to the knees in mire, under jungly tunnels dripping with wet, then into sloughs arm-pit deep. Every channel seemed filled to overflowing, yet down the rain poured, beating the surface of the river into yellowish foam, pelting us until we were almost breathless. Half a day's battling against such difficulties brought us, after crossing the river, once again to the dismal village of Mvumi.

We passed the night fighting swarms of black and voracious mosquitoes, and in heroic endeavours to win repose in sleep, in which we were partly successful, owing to the utter weariness of our bodies.

On the 13th we struck out of the village of Mvumi. It had rained the whole night, and the morning brought no cessation. Mile after mile we traversed, over fields covered by the inundation, until we came to a branch river-side once again, where the river was narrow, and too deep to ford in the middle. We proceeded to cut a tree down, and so contrived that it should fall right across the stream. Over this fallen tree the men, bestriding it, cautiously moved before them their bales and boxes; but one young fellow, Rojab—through over-zeal, or in sheer madness—took up the Doctor's box which contained his letters and Journal of his discoveries on his head, and started into the river. I had been the first to arrive on the opposite bank, in order to superintend the crossing, when I caught sight of this man walking in the river with the most precious box of all on his head. Suddenly he fell into a deep hole, and the man and box went almost out of sight, while I was in an agony at the fate which threatened the despatches. Fortunately, he recovered himself and stood up, while I shouted to him, with a loaded revolver pointed at his head, "Look out! Drop that box, and I'll shoot you."

All the men halted in their work while they gazed at their comrade who was thus imperilled by bullet and flood. The man himself seemed to regard the pistol with the greatest awe, and after a few desperate efforts succeeded in getting the box safely ashore. As the articles within were not damaged, Rojab escaped punishment, with a caution not to touch the box again on any account, and it was transferred to the keeping of the sure-footed and perfect pagazi, Maganga.

From this stream, in about an hour, we came to the main river, but one look at its wild waters was enough. We worked hard to construct a raft, but after cutting down four trees and lashing the green logs together, and pushing them into the whirling current, we saw them sink like lead. We then tied together all the strong rope in our possession, and made a line 180 feet long, with one end of which tied round his body, Chowpereh was sent across to lash it to a tree. He was carried far down the stream, but being an excellent swimmer, he succeeded in his attempt. The bales were lashed around the middle, and, heaved into the stream, were dragged through the river to the opposite bank, as well as the tent, and such things as could not be injured much by the water. Several of the men, as well as myself, were also dragged through the water; each of the boys being attended by the best swimmers; but when we came to the letter-boxes and valuables, we could suggest no means to take them over. Two camps were accordingly made, one on each side of the stream; the one on the bank which I had just left occupying an ant-hill of considerable height; while my party had to content itself with a flat, miry

"LOOK OUT, YOU DROP THAT BOX—I'LL SHOOT YOU."

marsh. An embankment of soil, nearly a foot high, was thrown up in a circle thirty feet in diameter, in the centre of which my tent was pitched, and around it booths were erected.

It was an extraordinary and novel position that we found ourselves in. Within twenty feet of our camp was a rising river, with flat, low banks; above us was a gloomy, weeping sky; surrounding us on three sides was an immense forest, on whose branches we heard the constant, pattering rain; beneath our feet was a great depth of mud, black and loathsome; add to these the thought that the river might overflow, and sweep us to utter destruction.

In the morning the river was still rising, and an inevitable doom seemed to hang over us. There was yet time to act—to bring over the people, with the most valuable effects of the Expedition—as I considered Dr. Livingstone's Journal and letters, and my own papers, of far greater value than anything else. While looking at the awful river an idea struck me that I might possibly carry the boxes across, one at a time, by cutting two slender poles, and tying cross sticks to them, making a kind of hand-barrow, on which a box might rest when lashed to it. Two men swimming across, at the same time holding on to the rope, with the ends of the poles resting on the men's shoulders, I thought, would be enabled to convey over a 70 lb. box with ease. In a short time one of these was made, and six couples of the strongest swimmers were prepared, and stimulated with a rousing glass of stiff grog each man, with a promise of cloth to each also if they succeeded in getting everything ashore undamaged by the water. When I saw with what ease they dragged themselves across, the barrow on their shoulders, I wondered that I had not thought of the plan before. Within an hour of the first couple had gone over, the entire Expedition was safe on the eastern bank ; and at once breaking camp, we marched north through the swampy forest which in some places was covered with four feet of water. Seven hours' constant splashing brought us to Rehenneko, after experiencing several queer accidents. We were now on the verge only of the inundated plain of the Makata, which, even with the last year's rain, was too horrible to think of undertaking again in cold blood.

We were encamped ten days on a hill near Rehenneko, or until the 25th, when, the rain having entirely ceased, we resolved to attempt the crossing of the Makata. The bales of cloth had all been distributed as presents to the men for their work, except a small quantity which I retained for the food of my own mess.

But we should have waited a month longer, for the inundation had not abated four inches. However, after we once struggled up to our necks in water it was useless to turn back. For two marches of eight hours each we plunged through slush, mire, deep sloughs, water up to our necks, and muddy cataclysms, swam across nullahs, waded across gullies, and near sunset of the second day arrived on the banks of the Makata River. My people are not likely to forget that night; not one of them was able to sleep until it was long past midnight, because of the clouds of mosquitoes, which threatened to eat us all up ; and when the horn sounded for the march of another day, there was not one dissentient amongst them.

It was 5 A.M. when we began the crossing of the Makata River, but beyond it for six miles stretched one long lake, the waters of which flowed gently towards the Wami. This was the confluence of the streams : four rivers were here gathered into one. The natives of Kigongo warned us not to attempt it, as the water was over our heads; but I had only to give a hint to the men, and we set on our way. Even the water—we were getting quite amphibious—was better than the horrible filth and piles of decaying vegetation which were swept against the boma of the village.

We were soon up to our armpits, then the water shallowed to the knee, then we stepped up to the neck, and waded on tiptoe, supporting the children above the water; and the same experiences occurred as those which we suffered the day before, until we were halted on the edge of the Little Makata, which raced along at the rate of eight knots an hour; but it was only fifty yards wide, and beyond it rose a high bank, and dry park-lands which extended as far as Simbo. We had no other option than to swim it; but it was a slow operation, the current was so swift and strong. Activity and zeal, high rewards, presents of money, backed by the lively feeling that we were nearing home, worked wonders, and in a couple of hours we were beyond the Makata.

Cheery and hopeful, we sped along the dry, smooth path that now lay before us, with the ardor and vivacity of heroes, and the ease and power of veterans. We rolled three ordinary marches into one that day, and long before night arrived at Simbo.

On the 29th we crossed the Ungerengeri, and as we came to Simbamwenni—the "Lion City" of Useguhha —lo! what a change! The flooded river had swept the entire front wall of the strongly-walled city away, and about fifty houses had been destroyed by the torrent. Villages of Waruguru, on the slopes of the Uruguru Mountains—Mkambaku range—had also suffered disastrously. If one-fourth of the reports we heard were true, at least a hundred people must have perished.

The Sultana had fled, and the stronghold of Kisabengo was no more! A deep canal that he had caused to be excavated when alive, to bring a branch of the Ungerengeri near his city—which was his glory and boast—proved the ruin of Simbamwenni. After the destruction of the place the river had formed a new bed, about 300 yards from the city. But what astonished us most were the masses of débris which seemed to be piled everywhere, and the great numbers of trees that were prostrate; and they all seemed to lie in the same direction, as if a strong wind had come from the south-west. The aspect of the Ungerengeri valley was completely changed—from a Paradise it was converted into a howling waste.

We continued our march until we reached Ulagalla, and it was evident, as we advanced, that an unusual storm had passed over the land, for the trees in some places seemed to lie in swathes.

A most fatiguing and long march brought us to Mussoudi, on the eastern bank of the Ungerengeri; but long before we reached it we realized that a terrific destruction of human life and property had occurred. The extent and nature of the calamity may be imagined, when I state that nearly ONE HUNDRED VILLAGES, according to Mussoudi's report, were swept away.

Mussoudi, the Diwan, says that the inhabitants had gone to rest as usual—as they had done ever since he had settled in the valley, twenty-five years ago—when, in the middle of the night, they heard a roar like many thunders, which woke them up to the fact that death was at work in the shape of an enormous volume of water, that, like a wall, came down, tearing the tallest trees

with it, carrying away scores of villages at one fell, sure
swoop into utter destruction. The scene six days after
the event—when the river has subsided into its normal
breadth and depth during the monsoons—is simply awful.
Wherever we look, we find something very suggestive of
the devastation that has visited the country; fields of
corn are covered with many feet of sand and débris; the
sandy bed the river has deserted is about a mile wide;
and there are but three villages standing of all that I
noticed when *en route* to Unyanyembe. When I asked
Mussoudi where the people had gone to, he replied, "God
has taken most of them, but some have gone to Udoe."
The surest blow ever struck at the tribe of the Wakami
was indeed given by the hand of God; and, to use the
words of the Diwan, "God's power is wonderful, and who
can resist Him!"

I again resort to my Diary, and extract the following:

April 30th.—Passing Msuwa, we travelled hurriedly
through the jungle which saw such hard work with us
when going to Unyanyembe. What dreadful odors and
indescribable loathing this jungle produces! It is so
dense that a tiger could not crawl through it; it is so
impenetrable that an elephant could not force his way!
Were a bottleful of concentrated miasma, such as we inhale
herein, collected, what a deadly poison, instantaneous in
its action, undiscoverable in its properties, would it be!
I think it would act quicker than chloroform, be as fatal
as prussic acid.

Horrors upon horrors are in it. Boas above our heads,
snakes and scorpions under our feet. Land-crabs, terra-
pins, and iguanas move about in our vicinity. Malaria
is in the air we breathe; the road is infested with "hot-
water" ants, which bite our legs until we dance and

squirm about like madmen. Yet, somehow, we are fortunate enough to escape annihilation, and many another traveller might also. Yet here, in verity, are the ten plagues of Egypt, through which a traveller in these regions must run the gauntlet:

1. Plague of boas.
2. Red ants, or "hot-water."
3 Scorpions.
4. Thorns and spear cacti.
5. Numerous impediments.
6. Black mud knee-deep.
7. Suffocation from the density of the jungle.
8. Stench.
9. Thorns in the road.
10. Miasma.

May 1st. Kingaru Hera.—We heard news of a great storm having raged at Zanzibar, which has destroyed every house and every ship,—so the story runs;—and the same destruction has visited Bagamoyo and Whinde, they say. But I am by this time pretty well acquainted with the exaggerative tendency of the African. It is possible that serious loss has been sustained, from the evidences of the effects of the storm in the interior. I hear, also, that there are white men at Bagamoyo, who are about starting into the country to look after me (?). Who would look after me, I cannot imagine. I think they must have some confused idea of my Expedition; though, how they came to know that I was looking for any man I cannot conceive, because I never told a soul until I reached Unyanyembe.

May 2nd. Rosako.—I had barely arrived at the village before the three men I despatched from Mvumi, Ugogo, entered, bringing with them from the generous American Consul a few bottles of champagne, a few pots of jam, and two boxes of Boston crackers. These were most welcome after my terrible experiences in the Makata Valley. Inside one of these boxes, carefully put up by the Consul, were four numbers of the 'Herald; one of which contained my correspondence from Unyanyembe, wherein were some curious typographical errors, especially in figures and African names. I suppose my writing was wretched, owing to my weakness. In another are several extracts from various newspapers, in which I learn that many editors regard the Expedition into Africa as a myth Alas! it has been a terrible, earnest fact with me; nothing but hard, conscientious work, privation, sickness, and almost death. Eighteen men have paid the forfeit of their lives in the undertaking. It certainly is not a myth— the death of my two white assistants; they, poor fellows, found their fate in the inhospitable regions of the interior.

One of my letters received from Zanzibar by my messengers states that there is an expedition at Bagamoyo called the "Livingstone Search and Relief Expedition." What will the leaders of it do now? Livingstone is found and relieved already. Livingstone says he requires nothing more. It is a misfortune that they did not start earlier; then they might with propriety proceed, and be welcomed.

May 4th.—Arrived at Kingwere's Ferry, but we were unable to attract the attention of the canoe paddler. Between our camp and Bagamoyo we have an inundated plain that is at least four miles broad. The ferrying of our Expedition across this broad watery waste will occupy considerable time.

May 5th.—Kingwere, the canoe proprietor, came about 11 A.M. from his village at Gongoni, beyond the watery plain. By his movements I am fain to believe him to be a descendant of some dusky King Log, for I have never seen in all this land the attributes and peculiarities of that royal personage so faithfully illustrated as in Kingwere. He brought two canoes with him, short, cranky things, in which only twelve of us could embark at a time. It was 3 o'clock in the afternoon before we arrived at Gongoni village.

May 6th.—After impressing Kingwere with the urgent necessity of quick action on his part, with a promise of an extra five-dollar gold piece, I had the satisfaction to behold the last man reach my camp at 3.30 P.M.

An hour later, and we are *en route*, at a pace that I never saw equalled at any time by my caravan. Every man's feelings are intensified, for there is an animated, nay, headlong, impetuosity about their movements that indicates but too well what is going on in their minds. Surely, my own are a faithful index to their feelings; and I do not feel a whit too proud to acknowledge the great joy that possesses me. I feel proud to think that I have been successful; but, honestly, I do not feel so elated at that as at the hope that to-morrow I shall sit before a table bounteous with the good things of this life. How I will glory in the hams, and potatoes, and good bread! What a deplorable state of mind, is it not? Ah, my friend, wait till you are reduced to a skeleton by gaunt famine and coarse, loathsome food—until you have waded a Makata swamp, and marched 525 miles in thirty-five days through such weather as we have had—then you will think such pabula, food fit for gods!

Happy are we that,—after completing our mission, after the hurry and worry of the march, after the anxiety and vexation suffered from fractious tribes, after tramping for the last fifteen days through mire and Stygian marsh, —we near Beulah's peace and rest! Can we do otherwise than express our happiness by firing away gunpowder until our horns are emptied—than shout our "hurrahs" until we are hoarse—than, with the hearty, soul-inspiring

" Yambos," greet every mother's son fresh from the sea? Not so, think the Wangwana soldiers; and I so sympathize with them that I permit them to act their maddest without censure.

At sunset we enter the town of Bagamoyo. " More pilgrims come to town," were the words heard in Beulah. " The white man has come to town," were the words we heard in Bagamoyo. And we shall cross the water tomorrow to Zanzibar, and shall enter the golden gate; we shall see nothing, smell nothing, taste nothing that is offensive to the stomach any more!

The kirangozi blows his horn, and gives forth blasts potential as Astolpho's, as the natives and Arabs throng around us. And that bright flag, whose stars have waved over the waters of the great lake in Central Africa, which promised relief to the harassed Livingstone when in distress at Ujiji, returns to the sea once again—torn, it is true, but not dishonoured—tattered, but not disgraced.

As we reached the middle of the town, I saw on the steps of a large white house a white man, in flannels and helmet similar to that I wore. I thought myself rather akin to white men in general, and I walked up to him. He advanced towards me, and we shook hands—did everything but embrace.

" Won't you walk in?" said he.

" Thanks."

" What will you have to drink—beer, stout, brandy? Eh, by George! I congratulate you on your splendid success," said he, impetuously.

I knew him immediately. He was an Englishman. He was Lieut. William Henn, R.N., chief of the Livingstone Search and Relief Expedition, about to be despatched by the Royal Geographical Society to find and relieve Livingstone. The former chief, as the Expedition was at first organized, was Lieut. Llewellyn S. Dawson, who, as soon as he heard from my men that I had found Livingstone, had crossed over to Zanzibar, and, after consultation with Dr. John Kirk, had resigned. He had now nothing further to do with it, the command having formally devolved on Lieut. Henn. A Mr. Charles New, also, missionary from Mombasah, had joined the expedition, but he had resigned too. So now there were left but Lieut. Henn and Mr. Oswell Livingstone, second son of the Doctor.

"Is Mr. Oswell Livingstone here?" I asked, with considerable surprise.

"Yes; he will be here directly."

"What are you going to do now?" I asked.

"I don't think it worth my while to go now. You have taken the wind out of our sails completely. If you have relieved him, I don't see the use of my going. Do you?"

"Well, it depends. You know your own orders best. If you have come only to find and relieve him, I can tell you truly he is found and relieved, and that he wants nothing more than a few canned meats, and some other little things which I dare say you have not got. I have his list in his own handwriting with me. But his son must go anyhow, and I can get men easily enough for him."

"Well, if he is relieved, it is of no use my going."

* * * * * *

At this time in walked a slight, young, gentlemanly man, with light complexion, light hair, dark, lustrous eyes, who was introduced to me as Mr. Oswell Livingstone. The introduction was hardly necessary, for in his features there was much of what were the specialities of his father. There was an air of quiet resolution about him, and in the greeting which he gave me he exhibited rather a reticent character; but I attributed that to a receptive nature, which augured well for the future.

"I was telling Lieut. Henn that, whether he goes or not, you must go to your father, Mr. Livingstone."

"Oh, I mean to go."

"Yes, that's right. I will furnish you with men and what stores your father needs. My men will take you to Unyanyembe without any difficulty. They know the road well, and that is a great advantage. They know how to deal with the negro chiefs, and you will have no need to trouble your head about them, but march. The great thing that is required is speed. Your father will be waiting for the things."

"I will march them fast enough, if that is all."

"Oh, they will be going up light, and they can easily make long marches."

It was settled, then. Henn made up his mind that, as the Doctor had been relieved, he was not wanted; but, before formally resigning, he intended to consult with Dr. Kirk, and for that purpose he would cross over to Zanzibar the next day with the 'Herald' Expedition.

At 2 A.M. I retired to sleep on a comfortable bed. There was a great smell of newness about certain articles in the bedroom, such as haversacks, knapsacks, portmanteaus, leather gun-cases, &c. Evidently the new Expedition had some crudities about it; but a journey into the interior would soon have lessened the stock of superfluities, which all new men at first load themselves with.

Ah! what a sigh of relief was that I gave, as I threw myself on my bed, at the thought that, "Thank God! my marching was ended."

CHAPTER XVI.

At 5 P.M., on the 7th of May, 1872, the dhow which conveyed my Expedition back to Zanzibar arrived in the harbor, and the men, delighted to find themselves once more so near their homes, fired volley after volley, the American flag was hoisted up, and we soon saw the house-roofs and wharves lined with spectators, many of whom were Europeans, with glasses levelled at us.

We drew ashore slowly ; but a boat putting off to take us to land, we stepped into it, and I was soon in presence of my friend the Consul, who heartily welcomed me back to Zanzibar; and soon after was introduced to the Rev. Charles New, who was but a day or two previous to my arrival an important member of the English Search Expedition—a small, slight man in appearance, who, though he looked weakly, had a fund of energy or ner-vousness in him which was almost too great for such a body. He also heartily congratulated me.

After a bounteous dinner, to which I did justice in a manner that astonished my new friends, Lieut. Dawson called to see me, and said :

"Mr. Stanley, let me congratulate you, sir."

Lieut. Dawson then went on to state how he envied me my success ; how I had "taken the wind out of his sails"

(a nautical phrase similar to that used by Lieut. Henn);
how, when he heard from my men that Dr. Livingstone
had been found, he at once crossed over from Bagamoyo to
Zanzibar, and, after a short talk with Dr. Kirk, at once
resigned.

"But do you not think, Mr. Dawson, you have been
rather too hasty in tendering your resignation, from the
mere verbal report of my men?"

"Perhaps," said he; "but I heard that Mr. Webb had
received a letter from you, and that you and Livingstone
had discovered that the Rusizi ran into the lake—that
you had the Doctor's letters and despatches with you."

"Yes; but you acquired all this information from my
men; you have seen nothing yourself. You have therefore
resigned before you had personal evidence of the fact."

"Well, Dr. Livingstone is relieved and found, as Mr.
Henn tells me, is he not?"

"Yes, that is true enough. He is well supplied; he
only requires a few little luxuries, which I am going to
send him by an expedition of fifty freemen. Dr. Livingstone is found and relieved, most certainly; and I have
all the letters and despatches which he could possibly
send to his friends."

"But don't you think I did perfectly right?"

"Hardly—though, perhaps, it would come to the same
thing in the end. Any more cloth and beads than he has
already would be an incumbrance. Still, you have your
orders from the Royal Geographical Society. I have not
seen those yet, and I am not prepared to judge what your
best course would have been. But I think you did wrong
in resigning before you saw me; for then you would have
had, probably, a legitimate excuse for resigning. I should
have held on to the Expedition until I had consulted with

those who sent me; though, in such an event as this, the order would be, perhaps, to 'Come home.'"

"As it has turned out, though, don't you think I did right?"

"Most certainly it would be useless for you to go to search for and relieve Livingstone now, because he has already been sought, found, and relieved; but perhaps you had other orders."

"Only, if I went into the country, I was then to direct my attention to exploration; but the primary object having been forestalled by you, I am compelled to return home. The Admiralty granted me leave of absence only for the search, and never said anything about exploration."

That evening I despatched a boy over to the English Consulate with letters from the great traveller for Dr. Kirk and Mr. Oswell Livingstone.

I was greeted warmly by the American and German residents, who could not have shown warmer feeling than if Dr. Livingstone had been a near and dear relation of their own. Capt. H. A. Fraser and Dr. James Christie were also loud in their praises. It seems that both of these gentlemen had attempted to despatch a private expedition to the relief of their countryman, but through some means it had failed. They had contributed the sum of $500 to effect this laudable object; but the man to whom they had entrusted its command had been engaged by another for a different purpose, at a higher sum. But, instead of feeling annoyed that I had performed what they had intended to do, they were among my most enthusiastic admirers.

The next day I received a call from Dr. Kirk, who warmly congratulated me upon my success. Bishop Tozer also came, and thanked me for the service I had rendered to Dr. Livingstone.

On this day I also discharged my men, and re-engaged twenty of them to return to the "Great Master." Bombay, though in the interior he had scorned the idea of money rewards, and though he had systematically, in my greatest need, endeavoured to baffle me in every way, received, besides his pay, a present of $50, and each man, according to his merits, from $20 to $50. For this was a day to bury all animosities, and condone all offences. They, poor people, had only acted according to their nature, and I remembered that from Ujiji to the coast they had all behaved admirably.

I saw I was terribly emaciated and changed when I presented myself before a full-length mirror. All confirmed my opinion that I was much older in my appearance, and that my hair had become grey. Capt. Fraser had said, when I hailed him, "You have the advantage of me, sir!" and until I mentioned my name he did not know me. Even then he jocosely remarked that he believed that it was another Tichborne affair. I was so different that identity was almost lost, even during the short period of thirteen months; that is, from March 23rd, 1871, to May 7th, 1872.

Lieut. Henn the morning after my arrival formally resigned, and the Expedition was from this time in the hands of Mr. Oswell Livingstone, who made up his mind to sell the stores, retaining such as would be useful to his father.

After disbanding my Expedition, I set about preparing another, according to Dr. Livingstone's request. What the English Expedition lacked I purchased out of the money advanced by Mr. Oswell Livingstone. The guns, fifty in number, were also furnished out of the stores of the English Expedition by him; and so were the ammunition, the honga cloth, for the tribute to the Wagogo, and the cloth for provisioning the force. Mr. Livingstone worked hard in the interests of his father and assisted me to the utmost of his ability. He delivered over to me, to be packed up, 'Nautical Almanacs' for 1872, 1873, 1874; also a chronometer, which formerly belonged to Dr. Livingstone. All these things, besides a journal, envelopes, note-books, writing-paper, medicines, canned fruits and fish, a little wine, some tea, cutlery and table ware, newspapers, and private letters and despatches, were packed up in air-tight tin boxes, as well as 100 lbs. of fine American flour, and some boxes of soda biscuits.

Until the 19th of May it was understood that Mr. Oswell Livingstone would take charge of the caravan to his father; but about this date he changed his mind, and surprised me with a note stating he had decided not to go to Unyanyembe, for reasons he thought just and sufficient.

Under these circumstances, my duty was to follow out the instructions of Dr. Livingstone, in procuring a good and efficient leader to take charge of the caravan as far as Unyanyembe.

In a few hours I succeeded in obtaining an Arab highly recommended from Sheikh Hashid, whom I engaged at an advance of $100. The young Arab, though not remarkably bright, seemed honest and able, but I left his further employment after reaching Unyanyembe to Dr. Livingstone, who would be able to decide then whether he was quite trustworthy.

The next day I collected the men of the new Livingstone Expedition together, and as it was dangerous to allow them to wander about the city, I locked them up in a courtyard, and fed them there, until every soul, fifty-seven in number, answered to their names.

In the meantime, through the American Consul's assistance, I obtained the services of Johari, the chief dragoman of the American Consulate, who was charged with the conduct of the party across the inundated plain of the Kingani, and who was enjoined on no account to return until the Expedition had started on its march from the western bank of the Kingani River. Mr. Oswell Livingstone generously paid him a douceur for the promise of doing his work thoroughly.

A dhow having been brought to anchor before the American Consulate, I then addressed my old companions, saying, " You are now about to return to Unyanyembe, to the ' Great Master.' You know him ; you know he is a good man, and has a kind heart. He is different from me ; he will not beat you, as I have done. But you know I have rewarded you all—how I have made you all rich in cloth and money. You know how, when you behaved yourselves well, I was your friend. I gave you plenty to eat and plenty to wear. When you were sick I looked after you. If I was so good to you, the ' Great Master ' will be much more so. He has a pleasant voice, and speaks kind. When did you ever see him lift his hand against an offender ? When you were wicked, he did not speak to you in anger—he spoke to you in tones of sorrow. Now, will you promise me that you will follow him—do what he tells you, obey him in all things, and not desert him ?"

" We will, we will, my master !" they all cried, fervently.

" Then there is one thing more. I want to shake hands with you all before you go—and we part for ever ;" and they all rushed up at once, and a vigorous shake was interchanged with each man.

" Now, let every man take up his load !"

In a short time I marched them out into the street,

and to the beach ; saw them all on board, and the canvas hoisted, and the dhow speeding westward on her way to Bagamoyo.

I felt strange and lonely, somehow. My dark friends, who had travelled over so many hundreds of miles, and shared so many dangers with me, were gone, and I—was left behind. How many of their friendly faces shall I see again ?

On the 29th, the steamer 'Africa,' belonging to the German Consulate, was chartered by a party of five of us, and we departed from Zanzibar to Seychelles, with the good wishes of almost all the European residents on the island.

We arrived at Seychelles on the 9th of June, about twelve hours after the French mail had departed for Aden. As there is only monthly communication between Mahé (Seychelles) and Aden, we were compelled to remain on the island of Mahé one month.

My life in Mahé is among the most agreeable things connected with my return from Africa. I found my companions estimable gentlemen, and true Christians. Mr. Livingstone exhibited many amiable traits of character, and proved himself to be a studious, thoughtful, earnest man. When at last the French steamer came from Mauritius, there was not one of our party who did not regret leaving the beautiful island, and the hospitable British officers who were stationed there. The Civil Commissioner, Mr. Hales Franklyn, and Dr. Brooks, did their utmost to welcome the wanderer, and I take this opportunity to acknowledge the many civilities I personally received from them.

At Aden, the passengers from the south were transferred on board the French mail steamer, the ' Mei-kong,' *en route* from China to Marseilles. At the latter port I was received with open arms by Dr. Hosmer and the representative of the 'Daily Telegraph,' and was then told how men regarded the results of the Expedition; but it was not until I arrived in England that I realised it.

Mr. Bennett, who originated and sustained the enterprise, now crowned it by one of the most generous acts that could be conceived. I had promised Dr. Livingstone, that twenty-four hours after I saw his letters to Mr. Bennett published in the London journals, I would post his letters to his family and friends in England. In order to permit me to keep my plighted word, and in order that there might be no delay in the delivery of his family letters, Mr. Bennett's agent telegraphed to New York the 'Herald' letters I had received from Dr. Livingstone at an expense of nearly £2,000.

*   *   *   •   *   *

And now, dear reader, the time has come for you and I to part. Let us hope that it is not final. A traveller finds himself compelled to repeat the regretful parting word often. During the career recorded in the foregoing book, I have bidden many farewells; to the Wagogo, with their fierce effrontery; to Mionvu, whose black-mailing once so affected me; to the Wavinza, whose noisy clatter promised to provoke dire hostilities; to the inhospitable Warundi; to the Arab slave-traders and half-castes; to all fevers, remittent, and intermittent; to the sloughs and swamps of Makata; to the brackish waters and howling wastes; to my own dusky friends and followers, and to the hero-traveller and Christian gentleman, David Livingstone. It is with kindliest wishes to all who have followed my footsteps on these pages that I repeat once more—Farewell.

CONCLUDING CHAPTER.

THE following correspondence, and especially the last letter, which was accompanied by a beautiful and valuable gold snuff-box set with brilliants, will be treasured by me as among the pleasantest results of my undertaking.

H. M. S.

SIR,   Foreign Office, August 1.
    I am directed by Earl Granville to acknowledge the receipt of a packet containing letters and despatches from Dr. Livingstone, which you were good enough to deliver to her Majesty's ambassador at Paris for transmission to this department; and I am to convey to you his Lordship's thanks for taking charge of these interesting documents.
I am, Sir,
Your most obedient humble servant,
ENFIELD.
HENRY M. STANLEY, Esq., 'New York Herald Bureau,'
        46, Fleet Street, London.

—••—

London, August 2.
    HENRY M. STANLEY, Esq., has handed to me to-day the diary of Dr. Livingstone, my father, sealed and signed by my father, with instructions written on the outside, signed by my father, for the care of which, and for all his actions concerning and to my father, our very

best thanks are due. We have not the slightest reason to doubt that this is my father's journal, and I certify that the letters he has brought home are my father's letters, and no others.

TOM S. LIVINGSTONE.

SIR, August 2, 1872.

I was not aware until you mentioned it that there was any doubt as to the authenticity of Dr. Livingstone's despatches, which you delivered to Lord Lyons on the 31st of July. But, in consequence of what you said I have inquired into the matter, and I find that Mr. Hammond, the Under-Secretary of the Foreign Office, and Mr. Wylde, the head of the Consular and Slave Trade Department, have not the slightest doubt as to the genuineness of the papers which have been received from Lord Lyons, and which are being printed.

I cannot omit this opportunity of expressing to you my admiration of the qualities which have enabled you to achieve the object of your mission, and to attain a result which has been hailed with so much enthusiasm both in the United States and in this country.

I am, Sir,
Your obedient,
GRANVILLE.

HENRY STANLEY, Esq.

SIR, Foreign Office, August 27.

I have great satisfaction in conveying to you, by command of the Queen, her Majesty's high appreciation of the prudence and zeal which you have displayed in opening a communication with Dr. Livingstone, and relieving her Majesty from the anxiety which, in common with her subjects, she had felt in regard to the fate of that distinguished traveller.

The Queen desires me to express her thanks for the service you have thus rendered, together with her Majesty's congratulations on your having so successfully carried on the mission which you fearlessly undertook. Her Majesty also desires me to request your acceptance of the memorial which accompanies this letter.

I am, Sir,
Your most obedient humble servant,
GRANVILLE.

GLOSSARY.

Boma	. . .	enclosure.
Bubu	. . .	black beads.
Diwan	. . .	elder, chief, or magistrate.
Doti	. .	four yards of cloth.
Dowa	. . .	medicine.
Fundo	. . .	ten necklaces, or ten khetes.
Ghulabio	. .	a species of bead.
Hafde	. . .	a species of bead.
Hamal	. . .	carrier.
Honga	. . .	tribute.
Ismahili	. .	a native name for a particular kind of cloth.
Kadunguru	. .	a brick-coloured species of bead.
Kaif-Halek	. .	" How do you do ?"
Kaniki	. . .	a blue cloth manufactured in India.
Knambi	. .	camp.
Khete	. . .	one necklace, or a tenth of a fundo.
Kichuma-chuma	.	" Little Irons," a disease of the liver.
Kirangozi	. .	guide.
Kitambi	. .	a cloth.
Kiti	. . .	stool.
Lakhio	. . .	a pink-coloured species of bead.
Lunghio	. .	blue beads.
Lunghio mbamba	.	small blue beads.
Lunghio rega	. .	large blue beads.
M	. . .	a prefix to denote a person of any country as M-jiji, a native of Jiji.
Manyapara	. .	elder, or sub-chief.
Matama	. .	Holcus sorghum, or the Arabic dourra.

Mbembu	. .	forest peach.
Merikani	. .	unbleached domestics manufactured in America.
Mganga .	.	? medicine man, or magic doctor.
Miezi-Mungu .		a Kisawahili term for " God."
Mtemi .	. ,	a term synonymous with king.
Mtoni .	. .	nullah.
Muhongo	. .	tribute.
Mulungu	. .	a native term for " God."
Mukunguru	. .	intermittent fever.
Mvuha .	. .	thunder.
Ngombe	. .	a cow.
Pagazi .	. .	a porter, or carrier.
Posho .	. .	food.
Sami-Sami	. .	the name of red beads.
Shamba .	.	a field.
Shash. .	.	a muslin cloth.
Sheikh .	, .	a title of courtesy given to an elderly man.
Shukka .	, .	two yards of cloth.
Sohari .	. .	a kind of colored cloth.
Sungomazzi	. .	large glass or china beads of the size of marbles.
Toujiri .	. .	the name for a particular kind of cloth.
U	. . .	a prefix to denote the country : thus U-jiji signifies the country of Jiji.
Uganga .	. .	medicine.
Wa-	. . .	a prefix to denote persons : thus Wa-jiji would signify people of Jiji.
Washensi	.	a term of contempt applied to the natives.
Yambo	.	" How are you ?"
Ziwa	.	a pool, or lake.
Ziwani	.	a pond.

APPENDIX.

———•◇•———

List of Camps from Bagamoyo to Ujiji and back to the Sea.

THROUGH UKWERE, UKAMI, AND UDOE TO USEGUHHA.

From Bagamoyo to—	h.	m.	From Msuwa to—	h.	m.
Shamba Gonera . .	1	30	Kisemo	4	30
Kikoka	3	40	Mussoudi	4	20
Rosako	5	0	Mikeseh	7	0
Kingaru	6	0	Muhalleh	6	45
Imbiki	4	30	Simbamwenni . .	3	0
Msuwa	4	30			

TO UGOGO.

USEGUHHA.			Rehenneko to—	h.	m
Ungerengeri River to—	h.	m	Camp on mountain .	3	30
Simbo	2	0	Kiora	3	40
Camp in plain . . .	4	10	Camp on river . . .	4	50
Makata River . . .	2	30	Madete	2	30
			Lake Ugombo . . .	3	0
USAGARA.			Matamombo . . .	6	0
Camp west of Makata .	0	5	Mpwapwa	7	0
Camp in plain . . .	4	30	Kisokweh	2	0
Camp „ . . .	2	0	Chunyo.	1	30
Rehenneko . . .	3	15			

FROM UGOGO TO UNYANYEMBE.

From Marenga Mkali to—		h.	m.
Mvumi, Little Ugogo		12	30
Mvumi, Great Ugogo		4	0
Matamburu	„	4	0
Bihawana	„	4	0
Kididimo	„	2	0
Pembera Pereh	„	10	0
Mizanza	„	5	30
Mukondoku	„	6	30
Munieka	„	5	0
Mabunguru Mtoni, U-yanzi		8	0
Kiti, Uyanzi		6	30
Msalalo		6	30

From Msalalo to—		h.	m
Welled Ngaraiso	. .	3	30
Kusuri	. . . .	3	I5
Mgongo Tembo	. .	3	3C
„ „ Mtoni		3	3C
Nghwhalah Mtoni	.	2	4C
Madedita	. . . .	2	30
Central Tura, Unyam-wezi	. . . .	3	0
Kwala River	. . .	7	0
Rubuga	. . . .	7	15
Kigwa	. . . . .	5	0
Shisa	. . . . .	7	0
Kwihara	. . . .	3	0

UNYANYEMBE TO MRERA, UKONONGO.

UNYAMWEZI.

From Kwihara to —		h.	m.
Mkwenkwe	. . .	1	30
Inesuka	. . . .	2	0
Kasegera	. . . .	3	0
Kigandu	. . . .	2	45
Ugunda	. . . .	7	0
Benta	. . . . .	3	15
Kikuru	. . . .	5	0
Ziwani	. . . . .	4	0
Manyara	. . . .	6	30

UKONONGO.

From Manyara to —		h.	m.
Gombe River	. . .	4	15
Ziwani	. . . . .	5	20
Tongoni	. . . .	1	30
Camp	. . . . .	5	15
Marefu	. . . . .	3	0
Utende	. . . . .	7	15
Mtoni	. . . . .	4	0
Mwaru	. . . . .	5	15
Mrera	. . . . .	5	13

FROM MRERA, UKONONGO TO UJIJI.

UKONONGO.

From Mrera to Mtoni	.	h.	m.
From Mrera to Mtoni	.	4	30
Misonghi	. . .	4	30
Mtoni	. . . .	6	0
Mpokwa in Utanda	.	4	45
Mtoni	. . .	3	0

UKAWENDI.

		h.	m
Mtambu River	. . .	4	30
Imrera	. . . . .	4	20
Rusawa Mts.	. . .	2	30
Mtoni	. . . . .	4	0
Mtoni	. . . . .	5	0

FROM MRERA, UEONONGO TO UJIJI—*continued.*

	h.	m
Camp in Forest . .	6	0
Camp in Forest . .	5	30

UVINZA.

Welled Nzogera . .	2	30
Camp in Forest . .	4	15
Siala on the Malagarazi	2	45
Ihata Island in the Malagarazi	1	30
Katalambula . . .	1	45

UHHA.

Kawanga in Uhha . .	5	30

	h.	m.
Lukomo ,, .	1	0
Kahirigi ,, .	4	0
Rusugi River . .	5	0
Lake Musunya. . .	4	0
Rugufu River . . .	4	30
Sunuzzi ,, . .	3	0
Niamtaga Ukaranga .	9	30

UJIJI.

Port of Ujiji . .	6	0

INDEX.

———◆◆———

A CATALOG OF SELECTED
DOVER BOOKS
IN ALL FIELDS OF INTEREST

A CATALOG OF SELECTED DOVER
BOOKS IN ALL FIELDS OF INTEREST

CONCERNING THE SPIRITUAL IN ART, Wassily Kandinsky. Pioneering work by father of abstract art. Thoughts on color theory, nature of art. Analysis of earlier masters. 12 illustrations. 80pp. of text. 5⅜ x 8½.   23411-8

ANIMALS: 1,419 Copyright-Free Illustrations of Mammals, Birds, Fish, Insects, etc., Jim Harter (ed.). Clear wood engravings present, in extremely lifelike poses, over 1,000 species of animals. One of the most extensive pictorial sourcebooks of its kind. Captions. Index. 284pp. 9 x 12.   23766-4

CELTIC ART: The Methods of Construction, George Bain. Simple geometric techniques for making Celtic interlacements, spirals, Kells-type initials, animals, humans, etc. Over 500 illustrations. 160pp. 9 x 12. (Available in U.S. only.)   22923-8

AN ATLAS OF ANATOMY FOR ARTISTS, Fritz Schider. Most thorough reference work on art anatomy in the world. Hundreds of illustrations, including selections from works by Vesalius, Leonardo, Goya, Ingres, Michelangelo, others. 593 illustrations. 192pp. 7⅛ x 10¼.   20241-0

CELTIC HAND STROKE-BY-STROKE (Irish Half-Uncial from "The Book of Kells"): An Arthur Baker Calligraphy Manual, Arthur Baker. Complete guide to creating each letter of the alphabet in distinctive Celtic manner. Covers hand position, strokes, pens, inks, paper, more. Illustrated. 48pp. 8¼ x 11.   24336-2

EASY ORIGAMI, John Montroll. Charming collection of 32 projects (hat, cup, pelican, piano, swan, many more) specially designed for the novice origami hobbyist. Clearly illustrated easy-to-follow instructions insure that even beginning papercrafters will achieve successful results. 48pp. 8¼ x 11.   27298-2

THE COMPLETE BOOK OF BIRDHOUSE CONSTRUCTION FOR WOODWORKERS, Scott D. Campbell. Detailed instructions, illustrations, tables. Also data on bird habitat and instinct patterns. Bibliography. 3 tables. 63 illustrations in 15 figures. 48pp. 5¼ x 8½.   24407-5

BLOOMINGDALE'S ILLUSTRATED 1886 CATALOG: Fashions, Dry Goods and Housewares, Bloomingdale Brothers. Famed merchants' extremely rare catalog depicting about 1,700 products: clothing, housewares, firearms, dry goods, jewelry, more. Invaluable for dating, identifying vintage items. Also, copyright-free graphics for artists, designers. Co-published with Henry Ford Museum & Greenfield Village. 160pp. 8¼ x 11.   25780-0

HISTORIC COSTUME IN PICTURES, Braun & Schneider. Over 1,450 costumed figures in clearly detailed engravings–from dawn of civilization to end of 19th century. Captions. Many folk costumes. 256pp. 8⅜ x 11¾.   23150-X

STICKLEY CRAFTSMAN FURNITURE CATALOGS, Gustav Stickley and L. & J. G. Stickley. Beautiful, functional furniture in two authentic catalogs from 1910. 594 illustrations, including 277 photos, show settles, rockers, armchairs, reclining chairs, bookcases, desks, tables. 183pp. 6½ x 9¼. 23838-5

AMERICAN LOCOMOTIVES IN HISTORIC PHOTOGRAPHS: 1858 to 1949, Ron Ziel (ed.). A rare collection of 126 meticulously detailed official photographs, called "builder portraits," of American locomotives that majestically chronicle the rise of steam locomotive power in America. Introduction. Detailed captions. xi+129pp. 9 x 12. 27393-8

AMERICA'S LIGHTHOUSES: An Illustrated History, Francis Ross Holland, Jr. Delightfully written, profusely illustrated fact-filled survey of over 200 American lighthouses since 1716. History, anecdotes, technological advances, more. 240pp. 8 x 10¾. 25576-X

TOWARDS A NEW ARCHITECTURE, Le Corbusier. Pioneering manifesto by founder of "International School." Technical and aesthetic theories, views of industry, economics, relation of form to function, "mass-production split" and much more. Profusely illustrated. 320pp. 6⅛ x 9¼. (Available in U.S. only.) 25023-7

HOW THE OTHER HALF LIVES, Jacob Riis. Famous journalistic record, exposing poverty and degradation of New York slums around 1900, by major social reformer. 100 striking and influential photographs. 233pp. 10 x 7⅞. 22012-5

FRUIT KEY AND TWIG KEY TO TREES AND SHRUBS, William M. Harlow. One of the handiest and most widely used identification aids. Fruit key covers 120 deciduous and evergreen species; twig key 160 deciduous species. Easily used. Over 300 photographs. 126pp. 5⅜ x 8½. 20511-8

COMMON BIRD SONGS, Dr. Donald J. Borror. Songs of 60 most common U.S. birds: robins, sparrows, cardinals, bluejays, finches, more–arranged in order of increasing complexity. Up to 9 variations of songs of each species.

Cassette and manual 99911-4

ORCHIDS AS HOUSE PLANTS, Rebecca Tyson Northen. Grow cattleyas and many other kinds of orchids–in a window, in a case, or under artificial light. 63 illustrations. 148pp. 5⅜ x 8½. 23261-1

MONSTER MAZES, Dave Phillips. Masterful mazes at four levels of difficulty. Avoid deadly perils and evil creatures to find magical treasures. Solutions for all 32 exciting illustrated puzzles. 48pp. 8¼ x 11. 26005-4

MOZART'S DON GIOVANNI (DOVER OPERA LIBRETTO SERIES), Wolfgang Amadeus Mozart. Introduced and translated by Ellen H. Bleiler. Standard Italian libretto, with complete English translation. Convenient and thoroughly portable–an ideal companion for reading along with a recording or the performance itself. Introduction. List of characters. Plot summary. 121pp. 5¼ x 8½. 24944-1

TECHNICAL MANUAL AND DICTIONARY OF CLASSICAL BALLET, Gail Grant. Defines, explains, comments on steps, movements, poses and concepts. 15-page pictorial section. Basic book for student, viewer. 127pp. 5⅜ x 8½. 21843-0

THE CLARINET AND CLARINET PLAYING, David Pino. Lively, comprehensive work features suggestions about technique, musicianship, and musical interpretation, as well as guidelines for teaching, making your own reeds, and preparing for public performance. Includes an intriguing look at clarinet history. "A godsend," *The Clarinet,* Journal of the International Clarinet Society. Appendixes. 7 illus. 320pp. 5⅜ x 8½. 40270-3

HOLLYWOOD GLAMOR PORTRAITS, John Kobal (ed.). 145 photos from 1926-49. Harlow, Gable, Bogart, Bacall; 94 stars in all. Full background on photographers, technical aspects. 160pp. 8⅜ x 11¼. 23352-9

THE ANNOTATED CASEY AT THE BAT: A Collection of Ballads about the Mighty Casey/Third, Revised Edition, Martin Gardner (ed.). Amusing sequels and parodies of one of America's best-loved poems: Casey's Revenge, Why Casey Whiffed, Casey's Sister at the Bat, others. 256pp. 5⅜ x 8½. 28598-7

THE RAVEN AND OTHER FAVORITE POEMS, Edgar Allan Poe. Over 40 of the author's most memorable poems: "The Bells," "Ulalume," "Israfel," "To Helen," "The Conqueror Worm," "Eldorado," "Annabel Lee," many more. Alphabetic lists of titles and first lines. 64pp. 5$^3/_{16}$ x 8¼. 26685-0

PERSONAL MEMOIRS OF U. S. GRANT, Ulysses Simpson Grant. Intelligent, deeply moving firsthand account of Civil War campaigns, considered by many the finest military memoirs ever written. Includes letters, historic photographs, maps and more. 528pp. 6⅛ x 9¼. 28587-1

ANCIENT EGYPTIAN MATERIALS AND INDUSTRIES, A. Lucas and J. Harris. Fascinating, comprehensive, thoroughly documented text describes this ancient civilization's vast resources and the processes that incorporated them in daily life, including the use of animal products, building materials, cosmetics, perfumes and incense, fibers, glazed ware, glass and its manufacture, materials used in the mummification process, and much more. 544pp. 6⅛ x 9¼. (Available in U.S. only.) 40446-3

RUSSIAN STORIES/RUSSKIE RASSKAZY: A Dual-Language Book, edited by Gleb Struve. Twelve tales by such masters as Chekhov, Tolstoy, Dostoevsky, Pushkin, others. Excellent word-for-word English translations on facing pages, plus teaching and study aids, Russian/English vocabulary, biographical/critical introductions, more. 416pp. 5⅜ x 8½. 26244-8

PHILADELPHIA THEN AND NOW: 60 Sites Photographed in the Past and Present, Kenneth Finkel and Susan Oyama. Rare photographs of City Hall, Logan Square, Independence Hall, Betsy Ross House, other landmarks juxtaposed with contemporary views. Captures changing face of historic city. Introduction. Captions. 128pp. 8¼ x 11. 25790-8

AIA ARCHITECTURAL GUIDE TO NASSAU AND SUFFOLK COUNTIES, LONG ISLAND, The American Institute of Architects, Long Island Chapter, and the Society for the Preservation of Long Island Antiquities. Comprehensive, well-researched and generously illustrated volume brings to life over three centuries of Long Island's great architectural heritage. More than 240 photographs with authoritative, extensively detailed captions. 176pp. 8¼ x 11. 26946-9

NORTH AMERICAN INDIAN LIFE: Customs and Traditions of 23 Tribes, Elsie Clews Parsons (ed.). 27 fictionalized essays by noted anthropologists examine religion, customs, government, additional facets of life among the Winnebago, Crow, Zuni, Eskimo, other tribes. 480pp. 6⅛ x 9¼. 27377-6

FRANK LLOYD WRIGHT'S DANA HOUSE, Donald Hoffmann. Pictorial essay of residential masterpiece with over 160 interior and exterior photos, plans, elevations, sketches and studies. 128pp. 9¼ x 10¾.   29120-0

THE MALE AND FEMALE FIGURE IN MOTION: 60 Classic Photographic Sequences, Eadweard Muybridge. 60 true-action photographs of men and women walking, running, climbing, bending, turning, etc., reproduced from rare 19th-century masterpiece. vi + 121pp. 9 x 12.   24745-7

1001 QUESTIONS ANSWERED ABOUT THE SEASHORE, N. J. Berrill and Jacquelyn Berrill. Queries answered about dolphins, sea snails, sponges, starfish, fishes, shore birds, many others. Covers appearance, breeding, growth, feeding, much more. 305pp. 5¼ x 8¼.   23366-9

ATTRACTING BIRDS TO YOUR YARD, William J. Weber. Easy-to-follow guide offers advice on how to attract the greatest diversity of birds: birdhouses, feeders, water and waterers, much more. 96pp. 5³⁄₁₆ x 8¼.   28927-3

MEDICINAL AND OTHER USES OF NORTH AMERICAN PLANTS: A Historical Survey with Special Reference to the Eastern Indian Tribes, Charlotte Erichsen-Brown. Chronological historical citations document 500 years of usage of plants, trees, shrubs native to eastern Canada, northeastern U.S. Also complete identifying information. 343 illustrations. 544pp. 6½ x 9¼.   25951-X

STORYBOOK MAZES, Dave Phillips. 23 stories and mazes on two-page spreads: Wizard of Oz, Treasure Island, Robin Hood, etc. Solutions. 64pp. 8¼ x 11.   23628-5

AMERICAN NEGRO SONGS: 230 Folk Songs and Spirituals, Religious and Secular, John W. Work. This authoritative study traces the African influences of songs sung and played by black Americans at work, in church, and as entertainment. The author discusses the lyric significance of such songs as "Swing Low, Sweet Chariot," "John Henry," and others and offers the words and music for 230 songs. Bibliography. Index of Song Titles. 272pp. 6½ x 9¼.   40271-1

MOVIE-STAR PORTRAITS OF THE FORTIES, John Kobal (ed.). 163 glamor, studio photos of 106 stars of the 1940s: Rita Hayworth, Ava Gardner, Marlon Brando, Clark Gable, many more. 176pp. 8⅜ x 11¼.   23546-7

BENCHLEY LOST AND FOUND, Robert Benchley. Finest humor from early 30s, about pet peeves, child psychologists, post office and others. Mostly unavailable elsewhere. 73 illustrations by Peter Arno and others. 183pp. 5⅜ x 8½.   22410-4

YEKL and THE IMPORTED BRIDEGROOM AND OTHER STORIES OF YIDDISH NEW YORK, Abraham Cahan. Film Hester Street based on *Yekl* (1896). Novel, other stories among first about Jewish immigrants on N.Y.'s East Side. 240pp. 5⅜ x 8½.   22427-9

SELECTED POEMS, Walt Whitman. Generous sampling from *Leaves of Grass*. Twenty-four poems include "I Hear America Singing," "Song of the Open Road," "I Sing the Body Electric," "When Lilacs Last in the Dooryard Bloom'd," "O Captain! My Captain!"–all reprinted from an authoritative edition. Lists of titles and first lines. 128pp. 5³⁄₁₆ x 8¼.   26878-0

THE BEST TALES OF HOFFMANN, E. T. A. Hoffmann. 10 of Hoffmann's most important stories: "Nutcracker and the King of Mice," "The Golden Flowerpot," etc. 458pp. 5⅜ x 8½. 21793-0

FROM FETISH TO GOD IN ANCIENT EGYPT, E. A. Wallis Budge. Rich detailed survey of Egyptian conception of "God" and gods, magic, cult of animals, Osiris, more. Also, superb English translations of hymns and legends. 240 illustrations. 545pp. 5⅜ x 8½. 25803-3

FRENCH STORIES/CONTES FRANÇAIS: A Dual-Language Book, Wallace Fowlie. Ten stories by French masters, Voltaire to Camus: "Micromegas" by Voltaire; "The Atheist's Mass" by Balzac; "Minuet" by de Maupassant; "The Guest" by Camus, six more. Excellent English translations on facing pages. Also French-English vocabulary list, exercises, more. 352pp. 5⅜ x 8½. 26443-2

CHICAGO AT THE TURN OF THE CENTURY IN PHOTOGRAPHS: 122 Historic Views from the Collections of the Chicago Historical Society, Larry A. Viskochil. Rare large-format prints offer detailed views of City Hall, State Street, the Loop, Hull House, Union Station, many other landmarks, circa 1904-1913. Introduction. Captions. Maps. 144pp. 9⅜ x 12¼. 24656-6

OLD BROOKLYN IN EARLY PHOTOGRAPHS, 1865-1929, William Lee Younger. Luna Park, Gravesend race track, construction of Grand Army Plaza, moving of Hotel Brighton, etc. 157 previously unpublished photographs. 165pp. 8⅞ x 11¾. 23587-4

THE MYTHS OF THE NORTH AMERICAN INDIANS, Lewis Spence. Rich anthology of the myths and legends of the Algonquins, Iroquois, Pawnees and Sioux, prefaced by an extensive historical and ethnological commentary. 36 illustrations. 480pp. 5⅜ x 8½. 25967-6

AN ENCYCLOPEDIA OF BATTLES: Accounts of Over 1,560 Battles from 1479 B.C. to the Present, David Eggenberger. Essential details of every major battle in recorded history from the first battle of Megiddo in 1479 B.C. to Grenada in 1984. List of Battle Maps. New Appendix covering the years 1967-1984. Index. 99 illustrations. 544pp. 6½ x 9¼. 24913-1

SAILING ALONE AROUND THE WORLD, Captain Joshua Slocum. First man to sail around the world, alone, in small boat. One of great feats of seamanship told in delightful manner. 67 illustrations. 294pp. 5⅜ x 8½. 20326-3

ANARCHISM AND OTHER ESSAYS, Emma Goldman. Powerful, penetrating, prophetic essays on direct action, role of minorities, prison reform, puritan hypocrisy, violence, etc. 271pp. 5⅜ x 8½. 22484-8

MYTHS OF THE HINDUS AND BUDDHISTS, Ananda K. Coomaraswamy and Sister Nivedita. Great stories of the epics; deeds of Krishna, Shiva, taken from puranas, Vedas, folk tales; etc. 32 illustrations. 400pp. 5⅜ x 8½. 21759-0

THE TRAUMA OF BIRTH, Otto Rank. Rank's controversial thesis that anxiety neurosis is caused by profound psychological trauma which occurs at birth. 256pp. 5⅜ x 8½. 27974-X

A THEOLOGICO-POLITICAL TREATISE, Benedict Spinoza. Also contains unfinished Political Treatise. Great classic on religious liberty, theory of government on common consent. R. Elwes translation. Total of 421pp. 5⅜ x 8½. 20249-6

MY BONDAGE AND MY FREEDOM, Frederick Douglass. Born a slave, Douglass became outspoken force in antislavery movement. The best of Douglass' autobiographies. Graphic description of slave life. 464pp. 5⅜ x 8½. 22457-0

FOLLOWING THE EQUATOR: A Journey Around the World, Mark Twain. Fascinating humorous account of 1897 voyage to Hawaii, Australia, India, New Zealand, etc. Ironic, bemused reports on peoples, customs, climate, flora and fauna, politics, much more. 197 illustrations. 720pp. 5⅜ x 8½. 26113-1

THE PEOPLE CALLED SHAKERS, Edward D. Andrews. Definitive study of Shakers: origins, beliefs, practices, dances, social organization, furniture and crafts, etc. 33 illustrations. 351pp. 5⅜ x 8½. 21081-2

THE MYTHS OF GREECE AND ROME, H. A. Guerber. A classic of mythology, generously illustrated, long prized for its simple, graphic, accurate retelling of the principal myths of Greece and Rome, and for its commentary on their origins and significance. With 64 illustrations by Michelangelo, Raphael, Titian, Rubens, Canova, Bernini and others. 480pp. 5⅜ x 8½. 27584-1

PSYCHOLOGY OF MUSIC, Carl E. Seashore. Classic work discusses music as a medium from psychological viewpoint. Clear treatment of physical acoustics, auditory apparatus, sound perception, development of musical skills, nature of musical feeling, host of other topics. 88 figures. 408pp. 5⅜ x 8½. 21851-1

THE PHILOSOPHY OF HISTORY, Georg W. Hegel. Great classic of Western thought develops concept that history is not chance but rational process, the evolution of freedom. 457pp. 5⅜ x 8½. 20112-0

THE BOOK OF TEA, Kakuzo Okakura. Minor classic of the Orient: entertaining, charming explanation, interpretation of traditional Japanese culture in terms of tea ceremony. 94pp. 5⅜ x 8½. 20070-1

LIFE IN ANCIENT EGYPT, Adolf Erman. Fullest, most thorough, detailed older account with much not in more recent books, domestic life, religion, magic, medicine, commerce, much more. Many illustrations reproduce tomb paintings, carvings, hieroglyphs, etc. 597pp. 5⅜ x 8½. 22632-8

SUNDIALS, Their Theory and Construction, Albert Waugh. Far and away the best, most thorough coverage of ideas, mathematics concerned, types, construction, adjusting anywhere. Simple, nontechnical treatment allows even children to build several of these dials. Over 100 illustrations. 230pp. 5⅜ x 8½. 22947-5

THEORETICAL HYDRODYNAMICS, L. M. Milne-Thomson. Classic exposition of the mathematical theory of fluid motion, applicable to both hydrodynamics and aerodynamics. Over 600 exercises. 768pp. 6⅛ x 9¼. 68970-0

SONGS OF EXPERIENCE: Facsimile Reproduction with 26 Plates in Full Color, William Blake. 26 full-color plates from a rare 1826 edition. Includes "The Tyger," "London," "Holy Thursday," and other poems. Printed text of poems. 48pp. 5¼ x 7. 24636-1

OLD-TIME VIGNETTES IN FULL COLOR, Carol Belanger Grafton (ed.). Over 390 charming, often sentimental illustrations, selected from archives of Victorian graphics—pretty women posing, children playing, food, flowers, kittens and puppies, smiling cherubs, birds and butterflies, much more. All copyright-free. 48pp. 9¼ x 12¼. 27269-9

PERSPECTIVE FOR ARTISTS, Rex Vicat Cole. Depth, perspective of sky and sea, shadows, much more, not usually covered. 391 diagrams, 81 reproductions of drawings and paintings. 279pp. 5⅜ x 8½. 22487-2

DRAWING THE LIVING FIGURE, Joseph Sheppard. Innovative approach to artistic anatomy focuses on specifics of surface anatomy, rather than muscles and bones. Over 170 drawings of live models in front, back and side views, and in widely varying poses. Accompanying diagrams. 177 illustrations. Introduction. Index. 144pp. 8⅜ x11¼. 26723-7

GOTHIC AND OLD ENGLISH ALPHABETS: 100 Complete Fonts, Dan X. Solo. Add power, elegance to posters, signs, other graphics with 100 stunning copyright-free alphabets: Blackstone, Dolbey, Germania, 97 more–including many lower-case, numerals, punctuation marks. 104pp. 8⅛ x 11. 24695-7

HOW TO DO BEADWORK, Mary White. Fundamental book on craft from simple projects to five-bead chains and woven works. 106 illustrations. 142pp. 5⅜ x 8. 20697-1

THE BOOK OF WOOD CARVING, Charles Marshall Sayers. Finest book for beginners discusses fundamentals and offers 34 designs. "Absolutely first rate . . . well thought out and well executed."–E. J. Tangerman. 118pp. 7¾ x 10⅝. 23654-4

ILLUSTRATED CATALOG OF CIVIL WAR MILITARY GOODS: Union Army Weapons, Insignia, Uniform Accessories, and Other Equipment, Schuyler, Hartley, and Graham. Rare, profusely illustrated 1846 catalog includes Union Army uniform and dress regulations, arms and ammunition, coats, insignia, flags, swords, rifles, etc. 226 illustrations. 160pp. 9 x 12. 24939-5

WOMEN'S FASHIONS OF THE EARLY 1900s: An Unabridged Republication of "New York Fashions, 1909," National Cloak & Suit Co. Rare catalog of mail-order fashions documents women's and children's clothing styles shortly after the turn of the century. Captions offer full descriptions, prices. Invaluable resource for fashion, costume historians. Approximately 725 illustrations. 128pp. 8⅜ x 11¼. 27276-1

THE 1912 AND 1915 GUSTAV STICKLEY FURNITURE CATALOGS, Gustav Stickley. With over 200 detailed illustrations and descriptions, these two catalogs are essential reading and reference materials and identification guides for Stickley furniture. Captions cite materials, dimensions and prices. 112pp. 6½ x 9¼. 26676-1

EARLY AMERICAN LOCOMOTIVES, John H. White, Jr. Finest locomotive engravings from early 19th century: historical (1804–74), main-line (after 1870), special, foreign, etc. 147 plates. 142pp. 11⅜ x 8¼. 22772-3

THE TALL SHIPS OF TODAY IN PHOTOGRAPHS, Frank O. Braynard. Lavishly illustrated tribute to nearly 100 majestic contemporary sailing vessels: Amerigo Vespucci, Clearwater, Constitution, Eagle, Mayflower, Sea Cloud, Victory, many more. Authoritative captions provide statistics, background on each ship. 190 black-and-white photographs and illustrations. Introduction. 128pp. 8⅞ x 11¾. 27163-3

LITTLE BOOK OF EARLY AMERICAN CRAFTS AND TRADES, Peter Stockham (ed.). 1807 children's book explains crafts and trades: baker, hatter, cooper, potter, and many others. 23 copperplate illustrations. 140pp. 4⅝ x 6.   23336-7

VICTORIAN FASHIONS AND COSTUMES FROM HARPER'S BAZAR, 1867–1898, Stella Blum (ed.). Day costumes, evening wear, sports clothes, shoes, hats, other accessories in over 1,000 detailed engravings. 320pp. 9⅜ x 12¼. 22990-4

GUSTAV STICKLEY, THE CRAFTSMAN, Mary Ann Smith. Superb study surveys broad scope of Stickley's achievement, especially in architecture. Design philosophy, rise and fall of the Craftsman empire, descriptions and floor plans for many Craftsman houses, more. 86 black-and-white halftones. 31 line illustrations. Introduction 208pp. 6½ x 9¼.   27210-9

THE LONG ISLAND RAIL ROAD IN EARLY PHOTOGRAPHS, Ron Ziel. Over 220 rare photos, informative text document origin (1844) and development of rail service on Long Island. Vintage views of early trains, locomotives, stations, passengers, crews, much more. Captions. 8⅞ x 11¾.   26301-0

VOYAGE OF THE LIBERDADE, Joshua Slocum. Great 19th-century mariner's thrilling, first-hand account of the wreck of his ship off South America, the 35-foot boat he built from the wreckage, and its remarkable voyage home. 128pp. 5⅜ x 8½.
40022-0

TEN BOOKS ON ARCHITECTURE, Vitruvius. The most important book ever written on architecture. Early Roman aesthetics, technology, classical orders, site selection, all other aspects. Morgan translation. 331pp. 5⅜ x 8½.   20645-9

THE HUMAN FIGURE IN MOTION, Eadweard Muybridge. More than 4,500 stopped-action photos, in action series, showing undraped men, women, children jumping, lying down, throwing, sitting, wrestling, carrying, etc. 390pp. 7⅞ x 10⅝.
20204-6 Clothbd.

TREES OF THE EASTERN AND CENTRAL UNITED STATES AND CANADA, William M. Harlow. Best one-volume guide to 140 trees. Full descriptions, woodlore, range, etc. Over 600 illustrations. Handy size. 288pp. 4½ x 6⅜.   20395-6

SONGS OF WESTERN BIRDS, Dr. Donald J. Borror. Complete song and call repertoire of 60 western species, including flycatchers, juncoes, cactus wrens, many more–includes fully illustrated booklet.   Cassette and manual 99913-0

GROWING AND USING HERBS AND SPICES, Milo Miloradovich. Versatile handbook provides all the information needed for cultivation and use of all the herbs and spices available in North America. 4 illustrations. Index. Glossary. 236pp. 5⅜ x 8½.
25058-X

BIG BOOK OF MAZES AND LABYRINTHS, Walter Shepherd. 50 mazes and labyrinths in all–classical, solid, ripple, and more–in one great volume. Perfect inexpensive puzzler for clever youngsters. Full solutions. 112pp. 8⅛ x 11.   22951-3

PIANO TUNING, J. Cree Fischer. Clearest, best book for beginner, amateur. Simple repairs, raising dropped notes, tuning by easy method of flattened fifths. No previous skills needed. 4 illustrations. 201pp. 5⅜ x 8½. 23267-0

HINTS TO SINGERS, Lillian Nordica. Selecting the right teacher, developing confidence, overcoming stage fright, and many other important skills receive thoughtful discussion in this indispensible guide, written by a world-famous diva of four decades' experience. 96pp. 5⅜ x 8½. 40094-8

THE COMPLETE NONSENSE OF EDWARD LEAR, Edward Lear. All nonsense limericks, zany alphabets, Owl and Pussycat, songs, nonsense botany, etc., illustrated by Lear. Total of 320pp. 5⅜ x 8½. (Available in U.S. only.) 20167-8

VICTORIAN PARLOUR POETRY: An Annotated Anthology, Michael R. Turner. 117 gems by Longfellow, Tennyson, Browning, many lesser-known poets. "The Village Blacksmith," "Curfew Must Not Ring Tonight," "Only a Baby Small," dozens more, often difficult to find elsewhere. Index of poets, titles, first lines. xxiii + 325pp. 5⅜ x 8¼. 27044-0

DUBLINERS, James Joyce. Fifteen stories offer vivid, tightly focused observations of the lives of Dublin's poorer classes. At least one, "The Dead," is considered a masterpiece. Reprinted complete and unabridged from standard edition. 160pp. 5³⁄₁₆ x 8¼. 26870-5

GREAT WEIRD TALES: 14 Stories by Lovecraft, Blackwood, Machen and Others, S. T. Joshi (ed.). 14 spellbinding tales, including "The Sin Eater," by Fiona McLeod, "The Eye Above the Mantel," by Frank Belknap Long, as well as renowned works by R. H. Barlow, Lord Dunsany, Arthur Machen, W. C. Morrow and eight other masters of the genre. 256pp. 5⅜ x 8½. (Available in U.S. only.) 40436-6

THE BOOK OF THE SACRED MAGIC OF ABRAMELIN THE MAGE, translated by S. MacGregor Mathers. Medieval manuscript of ceremonial magic. Basic document in Aleister Crowley, Golden Dawn groups. 268pp. 5⅜ x 8½. 23211-5

NEW RUSSIAN-ENGLISH AND ENGLISH-RUSSIAN DICTIONARY, M. A. O'Brien. This is a remarkably handy Russian dictionary, containing a surprising amount of information, including over 70,000 entries. 366pp. 4½ x 6⅛. 20208-9

HISTORIC HOMES OF THE AMERICAN PRESIDENTS, Second, Revised Edition, Irvin Haas. A traveler's guide to American Presidential homes, most open to the public, depicting and describing homes occupied by every American President from George Washington to George Bush. With visiting hours, admission charges, travel routes. 175 photographs. Index. 160pp. 8¼ x 11. 26751-2

NEW YORK IN THE FORTIES, Andreas Feininger. 162 brilliant photographs by the well-known photographer, formerly with *Life* magazine. Commuters, shoppers, Times Square at night, much else from city at its peak. Captions by John von Hartz. 181pp. 9¼ x 10¾. 23585-8

INDIAN SIGN LANGUAGE, William Tomkins. Over 525 signs developed by Sioux and other tribes. Written instructions and diagrams. Also 290 pictographs. 111pp. 6⅛ x 9¼. 22029-X

ANATOMY: A Complete Guide for Artists, Joseph Sheppard. A master of figure drawing shows artists how to render human anatomy convincingly. Over 460 illustrations. 224pp. 8⅜ x 11¼. 27279-6

MEDIEVAL CALLIGRAPHY: Its History and Technique, Marc Drogin. Spirited history, comprehensive instruction manual covers 13 styles (ca. 4th century through 15th). Excellent photographs; directions for duplicating medieval techniques with modern tools. 224pp. 8⅜ x 11¼. 26142-5

DRIED FLOWERS: How to Prepare Them, Sarah Whitlock and Martha Rankin. Complete instructions on how to use silica gel, meal and borax, perlite aggregate, sand and borax, glycerine and water to create attractive permanent flower arrangements. 12 illustrations. 32pp. 5⅜ x 8½. 21802-3

EASY-TO-MAKE BIRD FEEDERS FOR WOODWORKERS, Scott D. Campbell. Detailed, simple-to-use guide for designing, constructing, caring for and using feeders. Text, illustrations for 12 classic and contemporary designs. 96pp. 5⅜ x 8½.
25847-5

SCOTTISH WONDER TALES FROM MYTH AND LEGEND, Donald A. Mackenzie. 16 lively tales tell of giants rumbling down mountainsides, of a magic wand that turns stone pillars into warriors, of gods and goddesses, evil hags, powerful forces and more. 240pp. 5⅜ x 8½. 29677-6

THE HISTORY OF UNDERCLOTHES, C. Willett Cunnington and Phyllis Cunnington. Fascinating, well-documented survey covering six centuries of English undergarments, enhanced with over 100 illustrations: 12th-century laced-up bodice, footed long drawers (1795), 19th-century bustles, l9th-century corsets for men, Victorian "bust improvers," much more. 272pp. 5⅜ x 8¼. 27124-2

ARTS AND CRAFTS FURNITURE: The Complete Brooks Catalog of 1912, Brooks Manufacturing Co. Photos and detailed descriptions of more than 150 now very collectible furniture designs from the Arts and Crafts movement depict davenports, settees, buffets, desks, tables, chairs, bedsteads, dressers and more, all built of solid, quarter-sawed oak. Invaluable for students and enthusiasts of antiques, Americana and the decorative arts. 80pp. 6½ x 9¼. 27471-3

WILBUR AND ORVILLE: A Biography of the Wright Brothers, Fred Howard. Definitive, crisply written study tells the full story of the brothers' lives and work. A vividly written biography, unparalleled in scope and color, that also captures the spirit of an extraordinary era. 560pp. 6⅛ x 9¼. 40297-5

THE ARTS OF THE SAILOR: Knotting, Splicing and Ropework, Hervey Garrett Smith. Indispensable shipboard reference covers tools, basic knots and useful hitches; handsewing and canvas work, more. Over 100 illustrations. Delightful reading for sea lovers. 256pp. 5⅜ x 8½. 26440-8

FRANK LLOYD WRIGHT'S FALLINGWATER: The House and Its History, Second, Revised Edition, Donald Hoffmann. A total revision–both in text and illustrations–of the standard document on Fallingwater, the boldest, most personal architectural statement of Wright's mature years, updated with valuable new material from the recently opened Frank Lloyd Wright Archives. "Fascinating"–*The New York Times*. 116 illustrations. 128pp. 9¼ x 10¾. 27430-6

PHOTOGRAPHIC SKETCHBOOK OF THE CIVIL WAR, Alexander Gardner. 100 photos taken on field during the Civil War. Famous shots of Manassas Harper's Ferry, Lincoln, Richmond, slave pens, etc. 244pp. 10⅝ x 8¼. 22731-6

FIVE ACRES AND INDEPENDENCE, Maurice G. Kains. Great back-to-the-land classic explains basics of self-sufficient farming. The one book to get. 95 illustrations. 397pp. 5⅜ x 8½. 20974-1

SONGS OF EASTERN BIRDS, Dr. Donald J. Borror. Songs and calls of 60 species most common to eastern U.S.: warblers, woodpeckers, flycatchers, thrushes, larks, many more in high-quality recording. Cassette and manual 99912-2

A MODERN HERBAL, Margaret Grieve. Much the fullest, most exact, most useful compilation of herbal material. Gigantic alphabetical encyclopedia, from aconite to zedoary, gives botanical information, medical properties, folklore, economic uses, much else. Indispensable to serious reader. 161 illustrations. 888pp. 6½ x 9¼. 2-vol. set. (Available in U.S. only.) Vol. I: 22798-7
Vol. II: 22799-5

HIDDEN TREASURE MAZE BOOK, Dave Phillips. Solve 34 challenging mazes accompanied by heroic tales of adventure. Evil dragons, people-eating plants, blood-thirsty giants, many more dangerous adversaries lurk at every twist and turn. 34 mazes, stories, solutions. 48pp. 8¼ x 11. 24566-7

LETTERS OF W. A. MOZART, Wolfgang A. Mozart. Remarkable letters show bawdy wit, humor, imagination, musical insights, contemporary musical world; includes some letters from Leopold Mozart. 276pp. 5⅜ x 8½. 22859-2

BASIC PRINCIPLES OF CLASSICAL BALLET, Agrippina Vaganova. Great Russian theoretician, teacher explains methods for teaching classical ballet. 118 illustrations. 175pp. 5⅜ x 8½. 22036-2

THE JUMPING FROG, Mark Twain. Revenge edition. The original story of The Celebrated Jumping Frog of Calaveras County, a hapless French translation, and Twain's hilarious "retranslation" from the French. 12 illustrations. 66pp. 5⅜ x 8½. 22686-7

BEST REMEMBERED POEMS, Martin Gardner (ed.). The 126 poems in this superb collection of 19th- and 20th-century British and American verse range from Shelley's "To a Skylark" to the impassioned "Renascence" of Edna St. Vincent Millay and to Edward Lear's whimsical "The Owl and the Pussycat." 224pp. 5⅜ x 8½. 27165-X

COMPLETE SONNETS, William Shakespeare. Over 150 exquisite poems deal with love, friendship, the tyranny of time, beauty's evanescence, death and other themes in language of remarkable power, precision and beauty. Glossary of archaic terms. 80pp. 5³⁄₁₆ x 8¼. 26686-9

THE BATTLES THAT CHANGED HISTORY, Fletcher Pratt. Eminent historian profiles 16 crucial conflicts, ancient to modern, that changed the course of civilization. 352pp. 5⅜ x 8½. 41129-X

THE WIT AND HUMOR OF OSCAR WILDE, Alvin Redman (ed.). More than 1,000 ripostes, paradoxes, wisecracks: Work is the curse of the drinking classes; I can resist everything except temptation; etc. 258pp. 5⅜ x 8½. 20602-5

SHAKESPEARE LEXICON AND QUOTATION DICTIONARY, Alexander Schmidt. Full definitions, locations, shades of meaning in every word in plays and poems. More than 50,000 exact quotations. 1,485pp. 6½ x 9¼. 2-vol. set.
Vol. 1: 22726-X
Vol. 2: 22727-8

SELECTED POEMS, Emily Dickinson. Over 100 best-known, best-loved poems by one of America's foremost poets, reprinted from authoritative early editions. No comparable edition at this price. Index of first lines. 64pp. 5³⁄₁₆ x 8¼. 26466-1

THE INSIDIOUS DR. FU-MANCHU, Sax Rohmer. The first of the popular mystery series introduces a pair of English detectives to their archnemesis, the diabolical Dr. Fu-Manchu. Flavorful atmosphere, fast-paced action, and colorful characters enliven this classic of the genre. 208pp. 5³⁄₁₆ x 8¼. 29898-1

THE MALLEUS MALEFICARUM OF KRAMER AND SPRENGER, translated by Montague Summers. Full text of most important witchhunter's "bible," used by both Catholics and Protestants. 278pp. 6⅝ x 10. 22802-9

SPANISH STORIES/CUENTOS ESPAÑOLES: A Dual-Language Book, Angel Flores (ed.). Unique format offers 13 great stories in Spanish by Cervantes, Borges, others. Faithful English translations on facing pages. 352pp. 5⅜ x 8½. 25399-6

GARDEN CITY, LONG ISLAND, IN EARLY PHOTOGRAPHS, 1869–1919, Mildred H. Smith. Handsome treasury of 118 vintage pictures, accompanied by carefully researched captions, document the Garden City Hotel fire (1899), the Vanderbilt Cup Race (1908), the first airmail flight departing from the Nassau Boulevard Aerodrome (1911), and much more. 96pp. 8⅞ x 11¾. 40669-5

OLD QUEENS, N.Y., IN EARLY PHOTOGRAPHS, Vincent F. Seyfried and William Asadorian. Over 160 rare photographs of Maspeth, Jamaica, Jackson Heights, and other areas. Vintage views of DeWitt Clinton mansion, 1939 World's Fair and more. Captions. 192pp. 8⅞ x 11. 26358-4

CAPTURED BY THE INDIANS: 15 Firsthand Accounts, 1750-1870, Frederick Drimmer. Astounding true historical accounts of grisly torture, bloody conflicts, relentless pursuits, miraculous escapes and more, by people who lived to tell the tale. 384pp. 5⅜ x 8½. 24901-8

THE WORLD'S GREAT SPEECHES (Fourth Enlarged Edition), Lewis Copeland, Lawrence W. Lamm, and Stephen J. McKenna. Nearly 300 speeches provide public speakers with a wealth of updated quotes and inspiration–from Pericles' funeral oration and William Jennings Bryan's "Cross of Gold Speech" to Malcolm X's powerful words on the Black Revolution and Earl of Spenser's tribute to his sister, Diana, Princess of Wales. 944pp. 5⅜ x 8⅜. 40903-1

THE BOOK OF THE SWORD, Sir Richard F. Burton. Great Victorian scholar/adventurer's eloquent, erudite history of the "queen of weapons"–from prehistory to early Roman Empire. Evolution and development of early swords, variations (sabre, broadsword, cutlass, scimitar, etc.), much more. 336pp. 6⅛ x 9¼.
25434-8

AUTOBIOGRAPHY: The Story of My Experiments with Truth, Mohandas K. Gandhi. Boyhood, legal studies, purification, the growth of the Satyagraha (nonviolent protest) movement. Critical, inspiring work of the man responsible for the freedom of India. 480pp. 5⅜ x 8½. (Available in U.S. only.) 24593-4

CELTIC MYTHS AND LEGENDS, T. W. Rolleston. Masterful retelling of Irish and Welsh stories and tales. Cuchulain, King Arthur, Deirdre, the Grail, many more. First paperback edition. 58 full-page illustrations. 512pp. 5⅜ x 8½. 26507-2

THE PRINCIPLES OF PSYCHOLOGY, William James. Famous long course complete, unabridged. Stream of thought, time perception, memory, experimental methods; great work decades ahead of its time. 94 figures. 1,391pp. 5⅜ x 8½. 2-vol. set.
Vol. I: 20381-6 Vol. II: 20382-4

THE WORLD AS WILL AND REPRESENTATION, Arthur Schopenhauer. Definitive English translation of Schopenhauer's life work, correcting more than 1,000 errors, omissions in earlier translations. Translated by E. F. J. Payne. Total of 1,269pp. 5⅜ x 8½. 2-vol. set.
Vol. 1: 21761-2 Vol. 2: 21762-0

MAGIC AND MYSTERY IN TIBET, Madame Alexandra David-Neel. Experiences among lamas, magicians, sages, sorcerers, Bonpa wizards. A true psychic discovery. 32 illustrations. 321pp. 5⅜ x 8½. (Available in U.S. only.) 22682-4

THE EGYPTIAN BOOK OF THE DEAD, E. A. Wallis Budge. Complete reproduction of Ani's papyrus, finest ever found. Full hieroglyphic text, interlinear transliteration, word-for-word translation, smooth translation. 533pp. 6½ x 9¼. 21866-X

MATHEMATICS FOR THE NONMATHEMATICIAN, Morris Kline. Detailed, college-level treatment of mathematics in cultural and historical context, with numerous exercises. Recommended Reading Lists. Tables. Numerous figures. 641pp. 5⅜ x 8½.
24823-2

PROBABILISTIC METHODS IN THE THEORY OF STRUCTURES, Isaac Elishakoff. Well-written introduction covers the elements of the theory of probability from two or more random variables, the reliability of such multivariable structures, the theory of random function, Monte Carlo methods of treating problems incapable of exact solution, and more. Examples. 502pp. 5⅜ x 8½. 40691-1

THE RIME OF THE ANCIENT MARINER, Gustave Doré, S. T. Coleridge. Doré's finest work; 34 plates capture moods, subtleties of poem. Flawless full-size reproductions printed on facing pages with authoritative text of poem. "Beautiful. Simply beautiful."—*Publisher's Weekly.* 77pp. 9¼ x 12. 22305-1

NORTH AMERICAN INDIAN DESIGNS FOR ARTISTS AND CRAFTSPEOPLE, Eva Wilson. Over 360 authentic copyright-free designs adapted from Navajo blankets, Hopi pottery, Sioux buffalo hides, more. Geometrics, symbolic figures, plant and animal motifs, etc. 128pp. 8⅜ x 11. (Not for sale in the United Kingdom.) 25341-4

SCULPTURE: Principles and Practice, Louis Slobodkin. Step-by-step approach to clay, plaster, metals, stone; classical and modern. 253 drawings, photos. 255pp. 8⅛ x 11.
22960-2

THE INFLUENCE OF SEA POWER UPON HISTORY, 1660–1783, A. T. Mahan. Influential classic of naval history and tactics still used as text in war colleges. First paperback edition. 4 maps. 24 battle plans. 640pp. 5⅜ x 8½. 25509-3

THE STORY OF THE TITANIC AS TOLD BY ITS SURVIVORS, Jack Winocour (ed.). What it was really like. Panic, despair, shocking inefficiency, and a little heroism. More thrilling than any fictional account. 26 illustrations. 320pp. 5⅜ x 8½.
20610-6

FAIRY AND FOLK TALES OF THE IRISH PEASANTRY, William Butler Yeats (ed.). Treasury of 64 tales from the twilight world of Celtic myth and legend: "The Soul Cages," "The Kildare Pooka," "King O'Toole and his Goose," many more. Introduction and Notes by W. B. Yeats. 352pp. 5⅜ x 8½.
26941-8

BUDDHIST MAHAYANA TEXTS, E. B. Cowell and others (eds.). Superb, accurate translations of basic documents in Mahayana Buddhism, highly important in history of religions. The Buddha-karita of Asvaghosha, Larger Sukhavativyuha, more. 448pp. 5⅜ x 8½.
25552-2

ONE TWO THREE . . . INFINITY: Facts and Speculations of Science, George Gamow. Great physicist's fascinating, readable overview of contemporary science: number theory, relativity, fourth dimension, entropy, genes, atomic structure, much more. 128 illustrations. Index. 352pp. 5⅜ x 8½.
25664-2

EXPERIMENTATION AND MEASUREMENT, W. J. Youden. Introductory manual explains laws of measurement in simple terms and offers tips for achieving accuracy and minimizing errors. Mathematics of measurement, use of instruments, experimenting with machines. 1994 edition. Foreword. Preface. Introduction. Epilogue. Selected Readings. Glossary. Index. Tables and figures. 128pp. 5⅜ x 8½.
40451-X

DALÍ ON MODERN ART: The Cuckolds of Antiquated Modern Art, Salvador Dalí. Influential painter skewers modern art and its practitioners. Outrageous evaluations of Picasso, Cézanne, Turner, more. 15 renderings of paintings discussed. 44 calligraphic decorations by Dalí. 96pp. 5⅜ x 8½. (Available in U.S. only.)
29220-7

ANTIQUE PLAYING CARDS: A Pictorial History, Henry René D'Allemagne. Over 900 elaborate, decorative images from rare playing cards (14th–20th centuries): Bacchus, death, dancing dogs, hunting scenes, royal coats of arms, players cheating, much more. 96pp. 9¼ x 12¼.
29265-7

MAKING FURNITURE MASTERPIECES: 30 Projects with Measured Drawings, Franklin H. Gottshall. Step-by-step instructions, illustrations for constructing handsome, useful pieces, among them a Sheraton desk, Chippendale chair, Spanish desk, Queen Anne table and a William and Mary dressing mirror. 224pp. 8⅛ x 11¼.
29338-6

THE FOSSIL BOOK: A Record of Prehistoric Life, Patricia V. Rich et al. Profusely illustrated definitive guide covers everything from single-celled organisms and dinosaurs to birds and mammals and the interplay between climate and man. Over 1,500 illustrations. 760pp. 7½ x 10⅛.
29371-8

Paperbound unless otherwise indicated. Available at your book dealer, online at **www.doverpublications.com**, or by writing to Dept. GI, Dover Publications, Inc., 31 East 2nd Street, Mineola, NY 11501. For current price information or for free catalogues (please indicate field of interest), write to Dover Publications or log on to **www.doverpublications.com** and see every Dover book in print. Dover publishes more than 500 books each year on science, elementary and advanced mathematics, biology, music, art, literary history, social sciences, and other areas.